The Hip Hop Movement

The Hip Hop Movement

*From R&B and the Civil Rights
Movement to Rap and the
Hip Hop Generation*

Reiland Rabaka

LEXINGTON BOOKS
Lanham • Boulder • New York • Toronto • Plymouth, UK

Published by Lexington Books
A wholly owned subsidary of The Rowman & Littlefield Publishing Group, Inc.
4501 Forbes Boulevard, Suite 200, Lanham, Maryland 20706
www.rowman.com

10 Thornbury Road, Plymouth PL6 7PP, United Kingdom

British Library Cataloguing in Publication Information Available

Library of Congress Cataloging-in-Publication Data

Rabaka, Reiland, 1972–
The hip hop movement : from R&B and the civil rights movement to rap and the hip hop generation /
Reiland Rabaka.
pages cm
Includes bibliographical references and index.
ISBN 978-0-7391-8116-4 (cloth : alk. paper) — ISBN 978-0-7391-8243-7 (pbk. : alk. paper) —
ISBN 978-0-7391-8117-1 (electronic)
1. African Americans—Music—History and criticism. 2. Popular music—United States—History
and criticism. 3. Popular music—Social aspects—United States—History—20th century. 4. Rap
(Music)—History and criticism. 5. Hip-hop. I. Title.
ML3479.R28 2013
782.4216490973—dc23
2013000594

Printed in the United States of America

For my mother, Reverend Marilyn Giles, in deep and abiding love and respect. Her patience and perseverance, preaching and teaching, and all-around optimistic approach to life, even in the face of seemingly the most insurmountable odds, have made her "mother" to many and an honored elder in her community. To say that I am proud of her, that I admire and adore her, and that she is, as Stevie Wonder once sang, "the sunshine of my life," is simply not saying enough:

Ninakupenda mama. Asante sana mama. Mungu akubariki na akulinde. Wewe ni mwanga wa jua wa maisha yangu.

And, for the organic intellectuals (including rappers, spoke-word artists, neo-soulsters, MCs, DJs, b-girls, b-boys, graffiti-writers, students, etc.), activists, archivists, institutions, and organizations of the Hip Hop Movement:

Lift Every Voice and Sing . . .

Contents

Introlude

Acknowledgments

The Hip Hop Movement is a sequel of sorts. Obviously it continues the narrative begun in *Hip Hop's Inheritance* and further developed in *Hip Hop's Amnesia*. Part of the premise of the previous volumes is that rap music and hip hop culture are much more complex and complicated, more meaningful—literally, full of myriad meanings—than most hip hop scholars, fans, and critics give them credit for. More than music, rap is also a form of poetry, social commentary, political analysis, and cultural criticism. More than popular culture, hip hop culture is also *a new, post-Civil Rights Movement and post-Black Power Movement form of black popular culture and black popular music-based politics and social movement.* It is with this simultaneously historical, cultural, political, sociological, *and* musicological understanding that I conceive of *rap music as a "soundtrack"* and *hip hop as a "movement,"* rather than following the conventional conception of rap music and hip hop culture as merely an artistic expression of a "generation" born between the March on Washington and the beginning of Bill Clinton's presidency, roughly between 1963 and 1993. To reconceive of *rap music as a "soundtrack"* and *hip hop as a "movement"* is to conjure up and consciously conceive of rap music and hip hop culture, as well as the often overlooked cultural, social, and political movement it spawned, as *the accumulated politics and aesthetics of each and every African American movement and musical form that preceded it.*

Bearing all of this in mind, *The Hip Hop Movement* is meant to be a monument: a monument to the musicians and politicians, the musics and movements, the writers and revolutionaries, the preachers and teachers, the hipsters and hustlers and, most of all, the ghetto youth and suburban youth who paved the way for rap music, hip hop culture and, ultimately, *the Hip Hop Movement*. However, even more than a monument to hip hop's artistic ancestors, political antecedents, cultural inventors, and contemporary innovators, *The Hip Hop Movement* also stands as a testament to all the folk who contributed to my personal, professional, and radical political development. Every word, sentence, paragraph, and "remix" to follow bears the imprint of the diverse—although often disconnected—intellectual and political arenas and agendas I draw from and endeavor to establish critical dialogue with. As a consequence, the list of academics, organic intellectuals (including rappers, spoken-word artists, neo-soulsters, MCs, DJs, b-girls, b-boys, graffiti-writers, students, etc.), activists, archivists, institutions, and organizations to which I am indebted is, indeed, enormous. Such being the case, I hope I may be forgiven for deciding that the most appropriate way in which to acknowledge my sincere appreciation is simply to list them below without the protracted praise each has so solemnly earned.

My deepest gratitude and most heartfelt *asante sana* (a thousand thanks) is offered, first and foremost, to my family: my mother, Marilyn Giles; my father, Robert Smith I (deceased); my grandmothers, Lizzie Mae Davis (deceased) and Elva Rita Warren; my great aunt, Arcressia Charlene Connor; my older brother and his wife, Robert Smith II and Karen Smith; my younger brother, Dwight Randle Wellington Clewis; my nieces and nephews, Journée Clewis, Dominique Clewis, Kalyn Smith, Robert Smith III, Ryan Smith, and Remington Smith; my innumerable aunts, uncles, and cousins throughout the Americas, the Caribbean, and Africa; and, most especially *wangu malaika*, Dr. Stephanie Krusemark, whose incomparable intellect, extraordinary eloquence, grand sense of grace, soulful sophistication, and limitless love helped me research and write this book, as well as tend to my mind, body, heart, and soul (*nakupenda sana* Nzuri).

An undertaking as ambitious as *The Hip Hop Movement* would have been impossible without the assistance of colleagues and comrades, both far and wide. I express my earnest appreciation to the following fine folk, who each in their own special way contributed to the composition and completion of this book: Camille Paglia; Kariamu Welsh; Lucius Outlaw; Angela Y. Davis; Manning Marable (deceased); Rhonda Tankerson; Nedra James; Vickie Washington; the faculty, staff, students, and alumni of the Booker T. Washington High School for the Performing and Visual Arts (Dallas, Texas); the faculty, staff, students, and alumni of the University of the Arts (Philadelphia, Pennsylvania); the faculty, staff, students, and alumni of the Department of African American Studies at Temple University (Philadelphia, Pennsylvania); Rev. L.R. Davis and the congregation of Galilee Missionary Baptist Church (Dallas, Texas); Lamya Al-Kharusi; Denise Lovett; Adam Clark; Elzie Billops; Sigmund Washington; Patrick DeWalt; Awon Atuire; Stacey Smith; De Reef Jamison; Lynn Johnson; Anthony Lemelle; Troy Barnes;

Zachary Epps; Ursula Lindqvist; Tiya Trent; La'Neice Littleton; Howard Wallen; Timothy Allen; Vincent Harding; Marvin Lynn; David Stovall; Gloria Ladson-Billings; Daniel Solórzano; George Junne; Ward Churchill; Eva Torres Henry; Vicki Carter; Richard Hodges; Stacy and Sekou Robertson; Gail Dennis; Bernard Robertson; Bakari Kitwana; Oliver Wang; Mark Anthony Neal; Jared Ball; Adam Bradley; Nitasha Sharma; M.K. Asante Jr.; Chelsey Jennings; Mpozi Mshale Tolbert (deceased); Taharka Leophus King (deceased); the editorial board of the *Critical Africana Studies* book series (Martell Teasley, Christel Temple, and Deborah Whaley); the National Association for Ethnic Studies (NAES); and the Association for the Study of African American Life and History (ASALH).

I cannot adequately convey the depth of my gratitude to the National Council for Black Studies (NCBS) for providing me with the critical feedback and fora to deepen and develop my relationship with the wider world of American studies, critical race studies, cultural studies, popular music studies, women's studies, sexuality studies, postcolonial studies, black radical politics, and critical social theory. I have been presenting my research at NCBS's annual conferences for more than a decade and a half. Along with saying *maalum sana shukrani* (very special thanks) to NCBS in general, I would be remiss not to single out several members whose key contributions and intellectual encouragement have made the present volume possible. I, therefore, express my earnest appreciation to the following NCBS colleagues and comrades: Molefi Asante; Maulana Karenga; James Turner; Delores Aldridge; James Stewart; Martell Teasley; Mark Christian; James Conyers; Charles Jones; Sundiata Cha-Jua; Perry Hall; Shirley Weber; Barbara Wheeler; Alfred Young; Bill Little (deceased); Munasha Furusa; Akinyele Umoja; Fred Hord; Terry Kershaw; Jeffrey Ogbar; Scot Brown; Alan Colon; Abdul Nanji; Christel Temple; Patricia Reid-Merritt; Kevin Cokley; Salim Faraji; Cecil Gray; and Ricky Jones.

The faculty, staff, students, and alumni of the Department of Ethnic Studies and the Center for Studies of Ethnicity and Race in America (CSERA) at the University of Colorado at Boulder deserve special thanks for their patience and critical support. *Maalum sana shukrani* (very special thanks) to our steadfast staff, especially Sandra Lane and Jason Van Horn, for always being there and lending a helping hand. I am also deeply indebted to my colleagues and comrades who selflessly serve on the faculty in the Department of Ethnic Studies, each of whom has patiently listened to me rant and rave about both the positives and negatives of rap music and hip hop culture over the last couple of years. I say *maalum sana shukrani*, especially, to my mentor, brother, friend, colleague, confidant, and comrade, William King, who has consistently supported both my teaching and research endeavors over the years.

Several libraries, research centers, special collections, and archives hosted and helped me transform this book from an inchoate idea into its fully realized form. I am indelibly indebted to the directors, research fellows, and staffs of: the Hip Hop Archive and the W.E.B. Du Bois Institute for African and African American Research, Harvard University; Arthur A. Houghton Jr. Library, Harvard University; Arturo A. Schomburg Center for Research in Black Culture, New York Public Library; Nicholas Murray Butler Library, Columbia University; Institute for African American Affairs, New York University; Elmer Holmes Bobst Library, New York University; John Henrik Clarke Africana Library, Africana Studies and Research Center, Cornell University; Charles L. Blockson African American Collection, Temple University; Center for African American History and Culture, Temple University; Center for Africana Studies, University of Pennsylvania; August Wilson Center for African American Culture, Pittsburgh, Pennsylvania; Center for American Music, University of Pittsburgh; Center for Popular Culture Studies, Bowling Green State University; Center for Black Music Research, Columbia College, Chicago; Karla Scherer Center for the Study of American Culture, University of Chicago; Center for Popular Music, Middle Tennessee State University; Center for the History of Music Theory and Literature, Jacobs School of Music, Indiana University; African American Cultural Center, University of Illinois at Chicago; Bruce Nesbitt African American Cultural Center, University of Illinois at Urbana-Champaign; African American Cultural Center, North Carolina State University; H. Fred Simons African American Cultural Center, University of Connecticut at Storrs; Moorland-Spingarn Research Center, Howard University; John Hope Franklin Collection for African and African American Documentation, Rare Book, Manuscript, and Special Collections Library, Duke University; Carter G. Woodson Center for African American and African Studies, University of Virginia; Robert W. Woodruff Library, Atlanta University Center Archives; Manuscript Sources for African American History, Special Collections, Emory University; John L. Warfield Center for African and African American Studies, University of Texas at Austin; Center for African American Studies, University of Houston; African and African American Collection, University Library, University of California, Berkeley; Institute for Advanced Feminist Research, University of California, Santa Cruz; Ralph J. Bunche Center for African American Studies, University of California, Los Angeles; Blair-Caldwell African American Research Library, Denver Public Library; Center for Media, Arts, and Performance, Alliance for Technology, Learning, and Society (ATLAS) Institute, University of Colorado at Boulder; American Music Research Center, College of Music, University of Colorado at Boulder; Howard B. Waltz Music Library, College of Music, University of Colorado at Boulder; Department of Musicology, College of Music, University of

Colorado at Boulder; African American Materials, Special Collections, George Norlin Library, University of Colorado at Boulder.

The Hip Hop Movement could not have been researched and written without the music and inspiration of the following singer-songwriters, rapper-rhymewriters, and musician-magicians, several of whom were gracious enough to grant interviews: Abbey Lincoln; Taj Mahal; Otis Taylor; Sweet Honey in the Rock; Vinx; Sharon Jones; Sade; Cassandra Wilson; Tracy Chapman; Terence Trent D'Arby; Seal; Des'ree; Corey Harris; Lenny Kravitz; Ben Harper; Cody ChesnuTT; Lalah Hathaway; Mary J. Blige; Angie Stone; Eric Benét; Dionne Farris; Nadirah Shakoor; Erykah Badu; N'dambi; Carl Thomas; Raphael Saadiq; Alicia Keys; Maxwell; Hil St. Soul; Jaheim; Zap Mama; Bilal; Ledisi; Donnie; Macy Gray; Rahsaan Patterson; Les Nubians; Calvin Richardson; Nneka; Van Hunt; Jill Scott; Anthony Hamilton; Leela James; John Legend; India.Arie; Anthony David; Keyshia Cole; Musiq Soulchild; Jaguar Wright; Conya Doss; Chocolate Genius (a.k.a., Marc Anthony Thompson); Goapele Mohlabane; Dwele; Georgia Anne Muldrow; Aloe Blacc; Rhonda Nicole; Raheem DeVaughn; Chrisette Michele; Lyfe Jennings; Janelle Monáe; Meshell Ndegeocello; Michael Franti and Spearhead; Amel Larrieux; YahZarah; The Roots (especially Tariq "Black Thought" Trotter and Ahmir "Questlove" Thompson); Bahamadia; KRS-One; Public Enemy; Chuck D.; X-Clan; Rakim Allah; Tupac Shakur; Common; Talib Kweli; Mos Def (a.k.a., Yasiin Bey); Q-Tip; A Tribe Called Quest; De La Soul; The Jungle Brothers; Brand Nubian; Digable Planets; Arrested Development; Intelligent Hoodlum; Poor Righteous Teachers; Dream Warriors; Main Source; The Solsonics; NaS; OutKast; Goodie Mob; Cee-Lo Green; Little Brother; Phonte Coleman; Jean Grae; Dead Prez; M-1 (a.k.a., Mutulu Olugbala); K'naan; Medusa; The Coup; Paris; The Conscious Daughters; Wyclef Jean; Buju Banton; Gang Starr; Guru (a.k.a., Keith Edward Elam); and Lupe Fiasco.

My publisher and I would like to thank and openly acknowledge Chelsey Jennings, who graciously granted permission to use her collage for the book cover. Chelsey is an extraordinarily gifted artist, poet, and writer who skillfully melds aesthetics and politics. In my mind, her work symbolizes the hip hop aesthetic at its best—bold, full of color and rhythm, personal yet universal enough for us all to see our lives, loves, and struggles in it. *Asante sana*—thank you a thousand times for sharing your gift with us, Chelsey.

My editor, Jana Hodges-Kluck, and the Lexington Books editorial board deserve very special thanks (*maalum sana shukrani*) for seeing the potential in this book project and gently prodding me along during the many months it took me to revise the manuscript and prepare it for production. I would like to formally thank Jana and my publisher, Julie Kirsch, for the promptness and professionalism with which they have handled my book projects, and for their patience with my extremely erratic (if not a bit eccentric) research and writing regimen, which in this instance took me to dozens of university and public libraries, archives, and research centers. I am not by any means the easiest person to correspond with when I am working, but throughout the entire research, writing, and review process they calmly fielded my inquiries and coolly encouraged me to complete my book.

"DEAR MAMA": A LOVE LETTER TO MY MOTHER AND HER GENERATION

This book is offered as an emblem of my deep and abiding love and respect for my mother, Reverend Marilyn Giles, in celebration of her sixty-fifth birthday. One of my greatest sources of inspiration, my mother sacrificed more than I will ever fully comprehend for my brothers and me. Her patience and perseverance, preaching and teaching, and all-around optimistic approach to life, even in the face of seemingly the most insurmountable odds, has made her "mother" to many and an honored elder in her community. To say that I am proud of her, that I admire and adore her, and that she is, as Stevie Wonder once sang, "the sunshine of my life," is simply not saying enough. I am embarrassed to admit that I do not have the words to fully express the full depth of my feelings, my love and respect, for my mother. Perhaps it is best to say that each and every feeling or emotion cannot be put into words, that no matter what our grasp of a language is at best words and sentences only partially convey what we feel, what we really mean, and what we would really like to express. Suffice to say, I more than love my mother and I would like to super-celebrate her sixty-fifth birthday and the admirable life she leads. *Ninakupenda mama. Asante mama. Mungu akubariki na aku-linde. Wewe ni mwanga wa jua wa maisha yangu.*

This book, then, is as much my mother's as it is mine. She, before and more than anyone else, exposed me to the politics and musics of the Civil Rights Movement and Black Power Movement. In a way, *The Hip Hop Movement* is a love letter to my mother and her generation—the so-called "Baby Boomer Generation." With this work I would like to build or, rather, rebuild a bridge between the Baby Boomer Generation and the Hip Hop Generation. Or, more accurately within the context of African America, this book serves as a symbolic bridge swinging between the Civil Rights Movement, Black Power Movement and the, however unheralded, Hip Hop Movement. We need each other, and there is much that we can all lovingly learn from each other—just as I have learned from my beloved mother and, likewise, she seems to have picked up some things from me. Our futures, individually and collectively, depend on the transference of knowledge and culture from one generation to the next, from one movement to the next. Indeed, more than anything else, *The Hip Hop Movement* is a love letter to and remembrance of the unsung heroines and heroes, the neglected knowledge-bearers and cultural workers of the Civil Rights Movement, Black Power Movement, and Hip Hop Movement.

If, then, my most respected readers, any inspiration or insights are gathered from my journey through the musics and movements that influenced rap music, hip hop culture, and the Hip Hop Movement, I pray you will attribute them to each of the aforementioned. However, if (and when) you find foibles and intellectual idiosyncrasies, I humbly hope you will neither associate them with any of the forenamed nor, most especially, the members of the Hip Hop Movement. I, and I alone, am responsible for the flows and flaws to follow. As is my custom, then, I begin by softly saying, almost silently singing my earnest and eternal prayer: *Lift Every Voice and Sing.*

Introduction

Lift Every Voice and Sing and Rap

> Over the course of its career hip hop has developed a notorious and even self-perpetuating reputation as a spectacular cultural movement committed to defying the cultural and political mainstream. But as the borders of the Hip Hop Nation continue to expand, its biggest and most important battle is shaping up to be the one it is having with itself. Behind the explosive record sales, trend-setting cachet, and burgeoning economy is an intense struggle for the soul of the Hip Hop Movement. There has never been a consensus within hip hop about its purpose, identity, or destiny. In fact, the most robust debates about hip hop have always taken place within the movement. Hip Hop has and continues to be its most potent critic and courageous champion.
>
> —S. Craig Watkins, *Hip Hop Matters: Politics, Pop Culture, and the Struggle for the Soul of a Movement*

LIFTING EVERY VOICE AND SINGING AND RAPPING ABOUT THE HIP HOP MOVEMENT: ON THE AESTHETICS, POLITICS, AND SOCIAL MOVEMENTS OF POST-CIVIL RIGHTS MOVEMENT AND POST-BLACK POWER MOVEMENT AFRICAN AMERICA

Lift Every Voice and Sing. For more than a century "The Negro National Anthem," then "The Black National Anthem" and, more recently, "The African American National Anthem" has earnestly asked African Americans to lift their voices and sing, to tell their heartfelt stories and speak their special truths. However, with the rise of rap music and hip hop culture one wonders whether the hallowed "African American National Anthem" extends to hip hoppers, because it often seems as though the Civil Rights Movement and Black Power Movement generations would like for anyone

1

other than the Hip Hop Generation to lift their unique voices and sing—or, as is often the case with the Hip Hop Generation, lift their unique voices and sing *and* rap. James Weldon Johnson's poem "Lift Every Voice and Sing" was composed to celebrate Abraham Lincoln's birthday on February 12, 1900, and was initially used to introduce Booker T. Washington, who spoke at Johnson's Stanton School in Jacksonville, Florida, to commemorate the occasion. In 1905 Johnson's brother, John Rosamond Johnson, set the poem to music. With its references to enslavement, segregation, and lynching, its psalmic call for heaven and earth to "ring with the harmonies of liberty," and for African Americans to sing songs of hope and faith, "Lift Every Voice and Sing" was quickly adopted as an anthem by members of both the Black Women's Club Movement and New Negro Movement.[1]

In 1919 the National Association for the Advancement of Colored People (NAACP) officially adopted the song as "The Negro National Anthem." Also during the Harlem Renaissance years African American churches embraced "Lift Every Voice and Sing," going so far as to paste it in hymnals and reprint it on church programs. During the Civil Rights Movement years the song was frequently sung at protests, marches, and rallies. Moreover, during the Black Power Movement years Ray Charles released a jaw-dropping version of the song on his classic *A Message from the People* (1972) album, and former Motown diva Kim Weston offered a soulful version of the song on the 1972 WattStax Festival soundtrack. In 1990 a Melba Moore led star-studded choir, including Anita Baker, Stevie Wonder, Stephanie Mills, Dionne Warwick, Bobby Brown, the Clark Sisters, BeBe and CeCe Winans, Jeffrey Osborne, Howard Hewett, and Take 6, delivered an extremely popular version of the song that ultimately led Congressman Walter Fauntroy to have the song admitted into the Congressional Record as the official African American National Anthem.

With a national anthem that passionately implores African Americans to lift their voices and sing it is ironic that many, if not most, African American elders seem as though they would like to silence the Hip Hop Generation. Arguably the most misunderstood generation of African American youth in American history, one of the primary reasons the Hip Hop Generation is so misunderstood, I honestly believe, may have a lot to do with the often overlooked fact that rap music and hip hop culture actually reflect more than merely the ethos of a "generation"—they represent a movement, *the Hip Hop Movement*. In *Hip Hop Matters: Politics, Pop Culture, and the Struggle for the Soul of a Movement* (2005), S. Craig Watkins emphasized that what has been frequently called the "Hip Hop Generation" or the "Hip Hop Nation" is not only a movement but, he strongly stressed, a movement "unlike anything the world has ever seen":

The story of hip hop, like the story of millennial America, is infinitely more intriguing than typical accounts acknowledge. Most assessments of the Hip Hop "Generation" or "Nation" present a culture that is monolithic in its world-view or definable simply by age. But if the thirty-plus-year career of the movement suggests anything it is that hip hop belies the established definitions and caricatures that tend to celebrate or condemn the culture. Simply put, hip hop is unlike anything the world has ever seen. It is a vital source of creativity and industry for youth. Hip hop is consumed with pop celebrity and street credibility—and capable, many believe, of transforming young lives. (5)

It is hip hop's supporters' and detractors' belief in its ability to inspire both self-transformation *and* social transformation that speaks volumes about the ways in which what has been generally called the "Hip Hop Generation" or the "Hip Hop Nation" has evolved into a distinct movement that embodies the musical, cultural, social and political, among other, views and values of the post-Civil Rights Movement and post-Black Power Movement genera-tion. As illustrated in my previous volumes, *Hip Hop's Inheritance: From the Harlem Renaissance to the Hip Hop Feminist Movement* (2011) and *Hip Hop's Amnesia: From Blues and the Black Women's Club Movement to Rap and the Hip Hop Movement* (2012), rap music and hip hop culture are far from "monolithic in [their] worldview" or easily "definable simply by age." For example, *Hip Hop's Inheritance* examined women-centered rappers and hip hop feminists' "inheritance" from the Black Women's Liberation Move-ment and Feminist Art Movement, where *Hip Hop's Amnesia* explored the "amnesia" and outright ignorance surrounding the ways in which the Homo-sexual Hip Hop Movement has built on many of the major "queer" themes of the Harlem Renaissance, which frequently coupled critiques of racism, capi-talism, and colonialism with critiques of sexism, heterosexism, and black bourgeoisism.

Part of what my hip hop studies have sought to demonstrate is that rap music, hip hop culture, and the Hip Hop Movement are as deserving of critical scholarly inquiry as previous black popular musics, such as the spiri-tuals, blues, ragtime, jazz, rhythm & blues, rock & roll, soul, and funk, and previous black popular movements, such as the Black Women's Club Move-ment, New Negro Movement, Harlem Renaissance, Civil Rights Movement, Black Power Movement, Black Arts Movement, and Black Women's Libera-tion Movement. In equal parts *an alternative history of hip hop* and *a critical theory of hip hop*, this volume challenges those scholars, critics, and fans of hip hop who lopsidedly overfocus on commercial rap, pop rap, and gangsta rap while failing to acknowledge, as the "remixes" to follow reveal, that there are more than three dozen genres of rap music and many other socially and politically conscious forms of hip hop culture. At the outset, then, it is important to openly acknowledge that rap music and hip hop culture, much like earlier African American musical and cultural forms, for the most part, have been mediated through and commodified by what Frankfurt School critical theorists Max Horkheimer and Theodor Adorno called the "culture industry." In *Dialectic of Enlightenment* (1995), Horkheimer and Adorno asserted, "In the culture industry the individual is an illusion not merely because of the standardization of the means of production. He is tolerated only so long as his complete identification with the generality is unquestioned" (154).[2]

African Americans have always suffered high levels of dehumanization, generality, invisibility, and anonymity within *white, middle-class*, and *mainstream* America. Consequently, many, if not most, of the African American musical and cultural forms that have registered within the white world have frequently reinforced antiblack racist myths and stereotypes about African Americans, from blackface minstrelism to black exploitation movies, from country blues to gangsta rap. Because contemporary post-industrial-techno-capitalist society, in a sense, promotes and celebrates "mass identity," "unoriginality," and incessant (even if most times subconscious) embrace of capitalist views and values as the only socially acceptable forms of "identity," "originality," and "politically correct" views and values, popular music and popular culture have long revolved around generalities and faceless familiarities. As quiet as it has been kept, the most familiar images of African Americans in white America historically have been antiblack racist images, which is one of the reasons that for many white suburban youth a lot of commercial, pop, and gangsta rap seems simultaneously old and new, familiar and unfamiliar.

As Horkheimer and Adorno explained, "individuals have ceased to be themselves and are now merely centers where the general tendencies meet." The "general tendencies" and familiarities found in commercial, pop, and gangsta rap usually revolve around a wide range of antiblack racist myths and stereotypes surrounding black pathology, black inferiority, black hypersexuality, black rhythm, and black athleticism, and so forth. The ongoing extralegal nature of American apartheid has made it extremely difficult, if not impossible in many instances, for African Americans, especially black ghetto youth, to free themselves from the antiblack racist myths and stereotypes when it comes to black popular music and black popular culture.

It is as if the only way black ghetto youth can be "successful" within the world of contemporary black popular music and contemporary black popular culture is to "cease to be themselves" and become caricatures of themselves, "merely centers where the general tendencies [i.e., the antiblack racist myths and stereotypes] meet." Horkheimer and Adorno critically continued:

> In this way mass culture discloses the fictitious character of the "individual" in the bourgeois era, and is merely unjust in boasting on account of this dreary harmony of general and particular. The principle of individuality was always

full of contradiction. Individuation has never really been achieved. Self-preservation in the shape of class has kept everyone at the stage of a mere species being. Every bourgeois characteristic, in spite of its deviation and indeed because of it, expressed the same thing: the harshness of the competitive society. The individual who supported society bore its disfiguring mark; seemingly free, he was actually the product of its economic and social apparatus. Power based itself on the prevailing conditions of power when it sought the approval of persons affected by it. As it progressed, bourgeois society did also develop the individual. Against the will of its leaders, technology has changed human beings from children into persons. However, every advance in individuation of this kind took place at the expense of the individuality in whose name it occurred, so that nothing was left but the resolve to pursue one's own particular purpose. . . . The only reason why the culture industry can deal so successfully with individuality is that the latter has always reproduced the fragility of society. On the faces of private individuals and movie heroes put together according to the patterns on magazine covers vanishes a pretence in which no one now believes; the popularity of the hero models comes partly from a secret satisfaction that the effort to achieve individuation has at last been replaced by the effort to imitate, which is admittedly more breathless. It is idle to hope that this self-contradictory, disintegrating "person" will not last for generations, that the system must collapse because of such a psychological split, or that the deceitful substitution of the stereotype for the individual will of itself become unbearable for mankind. (155–56)

As Horkheimer and Adorno emphasized, distinct identity and authentic originality are virtually nonexistent, or in many senses simply not allowed, in contemporary post-industrial-techno-capitalist society. Capitalism's impact on contemporary African America could be said to be even more egregious and homogenizing than its impact on white America when antiblack racism and the fact that the majority of African America has been historically and currently remains working class and working poor. When antiblack racism is factored into Horkheimer and Adorno's critical theory of the culture industry (via critical race theory and Africana critical theory) it could be said that the "deceitful substitution of the [antiblack racist] stereotype for the [authentic African American] individual" has in and of itself "become unbearable" for contemporary African America, and that rap music and hip hop culture are simultaneously a cog in the wheel of the culture industry *and* also an important counter to the culture industry when both commercial, pop, and gangsta rap *and* political, alternative, and underground rap, among other rap genres, are taken into critical consideration.

For instance, when Horkheimer and Adorno observed that "Every bourgeois characteristic, in spite of its deviation and indeed because of it, expressed the same thing: the harshness of the competitive society," it is relatively easy to see how their critical theory of the culture industry is applicable to what I am wont to call *the hip hop industry*, and specifically several forms of rap music, especially gangsta rap. Essentially taking early commercially successful gangsta rappers such as Too $hort, Ice-T, N.W.A., Ice Cube, Snoop Dogg, and the Notorious B.I.G. as models, subsequent gangsta rappers such as DMX, Ja Rule, 50 Cent, the Game, Young Jeezy, and Rick Ross collectively seem to "express the same thing," which is in no uncertain terms indicative of the "harshness of the competitive" capitalist and antiblack racist society. Indeed, all of these rappers bear the "disfiguring mark[s]" of contemporary society, and each of them also, however unintentionally, demonstrates that their "effort[s] to achieve individuation has at last been replaced by the effort to imitate"—which is to say, "imitate" wealthy white businessmen, powerbrokers, pimps, drug dealers, hustlers, and, of course, gangsters.

Without placing too fine a point on it, even the most cursory listen to the latest commercial, pop, and gangsta rap will reveal that individuality and originality have been, for the most part, replaced by imitation, repetition, and often an overemphasis on technique. Even the more commercial rappers such as Jay-Z, NaS, Eminem, T.I., Kanye West, Lil' Wayne, Drake, and J. Cole seem to have rhymes that toy with and tug at what would otherwise be gangsta rap themes. Therefore, whether we engage commercial, pop, or gangsta rappers' work, most of these rappers' rhymes seem to "express the same thing" and, more or less, unambiguously embrace what we might call *the ghetto-gangsta-nigga-pimp-hoe-thug theme* (see "remix" 5). Consequently, a lot of the innovations and experimentations that have really and truly distinguished rap music and hip hop culture, and made it more than a mere passing musical and pop cultural fad, are found in political, alternative, and underground rap and hip hop communities. Horkheimer and Adorno's critical theory of the culture industry provides us with a lens through which to look at rap music, hip hop culture, and the Hip Hop Movement *dialectically*. Which is to say, exploring hip hop's controversies, contradictions, and contributions and how those controversies, contradictions, and contributions in many ways have roots in the controversies, contradictions, and contributions of previous black popular musics, black popular cultures, and black popular movements.

Usually when rap music and hip hop culture are discussed in the mass media, in churches, or even in the American academy, the focus is most often on commercial, pop, and gangsta rap, and especially nihilism, materialism, misogyny, and homophobia as expressed via these forms of rap. However, few in the mass media, in churches, and even in the American academy acknowledge the feminists, womanists, homosexuals, democratic socialists, antiwar activists, environmentalists, prisoners' rights activists, and animal rights activists, among others, who also identify as hip hoppers and who are leading their own respective *alternative* or *micro-hip hop movements*, such as the Hip Hop Feminist Movement, the Homosexual Hip Hop Movement, and the Hip Hop Environmentalist Movement, among others. It is these *micro-*

hip hop movements which, taken together, constitute the broader, multi-issue, *macro-Hip Hop Movement* or, more simply said, *the Hip Hop Movement*.

Hence, the Hip Hop Movement, as opposed to the "Hip Hop Generation" or the "Hip Hop Nation," is much more complicated and complex than previously noted, because movements—in the most generic historical, cultural, sociological, and political sense of the term—are nothing if they are not *moving away from*, and *moving toward* something. The Hip Hop Movement is obviously *moving away from* the various forms of American apartheid, oppression, and exploitation that characterized non-white America's past, especially black America's past. But, precisely what the Hip Hop Movement is *moving toward* seems to differ depending on who you ask, how you ask, when you ask, and which *micro-hip hop movement(s)* they are affiliated with. As alternative, underground, political, and other forms of noncommercial rap reveal—especially the work of rappers such as De La Soul, A Tribe Called Quest, Bahamadia, the Coup, the Roots, Missy Elliott, Blackalicious, Common, Mos Def, Talib Kweli, Wyclef Jean, Dead Prez, Pharoahe Monch, Little Brother, Lupe Fiasco, Jean Grae, K'naan, Wale, and Kid Cudi—rap music and hip hop culture are far from homogeneous. In fact, because of their high levels of heterogeneity and intense hybridity hip hoppers have rarely, if ever, reached consensus on exactly what hip hop culture and the Hip Hop Movement are and are not.

In a sense, the post-soul, post-funk, post-punk, post-disco, and post-electro *mélange* that has long distinguished rap music from other forms of black popular music has been frequently mirrored in the post-Civil Rights Movement *salmagundi* of hip hop's social movements and the post-Black Power Movement pastiche of hip hop's politics. In Watkins's (2005, 5) weighted words:

> Over the course of its career hip hop has developed a notorious and even self-perpetuating reputation as a spectacular cultural movement committed to defying the cultural and political mainstream. But as the borders of the Hip Hop Nation continue to expand, its biggest and most important battle is shaping up to be the one it is having with itself. Behind the explosive record sales, trend-setting cachet, and burgeoning economy is an intense struggle for the soul of the Hip Hop Movement. There has never been a consensus within hip hop about its purpose, identity, or destiny. In fact, the most robust debates about hip hop have always taken place within the movement. Hip Hop has and continues to be its most potent critic and courageous champion.

Perhaps more than anything else, this book is about the "intense struggle for the soul of the Hip Hop Movement." It grows out of the frustrations many hip hoppers (the author included) have surrounding the Hip Hop Generation's sometimes seeming lack of "purpose, identity, or destiny." Just as hip hoppers are more than merely a "generation" and actually part of a broader movement "unlike anything the world has ever seen," hip hoppers' seeming lack of "purpose, identity, or destiny" are often part of the myriad novel expressions that symbolize the new movement, politics, and culture that are, literally, "unlike anything the world has ever seen." The Hip Hop Movement is grounded in, and grows out of, black popular music and black popular culture in ways unlike any previous African American movement, but it is not simply hip hop music that distinguishes hip hoppers and their politics and new social movement.

Indeed, the African Americans born between, say, the 1963 March on Washington and the beginning of Bill Clinton's presidency in 1993 (circa 1963 to 1993), and who grew to maturity in the immediate aftermath of the Civil Rights Movement and Black Power Movement in the 1980s and 1990s, constitute a "generation" in the generic sense of the term. But, I assert once again, those of us who have been crudely clumped together and called the "Hip Hop Generation" are more than merely a generation, and our popular music and popular culture are more than merely "popular music" and "popular culture." Rap music and hip hop culture, however roguishly and politically incorrectly, register both the aspirations and frustrations of *the first generation of African American youth to come of age in a desegregated and awkwardly integrated, post-affirmative action America.*[3]

When viewed from an interdisciplinary perspective that incorporates history, political science, sociology, musicology, African American studies, and women's studies, among many others, the music and culture of the so-called "Hip Hop Generation" registers their unprecedented post-Civil Rights Movement and post-Black Power Movement politics and social visions which are, as Watkins put it, "unlike anything the world has ever seen." In a similar vein, in *The New H.N.I.C: The Death of Civil Rights and the Reign of Hip Hop* (2002), Todd Boyd insightfully observed:

> Hip hop is like an interdisciplinary academic community, combining the fields of sociology, psychology, political science, English, ethnomusicology, economics, American studies, and African American studies, and offering a choice of electives to its subscribers. The weight of all this is what makes hip hop something far beyond music, and far greater than the fashion, language, and ideology that express it. Hip hop is an unrivaled social force; it is a way of being. It is a new way of seeing the world and it is a collective movement that has dethroned civil rights and now commands our undivided attention. (13)

In complete agreement with Boyd, I would argue that what has been termed the "Hip Hop Generation" is actually "a collective movement," *the Hip Hop Movement.* Continuing his emphasis on *hip hop as a movement,* Boyd exclaimed that hip hop is "a social movement in and of itself" (16). Moreover, hip hop culture is "for all intents and purposes a modern-day social movement that forces us to redefine what we would normally allow as acceptable" with regard to popular music, popular culture, politics, and social struggle (18). Which is to say, the Hip Hop Movement, similar to the Black Power Movement in relationship to the Civil Rights Movement, extends and expands the African American movement tradition even as it obviously grows out of both the breakthroughs and setbacks of the Civil Rights Movement and Black Power Movement. Hence, instead of standing outside of the orbit of African American social movement history, the Hip Hop Movement—again, much like the Black Power Movement, as well as the Black Arts Movement and Black Women's Liberation Movement—is part of a post-Civil Rights Movement tradition of African American social, political, and cultural movements that have "remixed," if you will, conventional conceptions of African American popular movements by placing issues revolving around culture, education, women's rights, homosexual rights, prisoner's rights, animal rights, environmental rights, sexuality, and spirituality right alongside traditional issues surrounding racism, civil rights, social justice, American democracy, and poverty.

Similar to Boyd, in *Somebody Scream!: Rap Music's Rise to Prominence in the Aftershock of Black Power* (2008), Marcus Reeves argued that hip hop is a "community-based cultural movement" (ix). In the chapter titled "The New Afro-Urban Movement," Reeves briefly detailed the early history of hip hop with a focus on "old school" rap (21–37). Essentially covering rap music's roots in soul, funk, punk, disco, and electro, the chapter broadly sketched early rap history between 1975 and 1982 before giving way to a discussion of how early rappers such as the Sugarhill Gang, Kurtis Blow, the Funky 4 + 1, Afrika Bambaataa, and Grandmaster Flash and the Furious Five evolved rap from a "partycentric" music to a "streetcentric" or "ghettocentric" form of "anti-disco" and pro-black ghetto youth music that was "made to be *heard* more than for dancing" (22–25, 36, emphasis in original). As with Watkins and Boyd above, Reeves believes that rap music and hip hop culture are representative of both a "black musical revolution" *and* a "new Afro-urban movement" (35).

Obviously, then, over the last two decades many hip hop scholars have hinted at a Hip Hop Movement, but curiously none has yet to fully explore the origins and evolution of the Hip Hop Movement or what the movement's various popular musics (e.g., rap, neo-soul, and other forms of hip hop music) tell us about its distinct post-Civil Rights Movement and post-Black Power Movement popular culture, politics, and social justice agenda.[4] It is one thing to make passing mention of a "Hip Hop Movement" and wholly another thing to map the movement, chart its changes, and chronicle its roots, not merely in previous black popular movements, but also in previous black popular musics and black popular cultures. The Hip Hop Movement challenges conventional conceptions of black popular movements in light of the fact that it is simultaneously a sociopolitical movement *and* a musical movement, as it embodies both hip hop's politics *and* hip hop's aesthetics.

The five "remixes" (as opposed to chapters) to follow offer a critical theory and alternative history of rap music and hip hop culture by examining their roots in the popular musics and popular cultures of the Civil Rights Movement and the Black Power Movement. Moreover, the subsequent "remixes" reveal that black popular music and black popular culture have always been more than merely "popular music" and "popular culture" in the conventional sense and most often reflect a broader social, political, and cultural movement. For example, the spirituals registered African American protest during enslavement, the blues revealed African American desperation and resistance during the Reconstruction and post-Reconstruction years, and ragtime and jazz expressed the "New Negro" ethos during the New Negro Movement and Harlem Renaissance era.

As the ensuing "remixes" will reveal, the soundtracks of the Civil Rights Movement and Black Power Movement often tell us as much about these movements as their most eloquent leaders and participants. And, for those who might balk at the assertion that music can illustrate as much about a movement as its leaders, participants, and other more political and cultural artifacts should bear in mind Ron Eyerman and Andrew Jamison's contentions in "Social Movements and Cultural Transformation: Popular Music in the 1960s" (1995), where they stated, "In the 1960s songs contributed to a political movement, and were often performed at political demonstrations and collective festivals. Singers and songs were central to the cognitive praxis of these social movements, indeed, they may be central to all social movements in their formative stages" (451). Eyerman and Jamison continued, "During the early to mid-1960s the collective identity of what was then called The Movement was articulated not merely through organizations or even mass demonstrations, although there were plenty of both, but perhaps even more significantly through popular music. Movement ideas, images and feelings were disseminated in and through popular music and, at the same time, the movements of the times influenced developments, both in form and content, in popular music" (452).

The Hip Hop Movement remixes the history of hip hop by using Eyerman and Jamison's methodology and examining the ways in which rappers and neo-soulsters, among others, contribute to the "cognitive praxis" or, rather, the ideas *and* actions of the Hip Hop Movement, which are expressed through more than merely rap music, but also the broader popular culture, politics, and micro-movements that rap emerges from. Similar to 1960s singer-songwriters, rappers contribute to a social, political, and cultural movement, and "often perform . . . at political demonstrations and collective festivals" (e.g., the Million Man March, the Million Woman March, the Millennial Anti-War Movement, Hurricane Katrina relief efforts, Haitian earthquake relief efforts, the Occupy Wall Street Movement, etc.). Indeed, many would argue that rap music, perhaps more than any other aspect of hip hop culture, helped to popularize the politics and social justice agendas of the Hip Hop Movement, and that as with "The Movement" of the 1960s hip hoppers' collective identity, politics, and social agendas are "articulated not merely through organizations or even mass demonstrations, although there [have been] plenty of both, but perhaps even more significantly through popular music." Moreover, as with "The Movement" of the 1960s, the Hip Hop Movement's "ideas, images and feelings were disseminated in and through popular music and, at the same time, the movements of the times influenced developments, both in form and content," in hip hop music.

Where Eyerman and Jamison mostly focus on (ostensibly white) folk and rock music as expressions of "The Movement" of the 1960s, here my work focuses on the ways in which post-World War II black popular music not only reflected the politics and social justice agendas of post-World War II black popular movements, but also laid the foundation for the unrivaled relationship between rap music and the Hip Hop Movement. As Keli Goff argued in *Party Crashing: How the Hip Hop Generation Declared Political Independence* (2008), "Every generation is defined by something. For Americans born at the turn of the twentieth century, it was World War I. For their children, it was the Great Depression and World War II. And for their children's children—baby boomers—it was Vietnam, Watergate, and of course, the Civil Rights Movement" (11).

For African Americans born at the turn of the twenty-first century Reagan, Bush, Clinton, Bush Jr., the war on the poor, the war on drugs, the war on terrorism, gang violence, crack cocaine, police brutality, the rise of the prison industrial complex, the Rodney King beating, the O.J. Simpson trail, the Million Man March, the Million Woman March, the lynching of James Byrd, the murder of Amadou Diallo, and the callousness surrounding Hurricane Katrina, among many others, all helped to define the Hip Hop Generation. And, as will be witnessed in "remixes" 1 through 4, just as classic rhythm & blues and rock & roll represented the "cognitive praxis" of the Civil Rights Movement, and just as classic soul and funk registered the "cognitive praxis" of the Black Power Movement, rap, neo-soul, and other forms of hip hop music embody the "cognitive praxis" of the Hip Hop Movement. Although, I would be one of the first to admit that the Hip Hop Movement is as similar to the Civil Rights Movement and Black Power Movement as it is distinctly dissimilar to these movements in light of the fact that it is *a new, post-Civil Rights Movement and post-Black Power Movement form of black popular culture and black popular music-based politics and social movement.*

As will be discussed in greater detail in "remix" 5, in the most unprecedented manner imaginable, the Hip Hop Movement inverts *the black popular*

music-as-an-outgrowth-of-the-black popular movement tradition and, perhaps, starts a new tradition, a new form of politics and social movement
where future black popular movements may in fact spring from the alienation, cultural crises, political expressions, and social visions conveyed in
black popular music in particular, and black popular culture in general. Commenting on the distinct historical, cultural, legal, social, and political elements that have defined or, rather, radically redefined the Hip Hop Generation, Goff insightfully explained:

> Unlike previous generations that were defined by one or two major cultural
> touchstones, the post-Civil Rights Generation cannot point to a single unifying
> experience. Instead, it has been shaped by a variety of cultural landmarks,
> some triumphant, others tragic: the war on drugs, the war in Iraq, 9/11, the rise
> of hip hop, the rise of Oprah, the deaths of Tupac and Biggie, and the presiden-
> tial campaigns of Jesse Jackson and Barack Obama. What it has not experi-
> enced is legal segregation. This single fact has had a profound impact on the
> way the post-Civil Rights Generation views politics. . . . Post-Civil Rights
> black Americans are not defined by a universal social and political cause or
> movement as their parents and grandparents once were. Despite the best ef-
> forts of political strategists and the media to pigeonhole them, younger black
> Americans are staking out their own social and political identities. (12–13)

When Goff wrote that post-Civil Rights Movement and post-Black Power
Movement African American youth "are not defined by a universal social
and political cause or movement as their parents and grandparents once
were," her words help to highlight the fact that the Hip Hop Movement
registers as both an African American movement *and* an unprecedented
*multicultural, multiracial, multinational, multilingual, and multireligious
multi-issue movement* (see "remix" 5). Indeed, the Hip Hop Movement is not
concerned with a single "universal social and political cause or movement,"
because it is preoccupied with myriad post-Civil Rights Movement, post-
Black Power Movement, post-Women's Liberation Movement, post-Lesbian, Gay, Bisexual & Transgender Liberation Movement, post-Marxist,
postmodern, and postcolonial issues that, in many senses, transgress and
transcend "old school" social movement models and political paradigms,
African American or otherwise. As the first black popular movement to
emerge in the aftermath of the Civil Rights Movement and Black Power
Movement, the Hip Hop Movement simultaneously builds on and breaks
with the politics and social justice agendas of the previous black popular
movements. In many ways following in the footsteps of the militants of the
Black Power Movement and Black Arts Movement, hip hoppers emphasize
the political nature of black popular culture in general, and black popular
music in particular. Hence, those who quickly quip that invoking a "Hip Hop
Movement" is quite simply "hogwash" should bear in mind that the Hip Hop

Generation is not the first generation of black youth to not only note the political nature of black popular culture, but also to earnestly attempt to use the politics and social visions embedded in black popular culture in the interest of cultural criticism, political activism, and social (re)organization.[5]

RAP AND THE AFRICAN AMERICAN MOVEMENT MUSIC TRADITION

Over the last decade or so, there has been a great deal of discussion concerning rap music's connections to post-World War II forms of black popular music.[6] There have been scholarly studies of rap music's poetics, as well as several books centered around the "politics of rap music" or, rather, "rap music's politics."[7] Additionally, there have been studies that have examined the ways in which rap helped to revitalize the music industry at the end of the twentieth century, and other studies that have explored how certain forms of rap express regional culture, politics, and musical trends.[8] In spite of these very often innovative studies, most work within the world of hip hop studies seems to only superficially treat the wider historical, cultural, social, political, economic, and aesthetic contexts from which rap music initially and more directly emerged.

Even in light of all of its sonic, semantic, and social innovations, it is important to point to rap's musical and other aesthetic antecedents. Too often African American music is treated as though it exists outside of African American musical and other artistic traditions. This is not only unfortunate, it is extremely disingenuous, as it makes it seem as though each new form of black popular music is some sort of free-floating, "postmodern" sonic signifier, and not, as is most often the case, deeply connected to and undeniably indicative of the origins and evolution of African American musical history and culture. Therefore, in order to really and truly understand rap music much must be understood about the history, culture, and ongoing struggles of its primary producers: black ghetto youth in specific, and African Americans in general.

In often unrecognized ways, the origins and evolution of rap music have actually come to be treated or, rather, ill-treated much like African Americans—especially, black ghetto youth—in mainstream American history, culture, and society. To return to the theme of my previous volume, *Hip Hop's Amnesia*, there seems to be a serious *amnesia* surrounding the origins and evolution of rap music and the broader Hip Hop Movement that rap music reflects. Conceptually *amnesia*, which according to *Merriam-Webster's Dictionary* means "a partial or total loss of memory," offers us an interesting angle to revisit, reevaluate, and ultimately "remix" the origins and evolution of rap music and the Hip Hop Movement.

At this point it can be said with little or no fanfare that most work in hip hop studies only anecdotally explores the origins and evolution of rap music and hip hop culture. Consequently, hip hop studies stands in need of serious scholarly works that transcend the anecdotal and critically engage not only hip hop's musical history, but also its intellectual, cultural, social, and political history. If, as most hip hop studies scholars concede, rap music reflects more than merely the angst and ill will of post-Civil Rights Movement black ghetto youth and white suburban youth, among many other youths, then a study that treats rap music as a reflection of the Hip Hop Generation's—however "politically incorrect"—politics and social justice agenda is sorely needed. *The Hip Hop Movement* was researched, written, *and* remixed specifically with this dire need in mind.[9]

However, it should be sternly stated at the outset, *The Hip Hop Movement* is not merely about the ways that rap music reflects the Hip Hop Generation's politics and social justice agendas. As the sequel to *Hip Hop's Amnesia*, it is also a book about the *amnesia* surrounding the ways in which rap and other forms of hip hop music (e.g., neo-soul, reggaeton, gangsta rap, rock rap, metal rap, punk rap, rapcore, glitch hop, trip hop, krunk, snap music, and wonky music) builds on Civil Rights Movement and Black Power Movement popular music and popular culture. In *Rap Music and the Poetics of Identity* (2000), Adam Krims asserted that a full-length study of hip hop culture that "theorize[s] its embeddedness or expressive value within African American traditions" would be "eminently worth while" and a much-needed contribution to the literature on hip hop culture and rap music (2). But, he wrote, *Rap Music and the Poetics of Identity* "does not attempt to fill that gap" in hip hop studies. Hence, *The Hip Hop Movement* is not just another book about rap music and hip hop culture in some isolated, ahistorical, and apolitical sense, but arguably one of the first book-length studies to critically explore the musical, historical, cultural, social, and political roots of rap music and hip hop culture, which—as will be illustrated in the "remixes" to follow—unrepentantly, even if often unwittingly, reaches back to Civil Rights Movement and Black Power Movement politics, popular music, and popular culture.

Rap and other genres of hip hop music are based and ultimately build on earlier forms of *African American movement music*. Therefore, in order to really and truly understand rap and other forms of hip hop music—let alone whether there really is such a thing as *the Hip Hop Movement* currently underway—we must critically examine both the African American musics and the African American movements that these musics served as soundtracks for. This study will be primarily preoccupied with the ways in which post-World War II black popular music and black popular culture frequently served as a soundtrack for and reflected the populist politics of post-World War II African American social and political movements. Where many hip hop studies scholars have made clever allusions to the ways in which rap music and hip hop culture are connected to and seem to innovatively evolve previous forms of black popular music and black popular culture, *The Hip Hop Movement* moves beyond anecdotes and witty allusions and earnestly endeavors a full-fledged critical examination and reevaluation of *hip hop's inheritance* from the major African American musics *and* movements roughly between 1945 and 1980.

It is generally accepted that black popular music and black popular culture frequently reflect the conservatism *and* radicalism, the moderatism *and* militantism of the major African American movement (or movements, plural) of the milieu in which they initially emerged. Bearing this in mind, *The Hip Hop Movement* critically explores how "old school" black popular music—such as classic rhythm & blues, rock & roll, soul and funk, essentially from the end of World War II through to the emergence of rap music—were more or less *movement musics*. Which is to say, classic rhythm & blues, rock & roll, soul, and funk literally mirrored and served as mouthpieces for the Civil Rights Movement and Black Power Movement. Where *Hip Hop's Amnesia* examined classic blues, ragtime, and jazz, as well as the correlate African American sociopolitical movements that correspond with each of these classical black popular musics, *The Hip Hop Movement* will explore classic rhythm & blues, rock & roll, soul and funk, as well as the correlate African American sociopolitical movements that correspond with each of these more modern black popular musics.

There is, indeed, a serious need for more historically rooted, culturally relevant, and politically radical research within the world of hip hop studies. Too often fans and critics listen to, speak of, and write about rap music and hip hop culture as though contemporary black popular music and contemporary black popular culture are not in any way connected to a historical and cultural continuum that can be easily traced back to the black popular music and black popular culture of the Civil Rights Movement and Black Power Movement. Building on the sociology of music and politics of music-centered epistemologies and methodologies developed by Jon Michael Spencer (1990, 1996), Ron Eyerman and Andrew Jamison (1991, 1995, 1998), Nathan Davis (1996), Mark Mattern (1998), Murray Forman and Mark Anthony Neal (2004, 2011), Mellonee Burnim and Portia Maultsby (2006, 2012), Ian Peddie (2006), Courtney Brown (2008), William Banfield (2010), and William Roy (2010), *The Hip Hop Movement* is a study about music *and* sociopolitical movements, aesthetics *and* politics, as well as the ways in which African Americans' unique history, culture, and struggles have consistently led them to create musics that have served as the soundtracks or, more or less, the *mouthpieces* for their sociopolitical aspirations and frustrations, their sociopolitical organizations and micro-movements.

Obviously at this point many of my readers may be asking themselves a couple questions: "But, does rap music really reflect a movement? If there is really and truly such a thing as a 'Hip Hop Movement,' how come I haven't heard of it before? And, can a movement have sexist, heterosexist, or bourgeois elements and still be considered a movement?"

It is these questions that lie at the heart of this book, and which have burned and bothered me longer than I care to remember. It should be stated openly and outright: These are very valid questions. Indeed, they are critical questions that I am sincerely seeking to ask my generation, the so-called "Hip Hop Generation," throughout the following pages of this book. In a nutshell, what I have come to call the "Hip Hop Movement" actually does not rotely resemble any previous African American social and political movement. But, by the time my readers get to the fifth and final "remix" of this book they will see that, yet and still, there is a Hip Hop Movement afoot. As will be revealed in the five "remixes" to follow, truth be told, historic African American social and political movements are neither all identical nor have they all had the exact same goals. Rapid and radical changes in "mainstream" American history, culture, politics, economics, and society have made it such that there are great and often grave differences between successive generations of African Americans, including their overarching aspirations and frustrations. [10]

The Hip Hop Movement argues that many of these "great and often grave differences" are easily observed in the history of black popular music and black popular culture, and that, even more, black popular music and black popular culture are often incomprehensible without some sort of working knowledge of historic African American social and political movements. Taking this line of logic even further, *The Hip Hop Movement* contends that neither *hip hop's aesthetics* nor *hip hop's politics* can be adequately comprehended without some sort of working knowledge of historic African American social and political movements. Ultimately, then, this book, being a sequel to both *Hip Hop's Inheritance* and *Hip Hop's Amnesia*, is about "partial or total loss of memory" or, rather, *what has been forgotten but should be remembered* concerning the "old school" origins and evolution of rap music and the Hip Hop Movement.

However, *The Hip Hop Movement* is not simply about "hip hop's inheritance" and "hip hop's amnesia"—à la my previous volumes. It is also about what has not been "inherited" by, and the other forms of "amnesia" surrounding rap music and hip hop culture. It is a study about the Hip Hop Generation's "partial or total loss of memory" in terms of previous African American musics and movements, but also, and equally important here, it is a study about what hip hoppers' grandparents and parents have forgotten but should remember about previous African American musics and movements in relationship to the origins and evolution of rap music and hip hop culture.

In so many words it could and, perhaps, *should* be said that rap music and hip hop culture's real "old school" roots have been routinely overlooked largely in favor of 1980-onward examinations of black popular music and black popular culture. But, in many senses, the Hip Hop Movement and its various soundtracks represent a sometimes politically correct and socially acceptable rearticulation of the views and values of the Civil Rights Movement and Black Power Movement, and at other times it represents a sometimes politically incorrect and socially unacceptable remix or outright rejection of the views and values of the Civil Rights Movement and Black Power Movement.

THE HIP HOP MOVEMENT MIXTAPE MANIFESTO: ON THE FIVE REMIXES OF RAP MUSIC AND HIP HOP CULTURE TO FOLLOW

In lieu of "chapters" I have chosen to offer, quite literally, "remixes" of hip hop history and culture in the series of studies to follow. Opting for "remixes" instead of "chapters" speaks to the special efforts and intellectual labor-filled lengths I have gone through to really and truly make a contribution to the interdisciplinary and intersectional field of hip hop studies. From my point of view, hip hop studies is a wide-ranging and wide-reaching field of critical inquiry where contemporary black popular music and contemporary black popular culture are conceived of as "text" and (re)situated and (re)interpreted within the wider "context" of, first and foremost, African American and African diasporan history, culture, aesthetics, politics, and economics, and then ultimately broader national and international history, culture, aesthetics, politics, and economics.

Hence, within the world of hip hop studies, black popular music and black popular culture can be said to represent what Michel Foucault (1980, 81) called "an insurrection of subjugated knowledges," which he defined as ways of thinking and doing that have been eclipsed, devalued, or rendered invisible within the dominant institutions of power/knowledge, but which nonetheless counter, disrupt, and provide progressive alternatives to the dominant institutions of power/knowledge. It is important to emphasize, however, that Foucault's concept of "subjugated knowledges" actually has two distinct meanings:

> By subjugated knowledges I mean two things: on the one hand, I am referring to the historical contents that have been buried and disguised in a functionalist coherence or formal systemization. Concretely, it is not a semiology of the life of the asylum, it is not even a sociology of delinquency, that has made it possible to produce an effective criticism of the asylum and likewise of the prison, but rather the immediate emergence of historical contents. And this is simply because only the historical contents allow us to rediscover the ruptural effects of conflict and struggle that the order imposed by functionalist or

systematizing thought is designed to mask. Subjugated knowledges are thus
those blocs of historical knowledge which were present but disguised within
the body of functionalist and systematizing theory and which criticism—which
obviously draws upon scholarship—has been able to reveal. (81–82)

Here I wish to transpose Foucault's concept of "subjugated knowledges" and
apply it to rap music and hip hop culture in an effort to chronicle and clarify
the Hip Hop Movement's history, politics, and social justice agendas. Hence,
when Foucault contended that "only the historical contents allow us to rediscover the ruptural effects of conflict and struggle that the order imposed by
functionalist or systematizing thought is designed to mask," there is a sense
in which more nuanced and alternative histories of hip hop that "allow us to
rediscover the ruptural effects of conflict and struggle" within hip hop history and culture will enable us to move away from the "order imposed by
functionalist [commercial rap music-centered] or systematizing [commercial
hip hop culture-centered] thought is designed to mask." "Subjugate knowledges" within the world of hip hop are essentially "those blocs of historical
knowledge" which historically have been and remain "present but disguised"
and buried beneath the conventional histories of rap music and hip hop
culture, most of which have been and remain, for the most part, Eurocentric,
bourgeois, hyper-masculinist, and hyper-heteronormative, among others.

     All of this is to say that Foucault's double-sided concept of "subjugated
knowledges" is applicable to hip hop studies. And, in many senses, the
concept allows hip hop historians and hip hop critical social theorists to paint
a more detailed and discursively dense picture of the history, politics, and
aesthetics of rap music and hip hop culture because of its focus on forgotten,
uninherited, or outright erased aspects of marginalized hip hop communities'
thoughts and practices. The quotation above, however, is only one side of
Foucault's double-sided concept of "subjugated knowledges." He further explained:

> On the other hand, I believe that by subjugated knowledges one should under-
> stand something else, something which in a sense is altogether different,
> namely, a whole set of knowledges that have been disqualified as inadequate
> to their task or insufficiently elaborated: naïve knowledges, located low down
> on the hierarchy, beneath the required level of cognition or scientificity. I also
> believe that it is through the re-emergence of these low-ranking knowledges,
> these unqualified, even directly disqualified knowledges (such as that of the
> psychiatric patient, of the ill person, of the nurse, of the doctor—parallel and
> marginal as they are to the knowledge of medicine—that of the delinquent,
> etc.), and which involve what I would call a popular knowledge *(le savoir des
> gens)* though it is far from being a general commonsense knowledge, but is on
> the contrary a particular, local, regional knowledge, a differential knowledge
> incapable of unanimity and which owes its force only to the harshness with
> which it is opposed by everything surrounding it—that it is through the re-

appearance of this knowledge, of these local popular knowledges, these disqualified knowledges, that criticism performs its work. (82)

This book seeks to highlight and historize "a whole set of knowledges that
have been disqualified as inadequate to their task or insufficiently elaborated" within the world of hip hop studies and within the wider society. It seeks
to chronicle and, at times, critique, the "naïve knowledges, located low down
on the hierarchy, beneath the required level of cognition or scientificity" and
accepted hip hop history that emanate from rap music and hip hop culture's
roots in the black popular music, black popular culture, and black popular
movements that occurred between 1945 and 1980. The emphasis here, then,
is on the "parallel and marginal" histories and knowledges that have been
and remain at the heart of the history of rap music and hip hop culture, but
which have been hidden as a consequence of ahistorical, apolitical, Eurocentric, bourgeois, hyper-masculinist, and hyper-heteronormative, among other,
interpretations of rap music and hip hop culture.

In other words, *The Hip Hop Movement* seeks to set afoot a new version
of hip hop history and cultural criticism that is grounded in black popular
music, black popular culture, and black popular movement-based "popular
knowledges" that break through the borders and boundaries of Eurocentric,
bourgeois, hyper-masculinist, and hyper-heteronormative, among other,
forms of power, knowledge, and history. It aims to articulate a new, hip hop-
inspired "popular knowledge," a "particular, local, regional knowledge, a
differential knowledge incapable of unanimity and which owes its force only
to the harshness with which it is opposed by everything surrounding it." It is
through the reemergence of these new, hip hop-inspired "popular knowledges," these "parallel and marginal," "local [hip hop-based] popular knowledges, these disqualified knowledges," that *The Hip Hop Movement* ultimately advances an alternative history and critical theory of rap music, hip hop
culture, and the Hip Hop Movement. [11]

When black popular music and black popular culture are conceived of as
"subjugated knowledge" and "cognitive praxis" (as Eyerman and Jamison
emphasized above), then it is possible to perceive the ways that they historically have and currently continue to indelibly influence and inform race
relations, gender identity, sexual politics, class struggles, cultural conventions, social views, and broader political values. Revealingly, black popular
music and black popular culture are often relegated to the realm of "low
culture" (as opposed to "high culture"), which means they are frequently
overlooked and, accordingly, underscrutinized as "serious" sites of historical,
cultural, social, and political study. This lame line of logic also overlooks the
fact that black popular music and black popular culture, in their own sometimes warped and sometimes wicked ways, represent distinct sites of ideological and counter-ideological production, articulation, and contestation.

Hence, the five "remixes" of hip hop history and culture to follow aim to critically engage the ideological and counter-ideological currents and under-currents deeply embedded in Civil Rights Movement and Black Power Movement popular music and popular culture that have been, however un-heralded, handed down to rap music, hip hop culture, and the broader Hip Hop Movement.

To conceptually focus on *interdisciplinary and intersectional "remixes" of hip hop history and culture*, as opposed to taking a more musicological, monodisciplinary, and single-subject book-based approach to hip hop stud-ies, also enables me to illustrate the incredible intellectual depth and wide reach of rap music and hip hop culture's contributions to contemporary histo-ry, culture, aesthetics, politics, and society. At this point hip hop studies' interdisciplinary and intersectional emphasis is undeniably and rather easily detected in its use of myriad "remixed" epistemologies and methodologies from disciplines as far afield and far flung as: American studies; African American studies; women's studies; sexuality studies; critical race studies; cultural studies; postmodern studies; postcolonial studies; popular culture studies; and, of course, popular music studies—as well as more conventional disciplines such as: sociology; psychology; anthropology; history; philoso-phy; religion; political science; economics; linguistics; comparative litera-ture; communications; education; and, of course, musicology, among many others.

By the sheer fact of its ever-increasing cultural and sociopolitical impact over the last three decades, rap music and hip hop culture have proven to be much more than a passing postmodern cultural copycat or an erstwhile intel-lectual fad. As the "remixes" to follow will illustrate, the best hip hop intel-lectuals, artists, and activists are as adept at critiquing its flows and flaws as many of the most astute aficionados and entrants in other areas of critical, cultural, musical, or aesthetic inquiry. Moreover, as hip hop studies enters a new phase and heightens its critical acumen—which is to say, as it matures and moves to expand in new directions, as it discursively deepens and devel-ops even more extensive areas of investigation and interrogation—hip hop scholars and students must grapple with and seek to seriously grasp the multidimensionality and mayhem, serious contributions and controversies of not merely rap music and hip hop culture, but the wider Hip Hop Movement.

In other words, hip hop scholarship—as opposed to either uncritical "hip hop cheerleading" or hard-core "hip hop hateration"—must do a much better job of conceptually capturing, critically reflecting, and frequently refracting the music, aesthetics, politics, and culture it aims to interrogate—critique and/or appreciate. Hip hop scholarship should always and everywhere have the very same characteristics as the most exemplary rap music and hip hop culture: poetic license; loaded-language and value-laden lyrics; marvelous sense of melody; irresistible trunk-rattling rhythms; head-bobbing beats; sophisticated yet soulful samples; and a kind of *aural alchemy* or, rather, *musical magic* that inspires its listeners/readers to want more and more and to often place themselves within the world of the text. In a sense, more than anything else *The Hip Hop Movement* is emblematic of my ongoing efforts to bring some of the word wizardry, rhetorical acrobatics, aural innovation, and sonic experimentation of rap music and hip hop culture to the American academy, if not ultimately to the institutions of power/knowledge (à la Foucault) nationally and internationally.

The Hip Hop Movement is also emblematic of my ongoing efforts to wrestle with the creative cultural and political expressions of very often degraded, if not outright dehumanized and *de-Africanized*, past and present black ghetto youth. As a matter of fact, it could be said that this is a book about denigrated and much-misunderstood black ghetto youth—again, past and present—who have "knuckled and brawled" (to borrow a favorite phrase from the rhetorical genius Black Thought of the Roots) to have their long-muted and long-disregarded voices heard, views acknowledged, and values taken seriously, both intra-racially and inter-racially, as well as nationally and internationally.[12] Bearing this in mind, in the five "remixes" to follow my readers may detect that I am up to much more than merely making connections between classic rhythm & blues and "old school" rap, classic rock & roll and rock rap, classic soul and neo-soul, and classic funk and G-funk (i.e., "ghetto funk" or "gangsta funk").

There is admittedly, then, a deep sociopolitical dimension to this book, as each of the aforementioned musics will be "remixed" and (re)placed within the wider historical, cultural, social, and political contexts within which they initially emerged. Ultimately, this means that I will resituate and reinterpret these musics within the wider contexts of the sociopolitical movements they originally served as soundtracks or "mouthpieces" for. In this sense, I would like to openly acknowledge that I have several ulterior motives in the five "remixes" to follow: to expose and explore the "old school," Civil Rights Movement and Black Power Movement roots of rap music, hip hop culture, and the Hip Hop Movement; to examine African American femininity, masculinity, gender relations, sexual politics, cultural crises, and class struggles within the context of Civil Rights Movement and Black Power Movement popular music, popular culture, aesthetics, politics, and social activism in relationship to rap music, hip hop culture, and the Hip Hop Movement; to accent and amplify the unprecedented interracial alliances between African American and European American intellectual-artist-activists in Civil Rights Movement and post-Civil Rights Movement America; and, finally, to emphasize rap music and hip hop culture as "mouthpieces" for, and creative cultural expressions of the major post-Civil Rights Movement *multicultural, multiracial, multinational, multilingual, and multireligious multi-issue movement* of our era—*the Hip Hop Movement.*

In the five "remixes" that constitute the core of this text I seek to offer an intellectual-activist's version of a hip hop "mixtape"—à la Michael Eric Dyson (2007), Kevin Driscoll (2009), and Jared Ball (2005, 2009, 2011). However, what decidedly distinguishes my "mixtape manifesto"—to build on Ball's brilliant work—is that *The Hip Hop Movement* unerringly focuses on Civil Rights Movement and Black Power Movement popular music, popular culture, aesthetics, politics, and social activism in relationship to rap music, hip hop culture, and the Hip Hop Movement. Where the aforementioned works took a more or less theoretical and thematic angle in offering their intellectual-activist versions of a hip hop mixtape, *The Hip Hop Movement* endeavors a historical, sociological, political, musicological, and critical theoretical approach that, literally, highlights what rap music, hip hop culture, and the Hip Hop Movement—either directly or indirectly—"inherited" from Civil Rights Movement and Black Power Movement popular music, popular culture, aesthetics, politics, and social activism. [13]

As is well known, an authentic hip hop mixtape always and everywhere reflects the musical tastes and, to a certain extent, the political or even apolitical attitude of its compiler or, rather, its "mix-master," as we say in hip hop lingo. A hip hop mixtape can be a randomly selected compilation of the latest hot rap songs, or it can be a deeply contemplated conceptual mix of a wide range of songs—rap, classic soul, neo-soul, funk, jazz, blues, gospel, reggae, and rock, among other, songs—that are lyrically linked by a specific motif or mood. Recently, major rap artists, especially many of the more commercially successful rappers, have controversially used the mixtape format to release either more sordid or more sociopolitically conscious music that their more "mainstream" and pop chart-obsessed record labels have either passed on or do not want to be linked to—for instance: 50 Cent's *50 Cent is the Future* (2002) and *Automatic Gunfire* (2003); T.I.'s *Down with the King* (2004); Chamillionaire's *Mixtape Messiah* (2004); Talib Kweli's *Right About Now!* (2005); Young Jeezy's *Trap Or Die* (2005); 50 Cent's *Bullet Proof* (2005); Lil' Wayne's *Dedication* (2006); Little Brother's *Separate But Equal* (2006); Talib Kweli's *Liberation!* (2006); T.I.'s *The Leak* (2006); Drake's *Room for Improvement* (2006); Jay-Z's *An American Gangster Mixtape* (2007); Lil' Wayne's *Dedication 2* (2007), *Lyrical Homocide* (2007), *The Carter Files* (2007), and *New Orleans Millionaire* (2007); J. Cole's *The Come Up* (2007); Drake's *Comeback Season* (2007); Little Brother's *And Justice For All* (2008); Lil' Wayne's *Dedication 3* (2008), *The Carter Show* (2008), *It's Weezy Baby!* (2008), and *The Greatest Rapper Alive* (2008); Jay-Z's *A Prelude to Blueprint 3* (2009); J. Cole's *The Warm Up* (2009); Drake's *So Far Gone* (2009); T.I.'s *A Year & A Day* (2009); Jay-Z's *Creative Control* (2010); J. Cole's *Friday Night Lights* (2010); 50 Cent's *The Big 10* (2011) and *The Lost Tape* (2012); and Rick Ross's *Ashes to Ashes* (2010) and *Rich Forever* (2012).

In keeping with most aspects of rap music and hip hop culture, mixtapes are usually intensely personal and nothing if not revelatory manifestos specifically tailored to the tape's intended individual recipient or target audience. Hence, in "The Digital Mixtape Comes of Age" (2006), music critic Michael Resnick quoted the Library of America's editor in chief, Geoffrey O'Brien, as saying that the mixtape is "the most widely practiced American art form." With *The Hip Hop Movement* I seek to humbly share my mixtape manifesto about the real "old school" roots of rap music, hip hop culture, and the Hip Hop Movement; about the connections between classic rhythm & blues, rock & roll, soul, funk and rap; and, about the connections between the Civil Rights Movement, Black Power Movement, and Hip Hop Movement. The five extended "remixes" that constitute *The Hip Hop Movement*, therefore, seek to translate the energy and excitement, the contradictions and outright courting of controversy in rap music and hip hop culture's commercial, gangsta, political, alternative, and underground communities into book form, placing rap-styled remixes and homespun hip hop-inspired alternative histories, critical theories, and counter-narratives between the covers of a book and in the hands of the Hip Hop Generation.

As Russell Potter revealed in *Spectacular Vernaculars: Hip Hop and the Politics of Postmodernism* (1995), "[h]ip hop audiences do not, at any rate, merely *listen*—passive reception is no longer possible" (108, emphasis in original). The "remixes" of hip hop history and culture offered in *The Hip Hop Movement* are aimed at disrupting the long-standing amnesia-filled relationship most hip hop fans and critics have with the real "old school" roots of rap music and hip hop culture, especially Civil Rights Movement and Black Power Movement popular music, popular culture, aesthetics, politics, and social activism. If, indeed, "passive reception [of rap and other hip hop music] is no longer possible," then I would like to bring some of the same (pro)active ethos and intellectually assertive energy into the field of hip hop studies, where it is still very possible to passively claim to love rap music but actively hate black ghetto youth; where it remains possible to passively claim to love your mother and grandmother but actively hate your "baby-mama," girlfriend, or seemingly all hip hop women because they are perceived to be "skeezers," "hood rats," and "gold diggers"; and, finally, where it is still possible to passively claim to love *all* people but openly and assertively hate homosexuals.

Potter contended that "[h]ip hop itself is not merely *music* (though it is certainly that)," but even more, in a certain sense, hip hop is a novel kind of "cultural recycling center" (108, emphasis in original). Well, in a nutshell, *The Hip Hop Movement* is about the specific aspects of Civil Rights Movement and Black Power Movement popular music, popular culture, aesthetics, politics, and social activism that historically have been and currently continue to be radically "recycled" and "remixed" by rap music, hip hop culture, and the Hip Hop Movement. In keeping with the hip hop mixtape motif, the five "remixes" to follow offer alternative histories and critical theories of the "old school" roots of rap music and hip hop culture, classic rhythm & blues, rock & roll and the Civil Rights Movement, and classic soul, funk and the Black Power Movement in relationship to rap, other hip hop music, hip hop culture, and ultimately the Hip Hop Movement. Indeed, the real power of these "remixes" will hit home and be heartfelt only if my readers have a clear sense of what is at stake in each of the subsequent aural and intellectual excursions. Hence, here I will briefly outline the five "remixes" to follow.

Essentially divided into three parts that treat the two major forms of black popular music that serve as soundtracks for the Civil Rights Movement (i.e., classic rhythm & blues and rock & roll), the Black Power Movement (i.e., classic soul and funk), and the Hip Hop Movement (i.e., rap and neo-soul), *The Hip Hop Movement*'s five "remixes," literally, seek to *remix* the history of rap music and hip hop culture. "Part I," "The Soundtracks of the Civil Rights Movement, 1945–1965," features "remixes" 1 and 2. The first "remix," "Rhythm and Blues: From Classic Rhythm & Blues to Rap's Beats and Rhymes," will examine the ways in which the emergence of rhythm & blues after World War II, in many senses, paralleled the emergence of "old school" rap and early hip hop culture in the aftermath of the Black Power Movement. Returning to the notion that black popular music serves as a barometer in which to measure the cultural, social, and political climate in African America, in this "remix" classic rhythm & blues is explored as the black popular music mouthpiece of the Civil Rights Movement and the precursor of "old school" rap as the black popular music mouthpiece of the Hip Hop Movement. By (re)contextualizing classic rhythm & blues and (re)placing it within the social, political, cultural, and musical world(s) of its origins and early evolution we will be provided with new musical and extramusical "cognitive prax[es]" (à la Eyerman and Jamison's work) that will hopefully aid us in our efforts to historicize, decolonize, and repoliticize rap music, hip hop culture, and the Hip Hop Movement.

The second "remix," "Rock & Roll: From Classic Rock & Roll to Rock Rap," will explore the African American origins and evolution of rock & roll and rock rap. When and where we are willing to acknowledge that the Civil Rights Movement actually had two major popular music soundtracks, classic rhythm & blues *and* classic rock & roll, then and there it more clearly emerges as a model for the Hip Hop Movement, which also has two major popular music soundtracks, rap *and* neo-soul. Similar to the Civil Rights Movement, then, the Hip Hop Movement has an intra-cultural and African American-centered soundtrack, neo-soul and many of the more ghetto-centered forms of rap, and what could be seen as a more or less multicultural and white suburban youth-friendly soundtrack, commercial rap and pop rap, especially *rock rap*. Obviously the argument in "Part I" will not be that each and every form of rap or neo-soul conforms to classic rhythm & blues and classic rock & roll in relationship to the Civil Rights Movement, but that there are enough similarities between, for instance, classic rock & roll and commercial rap, especially rock rap, to make a case for critically engaging them as interracial arenas where black and white youths, among others, put forward messages and advanced ideals that have been not only informed by the Civil Rights Movement and the Hip Hop Movement, but in turn, even if only implicitly, have influenced the politics and aesthetics of these movements.

"Part II," "The Soundtracks of the Black Power Movement, 1965–1980" features "remixes" 3 and 4, which will treat classic soul and neo-soul, and classic funk and G-funk, respectively, as the "cognitive prax[es]" and cultural expressions of the Black Power Movement. More specifically, the third "remix," "Soul: From Classic Soul to Neo-Soul," surveys classic soul music as one of the major soundtracks of the Black Power Movement and the influence of both soul and the Black Power Movement on neo-soul, various forms of rap, and the Hip Hop Movement. Obviously classic soul has handed down a distinct aesthetic to neo-soul and, however unheralded, political rap as well. But, just what that aesthetic was and what it entailed, how it came to be and how it has influenced hip hoppers, is frequently glossed over.

The "soul aesthetic" was essentially the musical expression of the much-celebrated "black aesthetic" that was propagated by the members of the Black Arts Movement (e.g., Larry Neal, Amiri Baraka, Sonia Sanchez, Addison Gayle Jr., Nikki Giovanni, Hoyt Fuller, Maya Angelou, Haki Madhubuti, Gwendolyn Brooks, and Dudley Randall). However, most discussions of classic soul, even those that claim to be "scholarly," frequently fail to acknowledge and critically engage either the Black Arts Movement or the black aesthetic. What is more, there is a long-standing tendency to disassociate soul music's politics from the wider political world of the Black Power Movement. Similar to classic rhythm & blues in relationship to the Civil Rights Movement, soul expressed the lives, loves, losses, and struggles of African Americans during the Black Power Movement years. Because soul emerged at the intersection of two movements, the Black Power Movement *and* the Black Arts Movement, any serious analysis of soul music should situate it in the milieus of these movements, as well as connect the soul aesthetic with the broader black aesthetic. This "remix," therefore, strives to (re)contextualize soul in light of the aforementioned aesthetics and movements, as well as explore its contributions to neo-soul, alternative rap, and the Hip Hop Movement.

Growing out of the third "remix," the fourth "remix," "Funk: From P-Funk to G-Funk," investigates the origins and evolution of funk; its meaning, function, and significance for African Americans in the 1970s; and its enormous influence on the origins and evolution of rap music and hip hop culture.

Funk was audacious in its affirmation of post-Civil Rights Movement African American issues and ills, and was unapologetically aimed at working-class and poor black folk who were in desperate need of its expressions of both reality *and* fantasy. As one of the major foundations of rap, funk handed down more than most hip hoppers may realize, and it may not be going too far to suggest that rap cannot be adequately understood without a working knowledge of, not only funk's major figures (e.g., James Brown, Sly Stone, and George Clinton, etc.) and classic funk beats, but also the spiritual, sexual, cultural, social, and political messages that collectively permeate their music and that uniquely reflected the wider spiritual, sexual, cultural, social, and political world of African America in the 1970s.

"Part III," "The Soundtracks and Social Visions of the Hip Hop Movement, 1980–Present," features the final "remix," "The Hip Hop Movement: From Black Popular Music and Black Popular Culture To A Black Popular Movement," which brings the analyses of "remixes" 1 through 4 together and extends them to explore how rap music and hip hop culture articulate the—however sprawling and unconventional—politics and social visions of the Hip Hop Movement, what these politics and social visions tell us about the Hip Hop Generation and contemporary society, and how hip hoppers' unconventional politics and social visions over the last three and a half decades have been shaped by (even as they have undeniably shaped) the turn of the twenty-first century social, political, and cultural world. Perhaps one of the main reasons that rap music and the Hip Hop Movement's politics and social visions have been ignored and erased is because most social commentators, political analysts, and cultural critics have been surreptitiously, albeit eagerly, awaiting the second coming of the Civil Rights Movement and, similar to the Black Power Movement, the Hip Hop Movement has simply refused to play second fiddle and be forced to fit into the mold of previous black popular movements—no matter how great those previous movements and how much those movements may have inspired, even if often unwittingly, the Hip Hop Movement. Let us begin, then, by critically engaging rap music and the Hip Hop Movement's roots in and its "inheritance" from classic rhythm & blues and the Civil Rights Movement.

NOTES

1. For further discussion of James Weldon Johnson's life and legacy, "Lift Every Voice and Sing," and for the most noteworthy works that informed my interpretation here, see primary sources such as J.W. Johnson (1933, 2000, 2004), as well as important secondary sources such as Bond and Wilson (2000), Fleming (1987), Levy (1973), and Price and Oliver (1997).

2. My interpretation of the Frankfurt School has been informed by Bottomore (1984, 2002), Held (1980), Jay (1985, 1996), Kellner (1989, 1990a, 1990b, 1993), Tarr (2011), Wheatland (2009), and Wiggerhaus (1995). For further discussion of Max Horkheimer's life and critical theory, see primary sources such as Horkheimer (1972, 1974a, 1974b, 1978, 1993),

as well as secondary sources such as Abromeit (2011), Benhabib, Bonss, and McCole (1993), and Stirk (1992). And, for further discussion of Theodor Adorno's life and critical theory, see primary sources such as Adorno (1991, 1994, 1997, 2000), as well as secondary sources such as Huhn (2004), Müller-Doohm (2005), Schmidt (2007), and R. Wilson (2007). Because this book is equally *an alternative history of hip hop* and *a critical theory of hip hop*, it is unambiguously part of a larger intellectual archaeology project I have dubbed Africana Critical Theory (ACT), which emphasizes continental and diasporan African contributions to cultural criticism, radical politics, critical social theory, and progressive sociopolitical movements. This means, then, that it needs to be noted at the outset, and in agreement with David Held (1980, 14), "[c]ritical theory, it should be emphasized, does *not* form a unity; it does not mean the same thing to all its adherents" (emphasis in original). For instance, Steven Best and Douglas Kellner (1991, 33) employ the term "critical theory" in a general sense in their critique of postmodern theory, stating: "We are using 'critical theory' here in the general sense of critical social and cultural theory and not in the specific sense that refers to the critical theory of society developed by the Frankfurt School." Further, Raymond Morrow (1994, 6) has forwarded that the term *critical theory* "has its origins in the work of a group of German scholars [of Jewish descent] (collectively referred to as the *Frankfurt School*) in the 1920s who used the term initially (*Kritische Theorie* in German) to designate a specific approach to interpreting Marxist theory. But the term has taken on new meanings in the interim and can be neither exclusively identified with the Marxist tradition from which it has become increasingly distinct nor reserved exclusively to the Frankfurt School, given extensive new variations outside the original German context." Finally, in his study of Marx, Foucault, and Habermas's philosophies of history and contributions to critical theory, Steven Best (1995, xvii) uses the term *critical theory* "in the most general sense, designating simply a critical social theory, that is, a social theory critical of present forms of domination, injustice, coercion, and inequality." He, therefore, does not "limit the term to refer to only the Frankfurt School" (xvii). Ultimately this means that the term "critical theory" and the methods, presuppositions, and positions it has come to be associated with in the humanities and social sciences: (1) connotes and continues to exhibit an *epistemic openness* and style of radical cultural criticism that highlights and accents the historical alternatives and emancipatory possibilities of a specific age and/or sociocultural condition; (2) is not the exclusive domain of Eurocentric Marxists, neo-Marxists, post-Marxists, feminists, postfeminists, poststructuralists, postmodernists, and/or Habermasians; and, (3) can be radically reinterpreted and redefined to identify and encompass *classical and contemporary, continental and diasporan African praxis-promoting theory*. For further discussion of Africana critical theory of contemporary society, see Rabaka (2007, 2008, 2009, 2010a, 2010b, 2011, 2012, forthcoming).

3. Tellingly, a lot of the Hip Hop Movement's politics and social justice agendas have been informed by, not simply post-Civil Rights Movement racial politics but, more specifically, by post-affirmative action politics and ongoing institutional racism. For more detailed discussion of affirmative action and ongoing institutional racism, and for the most noteworthy works that informed my interpretation here, see T.H. Anderson (2004), Cahn (1995), Katznelson (2005), Kellough (2006), and Wise (2005).

4. In terms of other hip hop scholars who have hinted at or made reference to a "Hip Hop Movement," its politics and social justice agendas, see Alridge (2005), Bernard-Donals (1994), Clay (2006, 2012), Decker (1993), R. Jackson (1994), Kitwana (2002, 2004), Kun (2002), Shomari (1995), Stapleton (1998), L.Y. Sullivan (1997), and Trapp (2005).

5. For further, more detailed discussion of how the Hip Hop Generation not only note the political nature of black popular culture, but also earnestly attempt to use the politics and social visions embedded in black popular culture in the interest of cultural criticism, political activism, and social (re)organization, and for the most noteworthy works that informed my analysis here, see Dagbovie (2005, 2006), Ginwright (2004), Ogbar (2007), Spady, Alim, and Meghelli (2006), and Spady, Lee, and Alim (1999).

6. For examples of the hip hop scholarship that has explored the connections between rap and previous forms of black popular music, primarily jazz, rhythm & blues, and funk, see Bernard-Donals (1994), Demers (2003), Stewart and Duran (1999), J.B. Stewart (2005), Vincent (1996), and J. A. Williams (2010a, 2010b). Also, see the subsequent "remixes" 1 through

4, which correspond with the four major post-World World II and pre-rap forms of black popular music: rhythm & blues, rock & roll, soul, and funk, respectively.

7. For further discussion of rap music's poetics and politics, and for the most noteworthy works that informed my analysis here, see Bradley (2009), Hendershott (2004), Krims (2000), D.A. Murray (1998), Ogbar (2007), Pate (2010), I. Perry (2004), and Usher (2005).

8. For further discussion of the ways in which rap helped to revitalize the music industry at the end of the twentieth century, as well as the ways in which certain forms of rap express regional culture, politics, and musical trends, and for the most noteworthy works that informed my analysis here, see Basu and Lemelle (2006), Charnas (2010), Mitchell (2001), Negus (1999), Ogg (2001), and Watkins (2005).

9. It is important, here at the outset, to openly acknowledge that what we now call "hip hop" or "hip hop culture" initially had four fundamental elements, according to hip hop pioneer Afrika Bambaataa: MCing (i.e., "rapping"), DJing, break-dancing (i.e., "breaking"), and graffiti-writing (i.e., "writing"). According to Jeff Chang, in *Can't Stop Won't Stop: A History of the Hip Hop Generation* (2005), when hip hop "lost its way" Bambaataa ingeniously added a fifth fundamental element of hip hop culture: "knowledge" (90). It is extremely important, therefore, to acknowledge that instead of being "anti-intellectual," which is one of the common stereotypes about the Hip Hop Generation, one of the core elements of authentic hip hop culture is its emphasis on *the acquisition, production, and dissemination of knowledge*. Chang quoted Bambaataa as having stated that "real hip hop" is about having "right knowledge, right wisdom, right 'overstanding' and right sound reasoning—meaning that we want our people to deal with factuality versus beliefs, factology versus beliefs" (90). Although all five forms of the culture continue to survive today, in the early 1980s rap music, which synthesizes both MCing and DJing, entered into a love/hate relationship with corporate America and mainstream American popular culture (i.e., the American "culture industry" à la Horkheimer and Adorno's critical theory of the culture industry), effectively eclipsing break-dancing, graffiti-writing and, to a certain extent, the fifth fundamental element of "knowledge." In chapter 5 of my book *Hip Hop's Inheritance* I developed a critique of the "hyper-corporate colonization of hip hop culture" where I critically explored how late 1970s and early 1980s African American underclass and other working-class youth culture, which was initially thought to be nothing more than a mere passing ghetto fad and poor young folks' foolishness, evolved into an artistic and sociopolitical force of great significance, not only nationally but internationally (Rabaka 2011, 189–220). Hence, with its increasing cultural clout, by the mid-1980s corporate America began to take notice and perceive the "mad" money-making potential in hip hop culture, initially elevating rapping and break-dancing over the other five fundamental elements of hip hop culture. After a brief period of competing with rap music as the most identifiable public emblem or social symbol of hip hop culture, break-dancing fell to the wayside and the "hyper-corporate colonization of hip hop culture," mostly centering around all manner of schemes to market and commercialize rap music, began in earnest (Fricke and Ahearn 2002; Kugelberg 2007). It is important, yet and still, to emphasize the prominence of break-dancing and b-boys and b-girls (i.e., "break-dancing boys" and "break-dancing girls") in early hip hop culture. In fact, many of my readers may be too young to recall how break-dancing films—such as *Wild Style* (1983), *Breakin'* (1984), *Breakin' 2: Electric Boogaloo* (1984), *Beat Street* (1984), *Body Shock* (1984), *Krush Groove* (1985), and *Rappin'* (1985)—took the nation, and later the world, by storm. Along with several of the major scholarly studies of break-dancing and hip hop dance (e.g., Alford 1984; Bramwell and Green 2003; Franklin and Watkins 1984; Hazzard-Gordon 1990; Huntington 2007; Rajakumar 2012; Schloss 2009), I have relied on the following critically acclaimed documentaries for my interpretation of "breakin'" here: Celia Ipiotis's *Popular Culture in Dance: The World of Hip Hop* (1984), Israel's *The Freshest Kids: A History of the B-Boy* (2002), and Benson Lee's *Planet B-Boy: Breakdance Has Evolved* (2008). Moreover, graffiti-writing has made many inroads from the dark and dirty inner-city streets of its origins to several of the most prestigious contemporary art galleries around the world. But, truth be told, a greater appreciation of graffiti *as art* outside of the bourgeois "high art" versus "low art" distinctions germane to mainstream middle-class aesthetics remains desperately needed. For further discussion of the origins and evolution of hip hop-styled graffiti-writing, and for the major works which have influenced my interpretation here, see J. Austin (2001), Castleman

(1982), Cooper and Chalfant (1984), Felisbret and Felisbret (2009), Gastman and Neelon (2010), Hager (1984), S.A. Phillips (1999), Rahn (2002), and Wimsatt (2003). Finally, in terms of the fifth fundamental element of hip hop culture, "knowledge," a tug-of-war of sorts has been taking place between those who, on the one hand, see rap music as a pop cultural and commercial gold mine and those who, on the other hand, strongly believe that rap music should radically reflect the "knowledge," as well as the politics, culture, and impecunious communities, of its primary producers and practitioners: black ghetto youth. Needless to say, hip hop studies is part and parcel of the discourse and debates surrounding the fifth fundamental element of hip hop culture (i.e., "knowledge"), and this book is specifically aimed at addressing the "knowledge" that has been handed down to the Hip Hop Movement from previous generations of black ghetto youth via their popular music, popular culture, politics, and participation in black popular movements during the post-World War II, Civil Rights Movement, and Black Power Movement periods, roughly from 1945 to 1980.

10. For further discussion of the pre-Hip Hop Movement historic African American social and political movements, and for the most noteworthy works that informed my analysis here, see D.W. Aldridge (2011), V.P. Franklin (1984), Giddings (1984), V. Harding (1981), Hine and Thompson (1998), Kelley and Lewis (2000), Marable and Mullings (2000), Payne and Green (2003), Singh (2004), and Walters (1993).

11. The history and critical theory of the Hip Hop Movement elaborated in the five "remixes" to follow not only builds on Foucault's conception of "subjugated knowledges" but, perhaps even more importantly, on his discursively distinct conceptions of "archaeology" and "genealogy." For instance, my critical theory of hip hop culture critically follows Foucault's philosophical histories and/or historicist philosophies: from his critique of psychiatry in *The History of Madness in the Classical Age* (2009) to his critique of the evolution of the medical industry in *The Birth of the Clinic: An Archaeology of Medical Perception* (1994); from his critique of the evolution of the human sciences in *The Order of Things: An Archaeology of the Human Sciences* (1971) to his critique of the historical-situatedness of truth, meaning, and reason (i.e., the *episteme* of an epoch), and the very methodologies through which they are arrived at or comprehended in his extremely innovative *The Archaeology of Knowledge* (1974) (see also Foucault 1973).

According to Foucault (1994, 195), archaeology is distinguished from "the confused, under-structured, and ill-structured domain of the history of ideas." He, therefore, rejected the history of ideas as an idealist and liberal humanist, purely academic or ivory tower mode of writing that traces an uninterrupted evolution of thought in terms of the conscious construction of a tradition or the conscious production of subjects and objects. Against the bourgeois liberalism of the history of ideas approach, Foucaultian archaeology endeavors to identify the states and stages for the creation and critique of ongoing and open-ended or, rather, more nuanced knowledge, as well as the hidden rules and regulations (re)structuring and ultimately determining the form and focus of discursive rationality that are deeply embedded within and often obfuscatingly operate below the perceived borders and boundaries of disciplinary development, methodological maneuvers, or interpretive intention. At the outset of *The Order of Things* (1971), Foucault contended: "It is these rules of formation, which were never formulated in their own right, but are to be found only in widely differing theories, concepts, and objects of study, that I have tried to reveal, by isolating, as their specific locus, a level that I have called . . . archaeological" (xi).

Moreover, this critical theory of hip hop culture also draws from Foucault's more mature materialist genealogies, such as *Discipline and Punish: The Birth of the Prison* (1979), *The History of Sexuality, Vol. 1: The Will to Knowledge* (1990a), *The History of Sexuality, Vol. 2: The Use of Pleasure* (1990b), and *The History of Sexuality, Vol. 3: The Care of the Self* (1990c), where he deepened and developed his articulation of archaeology and evolved it into a unique conception of genealogy, which signaled an intensification of his critical theorization of power relations, social institutions, and social practices (see also Foucault 1977, 1984, 1988, 1996). However, my critical theory of hip hop culture does not understand Foucault's later focus on genealogy to be a break with his earlier archaeological studies as much as it is taken to represent a shift of discursive direction and, even more, an extension and expansion of his discursive domain. Similar to his archaeologies, Foucault characterized his later genealogical studies as a new method of investigation, a new means of interpretation, and a new mode of historical writing.

Truth be told, then, both of these Foucaultian methodologies endeavor to radically reinterpret the social world from a micrological standpoint that allows one to identify discursive discontinuity and discursive dispersion instead of what has been commonly understood to be continuity and uninterrupted identity evolution and, as a consequence, Foucault's methodologies enable us to grapple with and, in many instances, firmly grasp historical happenings, cultural crises, political power plays, and social situations in their complete and concrete complexity. Furthermore, both Foucaultian methodologies also attempt to invalidate and offer more nuanced narratives to commonly held conceptions of master narratives and great chains of historical continuity and their teleological destinations, as well as to hyper-historicize what has been long thought to be indelibly etched into the heart of human history. In other words, and more meta-methodologically speaking, in discursively deploying archaeology and/or genealogy Foucault sought to disrupt and eventually destroy hard and fast bourgeois humanist historical identities, power relations, and imperial institutions by critically complicating, by profoundly problematizing and pluralizing the entire arena of discursive formations and discursive practices—hence, freeing historical research and writing from its hidden bourgeois humanist social and political hierarchies, by disavowing and displacing the bourgeois humanist (and, therefore, "socially acceptable") subject, and critically theorizing modern reason and increasing rationalization through reinterpreting and rewriting the history of the human sciences.

Here, my intentions are admittedly less ambitious than those of Foucault, although, I honestly believe, they are just as relevant considering the state of contemporary culture, politics, and society. In *The Hip Hop Movement*, therefore, I seek to reinterpret and rewrite the history of contemporary cultural criticism, radical politics, critical social theory, and sociopolitical movements in light of the Hip Hop Movement's "inheritance" from and "amnesia" surrounding past black popular music, black popular culture, and black popular movements, as well as the Hip Hop Movement's contributions to future black popular music, black popular culture, and black popular movements. By identifying and critically analyzing the previous black popular music, black popular culture, and black popular movements that influenced the origins and evolution of rap music and the Hip Hop Movement, *The Hip Hop Movement* reinterprets and rewrites the conventionally conceived histories of rap music and hip hop culture, ultimately revealing that black popular music, black popular culture, and black popular movements historically have been and currently continue to be inextricable—constantly overlapping, interlocking, and intersecting, intensely infusing and informing each other. Black popular music, black popular culture, and black popular movements are not now and never have been created in a vacuum, but within the historical, cultural, social, political, and economic context of the United States. This means, then, that like previous black popular music, black popular culture, and black popular movements, rap music, hip hop culture, and the Hip Hop Movement are emblematic not only of contemporary African America, but also eerily indicative of the state of the "America dream" (or, for many U.S. citizens, the "American nightmare") at the turn of the twenty-first century.

12. With regard to Black Thought's famed phrase "knuckle and brawl," see the track "Long Time" on the Roots's *Game Theory* (2006) compact disc. He also used the phrase "knuckle and brawl" in his rhyme on the track "Duck Down!" on the Roots's *Tipping Point* (2004) compact disc. Obviously I have a particular predilection for a certain political rapper whose stage name is Black Thought (government name: Tariq Trotter) and who fronts the most famous acoustic hip hop band in the land. Those readers unaware of the Roots, their music *and* politics, and curious about message rap *and* acoustic hip hop music, should also spin the Roots's groundbreaking discs *Organix* (1993), *Do You Want More?* (1995), *Illadelphia Highlife* (1996), *Things Fall Apart* (1999), *The Roots Come Alive* (1999), *Phrenology* (2002), *Rising Down* (2008), *How I Got Over* (2010), and *Undun* (2011).

13. For further discussion of mixtapes, hip hop or otherwise, and for the most noteworthy works that informed my analysis here, see Batt-Rawden and DeNora (2005), K. Fox (2002), Geller (2008), Marshall (2003), Moore (2004), and Skågeby (2011).

I

The Soundtracks of the Civil Rights Movement, 1945–1965

Remix 1

Rhythm & Blues

From Classic Rhythm & Blues to Rap's Beats and Rhymes

To state that black song constituted a form of black protest and resistance does not mean that it necessarily led to or even called for any tangible and specific actions, but rather that it served as a mechanism by which Negroes could be relatively candid in a society that rarely accorded them that privilege, could communicate this candor to others whom they would in no other way be able to reach, and, in the face of the sanctions of the white majority, could assert their own individuality, aspirations, and sense of being. Certainly, if nothing else, black song makes it difficult to believe that Negroes internalized their situation so completely, accepted the values of the larger society so totally, or manifested so pervasive an apathy as we have been led to believe. . . . The African tradition of being able to verbalize publicly in song what could not be said to a person's face, not only lived on among Afro-Americans throughout slavery but continued to be a central feature of black expressive culture in freedom.
—Lawrence Levine, *Black Culture and Black Consciousness: Afro-American Folk Thought from Slavery to Freedom*

INTRODUCTION: ON THE SOUNDTRACKS OF THE CIVIL RIGHTS MOVEMENT AND THEIR INFLUENCE ON RAP AND THE HIP HOP MOVEMENT

As I have argued elsewhere, to understand either *hip hop's inheritance* or *hip hop's amnesia* it is important to critically comprehend rap music and hip hop culture within the context of African American history, culture, and struggle (see Rabaka 2011, 2012). While mainstream American history, culture, and politics have undoubtedly impacted rap music and hip hop culture, black ghetto youth have been, and remain, the primary producers and practitioners of hip hop music and culture. Consequently, the history, culture, and struggles of working-class and underclass black folk, especially black ghetto youth, should be at the heart of any serious analysis of rap music, hip hop culture, and the broader Hip Hop Movement. As a matter of fact, much of what historically has been, and currently continues to be called "black popular culture," is nothing more than black ghetto youth culture or, at the least, some derivation of it.[1]

Ironically, along with being the primary producers and practitioners of black popular culture, black ghetto youth have consistently served as the foot soldiers and very often the shock troops for the mostly middle-aged and middle-class leadership of post-enslavement black social and political movements: from the Black Women's Club Movement and the New Negro Movement through to the Harlem Renaissance and the Civil Rights Movement. For instance, with regard to the Civil Rights Movement, who can deny the role black ghetto youth played in the Montgomery Bus Boycott, the Voter Registration Movement, the Sit-In Movement, the Freedom Riders Movement, the Albany Movement, the March on Washington, or the Selma to Montgomery Marches? The point that I am making here has to do with the fact that black ghetto youth are often rendered *invisible* when and where we come to African American political thought and social movements. But, these same youths are usually rendered *hyper-visible* when and where we come to black popular culture, especially what is perceived to be the vices and vulgarities of black popular music.[2]

Needless to say, black popular music conveys more than vices and vulgarities. If one listens to it from a perspective that is sensitive to the lives and struggles of black ghetto youth, then—and, perhaps, only then—a whole new world, a whole new archive ripe for critical analysis is opened up. Often black ghetto youths' music, aesthetics, and politics are engaged, validated, or invalidated using either Eurocentric or black bourgeois criteria. This tendency reeks of the kind of dubious double standard that working-class and poor black folk have long resented when and where their music, aesthetics, and politics have been examined by bourgeois and petit bourgeois scholars and critics. By grounding my analysis in the lives and struggles of working-class and poor African American youth; by sincerely and sensitively attempting to understand the ways in which they have historically used music as a prime medium through which to express their views and values; and by (re)situating their sonic reflections within the wider contexts of African American political thought and social movements, and African American history, culture, and struggle more generally, here I will explore early rhythm & blues as the black popular music mouthpiece for black ghetto youths' contributions to and critiques of the Civil Rights Movement.

Ultimately I am undertaking this analysis to discover what Civil Rights Movement youth bequeathed to Hip Hop Movement youth. Therefore, this "remix" is not offered as a definitive or even a comprehensive history of classic rhythm & blues in relationship to the Civil Rights Movement, nor was it ever intended to be. Let me be real clear here: the main thrust or thesis of this "remix," and indeed this book, is that the Hip Hop Generation has inherited more from previous generations of African American youths'— especially black ghetto youths' musics, aesthetics, and politics—than readily admitted or otherwise understood. Part of the reluctance to acknowledge connections between past and present black ghetto youth has more to do with either the ignorance or amnesia surrounding working-class and poor African American youths' contributions to African American and mainstream American history, culture, and politics.

After all, the ghetto is supposedly a place where violence, vulgarity, poverty, illiteracy, promiscuity, and larceny reign supreme. In other words, to take this lame line of logic to its extreme, nothing of value can be found in or come out of the ghetto. Therefore, the contributions to African American and mainstream American history, culture, and politics that actually originated in and emerged from the ghetto are either attributed to the black bourgeoisie or treated as free-floating postmodern signifiers whose architects and origins are unknown. The simultaneous *invisibility* and *anonymity* with respect to black ghetto youths' contributions to African American and mainstream American history, culture, and politics have been sadly handed down to the Hip Hop Generation.[3]

Working-class and poor African American youths' lives are situated at the intersections of both black popular music and black popular movements because, on the one hand, they are the primary producers of black popular music and, on the other hand, they are frequently the primary preoccupation of black popular movements. On this last point, it might be helpful to, however briefly, consider the fact that each and every major post-enslavement African American social and political movement has been, more or less, black youth-centered—if not *black ghetto youth-centered.* Think about the Black Women's Club Movement's work with working-class and poor underage and unwed mothers, as well as their pre-schools and kindergartens for impoverished children. Think about the New Negro Movement's emphasis on employment and higher education opportunities for underprivileged African American youth, especially the black youth of the South, at the turn of the twentieth century. Think about how the 1954 *Brown vs. the Board of Education of Topeka* Supreme Court decision, which desegregated public schools in the United States, and how the long and arduous battle to implement that decision helped to spark the Civil Rights Movement. Although often uncommented on, a major motif that runs throughout each of these movements and their political activities decidedly revolves around the lives and struggles of African American youth, especially working-class and poor African American youth.

Indeed, the lives and struggles of African American youth have been consistently at the center of black popular movements. Furthermore, their contributions to black popular movements have always been multidimensional, meaning more than merely musical, artistic, or juvenile, but also political, cultural, intellectual, and spiritual. Yet and still, *the black popular music produced during the peak years of any post-enslavement black popular movement invariably seems to capture and convey the good and bad, the aspirations and frustrations, the thought and behavior of the black ghetto youth of the historical moment under consideration in ways that few other forms, aesthetic or otherwise, can.*

In short, working-class and poor African American youth's music, aesthetics, *and* politics at any given moment in African American history seems to serve as a crude kind of social, political, and cultural barometer, allowing us to measure the atmospheric pressure in black America. However, the foregoing should not be taken as a fast and firm embrace of subaltern theory as much as it should be understood to be a historical and cultural reality. Let's face it: there are more working-class and poor people in African America than any other class or group of people. Hence, my assertion that black politics and black popular culture are most often predicated on working-class and poor black folk's lives and struggles should not shock anyone.[4]

However, what may shock and awe many of my readers is the contention that black ghetto youth in particular have consistently contributed, not only to black popular culture, but also to black political culture. As I argued in *Hip Hop's Amnesia*, black ghetto youths' politics may not look like or sound like the Black Women's Club Movement, New Negro Movement, Civil Rights Movement, or Black Power Movement's politics, but, no mistake should be made about it, working-class and poverty-stricken African Americans have consistently contributed to African American political thought and social movements. Again, one of the best gauges of the distinct worldview, politics, and culture of black ghetto youth historically has been, and remains, black popular culture, especially black popular music.

In fact, black popular music has consistently served as the bridge between black political culture and black popular culture: black political culture being traditionally thought of as the domain of the black bourgeoisie, and black popular culture being traditionally thought of as the domain of working-class and underclass black folk. From my point of view, rap music and hip hop culture, however unheralded, build on this preexisting relationship between black popular culture and black political culture. To put it another way, almost inexplicably the music of black ghetto youth and the mores of the black bourgeoisie have traveled along parallel paths, seeming to cyclically coalesce in every major post-enslavement black popular movement, from the Black Women's Club Movement through to the Black Power Movement.[5]

In many ways the major forms of hip hop music—that is to say, rap and neo-soul—resemble the various genres of classic rhythm & blues that, between 1945 and 1965, served as sonic reflections of the politics and aesthetics, the frustrations and aspirations of the Civil Rights Movement. For example, who can deny the ways in which Motown Records, undoubtedly the most successful rhythm & blues record company of the Civil Rights Movement, paradoxically appealed to working-class and middle-class black America, as well as black and white America in general, during one of the most turbulent, class-divided, and racially-charged eras in U.S. history? Similar to contemporary black popular music—again, the most popular expressions being rap and neo-soul—classical black popular music was given entry into spaces and places that black people, especially black ghetto youth, were unambiguously denied entry. This, too, is a part of *hip hop's inheritance*, and black ghetto youth in particular continue to create music that is consumed and sometimes even seriously appreciated by middle-class black and suburban white America, even as middle-class black and suburban white America deny or, at the least, vocally despise black ghetto youths' ever-increasing impact on mainstream American culture, politics, and institutions.

Consisting of several hybrid styles of pre-World War II, World War II, and post-World War II black popular music, early rhythm & blues derived its essential elements from the spirituals, gospel, blues, ragtime, jazz, and jump blues. Initially called "race music," rhythm & blues began as an umbrella term for all styles of African American music produced and performed by African American musicians exclusively for African American entertainment. Which is to say, as Paul Oliver pointed out in *Broadcasting the Blues: Black Blues in the Segregation Era* (2006) and Karl Miller observed in *Segregating Sound: Inventing Folk and Pop Music in the Age of Jim Crow* (2010), just as pre-Civil Rights Movement American society was segregated, so too was the pre-Civil Rights Movement American music industry. As will be discussed below, this *sonic segregation* created the very conditions under which African Americans were able to evolve the African American musical aesthetic virtually free from the "crossover" and "pop" pretensions of later forms of rhythm & blues (and rhythm & blues-derived) music.

Evolving out of both the northern bebop jazz and jump blues styles and the southern boogie-woogie and "electric" or "urban" blues styles, what came to be called "rhythm & blues" in the late 1940s was a sonic synthesis of arguably each and every major form of African American music from enslavement through to the post-World War II period (Baptista 2000; Govenar and Joseph 2004; A. Shaw 1978). Similar to rap and other forms of hip hop music, classic rhythm & blues between 1945 and 1965 mixed or, rather, *remixed* African American musical history and culture. Like contemporary hip hop DJs and producers, early rhythm & blues musicians drew from disparate aspects of previous African American music and culture, in this instance pre-rhythm & blues music and culture, to create music and messages that reflected a rising racial, cultural, social, and political consciousness that reached back to the Black Women's Club Movement, New Negro Movement, and Harlem Renaissance, among other movements.

More than any previous form of black popular music, at its emergence rhythm & blues represented the wide range and wide reach of contemporary African American thought and culture (George 1988; Osborne and Hamilton 1980; A. Shaw 1986; Stamz 2010). Borrowing the frenzy feeling and aural otherworldliness from the spirituals, the blues feeling and tragicomic narrative tradition from the blues, the "exotic" and erotic sounds of the red-light district from ragtime, and the jive talk and updated juke joint sounds from jazz, early rhythm & blues symbolized the sound of African Americans in transition in mid-twentieth-century America. In other words, early rhythm & blues was *a music of motion*, the sound of a people on the move—figuratively, physically, socially, and politically speaking (Hildebrand 1994; O.A. Jackson 1995; Ripani 2006).

Retaining the tempo and drive of jump blues, early rhythm & blues' instrumentation was stripped down, and the overall emphasis was on the lyrics, not improvisation (à la jump blues and slightly later bebop). In essence, it was coded comedic or romantic lyrics sung over blues chord changes featuring an insistent backbeat. Distinguished from jump blues and bebop, early rhythm & blues openly embraced new technology, including the amplification and electrification of instruments. In fact, early rhythm & blues introduced and popularized the use of the electric bass in black popular music, in time evolving into a propulsive, dance beat-based music with unrelenting rhythms that seemed to perfectly mirror the migration, mores, and sociopolitical movements of mid-twentieth-century black America. It is important here at the outset to emphasize that throughout this "remix," and indeed throughout this book, the term "rhythm & blues" has two meanings, one musical and the other decidedly extramusical. [6]

Consequently, this "remix" will examine classic rhythm & blues in relationship to rap and other forms of hip hop music. Going back to the notion that black popular music in essence serves as a barometer by which to measure the political, social, and cultural climate in black America, here classic rhythm & blues represents the black popular music mouthpiece of the Civil Rights Movement, and rap and other forms of hip hop music represent the black popular music mouthpiece of the Hip Hop Movement. Frequently the connections between black popular music and black popular movements are downplayed and diminished in favor of ahistorical and apolitical analyses that whitewash black popular music and black popular movements.

By (re)contextualizing classic rhythm & blues and (re)placing it within the social, political, cultural, and musical world of its origins and early evolution we are provided with new musical and extramusical tools that could (and, indeed, should) aid us in our efforts to revive and repoliticize rap music and hip hop culture. Whether my readers believe that "hip hop is dead," as NaS infamously asserted, or that hip hop is alive and kicking, is all beside the point. What most of us can agree on is the fact that some aspects of hip hop have died or, at the least, have been lost. This moment in hip hop's history may very well be apart of its legendary ability to recycle and reinvent itself, or it may simply mean that there are new and novel contributions on the horizon that will once again jump-start hip hop culture. Whatever my readers believe to be the case, there simply is no getting around the fact that it is only by studying hip hop's death or, at the least, what it has lost during its decline that we can come to comprehend that intangible "something," that *je ne sais quoi* that so many of us deeply believe needs to be resuscitated and further developed to ensure rap music and hip hop culture's future.

FROM JUMP BLUES TO THE EMERGENCE OF RHYTHM & BLUES, FROM EARLY RHYTHM & BLUES TO THE EMERGENCE OF OLD SCHOOL RAP

The emergence of rhythm & blues coincided with the World War II migration of African Americans from the South to the Northeast, Midwest, and West to escape racial oppression and dehumanizing Jim Crow laws. African Americans also migrated from the South during this period in search of better economic, employment, and educational opportunities. Leaving their dream-destroying jobs as sharecroppers, general laborers, tenant farmers, washerwomen, and domestics, an estimated 5 million African Americans moved out of the South between 1940 and 1970.

However, these migrants quickly found out that the Northeast, Midwest, and West were not the "promised land." Although they did, for the most part, find higher-paying jobs, especially in the wartime industries, life in the new cities was generally just as segregated and devoid of civil rights as it was in the South. Antiblack racist redlining quarantined African Americans to segregated and impoverished communities (i.e., ghettos), effectively turning their dreams into seemingly never-ending nightmares as more and more black folk sought refuge from the new and unfamiliar forms of Northern racism in alcohol, drugs, promiscuity, gambling, and other illicit activities.[7]

By the end of the migration period between 1940 and 1970 African Americans had become a city-centered and urbanized population. In fact, as African Americans entered into the Black Power Movement years (1965 to 1975), more than 80 percent lived in cities. Fifty-three percent remained in the South. Furthermore, 40 percent lived in the North, and 7 percent in the West. It could probably go without saying that all of this would ultimately impact the origins and evolution of rap music, hip hop culture, and the Hip Hop Movement in the late 1970s and early 1980s.[8]

From rhythm & blues forward, virtually each and every major form of black popular music has been city-centered. But, astute African American music critics might also emphasize jazz's city-centered roots, and that is whether we discuss its southern city origins, New Orleans, or the midwestern city, Chicago, or northeastern city, New York, of its early evolution. Unlike the spirituals and the blues, which captured the sights, sounds, and sorrows of African American life during the enslavement, Reconstruction, and post-Reconstruction years, jazz, ragtime, and rhythm & blues reflected African Americans' simultaneous post-enslavement segregation, industrialization, and urbanization. No longer predominantly widespread throughout the rural regions of the South, the twentieth century symbolizes African Americans' transition into urban environments, whether North, South, East, Midwest, or West. However, even as they moved from rural regions to urban environments racism fiendishly followed them and reared its ugly head (and horns) at seemingly every tick and turn.[9]

Socially alienated, culturally isolated, and economically impoverished, segregated African American communities in the first half of the twentieth century created effervescent artistic practices and entertainment districts in every major city in the United States. In the context of their new cities, the more than five million black migrants transformed old rural traditions into new urban forms of African American expression and entertainment, inventing innovative musical styles predicated on a new city-centered set of criteria, cadences, and customs. The new city-centered aesthetic had a profound impact on African American music, as black musicians increasingly sought to incorporate the sights, sounds, sorrows, and celebrations of the city into their work. Hence, first urban blues, then jazz, and later rhythm & blues sonically signified city life, with its emphasis on regional customs, social conventions, local cuisine, communal rhythms, street noises, factory sounds, and, of course, new technologies—especially, the amplification and electrification of instruments. It was this synthesis of African American folk music and culture with the then emerging African American urban music and culture that led black musicians to the intense period of experimentation that ultimately birthed rhythm & blues.

Classic rhythm & blues has a hallowed place in the history of modern African American music because it is fundamentally the musical foundation, the bedrock on which all modern black popular music has built its house or, rather, its houses—or maybe even its mansions. In other words, every major form of modern African American (or African American-derived) music, from rock & roll and soul to funk and disco, has used the innovations of early rhythm & blues as sonic paradigms and points of departure (Banfield 2010, 2011; Ramsey 2003; Ripani 2006; A. Shaw 1986). By critically exploring the origins and evolution of early rhythm & blues we are provided with a musical Rosetta stone that will enable us to decipher the deep double entrendres and coded cultural messages buried within the basic structure of modern black popular music, including rap and neo-soul. In fact, I am convinced that we will have a greater appreciation of, and be able to offer more contributions to, as well as more constructive criticisms of, rap music and hip hop culture once we have a serious—as opposed to a superficial—sense of the history, culture, and struggles that coalesced to create the conditions under which rhythm & blues emerged. Needless to say, it is virtually impossible to fully understand early rhythm & blues without comprehending the ways in which it served as a harbinger and sonic symbol of the emergence, politics, and aesthetics of the Civil Rights Movement.

Where classic rhythm & blues represented the *sonic landscape* of African America between 1945 and 1965, the Civil Rights Movement represented the *sociopolitical landscape* of African America between 1945 and 1965. As argued in my previous volumes, *Hip Hop's Inheritance* and *Hip Hop's Amnesia*, African American music is more than merely music. It is also the spiritual, sexual, cultural, social, and political expression of an alienated and oppressed group which has historically had few other areas in which to fully express itself on its own terms. It is with this understanding that classic rhythm & blues may be interpreted as musical *and* spiritual, sexual, cultural, social, and political expression.

Moreover, when this line of logic is calmly conceded then it may also be openly acknowledged that classic rhythm & blues, along with its myriad extramusical implications, has long served as a musical paradigm *and* a political point of departure for contemporary hip hop music: from neo-soul, commercial rap, conscious rap, and reggaeton to glitch hop, trip hop, krunk, snap music, and wonky music. Just as each of these musics expresses elements of the politics, poetics, and aesthetics of the diverse hip hop communities they were created in, classic rhythm & blues conveys the politics, poetics, and aesthetics of the various communities it was created in. In fact, where classic rhythm & blues may be understood to be musical *and* spiritual, sexual, cultural, social, and political expression, the Civil Rights Movement can be interpreted as a decade-long synthesis and translation of classic rhythm & blues' extramusical expressions into action, into collective struggle and radical political praxis via the sit-ins, marches, demonstrations, and protests that came to be the signatures of the Civil Rights Movement. And, indeed, as the hands of history have revealed, black folk sitting-in, marching, demonstrating, and protesting within the world of 1950s and 1960s America was nothing else if not "radical."[10]

It may not be going too far afield to observe that even though most classic rhythm & blues scholars locate its origins in the rambunctious early rhythm & blues of Louis Jordan and the Tympany Five, who began performing and recording in 1938, it is equally important to acknowledge early rhythm & blues' roots in the African American protest music tradition. Undoubtedly one of the finest protest songs ever produced was Billie Holiday's "Strange Fruit," recorded in 1939, the same year that saw the senseless violence of World War II begin (although the United States would not enter into the war until 1941). By observing rhythm & blues' relationship to broader struggles for justice and social transformation in mid-twentieth-century America we will be able to more easily comprehend the ways in which black popular music represents more than music to the communities, musicians, and audiences who invented and continue to develop it. Hence, both Jordan and Holiday's work hints at the hallmarks of not only early rhythm & blues, but of black popular music for the remainder of the twentieth century. A closer look at Jordan's work demonstrates that he was more than a jump blues "jive clown."[11]

Over the years there has been a lot of ink spilled concerning the comedic nature of Jordan's colorful narratives and performances. Without in any way downplaying the freewheeling and outright fun-filled elements of his work, it is important not to lose sight of the undeniable fact that Louis Jordan was a serious musical and lyrical innovator. His songs were loaded with wry social commentary and coded cultural references. Interestingly, one of the most striking features of his slang-laden lyrics—as on his hit songs "I'm Gonna Leave You on the Outskirts of Town," "G.I. Jive," "Caldonia," "Buzz Me," "Choo Choo Ch' Boogie," "Ain't That Just Like A Woman," "Ain't Nobody Here But Us Chickens," "Boogie-Woogie Blue Plate," "Beans and Cornbread," "Saturday Night Fish Fry," "Blue Light Boogie," and "Weak Minded Blues"—was the fact that he did not sing in the traditional sense but instead rendered his stories in an unusual rapid-fire, semi-sung, semi-spoken vocal style. Jordan's rhyming semi-sung, semi-spoken narration deemphasized the lyrical melody while privileging highly syncopated phrasing and the percussive effects of alliteration and assonance. In other words, Louis Jordan arguably offered one of the earliest examples in American popular music of the slang-filled vocal stylings that eventually evolved into what we currently call rap music.

All of this means that rap music's roots, at least partially, can be traced back to the music that Louis Jordan helped to popularize and eventually helped to evolve into early rhythm & blues: jump blues. Jump blues was essentially the late 1930s and early 1940s synthesis of blues and jazz. Many interpreted the term "jump blues" to mean "bluesy jazz" or, rather, "jazzy blues," because by the late 1930s and early 1940s blues and jazz were simply two sides of the same coin, and most black musicians blurred the lines between these genres by being adept at playing both styles. Other than its emphasis on an updated and heavier rhythmic conception of big band-based swing, similar to "old school" rap jump blues was characterized by its boisterous vocalists, flamboyant performances, and frequently lighthearted songs about partying, dancing, drinking, and jiving. As is well known, these same themes predominate much of what has been termed "old school" rap. [12]

Bearing in mind that "old school" rap is one of those heatedly contested terms that means many different things to many different people, a brief explanation is in order. At the dawn of the twenty-first century it is commonplace for most members of the Hip Hop Generation who are in their teens or twenties to think of artists such as Run-D.M.C., the Fat Boys, Doug E. Fresh, or U.T.F.O., who were all the rage in the mid-1980s, as old school rappers. Obviously each of the aforementioned had very different rhyme techniques and rhythmic conceptions compared to turn of the twenty-first-century rap stars such as Lauryn Hill, NaS, Jay-Z, Missy Elliott, Eminem, and Lil' Wayne.

However, for those of us old enough to remember "real" old school rap, Run-D.M.C., LL Cool J, Salt-n-Pepa, Public Enemy, and Boogie Down Productions ain't old school rap. For us, "real" old school rap would be that first wave of rap artists who predated Run-D.M.C., LL Cool J, Salt-n-Pepa, Public Enemy, and Boogie Down Productions. Late 1970s and early 1980s rap artists, such as the Sugarhill Gang, the Sequence, Kurtis Blow, Grandmaster Flash & the Furious Five, the Treacherous Three, and Whodini, represent "real" old school rap in our hearts and minds because, truth be told, without seriously listening to and learning from these pioneering rap artists there simply is no way to fully comprehend, let alone honestly appreciate, how undeniably innovative mid-1980s rap artists such as Run-D.M.C., LL Cool J, Salt-n-Pepa, Public Enemy, and Boogie Down Productions truly were between 1984 and 1987. [13]

Needless to say, when and where I invoke old school rap throughout this "remix"—and, indeed, throughout this book—I am referring to those late 1970s and early 1980s rap artists who were essentially the architects of rap music during its most formative phase. Hence, here I am making a critical distinction between *the late 1970s and early 1980s pioneers of rap music* and *the mid-1980s popularizers of rap music*. With this distinction in mind, *pioneers of rap music* include not just the Sugarhill Gang, the Sequence, Kurtis Blow, Grandmaster Flash & the Furious Five, the Treacherous Three, and Whodini, but also often overlooked or underappreciated early rap artists such as Afrika Bambaataa, Paulette Tee and Sweet Tee, Spoonie Gee, Lady B, the Cold Crush Brothers, Lisa Lee, the Funky Four + One More, Sha Rock, and Fatback. In terms of *the mid-1980s popularizers of rap music*, a short list should include not only Run-D.M.C., LL Cool J, Salt-n-Pepa, Public Enemy, and Boogie Down Productions, but also the Fat Boys, the Beastie Boys,

Roxanne Shanté, the Real Roxanne, Stetsasonic, Mantronix, Doug E. Fresh, Marley Marl, Eric B. & Rakim, Schoolly D, Full Force, Ice-T, the Egyptian Lover, Newcleus, Dana Dane, MC Shan, and the World Class Wreckin' Cru.

Similar to jump blues artists between the late 1930s and the early 1940s, the pioneering old school rap artists of the late 1970s and early 1980s created rhyme after rhyme about partying, dancing, drinking, and jiving. The emphasis on partying, dancing, drinking, and jiving in both jump blues and old school rap can be easily explained by seriously considering the conditions under which both of these musical forms were created. Which is to say, both forms emerged in racially oppressed and economically impoverished environments, and both forms serve as *bridge musics* during periods of widespread musical *and* spiritual, sexual, cultural, social, and political transformation and transition in African America. Jump blues eventually evolved into rhythm & blues in the mid-1940s, where old school rap ultimately laid the foundation for the popularization and mainstream acceptance of rap music and hip hop culture in the mid-1980s.

Just as the emergence of old school rap can be linked to larger patterns of urbanization, industrialization, and automation in the last quarter of the twentieth century, jump blues' development can be traced to a series of transformations taking place in mid-twentieth-century American music, culture, politics, and society. As a consequence of the Great Depression (1929–1939) and the beginning of World War II in 1939, by the early 1940s the large big bands of the 1930s had to be cut back to small combos. African Americans in the 1940s, like most other Americans in the 1940s, continued to storm dance halls and watering holes on week nights and weekends, and they expected the small combos to keep the music just as "hot" and "jumpin'" as the big bands of the previous decade. In short, they wanted their music lively, loud, and danceable. This caused many of the combos to place greater emphasis on honking saxophonists and fiery, flamboyant, and seemingly frenzy-filled vocalists who could be heard over the rambunctious rhythms and hollering horn riffs. As a consequence of the honking saxophonists and shouting singers, early rhythm & blues musicians have been aptly characterized as "honkers and shouters."

In his brilliant book, *Honkers and Shouters: The Golden Years of Rhythm & Blues* (1978), Arnold Shaw explained that "[a]n expressiveness as extreme as the honking-falling down syndrome" popular among early rhythm & blues saxophonists was "unquestionably a social as well as a musical phenomenon" (171). In essence, he understood it to be an "expression of a threefold separation: from the sound of Western music; from white popular song; and from the Negro middle class to whom R&B was anathema." Ultimately, Shaw concluded, "the syndrome was a conscious or unconscious projection of the post-war segregation of black people, an abysmal expression of the separateness of the black ghettos." In fact, he went further, the "post-war world was one that Negroes viewed with a mixture of disgust and frustration. Not only were they isolated from the mainstream of society, they not infrequently suffered white violence" (171).[14]

The violence that African Americans endured during and after World War II was both physical and psychological, and early rhythm & blues reflected the torture and daily turmoil they experienced. Jump blues and its rhythm & blues offspring represented that bubbling stream of African American music during the interwar years that had been hailed as "city blues" and viewed as another step in the evolution of the urbanization of African American music. Jump blues and its early rhythm & blues offspring also, however uncomfortably, captured and conveyed a great deal about the mid-twentieth-century America it emerged in and, more tellingly, the African Americans who invented it, performed it, and lovingly listened to and identified with it. Although most African American historians have generally agreed that the Civil Rights Movement essentially began with the 1954 *Brown vs. the Board of Education* Supreme Court decision, it is extremely important to understand the fifteen-year period between 1939 and 1954—which is to say, from the beginning of World War II to the *Brown* decision—that undeniably laid the social, political, cultural, and musical foundation for what can be considered the peak years of the Civil Rights Movements between 1954 and 1965.

The Great Depression and World War II fundamentally changed the racial, cultural, social, and political consciousness of African Americans, just as they had irrevocably altered American society as a whole. A decade of economic depression further devastated an already impoverished and socially segregated people, coupled with the trials and tribulations of valiantly serving in a racially segregated military that was willing to fight for freedom abroad but not for freedom in the interests of African Americans at home, created a unique and perplexing historical moment. With America's preparation to join World War II, between 1939 and 1940 the U.S. economy was finally lifted out of the depths of the Depression.

However, when the United States went back to business it rebuilt its military just as it was prior to the Great Depression. Which is to say, the U.S. military continued its long-standing policy of segregation and other Jim Crow practices of racial discrimination and exclusion. Teams of unemployed white workers streamed into shipyards, aircraft factories, and other sites of war production, while the throngs of destitute and jobless African Americans were left standing at factory entrances day after dismal day. When African Americans were finally hired, no matter which jobs their education or hard-won skills qualified them for, they were usually quarantined to the most demeaning custodial positions.[15]

For the most part, African Americans did not fare any better when they sought employment in government jobs and government-funded training pro-

grams. For instance, black applicants were regularly rejected for government-funded training programs because training them was thought to be
pointless in light of their low prospects for finding skilled work. It was a
callous catch-22 that eventually saw the United States Employment Service
(USES) fill "whites-only" requests for defense industry workers. The U.S.
military accepted African American men in their proportion to the population, about 11 percent at the time, but placed them in segregated units and
assigned them to degrading service duties. More specifically, the navy limited African American servicemen to menial positions, while the marine corps
and the army air corps outright refused to accept them altogether.

In light of post-Great Depression segregation, in the larger society and in
the military, the Pittsburgh *Courier* called for a "Double V" campaign. Eventually adopted as a battle cry among African Americans in the early 1940s,
"Double V" stood for *victory over fascism abroad and victory over racism at
home*. Embracing the "Double V" mentality, during World War II African
Americans' simultaneous efforts to fight fascism *and* racism transformed the
worldviews of soldiers and civilians alike, and led to the further development
of African American civil rights efforts and organizations. A groundswell of
protests removed the muzzle that had been on their mouths, and in the 1940s
African Americans found the voices they had seemingly lost during the Depression years.[16]

A major catalyst for the change in African Americans' collective consciousness, A. Philip Randolph's 1941 March on Washington Movement
called on African Americans to organize their protests and direct them at the
national government. Indicating that he had ten thousand African Americans
prepared to march on the nation's capital, Randolph defiantly declared the
movement's motto: "We loyal Negro American citizens demand the right to
work and fight for our country." Throughout the spring and summer months
of 1941, Randolph's March on Washington Movement blossomed into the
largest mass movement of African Americans since Marcus Garvey's Universal Negro Improvement Association during its New Negro Movement and
Harlem Renaissance heydays in the 1920s.[17]

The 1940s March on Washington Movement demanded that President
Roosevelt issue an order forbidding companies with government contracts
from practicing racial discrimination. Randolph pushed for the complete
elimination of race-based exclusion from defense training programs and also
insisted that the USES provide work without regard to race. In short, Randolph wanted the president to abolish segregation in the armed forces.

The 1940s March on Washington Movement was a wide-ranging and
wide-reaching movement, and its powerful appeal garnered the support of
many African Americans who had never participated in social organization
and political activism. Increasing the pressure on the president, Randolph let
be known that as many as 50,000 African Americans had committed to

march on Washington. Roosevelt, deeply concerned that the March on Washington would seriously undermine America's effort to appear democratic before the world and give fodder to the Nazi fascists the United States claimed to be the opposite of, initially offered a set of superficial changes to appease African Americans. The March on Washington Movement would have none of it and firmly stood its ground. Consequently, they raised the stakes by increasing the number of African Americans who had committed to march on Washington to 100,000. By the close of June in 1941, Roosevelt raised the white flag and had his aides draft Executive Order 8802, effectively prompting Randolph to call off the march.

Even if only on a superficial or symbolic level, Roosevelt's order signaled an important change in African Americans' relationship with the government, and the government's relationship with African Americans. Perhaps the most meaningful lines of Executive Order 8802 read in part:

> WHEREAS there is evidence that available and needed workers have been barred from employment in industries engaged in defense production solely because of considerations of race, creed, color, or national origin, to the detriment of workers' morale and of national unity:
>
> NOW, THEREFORE, by virtue of the authority vested in me by the Constitution and the statutes, and as a prerequisite to the successful conduct of our national defense production effort, I do hereby reaffirm the policy of the United States that there shall be no discrimination in the employment of workers in defense industries or government because of race, creed, color, or national origin, and I do hereby declare that it is the duty of employers and of labor organizations, in furtherance of said policy and of this order, to provide for the full and equitable participation of all workers in defense industries, without discrimination because of race, creed, color, or national origin. (1)[18]

Although it was the first major blow to racial discrimination since Reconstruction, Executive Order 8802 was not the twentieth century's Emancipation Proclamation. Consequently, African American excitement over the order quickly faded when many industries, particularly those in the South, evaded the order's clear intent and almost exclusively engaged in token hiring. As they would repeatedly witness throughout the turbulent decades to come, in the 1940s African Americans learned a hard lesson that seems to have been passed down to the members of the Civil Rights Movement and the Black Power Movement: the U.S. government's high-sounding and hyperbole-filled articulations of antidiscrimination principles and the establishment of civil rights commissions and committees did not necessarily lead to the eradication of racial inequalities. Hence, words without deeds are as useless as fish without water.

Taken on its own terms or, better yet, placed within the context of African American history, culture, and struggle, black popular music—from the spirituals and the blues through to rap and neo-soul—can be seen as a form of *sonic protest* that is inextricable from the more conventional *sociopolitical protest* of black popular movements. As Shaw contended above, early rhythm & blues was "unquestionably a social as well as a musical phenomenon." Therefore, it is important not to negate the interconnections between black popular music and black popular movements.

Without in any way downplaying the ways in which gospel, blues, folk, and jazz served as soundtracks for the Civil Rights Movement, it is important to comprehend how early rhythm & blues was undeniably the most popular and socially salient soundtrack of the Civil Rights Movement, even though most people have a tendency to deprecate and diminish its connections to and significance for the movement. Part of the backlash against early rhythm & blues had to do with not only its "heavy" rhythms and "hard-driving" backbeats, but also its raw expressiveness and "hard life" lyrical content that, in the most unprecedented manner imaginable, dealt openly with love, lust, loss, poverty, delinquency, partying, drinking, city life, and fast cars. Similar to the rock & roll, soul, and funk music that built on the sonic breakthroughs and aural innovations of classic rhythm & blues, old school rap—and much of 1980s rap in general—offered countless songs that brashly, and frequently with brutal honesty, dealt with love, lust, loss, poverty, delinquency, partying, drinking, city life, and fast cars. This should be held in mind as we continue to explore rap's roots in early rhythm & blues and the Hip Hop Movement's roots in the Civil Rights Movement.

African American music, from the spirituals and the blues through to rap and neo-soul, seems to revolve around spirituality and sexuality, folk philosophy and new technology. To reiterate, black popular music often serves as a metaphor and medium of expression for black life, culture, and struggle. Consequently, the major issues and ills at any given moment in African America most often find their way into black popular music in particular, and black popular culture in general. At its core, black popular culture has always been a battlefield—a tug-of-war—between black conservatives and black radicals, between black traditionalists and black modernists, where each consistently vies to have its respective views and values accepted as the dominant expression of the African American experience.

In many ways, the emergence of rhythm & blues in mid-twentieth-century America is the musical and cultural culmination of African Americans' experiences from enslavement through to the 1941 March on Washington Movement, which actually continued to rally and call for nonviolent civil disobedience well after World War II had ended in 1945. Emphasizing the dialectic of *tradition* and *innovation* that is at the heart of early rhythm & blues—and, truth be told, all major forms of black popular music—in *Blues People: Negro Music in White America* (1963), Amiri Baraka asserted:

There was a kind of frenzy and extra-local vulgarity to rhythm & blues that had never been present in older blues forms. Suddenly it was as if a great deal of the Euro-American humanist façade Afro-American music had taken on had been washed away by the war. Rhythm & blues singers literally had to shout to be heard above the clanging and strumming of the various electrified instruments and the churning rhythm sections. And somehow the louder the instrumental accompaniment and the more harshly screamed the singing, the more expressive the music was. Blues had always been a vocal music, and it must be said that the instrumental accompaniment for rhythm & blues singers was still very much in the vocal tradition, but now the human voice itself had to struggle, to scream, to be heard. (171–72)

Taking the music as a metaphor for the Civil Rights Movement and African Americans' position in U.S. society between 1945 and 1965, it is difficult not to conclude that early rhythm & blues mirrored the movement and expressed African Americans' thoughts and feelings about post-World War II segregation, racial discrimination, and ongoing economic exploitation. One of the reasons early rhythm & blues expressed "a kind of frenzy and extra-local vulgarity . . . that had never been present in older blues forms" is probably because at the beginning of the postwar period African Americans honestly believed that by helping to topple German fascism they would also be contributing to the eradication of American racism. Nothing could have been further from the truth, and U.S. history during this period reveals America's reluctance and outright refusal to come to terms with the fact that it had been practicing its own form of fascism against African Americans for several centuries. What else is "fascism" if it is not in part, according to *Merriam-Webster's Dictionary*, the "belief in the supremacy of one national or ethnic group," and "a contempt for democracy" or, at the least, a contempt for extending democracy to all citizens without regard to race, gender, class, sexual orientation, or religious affiliation? To put it another way, there is a sense in which early rhythm & blues can be seen as sonic protest against American apartheid and America's "whites-only" democracy, which basically reduced the citizenry to *white haves* and *nonwhite have-nots*.

Listening to early rhythm & blues, "it was as if a great deal of the Euro-American humanist façade Afro-American music had taken on had been washed away by the war," and the music increasingly reflected African Americans' heightened cultural consciousness and new radical spirit (à la the 1940s March on Washington Movement). Almost as if directly responding to the whitewashing of jazz in the 1930s and early 1940s, especially under the guises of big band and "sweet" swing jazz, early rhythm & blues unrepentantly returned to its roots in the blues and advanced *a new, amplified, and electrified form of the blues*. Seeming to perfectly mirror the industrialization and urbanization taking place in the larger society, mid-twentieth-century blues—which is to say, rhythm & blues—emerged within a segregated world that was frequently lawless, loud, harsh, and often either erased or silenced authentic representations and interpretations of African American life and culture. Hence, Baraka observed, early rhythm & blues singers "literally had to shout to be heard above the clanging and strumming of the various electrified instruments and the churning rhythm sections. And somehow the louder the instrumental accompaniment and the more harshly screamed the singing, the more expressive the music was."

Early rhythm & blues was the music or, rather, the searing sounds of a people in search of their human, civil, and voting rights in the concrete jungles of segregated U.S. cities. The "clanging and strumming of the various electrified instruments and the churning rhythm sections" could be said to metaphorically represent the impact of industrialization and the automation of factory work on African American life and culture. Moreover, the "screamed . . . singing" can be taken as a defiant affirmation of African Americans' humanity and their dire need to be heard in the face of government-sanctioned segregation, Jim Crow laws, and myriad other forms of antiblack racism.

If, indeed, early rhythm & blues sounds harsh to our ears today, then we are only conceding how ingeniously it captured African Americans' struggle for human recognition and civil rights between 1945 and 1965. If the "clanging and strumming of the various electrified instruments and the churning rhythm sections" sound slightly off kilter and conflict with our understanding of what constitutes "good music," then perhaps that is because early rhythm & blues musicians created their music in the context of an increasingly urban and industrial segregated society, with all of the "clanging" and "churning" such a society harbors. Early rhythm & blues represented something raw and real, something working-class and poor black people could feel and know that it was created by one of their own specifically with them in mind. Hence, "somehow the louder the instrumental accompaniment and the more harshly screamed the singing, the more expressive the music was." Indeed, the African Americans who created early rhythm & blues and organized the Civil Rights Movement developed new music and new politics to express themselves—and, that is to say, to express themselves not as the larger society sanctioned and woefully wanted them to, but as they really were, in their full and indignant *ugly beauty* as Thelonious Monk put it on his classic album *Underground* in 1968.

All of this is to say, early rhythm & blues registers as a reclamation of the classic blues aesthetic and the antiracist ethos African Americans' unapologetically embraced during the Reconstruction, post-Reconstruction, Black Women's Club Movement, and New Negro Movement turn of the twentieth-century years. Whatever high hopes African Americans held concerning desegregation and integration during World War II soon soured in the years immediately following the fall of Nazi fascism in 1945. Early rhythm &

blues expressed the frustrations and ongoing aspirations of a people who had been repeatedly denied and brutally betrayed by their government. Crying seemed an inadequate response to the double-dealing African Americans had been consistently dealt after 350 years of enslavement and, at the time, close to 100 years of post-enslavement American apartheid. Instead of the sonic cry that was one of the distinguishing characteristics of classic blues, as jump blues evolved into early rhythm & blues the music eventually came to express a collective sonic scream or, quite literally, an unmitigated shout. The "shout" aesthetic of early rhythm & blues continues to reverberate throughout black popular music, including rap and neo-soul.

Even the early rhythm & blues instrumentalists seemed to "shout" and make their instruments mirror the human voice, saying with blue notes, coded sounds, and pulsating polyrhythms all the things they felt they could not say with their mouths. Early rhythm & blues' *musical shouting* is inextricable from the *spiritual shouting* that takes place in African American churches each and every Sunday morning, and both kinds of shouting are nothing if not cathartic releases, momentarily freeing the shouter from the inferiority complexes, racism, poverty, and other ills that have plagued African America since its inception. Hence, what has been long referred to as "the honking saxophonist" might actually be better explained by turning not simply to musicology but also to sociology and, even more, to early rhythm & blues saxophonists' segregated social world.

Along with the shouting and screaming so typical of early rhythm & blues singing, equally telling, Baraka contended, are the "uncommonly weird sounds that were made to come out of the instruments. The screaming saxophone is the most characteristic" (172). He importantly continued, "during the heyday of rhythm & blues, blues-oriented instrumentalists, usually saxophone players, would vie to see who could screech, or moan, or shout the loudest and longest on their instruments." In explaining the shouting and screaming in early rhythm & blues Baraka, perhaps, partially explained much about every major form of black popular music that rose in the aftermath of the classic rhythm & blues era between 1945 and 1965:

> The point, it seemed, was to spend oneself with as much attention as possible, and also to make the instruments sound as unmusical, or as *non-Western*, as possible. It was almost as if the blues people were reacting against the softness and "legitimacy" that had crept into black instrumental music with the advent of swing. In a way, this is what happened, and for this reason, rhythm & blues sat as completely outside of the mainstream as earlier blues forms, though without that mainstream this form of music might have been impossible. Rhythm & blues also became more of an anathema to the Negro middle-class, perhaps, than the earlier blues forms, which by now they might have forgotten, because it was contemporary and existed as a legitimate expression of a great

many Negroes and as a gaudy reminder of the real origins of Negro music. (172, emphasis in original; see also D. Miller 1995)

It would seem that early rhythm & blues' connections to old school rap could not be more pronounced. For example, notice how early rhythm & blues, to a certain extent, represented working-class and poor black peoples' interface and extremely interesting relationship with industry and technology (e.g., amplifying the saxophone and electrifying the lead, rhythm, and bass guitars). Where early rhythm & blues was one of the first forms of music to regularly use electric instruments, old school rap was one of the first forms of American music to regularly use digital technology, especially via drum machines and other computerized instruments. Moreover, much has been made of early hip hop DJs' ability to create new and unusual sounds on their respective instruments, which generally consisted of two turntables, a drum machine and, by 1982, the infamous Emulator sampling keyboard.

Paralleling early rhythm & blues saxophonists' screaming, screeching, and honking, early hip hop DJs' manipulation of music technology, as opposed to merely traditional musical instruments, also produced sounds that were considered quite controversial in the late 1970s and early 1980s. More specifically, I would like to suggest that early hip hop DJs'—such as DJ Kool Herc, Afrika Bambaataa, Grandmaster Flash, Grand Wizard Theodore, and Grand Mixer DXT—"scratching" represented a kind of sonic deconstruction and radical reconstruction much like that of the early rhythm & blues honking saxophonists. Obviously Adolphe Sax, the inventor of the saxophone, did not intend the instrument to be played the way the early rhythm & blues honkers did, just as, we can be certain, Thomas Edison, the inventor of the record player, never intended his invention to be used the way hip hop DJs have used turntables over the years. Early hip hop DJs' innovative use of technology enabled them to not only "scratch" and "sample" to reach unsettlingly high notes and odd sounds (à la the early rhythm & blues honkers and guitarists), but their unprecedented employment of drum machines allowed them to bring the *basso profondo*, extremely low notes, usually only heard in the recording studio or in an intimate club setting, to the boom boxes, headphones, and homes of not only black ghetto youth, but soon white suburban youth as well.

If, via early rhythm & blues, it was "almost as if the blues people were reacting against the softness and 'legitimacy' that had crept into black instrumental music with the advent of swing." Then, in a similar fashion, it could be observed that early hip hop DJing and old school rap registers as late-twentieth-century blues people's rejection of and resistance to the "softness and 'legitimacy'" that had increasingly whitewashed and watered down black popular music, from classic rhythm & blues to funk, with the infamous emergence of disco. As an aural effort to *whiten* and *lighten* the "heavy" rhythms and "hard-driving" backbeats, as well as the provocative and often overtly political messages in much of the black popular music of the postwar period—which is to say, from classic rhythm & blues and soul to funk and reggae—disco completely diminished the militant messages in black popular music and demanded that "everybody just dance!" and "get down to the boogie!"[19]

Without in any way denying disco's contributions to old school rap's party vibe and modified dance beats, it is important to make a distinction between the crossover schemes and hit record dreams of disco and the "in your face!" block party in the ghetto motif that marked most old school rap records. Evolving out of the increasingly groove-oriented sounds of 1970s soul and funk (especially the work of Isaac Hayes, Barry White, and Philadelphia International Records), disco emphasized the beat above everything else, including the lyrics and "good" singing. In contrast to the countless sociopolitical soul records that saw their release in the early 1970s—undisputed classics such as Donny Hathaway's "The Ghetto," Aretha Franklin's "Young, Gifted, and Black," Marvin Gaye's "Inner-City Blues," Curtis Mayfield's "Freddie's Dead," Gil Scott-Heron's "The Bottle," and the O'Jays' "For the Love of Money"—most disco songs were apolitical and primarily preoccupied with love, lust, sex, partying, and dancing.[20]

Taking its name from the fashionable discotheques of the 1970s, these clubs almost exclusively played upbeat dance music. While most of the discotheques were predominantly gay white clubs in New York City, the DJs in these clubs specifically picked not progressive rock or pop rock records, but soul and funk records that had heavy rhythms and hard grooves. Once popular in the disco clubs, these soul and funk records began to receive serious radio play and respectable sales. As a result, both black and white record companies and producers began to make records specifically with the disco clubs and their colorful clientele in mind. Of course, these records as a rule featured strong pop sounds and hummable hooks, so that they could achieve the greatest crossover success possible. In essence, to the ears of trained musicians, disco was pop music with bustling basslines and exaggerated dance beats.

Between 1975 and 1979, the unrelenting rhythms and ever-bubbling disco beat dominated the pop charts, and seemingly every musician of consequence began to make disco records: from rockers like the Rolling Stones and Rod Stewart, to soul artists such as Aretha Franklin and Curtis Mayfield, to blues artists like Johnnie Taylor and Z. Z. Hill. Several new disco artists became bona fide stars. For instance, Donna Summer, the Trammps, the Bee Gees, Chic, the Village People, the Andrea True Connection, and KC & the Sunshine Band. Moreover, considering how heavily disco drew from soul, several disco artists had serious commitments to both soul and disco, creating a subgenre of music generally referred to as "disco soul." Gloria Gaynor,

Gwen McCrae, Evelyn "Champagne" King, Loleatta Holloway, Sister Sledge, Vicki Sue Robinson, Linda Clifford, Double Exposure, the Trammps, and the incomparable Sylvester were the heart and soul of disco soul.

The more soul-oriented disco artists never forgot disco's roots in soul and funk and, consequently, they brought a great deal of gospel-influenced grit to their dance-floor ditties and party anthems. But, by the late 1970s disco began to fall out of favor as the post-Vietnam War period quickly turned into the economically ugly 1980s of Ronald Reagan's presidency. The 1980s were a particularly difficult period for working-class and poor African Americans, and in characteristic fashion black popular music during the early years of the decade carried over a lot of the feel-good and have-fun vibe of 1970s soul, funk, and disco.[21]

Just as early rhythm & blues supposedly contained "a kind of frenzy and extra-local vulgarity . . . that had never been present in older blues forms," similarly old school rap was repeatedly ridiculed as juvenile vulgarity obsessed with partying and material possessions. For example, the first hit rap record was the fun-filled and electro-beat driven "Rapper's Delight" by the Sugarhill Gang. The group, which consisted of three Englewood, New Jersey, rappers named Master Gee, Wonder Mike, and Big Bank Hank, was the brainchild of soul singer, producer, and Sugar Hill Records label owner Sylvia Robinson.

Robinson had become increasingly aware of the huge hip hop block parties and street jams occurring around the New York City area during the late 1970s. To cash in on what she initially thought was nothing more than a form of novelty music, Robinson produced the rappers over a track her Sugar Hill house band, which was called Positive Force, had cooked up. The track interpolated Chic's "Good Times," and after the record became a hit and went multiplatinum Chic's Nile Rodgers and Bernard Edwards sued the Sugarhill Gang for copyright infringement. It was the first of many legal battles rap artists, hip hop DJs, and hip hop producers would face over the years. Ultimately the lawsuit was settled out of court, leaving Rodgers and Edwards with a large share of the future royalties for "Rapper's Delight." Hence, even at its inception, rap's borrowing from other musics was as controversial as its "hedonistic" lyrics.[22]

The Sugarhill Gang's fourteen-minute "Rapper's Delight" was obviously the beginning of something big, something very big. At its earliest stages rap's influences are easily observed. "Rapper's Delight"—as well as the Sugarhill Gang's early albums *Rapper's Delight* (1980), *8th Wonder* (1982), *Rappin' Down Town* (1983), and *Livin' in the Fast Lane* (1984)—bears traces of vocalese or scatting from classic jazz and the proto-rap of jump blues and classic rhythm & blues. No matter how simple it may sound to our ears today, within the context of its time (circa 1979) "Rapper's Delight" was incredibly innovative. Its critical acclaim and worldwide success proved that rap was more than a mere novelty, and close to thirty-five years later no one can deny that rap has become one of the most influential musical genres in American history, ranking right up there alongside gospel, blues, jazz, rhythm & blues, and rock & roll. Although none of the Sugarhill Gang's other songs ever achieved the level of success of "Rapper's Delight," it really did not matter. "Rapper's Delight," with its rickety synthesized funk, disco, and electro sound, sparked a new musical genre that would eventually demonstrate that black ghetto youth could be just as serious as they could be silly, and just as creative as they could be destructive.

Similar to the Sugarhill Gang, the all-female rap group the Sequence recorded for Sugar Hill Records and, as with the Sugarhill Gang, their records were also mostly about relationships, partying, and dancing. The group is notable because its hit single "Funk You Up!" (1979) was the first rap record released by a female group and the second single released by Sugarhill Records. Originally formed in Columbia, South Carolina, by a group of high school cheerleaders, the group consisted of Cheryl Cook (a.k.a., Cheryl the Pearl), Gwendolyn Chisolm (a.k.a., Blondie), and lead singer/rapper Angie Brown Stone (a.k.a., Angie B.). Able to sustain their success better than the Sugarhill Gang, the Sequence had a minor hit with "And You Know That" (1980), and then a series of charting singles with "Funky Sound (Tear The Roof Off)" (1981), "Simon Says" (1982), "I Don't Need Your Love (Part One)" (1982), "Here Comes the Bride" (1982), "Love Changes" (1982), "I Just Want To Know" (1983), "Funk You Up '85" (1984), and "Control" (1985).[23]

Bringing a female perspective to old school rap, the Sequence's body of work challenges those who question whether women have contributed to rap music in specific, and hip hop culture in general. Considering the fickle tastes of early rap fans, it should be emphasized that Sugarhill Records' female group, the Sequence, actually fared better and had more hits than its male group, the Sugarhill Gang, during the early days of rap music. The Sequence's lead rapper/singer, Angie Stone, would increasingly focus on her singing, first filling the lead singer spot in Vertical Hold (peep their hit "Seems You're Much Too Busy" [1993]), before going solo and emerging as one of the premier voices of the Neo-Soul Movement (see Rabaka forthcoming). Equally important here is the fact that the first significant rap records actually featured rappers who were not native New Yorkers: the Sugarhill Gang was from Englewood, New Jersey, and the Sequence was from Columbia, South Carolina. Needless to say, hip hop history is a lot more complex and complicated than many folk (especially "serious hip hop heads") are willing to concede.[24]

While it is undeniable that one of the major motifs of old school rap revolves around partying and having a good time (à la soul, funk, and disco), it is extremely important not to overlook the early "love rap" of the Sequence (e.g., "Love Changes" [1982]) and Spoonie Gee (e.g., "Love Rap" [1979]). Moreover, it is equally important to emphasize the early "message rap" of Kurtis Blow (e.g., "The Breaks" [1980] and "Hard Times" [1980]), Melle Mel (e.g., "Superrappin'" [1980]), Lovebug Starski (e.g., "Positive Life" [1981]) and, of course, Grandmaster Flash & the Furious Five (e.g., "The Message" [1982]). Even during its first phase of development on record—the "on record" part here needs to be emphasized because, truth be told, rap's origins extend back far beyond late 1970s and early 1980s recordings—most rap songs revolved around three major themes: *partying*, *politicking*, and *romancing*. Which is to say, even at its outset rap music was more than merely party music, and while it eventually came to be associated with partying, to its inventors and most of its early practitioners it was music with a message. [25]

Similar to soul and funk, the multidimensional black popular musics it drew most heavily from, old school rap was music that was made for partying, politicking, and romancing. Seeming to perfectly embody all the elements of old school rap (i.e., the partying, politicking, and romancing), Kurtis Blow skillfully built on and went further than either the Sugarhill Gang or the Sequence. With his winning personality and unprecedented popularity (especially for a rapper in the early 1980s), Blow is an undisputed pioneer in the history of rap music. Perhaps more than any other figure in the early history of rap music he demonstrated that it was not a novelty or, rather more crudely, young black folk's foolishness. [26]

Blow was without question the first rapper to be taken seriously by the music industry, and his business acumen and list of hip hop firsts continues to inspire rappers more than thirty years after his exploits. For instance, he was really the first significant solo rapper on record; the first rapper to sign with and release an album on a major record label; the first rapper to have a single certified gold (i.e., his 1980 classic "The Breaks"); the first rapper to embark on a national and international concert tour; the first solo rap artist to make a music video; and the first rapper to establish rap's mainstream marketability and appeal by signing an endorsement deal with the Coca-Cola Company.

Although Blow's body of work is obviously important and his influence enormous, the truth of the matter is that his songs sound extremely dated at this point. His rapping technique, even though it was cutting edge at the time, just was not as innovative and ear-catching as the much more advanced MCs who both built on his style and chased him up the charts after his initial success. In this sense, Blow is a progenitor whose progeny, as if observing the "laws of nature" or Sigmund Freud's twisted Oedipus complex, went on to higher heights. However, as his best rhymes clearly indicate, Blow personified the essence of old school rap: accessibly partying, politicking, and romancing over the bangingest beats this side of funk and disco.

With his 1980 classic "The Breaks," Blow not only proved to the music industry that rap was not a novelty, but he also demonstrated to other emerging rappers that rap music could thematically cover a great deal of ground beyond partying. In other words, where the Sugarhill Gang placed the party theme on rap music's sonic palette, and Spoonie Gee and the Sequence could be said to have contributed the romance theme, Kurtis Blow added political rap to old school rap's sonic palette, as well as his distinctive spin on party rap and love rap. For instance, the wide-ranging lyrics to "The Breaks" run the gamut from rhymes about relationship troubles to tax troubles, from exorbitant phone bills to war. The song undeniably represents one of old school rap's defining and most enduring moments. His eponymous September 1980 debut album pushed the envelope even further by featuring rap, rock, and soul. The rock and soul songs sound like crossover filler, but the old school raps, especially "The Breaks," "Rappin' Blow (Part 2)," and "Hard Times," clearly illustrate that old school rap was not all fun and games. "Hard Times" in particular was a harbinger of things to come—that is to say, message rap, or what is currently called conscious or political rap.

Although it has been often overlooked in favor of Grandmaster Flash & the Furious Five's "The Message" (1982), Kurtis Blow's "Hard Times" addressed social and political issues two years before "The Message" was recorded and released. On "Hard Times" Blow delivered the most scathing rhymes of his career, seeming to channel the hundreds of blues and jazz musicians who sang about "hard times," poverty, and unemployment during the Great Depression and interwar years. Lyrically the song is not new, as African Americans have told countless tales of working-class and poor black folk's hardships via black popular music. However, musically "Hard Times" was quite new, because it opened up a whole new world where lyrics and music, hard-hitting rhymes and heavy rhythms coalesced to create a new form of social commentary and political critique in an era where most people seemed to just want to go along to get along and stood stupefied in the face of the callousness of the status quo.

Building on Blow's message rap, Grandmaster Flash & the Furious Five were the most influential message rappers of the old school rap era. Formed in the South Bronx in 1978, the group consisted of DJ Grandmaster Flash and five rappers, Melle Mel, Kidd Creole, Cowboy, Mr. Ness/Scorpio, and Rahiem. Placing a greater emphasis on the visual and performance aspects of their shows, the group's use of turntablism, break-beat DJing, colorful costumes, choreographed stage routines, and animated lyricism was a game-changing force in the early development of rap music. "The Message" was actually the third installment in a trilogy of message rap tracks that Grandmaster Flash & the Furious Five released between 1979 and 1983.[27]

Although frequently overlooked, Flash and the Five's 1979 Enjoy Records single, "Superappin'," partially served as a sonic blueprint for "The Message." However, "Superrappin'" was more focused on touting the skills of each of Flash's rappers, with the boasting and bragging style of old school rap on full display. In 1980 they released their Sugarhill Records debut, "Freedom," which built on the momentum of "Superrappin'" but decidedly shifted their lyrical focus further in the direction of social commentary. Flash and the Five commented on race in "Superrappin'," but in "Freedom" their lyrics were slightly more poignant even as they continued to emphasize partying and dancing to the funky modified electro-disco beat. After releasing "Birthday Party" and "The Adventures of Grandmaster Flash on the Wheels of Steel" in 1981, the latter track representing the first time that scratching and turntablism were put on record, Flash and the Five released "The Message."

Produced by Clifton "Jiggs" Chase and Ed "Duke Bootee" Fletcher, the latter cowrote the song with Melle Mel, "The Message" took what Kurtis Blow began with "Hard Times" to the next level. Instead of making a few passing references to racism and poverty (à la "Superappin'" and "Freedom"), "The Message" devoted every second of the song to political critique and social commentary. "The Message" was widely applauded and, as a result, Flash and the Five's debut album was titled *The Message* (1982). Seeming to meld the militant African American poetry tradition of the 1960s and 1970s (à la Amiri Baraka, Sonia Sanchez, Gil Scott-Heron, Nikki Giovanni, the Last Poets, and the Watts Prophets) with old school rap production techniques and beats, *The Message* contained party raps and love raps but was thematically united by the message (or, rather, quasi-message) tracks, such as "It's Nasty," "It's a Shame" and, of course, "The Message."

In the aftermath of Flash and the Five's "Message," countless rappers began to address social and political issues. "The Message," therefore, was not only a challenge to Reaganomics, but also a challenge to what was already perceived as the hyper-commercialization of rap music and hip hop culture in the early 1980s. Instead of boasting about their rap skills, dissin' their rivals ("sucker MCs!"), and asking audiences to wave their hands in the air and scream like they just don't care, after "The Message" rappers began to increasingly offer political critique and social commentary. Of course, "The Message" was not the end of braggadocio and swag in old school rap, which obviously continues to be a major part of rap in the twenty-first century. However, it did open up an alternative topical and lyrical universe that demonstrated to early rappers and hip hoppers that the hippest form of rap music does not cater to the whims and wishes of corporate America but instead stays in tune with the pulse of the people, especially poor black people.

Following in the tradition of "The Message" numerous rappers have addressed a wide variety of social and political topics, including everything from racism, gang violence, domestic violence, prostitution, drug addiction, and HIV/AIDS to U.S. foreign policy in Africa, Latin America, and the Middle East. It is important to understand the evolution of rap music and hip hop culture, especially in its first phase of development between 1979 and 1983. Many may find it ironic that message rap grew out of a musical style that was initially known for its preoccupation with love, sex, partying, and dancing, but rap's evolution only appears ironic if it is divorced from the history of black popular music and black popular culture. Black popular culture, and especially black popular music, has always expressed aspects of African American social and political thought. Mirroring classic rhythm & blues, message rap reflects a distinct form of contemporary African American protest and, as emphasized in the introduction to this book, *a new, post-Civil Rights Movement and post-Black Power Movement form of black popular culture and black popular music-based politics and social movement*—the Hip Hop Movement.

What needs to be understood here is that unlike most forms of political protest, *aesthetic protest* is very rarely a direct call to action. Even so, critical aesthetic representation of sociopolitical problems, political aesthetics, and social realism in the context of African American artistic traditions must be comprehended as constituting extremely powerful sociopolitical ideas and acts. Most hip hop critics might interpret instances of protest in rap songs as mere "complaint," but by the very fact that the alleged "complaint" is publicly articulated to such an eloquent extent that even rap music's most ahistorical and apolitical interpreters understand it to be "complaint" illustrates that rap protest, indeed, is a form of contestation of oppressive and exploitive conditions even when it does not directly translate into Civil Rights Movement-styled organized public demonstration. This is part of the distinct power of black popular music, if not black popular culture in general. Indirectly responding to hip hop critics' depoliticization of rap and helping to drive my point home about rap as protest even though it may not translate into "protest" in the conventional Civil Rights Movement-centered sense, in *Black Culture and Black Consciousness: Afro-American Folk Thought from Slavery to Freedom* (1977), Lawrence Levine offered remarkable insight:

> To state that black song constituted a form of black protest and resistance does not mean that it necessarily led to or even called for any tangible and specific actions, but rather that it served as a mechanism by which Negroes could be relatively candid in a society that rarely accorded them that privilege, could communicate this candor to others whom they would in no other way be able to reach, and, in the face of the sanctions of the white majority, could assert their own individuality, aspirations, and sense of being. Certainly, if nothing else, black song makes it difficult to believe that Negroes internalized their

situation so completely, accepted the values of the larger society so totally, or manifested so pervasive an apathy as we have been led to believe. . . . The African tradition of being able to verbalize publicly in song what could not be said to a person's face, not only lived on among Afro-Americans throughout slavery but continued to be a central feature of black expressive culture in freedom. (239–40, 247)

It is Levine's last sentence that directly connects with old school rappers' rhymes. When he reminds us that the "African tradition of being able to verbalize publicly in song what could not be said to a person's face not only lived on among Afro-Americans throughout slavery but continued to be a central feature of black expressive culture in freedom," he hints at how generation after jostling generation of African American musicians have, literally, used music as a medium to constructively critique their enslavers, oppressors, and abusers, both within and without African American communities. Long before "The Message" there were songs that critiqued and commented on African Americans' dire social conditions. For instance, the Last Poets' eponymous 1970 debut registered as a blistering proto-rap record that touched on everything from drug addiction and street violence to sex and revolution (e.g., "Run, Nigger," "Wake Up, Niggers," "Black Thighs," "When the Revolution Comes," and, of course, "Niggers Are Scared of Revolution"). The poetic equivalent to Marvin Gaye's *What's Goin' On?* (1971) and Sly & the Family Stone's *There's a Riot Goin' On* (1971), the Last Poets' ghetto-centered rhymes on the aforementioned album, as well as on *This Is Madness* (1971), *Chastisement* (1973), *At Last* (1974), and *Delights of the Garden* (1977), sadly remind us that little changed in the lives of African Americans between the early 1970s and the early 1980s.

It is also important for us to keep in mind that the contention that "black song constituted a form of black protest and resistance does not mean that it necessarily led to or even called for any tangible and specific actions." As with old school rap and the origins of the Hip Hop Movement, classic rhythm & blues' "protest and resistance" may not have nicely and neatly paralleled the "protest and resistance" emerging from the dominant African American sociopolitical movement of its epoch (i.e., the Civil Rights Movement). But, make no mistake about it, classic rhythm & blues folk, as Levine noted, indeed did protest and resist by way of black popular music and black popular culture, among other political and aesthetic avenues.

FROM RHYTHM & BLUES AND THE CIVIL RIGHTS MOVEMENT TO RAP AND THE HIP HOP MOVEMENT

As jump blues began to wane a new form of black popular music took center stage: vocal harmony groups, street corner groups, barbershop quartets or, more simply, *doo-wop groups*. Inspired by the stripped down trio sound and smooth singing of Nat King Cole, Johnny Moore's Three Blazers, and Charles Brown, the doo-wop concept actually reached all the way back to pre-World War II vocal groups, such as the Mills Brothers, the Ink Spots, the Delta Rhythm Boys, and the Charioteers. The first two groups, the Mills Brothers and the Ink Spots, had roots in the barbershop quartet, jazz, and pop traditions, frequently performing with the big bands of Duke Ellington, Glenn Miller, and Lucky Millinder. The latter two groups, the Delta Rhythm Boys and the Charioteers, began their careers as jubilee quartets, primarily singing spirituals, folk songs, and pop songs. Four core features character- ized pre-World War II vocal group singing, which consisted of a lead vocal- ist and supporting background singers: first, alternating lead vocals; second, closely harmonized choruses; third, imitation of instrumental tonality; and fourth, extreme contrasts in vocal range and timbre. It would be the postwar singers' innovative imitation of the sound of instruments that would provide their version of vocal harmony group singing with its catchy name: *doo-wop*.[28]

Here it is important to emphasize the two dominant streams running through the African American vocal harmony group tradition prior to the emergence of the postwar vocal harmony group tradition (i.e., *the doo-wop tradition*). Obviously the spirituals and African American folk songs pro- vided many of the prewar vocal harmony groups with their point of depar- ture, while pop, love, and novelty songs offered others their core repertoire. Hence, the same thread of the sacred and the secular, spirituality and sexual- ity found in 1960s and 1970s rhythm & blues, as well as 1980s-onward rap and neo-soul, can be traced back to postwar black popular music's roots in 1940s and 1950s rhythm & blues. Contemporary discussions concerning "commercial rap" versus "conscious rap" are particularly indebted to early rhythm & blues' gospel versus pop divide.

Taking its name from the incredibly close harmonies and creative scat singing of the background vocalists, "doo-wop" was a common phrase that 1950s vocal harmony groups used in their efforts to imitate musical instru- ments. Like rap music, doo-wop emerged from the lives and struggles of African American ghetto youth and, as a consequence, it reflected all of the limitations and idiosyncrasies of African American youth life and culture in the immediate postwar period. Although many have made fun of 1950s black ghetto youth singing "nonsense syllables," when these so-called "nonsense syllables" are placed within the wider context of postwar African American history, culture, and struggle alternative meanings and messages can be gleaned from doo-wop. As a matter of fact, I would be one of the first to admit that in a strict musicological sense phrases such as "doo-wop-wop, doo-wop-wop," "be-bop, be-bop, be-bop," "dang-dang-diggy-dang," and "shooby-dooby-doo" are nonsensical. However, in a sociological sense,

when dropped within the absurd world of postwar America, with its continued commitment to segregation, denial of decent African American education, and routine violation of African American civil rights, the nonsense
phrases of doo-wop seem to mirror, if not mimic, the high-sounding but
hollow words of 1950s U.S. government and society as a whole.[29]

Even doo-wop's most cynical critics have conceded that it has roots in the
hallowed harmonies and emotive phrasing of the spirituals and gospel. However, frequently these same critics fail to recognize that just as the spirituals
and gospel contained double meanings and masked messages, so too did doo-
wop. Doo-wop's double entendres and masked messages, whether perceived
as romantic or comedic, provided African American ghetto youth in the
1950s with one of the only avenues open to them at the time to express their
worldviews and distinct values.

Indeed, most doo-wop songs centered on love, but we should bear in
mind that African Americans creating and beautifully singing love songs in a
segregated postwar world, where less than a century prior it was basically
forbidden for African Americans to have families and against the law for
African Americans to enter into matrimony, was indeed political, if not decidedly defiant. This may also explain why rhythm & blues, soul, and neo-
soul are primarily perceived as *love-centered musics*. In other words, *black
love in a white-dominated world is always already political and an act of
undaunted defiance, because by loving each other African Americans not
only acknowledge the humanity of their special loved ones, but they also defy
the centuries of "civilized" and "scientific" discourse that has repeatedly
told them that they are not really and truly part of the human species—and
not really and truly American citizens.*

The 1950s were the peak years for youthful a cappella group harmony
sounds. The new music poured out of city parks and school gyms, and it
could also be heard on street corners and the stoops of overcrowded low-
income apartment buildings in the inner cities. Similar to rapping today, back
then singing was a diversion from the hard lives and harsh conditions most
African American youth faced in the ghetto. Although the African American
middle class made small but steady progress in the 1950s, the African
American masses, who were primarily poor and working-class folk, experienced very little change in their day-to-day lives. With this in mind, it is easy
to understand why these youths viewed a hit record and a successful career as
a singer as a viable way to get out of the ghetto.

Boldly building on the models and innovations of the pioneering interwar
vocal groups, throngs of African American teenagers (initially known as
"street-corner" groups) developed postwar harmony styles that directly cor-
responded with their musical tastes, cultural sensibilities, social values, political views, and lives as poor and working-class youth. Tellingly, the songs
they sang were, however juvenile to their critics, sonic reflections of their

aspirations and frustrations, their dreams and nightmares. More than any previous group of African American youths, the doo-woppers of the 1950s were able to draw from two parallel but distinct African American singing traditions.

The first tradition, as alluded to above, grew out of the spirituals and gospel and always seemed to privilege more of a "church sound" regardless of the thematic content of the song. The second tradition, which was also made mention of above, grew out of the blues and its more secular and sensual sounding offspring, such as jazz and jump blues. The more church-sounding music appealed to the masses of African Americans, who had been raised on the gospel vocal aesthetic, where—when it could be *whitened* and *lightened* and made to cross over—the more secular and sensual sounding music appealed to whites, who eventually began to accept a vanilla version of black popular music within the white popular music marketplace.

Doo-wop was not the first form of black popular music to "cross over" to white audiences; both the Mills Brothers and the Ink Spots crossed the color line in the 1930s and 1940s. However, it was *the first form of black popular music to spawn widespread white youth imitation of black popular music*, especially as it evolved into rock & roll. In keeping with the *sonic segregation* of the music industry in mid-twentieth-century America, which obviously mirrored the social segregation of mid-twentieth-century America, there were gospel sounding doo-wop songs for blacks and often a separate set of often placid pop sounding doo-wop songs for whites. A distinction between the more rhythm & blues-based doo-wop and the more "pop" sounding doo-wop—and black popular music in general—began to be embraced by fans and critics. In their classic essay, "The Doo-Wah Sound: Black Pop Groups of the 1950s" (1975), music critics Mike Redmond and Marv Goldberg offered an insightful analysis of the distinct differences between 1950s pop and rhythm & blues, essentially characterizing pop as

> the group singing the entire song in unison, or group members singing the chorus or phrase lines behind the lead. Or, in a variation, the group members singing a smooth, almost subdued blend of harmony without distinctive tenor to bass parts. In this format, the group provides a showcase for the lead and remains unobtrusively in the background. The material is presented in a cool—almost detached manner, and the subject matter is usually non-controversial in nature avoiding such topics as drinking, crime and associated societal problems, and overt sexuality. (22–23)

Clearly the pop music of the twenty-first century, including commercial or pop rap, continues to embrace much of the pop music formula of the 1950s, with the one important exception being that instead of "avoiding such topics as drinking, crime and associated societal problems, and overt sexuality," everything except social problems regularly turns up in contemporary pop music, especially sexuality. In other words, even though it has evolved a great deal over the last sixty years to include topics such as drinking, crime, and sexuality, the raising of serious social and political problems, at least in terms of contemporary black popular music, has been left to conscious, political, message, underground and alternative rappers, neo-soul singers, or spoken-word artists—all of whom, in one way or another, seem to, however incongruously, correspond with Redmond and Goldberg's definition of 1950s rhythm & blues. They explained:

> the R&B style employs a prominent, often intricate, background harmony pattern with distinguishable tenor and bass parts. The material is presented with an emotionally-charged reading reflecting the influence of gospel and blues music. The lyrical content of R&B songs is usually more representative of black cultural patterns of the period. Generally there are more variations in presentation and a greater tendency toward experimentation in R&B music— as opposed to the more stylized pop form. (23–24)

The first thing we might observe is that classic rhythm & blues, in contrast to much of the contemporary music put out under the "rhythm & blues" moniker, had "more variations in presentation and a greater tendency toward experimentation." Obviously when one listens to and really hears Atlantic, Chess, King, Motown, and Stax rhythm & blues from the 1950s and 1960s, what one is really listening to are the sounds of experimentation: the infectious sounds of Ray Charles synthesizing gospel, jazz, jump blues, and country & western; Etta James melding barrelhouse blues, jazz, and pop; James Brown masterminding his distinct mix of gospel, blues, jazz, and jump blues; Smokey Robinson & the Miracles, the Supremes, the Temptations, Martha Reeves & the Vandellas, the Four Tops, Mary Wells, and Marvin Gaye smoothing out the rough edges of early rhythm & blues; and Otis Redding, Carla Thomas, Wilson Pickett, and Sam and Dave fusing the grit of gospel, the bad luck tales of the blues, the jive of jump blues, and the earthiness of early rhythm & blues. With the shift toward the digitization of black popular music in the 1980s rhythm & blues, almost as a rule, suffered from overproduction. Its polished and super-slick sound frequently watered down the music (not to mention the messages in the music), making it sound more like mainstream pop, which was going through it own version of the post-disco digital revolution as well.

It was left to rap and neo-soul to present contemporary black popular music "with an emotionally-charged reading reflecting the influence of gospel and blues music," as well as the gutsy gospel aesthetic of classic rhythm & blues. Not only did rap and neo-soul represent a recommitment to the experimentalism that had marked the best rhythm & blues, soul, funk, and disco, its lyrical content has been consistently "more representative of [the] black cultural patterns of the [contemporary] period." To really understand rap and neo-soul, and the wider Hip Hop Movement they sonically represent, it is important to comprehend classic rhythm & blues as "representative of black cultural patterns of the period" in African American history, culture, and struggle between 1945 and 1965, which is also to say, during the immediate postwar years and the Civil Rights Movement era.

The entangled racial and commercial agendas of the recording and radio industries, as well as "mature," middle-class, and mainstream white America's response to the precipitous widespread popularity of African American and African American-derived musics, greatly influenced the evolution of rhythm & blues between 1954 and 1965. Along with that, there were concomitant currents internal to the African American community that were also equally influential on rhythm & blues' evolution between 1954 and 1965. Undoubtedly, the evolution of African American male vocal harmony group singing during the 1950s demonstrated that significant social, cultural, and demographic changes had converged to create unprecedented African American acceptance of a lighter and sweeter style of rhythm & blues (à la Nat King Cole, Charles Brown, Billy Eckstine, and the Four Toppers/Five Red Caps) that was more ballad-focused than previous forms of early rhythm & blues. Consequently, long before the recording industry took up a similar strategy in its efforts to reach the wallets of a wider white audience, African Americans' musical tastes favored a softer, slower, ballad-based form of rhythm & blues. In fact, in the late 1940s and early 1950s, these lighter and sweeter lyrical and musical stylings had periodically enabled a couple of the more sentimental sounding African American harmonizers—classic groups such as the Orioles ("It's Too Soon to Know"), the Five Keys ("The Glory of Love"), the Vocaleers ("Be True"), and the Harp-Tones ("Sunday Kind of Love")—to cross the color line and integrate the white pop charts.

By the middle of the 1950s the same sentimental and relatively safe sounding characteristics that put African American harmony groups on the pop charts in the late 1940s and early 1950s had paved the way for the wholesale crossover of several sets of upstarts who spearheaded a wave of *sonic desegregation* and *sonic integration* that has continued to this day. Groups such as the Moonglows, Spaniels, Penguins, Charms, Chords, and Crows all had major hits on the pop charts that, for all intents and purposes, put forward idealized and newfangled versions of male-female relationships that challenged the core characteristics of the African American male blues aesthetic, which revolved around sometimes subtle, and sometimes not-so-subtle, expressions of hyper-masculinity and outright misogyny. These changes in African American musical tastes were indicative of broader changes throughout African America in particular, and the United States more generally.

After World War II small crowds of well-meaning and mostly liberal white sociologists and cultural anthropologists marched into African America. When they came out and carefully reviewed their "scientific" findings they concluded that African Americans had created their own unique culture with identifiable value systems, codes of conduct, and standards of excellence. As a result of their distinct historical experiences and ongoing racial segregation in U.S. society, the urban African American masses incrementally evolved their own worldview, created their own cultural institutions, and put forward their own popular art forms geared toward expressing and legitimating their views and values. Among the myriad institutions that synthesized and publicized the post-war urban African American experience, few were more effective and effusive than rhythm & blues and its accompanying ethos and aesthetic.

Even though it was obviously distinctive, there is no denying the profound impact that mainstream and middle-class white America had on the daily existence, material conditions, and growing cultural consciousness of urban black America. Similar to other African American performers and artists—indeed, like most African Americans at the time—the exponents of rhythm & blues in the 1950s existed in a racially, culturally, psychologically, religiously, and musically segregated world. They existed and operated at the crossroads of a series of intersecting traditions, mostly African American but many European American as well; mainly southern, unsophisticated, and rural, but also increasingly northern, midwestern, western, and undeniably urban.

Their efforts to come to terms with their hybrid heritages were exemplified in their social, political, cultural, and religious expressions, and also reflected in their popular culture and, most especially, in their popular music. It was black popular music in the 1950s that increasingly came to sound like a vocalized version of "double-consciousness" which, it will be recalled, W.E.B. Du Bois famously identified as the core characteristic of the African American experience. In his classic *The Souls of Black Folk* (1903), Du Bois declared:

> After the Egyptian and Indian, the Greek and Roman, the Teuton and Mongolian, the Negro is a sort of seventh son, born with a veil, and gifted with second-sight in this American world,—a world which yields him no true self-consciousness, but only lets him see himself through the revelation of the other world. It is a peculiar sensation, this double-consciousness, this sense of always looking at one's self through the eyes of others, of measuring one's soul by the tape of a world that looks on in amused contempt and pity. One ever feels his two-ness,—an American, a Negro; two souls, two thoughts, two unreconciled strivings; two warring ideals in one dark body, whose dogged strength alone keeps it from being torn asunder.
>
> The history of the American Negro is the history of this strife,—this longing to attain self-conscious manhood, to merge his double self into a better and truer self. In this merging he wishes neither of the older selves to be lost. He would

not Africanize America, for America has too much to teach the world and Africa. He would not bleach his Negro soul in a flood of white Americanism, for he knows that Negro blood has a message for the world. He simply wishes to make it possible for a man to be both a Negro and an American, without being cursed and spit upon by his fellows, without having the doors of Opportunity closed roughly in his face. (3–4; see also Rabaka 2007, 2008, 2010a, 2010c)

Classic rhythm & blues, being the mid-twentieth-century culmination of black popular music up to that point, sonically and succinctly captures "double-consciousness." It represents the psychological, cultural, and musical aftermath of centuries of enslavement, racial colonization, social segregation, and American apartheid. It is what being emancipated and recurringly re-enslaved sounds like. It is the sound of African Americans expressing that "peculiar sensation," that "sense of always looking at one's self through the eyes of others, of measuring one's soul by the tape of a world that looks on in amused contempt and pity."

Classic rhythm & blues excruciatingly encompasses African Americans' feelings of perpetual "two-ness" and dividedness, their quests to see themselves as they actually are, not as others would like for them to be. Classic rhythm & blues, then, is fundamentally about truth, about black folk speaking their special truths to each other and to the world at large. Part of African Americans' distinct truth undeniably involves the struggle to come to terms with their "American[ness]" and their "Negro[ness]" (i.e., their "African-ness"), their "two souls, two thoughts," their "two unreconciled strivings," their "two warring ideals in one dark body, whose dogged strength alone keeps it from being torn asunder." How else can we explain Ray Charles's innovative Atlantic Records years, where he synthesized the pleading, frenzy-filled, and shouting sounds of the spirituals and gospel with the often calm cry and musical melancholia of the blues? Or Etta James's jocular gospel, blues, and jazz mix during her Chess Records years, where she seemed to combine the styles of countless black pop divas before her and unambiguously provide a sonic palette for seemingly each of the pop divas who would follow after her, from Aretha Franklin and Janis Joplin to Beyoncé and Christina Aguilera?

Classic rhythm & blues is a musical and cultural manifestation of African Americans' "dogged strength." It represents a secularization of the deep double entendres of the spirituals and the blues, and—as with all other forms of black popular music—it makes the music mean one thing to those who have not *lived* the music and wholly another to those who have. *Living the music* and having an authentic relationship—or, rather, "keeping it real"—with the culture and community, or the experiences, individuals, and institutions that one is singing or rapping about represents both the *leitmotif* and *sine qua non* of black popular music and black popular culture. In other words, both the artist and the audience have got to *feel* the realness of the lyrics and music. If the lyrics and music do not conjure up and sonically capture the African American experience in a highly original and thoroughly individual way they do not register as "real," or "authentic," or—dare I say— "soulful."

It is the mystical and almost magical category of "soul" that has determined the fate of more than a few would-be iconic African American artists. In African America, as in Africa, artists must do more than represent themselves. They must also "rep" (i.e., represent) their community and culture. They must speak the special truth of their community and culture to the wider world. No matter how technically proficient one may be on his chosen instrument, no matter how much facility one has to sing high or low, or rap fast or slow, without "soul"—that *je ne sais quoi* of both continental and diasporan African ethos and aesthetics—there would be nothing truly distinct or, more to the point, "African" about African American music.[30]

Classic rhythm & blues' expression of double-consciousness captured mid-twentieth-century African American existence at the intersection of its diverse and incessantly overlapping heritages, which represented African Americans' aspirations and frustrations in the two decades following World War II. On the one hand, by the 1950s both African America and European America regularly recognized that there was indeed something called "white" popular music—although, from a historical, cultural, and musicological perspective, the Great American Songbook, especially Tin Pan Alley pop, was greatly indebted to African American music, most notably blues, ragtime, and jazz.[31]

On the other hand, there was African American's creolized musical culture and customs, with their own collection of preferred devices and performance practices, most of which were traceable back to Africa, but all of which had been boldly re-created to speak to the special needs of Africans in America in the middle of the twentieth century. Situated somewhere between those slippery and sliding, theoretical, yet conventionally understood and embraced, black and white musical poles, the African American masses' musical tastes illusively reside. And, it is here, in between these two musical poles, that we may be able to better understand that black popular music at a specific historical moment provides us with an imperfect but nonetheless evocative index of African American cultural consciousness at the moment in question.

All of this is to say, urban African American culture was neither monolithic nor completely autonomous or somehow free from European American musical and cultural influences. Religious, gender, and generational differences were just as important in mid-twentieth-century African America as they were within the white world, even if widely shared racial and most often class characteristics produced fundamentally homogenous lived experiences and core values. Surely, then, African American ghetto culture in the postwar period and the Civil Rights Movement years, and especially as found in black popular culture and black popular music in the 1950s and 1960s, was not—as many liberal, and many not-so-liberal, white sociologists have argued—a "pathological" or, even worse, "pathogenic" response to African Americans' prolonged social predicament, racial oppression, and economic exploitation. Moreover, black ghetto culture in the postwar period and the Civil Rights Movement years was more than a fruitless attempt to apishly imitate the middle-class views and values of white America under less favorable conditions and in greatly reduced circumstances. On the contrary, it audaciously represented an unprecedented and wholly innovative act of agency on the part of working-class and poor black folk to construct an accessible and completely viable cultural arena for communal solidarity and individual achievement while simultaneously recording and releasing the accumulated discontent and defiance in the face of, literally, centuries of domination and discrimination.

Even more importantly, the African American worldview and the distinct culture it created over time, and through which it was able to evolve, was not inert, even as it firmly grounded itself and deepened its roots in the fertile soil of postwar black (and, to a certain extent, white) America. Needless to say, worldviews are transformed as people transform the world or, rather, as they appear to transform the world. As a consequence, the major modes of creation, re-creation, representation, and interpretation of the African American experience have changed with every apparent breakthrough and setback in African American life, culture, and struggle. The evolution and extraordinary popularity of rhythm & blues in the 1950s and 1960s revealed just such a process of re-creation and cultural adaptation to what many African Americans optimistically perceived to be the birth of a new era of "authentic" American democracy coupled with the requisite expanded opportunities.

Understanding jump blues as an early form of rhythm & blues, it is important to acknowledge that rhythm & blues was the first form of black popular music to emerge during the post-World War II period. As such it became the first form of black popular music to be exposed to the unrestrained mass consumerism that defined the latter half of the twentieth century. With the introduction of the transistor radio in 1954, white youth had unbridled access to the hot new and often sensual sounds coming out of black America, which they previously had only limited access to as a consequence of their parents' incessant surveillance of their musical and general listening choices. In fact, prior to the introduction of the television into mainstream American culture in the late 1940s and early 1950s, the old cumbersome radio console served as the undisputed centerpiece of suburban intra-familial entertainment.[32]

In many ways rhythm & blues' remarkable popularity in the 1950s was a double-edged sword. On the one hand, no matter what the song was really about, suburban white youth developed a distinct tendency to embrace rhythm & blues exclusively as dance music (à la England's Northern Soul Movement in the late 1960s and early 1970s). As was witnessed above, similar to most white youths' interpretation of old school rap, if not rap in general, in their minds classic rhythm & blues was the ultimate party music. Even though most of the lyrics revealed innocuous romantic ideas or registered a popular dance craze at the time, *many of the messages in classic rhythm & blues alluded to the same subversive topics put forward during African American enslavement, chief among them commitments to African American freedom and unity, as well as African American spiritual and physical transcendence.*

On the other hand, classic rhythm & blues bore the marks of Du Bois's double-consciousness in light of the fact that its lyrics, like contemporary rap and neo-soul lyrics, were impacted by African Americans' precarious position at the low end of the U.S. social, political, cultural, and economic hierarchy. The truth is, in this instance dissimilar to rap and neo-soul, the lyrics of classic rhythm & blues, once comprehended as part and parcel of a commodified product, quite simply could not directly comment on the most pressing problems confronting black America. However, with the *Brown vs. the Board of Education* victory and the beginning of the Civil Rights Movement in 1954, black America began to noticeably change, and as a consequence the content and style of the major forms of black popular music began to change as well.

From 1954 through to the emergence of soul as the major black popular music in the mid-1960s, at its most resonant rhythm & blues not only registered the hardships and frustrations of urban African American life and its core views and values, but it also expressed African America's most cherished postwar achievements and ongoing aspirations. Black popular culture, as with the more mainstream aspects of U.S. popular culture that African Americans embrace, serves a sociopolitical function when and where it offers an arena where African Americans can create and critique alternative views and values, as well as an arena where they can explore and express traditional African American views and values. In this sense, classic rhythm & blues reflected and increasingly articulated an idealized vision of not only loving and ultra-romantic African American relationships, but also a united and harmonious African America which, truth be told, was more a figment of classic rhythm & blues singer-songwriters' imaginations than a reality in the 1950s and 1960s.

However, the classic rhythm & blues singer-songwriters were not alone in imagining a united and harmonious African America, they were merely translating and transmitting the postwar optimism, spirit of determination, and political pulse of the people then running rampant throughout African America into black popular music. In fact, for the first time since jazz simultaneously served at the soundtrack for both the New Negro Movement and the Harlem Renaissance in the 1920s and 1930s, black popular music unambiguously and unapologetically served as the soundtrack for a black sociopolitical movement. Beginning with rhythm & blues and the Civil Rights Movement and continuing through to rap and the Hip Hop Movement, since the middle of the twentieth century every major form of black popular music has reflected and articulated, however incongruously, the core views and values of the major African American social and political movement of its era. And, even though it has been regularly ridiculed, rap continues to reflect and articulate the cultural maneuvers, micro-politics, and mini-movements of post-Civil Rights Movement and post-Black Power Movement African America.[33]

At this point it might be safe to say that in terms of rhythm & blues serving as the soundtrack for the Civil Rights Movement nothing drives this point home better than the triangular relationships between the Civil Rights Movement, the rise of Motown Records, and the inroads they both made in integrating black America into white America. Foreshadowing countless hip hoppers' biographies, the iconic founder of Motown Records, Berry Gordy, dropped out of a Detroit high school in the eleventh grade with dreams of becoming a professional boxer. His boxing career was short-lived, as he was drafted by the U.S. Army to serve in the Korean War in 1950. It was in the army that Gordy obtained his General Educational Development (GED) certificate.

Out of the army by 1953, Gordy gravitated toward music, especially jazz, regularly frequenting clubs and eventually opening up a record store. In the 1950s jazz was becoming more and more an acquired taste, being eclipsed first by jump blues and then ultimately by rhythm & blues. Needless to say, Gordy's jazz-centered record store did not last long. However, it did pique his interest in songwriting, music production, and music promotion. Financially devastated by the failure of his record store Gordy was forced to work in the Lincoln-Mercury plant, making cars on the assembly line. It was a pivotal experience for him, and later he would model his record company on Detroit's auto industry, attempting to achieve the same level of productivity and efficiency.[34]

After writing a string of hits for Jackie Wilson (e.g., "Reet Petite," "That Is Why [I Love You So], "I'll Be Satisfied," and "Lonely Teardrops"), Gordy created Anna Records in 1959 along with two of his sisters, Anna and Gwen Gordy, and his friend Billy Davis. In quick succession after Anna Records he established Tamla Records and later Jobete Music Publishing (named after his daughters: Joy, Betty, and Terry). On April 14, 1960, he incorporated his music business ventures under the name the Motown Record Corporation

("Motown," being a portmanteau of *motor* and *town*, is a well-known African American nickname for Detroit). Beginning with an artist roster that boasted classic rhythm & blues luminaries such as Smokey Robinson & the Miracles, Marv Johnson, Barrett Strong, Mable John, Eddie Holland, Mary Wells, and the Marvelettes, Gordy created what has been repeatedly referred to as "clean" rhythm & blues records that owed as much to white pop as they did black pop. Even though he greatly respected the raunchier and more mature aspects of 1950s rhythm & blues, Motown Records' rhythm & blues would emphasize anodyne youthful singers and songs, in effect deconstructing and reconstructing rhythm & blues to make it more palatable to a wider, whiter, and younger audience.[35]

Motown artists in the 1960s were essentially the antithesis of 1950s rhythm & blues artists. For instance, the contrasts between Smokey Robinson and Howlin' Wolf, or Mary Wells and Big Maybelle, or Marv Johnson and Muddy Waters are obvious. But, Motown's music was more than chocolate-covered pop fluff. By synthesizing black and white pop music, by coloring Motown songs with gospel beats and subdued church choir background singing, throbbing jazz-influenced bass lines, and blues-soaked guitar licks, Berry Gordy revolutionized rhythm & blues' sonic palette. Whatever he lacked in terms of technical proficiency at singing or playing a musical instrument, there simply is no deny Gordy's gargantuan sonic vision. In the 1960s Motown produced a wide range of music, all of which seemed to appeal to a broad audience and several different demographics. Ultimately, Motown created an extremely fluid and flexible sound—the much vaunted "Motown sound"—which, in the most unprecedented manner imaginable, allowed its music to have special meaning for, and appeal to mainstream pop music lovers and discerning black music lovers across the contentious regional, racial, cultural, social, political, and generational chasms afflicting America in the 1960s.[36]

According to Nelson George, in *Where Did Our Love Go?: The Rise & Fall of the Motown Sound* (2007), Gordy "preferred jazz musicians for his sessions, believing that they were both more technically assured and more creative than their blues-based counterparts" (37). Most of Motown's session musicians were actually local luminaries on Detroit's jazz scene: pianists Joe Hunter, Richard "Popcorn" Wylie, Earl Van Dyke, and Johnny Griffith; guitarists Dave Hamilton, Joe Messina, Marvin Tarplin, Melvin "Wah Wah Watson" Raglin, Robert White, Eddie Willis, and Dennis Coffey; bassists James Jamerson, Bob Babbitt, and Michael Henderson; drummers William "Benny" Benjamin, Uriel Jones, Richard "Pistol" Allen, and Frederick Waites; and percussionists Eddie "Bongo" Brown and Jack Ashford. To complement the supper club soul or uptown jazzy soul sound Gordy was going for, as early as 1960 he "hired members of the Detroit Symphony Orchestra to achieve the upscale R&B sounds" made popular by Nat King

Cole, Ray Charles, Jackie Wilson, Sam Cooke, and Aretha Franklin during her Columbia Records years (39). The strings had the "whitening and lightening" effect, smoothing out the rough edges of Motown's rhythm & blues and providing it with an identifiable sound virtually at the outset.[37]

From Gordy's point of view, black popular music, much like black people in the United States in the 1950s and 1960s, represented the recording industry's "bastard child and mother lode, an aesthetic and economic contradiction that was institutionalized by white record executives" (50). Hence, Motown's music became a metaphor for urban African American life, culture, and struggle in the 1960s. Gordy demonstrated to the American music industry, and eventually to the world, that African American youths were just like the "clean-cut" boy or girl next door, which was one of the major motifs of Motown's music, and especially the classic recordings by Smokey Robinson & the Miracles, the Supremes, the Temptations, Mary Wells, Marvin Gaye, Tammi Terrell, Stevie Wonder, Kim Weston, the Marvelettes, the Four Tops, Gladys Knight & the Pips, and Martha Reeves & the Vandellas.

As George observed, Motown made it clear that beneath "the glistening strings, Broadway show tunes, and relaxed vocal styles was a music of intense feeling" (50). Rhythm & blues, even the most "pop soul" sounding (à la Dionne Warwick, Walter Jackson, Barbara Lewis, Chuck Jackson, Maxine Brown, and Freddie Scott), was more than mere background music. It was a tool that could be used to break down barriers: musical, cultural, social, political, and economic barriers. Paralleling the emergence of the Civil Rights Movement, the rise of Motown sent a clear message to the white-dominated music industry: African Americans would no longer tolerate any form of segregation, neither social nor musical segregation. The message Motown sent to black America was equally provocative. Here was a company owned and operated by an African American armed only with a GED who challenged white corporate interests and white America's perception of African Americans, especially African American youths.

There is a certain kind of sick and twisted irony at play when one seriously ponders the parallels between the emergence of the Civil Rights Movement and the rise of classic rhythm & blues, specifically Motown and Motown sound-derived rhythm & blues. In a nutshell, both the Civil Rights Movement and classic rhythm & blues, for all intents and purposes, were *African American youth issues-centered* and *African American youth activism-centered*. In terms of the Civil Rights Movement: the 1954 *Brown vs. the Board of Education* victory obviously focused on African American youth, as it desegregated public schools; the March 1955 arrest of fifteen year-old Claudette Colvin, who was the first person on record to resist bus segregation in Montgomery, Alabama, alerted many African American adults to the adverse impact that segregation was having on African American youth and made many commit to the then inchoate Civil Rights

Movement; the August 1955 lynching of fourteen-year-old Emmett Till in Money, Mississippi, enraged even the most moderate African American adults, providing yet another reason to rise up against American apartheid; the September 1957 display of courage on the part of the "Little Rock Nine" (Melba Pattillo Beals, Minnijean Brown, Elizabeth Eckford, Ernest Green, Gloria Ray Karlmark, Carlotta Walls LaNier, Thelma Mothershed, Terrence Roberts, and Jefferson Thomas) as they integrated the all-white Central High School in Little Rock, Arkansas, flanked by gun-toting National Guardsmen, clearly made even more freedom-loving folk commit to the principles and practices of the Civil Rights Movement; the August 1958 sit-ins spearheaded by Clara Luper and the NAACP Youth Council accented the brimming youth activism in the Civil Rights Movement, as did the 1960 emergence of a full-blown Sit-In Movement led by African American college students; the May 1961 initiation of the Freedom Riders Movement, primarily led by the Congress of Racial Equality (CORE) and the Student Nonviolent Coordinating Committee (SNCC), ratcheted up youth radicalism during the movement years; the May 1963 Children's Crusade, led by James Bevel, in Birmingham, Alabama, accented even more youth issues and youth activism in the Civil Rights Movement; and certainly the September 1963 bombing of the 16th Street Baptist Church that took the lives of the schoolgirls Addie Mae Collins, Denise McNair, Cynthia Wesley, and Carole Robertson two weeks after the March on Washington sent shock waves through African America and helped to kick the Civil Rights Movement into an even higher gear. Again, African American youth—their lives and struggles—were squarely at the center of the Civil Rights Movement.[38]

During the same turbulent years that witnessed the backlash against African American youth and their valiant struggle for human, civil, and voting rights, Motown was tapping the teenage talent pool of Detroit's Brewster-Douglass housing projects. According to Nelson George (2007), the Brewster-Douglass housing projects were "low-rent yet well-kept public housing that served as home for the children of Detroit's post-World War II migration. For all intents and purposes, it was a ghetto, but for Detroit's blacks it was one with hope" (80). Berry Gordy's first great discovery from Detroit's public housing projects was Smokey Robinson & the Miracles, and soon thereafter a group of guys called the Primes and a companion girl group called the Primettes. The Motown machine quickly polished and rechristened the guy group as "The Temptations" and their sister group as "The Supremes."

Hence, similar to several contemporary rap stars (e.g., Jay-Z, NaS, Marley Marl, Kool G Rap, MC Shan, Roxanne Shanté, Mobb Deep, Trina, Lil' Wayne, Juvenile, Soulja Slim, and Jay Electronica, among countless others), the ghetto, and public housing projects in particular, provided classic rhythm & blues with the raw talent, tall tales, and innovative subaltern aesthetic that fueled much of its success. But, unlike rap, the ghetto origins, or the otherwise humble beginnings, of many classic rhythm & blues stars was masked to make them more appealing to middle-class and mainstream America. As is well known, a lot of rap is unapologetically ghetto-centered and often celebrates ghetto life and culture. For the most part, classic rhythm & blues production and promotion teams, especially those at Motown in the 1960s, downplayed the humble beginnings of the bulk of their stars, preferring to present them decked out in the glitz and glam fashions of the era. Needless to say, rap music and hip hop culture's hyper-materialism and bold bourgeoisisms did not develop in a vacuum, and Motown and Motown-sound derived music and branding has long served as a major point of departure for contemporary black popular music, especially rap and neo-soul.

Even though it was obviously an oppositional operation within the music industry of the 1960s, Motown was nonetheless deeply committed to the *modus operandi* and mechanisms of the U.S. mass market and, it should be strongly stressed, on the U.S. mass market's mostly anti-African American terms. This, of course, resembles most Civil Rights Movement members' open embrace of the "American Dream" without critically calling into question whether the "American democracy"—as articulated by the wealthy, white, slaveholding men who are recognized as the "Founding Fathers"— was a viable goal for African Americans (and other nonwhites) in the second half of the twentieth century. Consider for a moment, if you will, Martin Luther King's famous "I Have a Dream" speech, with its scattered references to the Constitution and the Declaration of Independence (M.L. King 1986, 217).

King undeniably critiqued "the architects of our republic" (i.e., the wealthy, white, slaveholding men who are recognized as America's "Founding Fathers"), but he also passionately embraced *their* American dream. As a matter of fact, King's dream—to use his own words—was "a dream deeply rooted in the American dream" (219). For several of the unsung soldiers of the Civil Rights Movement, such as Ella Baker, Malcolm X, and James Baldwin, King's articulation of the American dream did not sufficiently differentiate between white America and nonwhite America's conflicting conceptions of the American dream. As Britta Waldschmidt-Nelson's brilliant *Dreams and Nightmares: Martin Luther King, Jr., Malcolm X, and the Struggle for Black Equality in America* (2012) emphasized, the militants of the Civil Rights Movement were not as interested in the American dream as much as they were concerned with ending the "American nightmare"—to employ Malcolm X's infamous phrase—in which black America continued to be ensnared in 1960s America.[39]

In this sense, Berry Gordy's efforts to upset the white male-dominated music industry of the 1960s by drawing from the successful business models of white America was not out of the ordinary and perfectly mirrored the integrationist and middle-class mind-set of most of the black bourgeoisie during the Civil Rights Movement years. In the 1960s most African Americans were, as they remain today, largely working class and working poor. What Gordy and Motown provided the black masses with were sonic slices of African American life and culture, not necessarily as they actually were at the time but as the black bourgeoisie *and* the black masses wished them to be, and it was these, literally, phantasmagorical or surreal songs that both black and white America danced, romanced, partied, and politicked to during the Civil Rights Movement years.

Working-class and working-poor black folk—those humble human beings frequently treated like second-class citizens in segregated 1960s America—knew that Motown's music grew out of their loves, lives, and struggles. In short, they could genuinely relate to Motown music's timeless, clever, often tongue-in-cheek, and passionate stories of love, loss, loneliness, heartbreak, happiness, and community because in no uncertain terms these stories were *their* stories (as in the often heard refrain at African American dances, clubs, and house parties: "That's *my* song!"). It really did not matter to them how Gordy managed to create one of the most successful businesses in African American history. Simply said, they did not care about the backstory with all of its tales of trials and tribulations. What was new, exciting, and inspiring about Motown in the 1960s was that it consistently presented African Americans in general, and African American youth in specific, in dignified and sophisticated ways that the white male-dominated music industry—indeed, white America in general—had never dreamed of.

It could be said that Gordy challenged the mainstream American business model by deconstructing and reconstructing the received images of, and stereotypes about African Americans in general, and African American ghetto youth in specific. He, literally, refined, repackaged, and re-presented African Americans, and again African American ghetto youth in particular, employing business paradigms and procedures that were as far removed from African America, especially African American ghetto youth, as they were from the music business. Here, then, we have come back to our discussion concerning African American cultural adaptation or, rather, African American cultural appropriation.

No matter how far-fetched and mind-boggling it might sound, the truth of the matter is that Berry Gordy meticulously modeled his record company on Detroit's auto industry, selling a sumptuous black youthfulness, black hipness, and black sexiness employing one of the quintessential examples of mass production and consumption in America's market economy. The Motown Record Corporation was simultaneously new and familiar to most middle-class and mainstream-minded Americans, both black and white, because it used one of corporate America's most revered models. As Gerald Early explained in *One Nation Under a Groove: Motown and American Culture* (2004), Gordy's work on the assembly line at the Ford factory was pivotal:

> His job at the Ford plant, as Nelson George and other critics have pointed out, made him aware of two things: how production can be efficiently organized and automated for the highest quality. At Motown during the sixties, producers could also write songs and songwriters could produce, but artists—either singers or session musicians—were not permitted to do either. With this type of control, Motown put out a highly consistent product. . . . From his auto plant experience, Gordy also became aware that to keep his company going, it was necessary to provide a series of attractive rewards and incentives for hard work, as well as an elaborate system of shaming for laziness. A record company, like an auto company, requires an almost unbearable atmosphere of competition. Gordy believed in competition with the fervor of a fanatic. (This intense sense of contest not only created a celebrity system within the company but became a point of celebration about the company, a virtual mark of internal and external prestige.) Thus, producers with hit records at Motown were given more studio time, and the others had to fight for what was left. The hottest songwriters were allowed to work with the hottest singers. At company meetings, Gordy bluntly criticized any song or performance he considered inferior, not permitting the song to be released, thereby angering his producers and songwriters, but also spurring them to do better in order to curry his favor and approval. This system produced an unprecedented number of hit records in relation to the number of records released. (53–54)

Here we have a black record company owner using the production techniques of a white car company owner, Henry Ford, to mass produce a smoother, more or less white folk-friendly form of black popular music. It was not only ingenious, but it was also indicative of the desegregationist and integrationist ethos sweeping African America in the late 1950s and early 1960s. By re-creating and recasting African American ghetto youth in the anodyne and angelic image of mainstream and middle-class white youth, Motown was increasingly given entry into mainstream American popular culture at the exact same time that African Americans were desperately struggling to integrate into mainstream American society. In short, *1960s Motown music was implicitly Civil Rights Movement music without explicitly espousing traditional Civil Rights Movement themes, politics, and slogans.* This is where we come back to the double entendres and cultural codes contained in black popular culture in general, and black popular music in particular. Motown's *implicit politics* mirrored the Civil Rights Movement's *explicit politics*, and, what is more, contemporary black popular music's implicit politics continues to mirror contemporary black popular movements' explicit politics.

It is not my intention to argue that Motown agreed with or supported each and every social struggle, political campaign, and cultural movement afoot in black America in the 1960s. I am well aware of Berry Gordy's infamous reluctance to associate Motown with any organization or movement that could potentially negatively impact his company's commercial success. For instance, somewhat overstating his case I believe, in *Motown: Music, Money, Sex, and Power* (2002), Gerald Posner went so far to say that Berry Gordy "had no interest in politics or history. He did not read newspapers or books and had little sense of social destiny or moral responsibility stemming from his remarkable success" (172).

However, it should be quickly pointed out, Posner's interpretation directly contradicts Brian Ward's brilliant work in *Just My Soul Responding: Rhythm & Blues, Black Consciousness, and Race Relations* (1998), where he revealed that Gordy actually viewed "his own economic success as a form of progressive racial politics" (268). Bearing this in mind, it is not surprising that Gordy "did not wish to jeopardize his position" and the middle-of-the-road Motown brand by becoming "too closely associated with a still controversial black Movement for civil and voting rights." Hence, Posner's interpretation flies in the face of the facts and is quite simply untenable, if not outright wrongheaded.

Ward's painstaking research revealed that Gordy and Motown actually contributed to several 1960s civil rights organizations and causes: from the National Association for the Advancement of Colored People (NAACP) and the Congress of Racial Equality (CORE), to the Negro American Labor Council (NALC) and the 1963 March on Washington. Perhaps summing up Gordy and Motown's Civil Rights Movement moderatism best, Nelson George (2007, 54) wryly noted:

> Though he never spoke about the issue overtly, Berry's rise in the early 1960's linked him with the Civil Rights Movement. (Dr. Martin Luther King Jr., once visited Motown briefly, and Berry would release his "I Have A Dream" speech, along with a few other civil rights-related albums throughout the decade.) Naïvely, some saw Motown as the entertainment-business equivalent of the National Association for the Advancement of Colored People, or the Southern Christian Leadership Conference. To them Motown wasn't just a job; it was part of a movement.

This means, then, that the Hip Hop Generation is not the first generation of young black folk to conceive of its music as having deeper, implicit political meanings and being connected to the explicit political expressions of a broader social and cultural movement. No matter how "naïve" hip hoppers may appear to be to those who have little or no real relationship with rap music and hip hop culture—besides what they can glean from ultraconservative critics such as Bill O'Reilly, Rush Limbaugh, Sarah Palin, Glenn Beck, Sean Hannity, Laura Ingraham, Michael Savage, and Mark Levin, among many others—similar to the African American youth of the 1960s, rap is more than merely music. To paraphrase George above, it is part of a movement: *the Hip Hop Movement.* If, indeed, the African American youth of the 1960s conceived of their popular music as part of a movement, then isn't it highly hypocritical of them—now that they are parents, grandparents, and honored elders—to snicker at and chide their children and grandchildren for conceiving of their most beloved black popular music as part of an extramusical, social, political, and cultural movement?

The truth of the matter is that Motown's music and its entrepreneurial acumen were culled from urban African American communities that had long traditions of asserting their "implicit politics" through black popular culture, black popular music, and successful black businesses. By eventually becoming one of Detroit and the country's most successful producers of black popular music and most successful black businesses in the midst of a racially segregated American society, Motown was indeed perceived as "political," and that is regardless of whether or not we have consensus on whether Berry Gordy, Motown, or its individual artists comprehended it as such. As is the case in white America, black America has its own unique interpretive communities, customs of cultural appropriation, and political practices, which do not cater to the whims and wishes of megastars, music industry moguls, musicologists, sociologists, political analysts, and cultural critics. Speaking directly and eloquently to this issue in *Dancing in the Street: Motown and the Cultural Politics of Detroit* (1999), Suzanne Smith offered remarkable insight:

> Motown's role as a producer of black culture and its ambitions in the business world did not coexist without conflict and contradiction. At Hitsville, U.S.A., commercial concerns about the marketability of a recording often stalled and sometimes canceled projects that management deemed too politically controversial. The political climate at Motown Records was highly variable. Throughout the civil rights era the company wavered between willingness and caution when asked to produce recordings—musical or spoken-word—that involved overt political or racial messages. Sometimes an atmosphere of race consciousness prevailed, and other times a politically conservative ethos dominated.

> Motown's internal ambivalence about its relationship to the Civil Rights Movement was, however, only one side of the story. On the other side were popular music audiences, local artists, and national civil rights leaders, who had their own ideas and disagreements about the meanings of Motown's music and commercial success for the movement. At the national level debates about Motown's role in the struggle for racial justice mirrored larger divisions within the movement itself. From 1963 to 1973 . . . the national civil rights campaign shifted from the unified fight for integration—exemplified by the March on Washington—to a more fractious battle for Black Power. Given these transitions, Motown could not avoid becoming a contested symbol of racial progress. Motown's music symbolized the possibility of amicable racial integration through popular culture. But as a company, Motown represented the

possibilities of black economic independence, one of the most important tenets
of black nationalism. (18)

All of this means that the connections between classic Motown as a metaphor
and soundtrack for the Civil Rights Movement and contemporary rap as a
metaphor and soundtrack for the Hip Hop Movement are many. First, mention should be made of Smith's emphasis on the conflicts and contradictions
surrounding Motown as "a producer of black culture and its ambitions in the
business world." Motown's dilemma in the 1960s seems to prefigure the
commercial rap vs. conscious rap debates that have been an integral part of
the Hip Hop Movement since its inception. Many of the more critical members of the Civil Rights Movement believed that the "Motown sound" was
not the soundtrack to the Civil Rights Movement, but the soundtrack to
"selling out," black pop music that more or less encouraged African
Americans to abandon the core principles and practices of the Civil Rights
Movement. When rap music crossed out of the ghetto and into mainstream
America in the mid-1980s it was denounced by old school rap purists. Supposedly "real" rap music could not be understood by wealthy and white
America in general, and sheltered white suburban youth in specific.

Similar to Motown's brand of classic rhythm & blues, at its earliest stages
rap was increasingly censored and sanitized for a wider and whiter audience.
Which is to say, as with Motown in the 1960s, "commercial concerns about
the marketability" of many early rap recordings "often stalled and sometimes
canceled projects" 1980s music industry executives "deemed too politically
controversial," too racially charged, or too ghetto centered. Reflecting the
panorama of the cultural, social, and political views and values of the post-
Civil Rights Movement generation, from the mid-1980s onward rap music's
politics have been "highly variable," sometimes culturally conscious, politically progressive, and extremely critical of racism, and at other times rap
music has been extremely "politically conservative" and supportive of the
status quo, especially on issues revolving around women's rights and sexual
orientation.

Harking back to the jump blues era, a lot of early rap downplayed the
tragedy of black life during the Reagan and Bush presidencies (between 1980
and 1992) in favor of playing up the comedy of black life. Just as dance and
comedy songs helped to popularize rhythm & blues among a wider and
whiter audience between 1945 and 1965 (e.g., Louis Jordan, Bull Moose
Jackson, Screamin' Jay Hawkins, Nappy Brown, Little Richard, Chuck Berry, and Chubby Checker), after old school rap helped to establish the genre
and announce that it was more than a novelty between 1979 and 1983, by
1984 the Fat Boys' comedy rap came into vogue, paving the way for comedy
rap artists and groups such as the Beastie Boys, Heavy D & the Boyz, Biz
Markie, DJ Jazzy Jeff & the Fresh Prince, Kid 'N' Play, Chubb Rock, Sir

Mix-A-Lot, and Fu-Schnickens. Before gangsta rap arguably eclipsed all other forms of rap in the 1990s, comedy rap demonstrated that rap was not merely about dancing, romancing, and the hardships of ghetto life, but that it could also be light, tell funny stories, and make listeners laugh. Similar to classic rhythm & blues, the topical and lyrical range of rap music is a lot broader than many of its erstwhile critics realize, which is one of the reasons their criticisms frequently cause fury-filled and vitriolic responses from hip hoppers and their elder allies.

By bringing so many diverse groups together, at least in terms of a shared aural experience, classic Motown music foreshadowed and laid a foundation for every major form of black popular music that followed, including rap. Motown music in the 1960s, to put it poorly, was the rap music of its time. It captured the comedy and tragedy, and sonically signified the dancing and romancing of 1960s segregated black America in the process of desegregating and integrating into mainstream America. Moreover, Motown also symbolized black power brokers and black businesses in the process of desegregating and integrating into corporate America. With its increasingly young white clientele, in the 1960s Motown was both a metaphor for and the major black popular music soundtrack of the Civil Rights Movement. Its challenge to America's musical segregation mirrored African Americans' social and political challenges to America's racial segregation. Touching on this point in his essay "Crossing Over: 1939–1989" (1990), Reebee Garofalo importantly observed:

> In its early stages, the Civil Rights Movement, as embodied by Dr. Martin Luther King, Jr., had two predominant themes: non-violence and integration. As other, more militant tendencies developed in the black community, such a stance would soon appear to be quite moderate by comparison. At the time, however, it seemed to many that the primary task facing black people was to become integrated into the mainstream of American life. It was in this context that Motown developed and defined itself. . . . Gordy once commented that any successful Motown hit sold at least 70% to white audiences. Working closely with Smokey Robinson on the label's early releases, he laid rich gospel harmonies over extravagant studio work with strong bass lines and came up with the perfect popular formula for the early civil rights era: upbeat black pop, that was acceptable to a white audience, and irresistibly danceable. This was the "Motown sound." (90)

Similar to a lot of commercial or pop rap, in spite of classic Motown's more or less apolitical lyrics, many of its songs contained metaphors and came to have alternative meanings within the cultural, social, and political context of the Civil Rights Movement. Even the most apolitical lyrics can take on new meanings unfathomed by songwriters, singers, musicians, and record companies when the lyrics resonate with the cultural conventions, social sensibilities, and political praxes of a brutally oppressed people determined to rescue and reclaim their human, civil, and voting rights. For instance, a short list of classic Motown's songs that took on special meanings within the context of the Civil Rights Movement would most certainly include: Martha Reeves & the Vandellas' "Dancing in the Street," "Heat Wave," "Quicksand," and "Nowhere to Run"; Smokey Robinson & the Miracles' "I Gotta Dance To Keep From Crying," "The Tracks of My Tears," "Going to a Go-Go," "Abraham, Martin, and John," "Whose Gonna Take the Blame?," and "Tears of a Clown"; Marvin Gaye's "Can I Get a Witness?," "I'll Be Doggone," "Ain't That Peculiar?" and "I Heard It Through The Grapevine"; the Supremes' "Where Did Our Love Go?," "Stop in the Name of Love," "Love Child," "I'm Livin' in Shame," and "The Young Folks"; the Temptations' "Ain't Too Proud to Beg," "Beauty is Only Skin Deep," and "Ball of Confusion (That's What the World is Today)"; and, finally, the Four Tops "It's the Same Old Song" and "Reach Out I'll Be There."

Given the social and political situation during the early 1960s, Gordy's idea to create crossover "upbeat black pop" that was "irresistibly danceable" was yet another mark of his managerial and musical genius. Motown's predominantly white consumer base eventually made it one of the most influential record companies of the 1960s. When viewed from the "implicit politics" of black popular culture perspective we witness that as it increasingly exerted its influence on mainstream American popular music and popular culture Motown was transformed into a glowing symbol of the unprecedented economic and cultural opportunities available to African Americans during the Civil Rights Movement years. In this sense, Motown stars were understandably appropriated by most members of the Civil Rights Movement, who viewed them as more than musicians but, even more, as strategic cultural, social, and political icons. The fact that megastars such as Diana Ross, Smokey Robinson, Eddie Kendrick, and Mary Wells were all working-class and working-poor black youth raised in the brutal Brewster-Douglass housing projects prior to their Motown fame and fortune made them, for all intents and purposes, *icons of integration.* However, the success stories of the handful of African American ghetto youth that Motown took from rags to riches were frequently redeployed by white America in its efforts to quell legitimate critiques coming from the Civil Rights Movement concerning the mistreatment that the black masses continued to experience throughout the 1960s.

This means that America's culture wars are not new, and the use of black popular music and black popular culture as political footballs, as it were, is not new either. Culture wars were a major part of the Civil Rights Movement, and they have been and remain at the heart of the Hip Hop Movement. The initial backlash against rhythm & blues in the 1950s and 1960s foreshadowed almost identical attacks on early rap music and hip hop culture in the

1980s. However, by the time of rap's emergence America was a much more integrated society, and early rappers benefited from the struggles and gains of both the Civil Rights Movement and classic rhythm & blues. Similar to the ways in which Motown built on the evolution of rhythm & blues in the 1950s, the second wave of early rappers, roughly between 1983 and 1987, popularized rap and demonstrated its enormous commercial appeal.

Most conversations concerning rap's popularization almost immediately and understandably turn to Run-D.M.C. But, truth be told, it is debatable as to whether Run-D.M.C. would have been able to scale the lofty heights of the 1980s music industry were it not for Whodini, who made their mark slightly before Run-D.M.C. Coming on the scene a year ahead of Run-D.M.C., in many senses Whodini symbolizes not only the link between old school rap and the second wave of rappers who helped to popularize the genre between 1983 and 1987, but they also connect rap to rhythm & blues with their singing-rap style, which seemed to sidestep disco and electro in favor of *rhythm & blues-based rap*. The influence of old school rap on Whodini is obvious, but those with a sense of musical history will also be able to hear a heavy emphasis on rhythm & blues. Their classic albums, *Whodini* (1983), *Escape* (1984), *Back in Black* (1986), and *Open Sesame* (1987), not only boasted more sophisticated beats and rhymes compared to old school rappers, but their rhythm & blues-based rap made rap music more palatable to African American ghetto youth primarily accustomed to listening to rhythm & blues, soul, funk, and disco in the early 1980s.

Where Whodini's rhythm & blues-based rap prefigured new jack swing, a lot of their lyrics sound like precursors to the hyper-sexual braggadocio of both commercial and gangsta rap in the 1990s. Songs such as "Nasty Lady," "Freaks Come Out at Night," and "I'm a Ho" certainly sound tame when juxtaposed with the gangsta and hard-core rhymes of the 1990s (e.g., see Too $hort, 2 Live Crew, Poison Clan, Bitches With Problems [BWP], Freak Nasty and, of course, Ol' Dirty Bastard's rhymes), but within the context of the mid-1980s Whodini was as raunchy and racy as rap came. In hindsight, their lyrical and musical innovations sometimes sound more like proto-new jack swing than early rap, but that is part of what has garnered them an undisputed place in hip hop history.

As Nelson George jocularly observed in his chapter "new jack swing to Ghetto Glamour" from *Hip Hop America* (1999), new jack swing was essentially a hip hop-influenced form of high-tech funk that dominated rhythm & blues between 1987 and 1993 (114–28). It was a clear sonic sign that one of rhythm & blues' sonic babies—rap music—was beginning to influence it, and Whodini, perhaps more than any other early rap group, was a harbinger of rap's influence on all major forms of black popular music from 1980 onward. By the time gangsta rap and hard-core hip hop culture began to make new jack swing artists and groups—such as Bell Biv DeVoe (BBD),

Bobby Brown, Guy, Boyz II Men, Keith Sweat, Today, Wreckx-N-Effect, Color Me Badd, and the Force MD's—look "soft" and sound stale in the early 1990s, new jack swing had become so popular that the urban radio airwaves became oversaturated with a dumbed-down and overly polished new jack sound. To say the least, during its later years the music became increasingly bland and its pedestrian, blah-blah lyrics only made matters worse.[40]

Between 1983 and 1987 rap, in many senses, provided its listeners with a "real" alternative to much of what was passing as black popular music in the 1980s (e.g., Michael Jackson, Whitney Houston, Lionel Richie, Tina Turner, and Janet Jackson). Black pop musically retained its "blackness" and innovative edge, but lyrically it was as light, dross-laden, and computer-driven as white pop in the 1980s (e.g., Madonna, Cyndi Lauper, New Kids on the Block, George Michael, and Debbie Gibson). Considering how politically and economically challenging the 1980s were for black America, it is not surprising that rap increasingly reflected the "hard times" and hardships African Americans faced during Reagan's presidency.

Beginning with attacks on affirmative action and the dismantling of the Great Society legislation, and extending to the backlashes against the inauguration of the Martin Luther King holiday and Jesse Jackson's presidential runs, the 1980s proved to be a sobering decade that demonstrated that even though African Americans were now legally first-class citizens, they would continue to receive second-class treatment. Add to all of this the growing gang, crack, and HIV/AIDS epidemics plaguing African American communities in the 1980s, and all of a sudden a lot of early rap music and hip hop culture takes on new meanings—alternative meanings much like the classic rhythm & blues songs that implicitly expressed the explicit politics of the Civil Rights Movement.

Rap music between 1983 and 1987 also reflected the underbelly of black America. Where the Civil Rights Movement and classic rhythm & blues were preoccupied with love, freedom, justice, peace, and nonviolence, many interpreted 1980s and 1990s rap music and the emerging Hip Hop Movement as being preoccupied with hatred, profanity, promiscuity, crime, and violence. Rap has always been about more than cursing, drugs, drinking, sex, crime, and violence. And, when and where rap music appears to be preoccupied with vices it is important to connect it to the social, political, and cultural contexts it was created in.

"How people act and live," Cornel West contended in *Race Matters* (1993), are essentially "shaped—though in no way dictated or determined—by the larger circumstances in which they find themselves. . . . Life without meaning, hope, and love breeds a coldhearted, mean-spirited outlook that destroys both the individual and others" (12, 14). Obviously as rap evolved in the 1980s a lot of it came to increasingly express "a coldhearted, mean-spirited outlook"—just think about the mid-to-late 1980s proto-gangsta rhymes by Too $hort, Just-Ice, Schoolly D, Ice-T, Slick Rick, and the Geto Boys, among many others. But, mid- to late-1980s early gangsta rap is virtually incomprehensible without taking the "larger circumstances"—the wider cultural, social, political, and economic world—this music was created in and, truth be told, unambiguously reflected into serious consideration.[41]

Many historians and social scientists have characterized the 1980s as a particularly bleak period—economically and otherwise—for African Americans. The hope, faith, and love ethos of the Civil Rights Movement faded as new forms of conservatism and subtle racism swept across America. In the wake of the Civil Rights Movement a deeper sense of disappointment and social depression set in. After all of the struggling, marching, and sacrificing of the Civil Rights Movement, in the 1980s most African American youth felt as far away from the "American Dream" as their parents had during the movement years. These youth knew that their grandparents and parents risked life and limb so that they could have access to the "American Dream," and as more and more of them came to the realization that little had actually changed they registered a lot of their frustration and disappointment via rap music and other aspects of hip hop culture (e.g., break dancing, graffiti, cultural criticism, social organization, and political activism). West characterized the "horrifying meaningless, hopelessness, and (most important) lovelessness" in contemporary African American life and culture as "nihilism," importantly asserting:

> Like all Americans, African Americans are influenced greatly by the images of comfort, convenience, machismo, femininity, violence, and sexual stimulation that bombard consumers. These seductive images contribute to the predominance of the market-inspired way of life over all others and thereby edge out non-market values—love, care, service to others—handed down by preceding generations. The predominance of this way of life among those living in poverty-ridden conditions, with a limited capacity to ward off self-contempt and self-hatred, results in the possible triumph of the nihilistic threat in black America. (17)

Rap is primarily the musical and cultural expression of "those living in poverty-ridden conditions" after the strides of the Civil Rights Movement. Without any buffer between themselves and the pernicious effects of the hyper-consumer impulse of the American marketplace, a unique form of hip hop-styled *angst* has taken over. Hip hoppers' *angst* actually represents the feelings of depression and disappointment that most of black America feels but has not been able to adequately express via conventional cultural, social, and political channels. With this in mind, rap can be seen (or, rather, heard) as the anguished voice of the voiceless, and the deep (and often not-so-deep) thoughts of the supposedly thoughtless.[42]

The eclipse of optimism and the rise of pessimism among contemporary African American youth is deeply connected to the broader social scene and the inimical political economy of corporate America that affects all Americans. Within this world hip hoppers' *angst* is linked to the psychological scars and emotional wounds caused by the ongoing antiblack racist ideas, images, and actions that remain an integral part of post-Civil Rights Movement America. These ideas, images, and actions assault African American intelligence, African American ability, African American morality, and African American aesthetics each and every day in subtle and not-so-subtle ways.

Taken together, the accumulated scars and wounds contemporary African American youth suffer daily in antiblack racist environments give rise to an often-unarticulated moral outrage, insatiable anger, and impassioned pessimism aimed at post-Civil Rights Movement America's unwillingness to commit to the principles and social policies put forward during the Civil Rights Movement. Throughout the Civil Rights Movement this moral outrage, anger, and pessimism were, for the most part, expressed in new and unprecedented ways: civil disobedience; nonviolent demonstration; moral suasion; litigation; grassroots organization; economic boycott; and solicitation of allies. However, in hindsight many of the Civil Rights Movement's breakthroughs proved to be more symbolic and psychological than social or political, with the basic power structure ultimately staying the same. As quiet as it has been kept, hip hoppers inherited high levels of political depression and social disappointment from their grandparents and parents, which has led many of them to lash out at each other, especially African American women and homosexuals. Post-Civil Rights Movement depression and disappointment also led to lives of excess. Hence, rap song after rap song celebrates immoderate or, rather, overindulgent consumerism, partying, drinking, drug use, sex, and violence (particularly black-on-black violence).[43]

Bearing all of this in mind, a lot of early rap resembles ghetto-centered versions of corporate America's ethos in the 1980s and 1990s. Indeed, black ghetto youth are responsible for their reprehensible excessive behavior. But, corporate America must also be held accountable for its excessive profiting from, literally, everything under the sun. And, as more and more rappers rose in the public's eye in the 1980s, hip hoppers' views and values, however suspect within the world of mainstream America, cut across the country like lightning. Perhaps no rap group did more to bring hip hop into the homes and hearts of 1980s America than Run-D.M.C.

Building on old school rap and Whodini's breakthroughs, Run-D.M.C. raised the bar for rap, both creatively and commercially speaking. In terms of their creativity, there is a noticeable difference between Run-D.M.C. and all of the other rap acts who had come before them, including Whodini. Their first single, "It's Like That"/"Sucker M.C.'s," broke sonic barriers in 1983.

Run-D.M.C.'s minimalist instrumentation, hard beats, and hard-core rhymes announced a "new school" in rap music. Their wordplay and vocal dexterity, which always seemed to give their rhymes an improvisational and organic quality that harked back to jazz and jump blues, made their music stand out. Add their innovative use of drum machines and Jam Master Jay's production genius and you have a recipe for the most popular rap group between 1983 and 1987.[44]

Following fast on the heels of their Top 20 R&B hit, "It's Like That," Run-D.M.C. released their second single, "Hard Times"/"Jam Master Jay." Where "It's Like That"/"Sucker M.C.'s" can be characterized as early hard-core rap when situated within the socially and musically conservative context of the mid-1980s, "Hard Times" not only paid homage to Kurtis Blow (who penned and performed the song on his eponymous 1980 album), but it also paved the way for future message or political rap artists and groups such as Public Enemy, Boogie Down Productions, Paris, X-Clan, Arrested Development, Spearhead, Dead Prez, and Lupe Fiasco. More than any rap artist or group before them or active during their heyday, Run-D.M.C. registered rap's shifting musical, cultural, and political landscape in the mid-1980s.

By bolding displaying—instead of masking—the cultural, political, lyrical, and musical changes taking place within the world of hip hop in the mid-1980s, Run-D.M.C. garnered a wider audience for rap music by creating musical and lyrical contrasts between their tough and taut music and the humorous, happy, and disco/block party vibe of old school rap. Sasha Frere-Jones (1999) perceptively captured this contrast when he noted that Run-D.M.C. "weren't wearing those wack Village People costumes the Furious Five wore or those dopey matching red leather outfits the Treacherous Three and Fearless Four wore. They looked street in their matching Adidas suits (a style swiped from breakdancers), big Cazal eyeglasses, and those weird black fedoras. Sometimes they wore matching black leather suits. That was even cooler" (63).

Run-D.M.C.'s difference from other early rappers went further than their music and clothes. Where most early rappers had roots in the ghetto or, at the least, African American working-class culture, Run-D.M.C. had staunchly middle-class backgrounds. Just as Berry Gordy's middle-class background influenced his conception of rhythm & blues, Run-D.M.C.'s middle-class backgrounds significantly shaped their conception of hip hop and their execution of rap music. Undoubtedly, they had access to resources—although still limited compared to the hyper-privilege of white suburban youth in the 1980s—that black ghetto youth could not fathom. Run-D.M.C.'s middle-class upbringing not only shaped their music, but their bourgeois backgrounds also shaped their critics' and fans' perception of them. On this point, Frere-Jones further observed:

I had no idea where Hollis, Queens, was, and I assumed it had to be pretty hardcore, since Run-D.M.C. looked a lot tougher than that Deney Terrio style the Furious Five were kicking. It eventually emerged in interviews that Hollis wasn't exactly Beirut and that the band was solidly middle-class. Rap, like the blues, had gone missing and then been found miles away from its origin point (South Bronx, Mississippi Delta). Rap had been reread, reinforced, and made more itself by "outsiders."

Eventually De La Soul would drop the other shoe and make hip hop with clearly visible middle-class roots, but for now, rap's capacity for blunt confrontation and ghetto attitude was being expanded by guys who had been to college, for heck's sake, but were definitely not trying to make anyone feel more comfortable about using rap as entertainment. Perhaps their distance from ghetto aesthetics allowed Run-D.M.C. to pull off something their less advantaged forebears were too deep inside to see. Either way, rap was no longer folk music; it was now a portable, formal conceit and whoever could do it best would win. (63)

What sticks with me every time I come to this passage is the line, "[r]ap had been reread, reinforced, and made more itself by 'outsiders.'" I cannot help but think about how Berry Gordy basically began as a jazz-loving, middle-class "outsider" when he and his sisters founded what would ultimately blossom into the Motown Record Corporation in the early 1960s. However, unlike Gordy and Motown, Run-D.M.C. did not downplay or distort "rap's capacity for blunt confrontation" or its expression of a "ghetto attitude," even though they were "guys who had been to college"; bear in mind Gordy, in proto-hip hop fashion, dropped out of high school to pursue a boxing career.

Because of the lyrical and musical breakthroughs of late 1960s and 1970s rhythm & blues, rock & roll, soul, funk, punk, disco, and electro, rap inherited both a broader musical *and* lyrical palette. Lyrically speaking, black popular music has had a distinct working-class life and ghetto-centered lyrical tradition since the birth of the blues during the Reconstruction years. However, rhythm & blues was arguably one of the first forms of black popular music to address poverty-stricken life, love, lust, and loss while increasingly gaining a wider and whiter audience. In this sense, Run-D.M.C. and early rap's rise directly mirrors classic rhythm & blues' trajectory between 1945 and 1965.

Similar to Whodini, Run-D.M.C. sidestepped disco and electro, but instead of directly drawing from rhythm & blues (à la Whodini), they innovatively merged rap with hard rock. Like many middle-class kids in 1980s America, Run-D.M.C. had a relationship with rock music. But, unlike most middle-class white kids in the early 1980s, they were also immersed in rap music and hip hop culture. In fact, Joseph "Run" Simmons actually began his rap career under the name "the Son of Kurtis Blow," liberally borrowing from Blow, among other old school rappers. Run-D.M.C.'s throbbing bass beats, snatches of crunch guitar, uncluttered keyboard licks, and Jay Master Jay's patented scratching produced a new form of rap music that was basically as bare and brutal as the world most black ghetto youths experienced each and every day in the 1980s. Cutting through the music, the streetwise words of Run and Darryl "DMC" McDaniels made most old school rappers sound like disco-duped choirboys. Beginning with *Run-D.M.C.* (1984), the group increasingly incorporated more elements of hard rock while simultaneously staying on the cutting edge of rap production techniques and establishing tougher new lyrical topics.

By the time they released their second album, *King of Rock* (1985), they were not only the most influential, but also the most popular rappers in America. Their debut album went gold, something their mentor Kurtis Blow did a couple years before them. But, the hard rock-saturated *King of Rock* surpassed Blow's work when it became the first rap album to go platinum. Even though there was undoubtedly a greater flirtation with rock throughout *King of Rock*, it is important to emphasize that it is a rock-centered rap record that does not sound as though Run-D.M.C. was obsessed with crossing over to a wider and whiter audience. It is the distinct street-level rawness and realness of tracks like "You Talk Too Much," "You're Blind," and "It's Not Funny" that allow the entire album to slide into a category strictly reserved for classic rap records.

However, *King of Rock* was more than a rap record. It was equally a rap-centered rock record with big, banging beats and, tellingly, most open-eared rock critics have praised songs such as "Rock the House," "King of Rock," and "Can You Rock It Like This?" for bringing some much-needed soul to 1980s hard rock. Even at its earliest stages, then, much like jazz and rhythm & blues before it, rap music broke down sonic *and* social barriers. It did not necessarily perceive music in dichotomous black/white racial terms. Hence, Run-D.M.C. drew from the energy and excitement of hard rock and in turn produced one of the greatest early rap records of all time.

Unbelievably Run-D.M.C.'s next album, *Raising Hell* (1986), was an even bigger success than *King of Rock*. Building on and going far beyond the two previous albums, *Raising Hell* more seamlessly merged rap and rock with Rick Rubin nestled in the producer's chair. Working in tandem with Russell Simmons—Run's brother and Run-D.M.C.'s manager and the coproducer of their previous albums—Rubin innovatively added to the bare-bones minimalism that had heretofore characterized Run-D.M.C.'s music.

Adding more drum loops, more hooks, more riffs, and more scratching, *Raising Hell* was the most buoyant rap record ever produced by 1986. Layers and layers of sound were juxtaposed with the raw rhymes that everyone had come expect from Run and D.M.C. Rhyming about hip hop fashion ("My Adidas"), black pride ("Proud To Be Black"), and their intricate and awe-inspiring rhyme technique ("Peter Piper," "It's Tricky," and "Perfection"), among other topics, Run-D.M.C. and Rubin produced an album that was simultaneously innovative and accessible.

The icing on the cake was a hit cover version of Aerosmith's 1975 classic "Walk This Way," which featured Steven Tyler and Joe Perry reprising their roles "live" in the studio with Run-D.M.C. It was a music history-making match made in heaven. *Raising Hell* sold more than three million copies and provided rock-loving mainstream America with an accessible way to get into rap. Neither rap nor rock would ever be the same after Run-D.M.C.'s hell-raising *Raising Hell*.

In 1984, Run's brother, Russell Simmons, joined forces with Rick Rubin, who founded an indie rock label in his New York University dorm room: Def Jam Recordings. Together Rubin and Simmons transformed Def Jam into the most influential record label in hip hop history. Similar to Motown in the 1960s, between 1984 and 1992 Def Jam released one monster hit record after another, effectively building on Run-D.M.C.'s crossover success the way that Motown built on Nat King Cole, Ray Charles, Ruth Brown, Sam Cooke, Clyde McPhatter, LaVern Baker, and Jackie Wilson's success. Recalling Gordy's middle-class background, both Rubin and Simmons had bourgeois pedigrees. Moreover, by the early 1980s the not-so-unusual fact that they shared musical tastes and a deep desire to cross rap over to a wider audience made them a potent dynamic duo. The fact that Rubin is Jewish and Simmons is African American, and that they established the most influential record label in hip hop history, speaks volumes about how profoundly rhythm & blues and rhythm & blues-derived musics (e.g., rock & roll, soul, funk, and disco) altered the American music industry.[45]

Def Jam's interracial artists' roster harked back to the rhythm & blues indie labels of the 1950s and 1960s that, first, crossed rhythm & blues over into mainstream America, and then helped to do the same with rock & roll (e.g., Atlantic Records, Chess Records, Sun Records, Vee-Jay Records, Ace Records, Stax Records, and Philles Records). Eventually developing a deep roster that included rap icons such as LL Cool J, the Beastie Boys, Public Enemy, Slick Rick, EPMD, and 3rd Bass, it is interesting to note that Def Jam also signed both rhythm & blues (Oran "Juice" Jones and Alyson Williams) and rock (Slayer) artists. Seeming to put a 1980s, post-Civil Rights Movement spin on tried-and-true themes countless classic rhythm & blues songs celebrated, Def Jam's music demonstrated the wide range and wide reach of early rap. From the extremely popular street-smart romantic rhymes of LL Cool J, to the witty wordplay of the Beastie Boys, Slick Rick, and 3rd Bass, Def Jam catapulted rap into the center of American popular music and popular culture in the 1980s.

However, inverting the long-standing tendency to *lighten* and *whiten* black popular music, Def Jam in many senses rejected *the Motownization of black popular music* and decidedly *deepened* and *darkened* many aspects of its brand of rap music. For instance, opening up entirely new lyrical terrain within the world of rap music, Slick Rick's rhymes could be as misogynistic as they could be laugh-out-loud comedic. On songs such as "Treat Her Like a Prostitute," "Indian Girl (An Adult Story)," and "A Love That's True (Parts 1 and 2)" he tongue-twisted and turned his words to paint extremely demeaning portraits of women, while simultaneously playing up the perks of pimping. Indeed, he pioneered many of the *pimpisms* and *pimpology* that are currently the cornerstones of gangsta, porno, dirty, and hard-core rap on classic albums such as *The Great Adventures of Slick Rick* (1988) and *The Ruler's Back* (1991). Technically speaking, Slick Rick made a major contribution to rap music by ingeniously adding high levels of vocal drama to his increasingly expansive rhymes, adopting high voices for his female characters and a range of low-pitched voices for his male characters. Eventually dubbed "hip hop's greatest storyteller," his profanity-charged narratives— although chock-full of seemingly every vice and vulgarity imaginable—developed rap music's distinct style of storytelling.

Although certainly not free from their own neo-black nationalist brand of misogyny (e.g., "Sophisticated Bitch" and "She Watch Channel Zero"), Public Enemy deepened and darkened rap by building on the proto-gangsta rap of Run-D.M.C., LL Cool J, and Slick Rick (e.g., "You're Gonna Get Yours," "Miuzi Weighs a Ton," and "Timebomb"), but ultimately turned their attention toward pioneering political rap. In many ways mirroring the politicization of Motown artists such as Marvin Gaye, Stevie Wonder, Edwin Starr, Smokey Robinson, and Willie Hutch in the 1970s, who more or less implicitly espoused Black Power Movement politics, Public Enemy's Def Jam albums helped to redefine rap music and heighten hip hoppers' sense of African American history, culture, and struggle by consistently and critically addressing the most pressing social and political problems confronting black America between the late 1980s and the late 1990s. On classic albums such as *Yo! Bum Rush the Show* (1987), *It Takes a Nation of Millions to Hold Us Back* (1988), *Fear of a Black Planet* (1990), *Apocalypse 91 . . . The Enemy Strikes Black* (1991), and *Muse Sick-n-Hour Mess Age* (1994), with Chuck D commenting on the misery and tragedy, and Flava Flav on the comedy and absurdity of black life, Public Enemy showed the world that the Hip Hop Generation, indeed, did have a political conscience and serious social concerns.[46]

Rap music in the 1980s reflected the Hip Hop Generation's simultaneous acceptance and rejection of certain aspects of the Civil Rights Movement. On the one hand, early hip hoppers seemed to accept and sometimes openly celebrate the legal and psychological gains of the Civil Rights Movement: *Brown vs. the Board of Education*; the Montgomery Bus Boycott Movement; the March on Washington; Martin Luther King's Nobel Peace Prize; the Civil Rights Act of 1964; the Voting Rights Act of 1965; and the Fair Housing Act of 1968. On the other hand, coming of age in the aftermath of the radical rhetoric and militantism of the Black Power Movement, early hip hoppers also registered the Hip Hop Generation's frustrations with post-Civil Rights Movement racism and classism, among a host of other inimical issues. Particularly frustrating for early hip hoppers was the growing nostalgia concerning the Civil Rights Movement and the 1960s in general, which frequently omitted the insidious elements of desegregation and integration.

Indeed, African Americans struggled for and were legally granted their civil and voting rights in the 1960s. However, in the 1980s the United States remained segregated to a certain extent and as racial and economically divided as ever. Rap in the 1980s not only unveiled America's increasing decadence, but it also revealed that for many African American youth Martin Luther King's dream was a dream that had no bearing on the nonstop nightmare of their daily lives. Hence, a lot of 1980s rap was not so much a rejection of the Civil Rights Movement as much as it was a refutation of wholesale African American (among other nonwhites) assimilation under the guise of integration. Rap music's increasingly in-your-face aesthetics was a far cry from the innocuousness and piousness presented in 1960s Motown music. But, no mistake should be made about it, both 1960s Motown music and 1980s rap are linked because they served a similar function for black folk during intense periods of cultural development and social struggle: *they implicitly expressed via black popular music the explicit politics of black popular movements.*

After rhythm & blues the next major form of black popular music to emerge was rock & roll. Indeed, the origins and evolution of rock & roll reveal what I am wont to call the "black roots of what ultimately became white rock." As discussed above, even during it earliest stages rap groups and producers, such a Run-D.M.C. and Rick Rubin, developed rock-centered rap songs. Hence, in our efforts to really and truly understand the origins and evolution of rap music, hip hop culture, and the broader Hip Hop Movement it is important for us to understand rock & roll and, more specifically, the genesis and early development of rock & roll and its relationship to the Civil Rights Movement.

NOTES

1. The black ghetto youth-centered or "ghettocentric" nature of black popular culture and black popular music, essentially from the blues to rap, has been expertly explored by Back (2000), M.P. Brown (1994), Dyson (1997, 2002), M. Ellison (1985), L. Ford (1971), Forman (2000), N. Kelley (2002), R.D.G. Kelley (1994, 1997), Maultsby (2001), Maultsby and Burnim (1987), M.A. Neal (1997), and Rosenthal (1988b).

2. In *The Hip Hop Generation Fights Back!: Youth, Activism, and Post-Civil Rights Politics* (2012), Andreana Clay contended that "[s]ocial movement representations of youth suggest that young people have always been at the center of political activism and social change. Youth

have been characterized as the backbone of the Civil Rights, Feminist, Anti-War, and Gay and Lesbian Liberation Movements" (3). However, "[l]ittle research has been conducted on adolescence as a significant identity from which to frame social justice organizing," even though "[n]ew social movement scholars have long focused on the importance of identity to social movement activism" (3). In terms of what I am calling the "Hip Hop Movement" here, it is important to understand that for many members of the "Hip Hop Generation" hip hop is much more than rap music, and certainly much more than commercial, pop, and gangsta rap. Indeed, for many hip hoppers, hip hop is a culture and a wider way of life that can not be simply reduced to rap music and videos. By the time we arrive at the fifth "remix" to follow we will see that there is such a thing as a "hip hop identity" and that the distinct "hip hop identity" is being used to "frame social justice organizing" around issues deemed relevant to the Hip Hop Generation. For further discussion of black ghetto youth's contributions to past and present African American political culture and social movements, see Bynoe (2004), Chong (1991), Ginwright (2006), Ginwright and James (2002), Joseph (2006a, 2006b), A.B. Lewis (2009), Morris (1981, 1984), Ogbar (2004, 2007), Ransby (2003), Van Deburg (1992), and Williamson (2003).

3. My interpretation of the ghetto, and more specifically the black ghetto, has been informed by Geschwender (1971), Glasgow (1981), Hannerz (1969), Hilfiker (2002), N. Jones (2010), Kusmer (1976), Lightfoot (1968), McCord (1969), Meister (1972), Osofsky (1996), Owens (2007), Polikoff (2005), Rainwater (2006), H.M. Rose (1971, 1972), Schulz (1969), Spear (1967), Tabb (1970), Venkatesh (2000, 2006), Vergara (1995), R.L. Warren (2008), and D. Wilson (2007).

4. My interpretation of working-class and poor African Americans' lives and culture has been informed by E. Anderson (1981, 1990, 1999, 2008), Halpern (1997), Halpern and Horowitz (1996), Huntley and Montgomery (2004), Jaynes (1986), B. Kelly (2001), R.D.G. Kelley (1994, 1997), Lewis and Looney (1983), Lewis-Colman (2008), K.L. Phillips (1999), Roll (2010), and W.J. Wilson (1987, 1997, 1999, 2009).

5. My contention that black popular music has consistently served as the bridge between black political culture and black popular culture, as well as a crude kind of social, political, and cultural barometer allowing us to measure the atmospheric pressure in black America, has been indelibly influenced by Abbott and Seroff (2002), Baraka (1963, 1969, 1987, 1994, 2009), Burnim and Maultsby (2006, 2012), R. Ellison (1964, 1995a, 1995b, 2001), Ellison and Murray (2000), A.C. Jones (1993), Jones and Jones (2001), Lornell (2010), A. Murray (1973, 1976, 1996, 1997), M.A. Neal (1998, 2002, 2003), Ramey (2008), and C. Small (1998a, 1998b).

6. My emphasis on classic rhythm & blues having two meanings, one musical and the other extramusical, between 1945 and 1965 has been influenced by several early rhythm & blues musicologists; see Caponi-Tabery (1999, 2008), Eastman (1989), Govenar and Joseph (2004), McCourt (1983), Ripani (2006), and A. Shaw (1978, 1986).

7. For further discussion of the African American migration during the early- to mid-twentieth century that significantly impacted the emergence of the Civil Rights Movement and its rhythm & blues soundtrack, see Arnesen (2002), D.L. Baldwin (2007), Blocker (2008), Groh (1972), Grossman (1991), Hahn (2003), Johnson and Campbell (1981), Lemann (1991), Marks (1989), Tolnay and Beck (1992), Trotter (1991), and Wilkerson (2010).

8. My interpretation of African American migration between 1940 and 1970 has been informed by Askin (1970), Dodson and Diouf (2004), Gill (1975), Gregory (2005), L.L. Harris (2012), and A. Harrison (1991).

9. The emphasis here on the city-centered nature of post-World War II black popular music, from bebop to hip hop, has been influenced by Banfield (2010), DjeDje and Meadows (1998), Forman (2002), Goosman (2005), M.A. Hunter (2010), Kochman (1972), Peretti (1992, 2009), Ramsey (2003), and L. Thomas (2008).

10. My assertion that the Civil Rights Movement can be interpreted as a decade-long synthesis and translation of classic rhythm & blues' extramusical expressions into action, into collective struggle and radical political praxis, has been indelibly influenced by D. Brackett (2005), Carawan and Carawan (2007), D.C. Carter (2009), Dunson (1965), Garofalo (1992), Guralnick (1986), Sanger (1995), S.E. Smith (1999), Ward (1998, 2001, 2004), and Werner (2004, 2006).

11. My interpretation of Louis Jordan and his distinct brand of jump blues has been informed by Chilton (1992) and Eastman (1989), and my interpretation of Billie Holiday's "Strange Fruit" has been influenced by Gourse (1997), Margolick (2000), and Simien (2011).

12. For further discussion of the origins and evolution of jump blues, and for the most noteworthy works that influenced my interpretation here, see Bogdanov, Woodstra, and Erlewine (2003a, 2003b), Caponi-Tabery (1999, 2008), Gulla (2008), McCourt (1983), and D. Miller (1995).

13. My interpretation of "old school" rap and early hip hop culture has been informed by Fricke and Ahearn (2002), George (1989, 1999), Hewitt and Westwood (1989), Kugelberg (2007), Light (1999), Ogg (2001), and Woodstra, Bush, and Erlewine (2008).

14. For further discussion of the "white violence" (or, rather, antiblack racist violence) against African Americans during and immediately after World War II, and for the most noteworthy works that informed my analysis here, see Berry (1994), A.V. Collins (2012), Markovitz (2004), Nevels (2007), O'Brien (1999), Reddy (2011), H. Shapiro (1988), Waldrep (2001, 2002, 2006, 2009), and A.L. Wood (2009).

15. For further discussion of the antiblack racism of, and segregationist policies in the U.S. military during and immediately after World War II, and for the most noteworthy works that informed my analysis here, see Becton (2008), Brandt (1996), R.B. Edgerton (2001), Hope (1979), and Kimbrough (2007).

16. For further discussion of the "Double V" campaign and its transformative impact on the worldviews of African American soldiers and civilians alike during and immediately after World War II, and for the most noteworthy works that informed my analysis here, see Bailey and Farber (1993), Jefferson (2008), E.L. Perry (2002a, 2002b), K.L. Phillips (2012), Scott and Womack (1998), Washburn (1986,) and Wynn (2010).

17. For further discussion of A. Philip Randolph's life, legacy, and 1940s March on Washington Movement, and for the most noteworthy works that informed my analysis here, see J. Anderson (1973), Bynum (2010), D.S. Davis (1972), Kersten (2007), Marable (1980), C.C. Miller (2005), Pfeffer (1990), and S.E. Wright (1990).

18. Lynne Ianniello's *Milestones Along the March: Twelve Historic Civil Rights Documents, from World War II to Selma* (1965) continues to provide one of the best overviews of key civil rights legislation and is highly recommended to those seeking an understanding of the evolution of civil rights legislation between 1945 and 1965.

19. For further discussion of disco music and culture, and for the most noteworthy works that informed my analysis here, see Andriote (2001), Echols (2010), Haden-Guest (1997), Jones and Kantonen (2000), T. Lawrence (2003), J. Morgan (2011), and P. Shapiro (2005b).

20. A more detailed discussion of sociopolitical soul songs is provided in "remix" 3.

21. For further discussion of the Reagan administration's impact on black America, and for the most noteworthy works that informed my analysis here, see Bothmer (2010), Brownlee and Graham (2003), Bunch (2009), Detlefsen (1991), Ehrman (2005), Hudson and Davies (2008), Laham (1998), Martin (2011), Schaller (1992), and Shull (1993).

22. For further discussion of Sugar Hill Records and the Sugarhill Gang, and for the most noteworthy works that informed my analysis here, see Chang (2005), Greenberg (1999), P. Shapiro (2005a, 351–52), and Woodstra, Bush, and Erlewine (2008, 83).

23. For further discussion of the Sequence, and for the most noteworthy works that informed my analysis here, see Bogdanov, Woodstra, Erlewine, and Bush (2003, 428), Greenberg (1999), and Woodstra, Bush, and Erlewine (2008, 77).

24. According to Jeff Chang in Oliver Wang's *Classic Material: The Hip Hop Album Guide* (2003), former soul singer and Sugar Hill Records label owner Sylvia Robinson initially faced great difficulty finding youths who were willing to record their raps (63–65, 84–86).

25. My emphasis on early rap music as "music with a message" has been informed by Allen (1996), Chang (2005), Decker (1993), Fernando (1999), Keyes (2002), Krohn and Suazo (1995), Light (1999), W.E. Perkins (1996), T. Rose (1994), Szwed (1999), and R.F. Thompson (1996).

26. For further discussion of Kurtis Blow's life and musical legacy, and for the most noteworthy works that informed my analysis here, see George (1999), Price (2006, 118, 167–68), P. Shapiro (2005a, 36–37), T. Terrell (1999), Woodstra, Bush, and Erlewine (2008, 10).

27. My interpretation of Grandmaster Flash & the Furious Five and their pioneering message rap has been informed by Allen (1996), Bynoe (2006, 159–61), Chang (2005, 167–214), Price (2006, 1–19, 156), P. Shapiro (2005a, 161–64), Szwed (1999), T. Terrell (1999), and Wang (2003, 84–86).

28. For further discussion of vocal harmony groups, street corner groups, barbershop quartets or, more simply, *doo-wop groups*, and for the most noteworthy works that informed my analysis here, see Friedman and Gribin (2003), Gribin and Schiff (1992, 2000), B. Morrow (2007), Pruter (1996), Rosalsky (2000), Runowicz (2010), and Santiago and Dunham (2006).

29. My interpretation of the cultural, social, and political world doo-wop emerged from and, more or less, mirrored has been informed by L. Abbott (1992), Averill (2010), Baptista (2000), Goosman (1992, 1997, 2005), Kaplan (1993), Lornell (1995), Naison (2004), Ripani (2006), and Stebbins (1996).

30. For further discussion of authenticity, "realness," and "soulfulness" within the world of black popular music and black popular culture, and for the most noteworthy works that informed my analysis here, see Banfield (2010), Bracey (2003), Moten (2003), Nielsen (1997), and R.F. Thompson (1983).

31. For further discussion of black popular music's contributions to the Great American Songbook, especially Tin Pan Alley pop, and for the most noteworthy works that informed my analysis here, see Abbott and Seroff (2002), Appell and Hemphill (2006), Bennett, Shank, and Toynbee (2005), Kempton (2003), Rubin and Melnick (2001), and Sanjek and Sanjek (1996).

32. A couple of the most noteworthy works that informed my interpretation of American radio and television history and culture here include Castleman and Podrazik (2003), G.R. Edgerton (2007), Magoun (2007), Rudel (2008), and J. Walker (2001).

33. For further discussion of the contention that since the middle of the twentieth century every major form of black popular music has reflected and articulated, however incongruously, the core views and values of the major black popular movement of its era, and for the most noteworthy works that informed my analysis here, see Banfield (2010, 2011), Burnim and Maultsby (2006, 2012), D.C. Carter (2009), Floyd (1995), Peretti (2009), Ramsey (2003), T.V. Reed (2005), Roach (1973), Rublowsky (1971), Sanger (1995), Schenbeck (2012), Southern (1997), E.L. Stewart (1998), and Tudor and Tudor (1979).

34. For further discussion of Berry Gordy's life and legacy, and for the most noteworthy works that informed my analysis here, see Abbott (2000), George (2007), Gordy (1994), Hirshey (1984), and Singleton (1990).

35. For further discussion of Motown's origins and early evolution, and for the most noteworthy works that informed my analysis here, see Benjaminson (1979), Dahl (2001), S. Davis (1988), Early (2004), Flory (2006), George (2007), Morse (1971), S.E. Smith (1999), Waller (1985), and A. White (1985).

36. For further discussion of the much-celebrated "Motown sound," and for the most noteworthy works that informed my analysis here, see K. Abbott (2000), Carasik (1972), Early (2004), Flory (2006), Fuller and Mack (1985), George (2007), E.E. Jones (2008), and Lüthe (2010).

37. It is interesting to observe that around the same time that Motown was "whitening and lightening" its rhythm & blues, over in Chicago Leonard and Phil Chess's Chess Records was pushing Etta James, undoubtedly their most famous rhythm & blues/soul singer, in a pop or "cross over" direction. Recording thirteen albums for Chess between 1960 and 1978, James's first four Chess albums—which is to say, *At Last!* (1960), *The Second Time Around* (1961), *Etta James Sings for Lovers* (1962), and *Etta James Top Ten* (1963)—were each in their own way string-ladened, early "pop soul" or "soft soul" records. By the time she recorded and released more soulful and musically mature albums such as *The Queen of Soul* (1965), *Call My Name* (1966), *Tell Mama* (1968), *Etta James Sings Funk* (1970), and *Losers Weepers* (1971), James had reinvented and re-branded herself as one of the undisputed "Queens of Soul" (alongside the likes of Nina Simone, Tina Turner, Carla Thomas, Patti LaBelle, Gladys Knight, Roberta Flack, Millie Jackson, and, of course, Aretha Franklin) and indelibly etched her name into the annals of black popular music. For further discussion of Chess Records, see R. Cohen (2004), Cohodas (2000), and Collis (1998). And, for further discussion of Etta James's life and music, see Gulla (2008, 147–66), B. Jackson (2005), and E. James (1995).

38. Several historical works on the Civil Rights Movement informed my narrative here, among them Blake (2004), Branch (1988, 1998, 2006), Bullard (1993), Carson, Garrow, Gill, Harding, and Hine (1997), De Schweinitz (2009), Dierenfield (2008), Kelley and Lewis (2000), Lawson and Payne (2006), E. Levine (1993), Morris (1981, 1984), Weisbrot (1990), and J. Williams (1987).

39. In his famous, or I should say infamous, "The Ballot or the Bullet" speech in *Malcolm X Speaks* (1990), Malcolm X sternly stated: "No, I'm not an American. I'm one of the 22 million black people who are victims of Americanism. One of the 22 million black people who are victims of democracy, nothing but disguised hypocrisy. So, I'm not standing here speaking to you as an American, or a patriot, or a flag-saluter, or a flag-waver—no, not I. I'm speaking as a victim of this American system. And I see America through the eyes of the victim. I don't see any American dream; I see an American nightmare" (26). For further discussion of Malcolm X's critique of the "American Dream" and Martin Luther King's, as well as other Civil Rights Movement moderates', embrace of the "American Dream," see Cone (1991), Howard-Pitney (2004), Malcolm X (1971, 1991, 1992a, 1992b), Marable (2011), and W.W. Sales (1994).

40. My interpretation of new jack swing has been informed by Cepeda (2004), Lena (2006), Price, Kernodle, and Maxile (2011, 665–67), and Ripani (2006).

41. For further discussion of the poetics, politics, and overall aesthetic of gangsta rap and hard-core hip hop culture in relationship to the Civil Rights Movement, Black Power Movement, and Hip Hop Movement, see "remix" 4, "Funk: From P-Funk to G-Funk," in the present volume.

42. My interpretation of hip hop-style *angst* in 1980s rap music and hip hop culture has been influenced by E. Allen (1996), Donahue (2001), Krohn and Suazo (1995), J.B. Stewart (2005), and L.Y. Sullivan (1997).

43. It is interesting to observe that many classic funk songs between 1970 and 1980 in many senses celebrate overindulgent consumerism, partying, drinking, drug use, and sex—that is to say, five out of the six excesses identified here that seem to run through the history of rap music and hip hop culture. Hence, core elements of the classic funk aesthetic have obviously been handed down to the Hip Hop Generation and inform their distinct post-soul, post-funk, post-disco *hip hop aesthetic*, especially via commercial and gangsta rap and hard-core hip hop culture. For further discussion of the classic funk aesthetic and its enormous influence on the origins and evolution of rap music and hip hop culture, see "remix" 4, "Funk: From P-Funk to G-Funk," in the present volume.

44. For further discussion of Run-D.M.C., as well as their enormous impact on rap music and hip hop culture in the 1980s, and for the most noteworthy works that informed my analysis here, see Adler (1987, 2002), T. Brown (2007), Chang (2005), Frere-Jones (1999), George (1999), McDaniels (2001), Ro (2005), J. Simmons (2000), and Thigpen (2003).

45. For further discussion of Rick Rubin, Russell Simmons, and Def Jam, as well as their enormous impact on rap music and hip hop culture, and for the most noteworthy works that informed my interpretation here, see Adler and Charnas (2011), Baughan (2012), J. Brown (2009), Gueraseva (2005), Ogg (2002), and R. Simmons (2001).

46. For further discussion of Public Enemy, as well as their enormous impact on rap music and hip hop culture, and for the most noteworthy works that informed my interpretation here, see Chuck D (1997), Danielsen (2008), Eiswerth (1996), Hamrick (1991), Myrie (2008), Shabazz (1999), Walser (1995), and Weingarten (2010).

Remix 2

Rock & Roll

From Classic Rock & Roll to Rock Rap

By applying the term "rock & roll" to what he played, a phrase that often appeared in black music as a euphemism for fucking, [Alan] Freed tried, with some initial success, to disguise the blackness of the music. In the 1950s, "rhythm & blues," like "Negro," meant blacks. Calling it rock & roll didn't fool everybody, as Freed would ultimately find out, but it definitely dulled the racial identification and made the young white consumers of Cold War America feel more comfortable. If rhythm & blues was ghetto music, rock & roll, at least in name, was perceived to be "universal music" (a key term in the history of black music's purchase by whites). That term made it acceptable for whites to play the music removing the aura of inaccessibility. . . . This is not to downplay the impact white covers of black material had on white teens and their attitude toward the music, but the term "rock & roll"—perhaps the perfect emblem of white Negroism—was in itself powerful enough to create a sensibility of its own.

—Nelson George, *The Death of Rhythm & Blues*

INTRODUCTION: THE HIDDEN AFRICAN AMERICAN HISTORY OF ROCK & ROLL

Similar to the Hip Hop Movement, the Civil Rights Movement had more than one musical mouthpiece in which to implicitly express its politics, social visions, and cultural values. Although it is generally accepted that classic rhythm & blues provided the major black popular music soundtrack for the Civil Rights Movement, a growing body of research reveals that rock & roll, which basically began as on offshoot of classic rhythm & blues, also served as a sonic symbol of the youthful ambitions and dejections of the Civil

97

Rights Movement. Where classic rhythm & blues essentially represents the internal or intra-communal politics of the Civil Rights Movement, rock & roll could be said to register as the external or extra-communal politics of the Civil Rights Movement.

During the same time period that African Americans began to physically defy social segregation via the Civil Rights Movement, their music began to musically defy sonic segregation via rhythm & blues and later its multicultural musical offspring: *rock & roll.* The black roots of what is now considered "white rock" are usually explored in the blues tradition, and more specifically in the music of luminaries like Robert Johnson, Charley Patton, Muddy Waters, Howlin' Wolf, Big Mama Thornton, T-Bone Walker, Big Maybelle, and Elmore James. However, even as the black roots of rock & roll are acknowledged via the blues tradition the early African American rock & rollers who not only electrified and amplified the blues, but who also synthesized it with gospel, jazz, jump blues, doo-wop, rhythm & blues, and country & western to birth rock & roll are erased from rock history at the very moment they should be at the heart of the discussion.

When African Americans' distinct contributions to the origins and evolution of rock & roll are either erased or attributed to white rock & rollers who came later and who, for the most part, copied black rock & roll styles, then and there rock history mirrors conventional Eurocentric interpretations of U.S. history, culture, politics, and society. Moreover, without unambiguously understanding how deeply early rock & roll was identified with African American music, life, and culture contemporary rock critics and fans cannot possibly fathom how rebellious and outright offensive early white rock & rollers' music was to white America in the 1950s. Writing directly about the "rock & roll controversy" and all of its racial undercurrents in *The Death of Rhythm & Blues* (1988), Nelson George explained:

> By applying the term "rock & roll" to what he played, a phrase that often appeared in black music as a euphemism for fucking, [legendary white disc jockey Alan] Freed tried, with some initial success, to disguise the blackness of the music. In the 1950s, "rhythm & blues," like "Negro," meant blacks. Calling it rock & roll didn't fool everybody, as Freed would ultimately find out, but it definitely dulled the racial identification and made the young white consumers of Cold War America feel more comfortable. If rhythm & blues was ghetto music, rock & roll, at least in name, was perceived to be "universal music" (a key term in the history of black music's purchase by whites). That term made it acceptable for whites to play the music removing the aura of inaccessibility. . . . This is not to downplay the impact white covers of black material had on white teens and their attitude toward the music, but the term "rock & roll"—perhaps the perfect emblem of white Negroism—was in itself powerful enough to create a sensibility of its own. (67)

We need to understand why the real roots of rock & roll needed to be disguised in order for the music to be seen as "universal." Why was it necessary to "disguise the blackness of the music?" How has several decades of "disguis[ing] the blackness" of rock & roll ultimately robbed African Americans of yet another one of their major contributions to U.S. history and culture? Also, how has the hidden black history of rock & roll altered our perception of it as a soundtrack for the Civil Rights Movement? Indeed, the politics of black popular music are even more profound when we take into consideration classic rhythm & blues and arguably the most famous and unquestionably the first great rhythm & blues-derived music: rock & roll.

When and where we are willing to acknowledge that the Civil Rights Movement actually had two major soundtracks, rhythm & blues and rock & roll, then and there it more clearly emerges as a model for the Hip Hop Movement, which also has two major soundtracks, rap *and* neo-soul. Similar to the Civil Rights Movement, the Hip Hop Movement has an intra-cultural and African American-centered soundtrack, neo-soul and many of the more ghetto-centered and socially conscious forms of rap, and what could be seen as a more or less multicultural and white folk-friendly soundtrack, commercial rap and pop rap, especially *rock rap*. Obviously the argument here is not that each and every form of rap or neo-soul conforms to classic rhythm & blues and rock & roll in relationship to the Civil Rights Movement. On the contrary, the main argument here is that there are enough similarities between, for instance, rock & roll and commercial rap, especially rock rap, to make a case for critically engaging them as interracial arenas where black and white youths, among others, put forward messages and advanced ideals that have been not only informed by the Civil Rights Movement and the Hip Hop Movement, respectively, but in turn, even if only implicitly, have influenced the rhetoric, politics, and aesthetics of these movements.

An issue of "inaccessibility" continues to keep white fans from fully embracing the sonic experimentalism and social commentary of neo-soul. Much like rhythm & blues during the Civil Rights Movement era it is perceived as "ghetto music" or mocked as "baby-making music." Where, after years of being labeled "ghetto music," rap via commercial rap, pop rap, and rock rap has come to be considered "universal music" to a certain extent, in many ways occupying the place held by rock & roll during the Civil Rights Movement. Consequently, this "remix" explores rock & roll as the second major soundtrack for the Civil Rights Movement and the ways that rock rap fulfills a similar function for the Hip Hop Movement. The emphasis here will be on the ways in which rock rap's relationship with the Hip Hop Movement, even if often unwittingly and often unacknowledged, builds on rock & roll's relationship to the Civil Rights Movement.

THE BLACK ROOTS OF WHITE ROCK:
FROM RHYTHM & BLUES TO ROCK & ROLL

Similar to rap in the 1980s, as rhythm & blues grew in popularity among white youth in the 1950s it was increasingly imbued with their musical and extramusical meanings. In the segregated social world of 1950s America, almost anything emerging from or unambiguously associated with black America was looked at in a negative light. As a consequence, as with the blues backlash and the jazz controversy in the 1920s and 1930s, there was an uproar over rhythm & blues' influence on white youth in the 1940s and 1950s. Presaging the resistance to rap in the 1980s and 1990s, white adults in the 1940s and 1950s became increasingly concerned about what they perceived to be the complete disregard for traditional American values surrounding authority, sobriety, chastity, and family in rhythm & blues. For most white adults, rhythm & blues promoted violence, delinquency, promiscuity, drugs, and heavy drinking.[1]

Even after legendary white disc jockey Alan Freed's, among others', efforts to whiten and lighten rhythm & blues for the pop music market, resistance increased and intensified. Part of the unpleasantness surrounding rhythm & blues and its whitened and lightened offspring, which Freed dubbed "rock & roll," was the simple but long overlooked fact that, as Greil Marcus noted in *Mystery Train: Images of America in Rock 'n' Roll Music* (1975), most of "the first rock & roll styles were variations on black forms that had taken shape before the white audience moved in" (166). That is to say, although rock & roll, classic rock, and contemporary rock are most often understood to be "white music" within the context of contemporary American popular music and popular culture, like so much within the American social and cultural world, rock's origins and early evolution owe a great deal to African American life and culture.[2]

Those of us living in Obama's America and its aftermath are quite aware of how fashionable it has become to tout how multicultural America historically has been and currently continues to be. Similar to jazz, rock & roll is frequently raised up as a prime example of America's distinct multiculturalism. Indeed, at its inception rock & roll was deeply multicultural. However, any serious analysis of rock & roll's core characteristics should strive to equitably and accurately allocate its various early influences, many of which are undeniably indebted to black popular music.

The origins of rock & roll have been regularly described as a combination of rhythm & blues and country & western. Unquestionably, rhythm & blues and country & western were the primary musical genres that factored into rock & roll's genesis, but rock & roll drew from more than rhythm & blues and country & western. It also borrowed from all of the musics that rhythm & blues and country & western adapted, most importantly gospel, blues, folk, jazz, and jump blues. As Robert Palmer went even further to point out in "The Church of the Sonic Guitar" (1991), rock & roll also appropriated elements of Caribbean and Latin American music:

> The cliché is that rock & roll was a melding of country music and blues, and if you are talking about, say, Chuck Berry or Elvis Presley, the description, though simplistic, does fit. But the black inner-city vocal group sound [i.e., the doo-wop sound] . . . had little to do with either blues or country in their purer forms. The Bo Diddley beat . . . was Afro-Cuban in derivation. The most durable . . . bass riff in Fifties rock & roll . . . had been pinched . . . from a Cuban *son* record. The screaming, athletic saxophone playing . . . was straight out of Forties big band swing. . . . Traditional Mexican rhythms entered the rock & roll arena through Chicano artists. . . . Rock & roll proved an All-American, multi-ethnic hybrid, its sources and developing sub-styles too various to be explained away by "blues plus country" or any other reductionist formula. (652; see also Palmer 1995, 1996)

As important as it is to acknowledge rock & roll's wide range of influences, then, it is equally important to observe that African Americans contributed more musical building blocks to rock's foundation than any other cultural group. Moreover, African American musicians provided the models for the majority of the early rock & rollers (e.g., Joe Turner, Ruth Brown, the Crows, Ike Turner, Jackie Brenston, the Penguins, the Coasters, the Platters, Big Mama Thornton, Hank Ballard & the Midnighters, Clyde McPhatter & the Drifters, Fats Domino, Little Richard, Chuck Berry, and Bo Diddley). Hence, going back to the rhythm & blues plus country & western equals rock & roll equation (i.e., R&B + C&W = R&R), in *Rockin' Out: Popular Music in the U.S.A.* (2011) Reebee Garofalo critically asserted that "one might infer that R&B and C&W contributed equally to the new genre" (82). But, "such an inference invariably undervalues the African American contribution." Garofalo continued:

> When rock & roll erupted full-blown in the national pop market in 1956, it presented itself as an integrated phenomenon with performers such as Bill Haley and Elvis Presley sharing the stage equally with artists like Fats Domino, Little Richard, and Chuck Berry. Accordingly, Steve Perry painted the early history of rock & roll in racially glowing terms: "From 1955-1958, the roster of popular rock & rollers was more racially equal than at any time before or since. Chuck Berry, Little Richard, the Coasters, the Platters, Fats Domino, Lloyd Price—major stars all, and on a rough par with the likes of Bill Haley, Jerry Lee Lewis, and Buddy Holly." But this only happened after it had begun to expand to disruptive proportions among mainstream fans. (82)

Here we have come back to Greil Marcus's contention that "[m]ost of the first rock & roll styles were variations on black forms that had taken shape before the white audience moved in." Without in any way disparaging the seminal contributions of white rock & roll legends such as Bill Haley, Jerry Lee Lewis, Buddy Holly, Carl Perkins, and Elvis Presley, it is important to understand that part of what made them so controversial within the context of 1950s America is the fact that they were white men who played vanilla versions of what sounded to most folk like rhythm & blues by another name. In other words, they were seemingly proponents of musical integration in the midst of an African American-led movement aimed at social integration. Whether consciously or unconsciously, early white rock & rollers' challenges to musical segregation were taken by many to be challenges to social segregation.[3]

Without acknowledging how profoundly early rock & roll was identified with African American music, particularly rhythm & blues, many contemporary rock critics and fans unwittingly fail to concede what many of the most rabid racists of the Civil Rights Movement era openly acknowledged. It is hard to understand how racists can concede what many self-described white "liberals" and "progressives" fail to take into serious consideration. This is one of the reasons that even as we acknowledge and identify the influences on early rock & roll we should never lose sight of the fact that at its core it is primarily a synthesis of African American music, among other African diasporan musics. In fact, the majority of the musics that make up rock & roll's sonic DNA are either African American (e.g., gospel, blues, jazz, jump blues, doo-wop, and rhythm & blues) or African diasporan (e.g., *rumba*, *son*, among other Cuban and Caribbean musics).

Again, as much as we are open to acknowledging rock & roll's multicultural origins, it is important to observe the centrality of African Americans during its most formative phase. Without placing African Americans front and center in our discussions concerning the origins and early evolution of rock & roll, then rock history looks like little more than yet another whitewashed version of American history where African American contributions are appropriated and attributed to yet another set of white "Founding Fathers" (i.e., Bill Haley, Jerry Lee Lewis, Buddy Holly, Carl Perkins, and, of course, Elvis Presley). In this sense, as Garofalo emphasized, "in the well-intentioned and largely accurate celebration of rock & roll's mongrel character, it is important not to lose sight of the fact that most of its formative influences, as well as almost all of its early innovators, were African American. Among the artists who could have been considered rock & roll musicians prior to 1955, there was only one white act that made a national impact—Bill Haley & His Comets" (83).

Before it was whitened and lightened and renamed "rock & roll" by Alan Freed, rhythm & blues articulated how African Americans lived, loved, laughed, cried, and died, first and foremost, to each other and, eventually, to the wider world. It was, as Arnold Shaw perceptively put it in *Honkers and Shouters: The Golden Years of Rhythm & Blues* (1978), the sound of a newfound freedom, a "liberated music, which in its pristine form represented a break with white, mainstream pop. Developing from black sources, it embodied the fervor of gospel music, the throbbing vigor of boogie-woogie, the jump beat of swing, and the gutsiness and sexuality of life in the black ghetto" (xvii). Encapsulating the full range of mid-twentieth-century African American emotions and expressions, spirituality and sexuality, and politics and aesthetics, classic rhythm & blues represents a defining musical moment and an audible emblem of how intensely African American culture and politics changed during the first two decades of the postwar period (circa 1945 to 1965). By synthesizing so many different strands of previous black popular musics with white pop and country & western, as it developed classic rhythm & blues boldly demonstrated that African Americans did not, at least sonically speaking, recognize the color line and ultimately unrepentantly refused to be confined to the crude category of "race records," which was the term that had been used to designate black popular music since the classic blues era of the 1920s. All of which is to say, in several senses even before the inauguration of rock & roll classic rhythm & blues represented African Americans' rejection of not only pre-World War II musical categories, but also pre-World War II race relations and cultural conventions.

With its remarkable synthesis of gospels' jubilation, big beats, hand-clapping, tambourine-banging, and call and response; the blues' hoarse-voiced vulnerableness, impassioned uneasiness, and anguish-filled tales of wickedness and woe; jazz's emphasis on improvisation, syncopation, and elation; and jump blues' electrification, amplification, and unrestrained celebration, rhythm & blues unapologetically announced a new, even more emboldened spirit in black America between 1945 and 1965. To be sure, black Americans still had the blues between 1945 and 1965, but in the immediate aftermath of World War II they believed they had reasons to be optimistic. Hence, their new postwar blues had a dance beat. It was sung in a way that recalled gospel and jazz vocal stylings just as much as the blues vocal tradition. Indeed, rhythm & blues was blues undergirded by the hip new vernacular-inflected rhymes and dynamic double-time rhythms of black America in the postwar period.

If country blues was bad luck music and city blues the electrified and amplified sound of migration and urbanization, then classic rhythm & blues was the music of momentary freedom and a night full of fun. If country blues was rural song and city blues urban song, then classic rhythm & blues was unmistakably inner-city song, the swelling and sweaty sound of African American ghettos in every major city in America. If rural blues symbolized individual expression and yearning, and urban blues a longing for rural life and romance, then classic rhythm & blues was the collective sound of a people discovering happiness and newfound joy whenever and wherever possible in their new homes-away-from-home. If country blues musicians howled and city blues musicians crooned, then classic rhythm & blues artists shouted, yelled, screamed, and cried, in the process deconstructing and re-constructing conventional notions of both rhythm *and* blues.

Prior to the emergence of rhythm & blues, rural blues featured vocals and guitar, with added harmonica on occasion, and urban blues featured vocals backed by guitar, piano, bass, and drums. In contrast, classic rhythm & blues was characterized by impassioned, blues-drenched, vernacular-laden vocals backed by a combo consisting of electrified and amplified instruments, in-cluding honking saxophones, wailing guitars, and bubbling basses. The "im-passioned, blues-drenched, vernacular-laden vocals," "honking saxophones," and "wailing guitars" blaring over the equally unbridled and often awry rhythm sections of the classic rhythm & blues combos eventually took on many meanings, perhaps none more telling than the one ascribed to the music by Arnold Shaw. "Psychologically," he asserted, classic rhythm & blues "was an expression of a people enjoying a new sense of freedom, hemmed in though that freedom was by ghettos" (xvi). He went further, "R&B discs helped blacks establish a new identity—the kind that led a little old lady [i.e., Rosa Parks—who was actually only forty-three at the time] to refuse to yield her seat to a white in an Alabama bus; that led to the rise of Martin Luther King Jr.; and that resulted in the 1954 Supreme Court ruling on school desegregation" (xvi).

Tapping into African Americans' "new sense of freedom" and "new iden-tity" as expressed through rhythm & blues many white youth in the 1950s were inspired to develop their own new identities and reevaluate their rela-tionships with mainstream American music, culture, and values. Whether or not they made the connection between African Americans' "new sense of freedom" and "new identit[ies]" and the burgeoning Civil Rights Movement, many white youth in the 1950s were increasingly attracted to the exhilarating and, from their point of view, unusually exotic and erotic sounds of rhythm & blues. However, as rhythm & blues evolved into rock & roll in the mid-1950s, according to Peter Guralnick in *Feel Like Going Home: Portraits in Blues and Rock 'n' Roll* (1999), "rock & roll represented not only an implicit social commitment but the explicit embrace of a black subculture which had never previously risen to the surface" of white America (22). This means, then, that some white youth indeed did connect rhythm & blues and its rock & roll offshoot with the Civil Rights Movement, and for many of them a commitment to rock & roll surreptitiously signified a commitment to civil rights and social justice. [4]

While bearing in mind the musical origins of rock & roll, it is also impor-tant to accent the social, political, and cultural world rock & roll emerged in. It may be difficult for many of my readers to grasp just how deeply conserva-tive the Cold War world was, but a lot of rock & roll's rebelliousness will be lost without understanding the kind of close-mindedness, hysteria, and undisguised hatred this period engendered. Anything not sanctioned by the established order was deemed part of the "communist plot" to destroy America.

Hence, first rhythm & blues, and then rock & roll were regularly derided as "un-American noise" created for the sole purpose of brainwashing white youth and bringing America to its knees. It is interesting to reflect on mainstream America's perception of the power of black popular music during the postwar period. While black people have long been viewed as socially, politically, and culturally inconsequential and impotent in the broader sweep of America's master narrative, their music has been consistently conceived of as possessing special, almost *black magical* powers. Similar to rap, the "more attractive R&B became to white youth, the more controversial it became," contended Glenn Altschuler in *All Shook Up: How Rock & Roll Changed America* (2003, 19). "White teenagers were listening," he continued, "but as they did a furor erupted over R&B. Good enough for blacks, apparently, the music seemed downright dangerous as it crossed the color-line" (18).

When it crossed the color line rhythm & blues was whitened and lightened and ultimately became "rock & roll," and for many in mainstream and "mature" America rock & roll was nothing more than a metaphor for African American desegregation and integration. As a consequence, rock & roll initially elicited unambiguous antiblack racist responses seemingly from all quarters of the country. For example, in the *New York Times* in 1956, noted psychiatrist Francis Braceland asserted that rock & roll was essentially a "cannibalistic and tribalistic" form of music that appealed to white youths' immaturity, social uncertainty, base passions, and brewing spirit of rebelliousness (8). Because white youth were, in the most unprecedented manner imaginable in Cold War America, emulating African Americans' newfound social assertiveness and musical expressiveness, he concluded that rock & roll was basically a "communicable disease" inexplicably infecting white youth with its supposedly vulgar and vice-laden cultural, social, and highly-sexual views and values.

Another critic who was particularly concerned about the African American musical roots of rock & roll, the Right Reverend John Carroll, speaking to the Teachers Institute of the Archdiocese of Boston in 1956, exclaimed that "[r]ock & roll inflames and excites youth like jungle tom-toms. . . . The suggestive lyrics are, of course, a matter for law enforcement" (32). Moreover, in their best-selling book, *U.S.A. Confidential* (1952), journalists Jack Lait and Lee Mortimer also made several unveiled antiblack racist references to rock & roll's African American roots, directly linking the increase in white juvenile delinquency

> with tom-toms and hot jive and ritualistic orgies of erotic dancing, weed-smoking and mass mania, with African jungle background. Many music shops purvey dope; assignations are made in them. White girls are recruited for

colored lovers. . . . We know that many platter-spinners are hopheads [i.e.,
drug addicts]. Many others are Reds, left-wingers, or hecklers of social convention. . . . Through disc jockeys, kids get to know colored and other musicians; they frequent places the radio oracles plug, which is done with design . . . to hook juves [i.e., juveniles] and guarantee a new generation subser-
vient to the Mafia. (37–38)

Lait and Mortimer's criticisms reveal that many of the very same vices that
are currently hurled at rap music were already in play in the 1950s. Notice
here how rock & roll, like rap, was allegedly connected to and supposedly
promoted gibberish ("hot jive"), promiscuity ("ritualistic orgies" and "assig-
nations"), miscegenation ("[w]hite girls are recruited for colored lovers"),
drug abuse ("weed-smoking," "dope," and "hopheads"), and violence and
criminality ("the Mafia"). Unwittingly, Lait and Mortimer give credence to
my contention that black popular music has always been and remains more
than merely music. As one of the few mediums through which African
Americans have had to more or less fully express themselves, it may be the
case that they have imbued their music with more energy, ideals, and allego-
ries than most other aspects of African American life and culture. Even
though many African Americans and the white youth who are attracted to
black popular music have long had a tendency to see it simply as music in a
socially, politically, and culturally neutral sense, the protectors of the established order in America have consistently viewed black popular music as a
threat and serious challenge to their conventional conservative views and
values.

Black popular music, for what ever else it might represent, has been and
remains "political" in light of the fact that it has consistently conveyed
African American perspectives—conservative, liberal, radical, and, occasionally, revolutionary perspectives—on major social, political, and cultural
issues. Although the United States has long imperiously claimed that it is the
most democratic country in the world, the very fact of African Americans
freely and fully expressing themselves has always been and remains extremely controversial. No matter what black popular music might symbolize to
others, for African Americans, especially working-class and working-poor
black folk, it has long been one of the few mediums through which to document, dissent, and express their distinct thoughts and views on the most
pressing social, political, and cultural problems confronting African America. In this sense, to reiterate, black popular music at any given moment in
African American history invariably tells us a great deal about African
Americans' inner thoughts and inner worlds at the specific historical moment
in question.

However, when the fact that black popular music, for the most part, has
consistently served as the soundtrack for virtually every major event in U.S.

history—from the Civil War through to the Civil Rights Movement (and beyond)—it can be conceived of as not merely the soundtrack for African American historical events and popular movements, but also the soundtrack for mainstream American culture, politics, and society. This contention is even more pronounced in the decades leading up to the incremental integration of African Americans into mainstream American society. For instance, as with contemporary white hip hoppers, white rock & rollers in the 1950s were hardly the first group of white youth to use black popular music and black popular culture as avenues to express their angst and dissent. As I discussed in detail in *Hip Hop's Amnesia*, during the 1920s countless white youth—calling themselves the "Lost Generation"—appropriated jazz and new "Jazz Age" (F. Scott Fitzgerald's term) styles of speaking, dancing, dressing, flirting, smoking, and drinking to define and express themselves in an increasingly indifferent, urban, and industrialized society.

By the 1930s the Jazz Age gave way to the big band and swing era, and along with its new sense of syncopated music, fashion, and socializing, similar to their Jazz Age predecessors, the "swing kids" of the 1930s understood their commitment to swing to be a form of rebellion against the establishment. Like the white rock & rollers and white hip hoppers who would faithfully follow in their footsteps, the swing kids of the 1930s conspicuously appropriated black popular culture-influenced forms of fashion, language, dance, aesthetics, and other African American elements in their efforts to defy the prevailing cultural conventions and socially sanctioned views and values of their epoch.

In the 1940s bebop and jump blues provided a new generation of white youth—most notably the Beat Generation—with a platform in which to dissent and distance themselves from their parents and the prevailing conservative culture and segregationist social policies of the time. Hence, long before rock & roll in the 1950s, white parents were increasingly exasperated and consistently concerned about how the obviously black music, dance steps, clothes, language, and behavior that their children were enthusiastically embracing was corrupting them and ruining their relationship with the much-vaunted lily-white morals and values of mainstream America. As Peter Guralnick (1999, 18) coyly contended: "If rock & roll had had no other value it would have been enough merely to dent the smug middle-class consciousness of that time and throw into confusion some of the deadening rigidity of that world. For that was what it unmistakably did."

Far from out of the ordinary, then, white rock & rollers in the 1950s tapped into *the tradition of white youth appropriation of black popular music and black popular culture* that had consistently, albeit ironically, found that black popular music and black popular culture offered the most effective vehicles for verbalizing white youths' discontent and estrangement. With all of this in mind, there can be little doubt that white rock & rollers' fascination with, first, rhythm & blues and then what ultimately evolved into rock & roll was part and parcel of *the tradition of white youth appropriation of black popular music and black popular culture*. Moreover, their attraction to post-World War II black popular music and black popular culture noticeably encompassed many of the same rebellious tendencies and, truth be told, subtle antiblack racist fantasies that characterized previous white youths' enthusiastic appropriations of black popular music and black popular culture. Candidly writing about his own and his friends' youthful fascination with the blues, which he acknowledged as the foundation of both rhythm & blues and rock & roll, Guralnick gushed:

> There are lots of reasons, of course, why blues should attract a white audience of some proportions. There is, to begin with, the question of color. Most of us had never known a Negro. That didn't stop us, however, from constructing a whole elaborate mythology and modeling ourselves in speech and dress and manner along the lines of what we thought a Negro would be. Norman Mailer has expressed this attraction well in "The White Negro." It was, really, the whole hipster pose. . . . Blues offered the perfect vehicle for our romanticism. What's more, it offered boundless opportunities for embroidery due to its exotic nature, the vagueness of its associations, and certain characteristics associated with the music itself. For one thing it was an undeniably personal music; whatever the autobiographical truth of the words, each singer undoubtedly conveyed something of himself in his song. Then, too, the lyrics in addition to being poetically abstract, were often vague and difficult to understand; the singer made a habit of slurring syllables or dropping off the end of a verse, and the quality of the recording, often from a distance of thirty-five years, added to the aura of obscurity. The life of the singer, too, was shrouded in mystery. Blind Lemon Jefferson, Sleepy John Estes, Jaybird Coleman, Funny Paper Smith, and Bogus Blind Ben Covington: bizarre names from a distant past about whom literally no facts were known. We were explorers in an uncharted land. (22–23)

While Guralnick's deep respect for the blues is obvious, he and his friends' subtle antiblack racism is also equally obvious. For instance, notice that he and his friends begin their explorations of African American music, not with a focus on the overall quality and core characteristics of the music, but precisely where almost all Eurocentric engagements of African American life and culture begin—with "the question of color." This is odd, indeed.

Completely flying in the face of white liberals' claims to "color-blindness" that would rise to prominence in the "politically correct" last quarter of the twentieth century, Guralnick highlights white America and, even more, liberal white America's preoccupation with race and skin color when and where they come to African Americans and their culture. In other words, from a Eurocentric point of view, whites are raceless and blacks are the epitome of race (that is, whatever whites decide "race" is at that specific moment). Hence, when it is all said and done, for many, if not most whites, African Americans are always already overdetermined by their race, and since "race" is whatever whites say it is at any given moment, African Americans are whoever and, literally, whatever whites say they are at any given moment.

Thus, even though Guralnick and his friends "had never known a Negro," that extremely telling fact in the midst of the Civil Rights Movement did not stop them "from constructing a whole elaborate mythology" surrounding "what [they] thought a Negro would be." Acknowledging their romanticization and exotification of African Americans, as well as African American music and culture, Guralnick and his gang—obviously inadvertently, albeit injuriously nonetheless—let's face it: *unconscious racism* is just as wounding and dehumanizing as *conscious racism*—continued the long-standing tradition of white appreciation and white celebration of black music while simultaneously disregarding black humanity. The "bizarre[ly] name[d]" blues musicians and their lives "shrouded in mystery" may not have been so "bizarre" or "mysterious" had Guralnick and his crew simply taken the time to cross the "color line" and to learn about and, even more, befriend African Americans during one of the most turbulent periods in their peculiar history.

By the middle of the twentieth century African Americans had produced several highly competent historians who had published watershed work. If Guralnick and his guys sincerely wished to know more about African Americans they could have easily acquired a copy of W.E.B. Du Bois's *The Souls of Black Folk* (1903), *The Gift of Black Folk* (1924), or *Black Folk: Then and Now* (1939), or Carter G. Woodson's *The Negro in Our History* (1922), or John Hope Franklin's *From Slavery to Freedom: A History of American Negroes* (1947) the same way they eagerly sought out extremely obscure blues, rhythm & blues, and rock & roll records by African Americans. What is at issue here is the simple fact that the long-standing tradition of white youth appropriation of black popular music and black popular culture has regularly involved privileging African American music over African American history, African American art over African American ideals, and African American athleticism over African American intellectualism.

As African Americans moved further and further away from their rural roots, their music seemed to sonically move further and further away from its roots in the blues. And the more black popular music was electrified and amplified, and laced with exciting lyrics about (ostensibly black) life in the city, the more the music seemed to appeal to the unpredictable and often prickly sensibilities of white youth. For the most part, according to David Szatmary in *Rockin' in Time: A Social History of Rock &Roll* (2010), the "white teens who bought R&B records favored a few showmen who delivered the most frenetic, hard-driving version of an already spirited rhythm

& blues that became known as rock & roll" (16). However, very similar to rap music, white youth "especially idolized young R&B performers with whom they could identify." Hence, the very same kind of black youthfulness, black hipness, and black sensuousness that would come to characterize Motown's brand of rhythm & blues—if not rhythm & blues in general—in the 1960s was at the heart of white youths' initial attraction to rock & roll in the 1950s.

As Szatmary importantly shared, by 1955 "Muddy Waters had turned forty, Howlin' Wolf was forty-six, Sonny Boy Williamson was fifty-six, John Lee Hooker was thirty-five, B.B. King was thirty, and Elmore James was thirty-seven" (16). Even though each of the aforementioned obviously pioneered and laid the musical foundation for what is now known as "rock & roll," it was a later group of much younger African American performers who actually popularized and further developed the new, more "frenetic" and "hard-driving version" of rhythm & blues. A short list of the young African American rock & rollers with whom white youth strongly identified in the 1950s should surely include: Chuck Berry, Bo Diddley, Peggy Jones ("Lady Bo"), Fats Domino, Little Richard, Lloyd Price, Big Mama Thornton, Larry Williams, Etta James, Screamin' Jay Hawkins, Ruth Brown, Chubby Checker, Hank Ballard & the Midnighters, LaVern Baker, the Coasters, the Drifters, the Platters, the Chords, the Crystals, the Five Satins, the Flamingos, the Penguins, the Ronettes, and the Shirelles.[5]

As rhythm & blues via rock & roll began increasingly—even if only implicitly—to reflect the integrationist impulse of the Civil Rights Movement, white youth moved from mere rock & roll listeners to undeniable rock & roll innovators and icons. Bill Haley, Elvis Presley, Jerry Lee Lewis, Wanda Jackson, Buddy Holly, Carl Perkins, Roy Orbison, Gale Storm, Rick Nelson, Gene Vincent, the Chordettes, and the Teen Queens were among the white youth who crossed the color line and helped to musically desegregate the American music industry in the 1950s. Elvis Presley, perhaps the most noted of the first wave of white rock & rollers, openly exclaimed in a 1956 interview with Kays Gary in the *Charlotte Observer*, "colored folks been singing and playing it [i.e., rock & roll] just like I'm doing now, man, for more years than I know. They played it like that in the shanties and in their juke joints and nobody paid it no mind until I goosed it up. I got it from them."

What Elvis and the other white rock & roll musicians of the 1950s appropriated from black popular music ultimately provided white youth in general with an unprecedented way to express the differences between themselves and their parents, as well as the power brokers most of their parents worked for, and unapologetically idolized. It was as if those "mysterious" and "bizarre[ly] named" African American blues, jump blues, and rhythm & blues musicians' distinct differences—racial, cultural, social, political, and spiritual differences—somehow or another provided an unfettered and, for all intents and purposes, perfect vehicle through which white youth could register their differences. Hence, when Elvis admitted that he "got it from them," meaning African Americans, in so many words he was revealing that black popular music and black popular culture had provided white youth with a musical model, vernacular-inflected vocabulary, dynamic dance steps, flamboyant sense of fashion, and possibly even a new political vision. Guralnick (1999, 18), perhaps, captured the change in the air best when he wrote, "[w]hat I think was happening quite clearly was the convergence of two warring cultures." We should be clear here, he did not have in mind African American culture versus mainstream white culture but, more tellingly, black popular culture-informed white youth culture versus conservative white adult culture.

"Just as James Dean and Marlon Brando came to represent our unarticulated hurt," Guralnick assuredly explained, "just as it was *The Catcher in the Rye* and *The Stranger* that gave us our literary heroes—the existential ciphers that refused to speak when spoken to—rock & roll provided us with a release and a justification that we had never dreamt of" (18). Drawing directly from rhythm & blues and indirectly from the Civil Rights Movement—that is, since rhythm & blues sonically captured and reflected, and was the most widely recognized soundtrack of, the Civil Rights Movement—white rock & rollers in the 1950s found "a release and a justification that [they] had never dreamt of," not in the much-vaunted mores of middle-class white America, but ironically in the despised popular music, vibrant dance moves, "uncouth" colloquialisms, bold "bad" attitudes, and populist politics of black America. Putting into words white youths' attraction to what was quickly becoming rhythm & blues' surreptitiously civil rights-saturated biracial sonic baby, rock & roll, Guralnick asserted:

> The very outrageousness of its poses, the swaggering sexuality, the violence which the radio of that day laid at its door, its forbidden and corrupting influence—that was the unfailing attractiveness of rock & roll. The hysteria of its terms, the absurdity of its appeal—Fats Domino bumping a piano offstage with his belly; Jerry Lee Lewis' vocal gymnastics and theatrical virtuosity; Elvis' very presence and Carl Perkins' "Get off of my blue suede shoes"; with Chuck Berry all the while merrily warning, "Roll over Beethoven"—how could we deny it entrance into our lives? The ease with which you could offend the adult world, the sanctimoniousness of public figures and the turnabout that came with success . . . above all the clear line of demarcation between *us* and *them* made it impossible for us to turn our backs and ignore this new phenomenon. (18, 20, emphasis in original)

To reiterate, the white rock & rollers of the 1950s were not the first generation of white youth to embrace and explore their identity, sexuality, and burgeoning politics via black popular music and black popular culture. But, unmistakably, something wholly different happened in the 1950s. Unlike the Lost Generation of the 1920s and the swing kids of the 1930s and 1940s, and more akin to the Beat Generation of the 1950s, the white rock & rollers of the 1950s seemed to implicitly embrace and be in tune with some of the more popular principles and practices of the major African American social and political movement of their era: the Civil Rights Movement. However, in keeping with their audacious "*us* and *them*" attitude—meaning, "*us*" white youth and "*them*" white adults—even as they drew from the spirit of the Civil Rights Movement white youth, for the most part, turned inward to their own "unarticulated hurt," angst, and alienation.

Without in any way downplaying white youths' "unarticulated hurt," angst, and alienation in the 1950s, it is important to call into question whether they sufficiently considered African Americans' increasingly highly-articulated and excruciating hurt, angst, alienation, and horrifying experiences in light of racial oppression and segregation. By the very fact that they were ingeniously and, in some senses, therapeutically using what in essence began as a form of black popular music to express their "unarticulated hurt," angst, and alienation, it would seem that white youth were deeply indebted to African Americans. However, as white youth increasingly became the voices and faces of rock & roll, African American rock & rollers faded and, in many cases, were deceitfully forced into the background, and rock & roll was in essence *resegregated* as opposed to genuinely desegregated.

Consequently, hit song after hit song, rock history began to mirror the Eurocentric master narratives of American history, which have consistently racially colonized and plainly plagiarized the contributions of African Americans and fraudulently attributed them to white "Founding Fathers" in specific, and white America more generally. As Glenn Altschuler (2003, 48–49) correctly observed, even though "[m]any whites in the music industry recognized that rock & roll was a metaphor for integration," it "did not always raise the racial or political consciousness of fans." In fact, he candidly contended, "[s]ome listeners remained blissfully ignorant of the racial connotations of rock & roll," as vanilla version after vanilla version of rhythm & blues hits were copied or, rather, "covered" and began to dominate the radio airwaves.

On the one hand, rhythm & blues and rock & roll can be viewed as the soundtracks of the Civil Rights Movement. What began as rhythm & blues and eventually evolved into rock & roll subtly and frequently unwittingly expressed aspects of the social mission and political sentiments of the Civil Rights Movement. And as rock & roll garnered more and more white fans, and soon the participation of young white musicians, however, the music, its modes of communication, and the virtually integrated popular culture that quickly sprang up around it progressively challenged American apartheid and the long-standing color line. The increase in rhythm & blues on radio airwaves that previously adhered to sonic segregation ("white music only") policies that mirrored the social segregation ("white people only") policies of the larger society, as well as integrated rhythm & blues and rock & roll concerts and dances, steadily exposed postwar white youth to positive or, at the least, more realistic representations of African American life and culture.

In an nation where long-held antiblack racist stereotypes and more than a century of blackface minstrelism-informed misconceptions had regularly blocked the development of serious social dialogue and cultural understanding between African Americans and European Americans, the rock & roll phenomenon initially gave many African Americans high hopes that American apartheid, that the stigma of enslavement, that the long and degrading shadow cast by blackface minstrelism might finally come to an end. At long last, African American culture, via rock & roll, was being presented to mainstream American society in dignity-endorsing and unambiguously uplifting ways that ran counter to the antiblack racist assumptions that were previously projected onto African American life, culture, and aesthetics. Bearing all of this in mind, rock & roll indeed did contribute to white youths' (and, perhaps, many white adults') reevaluation of race relations and the emerging Civil Rights Movement.

On the other hand, however, echoing Altschuler's caveat above, in *Race, Rock, and Elvis* (2000), Michael Bertrand cautions us to keep in mind that "rock & roll was not a panacea that magically cured the South's [and the nation's] racial ills" (55). By the 1950s, America had been suffering with its antiblack racist affliction for several centuries and, as with any serious illness, time, patience, aggressive treatment, and consistent recuperative care were desperately needed. Bertrand adamantly further asserted:

> Shifting tastes in musical preference did not necessarily obliterate racism. It would be naïve to think that the cultural process functioned in such a rapid, thorough, and uniform fashion. One generation could not completely reverse what had taken centuries to develop. Racism in the United States, moreover, has never been simply a history of attitudes and prejudices. It has been, more importantly, the product of an exploitative economic and political system whose institutions favor wealthy white males. The persistent realities of inadequate and subservient employment opportunities, substandard housing, poor healthcare, and inferior public education not only oppressed the black community but also reiterated the second-class nature of its existence. One must use caution, therefore, in alleging that popular music miraculously healed [the nation and] the region's divisions. Rock & roll did not directly influence the existing social structure, and it did not command or seek the power to abolish institutional discrimination and inequality. As forces for substantive and lasting change in the racial realm, commercial music and culture of the period were limited. (55)

There is only so much music can do to impact and, more to the point, *enact* social change. And, no matter how aurally insurgent any form of music might be at its inception, if it is hyper-commodified, if it is increasingly used to tout the latest corporate product or teen dance craze, and if by some perplexing turn of events it is distanced and completely disassociated from its social, political, spiritual, cultural, and musical roots in the lives and struggles of a racially oppressed and economically exploited group, then that music becomes, for all intents and purposes, a part of the very system and social conventions it was created to critique and contest. Guralnick (1999, 34), as perceptive as ever, dispiritedly declared that "[r]ock & roll today, to my mind at least, is a middle-class phenomenon almost exclusively." More-over, it may not be stretching his statement too far to say that it could actually be read as "[r]ock & roll today . . . is a [*white*] middle-class phenom-enon almost exclusively." The truth of the matter is that race, racism, and antiracism were actually intrinsic to rock & roll at its inception, and the history of its first decade—from the Chords "Sh-Boom" in 1954 through to the Rolling Stones' acclaimed eponymous debut in 1964—is dotted with either unsuspecting or subtle reflections on and references to race, racism, and antiracism during the Civil Rights Movement years.[6]

In contrast to the often-unacknowledged fact that, not only did almost all of the early African American rock & rollers have working-class and pover-ty-stricken backgrounds, but, as Bertrand (2000, 22) importantly observed, "virtually all the [early white rock & roll] artists were from working-class backgrounds" as well. How, then, did "[r]ock & roll today" eventually grow into "a [*white*] middle-class phenomenon almost exclusively?" Indeed, something was lost in translation as rock & roll was distanced and almost completely disassociated from its roots in rhythm & blues and black America and increasingly bleached to make it more appealing to the "*us*" white youth and "*them*" white adults attitude so prevalent in white youth popular music and culture from the late 1950s onward.

There is something at once extremely disturbing and undeniably depress-ing when Guralnick (1999, 32), in his characteristic uncontrived prose style, stated: "In the end everything gets absorbed into the cultural mainstream, and rock & roll was no different. . . . They've even gone and changed the name, and what was once a kind of secret metaphor (like 'ball' and 'Miss Ann' and 'brown-eyed handsome man') has become instead just another explicit An-glo-Saxon epithet." I am in complete agreement with Guralnick when he bemoans the fact that rock & roll has been essentially reduced to yet another "explicit Anglo-Saxon epithet," robbed of the rudeness, radicalness, and allu-sive antiracism that marked its origins. However, in my mind at least, the question continues to beg: "Does everything really and truly get 'absorbed into the cultural mainstream'?" And, a corollary question creeps in here:

"Did *every* (or, rather, *all*) aspects of rock & roll get 'absorbed into the cultural mainstream?'"

Truth be told, for the most part African Americans, even in the aftermath of the Civil Rights Movement, certainly have not been "absorbed [and genuinely accepted as opposed to assimilated] into the cultural mainstream," even though each and every major form of black popular music (from the spirituals and the blues through to rap and neo-soul), to a certain extent, has found high levels of acceptance in the American music industry, if not in American popular culture more generally. In other words, "real" rock & roll actually has not been "absorbed into the cultural mainstream," because "real" rock & roll, as Guralnick intimated above, was "a kind of secret metaphor" that clandestinely conveyed ·as much about black ghetto youths' "unarticulated hurt," angst, and alienation as it did white suburban youths' "unarticulated hurt," angst, and alienation. What actually has been "absorbed into the cultural mainstream" is a vanilla version of rock & roll, an often bland and highly bleached form of black popular music that continues the long-standing white American tradition of accepting those aspects of African American life and culture that are highly colonizable and commodifiable, but unrepentantly rejecting those subversive elements of African American life and culture that do not quickly coincide with blackface minstrelesque and assimilation-obsessed antiblack racist misconceptions and misrepresentations of African Americans. In this sense, rock & roll, "real" rock & roll, Guralnick lamented, "was over before it even had a chance to slyly grin and look around," and "[i]n its place came a new all-synthetic product" that is often as inept as it is ahistorical and apolitical (20).

RAGE AGAINST THE MACHINE: THE POETICS AND POLITICS OF ROCK RAP

Entangled in the racial and cultural politics of the 1950s, rock & roll was frequently credited with and vehemently criticized for advocating integration and providing new economic opportunities for African Americans while simultaneously injecting African American culture and values into mainstream America. In light of the African American origins and early evolution of rock & roll, it quickly became one of the most contentious topics in popular discourse. White Southerners, in particular, associated the music with stereotypical antiblack racist ideas about African Americans as either subhuman, at best, or nonhuman, at worst. They projected and, consequently, heard echoes of "black emotionalism" and "black expressivism" coupled with "black exoticism" and "black eroticism."

In the face of all of this, we should never lose sight of the fact that rock & roll was also big business—very big business—and, consequently, it was susceptible to the whims and wishes of the white youth-dominated American music market. Preoccupied with the unprecedented profits that rock & roll generated, by the late 1950s and early 1960s the mostly white male music industry moguls did everything they could to avoid controversy and commotion. As a result they exploited countless African American rhythm & blues and rock & roll musicians by encouraging white roll & rollers to copy or, rather, "cover" African American rhythm & blues and rock & roll hits. In the process what began as a black musical expression and eventually evolved into an interracial musical expression was ultimately whitewashed into an inoffensive "[*white*] middle-class phenomenon almost exclusively."[7]

Seeming to permanently Clorox the complexion and soul of rock & roll in the minds of the American masses, from the early 1960s onward white rock & rollers would be perfunctorily privileged and promoted over black rock & rollers as "real" and the most righteous rock & roll. Only occasionally in the post-1950s history of rock would African Americans register as "authentic" rock musicians (e.g., Jimi Hendrix, Buddy Miles, Sly & the Family Stone, Swamp Dogg, Funkadelic, Prince, Bad Brains, Sound Barrier, Fishbone, Terence Trent D'Arby, Tracy Chapman, Living Colour, 24-7 Spyz, Follow For Now, Lenny Kravitz, Seal, Ben Harper, Meshell Ndegeocello, Michael Franti, Chocolate Genius, Eagle-Eye Cherry, Cree Summer, Amel Larrieux, Van Hunt, and Cody ChesnuTT). But, truth be told, as observed in Raymond Gayle's groundbreaking documentary *Electric Purgatory: The Fate of the Black Rocker* (2010), most modern white rock & roll youth have never even heard of half of the aforementioned, let alone seriously listened to their distinct brands of rock. In other words, paralleling the historical experiences of African Americans, rock & roll was racialized and colonized in the interest of whites, and suburban white youth in particular. Like so many other contributions African Americans have made to American culture, rock & roll went from being rejected, to accepted, to claimed as "white property" and integral to white popular culture. As Altschuler (2003, 34) stated:

> For African Americans, rock & roll was a mixed blessing. At times a force for integration and racial respect, rock & roll was also an act of theft that in supplanting rhythm & blues deprived blacks of appropriate acknowledgement, rhetorical and financial, of their contributions to American culture. Rock & roll deepened the divide between the generations, helped teenagers differentiate themselves from others, transformed popular culture in the United States, and rattled the reticent by pushing sexuality into the public arena.

Considering the African American origins and early evolution of rock & roll and its gradual appropriation by white youth, it is extremely interesting to engage rock's contributions to and connections with rap music, and especially the "rock rap" genre. Just because rock was ultimately musically colonized and disassociated from its roots in black America does not mean that African

Americans have forgotten who created it and the double meanings of the music during its early years. In fact, to my ears, many African American rock rap artists and songs ingeniously critique rock's "theft" (Altschuler's apt term above) from African Americans. But because there is such an acute amnesia surrounding the African American origins and early evolution of rock & roll, white rock rap fans are oblivious to most of these critiques. For example, there is a sense in which Run-DMC's first four albums—*Run-D.M.C.* (1984), *King of Rock* (1985), *Raising Hell* (1986), and *Tougher Than Leather* (1988)—can be viewed as solid critiques of the whitewashing of rock. Taken together Run-D.M.C.'s first four albums not only represent African American youths' reclamation of rock, but these classic albums also ingeniously popularized rap in the process.

For the record, Run-D.M.C.'s eponymous debut featured the first foray into rock rap. The group was formed in 1982 in Queens, New York, and from its inception it seemed to synthesize snatches of hard rock with early rap. Predating both the Red Hot Chili Peppers' self-titled debut album in August of 1984 and the Beastie Boys' *Rock Hard* EP in 1985, "Rock Box" from Run-D.M.C.'s March 1984 debut was an early rap/hard rock hybrid that merged rap's big beats and mind-boggling rhymes with the head-banging tension and hyper-testosterone guitar gimmickry of heavy metal. [8]

Taking the early rap/hard rock synthesis even further on their sophomore effort, *King of Rock*, released in January of 1985, Run-D.M.C. unambiguously challenged the misconception that African American youth were not interested in rock. Coinciding with the mercurial rise of 1980s black rock artists and groups, such as Prince, Bad Brains, Sound Barrier, Fishbone, Terence Trent D'Arby, Tracy Chapman, Living Colour, 24-7 Spyz, and Lenny Kravitz, Run-D.M.C. demonstrated that rap could appeal to both black and white, rap and rock fans. In fact, many of the more observant in the 1980s music industry began to think of rap as "the new rock" because of its ability to express the "unarticulated hurt," angst, and alienation of U.S. youth at the end of the twentieth century.

By the time they released their rock rap masterpiece *Raising Hell* in July of 1986, which featured a rock rap version of Aerosmith's "Walk This Way" with Steven Tyler and Joe Perry reprising their roles from their 1975 hit, Run-D.M.C. had completely altered the course of American popular music. Their music countered many of the early misconceptions about rappers and rap music in light of the fact that they were not black ghetto youth, but black bourgeois youth who not only listened to rap but rock as well. However, their bourgeois backgrounds did not make them immune to what was happening in the ghetto during the economically depressing Reagan years (1980 to 1988). Songs such as "Hard Times," "It's Like That," "You're Blind," "It's Not Funny," "You Be Illin'," and "Proud To Be Black" helped to register the distinct differences between Run-D.M.C. and the black ghetto youth-centered versions of rock rap and the later more popular white suburban youth-centered versions of rock rap, which have been mostly apolitical, comical, and more or less party-oriented almost as a rule.

Eerily mirroring the *musical colonization* and *musical depoliticization* of rock & roll in the late 1950s and early 1960s, after Run-D.M.C.'s third album, *Raising Hell*, achieved triple-platinum status and established rock rap as a viable genre within the wider music industry, scores of white suburban youth tried their hands at rock rap. Undoubtedly the most successful and most talented white rock rap group to emerge in the 1980s was the Beastie Boys. Although they began as a hard-core punk band in 1979, in the post-punk early 1980s they switched gears and transformed themselves into a rock rap group. By the time they released their legendary *Rock Hard* EP in 1985 they were poised to take the music industry by storm in that there were, literally, millions of white suburban youth who, just like the Beastie Boys, loved hard rock and had a growing affection for rap.[9]

As the first significant white rap group, the Beastie Boys received a great deal of attention. Their first album, *Licensed to Ill*, was released in November of 1986 to much fanfare. If one were able to sidestep all of the claims of cultural banditry leveled against them, there was still their tongue-in-cheek, over-the-top caricatures of both b-boys and frat boys to be contended with. As simultaneously offensive and entertaining as anything that had ever been released during the early years of rap, with their simultaneously gonzo sense of humor and gleeful delivery, the Beastie Boys joked, jostled, and rhymed their way to the top, surpassing their idols Run-D.M.C. and the Fat Boys and going a music history-making nine-times platinum in the process.

Licensed to Ill was an innovative amalgam of b-boy jive, frat-boy jokes, parody-filled wordplay, heavy metal riffs, and banging hip hop beats. Where the Fats Boys were "black folk-funny" (peep *Fat Boys* [1984], *The Fat Boys are Back!* [1985], *Big & Beautiful* [1986], *Crushin'* [1987], and *Coming Back Hard Again* [1988]), the Beastie Boys were "white folk-funny" and, similar to their heir apparent, Eminem (peep *The Slim Shady LP* [1999], *The Marshall Mathers LP* [2000], and *The Eminem Show* [2002]), often their sense of humor was as controversial as it was misogynist. For example, many African American hip hoppers have questioned whether the Beastie Boys' parodies of b-boys (who were predominantly African American in the mid-1980s) hinged on the very same antiblack racist myths and stereotypes that fueled Al Jolson's famous (and, for black folk, infamous) blackface minstrel routines at the turn of the twentieth century.

It was one thing, the critics claimed, if the Beastie Boys wished to poke fun at their own culture and community by making a mockery of highly educated and extremely privileged frat boys and the infamous "lager lads" who seem to solidly populate each and every college in the country. However, it was wholly another thing to parody poorly educated black ghetto youths' walking, talking, dancing, speaking, dressing, and rapping styles. Many early African American hip hoppers began to question whether the Beastie Boys were friends or foes, or merely modern-day blackface minstrels without the blackface. [10]

In terms of the misogynistic elements of the Beastie Boys' music, there was not only obviously sexists songs such as "She's On It," "She's Crafty," "Girls," "To All The Girls," "Egg Man," "Hey Ladies," "Ask for Janice," "Netty's Girl," and "Auntie Jackie's Poom Poom Delicious," but also the high levels of misogyny on display in their music videos and at their controversial concerts. Featuring female audience members gleefully dancing in go-go cages, at their concerts the Beastie Boys developed the sadistic habit of pouring beer on (go-go) caged young women. To make the situation even more misogynistic, the Beastie Boys routinely taunted female concertgoers with an enormous ten-foot tall inflatable penis, which to most older rock fans looked like an exact replica of the one the Rolling Stones infamously used on their mid-1970s concert tours. Hence, like many of the hard rock and heavy metal bands they idolized, the Beastie Boys' phallocentrism was unmistakable.

When the discussion concerning misogyny in rap music arises it is interesting to note that it usually centers around gangsta rap and hard-core hip hop culture, which is generally accepted as the exclusive domain of black ghetto youth. However, I believe that it is also important to observe the misogynistic elements in predominantly white suburban youth-focused forms of rap music, and especially comedy rap and rock rap in this instance. Undoubtedly the Beasties Boys' body of work raised the profile of both comedy rap and rock rap. After *License to Ill* they released several innovative and critically acclaimed albums in the comedy rap and rock rap genres: *Paul's Boutique* (1989), *Check Your Head* (1992), *Ill Communication* (1995), and *Hello Nasty* (1998). Each of these albums contains questionable gender politics and frequently unrepentantly expresses patriarchal attitudes and extremely sexist sentiments. However, for some reason the Beastie Boys and the throngs of white suburban youth—and, occasionally, white working-class youth—who followed in their footsteps have been basically given a pass when and where critics come to misogyny in their beloved music. [11]

Misogyny is immoral, and it should be condemned when it rears its ugly head and horns in rap music and hip hop culture without regard to the genre of rap or the race of the rapper. I have a hard time accepting that the gangsta rappers are any more misogynist and morally repugnant than the prominent white rock rappers and comedy rappers. In other words, 3rd Bass, Kid Rock, 311, the Insane Clown Posse, Korn, the Bloodhound Gang, Limp Bizkit, Linkin Park, Hed PE, and Eminem have all at one time or another spewed outright misogynist or subtly sexist lyrics. Why, then, is the blame for misogyny in rap music placed squarely on black ghetto youth, and primarily gangsta rappers? And, even as I write all of this I continue my condemnation of misogyny in gangsta rap. I simply refuse to hold up gangsta rap as an "especially egregious" form of misogyny in American popular culture and then cavalierly turn a blind eye to misogyny and other associated expressions of patriarchy in countless white suburban youth-centered forms of popular culture, especially horror movies, video games, cage fighting, and TV shows aimed at white suburban youth. [12]

If there is one thing that we can all agree on when it comes to the Beastie Boys, it would have to be the fact that they brought an insatiable passion for parodying pop culture, sophisticated satire of several subcultures, and wicked sense of wordplay to rock rap and comedy rap. Whether one turns to *Licensed to Ill* and *Paul's Boutique* or *Check Your Head* and *Ill Communication*, one of the overarching themes of their work is centered around parody and (especially on *Paul's Boutique*) pastiche. However, because their parodies were so solid, many critics believe that the Beastie Boys ultimately became a part of the very pop culture industry they made their name mocking and (tongue-in-cheek) critiquing. Even still, the Beastie Boys fared much better than Run-D.M.C., whose career seemed to go into a tailspin after the Beastie Boys' *Licensed to Ill* in 1986 and the rise of political rap via Boogie Down Productions' *Criminal Minded* and Public Enemy's *Yo! Bush Rush The Show*, both released to critical acclaim in 1987.

Seeking to ride the momentum of the rock rap movement they started and that the Beastie Boys took to the next level, in 1988 Run-D.M.C. released their much-anticipated *Tougher Than Leather*. Hoping that their fourth album would outsell the Beastie Boys' at that point quintuple-platinum *Licensed to Ill*, Run-D.M.C.'s characteristic merging of rap with hard rock began to fall out of favor even as the Beastie Boys' rock rap blend racked up unprecedented rap record sales. Recalling the black backlash against rock & roll in light of white youths' almost complete colonization of the genre by the mid-1960s, after the Beastie Boys' rock rap success with white suburban youth many black hip hoppers began to look at rock rap as a form of passé pop rap. Hence, even though they started the rock rap genre, by the time Run-D.M.C. released *Tougher Than Leather* with hard-hitting rock rap songs, such as "Miss Elaine," "Papa Crazy," "Mary, Mary" and "Soul to Rock & Roll," to the more ghetto-centered rap fans of the late 1980s these songs sounded like "white boy" (or, even more pejoratively at that time, "Beastie Boy") rock rap music. Ironically *Tougher Than Leather* sold well enough among white suburban rap and rock fans that the album did achieve platinum status for sales exceeding one million copies.

After Run-D.M.C. and the Beastie Boys' phenomenal rock rap success several rock rap groups took the American music industry by storm. The 1990s saw the rise of iconic rock rap groups such as Biohazard, Rage Against the Machine, 311, Korn, Limp Bizkit, Kid Rock, the Insane Clown Posse,

Linkin Park, and Hed PE. Rock rap was such an unprecedented force in rap as it transitioned from the 1980s to the 1990s that many rap fans have forgotten the miscellaneous rock rap tracks by the Fat Boys ("Rock-N-Roll"), LL Cool J ("Go Cut Creator Go"), Whodini ("Fugitive"), Public Enemy ("Sophisticated Bitch" and "Bring the Noise"), and the D.O.C. ("Beautiful But Deadly"). Moreover, on his 1987 debut album, *Rhyme Pays*, Ice-T even went so far as to sample Black Sabbath's "War Pigs" on the title track ("Rhyme Pays"). Continuing his rock/rap mash-up, on his sophomore effort, *Power*, Ice-T mixed in Heart's "Magic Man" on the classic track "Personal," and on his third album he used snatches of Black Sabbath's 1970 classic eponymous track.

Similar to Run-D.M.C., Ice-T was a serious fan of hard rock and heavy metal. After a series of seminal and well-received early gangsta rap albums—for example, *Power* (1988), *The Iceberg/Freedom of Speech* (1989), and *O.G.: The Original Gangster* (1991)—in 1992 Ice-T released the controversial *Body Count* album with his new rock rap group of the same name. Although the rock rap track "Body Count" that appeared on the *O.G.* album was full of hard-hitting social commentary, the album-length *Body Count* project was something of a disappointment. If one is able to somehow circumvent the commotion caused by the "Cop Killer" track, which was actually little more than a bare-bones rap-cum-thrash metal chant, the bulk of the album's tracks are rather aimless at best and sophomoric at worst. For example, on the "Evil Dick" track Ice-T's penis (yes, his penis) tells him to never "sleep alone," which is to say, be promiscuous; on the "KKK Bitch" track he violently invades a Ku Klux Klan meeting and ends up "screwing" (his term) the Grand Dragon's daughter; on the "Voodoo" track he lamely plays into antiblack racist myths when he rhymes about a "witch doctor" crippling him with a "voodoo doll"; and, finally, on the "Mama's Gotta Die Tonight" track he takes his misogyny to the next level when he murders his mother because she is a racist.[13]

In contrast to the aimlessness of Ice-T's Body Count band was the focused, fiery, provocative, and often-polemical rock rap of Rage Against the Machine. Equally influenced by the Last Poets, the Ramones, Bad Brains, the Sex Pistols, Public Enemy, Fishbone, the Beastie Boys, KRS-One, the Red Hot Chili Peppers, Gil Scott Heron, the Clash, Run-D.M.C. and Led Zeppelin, Rage Against the Machine synthesized the searing rhymes of political rap with the hyper-testosterone of punk, hard rock, and heavy metal. The incredible synergy between rapper-singer Zack de la Rocha and guitar wunderkind Tom Morello created what sounds to my ears like the most skillful and successful marriage of political rap and hard rock ever recorded. Their eponymous 1992 debut set a new standard for rock rap, but sadly few followed their lead. Delivering his rhymes in an innovative oscillating *marcato*, *staccato*, and *legato* emotionally charged chanting style, de la Rocha merged the political punch of Gil Scott Heron, Chuck D, and KRS-One with the tortured vocals of Johnny Rotten, Sid Vicious, and Joe Strummer.[14]

Critiquing everything from cultural imperialism and corporate America to government oppression and American militarism, Rage Against the Machine developed a musical Molotov cocktail of political rap, post-punk, hard rock, and heavy metal that sonically bombed and blew up suburban America. They had a sound that was wholly their own. Perhaps the most stunning aspect of Rage Against the Machine's recordings is centered around the ways in which de la Rocha's far-reaching and often ultraradical rhymes were amazingly matched by Morello's spectacular guitar playing, which seemed to channel the spirits and sparks of a wide range of "guitar gods," such as Jimi Hendrix, Carlos Santana, Jimmy Page, Tony Iommi, Eddie Hazel, Ace Frehley, Adrian Smith, Dr. Know, and Vernon Reid.

Compared to the horribly ahistorical and extremely apolitical, albeit incredibly angst-filled, rock rap of the 1990s, Rage Against the Machine's trilogy—*Rage Against the Machine* (1992), *Evil Empire* (1996), and *The Battle of Los Angeles* (1999)—captured the essence of what rap in general, and rock rap in particular, was about and sounded like when it was grounded in and grew out of broader social and political struggles. Those who question whether or not rap music really and truly reflects the politics (and polemics) of the Hip Hop Movement need look no further than Rage Against the Machine. They used their music to not only critique and protest what they were against, but to support and raise awareness about countless progressive causes. For example, throughout their career Rage Against the Machine has supported and hipped millions of youths to: the Zapatista Army of National Liberation; UNITE (Union of Needletrades Industrial and Textile Employees); the Committee to Support the Revolution in Peru; the Peruvian revolutionary organization Shining Path; political prisoner Abimael Guzmán; Rock for Choice; the Anti-Nazi League; the United Farm Workers; the child-care organization Para Los Niños; Fairness and Accuracy in Reporting; the National Commission for Democracy in Mexico; Women Alive; the Free Tibet Movement; AK Press; Amnesty International; the Hollywood-Sunset Free Clinic; Indymedia; Parents for Rock and Rap; the Popular Resource Center; RE: GENERATION; Refuse and Resist; Voices in the Wilderness; political prisoner Leonard Peltier; and political prisoner Mumia Abu-Jamal.

Deeply inspired by Public Enemy's innovative frontman, Chuck D, Zack de la Rocha wrote classic hard-hitting rhyme after hard-hitting rhyme that went beyond the standard rock rap lyrical fare, which for the most part seemed obsessed with life in the suburbs, sex, drugs, and drinking. With songs such as "Settle for Nothing," "Bullet in the Head," and the particularly vitriolic "Wake Up," Rage Against the Machine conducted clinics in the art of slowly building tension and allowing the music to breathe and modulate until it finally exploded in an indescribable display of out-and-out passion, politics, and poetry. Based, in part, on the speeches and writings of Martin Luther King and Malcolm X, as well as inspired by Muhammad Ali's courageous stand against the Vietnam War, "Wake Up" exposed an entire generation of white suburban youth to the Civil Rights Movement and the Federal Bureau of Investigation's (the FBI's) infamous COINTELPRO (an acronym for Counter Intelligence Program).

In brief, COINTELPRO's sole purpose—according to J. Edgar Hoover's many detailed directives to FBI agents between 1956 and 1971—was to "expose, disrupt, misdirect, discredit, or otherwise neutralize" seditious movements and their leaders. Focusing on individuals and organizations deemed "subversive" by the post-McCarthyist conservative forces who conceived of themselves as working in the best interest of middle-class white America, the FBI's records indicate that 85 percent of all of COINTELPRO's work targeted communist and socialist organizations; individuals and organizations associated with the Civil Rights Movement, including Martin Luther King, as well as other individuals associated with the Southern Christian Leadership Conference, the National Association for the Advancement of Colored People, the Congress of Racial Equality, the Student Nonviolent Coordinating Committee, and several other civil rights organizations; the Nation of Islam; Elijah Muhammad; Malcolm X; Stokely Carmichael; Angela Davis; the Black Panther Party; the Us Organization; the American Indian Movement; a wide range of "New Left" organizations, including Students for a Democratic Society and the Weather Underground; the National Lawyer's Guild; individuals and organizations associated with the Anti-War Movement, the Women's Liberation Movement, the Chicano Movement, and the Homosexual Liberation Movement. Tellingly, only 15 percent of COINTELPRO's work was directed at marginalizing and subverting white supremacist and domestic terrorist groups, such as the Ku Klux Klan, various White Citizens Councils, the American Nazi Party, and the National States' Rights Party. [15]

Where fans of most of the other rock rap bands talked incessantly of their favorite band's music, with Rage Against the Machine there was constant chatter about the radical political lyrics *and* the music. As has been repeatedly said of Public Enemy, Rage Against the Machine's music made its listeners think and feel just as much as it made them bob and weave and dance with abandon. With songs like "Bombtrack," "Killing in the Name," "Bullet in the Head," "People of the Sun," "Bulls on Parade," "Vietnow," "Guerilla Radio," and "Voice of the Voiceless," Rage Against the Machine eventually came to represent to rock rap what Public Enemy represented to political rap. Challenging the ahistorical, apolitical, and hyper-privileged mind-set of many white hip hoppers, Public Enemy, Rage Against the Machine, and several of the more popular politically-inclined rap artists and groups, such as KRS-One, Gang Starr, De La Soul, A Tribe Called Quest, Poor Righteous

Teachers, Arrested Development, Digable Planets, and the Disposable Heroes of Hiphoprisy, used rap music and hip hop culture as a consciousness-
raising tool.

If Rage Against the Machine represented one of the undisputed peaks of
rock rap in the 1990s, several other rock rap groups, while competent,
seemed more interested in cashing in on rap's growing popularity than actually making a serious contribution to rock rap as a genre. Moreover, most
other rock rap artists' music was woefully devoid of anything that might be
considered "political lyrics" or "social commentary." Considering the mixed
or biracial backgrounds of both Zack de la Rocha and Tom Morello it is
intriguing to ponder the part race and culture may have played in their burgeoning political views.

As is well known, de la Rocha is the son of German-Irish American
anthropologist Olivia de la Rocha and famed Mexican American visual artist
Robert "Beto" de la Rocha. Morello is the son of Irish-Italian American
schoolteacher Mary Morello and Kenyan ambassador to the United Nations
Ngethe Njoroge. De la Rocha has spoken openly about the constant racism
he experienced growing up in Irvine, California, and likewise Morello reportedly experienced a lot of racism growing up in Libertyville, Illinois, a suburb
of Chicago. Morello, consequently, developed his radical political leanings
early in life, penning anarchist and antiapartheid essays for his high school
newspaper and eventually earning a Bachelor of Arts degree in political
science and social studies from Harvard University in 1986.

Obviously race and racism impacted Rage Against the Machine's dynamic duo—de la Rocha and Morello—in ways that few other rock rap artists
fully fathomed. Instead of downplaying race and racism in a decade, the
1990s, which witnessed the Clarence Thomas-Anita Hill hearings, the Rodney King beating, the Los Angeles uprising, the O.J. Simpson trial, the
Million Man March, and the Million Woman March, Rage Against the Machine made eye-opening connections between racism, capitalism, and U.S.
imperialism. Although several other rock rap groups may have sold more
albums than Rage Against the Machine, when all the smoke clears and all the
dust settles they remain paragons of 1990s rock rap by the very fact that they
were *inventively musical* and *unapologetically political* in an era of much
musical schlock and intense political apathy.

Even with the rise and increasing popularity of rock rap throughout the
1990s, for the most part rap music was almost wholly identified with black
ghetto youth. Here we have to ask a series of critical questions: Why didn't
rap fall to the same fate as rock & roll? In other words, after the Beastie
Boys, Kid Rock, 311, Linkin Park, and Limp Bizkit's unprecedented success,
why wasn't rap overrun with a bunch of blond-haired and blue-eyed rappers
from every lily-white suburban corner of the country? Furthermore, what
was it about the Beastie Boys' brand of rock rap that—obviously considering

their record sales—appealed to a wider audience than (the actual inventors of rock rap) Run-D.M.C.'s rock rap albums, including their ill-fated *Tougher Than Leather*? How do race and racial politics play themselves out in rap music and hip hop culture, especially when and where we come to white rappers and white rap fans' consumption of rap music? Would the Beastie Boys have been as successful if their early rhymes were as political (à la Public Enemy or Rage Against the Machine) as they were comical? Why have rap music and hip hop culture thus far failed to produce a really and truly radical political white rapper on the level of the white rock rappers and white comedy rappers?[16]

Truth be told, there simply are no easy answers to these questions. However, I have a sneaking suspicion that several of the answers actually lie in the ways in which rap music in specific, and hip hop culture more generally, has "inherited" a lot of the post-Civil Rights Movement myths surrounding race and what it means to be black, especially poor and black. The very same black youthfulness, black hipness, and black sexiness that made Motown a major force in the music industry in the 1960s was carried over to rap music in the 1980s and 1990s. Part of rap's charm in its first two decades was the fact that it was simultaneously familiar and unfamiliar: *familiar* insofar as it sampled music, movie themes, commercial jingles, cartoons, and other sounds from American popular culture that most people, black and white, could easily identify with and have heard, literally, hundreds of times; and it was *unfamiliar* in light of the fact that it took the gritty and often grisly tales of life in the ghetto handed down from almost every major form of black popular music, from the blues all the way through to funk, and gave voice to the ongoing horror, hurt, and hardships most African Americans continued to endure in the aftermath of the progressive sociopolitical movements of the 1960s.

Rap music's "realness," if you will, in many senses has always been predicated on an intense understanding of and identification with poor and working-class people's lives, loves, lusts, and losses. By the very fact that rock rap, for the most part, has been and remains preoccupied with life in the suburbs, and while it uniquely registers with white suburban youth, after Run-D.M.C. and the Beastie Boys' groundbreaking efforts in the mid-1980s it did not seem to resonate as much with black ghetto youth. Although often overlooked in favor of its racial politics, similar to both rhythm & blues and rock & roll at their inceptions, rap has always been *a populist form of popular music*, and hip hop culture has always been *a populist form of popular culture*. Bearing this in mind, rap music and hip hop culture could be said to be simultaneously universal and particular: *universal* in light of their populism, and *particular* insofar as the bulk of their populism historically has been and currently remains predicated primarily on the experiences of black ghetto youth.

Helping to elaborate on the universality and integration of rap music and hip hop culture into mainstream American popular culture, in his eye-opening book, *Other People's Property: A Shadow History of Hip Hop in White America* (2007), Jason Tanz decidedly declared, "over the past couple of decades, just about every element of mainstream American culture has, in one way or another, fucked with hip hop" (x). Just as rhythm & blues and rock & roll can be viewed as musical metaphors for the politics and social vision of the Civil Rights Movement, there is a sense in which rap music can be viewed as a metaphor for the politics and social vision of the Hip Hop Movement. Whether or not we agree with the politics and social vision of the Hip Hop Movement, that should not stop us from acknowledging that the various genres of rap serve as soundtracks for the movement.

Since the early 1980s rap has increasingly caught the eyes and ears of mainstream America and, consequently, there is a sense in which certain aspects of rap music and hip hop culture have resonated with the wider American world. Hence, Tanz wryly went on, "[o]ur television shows are spiced with hip hop humor, presidential candidates drop knowing references to the Atlanta hip hop duo Outkast, and gangsta rapper Snoop Dogg appears next to Lee Iacocca in advertisements for Chrysler automobiles. Just like previous paradigm-shifters before it—from jazz to rock to punk—hip hop culture, which once felt alien and potentially revolutionary, has been fully integrated into American life" (x). Accordingly, any doubts about hip hop's wide appeal and, more specifically, what the Hip Hop Movement "inherited" from the Civil Rights Movement and its major soundtracks can be quickly laid to rest—although I am certain distinguished folk like Rosa Parks, Martin Luther King, and Bayard Rustin had a different kind of "integration" in mind when they risked their lives for social justice and to redefine American democracy.

Tanz's work is extremely telling, especially when he emphasized that even though hip hop "once felt alien and potentially revolutionary" to most of mainstream America (including the black bourgeoisie), by the turn of the twenty-first century it had been "fully integrated into American life." Rap music and hip hop culture have, literally, achieved entry into mainstream American society in ways that the black ghetto youth who, for the most part, initiated and intensely evolved the music and culture have not. This brings us to the question of how truly "desegregated" and "integrated" is twenty-first-century America, especially under the Obama administration and Tea Party hateration?

The integrationist ethos of the Civil Rights Movement obviously, even if mostly through osmosis, impacted the popularity and white youth's perception and consumption of rhythm & blues and rock & roll in the 1950s and 1960s. And, it will be recalled, both rhythm & blues and rock & roll "once felt alien and potentially revolutionary" during their early years prior to being "fully integrated into American life." In the aftermath of the Civil Rights Movement it would seem that increased musical integration has taken the place of increased social integration. However, it is important to point out that black popular music (e.g., blues, ragtime, and jazz) achieved high levels of popularity in mainstream America prior to the emergence of the Civil Rights Movement. So, even though rap may be "new" in a musical sense, it occupies a preexisting, shall we say, "old" space in mainstream American popular culture in a sociopolitical sense.

As I discussed in *Hip Hop's Amnesia*, even within the context of pre-Civil Rights Movement Jim Crow laws and wholesale segregation black popular music and black popular culture often "crossed over" to white America. Even more, to continue questioning, we must ask how truly new and novel are rap music and hip hop culture if they occupy positions suspiciously similar to each and every form of black popular music and black popular culture that preceded them? In other words, contemporary black popular music and contemporary black popular culture, arguably best represented by rap music and hip hop culture, are more or less *aesthetically accepted* but *politically rejected*.[17]

As Tanz hinted at above, rap music and hip hop culture really register within mainstream America when and where they appear to be politically neutral, "black" or "racial" in white user-friendly or Eurocentrically acceptable ways, and "gendered" or "feminine" in ways which do not challenge misogyny and patriarchy (i.e., *not* à la Sarah Jones's jaw-dropping "Your Revolution," a.k.a. "Your Revolution Will Not Happen Between These Thighs!" [in A. Olson 2007, 8–10]). Tanz (2007) characteristically continued his "shadow history" tongue-in-cheek critique of white folks'—especially suburban white youths'—fascination with rap music and hip hop culture:

> It is, in a sense, an old story. The artistic expression of black struggle has always captivated white listeners, ever since groups of slaves converted their plantation woes into musical lamentations. The urge of sheltered suburban kids to turn to abrasive, foreign music—from rock to punk to techno—as an outlet for their own frustrations and fantasies is almost as old as the suburbs themselves. And every generation has discovered new technology by which to infuriate and befuddle its parents, a goal that rap music has proven singularly successful at achieving. But hip hop is a unique phenomenon. Unlike rock, which did not gain a foothold in popular culture until Elvis Presley gave a white face to its potentially threatening rhythms, rap's performers and narratives have remained defiantly black for more than two decades. Even more importantly, it is understood to be more than mere entertainment. More than any other musical form before it, hip hop promises to provide insight into the lives and thoughts of an entire community of black Americans.
>
> If our culture is an expression of our deepest fears, anxieties, and fantasies, then what does it say that hip hop has become our national soundtrack? In

1970, Tom Wolfe coined the expression "radical chic" to describe a cadre of moneyed white elites that entertained itself by throwing dinner parties for the Black Panthers. Today, that prospect seems neither radical nor particularly chic. To an unprecedented degree, our popular culture consists of white people entertaining themselves with—and identifying with—expressions of black people's struggles and triumphs. Racial dissonance has become an immutable fact of our everyday life. Rappers Method Man and Redman shill for Right Guard deodorant; soccer moms shout "you go, girl!" at one another; white kids wear FUBU, a black-owned clothing label whose name stands for "For Us, By Us." (x–xi; see also 99–199; Wolfe 1970)[18]

After importantly acknowledging the African American roots of rock music ("rock, which did not gain a foothold in popular culture until Elvis Presley gave a white face to its potentially threatening rhythms"), Tanz emphasized that what might be the most extraordinary aspect of rap music and hip hop culture—especially in light of the hard-core *vanillaization* and commercialization of blues, jazz, and rock—may very well be the fact that "rap's performers and narratives have remained defiantly black for more than two decades." Rap's "defiantly black" discourse is actually what makes it "more than mere entertainment." Even with all of the blackface minstrelesque motifs in contemporary rap music and hip hop culture, yet and still, there remain remnants of both black conservatism *and* black radicalism that sometimes hark back to the Black Women's Club Movement and the New Negro Movement and, at other times, evoke the aesthetic exoticism and artistic activism of the Harlem Renaissance and the Bebop Movement. Yet, in even more ways, rap music and hip hop culture resemble remixed versions of the moderatism of the Civil Rights Movement and the militantism of the Black Power Movement, not to mention the radical political aesthetic of the Black Arts Movement and the neo-minstrelist aesthetic of the blaxploitation (i.e., "black exploitation") films and soundtracks on the 1970s.

Observe that Tanz's work squarely places rap music and hip hop culture within both the African American music and the African American movement traditions, and I could not agree with him more when he stated, "[m]ore than any other musical form before it, hip hop promises to provide insight into the lives and thoughts of an entire community of black Americans." Hence, rap frequently blurs the lines between aesthetics and politics by being "defiantly black" and decidedly ghetto-centered (or, rather, "ghettocentric") in an era—1980 to the present—where most of mainstream America and the African American middle class sought to distance themselves from discussions of race, racial oppression, and racialized economic exploitation (i.e., the long-standing antiblack racist character of U.S. capitalism and the labor industry). Instead of sounding like leftover or "lost" tracks from a Last Poets or Watts Prophets album, rappers' engagement of race, racism, class, and capitalism is sometimes serious and sometimes playful, sometimes inspiring and, truth be told, sometimes extremely infuriating. However, what should be emphasized after all of rap's critics and defenders have had their say is that rap has unrepentantly remained "defiantly black" and decidedly ghettocentric in post-Civil Rights Movement and post-Black Power Movement America, even as most hip hoppers' parents and grandparents seemed to retreat from race, race consciousness, and serious critiques of racial oppression and economic exploitation between 1980 and the present. Here we have yet another distinguishing feature of the Hip Hop Movement and its admittedly problematic aesthetics, poetics, and politics.

Special attention should be paid to the often-overlooked fact that although the Hip Hop Movement's politics do not rotely resemble the Civil Rights Movement or the Black Power Movement's politics, it is, in its own unique way, political—in fact, I would go so far as to say, *extremely political*, insofar as its politics were initially and currently continue to be put forward during a so-called "postracial," "postfeminist," "post-Marxist," "post-Civil Rights Movement," "post-Black Power Movement," and "post-Women's Liberation Movement" period. To be "defiantly black" in an era of antiblack racist and antipoor people Reaganism and Bushism is to challenge the very foundations on which modern white America was built. To be "defiantly black" in the last quarter of the twentieth century—which is to say, even after the unprecedented black radicalism of the Black Power Movement—is to challenge the very foundations on which modern African America was built. To be "defiantly black" in the aftermath of the epoch-making success of white rock rappers and white comedy rappers is to rescue and reclaim rap music and hip hop culture for black ghetto youth and refuse to allow rap to be musically colonized the way jazz was in the 1930s and 1940s and rock was in the 1950s and 1960s. And, lastly, to be "defiantly black" in the midst of Obama's America is to challenge the long-lingering myth and lily-white lie that African American life actually improved simply because an African American was elected the president of the United States of America.

If the Hip Hop Movement surreptitiously inherited nothing else from the Civil Rights Movement, the Black Power Movement, and their various soundtracks it has been its ability to distinguish between black conservatism and black radicalism, which is to say, *African American upper-class and middle-class policies and programs* and *African American working-class and underclass-focused policies and programs*. One doesn't have to be Cornel West, Michael Eric Dyson, or Tavis Smiley to see that many of Obama's policies and programs actually do not speak to the special needs of working-class and poor people, especially working-class and poor black folk. In point of fact, Obama most often emphasizes the American middle class a lot more than he does America's working class and working poor, African American or otherwise. The concern here has nothing to do with the color of Obama's skin, who his parents were, or where he was born, but—and here's the real rub—it has more to do with the ongoing poor quality of the majority of African Americans' births, lives, and deaths during his presidency and administration. It would seem that Jean-Baptiste Alphonse Karr's old adage "plus ça change, plus c'est la même chose"—that is, "the more it changes, the more it's the same thing" or, the more noted translation, "the more things change, the more they stay the same"—is applicable to African America now more than ever before.

Tanz was completely correct when he contended, "[t]o an unprecedented degree, our popular culture consists of white people entertaining themselves with—and identifying with—expressions of black people's struggles and triumphs. Racial dissonance has become an immutable fact of our everyday life." Let's "keep it real" and, even more importantly, *keep it critical* here: Wasn't blackface minstrelism a telltale sign of "racial dissonance" in antebellum, Civil War, Reconstruction, and post-Reconstruction America? Weren't the artistry and activism of the Harlem Renaissance indicative of the "racial dissonance" in America between 1920 and 1940? Wasn't the rise and widespread popularity of rhythm & blues and rock & roll in the 1950s and 1960s a sonic symbol of the national struggle against "racial dissonance" in America, undoubtedly best embodied by the Civil Rights Movement? Who can deny that the soul music of the 1960s and 1970s, by *decommercializing* and *repoliticizing* rhythm & blues, served as an obvious aural rebellion against "racial dissonance" in America and an extremely intimate and innovative soundtrack for the Black Power Movement?

It might be uncomfortable for many of my readers to sincerely grapple with and seek to grasp the physical, psychological, spiritual, and emotional implications of the long-standing reality of "white people entertaining themselves with—and identifying with—expressions of black people's struggles and triumphs," but it is only when we earnestly engage this issue that we can come to terms with both the sonic and social salience of rap music and hip hop culture. In short, the Hip Hop Movement represents a kind of continuation of African American social commentary and political critique via one of the only avenues black youth have available to them to make such commentary and critique. Recall, both rhythm & blues and rock & roll served a similar function for the black youth of the 1950s and 1960s.

In so many words, Tanz and I are saying that black suffering and black social misery, black oppression and black exploitation have become a major part—if not the motor inside of the merciless, macabre-making machine—of the U.S. entertainment industry. From nineteenth-century blackface minstrelism all the way through to the twenty-first century frequently minstrelesque musings of gangsta rappers and hard-core hip hoppers, African Americans' lives and labors, African Americans' hardships and historic endurance of racial hatred, African Americans' historic trauma and contemporary drama have all at one time or another ironically and thoroughly entertained white

America. This point hits home even harder when we seriously consider the ways in which white youth have been and remain utterly entertained by "hard-core," "dirty" and, especially, "gangsta" rap.

The argument here is not that black suffering and black social misery are completely absent in the forms of rap that are heavily consumed by white suburban youth, but that even though hard-core, dirty, and gangsta rap all clearly harbor questionable sexual, cultural, social, and political positions they nonetheless contain commentary on and critiques of black suffering and black social misery. Social commentary and political critique are not the exclusive domain of any single form of rap and, in fact, all forms of rap— including pop, rock, comedy, and gangsta rap—contain semblances of social commentary and political critique. In keeping with the central focus of this "remix," which has primarily involved engaging rock & roll as a musical metaphor for the politics and social vision of the Civil Rights Movement and classic rock's contributions to rock rap, it might be fitting to conclude with a discussion of the evolution of rock rap in the aftermath of Rage Against the Machine's radical politicization of the genre in the 1990s.

THE RE-AFRICAN AMERICANIZATION OF ROCK: MOS DEF, MICHAEL FRANTI, AND POST-RAGE AGAINST THE MACHINE POLITICAL ROCK RAP

Following Rage Against the Machine's radical politicization of rock rap in the 1990s, there was a concerted effort to reclaim the African American origins and early evolution of both rock & roll and rock rap by noted political rap artists such as Mos Def and Michael Franti, among others. After his pioneering partnership with Talib Kweli and DJ Hi-Tek on the 1997 political rap classic *Black Star*, Mos Def's 1999 solo album, *Black on Both Sides*, took the rap world by storm. Conceived of as a return to the "old school" roots of rap, *Black on Both Sides* was a musical manifesto aimed at rescuing rap from *the ghetto-gangsta-nigga-pimp-hoe-thug theme* redundancy that was threatening the future of the art form. Growing out of the Native Tongues Posse's preoccupation with the entire history of black popular music (à la the avant-garde jazz-centered Association for the Advancement of Creative Musicians [AACM]), Mos Def's work fit within the framework of the Native Tongues' aesthetic with its emphasis on political critique, social commentary, and use of "live" musical instruments on his backing tracks. Similar to other Native Tongues members, such as the Jungle Brothers, A Tribe Called Quest, Queen Latifah, De La Soul, and Monie Love, his brand of rap drew heavily from the jazz poetry, soul, and funk aesthetics of the 1960s and 1970s. [19]

Displaying remarkable rhyme skills with intricate wordplay, *Black on Both Sides* was as lyrically eclectic as it was musically eclectic. Ranging from rhymes about religion ("Fear Not of Man"), racism ("Mr. Nigga"), environmental racism ("New World Water"), racial profiling ("Speed Law"), the state of rap ("Hip Hop"), and his mother's wisdom ("Umi Says"), Mos Def's political critique and social commentary provided a clear contrast to *the ghetto-gangsta-nigga-pimp-hoe-thug theme* clichés of gangsta rap. However, gangsta rap was only one of many other forms of rap that Mos Def believed was blocking rap's discursive development. On the track "Rock N Roll" he not only provided the most articulate and forceful rap-styled statement concerning the African American origins and early evolution of rock & roll, but he also critiqued what was quickly becoming the clichés of rock rap—namely, its preoccupation with life in the suburbs, sex, drinking, and drugs.

"Rock N Roll" was a career-defining track. In one fell swoop Mos Def brazenly reclaimed rock for black ghetto youth and exposed both black ghetto youth and white rock rap fans to the African American origins and early evolution of rock & roll with copious references to Chuck Berry, Bo Diddley, and Little Richard. Beginning his sonic history of rock & roll with African American enslavement and the spirituals (referencing "plantations," "cotton money," and chained ankles and feet), from Mos Def's point of view rock & roll was unquestionably an all-encompassing form of black popular music that included the music of blues musicians John Lee Hooker and Albert King, jazz musicians Nina Simone and John Coltrane, and soul musicians James Brown and Otis Redding. While also referencing Motown, Jimi Hendrix, Bad Brains, and Fishbone, Mos Def lyrically deconstructed accepted whitewashed interpretations of rock & roll and offered an African American-centered reinterpretation of rock that openly critiqued classic white rockers Elvis Presley and the Rolling Stones, as well as contemporary white rock rappers Limp Bizkit and Korn's cultural theft of African American music and styles.

By placing "Rock N Roll" on an album titled *Black on Both Sides*, Mos Def demonstrated that both rock and rap are forms of black popular music. He also illustrated that political rap was not merely concerned with conventional social and political issues impacting African Americans (e.g., racism, racial profiling, police brutality, economic exploitation, etc.), but also with the politics of black popular music. This is where rock rap reconnects with early African American rock & roll and highlights how contemporary African American rock artists such as Nona Hendryx, Bad Brains, Sound Barrier, Fishbone, Living Colour, 24-7 Spyz, Meshell Ndegeocello, and other members of the Black Rock Coalition conceive of their commitment to rock, not merely as a musical act, but also as a decidedly political act. Consequently, the early distinctly black, civil rights-saturated politics of rock & roll (circa 1954 to 1964) has been handed down to the African American rock artists of the Hip Hop Generation, and even contemporary black rockers not usually associated with rap music often display their solidarity with black ghetto youth, rap music, hip hop culture, and the Hip Hop Movement by featuring rappers, spoken-word artists, and hip hop (or, at the least, hip hop-influenced) beats in their music (e.g., Prince, Terence Trent D'Arby, Tracy Chapman, Lenny Kravitz, Cassandra Wilson, Seal, and Ben Harper). [20]

Mos Def's tracks like "Hip Hop," "Rock N Roll," "Habitat," and "Mathematics" went far to illustrate both the political nature of contemporary black popular music and the expansive nature of political rap. Hence, *Black on Both Sides* not only contested *the ghetto-gangsta-nigga-pimp-hoe-thug theme* of commercial and gangsta rap, but it also unambiguously showed that black ghetto youth had a sense of the political history of black popular music, especially rock, at a time when most African American adults seemed quite content to lazily label rock "white folk's music" or, even more frequently, "white kids' music." When political rock rap is connected with the political (and often radical political) elements in contemporary African American rock, black youths' efforts to repoliticize both rap and rock are easily apparent.

Continuing his reclamation of black rock via rap, Mos Def's second album, *The New Danger* (2004), was a full-fledged rock rap album. Featuring luminaries like guitarist Dr. Know of Bad Brains, keyboardist Bernie Worrell of both Parliament and Funkadelic, bassist Doug Wimbish of both the Sugar Hill Records house band and Living Colour, and drummer Will Calhoun of Living Colour, his new star-studded rock rap band, which he dubbed Black Jack Johnson, rocked and ripped through a sprawling set of songs that, although often lacking the lyrical and conceptual cohesion of *Black on Both Sides*, touched on several topical issues nonetheless. Ranging from half-sung/half-rapped songs about the reemergence of blackface minstrelism ("The Boogie Man Song"), ghetto life ("Freaky Black Greetings" and "Ghetto Rock"), the state of rap music and hip hop culture ("The Rape Over" and "Grown Man Business"), and the senselessness of war ("War"), the minimalism of Mos Def's lyrics provided a clear contrast with the *rock & soul* (as opposed to "rock & roll") sound of his mostly live backing tracks.

In combining rap, rock, and soul, in some senses Mos Def grounded his rock rap in an alternative aesthetic universe compared with the one most frequented by other rock rappers. Songs such as "Bedstuy Parade & Funeral March," "Sunshine," and the nearly ten-minute epic "Modern Marvel," with a sampled Marvin Gaye wailing in the background, deftly demonstrated the range and reach of contemporary black popular music and how rock rap could be reconstructed to speak to the special needs of black ghetto youth. Part of what enabled rock & roll to be so quickly and so thoroughly musically colonized in the late 1950s and early 1960s was the fact that after a while it ceased to reflect African American realities, especially black ghetto youths' lives, loves, and struggles. When one listens to the music of contemporary

African American rock artists like Fishbone, or Tracy Chapman, or Lenny Kravitz, or Ben Harper, one can hear distinct echoes of contemporary African American life and struggle. In this sense, although it does not rotely resemble each and every political expression of the Civil Rights Movement or aesthetic expression of early rock & roll in relationship to the Civil Rights Movement, rock rap nonetheless expresses important aspects of the Hip Hop Movement's politics, poetics, and aesthetics.

As with rock & roll at its inception during the early years of the Civil Rights Movement, Run-D.M.C.'s 1980s rock rap reflected African Americans' reality, and especially black ghetto youths' lives, loves, and struggles. But, beginning with the Beastie Boys' *Licensed to Ill* in 1986, as more and more white suburban youth appropriated rock rap to express their angst and issues, and as rock rap was pushed and pulled in every direction in the mid-1980s music marketplace, it was commodified, de-politicized, and recast as "suburban rap" in contrast to "ghetto rap" (i.e., forms of rap such as political, gangsta, dirty, and hard-core rap). Similar to most things in American popular culture, and American culture more generally, like rock & roll in the late 1950s and early 1960s rap was (and remains) racialized. As quiet as it has been kept, certain forms of music are associated with specific racial and cultural groups in America, and there have been a rare few musicians who have challenged the ongoing musical segregation that continues to plague the United States in the twenty-first century.[21]

However, many of the rock rappers, both black and white, in their own off-kilter and clumsy ways have consistently contested musical segregation by merging and mixing musics traditionally thought to be incompatible at best, or complete opposites at worst. Here we have yet another way in which rap, in this instance rock rap, seems to have absorbed much from the Civil Rights Movement and its rock & roll soundtrack. In fact, it could be argued that where desegregation and integration were major political goals of the Civil Rights Movement that were reflected in both classic rhythm & blues and classic rock & roll, the Hip Hop Movement's sociopolitical goals of social justice, economic justice, environmental justice, religious tolerance, and authentic multiculturalism are frequently reflected in political rock rap and it correlate subculture.

Mos Def was not the only alternative or political rapper to build on Rage Against the Machine's radical politicization of rock rap. Certainly Q-Tip's *Kamaal the Abstract* (2002) and *The Renaissance* (2008) featured innovative political rock rap tracks, as did Pharoahe Monch's *Internal Affairs* (1999). Synthesizing the alternative rap aesthetic with the alternative rock aesthetic, both Lupe Fiasco (see his *Food & Liquor* [2006], *The Cool* [2007], *Lasers* [2011], and *Food & Liquor II: The Great American Rap Album, Pt.1* [2012]) and Kid Cudi (see his *A Kid Named Cudi* [2008], *Man on the Moon* [2009], *Man on the Moon II* [2010], *WZRD* [2012], and *Man on the Moon III* [2013]) have released often left-of-field political rock rap tracks. However, arguably more than any of the aforementioned it was the music and politics of Michael Franti & Spearhead that consistently breathed new life into the political rock rap genre in the first decade of the twenty-first century and reconnected it to its roots in the Civil Rights Movement and both its rhythm & blues and rock & roll soundtracks.

Beginning his career as a member of the Beatnigs—an alternative group that mixed industrial music, punk, and rap on their eponymous 1988 album—Michael Franti later released a more rap-centered album, *Hypocrisy Is the Greatest Luxury* (1992), with his new avant-garde political/jazz rap group the Disposable Heroes of Hiphoprisy. However, it was with his third group, Spearhead, that his alternative vision of rap music, hip hop culture, love, life, and political struggle really came together. Simultaneously a jazz rap, funk rap, political rap, and alternative rap album, Spearhead's stunning debut *Home* (1994) touched on a wide range of topics, most of which targeted issues in the African American community, but it also addressed many issues that plagued U.S. society in the 1990s more generally. Franti's lyrics were thought-provoking in a way unlike many other political rappers, perhaps, partly owing to his characteristic radical humanism. Although often compared to Arrested Development, A Tribe Called Quest, De La Soul, Digable Planets, and the Roots, Franti's social commentary and use of live instruments drew from the Native Tongues aesthetic even as it pushed and pulled it in new lyrical and musical directions.[22]

Similar to other emerging 1990s political rap artists, such as Gang Starr, Paris, X Clan, Poor Righteous Teachers, Mos Def, Talib Kweli, Common, the Coup, and the Roots, Spearhead offered an alternative to *the ghetto-gangsta-nigga-pimp-hoe-thug theme* of commercial and gangsta rap. But, Franti's music was also distinguished by its increasingly upbeat and sunny disposition, which was in stark contrast to his often dark, brooding Isaac Hayes and Barry White-sounding baritone delivery. Reaching deep into the dark recesses of black ghetto youths' reality, Franti painted affecting portraits of racism, poverty, and crime on the one hand (e.g., "Hole in the Bucket," "Runfayalife," "Crime To Be Broke in America," and "Caught Without an Umbrella"), and uplifting pictures of African American life and culture on the other hand (e.g., "Love Is Da Shit," "Piece O' Peace," and "Red Beans & Rice"). His simultaneously hard-hitting and optimistic lyrics, as well as his live band and neo-soul-sounding background singers, made Franti one of the most innovative political rappers of the 1990s.

Spearhead's second album, *Chocolate Supa Highway* (1997), continued Franti's synthesis of socially conscious rap and neo-soul instrumentation and background vocals, but it importantly added elements of dancehall reggae and trip hop to the mix. Wrapping his positive and politically oriented baritone-bathed rhymes around the combustible beats of his live band, Franti's new reggae and trip hop vibe further distinguished his brand of rap from gangsta rappers, and other political rappers as well. Lyrically and musically Franti seemed to channel a lot of the political energy of the Civil Rights Movement and Black Power Movement, and songs such as "Africa Online," "Chocolate Supa Highway," and "Keep Me Lifted," recalled several of the progressive soul singer-songwriters of the 1960s and 1970s. Tracks like "Food for Tha Masses," "Madness in Tha Hood," and "Life Sentence" invoked the politics, poetics, and music of classic soul and funk luminaries like Curtis Mayfield, Gil Scott Heron, Marvin Gaye, the Last Poets, Bill Withers, and the Watts Prophets. But, at the same time, the tracks on *Chocolate Supa Highway* also seemed to parallel the radical politics of Civil Rights Movement and Black Power Movement icons and organizations such as Ella Baker, Bayard Rustin, Stokely Carmichael, George Jackson, Angela Davis, the Student Nonviolent Coordinating Committee, the Revolutionary Action Movement, the Organization Us, and, most obviously, the Black Panther Party. Hence, it was not simply the music of the Civil Rights Movement and Black Power Movement that influenced Franti & Spearhead, but the politics and social visions of these movements as well.

By the time he released *Stay Human* in 2001, Franti had once again reinvented himself and his music. On *Stay Human* he revealed his new sonic persona as a radical political rock rapper with a predilection for neo-soul and funky bass lines. Drawing from the brilliant and often biting social commentary of Curtis Mayfield and Bill Withers, the frequently wistful and bluesy narratives of Roberta Flack and Swamp Dogg, the sophisticated soul of Stevie Wonder, Donny Hathaway, and Marvin Gaye, and the incendiary poetry of Amiri Baraka, Sonia Sanchez, Haki Madhubuti, and Nikki Giovanni, *Stay Human* blurred the lines between alternative rap and alternative rock with its stripped-down acoustic *rock & soul* (as opposed to "rock & roll") sound. Emphasizing nonviolence, tolerance, and perseverance, as well as critiquing serious social issues such as the death penalty, police brutality, poverty, homophobia, and racism, similar to *Home* and *Chocolate Supa Highway*, *Stay Human* offered an accessible, love-inspired radical humanist alternative to *the ghetto-gangsta-nigga-pimp-hoe-thug theme* of commercial and gangsta rap. However, it also offered a sometimes sunny and "hippie" or psychedelic sounding alternative to the increasing blandness, bleakness, and suburbia-centeredness of mainstream rock at the turn of the twenty-first century.

Like Mos Def's *Black on Both Sides*, *Stay Human* was both a return to rap's roots and a reclamation of the African American roots of rock. Recalling the militancy of Run-D.M.C.'s early rock rap and Public Enemy's early political rap while simultaneously combining the alternative rap and alternative rock aesthetics, Franti's radical political rhymes gave voice to several of the key issues on the Hip Hop Movement's burgeoning social justice agenda: spirituality; sexuality; freedom; the deconstruction and reconstruction of

American democracy; American militarism; pacifism; multiculturalism; transnationalism; neocolonialism; antiracism; women rights; homosexual rights; religious tolerance; police brutality; political corruption; poverty; environmental justice; HIV/AIDS; and so forth. Essentially reflecting on what it means to be human at the opening of the twenty-first century, *Stay Human* tapped into the spirit of tolerance and togetherness of the Civil Rights Movement, Anti-War Movement, and Hippie Movement without sounding like a cluttered and clumsy "retro-soul," "retro-rock," or "retro-rap" record. After repeated listening, and even considering its emphasis on what might be considered the major civil rights issues of the twenty-first century, *Stay Human* is ultimately an album about hip hop-style radical humanism and human rights—and the ways in which progressive political messages are frequently woven deep into the fabric of fun-filled and funky neo-soul sounding songs is part of the music's lasting charm.[23]

Continuing his music history-making metamorphosis from alternative political rapper to alternative political rock rapper, on *Songs from the Front Porch* (2002), *Everyone Deserves Music* (2003), and *Love Kamikaze* (2005), lyrically and musically Franti displayed the influence of Prince, Fishbone, U2, Tracy Chapman, Red Hot Chili Peppers, Lenny Kravitz, and Ben Harper, among other occasional political rock artists. Rhyming and increasingly singing in a surprisingly beautiful baritone voice over alternative rock backing tracks, when his provocative and politically charged lyrics are contrasted with the rock, funk, soul, and hip hop aesthetic of the music Franti reemerges as a *rapper-singer-songwriter*. Similar to many of the major rock and soul singer-songwriters of the 1960s and 1970s, Franti blurs the boundaries between politics and aesthetics, between black music and white music. And, like the Motown aesthetic of the 1960s, Franti seems to understand the value of his music reaching across racial, cultural, and political chasms and bringing people together. In much the same way that the Hip Hop Movement seeks to break down musical, social, political, and cultural barriers, Franti's music is a genre-bending and mind-boggling metaphor for rap music and hip hop culture's constantly changing musical and political landscape.

Heightening the radical humanist impulse that has run through his music since his very first release, *Everyone Deserves Music* was a particularly affecting album in that by the time it was released in 2003 most rappers had begun to regularly recycle themselves and the neo-minstrel *ghetto-gangsta-nigga-pimp-hoe-thug theme* that had come to dominate commercial rap. Franti's music was fresh in that it seemed to go back in order to go forward (i.e., *sankofa*). A lot of *Everyone Deserves Music* has the funk-disco-electro feel of early rap. But, the lyrics could not be mistaken for any time period other than the turn of the twenty-first century, as Franti's rhymes frequently offer mini-State of the Union addresses. From the title track "Everyone Deserves Music" and "Pray for Grace" to "Love, Why Did You Go Away?" and

"Love Invincible," love, compassion, and community building were at the conceptual core of the album, and even though we have all heard, literally, hundreds and hundreds of love songs what makes Franti's work different is his insatiable love for all humanity, even those human beings he fundamentally disagrees with on key issues. This is where the work of Martin Luther King, Ella Baker, and Bayard Rustin seems to allusively live on in the heads and hearts of the Hip Hop Generation.

Franti's commitment to nonviolence, tolerance, and perseverance did not fall out of the sky, and the same can be said about his affinity for message-oriented rock music. When we consider the politics and social vision of the Civil Rights Movement as articulated by Ella Baker, Martin Luther King, Bayard Rustin, the NAACP, the Congress of Racial Equality, and the Student Nonviolent Coordinating Committee, among many other 1960s civil rights icons and organizations, we have hard historical evidence of an African American youth-led nonviolent movement for social change. Similar to the Civil Rights Movement, then, the broader Hip Hop Movement, especially as conceived of and articulated by Mos Def, Michael Franti, and other political rappers, is primarily an African American youth-led movement dedicated to the deconstruction and reconstruction of American democracy, society, and culture. Moreover, when we consider the early message-oriented rock & roll of Chuck Berry, Bo Diddley, Little Richard, Fats Domino, and Ike Turner, we have examples of some of the models that obviously influenced the political rockers of the 1960s and 1970s, who in turn ultimately influenced Franti and other contemporary political rock rappers.

All of this is to say, the Civil Rights Movement and its integrationist-oriented rock & roll soundtrack seems to have profoundly influenced Franti, among many other rappers and hip hoppers, and that influence is not in any way diminished simply because the larger public either refuses to acknowledge that influence or simply fails to fully understand the politics of black popular music, including early rock & roll. Hence, Franti's long-standing love, nonviolence, tolerance, and perseverance theme is actually a core characteristic of the Civil Rights Movement and its integrationist-oriented early rock & roll soundtrack that was, even if unrecognized by the mostly Euro-centric rock historians, handed down through the African American rock tradition. As a matter of fact, a love, nonviolence, tolerance, and perseverance motif can be easily observed in the music of iconic African American rockers such as Jimi Hendrix, Buddy Miles, Sly & the Family Stone, the Isley Brothers, Swamp Dogg, Funkadelic, LaBelle, Nona Hendryx, Bad Brains, Fishbone, Prince, Living Colour, Terence Trent D'Arby, Tracy Chapman, Lenny Kravitz, Meshell Ndegeocello, and Ben Harper, among many others. What makes Franti's music really and truly distinct among this distinguished cast of characters is his rootedness in rap music and his liberal use of the evolving hip hop aesthetic beyond *the ghetto-gangsta-nigga-pimp-hoe-thug theme* that currently dominates commercial rap.

Amplifying his hip hop-style radical humanism, *Yell Fire!* (2006) skillfully balanced Franti's national and international concerns. Featuring gentler and wiser lyrics over even harder rock/reggae/funk/hip hop rhythms, *Yell Fire!* further merged the alternative rap aesthetic with the alternative rock aesthetic. Commenting on everything from war and world peace to the joys of love and life, Franti's new chanting/singing style owed as much to Jamaican reggae and African American rock as it did to rap and neo-soul. Once again recalling the integrationist ethos of the Civil Rights Movement, Franti's lyrics brilliantly reflected the overall compassion and musical multiculturalism concept that undergirded the album. Coupling moral outrage and righteous indignation with empathy and vulnerability, ironically the more guitar-centered Franti's music became the more alternative issues and African American-centered it seemed. Songs such as "I Know I'm Not Alone," "Sweet Lies," "What I've Seen," "Tolerance," and "Is Love Enough?" seem to summon the Civil Rights Movement and its rock & roll soundtrack just as much as they do the progressive politics of the dawn of the twenty-first century.

Similar to Martin Luther King, Michael Franti seems to have increasingly gravitated toward a principled antiwar stance that is linked to a serious critique of racism and poverty. Although his early political raps focused on racism, then later racism and poverty, by the time he released the radical political rock rap *Stay Human* album Franti was simultaneously critiquing militarism, heterosexism, racism, misogyny, and poverty, among many other issues. This is an important point, because when Franti's post-*Stay Human* music is read against the backdrop of Martin Luther King's famous antiwar speeches and sermons, all of which connected America's increasing militarism with racism and poverty, yet another connection is made between a major voice of the Civil Rights Movement and a major voice of the Hip Hop Movement. Reading or listening to King's many antiwar speeches and sermons, such as "A Time To Break Silence" (April 4, 1967), "Why I Am Opposed to the War in Vietnam" (April 30, 1967), "A Knock at Midnight" (June 25, 1967), "Standing by the Best in an Evil Time" (August 6, 1967), "Thou Fool" (August 27, 1967), "Mastering Our Fears" (September 10, 1967), "But, If Not . . ." (November 5, 1967), "The Meaning of Hope" (December 10, 1967), "Drum Major Instinct" (February 4, 1967), and "Unfulfilled Dreams" (March 3, 1968), one can quickly come to the conclusion that Franti's antiwar activism is not in any way foreign to African America, but deeply connected to a tradition that can actually be traced back to W.E.B. Du Bois and Bayard Rustin's early pacifism and antiwar activism.[24]

Franti's antiwar songs such as "Bomb the World," "I Know I'm Not Alone," and "What I've Seen" are linked to a longer and larger narrative of

African American antiwar activism. And, just as Martin Luther King's anti-
war activism was different from that of W.E.B. Du Bois and Bayard Rustin's
antiwar activism, Michael Franti and the Hip Hop Movement's antiwar activism differs from that of Martin Luther King and the Civil Rights Movement.
Obviously the Hip Hop Movement has inherited more from the Civil Rights
Movement and its soundtracks than previously acknowledged. Something
similar can be said concerning the Hip Hop Movement's inheritance from the
Black Power Movement and its major soundtracks. Hence, "remixes" 3 and 4
will be devoted to examining what the Black Power Movement and its major
soundtracks contributed to rap music, hip hop culture, and the Hip Hop
Movement.

NOTES

1. For further discussion of the blues backlash and the jazz controversy in the 1920s and
1930s, see my analysis in "remixes" 2 and 3 in Rabaka (2012, 19–166).
2. My interpretation of the African American origins and evolution of rock & roll, which
eventually came to be called "rock" by the late 1960s, has been informed by Altschuler (2003),
Crazy Horse (2004), Gillet (1996), Kirby (2009), Lauterbach (2011), Mahon (2004), Othello
(2004), Scrivani-Tidd, Markowitz, Smith, Janosik, and Gulla (2006), Tosches (1999), and
Wald (2009).
3. For further discussion of the ways in which early rock & roll was viewed as an implicit
expression of the politics and social justice agenda of the Civil Rights Movement, and how
early white rock & rollers' music in specific was seen as a challenge to both the musical
segregation *and* social segregation of 1950s and early 1960s America, see Aquila (2000), Bell
(2007), Bertrand (2000), Daniel (2000), Delmont (2012), Francese and Sorrell (2001), and
Knowles (2010).
4. My interpretation here and throughout this section is based on a number of works that
not only view rhythm & blues as the foundation of and inspiration for rock & roll, but that
connect the emergence and early development of rock & roll with cultural, social, and political
changes as a result of the rising Civil Rights Movement. The most noteworthy among the
works I have relied on here include Broven (2009), M. Campbell (2007), Daniel (2000), Escott
(1991, 1999), M. Fisher (2007), Kirby (2009), Redd (1974), Salem (1999), and A. Shaw (1969,
1987).
5. Although there has not been a book published that specifically focuses on the African
American origins and early evolution of rock & roll, several more general rock histories
informed my interpretation here, including Aquila (2000), Delmont (2012), Escott (1999),
Friedlander (2006), Kirby (2009), Lauterbach (2011), Palmer (1995, 1996), and Stuessy and
Lipscomb (2012).
6. Several works factored into and influenced my interpretation here, the most noteworthy
among them Daniel (2000), Delmont (2012), Lawson (2010), Palmer (1995), and Petigny
(2009).
7. For further discussion of white rock & roll cover versions of black rhythm & blues
songs, and for the most noteworthy works that informed my analysis here, see Aquila (2000),
Bell (2007), Crazy Horse (2004), Daniel (2000), Escott (1999), Lauterbach (2011), J. Miller
(1999), Othello (2004), Palmer (1995), Redd (1974, 1985), and Tosches (1999).
8. My interpretation of Run-D.M.C.'s first four albums (*Run-D.M.C.* [1984], *King of Rock*
[1985], *Raising Hell* [1986], and *Tougher Than Leather* [1988]), as well as their enormous
impact on rap music and hip hop culture in the 1980s, had been informed by Adler (1987,
2002), T. Brown (2007), Chang (2005), Frere-Jones (1999), George (1999), McDaniels (2001),
Ro (2005), J. Simmons (2000), and Thigpen (2003).

9. My interpretation of the Beastie Boys' early years has been informed by Batey (1998), Heatley (1999), Light (2005), and Zwickel (2011).

10. Those seeking a more detailed discussion of the often unacknowledged connections between certain forms of rap music and hip hop culture and blackface minstrelism are urged to see my book, *Hip Hop's Inheritance*, and specifically chapter 2, "Civil Rights by Copyright!: From the Harlem Renaissance to the Hip Hop Generation" (Rabaka 2011, 49–82).

11. My interpretation of the Beastie Boys' post-*Licensed to Ill* albums and peak years— specifically *Paul's Boutique* (1989), *Check Your Head* (1992), *Ill Communication* (1995), and *Hello Nasty* (1998)—has been informed by LeRoy (2006), Light (2000, 2005), Luck (2002), Rocco (2000), and Zwickel (2011).

12. For further discussion of the ever-elusive "white rapper" and white privilege within the world of hip hop, and for the most noteworthy works that informed my analysis here, see Calhoun (2005), Cobb and Boettcher (2007), Cutler (2003), R. Ford (2004), Fraley (2009), Gan, Zillman, and Mitrook (1997), Hess (2005), Kitwana (2005), J. Scott (2004), V. Stephens (2005), and Yousman (2003).

13. My interpretation of Ice-T and his gangsta and rock rap has been informed by Brennan (1994), Hamm and Ferrell (1994), Ice-T (1994, 2011), E. Quinn (2000b), and Sieveng (1998).

14. For further discussion of Rage Against the Machine and their enormous influence on the rock rap genre, and for the most noteworthy works that informed my analysis here, see Devenish (2001), Finley (2002), Galiana (1997), Stenning (2008), Tollemer (2009), and Viesca (2004).

15. For further discussion of the FBI's infamous Counter Intelligence Program (COINTELPRO), especially its assault on African America from the beginning of World War I in 1914 to the end of the Vietnam War in 1975, and for the most noteworthy works that informed my analysis here, see Blackstock (1988), Churchill and Wall (1988, 2002), J.K. Davis (1992), Drabble (2004, 2007, 2008), Jeffreys-Jones (2007), O'Reilly (1983, 1989, 1994), and T. Weiner (2012).

16. My interpretation of white rappers, white hip hoppers, and white privilege within the world of hip hop has been informed by Cutler (2003, 2007), Diner (2006), Harkness (2011), Hess (2005), Johnson, Trawalter, and Dovidio (2000), Kitwana (2005), J. Scott (2004), R.E. Sullivan (2003), and Tanz (2007).

17. For further discussion of the "cross over" phenomenon in African American musical history and culture, especially the ways in which black popular music has influenced white popular music and has been more or less *aesthetically accepted* but *politically rejected*, see Awkward (2007), Garofalo (1990, 1992), Guralnick (1986, 1989, 1999), Kempton (2003), Phinney (2005), Ripani (2006), A. Shaw (1970, 1978, 1986, 1987), and Werner (2006).

18. Tanz's telling reference to African Americans' invention of or, at the least, key contributions to the origins and early evolution of rock & roll should not be overlooked. Again, there is a very tired tendency to view rock music as the exclusive domain of and soundtrack for white America, negating the historical fact that at its outset it was almost wholly a black musical expression. As countless musicologists have observed, rock & roll's primary musical points of departure were blues, folk, jazz, country, gospel, jump blues, boogie-woogie, doo-wop, and rhythm & blues. If, indeed, rock began primarily as a synthesis of the aforementioned musics, and if the bulk of its early pioneers were in fact African Americans (e.g., Sister Rosetta Tharpe, Ike Turner & the Kings of Rhythm, Big Mama Thornton, Big Joe Turner, Chuck Berry, Bo Diddley, Etta James, Fats Domino, Little Richard, the Ink Spots, the Mills Brothers, the Platters, the Coasters, and the Drifters), then it is imperative that we highlight the African American origins and early evolution of rock & roll. For further discussion of the African American origins and early evolution of rock & roll, especially the ways in which early rock & roll was grounded in and grew out of early rhythm & blues, and for the most noteworthy works that informed my analysis here, see Altschuler (2003), Aquila (2000), Bertrand (2000), Crazy Horse (2004), Delmont (2012), M. Fisher (2007), Guralnick (1986, 1989, 1999), Lauterbach (2011), Mahon (2004), Merlis and Seay (1997), Othello (2004), Redd (1974, 1985), and A. Shaw (1969, 1987).

19. My interpretation of Mos Def and the Native Tongues Posse has been informed by Beckman and Adler (1991), Bynoe (2006), Crazy Horse (2004), Hess (2007a, 2010), Keyes

(2002), Price (2006), T. Rose (1994), Wang (2003), and J. Wood (1999). And, for further discussion of the Association for the Advancement of Creative Musicians (AACM) and its use of the whole history of black popular music, see G. Campbell (2006), de Jong (1997), G. Lewis (2008), Mittleman (1996), and Pierrepont (2007).

20. Arguably the preeminent organization dedicated to rescuing, reclaiming, and sharing the African American origins and ongoing evolution of rock & roll, the Black Rock Coalition (BRC) "was created in the fall of 1985 in New York City with the purpose of creating an atmosphere conducive to the maximum development, exposure and acceptance of black alternative music. The BRC seeks to foster cooperation among musicians and like organizations through networking and shared resources. The BRC opposes those racist and reactionary forces within the American music industry which undermine and purloin our musical legacy and deny black artists the expressive freedom and economic rewards that our Caucasian counterparts enjoy as a matter of course." The BRC manifesto further declared, "Rock & roll, like practically every form of popular music across the globe, is black music and we are its heirs. We, too, claim the right of creative freedom and access to American and international airwaves, audiences, markets, resources and compensations, irrespective of genre. The BRC embraces the total spectrum of Black music. The BRC rejects the arcane perceptions and spurious demographics that claim our appeal is limited. The BRC rejects the demand for Black artists to tailor their music to fit into the creative straitjackets the industry has designed. We are individuals and will accept no less than full respect for our right to be conceptually independent" (see "The Black Rock Coalition Manifesto" at http://blackrockcoalition.org/mission/manifesto/). For further discussion of the Black Rock Coalition, see Crazy Horse (2004) and Mahon (2000, 2004).

21. A number of scholars have noted the racialization of rap music and hip hop culture and the ways in which racial stereotypes play themselves out within the world of hip hop. For example, see Gan, Zillman, and Mitrook (1997), M.P. Jeffries (2011), Johnson, Trawalter, and Dovidio (2000), Ogbar (2007), Peterson, Wingood, DiClemente, Harrington, and Davies (2007), Rudman and Lee (2002), Watkins (2005), and Yousman (2003).

22. My interpretation of Michael Franti & Spearhead has been informed by Brahinsky (2008), Chang (2003), DiNovella (2002), Franti (2006), Gregg (2002), Griffin (1994), R. Jones (2003), Reed, Franti, and Adler (1992), C.E. Rogers (1996), Sachdev and Freeman (2005), Tatum (1995), and Wilshire (2006).

23. For further discussion of my conception of "hip hop-style radical humanism" or, more simply, *hip hop radical humanism*, see Rabaka (2011, 72–78; 2012, 209–24).

24. For further discussion of Martin Luther King's antiwar speeches and sermons, see Branch (1988, 1998, 2006), Garrow (2004), and M.L. King (1986, 1992, 2001).

II

The Soundtracks of the Black Power Movement, 1965–1980

Remix 3

Soul

From Classic Soul to Neo-Soul

Despite an observable tendency for differing factions to claim the entire movement as their own, the multifaceted nature of Black Power was one of its most significant characteristics. One important mode of Black Power expression was cultural. Playwrights, novelists, songwriters, and artists all had their chance to forward a personalized vision of the militant protest sentiment. They used cultural forms as weapons in the struggle for liberation and, in doing so, provided a much needed structural underpinning for the movement's more widely trumpeted political and economic tendencies.
—William Van Deburg, *New Day in Babylon: The Black Power Movement and American Culture, 1965–1975*

INTRODUCTION: ON THE SOUNDTRACKS OF THE BLACK POWER MOVEMENT AND THEIR INFLUENCE ON RAP AND THE HIP HOP MOVEMENT

Similar to the Civil Rights Movement, the Black Power Movement also had two major soundtracks: soul and funk. Placing a greater emphasis on rhythm & blues' gospel roots, soul was partly a musical, and partly a political response to the whitening and lightening of both rhythm & blues and rock & roll. Moving away from the pop elements and the obsession with crossing over so common in rhythm & blues in the early 1960s, at its emergence in the mid-1960s soul privileged gospel over blues and jazz. Where classic rhythm & blues could be said to have electrified and amplified the blues, classic soul could be said to have intensified the spiritual, sexual, social, political, and cultural components of classic rhythm & blues. Indeed, all of these elements were present in classic rhythm & blues, but they were most often buried beneath a barrage of pop chart-obsessed pretensions, which ultimately white-washed the music and made it sound like little more than black singers imitating white singers. Soul, as with its sister sound—funk—was a sonic challenge that openly emphasized the "African" elements of African Americans' musical and cultural history.[1]

Moreover, soul also expressed African Americans' growing disillusion-ment with both the broken and unfulfilled promises of American democracy during its peak years between 1965 and 1975. After more than a decade of nonviolent sitting-in, marching, freedom-riding, demonstrating and protest-ing, many African Americans, especially black ghetto youth, observed that little had actually changed in American society. Even after the signing of high-sounding civil rights legislation—for example, *Brown v. the Board of Education* (1954), *Gideon v. Wainwright* (1963), *Heart of Atlanta v. the United States* (1964), the Civil Rights Act of 1964, the Twenty-Fourth Amendment (1964), and the Voting Rights Act of 1965—American apart-heid seemed as alive and pernicious as ever.[2] As a consequence, soul lyrics reflected the spiritual, sentimental, and sensual, as well as—in clear contrast to most classic rhythm & blues—the social, political, and cultural. Inspired by both the Civil Rights Movement and the Black Power Movement, then, soul lyrics carried over classic rhythm & blues' focus on love, lust, and loss but distinctively expanded black popular music's sonic palette to include social commentary, political critique, and copious cultural references. In this sense soul music is distinguished from rhythm & blues in light of both its broadened lyrical content and grittier, gospel-influenced musical elements.

Soul was the unsanctioned sound of primarily black ghetto youth express-ing not only their adolescent love (à la Motown-styled rhythm & blues), but also their discontent with both American democracy and the increasing mod-eratism of the Civil Rights Movement. Serving as a major mouthpiece for the rhetoric, politics, and aesthetics of the Black Power Movement, much like 1980s and 1990s political rap and neo-soul, classic soul sought to decolonize and repoliticize black popular music, if not black people more generally. Essentially mirroring the Black Power Movement's efforts to radicalize African American politics in the aftermath of the mixed results and mostly disappointing outcomes of the Civil Rights Movement, soul represented a radicalization and, truth be told, a *re-African Americanization* of black popu-lar music in the 1960s and 1970s. Because of the often overtly political nature of a lot of soul music, and considering the ways in which both neo-soul and political rap artists draw from classic soul aesthetics and Black Power politics, it is important to understand the larger social, political, and cultural landscape in which soul emerged.

Obviously classic soul has handed down a distinct aesthetic to neo-soul and, however unheralded, political rap as well. But, just what that aesthetic was and what it entailed, how it came to be and how it has influenced hip hoppers, is frequently glossed over. The "soul aesthetic" was essentially the musical expression of the much-celebrated "black aesthetic" that was propagated by the members of the Black Arts Movement. However, most discussions of classic soul, even those that claim to be "scholarly," frequently fail to acknowledge and critically engage either the Black Arts Movement or the black aesthetic. What is more, there is a long-standing tendency to disassociate soul music's politics from the wider political world of the Black Power Movement. Similar to rhythm & blues in relationship to the Civil Rights Movement, soul expressed the lives, loves, and struggles of African Americans during the Black Power Movement years. Because soul emerged at the intersection of two movements, the Black Power Movement *and* the Black Arts Movement, any serious analysis of soul music should situate it in the milieus of these movements, as well as connect the soul aesthetic with the broader black aesthetic. This "remix," therefore, examines soul music as one of the major soundtracks of the Black Power Movement and the influence of both soul and the Black Power Movement on neo-soul, various forms of rap, and the Hip Hop Movement.

"BLACK IS BEAUTIFUL!": THE BLACK POWER MOVEMENT, THE BLACK ARTS MOVEMENT, AND THE EMERGENCE OF THE BLACK AESTHETIC OF THE 1960S AND 1970S

In order to critically understand the Black Arts Movement and the black aesthetic, it is important, first and foremost, to engage the myriad meanings of the Black Power Movement, its central message and mission. However, identifying the essential message and mission of the Black Power Movement has proved to be extremely difficult in light of the fact that "Black Power" actually meant many different things to many different individuals and organizations. As a matter of fact, one could go so far as to say that there was no such thing as the Black Power Movement, singular, but rather something more akin to Black Power Movements, plural. *Black Power studies* is an emerging, discursively diverse and conceptually contentious arena within African American studies that seeks to document and develop a critical re-evaluation of the Black Power Movement. Because of the wide range of issues Black Power Movement members and organizations addressed, Black Power studies is a highly heterogeneous field, one that, much like the Black Power Movement itself, challenges the homogenization of the interpretation and appreciation of African American history, culture, and struggles in general, and Black Power Movement histories, cultures, and struggles in particular. Needless to say, even with all of its discursive diversity, several central questions and concerns, recurring themes and theories emerge that have enabled Black Power studies scholars and students to capture the contours of the movement.[3]

In *New Day in Babylon: The Black Power Movement and American Culture, 1965-1975* (1992), William Van Deburg declared: "Black Power was a revolutionary cultural concept that demanded important changes in extant patterns of American cultural hegemony. Its advocates hoped that this revolution eventually would reach the very core of the nation's value system and serve to alter the social behavior of white Americans" (27). In order to challenge and change "American cultural hegemony," however, Black Power advocates—faithfully following Malcolm X and Frantz Fanon—argued that African Americans needed *psychological liberation* and to undergo a *protracted process of decolonization and reeducation*—what I have termed elsewhere, *revolutionary re-Africanization.*[4] Before they could "alter the social behavior of white Americans," Black Power advocates asserted, black folk "had to be awakened, unified, and made to see that if they were to succeed they must define and establish their own values while rejecting the cultural prescriptions of their oppressors" (Van Deburg 1992, 27).

All of this is to say that *self-discovery, self-definition, self-determination,* and *self-defense* were at the heart of the Black Power Movement, its central message and mission. In fact, we could go so far as to say that the Black Power Movement might be more properly called *the Black Empowerment Movement*, because it was not a movement that had as its end-goal "black supremacy"—an oxymoron if ever there were one—but a bona fide multiracial and multicultural democracy. For example, in arguably one of the most widely read works of the movement, *Black Power: The Politics of Liberation in America* (1967), Stokely Carmichael and Charles V. Hamilton strongly stressed that the "ultimate values and goals" of the Black Power Movement "are not domination or exploitation of other groups, but rather an effective share in the total power of society" (47).[5]

Twenty-first-century discussions of the Black Power Movement often degenerate into debates revolving around "Malcolm X's advocacy of black rage and violence," or Frantz Fanon as "the prophet of Third World violence," or "the Black Panther Party's glorification of senseless violence" without in any way attempting to understand that each of the aforementioned made undeniable distinctions between *counterrevolutionary violence, state-sanctioned violence*, and *self-defensive violence*—in other words, *the violence of domination* and *the violence of liberation* or, rather, *the violence of the oppressor* and *the violence of the oppressed.*[6] It is not as though black folk just woke up one morning and said, "Hey, it's time to go out there and get whitey!" That, quite simply, is not what happened. Truth be told, many of the gross misinterpretations of the Black Power Movement are actually symptomatic of most people's (including many black people's) general lack of knowledge concerning African American history, culture, and struggle, especially during the 1960s and 1970s.

The early advocates of Black Power came to the conclusion that the *nonviolence, civil disobedience,* and *passive resistance* strategies and tactics of the Civil Rights Movement had been exhausted, and that the time for masking and muting ongoing black suffering and black social misery, as well as black anger and black outrage aimed at racial and economic injustice, had long passed. After centuries of antiblack racist oppression, exploitation, and violence, Black Power advocates decided it was time for *black solidarity, black self-love,* and *black self-defense.* "They proclaimed that," Van Deburg (1992, 27) wrote, "blacks were indeed beautiful. Also claimed was the right to define whites." It is difficult at this point to determine what caused white America of the 1960s and 1970s more angst and ire: blacks' radical redefinition of themselves and their blackness, or blacks' radical redefinition of whites and their whiteness.

In *Waiting 'Til the Midnight Hour: A Narrative History of Black Power in America,* Peniel Joseph (2006b, 163) contended that Stokely Carmichael's "calls for blacks to organize a national Black Panther political party . . . placed racial solidarity ahead of interracial alliances—he dared white and black liberals to 'prove that coalition and integration are better alternatives.'" Carmichael's critique of the increasing obsolescence of civil rights strategies and tactics had a resounding—indeed, *black radicalizing*—effect on Black Power political culture. After all, Carmichael not only issued the call for the formation of "a national Black Panther political party," but he and his Student Nonviolent Coordinating Committee (SNCC) comrades also provided the Black Power Movement with its name. As is well known, it was Carmichael who popularized the "Black Power" slogan during an impassioned speech delivered in the course of the 1966 "March Against Fear" in Mississippi (142–62). However, as Joseph's judicious research highlights, throughout the Black Power period Carmichael went through great pains to explain that *"Black Power" was not about hating white people, but about loving black people.*

Whites, to put it plainly, were not the focus of Black Power, and most Black Power proponents believed that whites' narrow-minded and knee-jerk reactions to the movement had more to do with their own, whether conscious or unconscious, deep-seated hatred of and historical amnesia concerning African Americans, their history, culture, and post-Civil Rights Movement struggles. What is more, Black Power radicals averred, whites' histrionic and hyper-negative reactions to the Black Power Movement also seemed to be symptomatic of their unacknowledged uneasiness about the epoch-making calls for *black solidarity, black self-love,* and *black self-defense* coming from black folk coast to coast. With respect to Carmichael's conception of Black Power, Joseph astutely observed:

> For Carmichael, Black Power did indeed promote universalism, but it did so in black. That is to say Black Power recognized power's ability to shape politics, identity, and civilization, and sought to extend these privileges to African Americans—a group that was too often excluded from even the broadest interpretations of whose interests constituted those of humanity. While critics feared that Black Power hinted at a perverse inversion of America's racial hierarchies, Carmichael envisioned something both more and less dangerous—a black community with the resources, will, and imagination to define the past, present, and future on its own terms. (172)

When one takes a long and hard look at the history of the Black Power Movement it is easy to see it as the logical evolution of the Civil Rights Movement's efforts to attain liberty, dignity, and equality for black folk in America. To be sure, Black Power militants greatly differed in semantics and tactics when compared with the civil rights moderates, but it must be borne in mind that in the final analysis the core concerns of the two movements were more congruous and complementary than conflictual and contradictory. Where the Civil Rights Movement was reformist and moderate, the Black Power Movement was radical and militant. In fact, the Black Power Movement ushered in a whole new age of unprecedented *black radicalism* in the wake of the woes of the Civil Rights Movement. Its goals extended well beyond Civil Rights Movement conceptions of "integration" and "assimilation," and it was not preoccupied with the reaffirmation of African Americans' civil rights and the U.S. government's public admission that it had a legal and ethical obligation to protect the constitutional rights of its black citizens.

Black Power proponents daringly demanded access to the fundamental operative force in U.S. history, culture, society, and politics: *power*—physical and psychological, social and political, economic and educational, cultural and aesthetic, and so forth. Following Malcolm X, they argued that they would gain *power* "by any means necessary." Moreover, Malcolm X admonished blacks to focus their energies and resources on improving their own conditions rather than exhorting whites to allow them to integrate into mainstream America. He also preached black self-defense, repeatedly reminding his audiences that blacks have a constitutional right to retaliate against anti-black racist violence.[7] Black Power radicals challenged whites' constant claims that they (i.e., Black Power radicals) had essentially reversed America's racial hierarchy by deconstructing the "myth of black racism." From Malcolm X to Stokely Carmichael, from Maulana Karenga to Amiri Baraka, and from the Black Panther Party to the Republic of New Afrika, the Black Power period offered up innumerable contestations of the "myth of black racism," and William Van Deburg's (1992, 21) weighted words continue to capture this quandary best:

To the militant mind, white racism had no valid black analogue. By definition, racism involved not only exclusion on the basis of race, but exclusion for the purpose of instituting and maintaining a system of arbitrary subjugation. Throughout American history, whites, not blacks, had been the chief supporters of this corrupt ideology. Black people had not lynched whites, murdered their children, bombed their churches, or manipulated the nation's laws to maintain racial hegemony. Nor would they. To adopt the ways of the white racist as their own would be counterproductive and, for a minority group, self-destructive. What whites called black racism was only a healthy defense reflex on the part of Afro-Americans attempting to survive and advance in an aggressively hostile environment.

It is important here to emphasize, once again, that Black Power was not about *hating* white people, but about *loving* black people, and defending them against antiblack racist assaults (again, both physical and psychological). When the history of antiblack racist violence in the United States is taken into serious consideration then, and perhaps only then, does Van Deburg's contention that Black Power proponents' stance on self-defensive violence as "a healthy defense reflex on the part of Afro-Americans attempting to survive and advance in an aggressively hostile environment" make any sense. Even though Malcolm X's words on black self-love and black self-defensive violence were held as prophecy by most Black Power radicals, more often than not, in practice the activist expressions of their movement followed more carefully defined and, for the most part, more familiar African American sociopolitical movement methods (e.g., boycotts, direct-action protests, street rallies, marches, demonstrations, conferences, concerts, etc.). In fact, according to Van Deburg, although the Black Power Movement "was not exclusively cultural . . . it was essentially cultural. It was a revolt in and of culture that was manifested in a variety of forms and intensities" (9). [8]

In so many words, it could be said that at its core the Black Power Movement was essentially an *African American cultural revolution*. This, of course, is where the cultural aesthetic radicalism of the Black Arts Movement comes into play. Mirroring the Harlem Renaissance in relationship to the New Negro Movement, the Black Arts Movement was the artistic wing of the Black Power Movement, but it also served a role that seemed to situate it within a distinct historical and cultural continuum. As discussed in *Hip Hop's Inheritance* and *Hip Hop's Amnesia*, it would seem that there is a discernible pattern with respect to African American cultural aesthetic movements. Recall that the Harlem Renaissance only emerged when the younger New Negroes of the New Negro Movement believed that an embourgeoisement of the movement had taken place and that Booker T. Washington and W.E.B. Du Bois's articulations of New Negro politics had run their course. There was, indeed, a discernible shift away from politics in the traditional civil rights sense and greater emphasis placed on New Negro culture, poetics, and aesthetics. This is extremely telling insofar as the emphasis on cultural aesthetics appears to arise only after what is perceived to be a political impasse in the more mainstream African American civil rights and social justice struggle. Clearly something very similar occurred when we consider that the young militants of the Black Arts Movement were extremely frustrated with the Civil Rights Movement's strategies and tactics of *nonviolence, civil disobedience,* and *passive resistance* in light of seemingly ever-increasing displays of white supremacy and antiblack racist exploitation, oppression, and violence by the mid-1960s.

Although in African American studies it is generally accepted that the Black Arts Movement represented the cultural aesthetic arm of the Black Power Movement, it is important to observe that unlike the Harlem Renaissance, which is widely considered the cultural aesthetic outlet of the New Negro Movement, and much like the Hip Hop Movement that arose in its aftermath, the Black Arts Movement blossomed in a wide range of locations. In fact, virtually every community and college campus with a substantial African American presence between 1965 and 1975 offered up its own unique Black Arts Movement-inspired organizations and theaters, with neo-black nationalist writers, actors, dancers, musicians, and visual artists. For instance, noted Black Arts Movement organizations and institutions of the era included: the Umbra Poets Workshop, the New Lafayette Theater, and the Black Arts Repertory Theater and School in New York, New York; the Committee for a Unified Newark and the Spirit House in Newark, New Jersey; BLKARTSOUTH, the Free Southern Theater, and the Southern Black Cultural Alliance in New Orleans, Louisiana; the Sudan Arts South/ West in Houston, Texas; the Theater of Afro-Arts in Miami, Florida; the Black Arts Workshop in Little Rock, Arkansas; the Black Belt Cultural Center and the Children of Selma Theater in Selma, Alabama; the Blues Repertory Theater in Memphis, Tennessee; the Last Messengers in Greenville, Mississippi; the Kuumba Theater, the Association for the Advancement of Creative Musicians, the Organization of Black American Culture, and the African Commune of Bad Relevant Artists in Chicago, Illinois; the Black Arts Group in St. Louis, Missouri; Black Arts/West and the Black House in San Francisco, California; the Watts Writers Workshop, the Underground Musicians Association, the Union of God's Musicians and Artists Ascension, and the Pan-Afrikan Peoples Arkestra in Los Angeles, California; and Broadside Press in Detroit, Michigan.[9]

Where many Black Power Movement radicals conceived of it as a movement for black political and economic independence, others understood it to be more of a revolutionary political struggle against racism, capitalism, and other forms of imperialism in the United States and throughout the wider world. However, yet another wing of the Black Power Movement interpreted it as a black consciousness-raising and cultural nationalist movement, emphasizing *African roots* and *African American fruits*. It is this latter group of Black Power proponents who created and crusaded on behalf of the Black Arts Movement. Similar to the Black Power Movement, Black Arts intellectuals, artists, and activists embraced a wide range of political and cultural ideologies: from pre-colonial or indigenous African worldviews and religions to revolutionary Marxist-Leninism; from Malcolm X-style Islamic radicalism to Frantz Fanon-inspired revolutionary decolonization; and, from Maulana Karenga's articulation of Kawaida philosophy to the Black Panther Party's emphasis on black folk wisdom and black popular culture. As Van Deburg (1992, 9) perceptively put it:

> Despite an observable tendency for differing factions to claim the entire movement as their own, the multifaceted nature of Black Power was one of its most significant characteristics. One important mode of Black Power expression was cultural. Playwrights, novelists, songwriters, and artists all had their chance to forward a personalized vision of the militant protest sentiment. They used cultural forms as weapons in the struggle for liberation and, in doing so, provided a much needed structural underpinning for the movement's more widely trumpeted political and economic tendencies.

This means, then, that despite the jaw-dropping range of what would be otherwise considered conflicting ideological positions, Black Arts advocates generally held a collective belief in African American liberation and African Americans' right to self-definition and self-determination. However, in order to really and truly define or, rather, *redefine* themselves, ironically, 1960s and 1970s black cultural aesthetes came to the startling conclusion that blacks would have to radically deconstruct whites and their much-vaunted whiteness. Here, we have come back to the diabolical dialectic of white superiority and black inferiority, and the precise reason why Black Arts advocates, almost as a rule, employed their "cultural forms as weapons in the struggle for liberation."

In *The Wretched of the Earth* (1968) which has long been said to have been one of the "handbooks" of the Black Power Movement, Frantz Fanon famously argued: "Decolonization is the veritable creation of new men. But this creation owes nothing of its legitimacy to any supernatural power; the 'thing' which has been colonized becomes man during the same process by which it frees itself" (36–37). In other words, the racially colonized could only rescue and reclaim their long-denied humanity by "a complete calling into question of the colonial situation," which had been created and administered by whites, for the benefit of whites, and to the detriment of nonwhites, and we are speaking here especially of blacks (37).

Black Arts radicals sought to either recover or discover an authentic national African American culture free from white capitalist commodification and consumer culture. This authentic national African American culture was believed to be buried in African American folk philosophy and popular culture because the masses of black folk were understood to have had little or no lasting contact with white bourgeois culture and values. [10] Hence, although discussing revolutionary decolonization in Africa, Fanon's words deeply resonated with Black Power and Black Arts radicals, especially when he wrote: "While at the beginning the native intellectual used to produce his work to be read exclusively by the oppressor, whether with the intention of charming him or of denouncing him through ethnic or subjectivist means, now the native writer progressively takes on the habit of addressing his own people. . . . This may be properly called a literature of combat, in the sense that it calls on the whole people to fight for their existence as a nation" (240). Fanon's words here capture the evolution of many Black Arts intellectuals and artists as they shifted from the moderatism of the Civil Rights Movement to the militancy of the Black Power Movement.

Obviously from the point of view of people who are critically conscious of their oppression, politics and aesthetics are frequently combined, in a sense, searingly synthesized in ways often unimaginable and/or incomprehensible to people, particularly politicians, artists, and critics, who know nothing about the kinds of half-lived lives and dire struggles that oppression and incessant exploitation breed. This is precisely why the discourse on the development of a black aesthetic specific to the special needs of black folk during the 1960s and 1970s was such a major preoccupation for the Black Arts Movement. It could be argued that at the conceptual core of the Black Arts Movement was an incendiary effort to, literally, *decolonize* every aspect of African American expressive culture or, rather, *the art of black expression*. When Fanon wrote of the creation of a decolonized and/or decolonizing "literature of combat" that "calls on the whole people to fight for their existence as a nation," Black Arts insurgents solemnly took his words to heart because they too were waging a war on behalf of "a nation"—a *black nation*.

As Larry Neal's classic essay "The Black Arts Movement" (1968) revealed, Fanon's philosophy was a key contribution to Black Arts aesthetes' conceptualization and articulation of a black aesthetic, and it is not difficult to understand why when we turn to *The Wretched of the Earth* (29, 34, 37). According to Fanon, the art of an oppressed or colonized people is always already political, and his conception of a "literature of combat" strongly stressed that anticolonial intellectuals and artists' "combat" must be more than merely intellectual warfare or radical rhetoric—it must connect ideas with action or, rather, radical political theory with revolutionary social praxis. In his own weighted words:

> The colonized man who writes for his people ought use the past with the intention of opening the future, as an invitation to action and a basis for hope. But to ensure that hope and give it form, he must take part in action and throw

himself body and soul into the national struggle. You may speak about everything under the sun; but when you decide to speak of that unique thing in
man's life that is represented by the fact of opening up new horizons, by
bringing light to your own country, and by raising yourself and your people to
their feet, then you must collaborate on the physical plane. (Fanon 1968, 232)

It is not a blind hatred of the colonizer that motivates the anticolonial intellectual, artist, and activist, but instead a deep desire to provide their colonized comrades, the wretched of the earth, with "an invitation to action and a
basis for hope." Fanon understood the colonizer's literature and art to be
nothing but so many subtle, or not-so-subtle, contributions to the continuance
of colonization, and a lame literature and art that was/is neither created for,
nor in the anti-imperial interests of the colonized masses. This is also to say
that Fanon viewed the colonizer's literature and art as, quite literally, *the art
of imperialism*. That is why he contended that intellectuals and artists actively involved in the decolonization process, to reiterate, "ought use the past
with the intention of opening the future, as an invitation to action and a basis
for hope." In other words, the art of the oppressed, which at its best is *the art
of social transformation and human liberation*, must have a solid sense of
history that heuristically brings the oppressed from the periphery to the center. Additionally, anticolonial intellectuals and artists' "histories," if you will,
must do much more than rattle off tragedy after tragedy; they must also point
to triumphs and astutely inspire the oppressed to continue to struggle (*a luta
continua*). Hence, the literature and art of the oppressed, in several senses,
serve as *counter-histories* and *critical theories* that challenge the dominant
discourse and ideological arrangements.

Equally emphasized and expatiated by Fanon in *The Wretched of the
Earth* (1968) was his heartfelt belief that anticolonial intellectuals, artists,
and activists' work (or "combat," as he aptly put it above) must provide
"political education" to the colonized people. His words to anticolonial intellectuals, artists, and activists were unequivocal, with respect to revolutionary
decolonization, authentic human liberation, and truly democratic social transformation, he sternly stated: "You will not be able to do all this unless you
give the people some political education" (180). He went even further, exhorting anticolonial intellectuals, artists, and activists to always bear in mind
that "[e]verything can be explained to the people, on the single condition that
you really want them to understand" (189). Here it is important to take this
one step further and critically engage Fanon's distinct definition of "political
education," because it had a profound impact on the radicals and radicalism
of both the Black Power Movement and Black Arts Movement. He intrepidly
announced:

Now, political education means opening their minds, awakening them, and
allowing the birth of their intelligence; as [Aime] Cesaire said, it is "to invent

souls." To educate the masses politically does not mean, cannot mean, making
a political speech. What it means is to try, relentlessly and passionately, to
teach the masses that everything depends on them; that if we stagnate it is their
responsibility, and that if we go forward it is due to them too, that there is no
such thing as a demiurge, that there is no famous man who will take responsibility for everything, but that the demiurge is the people themselves and the
magic hands are finally only the hands of the people. (197) [11]

It is easy to see why so many Black Power and Black Arts advocates were
attracted to Fanon's philosophy. When he wrote of "opening their [i.e., 'the
masses'] minds, awakening them, and allowing the birth of their intelligence," one does not have to go far to understand how such an assertion
would resonate with Black Power and Black Arts radicals, especially those
who became major players in the Black Studies Movement. [12] Fanon's philosophy of education is one that centers Africa and its diaspora and unapologetically emphasizes African and African diasporan agency, trans-historical-
ly and globally. When he wrote "[t]o educate the masses politically does not
mean, cannot mean, making a political speech," it takes us right back to
Black Power and Black Arts proponents' critiques of the Civil Rights Movement as little more than a bunch of political pandering and religious rhetoric,
as opposed to "real" or revolutionary struggle, for African American civil
rights and social justice.

This last point also enables us to see that when Black Power and Black
Arts radicals read "there is no famous man who will take responsibility for
everything," their critiques of Martin Luther King, and his leadership of the
Civil Rights Movement in specific, were grounded in a growing frustration
with what they perceived to be the demiurgical discourse in which the Civil
Rights Movement seemed to be caught at the time. Black Power and Black
Arts insurgents' politics and aesthetics were preoccupied with providing the
black masses with counter-histories, critical theories, and radical political
education that decidedly demonstrated, in Fanon's weighted words, that "the
demiurge is the people themselves and the magic hands are finally only the
hands of the people." In other words, Black Power and Black Arts activists
desired nothing more than to prove that there was, quite simply, no social
justice or civil rights "Wizard of Oz."

In a nutshell, this is what the discourse surrounding the black aesthetic
was about. Although a heatedly debated concept between 1965 and 1975,
with often widely differing definitions, the black aesthetic could be said to
collectively include: a corpus of oral and written fiction and non-fiction that
proclaimed the distinctiveness, beauty, and sometimes the supposed superiority of African American thought, culture, and aesthetics; an assemblage of
radical political principles openly opposed to white supremacy and antiblack
racism which promoted black unity and solemn solidarity with other oppressed nonwhites, such as Native Americans, Asian Americans, Mexican

Americans, and other Latinos; and, an ethical exemplar and aesthetic criteria outlining "authentic" and "inauthentic" African American literature and art. Above all else, the black aesthetic strongly stressed that "authentic" black art has always been and must remain *historically grounded, politically engaged, socially uplifting*, and *consciousness-raising*. [13]

There is widespread consensus that the black aesthetic provided the major theoretical thrust of the Black Arts Movement. The unrelenting search for and definition and redefinition of the black aesthetic gave way to a set of distinctive discursive formations and discursive practices that continue to reverberate through neo-soul, rap music, and the Hip Hop Movement (e.g., see the work of Public Enemy, KRS-One, X Clan, Poor Righteous Teachers, Paris, the Jungle Brothers, A Tribe Called Quest, De La Soul, Queen Latifah, Brand Nubian, Arrested Development, Digable Planets, Meshell Ndegeocello, the Coup, Lauryn Hill, Wyclef Jean, Michael Franti & Spearhead, Erykah Badu, NaS, Common, Amel Larrieux, Mos Def, Talib Kweli, Jill Scott, the Roots, India.Arie, Dead Prez, Georgia Anne Muldrow, Kanye West, Conya Doss, Lupe Fiasco, and Nneka). In fact, one of the more innovative aspects of the discourse on the black aesthetic revolved around its unambiguous critique of "Western cultural aesthetics." For instance, in "The Black Arts Movement" (1968), Larry Neal articulated the collective ambitions of the advocates of the black aesthetic:

> The Black Arts Movement is radically opposed to any concept of the artist that alienates him from his community. This movement is the aesthetic and spiritual sister of the Black Power concept. As such, it envisions an art that speaks directly to the needs and aspirations of black America. In order to perform this task, the Black Arts Movement proposes a radical reordering of the Western cultural aesthetic. It proposes a separate symbolism, mythology, critique, and iconology. The Black Arts and the Black Power concepts both relate broadly to the Afro-American's desire for self-determination and nationhood. Both concepts are nationalistic. One is concerned with the relationship between art and politics; the other with the art of politics. (29)

Emphasis should be placed on the fact that the Black Arts activists understood their movement to be "the aesthetic and spiritual sister of the Black Power concept." Which is also to say, there was a deliberate division of labor between those who were primarily "concerned with the relationship between art and politics" (i.e., the Black Arts Movement) and those who were preoccupied with "the art of politics" (i.e., the Black Power Movement). This is an extremely important point, not simply because it reveals the sophistication of 1960s and 1970s African American aesthetic and political culture but, even more, because it highlights one of the major differences between the Black Arts Movement and the Harlem Renaissance: Black Arts Movement members' artistry was not a reaction to the nadir of "Negro" life or leadership between 1965 and 1975, but an audacious call to action that was inextricable from the radical politics of the broader Black Power Movement—a social and political movement that arose in the aftermath of the Civil Rights Movement, which many consider, in light of the signing of the Civil Rights Act of 1964 and the Voting Rights Act of 1965, the most successful social justice movement in African American history. In fact, James Smethurst has eloquently argued in *The Black Arts Movement: Literary Nationalism in the 1960s and 1970s* (2005), "It is a relative commonplace to briefly define Black Arts as the cultural wing of the Black Power Movement. However, one could just as easily say that Black Power was the political wing of the Black Arts Movement" (14).

As discussed in *Hip Hop's Inheritance* and *Hip Hop's Amnesia*, in some senses it could be said that most of the radicals of the Harlem Renaissance felt that their aspirations were increasingly out of sync with those of the wider New Negro Movement of the 1920s and 1930s. If this is conceded, then, we are given grounds to argue that the Black Arts Movement may very well have been *the first national African American cultural aesthetic movement to have consciously mirrored a national African American social and political movement*. At no other point in African American history, culture, and struggle have so many black writers and artists collectively responded to the call of black radical politics and a black revolutionary social movement—save perhaps, and this is said quite solemnly, the innumerable "slave narratives" and radical abolitionist writings contributed by African Americans to the Abolitionist Movement (e.g., Olaudah Equiano, Phillis Wheatley, David Walker, Nat Turner, George Moses Horton, Sojourner Truth, Maria Stewart, Harriet Jacobs, William Wells Brown, Henry Bibb, Sarah Forten, Henry Highland Garnet, Victor Séjour, Frederick Douglass, James Whitfield, Frances Harper, and Harriet Wilson). However, my more critical readers might observe, neither the Abolitionist Movement nor the Harlem Renaissance were exclusively or unapologetically *for black folk* and *in the interest of black folk* in the ways in which the Black Arts Movement unequivocally was. [14]

Here it is equally important to understand that when Neal wrote that the Black Arts Movement was "the aesthetic and spiritual sister of the Black Power concept," he was also hinting at the ways in which the two movements discursively dovetailed virtually from their inceptions. This is to say, going back to Smethurst's comment, during the Black Power period "black radical politics" was not automatically privileged over "black art," but black politics and black art were understood to be complementary. As a matter of fact, between 1965 and 1975 there was a kind of symmetry between "art and politics" and "the art of politics" that had not been achieved before or since the Black Power Movement and Black Arts Movement. Directly commenting on what I have termed the "discursive dovetailing" between the Black Power Movement and Black Arts Movement, Larry Neal (1968, 29) shared:

> Recently, these two movements have begun to merge: the political values inherent in the Black Power concept are now finding concrete expression in the aesthetics of Afro-American dramatists, poets, choreographers, musicians, and novelists. A main tenet of Black Power is the necessity for black people to define the world in their own terms. The black artist has made the same point in the context of aesthetics. The two movements postulate that there are in fact and in spirit two Americas—one black, one white. The black artist takes this to mean that his primary duty is to speak to the spiritual and cultural needs of black people. Therefore, the main thrust of this new breed of contemporary writers is to confront the contradictions arising out of the black man's experience in the racist West. Currently, these writers are reevaluating Western aesthetics, the traditional role of the writer, and the social function of art. Implicit in this reevaluation is the need to develop a "Black Aesthetic." It is the opinion of many black writers, I among them, that the Western aesthetic has run its course: it is impossible to construct anything meaningful within its decaying structure. We advocate a cultural revolution in art and ideas. The cultural values inherent in Western history must either be radicalized or destroyed, and we will probably find that even radicalization is impossible. In fact, what is needed is a whole new system of ideas.

The Black Arts Movement sought to offer "a whole new system of ideas" that would complement the radical politics of the Black Power Movement. It was, as Neal explicitly stated, a "cultural revolution in art and ideas" that took very seriously the notion that *black artists' work should be historically rooted, socially relevant, politically radical, and reflect the ongoing struggles of the black community (or, rather, the black nation)*. In fact, it could be said that the Black Arts Movement in several senses represented the 1960s and 1970s blossoming of the aspirations of the radical New Negroes of the Harlem Renaissance of the 1920s and 1930s insofar as the radical New Negroes were more or less the African American avant-garde of their era. It is relatively easy to see, as the work of Fred Moten (2003), Aldon Nielsen (1997), Mike Sell (2008), and Danie Widener (2010) emphasized, that the Black Arts Movement was the Black Power Movement's avant-garde.

Above when Neal wrote that the Black Arts advocates believed that "the Western aesthetic has run its course: it is impossible to construct anything meaningful within its decaying structure," his words simultaneously connected the Black Arts Movement to many of the aesthetic ambitions of the radical New Negroes of the Harlem Renaissance and more mainstream American avant-gardism.[15] With respect to its connection to the radical New Negroes of the Harlem Renaissance, when Neal asserted that the Black Arts Movement is "radically opposed to any concept of the artist that alienates him from his community" and we observe the myriad ways in which Black

Arts activists frequently connected their work to and/or took their aesthetic cues from black popular culture, and when we recall that one of the major missions of the radical New Negroes was to document and celebrate the life and culture of the "low-down folks" (as Langston Hughes put it in 1926) as opposed to simply black bourgeois life and culture during the Renaissance years, we are presented with ample evidence of *the "low-down folk culture" link* between the Black Arts Movement and the radical New Negroes of the Harlem Renaissance. Both cultural aesthetic movements sought to document and celebrate the lives and struggles of the "low-down folks," which is something that has consistently distinguished African American cultural aesthetic movements (including the Hip Hop Movement) from most other cultural aesthetic movements in U.S. history. [16]

In terms of the ways in which the Black Arts Movement simultaneously converged with and decidedly diverged from more mainstream avant-gardism in the United States it is important to observe what could be interpreted as Neal's proto-postmodern critique of the Western cultural aesthetic. When he wrote that the Black Arts Movement "proposes a radical reordering of the Western cultural aesthetic. It proposes a separate symbolism, mythology, critique, and iconology," his words undoubtedly prefigured both postmodern and postcolonial critiques of European modernist aesthetics. Moreover, when Neal wrote "the Western aesthetic has run its course: it is impossible to construct anything meaningful within its decaying structure," his critique further prefigured and innovatively invoked more mainstream American avant-gardist critiques associated with the postmodern and postcolonial critics of the 1980s and 1990s.

Let me be clear here: it is not my intention to argue that the Black Arts Movement was a "postmodern" or "postcolonial" movement, which it most certainly was not. Instead here my main intention is to emphasize the ways in which even when placed within the continuum of more mainstream American avant-gardism the Black Arts Movement is decidedly distinguished in light of its unrelenting and unrepentant critique of white supremacy and antiblack racism, combined with its critiques of U.S. capitalism, militarism, and hedonism, among other issues and ills. In fact, it would be difficult, if not impossible, to find American cultural aesthetic movements besides the Harlem Renaissance, the Black Arts Movement, and the Hip Hop Movement that have sincerely documented and celebrated black "low-down folks'" lives, culture, and struggles.

Neal's above assertion that Black Arts intellectuals and artists were "re-evaluating Western aesthetics, the traditional role of the writer, and the social function of art" not only illustrates that the Black Arts Movement was an avant-garde movement, but also that the inner-workings of the aesthetic wing of the Black Power Movement were much more complicated and complex than previously acknowledged. His contention that "[i]mplicit in this reevaluation is the need to develop a 'Black Aesthetic'" directly contradicts long-standing claims that the Black Arts Movement was essentially anti-intellectu-al or, what is more, a movement predicated on *black anti-intellectualism*. Such claims not only negate the glaring fact that the Black Studies Move-ment evolved out of the Black Power Movement and Black Arts Movement, but they also fail to fully engage Black Arts aesthetes' almost obsessive preoccupation with intensely interrogating and critically theorizing "the tra-ditional role of the writer" and "the social function of art" and their relation-ship with African American history, culture, and ongoing struggle. From an African American studies perspective, and especially from the point of view of Africana critical theory, this is undoubtedly one of the most distinctive features of the movement when compared with the Harlem Renaissance.

FROM CLASSIC SOUL QUEENS TO NEO-SOUL SISTERS: THE SOUL AESTHETIC, WOMEN-CENTERED SOUL MUSIC, AND THE POLITICS OF BLACK POPULAR MUSIC DURING THE BLACK POWER MOVEMENT

Emerging within the context of the Black Arts Movement's reevaluation of the "social function of art," soul music was a sonic expression of the aspira-tions and frustrations of the Black Power Movement. It was an integral part of post-Civil Rights Movement African Americans' efforts to "define the world in their own terms." It was the sound of African American musicians embracing what Neal described above as their "primary duty . . . to speak to the spiritual and cultural needs of black people." In stark contrast to the pop chart-obsessed and increasingly bland sounding rhythm & blues of the mid-1960s, soul refocused black popular music on the "spiritual and cultural needs of black people."

By focusing on the "spiritual and cultural needs of black people," similar to rap and neo-soul for many contemporary black ghetto youth, soul was more than music. It was a way of life and emblematic of the wide spectrum of black popular culture between 1965 and disco music's rise to national prominence in the late 1970s. Thus, beyond its musical meanings, soul had several extramusical expressions and was frequently associated with a wide range of black popular cultural forms between 1965 and 1977, including Black Power Movement and Black Arts Movement-influenced: language, literature, theater, dance, visual art, fashion, hairstyles, film, and food, among others.

For instance, soul fashions included either African or African-derived clothing and accessories, khaki safari jackets, leisure suits, colorful bell-bottom pants, berets, leather jackets and vests, platform shoes, and wide-brimmed hats. Soul was also associated with natural hairstyles, including

Afros, cornrows, blowout combs, fist picks, colorful hair beads, and African-based crops. Moreover, soul was connected with African American nonverbal communication practices, which encompassed rhythmic greeting rituals, complex and coded handshakes, swagger-filled walking styles, and other inimitable and dynamic body motions. And, lastly, with respect to language, as Geneva Smitherman observed in *Black Language and Culture: Sounds of Soul* (1975), soul was said to be at the heart of the coded colloquialisms of black ghetto youth and the radical rhetoric of Black Power Movement militants.[17]

Soul musicians and DJs popularized not only the word "soul," but also several key phrases that supposedly connoted the "soul aesthetic." Both within everyday language use and in musical contexts, soul linguistics seemed to be heavily based on the African American preaching and gospel singing traditions, especially both traditions' use of call-and-response. For example, soul musicians' lyrical and overall musical delivery frequently reflected the dramatic performance styles of African American preachers, who regularly use a wide range of improvisatory techniques—including vocal inflections, varying timbres, word and riff repetition, and the punctuation of the end of phrases with shouts, grunts, groans, and moans—to systematically build the intensity to an unfathomed degree that transfigures what began as a sermon into an epic *sermon-song*. Hence, the preacher and congregation paradigm, with its patented call-and-response tradition so prevalent in African American church culture and gospel music, was secularized and popularized by soul musicians (especially in the work of icons such as Ray Charles, Etta James, James Brown, Aretha Franklin, Curtis Mayfield, Donny Hathaway, Otis Redding, Wilson Pickett, Solomon Burke, Gladys Knight & the Pips, and the Staples Singers). Furthermore, just as Sunday morning sermons were peppered with soulful interjections such as "Amen brother, God be praised!" and "Tell the truth and shame the devil!," classic soul music—especially live performances—as augmented with exclamations such as "Tell it like it is!," "Ain't it the truth!," "Can you dig it?," and "Right on!"

Soul was obviously more than music. It was the first post-Civil Rights Movement black popular culture, and as such it was part of African Americans' ongoing efforts to deconstruct and reconstruct what it meant to be unapologetically "black" or "African American" as opposed to "Negroes" or "colored people." In this sense, soul signified the views and values of arguably the first generation of black ghetto youth since the radical New Negroes of the Harlem Renaissance to be in open revolt against the middle-aged, middle-class, and middle-of-the-road establishments of both white and black America. To be a "soul man" (à la Sam and Dave) or "a natural woman" (à la Aretha Franklin), or to be, more generally speaking, a "soul brother" or "soul sister" meant that you identified with working-class and underclass African Americans, among other nonwhite working-poor people.

With the politicization of black popular culture came the politicization of black popular music and, as Brian Ward (1998, 333) asserted, during soul's heyday "popular music and its heroes did help to shape the ways in which people—especially young people—perceived the world, sorted out its heroes from its villains, and evaluated the relationship between its rights and its wrongs." Hence, no matter how preoccupied white America is with soul love songs, it is equally important to acknowledge that for most African American youth, past and present, soul music is in equal measures concerned with both *black love* and *black liberation*. Having roots in the early gospel-influenced rhythm & blues experiments of Ray Charles, James Brown, and Sam Cooke, among others, soul music's politics can be traced back to the late 1950s and early 1960s love songs sung in a gospel style that often subtly depicted the hardships of African American life and romance as a consequence of segregation, poverty, poor education, and substandard housing (e.g., Ray Charles's "The Sun's Gonna Shine" and "The Midnight Hour"; James Brown's "Why Does Everything Happen To Me?" and "Messing With The Blues"; and Sam Cooke's "Wonderful World"). However, soul music's politics also have roots in the more obvious early gospel-influenced rhythm & blues songs that are not love songs and that unambiguously expressed the hardships and horrors of African American life in light of American apartheid (e.g., Ray Charles's "Greenbacks," "Hard Times," and "Losing Hand"; Sam Cooke's "Chain Gang" and "A Change is Gonna Come"; Lloyd Price's "Stagger Lee," and Jerry Butler's "I'm Telling You").

Many black popular music scholars have argued that Sam Cooke's "A Change is Gonna Come" marked the transition from rhythm & blues to soul. Growing out of years of quiet reflection on segregation and other civil rights abuses, Cooke was inspired to compose and record "A Change is Gonna Come" after hearing Bob Dylan's epochal "Blowin' in the Wind." Touching on everything from poverty to segregation, the simultaneously gospel-tinged vocals and orchestral/pop sounding background music made "A Change is Gonna Come" a harbinger of a new genre of black popular music.

Musically speaking, soul obviously continued the evolution of rhythm & blues, which reached back to the early 1940s and which synthesized elements of gospel, blues, jazz, and doo-wop. But, vocally and lyrically speaking, soul was something altogether new: *vocally*, it secularized the gospel sound, bringing a spirit-filled folksiness to black popular music and, *lyrically*, it extended the topical range and political character of black popular music. "If you're going to come away from a party singing the lyrics of a song," Curtis Mayfield contended in *Soul* magazine in 1969, "it is better that you sing of self-pride like 'We're A Winner' instead of "Do the Boo-ga-loo!'"

Prior to the release of Cooke's "A Change is Gonna Come" in December of 1964, in July of that year Curtis Mayfield & the Impressions released an album titled *Keep On Pushing* that featured two falsetto-filled tracks that were almost immediately adopted as "movement songs": the title track, "Keep On Pushing," and the immortal "Amen." The next year Mayfield & the Impressions released *People Get Ready*, which featured a set of songs that further developed the soul aesthetic, including the title track, "People Get Ready," "Woman's Got Soul," and "Just Another Dance." As adept at composing love songs as he was at penning "message songs" (e.g., "Gypsy Woman," "Minstrel and Queen," "I'm So Proud," "We're A Winner," "Little Brown Boy," "This Is My Country," "Choice Of Colors," "Mighty Mighty [Spade & Whitey]"), Mayfield provided one of the major models for soul musicians.[18]

Although she is primarily known for her soul love songs, similar to Mayfield, Aretha Franklin's music also took on an increasingly political tone in the 1960s and 1970s. A list of several of the often overlooked message songs Franklin released include: "Hard Times," "God Bless The Child," "Nobody Knows the Way I Feel This Morning," "If I Had a Hammer," "A Change is Gonna Come," "Ain't Nobody (Gonna Turn Me Around)," "People Get Ready," "Son Of A Preacher Man," "When The Battle Is Over," "Young, Gifted and Black," "Border Song (Holy Moses)," "Bridge Over Troubled Water," and, many would argue, the entire *Amazing Grace* (1972) album. According to Ward (1998, 400), Franklin's father, Reverend C.L. Franklin, was "a good friend of Martin Luther King," and it was King himself who coaxed Aretha into "Movement work." Therefore, it should not come as a great surprise that "her presence in and around the Movement increased dramatically in the late 1960s." Moreover, no one should be shocked that Franklin consistently sang protest songs and supported both the Civil Rights Movement and the Black Power Movement.

As Jerry Wexler revealed in an interview quoted in Mark Bego's *The Aretha Franklin: Queen of Soul* (1990), "[s]he devoted an enormous piece of her life to Martin Luther King, yet she never became merely a sloganeer or polemicist. She acted out of the purest wellsprings of faith and belief" (108–9). Echoing Ward and Wexler, historian Craig Werner, in *Higher Ground: Stevie Wonder, Aretha Franklin, Curtis Mayfield, and the Rise and Fall of American Soul* (2004), asserted:

> Because of her father's friendship with King and Detroit's black political establishment, Aretha had more direct contact with the Movement. She idolized King and took pride in Detroit's "Great March to Freedom," a Midwestern counterpart of the more famous 1963 March on Washington that her father helped to organize. Joining Mahalia Jackson and Dinah Washington at a Chicago benefit for the Birmingham Movement, Aretha mesmerized the overflowing audience at McCormack Place with a rendition of "Precious Lord (Take My Hand)." (67)

This means, then, although often erased or rendered invisible, Aretha Franklin's protest music began long before 1972, the year she released both *Young, Gifted and Black* and *Amazing Grace*. As noted above, even during her early Columbia Records years between 1960 and 1966 she recorded and released a number of tracks that can certainly be considered protest songs when they are placed within the context of the Civil Rights Movement and, later, the Black Power Movement. Her early recordings such as "Hard Times," "God Bless The Child," "Nobody Knows the Way I Feel This Morning," and "If I Had a Hammer" were as much message songs as anything Curtis Mayfield & the Impressions cut during the same period—and, similar to Franklin, Mayfield's message songs between 1960 and 1966 were often isolated efforts on albums that owed as much to the jazz, pop, and supper club singing traditions as they did to the emerging soul sound (e.g., see Mayfield's *The Impressions* [1963], *The Never Ending Impressions* [1964], *Keep On Pushing* [1964], *People Get Ready* [1965], *One By One* [1965], and *Ridin' High* [1966]). However, Franklin's gender and both the Civil Rights Movement and Black Power Movement's embrace of simultaneously patriarchal and Eurocentric gender roles seems to have blinded most folk, especially black popular music scholars and critics, from seeing her distinct brand of protest music. [19]

Franklin's politics and modes of protest may not mirror male soul musicians' politics and modes of protest, but that does not in any way negate the fact that she indeed did produce songs that offered social commentary and political critique. As a matter of fact, there is a sense in which Franklin's pioneering protest music went above and beyond the other mostly male architects of soul music when we seriously consider that her songs became anthems for the Women's Liberation Movement, as well as both the Civil Rights Movement and the Black Power Movement. Hence, as Pamela Greene argued in "Aretha Franklin: The Emergence of Soul and Black Women's Consciousness in the Late 1960s and 1970s" (1995), along with her Civil Rights Movement and Black Power Movement-related songs, Franklin also released several songs that were adopted as anthems of the Women's Liberation Movement, including: "Respect," "Do Right Woman, Do Right Man," "Satisfaction," "(You Make Me Feel Like) A Natural Woman," "Chain of Fools," and "Think."

"I don't make it a practice to put my politics into my music," Franklin coyly contended in her autobiography, *Aretha: From These Roots* (1999, 155). However, she was all too aware of the fact that her chart-topping version of Otis Redding's "Respect" resonated with blacks *and* whites, males *and* females, businessmen *and* housewives all across the country. At the time of its release, she recalled in her autobiography, the song touched "the need of a nation, the need of the average man and woman in the street, the businessman, the mother, the fireman, the teacher—everyone wanted respect. It was also one of the battle cries of the Civil Rights Movement. The song took

on monumental significance. It became the 'Respect' women expected from
men and men expected from women, the inherent right of all human beings"
(155).

Situated at the intersection of three social and political movements (i.e.,
the Civil Rights Movement, Black Power Movement, and Women's Liberation Movement), "Respect," once again, demonstrates both the duality and
universality of black popular music and black popular movements. Remarking on the song's broad appeal and variable meanings in a *Rolling Stone*
interview, famed Atlantic Records audio engineer Tom Dowd, who recorded
and mixed the classic track, added that "[i]t could be a racial situation, it
could be a political situation," or "it could be just the man-woman situation,"
but, no matter what the situation, it was a song that "[a]nyone could identify
with it. It cut a lot of ground."

Similar to the apolitical stance and pop sheen Berry Gordy attempted to
stamp Motown's music with throughout the 1960s, Aretha tried her best to
avoid "put[ting] [her] politics into [her] music." But, her magical melisma
and unbridled *Übermensch* blending of gospel, blues, jazz, rhythm & blues,
rock & roll, and country & western vocalizations, not to mention the extremely turbulent nature of the times, made even her most middle-of-the-road
and pop-sounding songs take on multiple political meanings. Therefore, it
wasn't merely the words she sang, but the black church folk-influenced
fervency with which she sang the words she sang that gave her listeners the
distinct impression that the power and passion in her voice were the culmination of centuries of African American love, loss, and struggle for liberation
and social transformation.

Observe that prior to hinting at its anthemic status for the sister-soldiers
of the Women's Liberation Movement, above Franklin noted that "Respect"
quickly became "one of the battle cries of the Civil Rights Movement." Her
contention that the song "took on monumental significance" for many different people, from any different walks of life, was corroborated by Werner
(2004, 134), who revealingly wrote:

> "Respect" burst like a howitzer shell over a nation braced for another round of
> summertime riots. Angry over the failure of the Movement's southern victo-
> ries to translate into meaningful change in their own communities, rioters had
> taken to the streets in dozens of cities in the North and West the previous two
> years. The defeat of Martin Luther King's Chicago campaign transmitted an
> unambiguous message to the residents of Newark, Watts, and Paradise Valley
> as well as those manning the frontlines on the south shore of Lake Michigan.
> Many turned their backs on the Civil Rights Movement's nonviolent and inter-
> racial ideals in favor of the emerging Black Power Movement. But even many
> who weren't impressed with Black Power ideology responded powerfully to
> the emotional punch of slogans like "Black Is Beautiful" and "Power to the

People." "R-E-S-P-E-C-T" spelled the same thing to them, without the ideological baggage and with a gospel call to freedom on the backbeat.

Not called the "Queen of Soul" for nothing, it seems that Aretha was right
when she reluctantly admitted that "Respect" "took on monumental significance." In light of the deep disillusionment much of black America experienced in the aftermath of the Civil Rights Movement, many knew that more
needed to be done in order to achieve a real and lasting multicultural democracy in America. As Dowd shared, the racial and political connotations of
"Respect" were almost inherent in the song and the intense gospel-influenced
manner in which it was sung—and that is whether or not Aretha intended
those connotations. Let's face it: In the end most people hear what they want
to hear in black popular music. But, I would heartily agree with those who
hold that women's interpretation of women's art—in this instance, African
American women's interpretation of an African American woman's art—is
especially meaningful. Hence, along with the racial and political interpretation of "Respect" there was the equally popular black women-centered interpretation of the song.

In *Black Feminist Thought: Knowledge, Consciousness, and the Politics
of Empowerment* (1990), Patricia Hill Collins asserted that "[e]ven though
the lyrics can be sung by anyone, they take on special meaning when sung by
Aretha in the way that she sings them. On one level the song functions as a
metaphor for the conditions of African Americans in a racist society" (108).
This is obviously the way many Black Power Movement participants interpreted the song, as well as those African Americans "who weren't impressed
with Black Power ideology" and all of its "ideological baggage," but who
continued their commitments to the principles and practices of the waning
Civil Rights Movement. On another level, however, "Respect" also serves as
a metaphor for the conditions of African American women in a simultaneously racist *and* sexist society. "Aretha's being a black woman enables the
song to tap a deeper meaning," continued Collins. "Within the blues tradition, the listening audience of African American women assumes 'we' black
women, even though Aretha as the blues singer sings 'I'" (108).

The collective "I" of classic soul music—the musical "I" that was actually a political "we"—should be borne in mind because it was inherited by,
first, "hip hop soul" and then, later, contemporary "neo-soul" divas. Which is
to say, a very similar kind of "I"/"we" convergence—an individual artist
serving as a symbol for the collective loves, lives, and struggles of African
American women—continues to reverberate and boom in contemporary
women-centered black popular music, especially women-centered rap and
neo-soul. But, as it was with Aretha Franklin's classic soul songs, the political and unambiguously African American women-centered nature of African
American women's music is often either downplayed or erased altogether. In

fact, the music criticism centered around African American women's work frequently mirrors the racial myth and sexual stereotype-styled approach to African American women's loves, lives, and struggles prevalent within the broader social, political, and cultural world.[20]

Hence, whatever Aretha Franklin's music might have meant to the wider Women's Liberation Movement of the 1960s and 1970s, it had special meaning for the African American women of the period. Many African American women's deep identification with Aretha grew out of their ability to relate to her life, music, and unapologetic commitment to the social and political movements of the era. As discussed above, Franklin enjoyed a close friendship with Martin Luther King and regularly sang at and supported Civil Rights Movement activities. According to Mark Bego (1990), with her "sense of pride and her dignified stance," perhaps more than any other figure associated with soul music, the Civil Rights Movement, and the Black Power Movement, Aretha "represented the new black woman of the late 1960s. In her own way she embodied the social and cultural change that was taking place in the country, merely by being herself without pretense. Respected by black *and* white America, she was the 'natural woman' that she sang about" (108, emphasis in original).

In terms of her personal life, many African American women in the 1960s and 1970s related to the fact that, as Franklin revealed in her autobiography, she had been an unwed teen mother. Making neo-soul divas Erykah Badu and Lauryn Hill's unwed and much discussed pregnancies in the late 1990s look extremely tame in comparison (bear in mind that both Badu and Hill were over twenty-five at the time of their pregnancies and their children's births), Franklin had her first child, Clarence Franklin, on March 30, 1956, five days after her fourteenth birthday, and her second child, Edward Franklin, in January of 1957 at the age of fifteen. Franklin's much publicized abusive marriage to Ted White between 1961 and 1969 also endeared her to African American women, many of whom—very similar to "Sister Aretha"—knew firsthand the hardships of black womanhood, black wifehood, and black motherhood, as well as the hurt and seemingly constant heartbreaks of unrewarding relationships. Therefore, Aretha's Atlantic Records albums have a special place within the world of black popular music in general, and African American women's popular music in particular.

Instead of being the Motown and Brill Building "girl next door"—which always meant, however clandestinely, the *white girl* next door—Aretha's early Atlantic albums between 1967 and 1972 bristled with a gutsy, gospel-influenced intensity and unparalleled passion that were unmistakably *African American* and *womanist* in the sense that the sound of her voice seemed to capture and echo centuries of enslavement, hush harbors, ring shouts, tent revivals, healing crusades, brutal beatings, and incessant sexual violence, as well as quiet determination, abolitionism, armed rebellion, civil rights struggle, and individual African American women's triumph over untold personal tragedy. Her Atlantic albums *I Never Loved a Man the Way I Love You* (1967), *Aretha Arrives* (1967), *Lady Soul* (1968), *Aretha Now* (1968), *Aretha in Paris* (1968), *Soul '69* (1969), *This Girl's in Love with You* (1970), *Spirit in the Dark* (1970) *Aretha Live at Fillmore West* (1971), *Young, Gifted and Black* (1972), *Amazing Grace* (1972), and *Oh Me, Oh My: Aretha Live in Philly* (1972), a total of twelve music history-making albums, endeared Aretha Franklin to African American women in the late 1960s and early 1970s in ways that few who are not African American *and* female fully understand. However, it could be argued even further that working-class and underclass African American women—the very same women who form the primary demographic for contemporary neo-soul divas' work—had an especially remarkable relationship with Aretha and her music. In Werner's (2004, 213) words:

> Those who'd grown up in the "Age of Aretha" kept right on living their lives to the rhythms of "Baby, I Love You," "Since You've Been Gone (Sweet Sweet Baby)," "Spirit in the Dark," and "Respect." That was especially the case for black women, who'd always seen Sister Ree from a slightly different angle than anyone else. While feminists, revolutionaries, and Vietnam veterans all responded to the metaphorical possibilities of Aretha's music, the ghetto women whom black novelist Paule Marshall called "poets in the kitchen" understood her as one of their own—if not quite a ghetto girl, certainly the voice of the girls in the ghetto. Aretha's struggles for self-acceptance, her fiery insistence that her man do the right thing, her melting sensuality, her never-easy knowledge that at the end of the day Jesus would give her the strength to weather the storm: all of it remained as real for Aretha's African American sisters in the late seventies as it had been five or ten years earlier. As the black feminist (or womanist, to use Alice Walker's preferred term) movement emerged in the late seventies, Aretha became an icon. The first generation of black women to articulate womanism's aims and values was Aretha's. They'd grown up with the Civil Rights Movement and benefited from the movement's assault on Jim Crow.

It is important to understand that even though "feminists, revolutionaries, and Vietnam veterans all responded to the metaphorical possibilities of Aretha's music," it was "the ghetto women" who claimed "her as one of their own—if not quite a ghetto girl, certainly the voice of the girls in the ghetto." The same thing could be said about several contemporary neo-soul sisters and their music. For example, while neither Lauryn Hill nor Alicia Keys are "ghetto girls" in the strict sense of the term, their music has been consistently appropriated by working-class and underclass African American women. Undoubtedly, however, the modern-day soul sister who most recalls Aretha Franklin within the world of contemporary soul is the incomparable Mary J. Blige.

Blige's similarities with Franklin are not purely stylistic, as Blige's hip hop-style histrionics actually owe as much to Nina Simone, Etta James, Gladys Knight, Patti LaBelle, Mavis Staples, Roberta Flack, Millie Jackson, Chaka Khan, Minnie Riperton, Angela Bofill, Sade, and Anita Baker, among others, as they do to Franklin. But, in a broader sense, it was Blige's ability to weave old and new genres of black popular music into her own unique, extremely angst-filled autobiographical style that points to Franklin's enormous influence on her music. Like Franklin, Blige seemed to use her music to exorcise her personal demons—demons that seemed to haunt many working-class and underclass African American women at the turn of the twenty-first century (e.g., abusive relationships, drug addiction, alcoholism, body image issues, and depression). Where Franklin's Atlantic albums between 1967 and 1972 undeniably offered an alternative to the Diana Ross-styled "girl next door" image manufactured by Motown in the 1960s, Blige offered a *counter-image* and *counter-sound* to the Whitney Houston, Janet Jackson, and Mariah Carey black pop diva sound that dominated the 1980s and 1990s.

Franklin not only brought a grittier and heavier gospel-influenced sound to black popular music in the late 1960s and early 1970s, but she also either composed or appropriated songs that spoke directly to working-class and underclass African American women's loves, lives, and struggles. In this sense, one of the great ironies of Franklin's Atlantic albums between 1967 and 1972 is that even as they innovatively merged gospel inflections and nonverbal vocalizations (e.g., yelps, howls, moans, grunts, and groans) with the Stax Records-style southern soul sound, lyrically her music actually harked back and held on to themes and topics that were taken up by classic blues queens and classic jazz divas such as Ma Rainey, Bessie Smith, Billie Holiday, Dinah Washington, and Nina Simone. All of the forenamed are as famous for their protest songs as they are for their love songs. Therefore, the tradition Franklin extended, expanded, and handed down to hip hop women reaches all the way back to the very first form of (post-enslavement) black popular music: the blues.[21]

Similar to Franklin, Blige's innovation was more musical than lyrical. Lyrically, her music continues the Ma Rainey, Bessie Smith, Billie Holiday, Dinah Washington, and Nina Simone tradition of "telling it like it is" from an African American woman's point of view. But musically speaking, Blige's music was extremely innovative in that it was the first to successfully merge rap music and hip hop beats with the classic soul vocal sound. Born in the Bronx, New York, on January 11, 1971, to a nurse, Cora Blige, and a struggling jazz musician, Thomas Blige, both of Mary J. Blige's parents contributed to her musical development.

Her mother was a serious fan of soul music and exposed Mary to Aretha Franklin, Gladys Knight, Patti LaBelle, Margie Joseph, Chaka Khan, and Jean Carne, among many others. Blige has repeatedly said that her father taught her how to sing and exposed her to jazz songstresses such as Billie Holiday, Ella Fitzgerald, Dinah Washington, Nina Simone, Abbey Lincoln, Betty Carter, and Esther Phillips, among others. Spending a considerable part of her childhood on the outskirts of Savannah, Georgia, Blige sang in a Pentecostal church choir in Richmond Hill, Georgia. When her family moved back to New York they resided in the Schlobohm housing projects in Yonkers, where she lived in extremely cramped conditions with her mother, older sister, two aunts, and several cousins.[22]

The harsh conditions Blige grew up in, as well as the trials and tribulations of women's lives within the world of hip hop, were reflected on her street-smart debut album, *What's the 411?* (1992). Combining elements of rap and new jack swing with classic rhythm & blues and classic soul, *What's the 411?* was one of the first albums to demonstrate how *rap-influenced rhythm & blues* sounded. But, it was Blige's often stunning blend of classic soul's vocal sound with hip hop beats that made tracks such as "Real Love," "Sweet Thing," "You Remind Me," "Reminisce," and "Love No Limit" a new kind of soul rather than another over-digitized and extremely bland early 1990s rhythm & blues production. Compared with Mariah Carey's eponymous debut in 1990 and her sophomore effort *Emotions* in 1991, both of which demonstrated Carey's remarkable Minnie Riperton and Jean Carnesque five-octave vocal range, *What's the 411?* was a decidedly "rawer," "realer," and soul-centered affair. With her backwards baseball caps, baggy pants, Malcolm X medallions, combat boots, and copious colloquialisms, Blige was *a ghetto girl speaking on behalf of ghetto girls.* Instead of ignoring the increasing popularity of rap music and hip hop culture in the early 1990s, Blige openly embraced the hip hop aesthetic, even trying her hand at rapping on *What's the 411?*[23]

On *What's the 411?* Blige brought the ghetto realism of rap to rhythm & blues and in the process helped to birth neo-soul. According to Nathan Brackett and Christian David Hoard, in *The New Rolling Stone Album Guide* (2004), Blige's "tough girl persona and streetwise lyrics" gave the album "a gritty undertone and a realism missing from much of the devotional love songs ruling the charts at that time" (83). Even when compared with other black popular music divas who burst onto the scene in the 1990s—for example, songstresses such as Toni Braxton, Brandy, Monica, Aaliyah, and Faith Evans—Blige's life and music continued to distinguish and endear her. Even as her sophomore effort *My Life* (1994) scaled back the hip hop beats, and most of the rap influences were pushed to the background, Blige's music continued to resonate with hip hop women with its often tortured tales of love, loss, and ghetto life. In spite of the overarching blues motif that shades and colors the music, the major preoccupation of the album revolves around sadness *and* happiness. Tracks such as "Be Happy" and "You Bring Me Joy" are as integral to the album's success as the more noted neo-soul ballads "I'm Going Down" and "My Life."

Either writing or cowriting every track on *My Life*, except for Norman Whitfield's "I'm Going Down" and Cedric "K-Ci" Hailey and Dalvin De-Grate's "No One Else," Blige produced a classic soul-sounding album that certainly was not her parents' soul but nonetheless a new kind of soul that linked the anguished women-centered classic soul of Doris Duke (*I'm A Loser* [1969] and *A Legend in Her Own Time* [1971]), Ann Peebles (*Straight From the Heart* [1972] and *I Can't Stand the Rain* [1973]), and Denise LaSalle (*Trapped By A Thing Called Love* [1972] and *On The Loose* [1973]), with her hip hop-influenced soul hybrid and the neo-soul sisters who would follow her lead. After the certified three-times platinum success of *My Life*, Blige went on to release a series of neo-soul albums that continued to synthesize the classic soul vocal sound pioneered by Aretha Franklin, Etta James, Carla Thomas, Brenda Holloway, Gladys Knight, Bettye LaVette, and Millie Jackson with hip hop beats and production techniques. Ultimately what connects *Share My World* (1997), *Mary* (1999), *No More Drama* (2011), *Love & Life* (2003), *The Breakthrough* (2005), *Growing Pains* (2007), *Stronger with Each Tear* (2009), and *My Life II* (2011) with *What's the 411?* and *My Life* is Blige's consistently soulful singing and her simultaneously ghetto-centered and women-centered lyrics. Therefore, Mary J. Blige has been hailed as the "Queen of Hip Hop Soul" and one of the foundational figures in the emergence of neo-soul.

Another one of the founding figures of neo-soul is the genre-jumping multi-instrumentalist Meshell Ndegeocello. In 1993 Ndegeocello released the groundbreaking *Plantation Lullabies*, which continued the protest song tradition of Aretha Franklin in much the same way that the bulk of Mary J. Blige's work continued Franklin's gospel-influenced love song tradition. Bursting the musical and lyrical boundaries surrounding African American music in the 1990s, *Plantation Lullabies* was a protest record in several different senses.

On the one hand, *Plantation Lullabies* can be interpreted as a critique and contestation of the rigid, mostly white male music critic-created categories that African American women's music is regularly quarantined to and judged by. Featuring jazz, rhythm & blues, rock & roll, soul, funk, reggae, disco, electro, techno, and rap-influenced tracks, similar to Blige's early work, Ndegeocello refused to allow anything other than her muse to dictate the content and direction of her music. On the other hand, Ndegeocello's music registers as protest when the regular references to contemporary African American life and struggle are taken into consideration. Songs such as "I'm Diggin' You (Like an Old Soul Record)," "Shoot'n up and Gett'n High," "Dred Loc," "Step into the Projects," and "Soul on Ice" capture black ghetto youths' loves, lives, and struggles in the early 1990s like few other non-rap albums do. Perhaps the most remarkable aspect of *Plantation Lullabies* is the ingenious way in which Ndegeocello remixes African American racial, sexual, and political identities and issues.[24]

Often coupling her critiques of racism and sexism with critiques of African American self-hatred and cultural misorientation as a consequence of antiblack racism, Ndegeocello's music opens the window to an alternative African American world. Taking up everything from prison and prostitution to poverty and homosexuality on innovative albums such as *Peace Beyond Passion* (1996), *Bitter* (1999), *Cookie: The Anthropological Mixtape* (2002), *Comfort Woman* (2003), *The World Has Made Me the Man of My Dreams* (2007), *Devil's Halo* (2009), *Weather* (2011), and *For a Sovereign Soul: A Dedication to Nina Simone* (2012), Ndegeocello's sonic protest recalls not only Aretha Franklin's protest music, but also that of the *nonpareil* Nina Simone. In fact, similar to Franklin, Nina Simone is as famous for her protest songs as she is for her lush love songs.

Simone can be considered a "soul" singer when we observe her gospel-influenced singing and the sheer range of raw emotions she was able to capture and often conjure up, rather than strictly based on the unconventional but nonetheless "soulful" sound of her music. Prefiguring Ndegeocello's music, Simone synthesized gospel, blues, European classical, folk, jazz, pop, rhythm & blues, rock & roll, soul, and funk into her own distinct signature sound. Although often characterized as an innovative and eclectic jazz diva, Simone was as adept at folk and blues as she was at rhythm & blues and soul (e.g., see *Folksy Nina* [1964], *Broadway-Blues-Ballads* [1964], *Pastel Blues* [1965], *The High Priestess of Soul* [1966], *Nina Simone Sings the Blues* [1967], and *Nina Simone and Piano* [1968]). In *I Put a Spell on You: The Autobiography of Nina Simone* (1991) she stated, "[t]o me 'jazz' meant a way of thinking, a way of being, and the black man in America was jazz in everything he did—in the way he walked, talked, thought and acted. Jazz music was just another aspect of the whole thing, so in that sense because I was black I was a jazz singer, but in every other way I most definitely wasn't" (68–69).[25]

Simone's words capture the ways in which African American music in general, and—even though she said "the black *man* in America"—African American women's music in particular, has been consistently misnamed and forced to fit into white male music critic-created categories. Similar to Ndegeocello and a whole host of past and present black divas, Simone eschewed the lazy labeling so often associated with black popular music, and she was especially peeved by the constant comparisons between her music and that of other black divas that, from her point of view, always seemed to rob her and whoever she was being compared with of the distinctiveness and magic of their music. Directly addressing this issue in her autobiography, she asserted:

Because of "Porgy" people often compared me to Billie Holiday, which I hated. That was just one song out of my repertoire, and anybody who saw me perform could see we were entirely different. What made me mad was that it meant people couldn't get past the fact we were both black: if I had happened to be white nobody would have made the connection. And I didn't like to be put in a box with other jazz singers because my musicianship was totally different, and in its own way superior. Calling me a jazz singer was a way of ignoring my musical background because I didn't fit into white ideas of what a black performer should be. It was a racist thing; "if she's black she must be a jazz singer." It diminished me, exactly like Langston Hughes was diminished when people called him a "great black poet." Langston was a great poet period, and it was up to him and him alone to say what part the color of his skin had to do with that. (69)

It is important to note that Simone "didn't like to be put in a box with other jazz singers" because, she strongly stressed, "my musicianship was totally different." This is a theme that runs throughout African American women musicians' interviews and autobiographies, from Billie Holiday's classic *Lady Sings the Blues* (1956) all the way through to Etta James's *Rage to Survive: The Etta James Story* (1995) and Aretha Franklin's *Aretha: From These Roots* (1999). In this sense, then, many African American women musicians' contestation of the lazy labeling that often diminishes their distinctiveness could be understood as a form of protest against an antiblack racist *and* sexist society that frequently fails to acknowledge African American women on their own terms, as opposed to Eurocentric terms that see black women as nothing more than white women in blackface or chocolate-covered white women. However, similar to Franklin, Simone's sonic protest registered on both the *personal* level and the *political* level, to play on the "the personal is political" slogan of the Women's Liberation Movement. In other words, her sonic protest was simultaneously and amazingly *African American women-centered* and *Civil Rights Movement-centered*.

Simone's growing commitment to the Civil Rights Movement led her to record some of the most incendiary protest music of the 1960s and 1970s. Under contract to record for Columbia Pictures' subsidiary Colpix Records between 1959 and 1963, Simone recorded several protest songs that mirrored the major issues and events of the Civil Rights Movement. For instance, *The Amazing Nina Simone* (1959) featured a stunning rendition of the gospel song "Children Go Where I Send You," which many took as a coded message of encouragement to civil rights workers; *Nina Simone at Town Hall* (1959) featured the folk song "Black Is the Color of My True Love's Hair" and an original composition "Under the Lowest"; *Forbidden Fruit* (1960) featured "Work Song," which critiqued chain gangs; *Nina Simone at the Village Gate* (1962) featured "House of the Rising Sun," "Brown Baby," and

"Zungo," each of which unambiguously painted sonic portraits of African American life and culture in the early 1960s.

When Simone signed a new recording contract with the Netherlands-based Philips Records in 1964 her music took on an even greater political tone. In response to the brutal murder of NAACP field secretary Medgar Evers on June 12, 1963, and the 16th Street Baptist Church bombing on September 15, 1963, in Birmingham, Alabama, which claimed the lives of Addie Mae Collins (age 14), Denise McNair (age 11), Carole Robertson (age 14), and Cynthia Wesley (age 14) and injured two dozen other churchgoers, Simone's first Philips album, *Nina Simone in Concert* (1964), featured two new subversive songs, "Mississippi Goddam" and "Old Jim Crow." Her *Pastel Blues* (1965) featured "Strange Fruit" and "Sinnerman"; *Let It All Out* (1966) featured "The Ballad of Hollis Brown" and the African American working-class women-centered song "Images"; and the albums *Wild Is the Wind* (1966), *The High Priestess of Soul* [1967], and *Nina Simone Sings the Blues* [1967] contained several tracks that reflected Simone and African America's embrace of aspects of the more militant politics that characterized the Black Power Movement in the late 1960s and early 1970s. As a matter of fact, in *The Sound of Soul* (1969), Phyl Garland quoted H. Rap Brown—one of the most noted and controversial militants of the Black Power Movement and, more specifically, the new chairman of the revamped SNCC—in 1967 lionizing Simone as "the singer of the Black Revolution because there is no other singer who sings real protest songs about the race situation" (183). Essentially corroborating Brown's contention, Brain Ward's painstaking scholarship in *Just My Soul Responding* (1998) painted a very vivid picture of Simone's music and politics in relationship to the Civil Rights Movement and its evolution into the Black Power Movement:

> Simone's level of involvement was unmatched by any of the major figures of rhythm & blues in the early-to-mid 1960s, and it was probably not coincidental that she was actually outside the main run of soul artists. Simone was a classically trained singer-pianist; a Julliard [*sic*] graduate whose predilection for mixing Bach fugues, jazz, blues, folk and gospel frequently confounded attempts by critics, record label executives, producers, and nightclub owners to assign her to any of the stylistic slots routinely reserved for black artists. "I didn't fit into white ideas of what a black performer should be. It was a racist thing," she later wrote. Her distinctive hybrid stylings also meant that her principal black audience comprised mainly intellectuals and Movement workers who appreciated her candid lyrics and personal commitment. Her other fans were mostly white folk, jazz, and blues aficionados, many of whom were Northern college students or budding bohemians. They also tended to be racial liberals and as such were untroubled by Simone's politics. (303)

To reiterate, Simone's sonic protest registered on both the *personal* level and the *political* level, and part of her personal protest as a recording artist "frequently confounded attempts by critics, record label executives, producers, and nightclub owners to assign her to any of the stylistic slots routinely reserved for black artists." As will be discussed below, as if channeling Nina Simone's musical audacity and aural eclecticism, Ndegeocello occupies a place in the annals of neo-soul that often seems almost identical to the indescribable and undefinable place Simone occupied in relationship to 1960s and 1970s soul. Both Simone and Ndegeocello's sonic protest grew more complex and, at times, more direct as the social, political, and cultural struggles engulfing their respective epochs further unfolded.

"After the murder of Medgar Evers, the Alabama bombing and 'Mississippi Goddam' the entire direction of my life shifted," Simone (1991, 91) importantly recounted. She further stated, "for the next seven years I was driven by civil rights and the hope of Black Revolution. I was proud of what I was doing and proud to be part of a movement that was changing history." Moving her music even further away from the unchallenging and unrewarding music favored by mainstream America in the 1960s, Simone shared, "although being a performing artist sounded like something grand and wonderful, up to then it felt like just another job." But, "[t]hat changed when I started singing for the movement. . . . It made what I did for a living something much more worthwhile." Instead of the world of popular music seeming like a "nothing world" where she "didn't have much respect for popular audiences because they were so musically ignorant," after she began to record Civil Rights Movement-centered music her relationship with her music, her audiences, and the movement drastically changed. Performing her music no longer felt like "just another job." Describing the far-reaching changes that took place in her life and music during the Civil Rights Movement and Black Power Movement years, Simone observed:

> As I became more involved in the movement this attitude I had towards my audiences changed, because I admired what they were achieving for my people so much that the level of their music education didn't come into it anymore. They gave me respect too, not only for my music—which they loved—but because they understood the stand I was making. They knew I was making sacrifices and running risks just like they were, and we were all in it together. Being a part of this struggle made me feel so good. My music was dedicated to a purpose more important than classical music's pursuit of excellence; it was dedicated to the fight for freedom and the historical destiny of my people. I felt a fierce pride when I thought about what we were all doing together. So if the movement gave me nothing else, it gave me self-respect. (91)

Simone's "fierce pride" and new sense of "self-respect" were documented in most of the songs she recorded in the mid- to late-1960s and early 1970s. As a matter of fact, by the time she signed with RCA Records in 1967 she had produced a patchwork of political songs that were virtually unrivaled in black popular music. However, similar to Aretha Franklin's music, Simone's new sense of "self-respect" embedded in her mid- to late-1960s and early 1970s music seemed to resonate with the emerging Women's Liberation Movement as much as it did the Civil Rights Movement and the Black Power Movement. Songs such as "Images" (from *Let It All Out*) and "Four Women" (from *Wild Is the Wind*) endeared Simone to African American women in a special way: "Images" emphasized African American working-poor women's beauty and need for self-love and self-respect in spite of their dream-destroying jobs and the overall ugliness of most of their lives; and "Four Women" was an epic musical history of stereotypical antiblack racist and sexist images of African American women from enslavement through to the Black Power Movement.

By broaching the subject of black women's brutal treatment during and after African American enslavement, with "Four Women" Simone made one of her greatest contributions to African American women's protest song tradition. For instance, "Aunt Sarah" is the first of the four women described in the song. Simone's "Aunt Sarah" is obviously a critique of the supposedly asexual and apolitical "Aunt Jemima" character, which was inspired by Billy Kersands's popular 1875 blackface minstrel song "Old Aunt Jemima."[26] In a sense the allegedly asexual and unappealing "Aunt Sarah" is the mother of "Safronia," the second woman depicted in "Four Women." Simone details how Safronia's "father was rich and white" and he "forced [her] mother late one night." The racial *and* sexual violence of African American enslavement and its aftermath during the Reconstruction years produced a mixed race people who were forced to live "between two worlds," as Simone bitterly sang. As if putting Du Bois's analysis of double-consciousness, the color line, and second sight in *The Souls of Black Folk* to music, by giving the second of the four women the name "Safronia"—moving beyond the more obvious interpretation that connects the name to the lavender-colored saffron flower and linking it to "sapphire," as in the name of the precious blue stone—Simone connects the hardships and horrors of enslaved African American foremothers with the blues of the classic blues queens of the Jazz Age and the rhythm & blues divas of her own epoch during the Civil Rights Movement and Black Power Movement years.

Safronia's life and struggles "between two worlds" led to "Sweet Thing," the third character Simone depicted in "Four Women." Sweet Thing conceptually captures the centuries of racial oppression, economic exploitation, and sexual violence against African American women. While she is, to a certain extent, accepted by both whites and blacks because her skin is "fair" and her hair is "fine," ultimately Sweet Thing is a reminder of the centuries of anti-black racist rape African American women endured, as well as their ongoing misuse and abuse. Sweet Thing, as her name clearly implies, is almost completely reduced to her sexuality, to her body, and to her ability to tease and please men. Similar to Safronia, Sweet Thing is caught "between two worlds," and it is her foremothers and mothers' sexuality and their sexual exploitation that continues to haunt her identity and sexuality.

Recalling the "tragic mulatto," because even though her skin is "fair" and her hair is "fine," Sweet Thing is accepted neither in white nor black America on account of the fact that she has been hyper-sexualized, objectified, and reduced to a life of prostitution, in the end her life is extremely tragic. As with the "tragic mulatto" characters in Nella Larsen's *Passing* (1929), Fannie Hurst's *Imitation of Life* (1933), and Harper Lee's *To Kill a Mockingbird* (1960), Simone's Sweet Thing is ultimately rejected by both white and black America consequent to the very "miscegenation" and the same sordid interracial sex that produced her and, truth be told, the bastardization of the bulk of black America.[27] The fourth and final woman Simone depicted in "Four Women" is named "Peaches." A peach is typically thought of as being soft and sweet. Simone's Peaches openly admits, "I'm awfully bitter these days, 'cause my parents were slaves." Coming full circle with her narrative and essentially painting a sonic picture of black women as being in bondage both during enslavement and afterward in so-called "freedom," Peaches invokes violence against enslavement and black women's continued colonization: "I'll kill the first mother [as in "motherfucker"] I see!" Peaches's abrasive language and audible impatience linked her to the Black Power Movement, which was known for, literally, cursing the established order, and referring to police officers as "pigs" and racist whites as "crackers," "rednecks," and "peckerwoods."[28]

Simone's sonic protests did not go unnoticed by classic soul artists, who considered her an erstwhile and extremely eclectic soul sister. Building on her Colpix and Philips years, Simone's RCA years between 1967 and 1974 produced even more searing message music which seemed to be perfectly in tune with many aspects of the Black Power Movement and Women's Liberation Movement. For example, on *Nina Simone Sings the Blues* (1967), she recorded a hard-hitting protest poem written by her close friend Langston Hughes titled "Backlash Blues"; *Silk & Soul* (1967) featured the civil rights anthem "I Wish I Knew How It Would Feel to Be Free" and the critique of racism "Turning Point"; *'Nuff Said* (1968), which was recorded three days after Martin Luther King's assassination on April 4, 1968, featured a song dedicated to the slain civil rights leader titled "Why? (The King Of Love Is Dead)"; *To Love Somebody* (1969) featured "I Shall Be Released," as well as the epic "Revolution (Part 1)" and "Revolution (Part 2)"; and, finally, *Black Gold* (1970) featured the epochal "To Be Young, Gifted and Black," which was dedicated to her recently deceased confidante, playwright, and political essayist, Lorraine Hansberry.

Of all of Simone's protest songs, it was "To Be Young, Gifted and Black" that seemed to resonate most with the classic soul crowd. For instance, almost immediately after hearing Simone's version of the song, one of the true unsung heroes of classic soul, Donny Hathaway, recorded a version of "To Be Young, Gifted and Black" that was featured on his debut album *Everything Is Everything* in 1970. Two years later Aretha Franklin, the undisputed "Queen of Soul," not only recorded a jaw-dropping version of "To Be Young, Gifted and Black," but she titled her Grammy Award-winning 1972 album *Young, Gifted and Black*. Hence, even if most music critics refuse to acknowledge Nina Simone as a classic soul diva, her contemporaries did. Soul was more than merely Atlantic, Chess, Motown, and Stax. Indeed, soul was more than even the iconic artistry of James Brown, Aretha Franklin, Curtis Mayfield, Etta James, Otis Redding, and Marvin Gaye. It was a broad cultural and musical category that often defied nice and neat definitions, similar to other Black Power Movement and Black Arts Movement concepts, such as "Black Power" and the "black aesthetic."

All of this is to say that soul, like neo-soul, is a wide-ranging and wide-reaching arena that seemingly from the very first songs of the genre distinguished itself from rhythm & blues and rock & roll in light of the fact that its major mediums were both love songs *and* protest songs undergirded by lyrics that directly grew out of and incessantly referenced the African American experience, gospel-influenced vocals, and musical motifs that drew from the entire spectrum of black popular music, including ragtime and rock & roll, as well as elements of folk and country & western. Along with Meshell Ndegeocello there are several other neo-soul sisters who have followed in the mercurial musical footsteps of Nina Simone and refused to be boxed in by the mostly white male music critic-created categories and conceptions of "good" and "bad" black music. For the most part sidestepping pop pretensions and the constant pressure from record labels to create "hit" songs, progressive neo-soul sisters such as Des'ree, Erykah Badu, Jill Scott, India.Arie, Macy Gray, Amel Larrieux, N'dambi, Conya Doss, and Georgia Anne Muldrow demonstrate that often unsung classic soul divas like Nina Simone, Esther Phillips, Fontella Bass, Mitty Collier, Sugar Pie DeSanto, Bettye LaVette, Brenda Holloway, Lorraine Ellison, Ann Sexton, and Loleatta Holloway are just as influential on their music as Aretha Franklin, Etta James, Carla Thomas, and other more noted classic soul queens.

In focusing on the ways in which *African American women's sonic protest has almost always reflected African American social protest*, it is important to emphasize the enormous influence both Aretha Franklin and Nina Simone's protest songs have had on neo-soul singer-songwriters in general, and neo-soul sisters in particular. It should be stated outright: African American women's political protest and social critique frequently differs from both African American men and European American women's political protest and social critique. Elite and college-educated African American women's political protest and social critique decidedly differs from that of working-class and poor African American women. Furthermore, classic soul queens' protest and critique in many senses diverges from neo-soul sisters' protest and critique. But, it is important not to overlook the fact that virtually since their inception both classic soul and neo-soul have offered political protest and social critique. Moreover, Aretha Franklin and Nina Simone have provided neo-soul sisters with lyrical, musical, *and* political models, and only the most ahistorical and apolitical interpretations of neo-soul sisters' music can miss the obvious connections.

Just as there is no monolithic form of black feminism or womanism that each and every black woman adheres to, there is no single form of political protest and social critique that each and every black woman embraces. As Deborah King contended in "Multiple Jeopardy, Multiple Consciousness: The Context of a Black Feminist Ideology" (1988), what provides the diverse forms of black feminism with discursive coherence is the fact that "black feminist ideology fundamentally challenges the interstructure of the oppressions of racism, sexism, and classism both in the dominant society and within movements for liberation" (72). Indeed, she continued,"[i]t is in confrontation with multiple jeopardy that black women define and sustain a multiple consciousness essential for our liberation, of which feminist consciousness is an integral part."

African American women's political protest and social critique is as diverse as African American women's lives and struggles, as well as their complexions, body types, heights, and hair textures. Class, cultural geography, social ecology, spirituality, and sexuality impact black women's views and values just as much as their race and gender. Hence, King's conception of "multiple jeopardy" directly speaks to my emphasis on the alternative forms of black feminism found in classic soul women and contemporary neo-soul women's lyrics, music, politics, and lifestyles. "In the interactive model, the relative significance of race, sex, or class in determining the conditions of black women's lives is neither fixed nor absolute but, rather," King continued, "is dependent on the socio-historical context and the social phenomenon under consideration. These interactions also produce what to some appears a seemingly confounding set of social roles and political attitudes among black women" (49).

Contemporary neo-soul women are extending and expanding a tradition that reaches back to classic soul women and, again, not simply Aretha Franklin and Nina Simone, but also often unsung classic soul queens such as Etta James, Carla Thomas, Tina Turner, Barbara Lynn, Patti LaBelle, Esther Phillips, Irma Thomas, Martha Reeves, Fontella Bass, Mitty Collier, Sugar Pie DeSanto, Bettye LaVette, Laura Lee, Gladys Knight, Brenda Holloway, the Sweet Inspirations, Mavis Staples, Lorraine Ellison, Linda Jones, Roberta

Flack, Millie Jackson, Ann Peebles, Candi Staton, Margie Joseph, Doris Duke, Loleatta Holloway, Tommie Young, Ann Sexton, Denise LaSalle, and Betty Wright, among many others. All of these women's "multiple consciousness" of the ways in which they are oppressed and exploited on the basis of their race, gender, class, and sexuality led them to develop *a distinct African American women-centered style of insurgent intersectional critique via soul music.* After listening to classic soul women and contemporary neo-soul women's work, who can deny that this is precisely what the classic soul women did during their day and what many contemporary neo-soul sisters are doing during our day—which is to say, using soul music as a medium through which to protest and critique as well as express their happiness and sadness, their joys and blues?

Obviously there are countless hip hop women, both women-centered rappers and neo-soul singers, who have continued the sonic protest and social critique tradition that classic soul queens carried over from classic blues queens. Hip hop women, such as MC Lyte, Queen Latifah, Lauryn Hill, Jean Grae, Harmony, Yo-Yo, Jill Scott, Amel Larrieux, Alicia Keys, Eve, Ledisi, Erykah Badu, Angie Stone, Missy Elliott, Meshell Ndegeocello, Nneka, and Georgia Anne Muldrow, have effectively built on and, in several instances, gone beyond many of the issues and ills that the classic soul women collectively addressed in their work. For instance, Eve engaged the issue of domestic violence with her 1999 hit song and video "Love is Blind," and over a decade later Rihanna continued the critique of domestic violence with her controversial song and video "Man Down." Mary J. Blige has consistently addressed the issue of domestic violence and abusive relationships in her music (see *My Life, Share My World, Mary,* and *No More Drama*). Alicia Keys delivered a subtle critique of the ways the prison system (i.e., now the notorious "prison industrial complex") continues to impact African Americans and African American relationships with her runaway hits "Fallin'" and "A Woman's Worth."

Several neo-soul sisters, deftly demonstrating the transgender and transcendent range and reach of hip hop womanism, have even gone so far as to critique the hardships African American men face as a consequence of their race, gender, class, and sexuality. For example, Erykah Badu's "Other Side of the Game" and "A.D. 2000" (for Amadou Diallo), Jill Scott's "Brotha," Angie Stone's "Soul Brotha," and Marsha Ambrosius's "Far Away" each acknowledge many of the major issues confronting hip hop men and lovingly celebrate their "brothas'" triumph over tragedy. Moreover, Meshell Ndegeocello, seeming to directly follow in the footsteps of Nina Simone in relationship with the Civil Rights Movement and Black Power Movement, has consistently used her music to address issues plaguing the Hip Hop Movement in general, and hip hop women in specific. However, what makes Ndegeocello's music distinctive, even when compared with Angie Stone or

Erykah Badu, or Jill Scott or India.Arie's music, is not simply her innovative amalgam of the entire spectrum of black popular music, including rock & roll and rap, but her willingness to lyrically explore homosexual hip hoppers' loves, lives, and struggles within the world of hip hop and within the broader context of African America.

In "Meshell Ndegeocello: Musical Articulations of Black Feminism" (2007), Martha Mockus asserted that "[c]entral to her [Ndegeocello's] musical ethnography are political convictions about the search for freedom and the struggles against capitalism, racism, sexism, and homophobia in African American cultural history" (82). With musical politics that directly mirror a combination of the political agendas of the Civil Rights Movement, Black Power Movement, Women's Liberation Movement, and Homosexual Liberation Movement, Ndegeocello's work is both musically and lyrically groundbreaking. For the most part, her music centers around both heterosexual and homosexual love, as well as heterosexual and homosexual struggles. As critical as she seems to be appreciative of rap and other aspects of hip hop culture (see, "Dead Nigga Blvd. [Part 1]" and "Dead Nigga Blvd. [Part 2]" on *Cookie*), Ndegeocello pushes the discourse on rap music and hip hop culture beyond merely noting its misogyny and homophobia by connecting sexism and heterosexism in rap music and hip hop culture to larger, superstructural sexism and heterosexism in mainstream American history, culture, politics, and society.

With her raspy singing, rapping, and poetry reading, Ndegeocello challenges how a neo-soul singer should sound and what she should sing about. In a sense, when her body of work to date is carefully and critically studied one walks away with the distinct impression that Ndegeocello is audaciously deconstructing and reconstructing what it means to be a "soul" singer at the turn of the twenty-first century. A true trailblazer with a profound respect for tradition, Ndegeocello's music—like the often uncategorizable and equally experimental music of Nina Simone, Betty Carter, Abbey Lincoln, Nona Hendryx, and Cassandra Wilson—is simultaneously within the tradition of eclectic African American songstresses and equally within the tradition of the more mainstream classic soul divas who pioneered and popularized women-centered soul music in the 1960s and 1970s.

As a matter of fact, in "The Last Maverick: Meshell Ndegeocello and the Burden of Vision" (2004), Amy Linden lauded, "[f]rom the moment she stepped in the arena, with her potent debut *Plantation Lullabies*, and continuing through her latest release *Cookie: The Anthropological Mixtape*, Meshell Ndegeocello has defied categorization and sent any number of critics and industry executives scrambling to dig deeper into their respective trick bags to find a neat, simplistic description that would suit her. Or maybe just suit them" (206). Linden colorfully continued:

She's been lumped in with progressive artists, both black and white, female musicians, gay musicians, gay single mother musicians, pop, jazz, funk, rock, R&B, hip hop, and any possible netherland that manages to bridge all of those and anything else that might slip between the cracks. She carries the double-edged sword of not only being a female musician but a black one who is not traditionally R&B or hip hop—the two entry-level positions most accessible to women of color. Defiantly, Meshell answers to no one except for what she instinctively senses sounds good and feels right. She's recorded with a disparate array of musicians from Scritti Politti, to Roy Hargrove, Citizen Cope, and John Mellencamp and seems as at ease being the focus of the record as she does keeping it rock steady in the background. She is that most odd of birds: a star who behaves like a session player and a session player with the undeniable charisma and chops to become a star. Meshell's ability—hell, one might even declare it a mission—to make music that does what it needs to do regardless of what it happens to sound like has been instrumental (no pun intended) in sealing her position as one of the most consistently inconsistent artists of the past ten years. That is a good thing, unless, of course, you have the unenviable task of creeping over to the studio to let someone know that, "Wow, you know, I'm not really sure I hear a single." (206–7)

Drawing from everything from blues and jazz to rock & roll and soul, from reggae and rap to gospel and rhythm & blues, Ndegeocello—constantly "def[ying] categorization" and undoubtedly "one of the most consistently inconsistent artists of the past ten years"—has a whopping ten career Grammy Award nominations. She is arguably one of the most noted contemporary exponents of the special truths that classic soul women spoke to the world via both their love songs and protest songs. It has been, and remains, her willingness to take up taboo topics and insurgently embrace sonic experimentation that places her squarely in the tradition established by the classic soul queens and the long line of black pop divas who rose in their wake. However, for as lush as Ndegeocello's love songs are, it is her consistent cultural, social, and political realism in the face of the high levels of musical fakery and lyrical lameness that makes even her most "romantic" songs sound like sonic protests against the overproduced melodrama and mundanity that passes for "good" music nowadays.

In a world where most of the rap music that we hear on the radio seems overly preoccupied with sex, drinking, drugs, and clubs, neo-soul sisters' continued commitment to "real love," as Blige famously sang, as well as their social commentary concerning myriad issues plaguing African America speaks volumes about the ways in which neo-soul sisters are continuing not only the soul love song tradition, but also the soul protest song tradition handed down by the classic soul queens. Neo-soul divas such as Des'ree, Angie Stone, Erykah Badu, Lauryn Hill, Jill Scott, Amel Larrieux, India.Arie, Goapele, Ledisi, N'dambi, Nneka, Conya Doss, and Georgia Anne Muldrow, among many others, collectively seem as concerned with "real

love" as they are with "keeping it real" and "telling it like it is" with respect
to cultural, social, and political issues. Indeed, as Daphne Brooks observed in
"'All That You Can't Leave Behind': Black Female Soul Singing and the
Politics of Surrogation in the Age of Catastrophe" (2007), these neo-soul
women's "work creates a particular kind of black feminist surrogation"
(183). That is to say, "an embodied cultural act that articulates black wom-
en's distinct forms of palpable sociopolitical loss and grief, as well as spirited
dissent and dissonance. Their combined efforts mark a new era of protest
singing that sonically resists, revises, and reinvents the politics of black
female hyper-visibility in the American cultural imaginary."

Similar to the classic soul queens, contemporary neo-soul sisters frequently blur the lines between the spiritual and the sexual, the personal and
the political, the public and the private by embedding their sonic protests and
social critiques in songs that seem to fall squarely within the world of rhythm
& blues—both flamboyant and flaccid—balladry. The public and sociopolitical voices of African American women's discontent is often difficult to detect in black popular music in particular, and black popular culture more
generally, because of a unique form of what could be characterized as "double-consciousness" (à la W.E.B. Du Bois in *The Souls of Black Folk*) in
which African American women self-consciously struggle to avoid being
labeled "the angry black woman" both intraracially and interracially—that is
to say, by both African American men and the ever-onlooking white world at
large. Brooks broached this extremely taboo topic, audaciously asserting that
"[c]rafting a voice of black female discontent in black female popular culture
is, however, a slippery slope if one aims to avoid the caricature of 'the angry
black woman'—immortalized by everyone from Hattie McDaniel's simmer-
ing and contemptuous cinematic characters to the sour squint of genius comic   La-
Wanda Page, or of late, the wickedly 'sick and tired' stand-up of Wanda
Sykes" (184). Moving from African American women's discontent in black
popular culture to African American women's discontent in black popular
music, and directly hitting at the heart of our discussion here, Brooks continued:

> In contemporary pop music, black female (sociopolitical) discontent is even
> trickier to trace. Certainly eclectic performer Nina Simone's songbook ranged
> from the sly, oblique, and ironic critique in classics such as "I Hold No
> Grudge" ("I hold no grudge/There's no resentment und'neath/I'll extend the
> laurel wreath and we'll be friends/But right there is where it ends") to the
> searing political satire of the civil rights "showtune" "Mississippi Goddam."
> But while Simone and Odetta remain forebears of a certain kind of critical
> voice that emerged as the cultural arm of the Civil Rights Movement and Anti-
> War Movement, twenty-first- century black female pop stars—save for folkies
> like Tracy Chapman, bohemian rebels like Meshell Ndegeocello, or sharp and

powerful emcees like early MC Lyte, Lauryn Hill, and Jean Grae—are more
likely to couch their dissatisfaction in domestic, romantic, and/or gospel-relig-
ious R&B zones. (185)[29]

We see here, then, that "attitude"—especially an antiracist, antisexist, and
sometimes even an obscured anticapitalist attitude—is an important ingredi-
ent in African American women's popular music and popular culture. Hence,
to reiterate, classic soul queens handed down more than merely music to neo-
soul divas in specific, and contemporary hip hop women in general. A women-centered social outlook and political "attitude," although often overlooked, is a unique part of hip hop women's "inheritance" from soul women.
Again, because black popular music is more than merely music, *hip hop's
inheritance* from previous forms of black popular music is simultaneously
musical *and* extramusical.

Here it is important to emphasize the ways in which black popular music
has consistently revealed the social, political, and cultural desires of African
Americans, as well as the astonishing irony that these sonically registered
desires remain largely overlooked and undertheorized in a wide range of
academic disciplines, including African American studies, American studies,
cultural studies, ethnic studies, and popular music studies. An equally indict-
ing observation could be made about the ways in which classic soul queens
and neo-soul sisters' discontent, and, more specifically, African American
women's discontent in popular music and popular culture has been largely
overlooked and undertheorized in women's studies. All of this is to say, very
few critics have critically engaged the ways in which blues women, jazz
women, rhythm & blues women, rock & roll women, soul women, funk
women, disco women, and hip hop women, as well as their legions of female
fans, have historically and currently continue to contribute to black femi-
nism/womanism and produce public records of African American women's
deep-seated social, political, cultural, spiritual, and sexual desires. In other
words, African American women's musical subcultures—from classic blues
all the way through to contemporary neo-soul—insist that we take them a lot
more seriously in light of the fact that they, however "unconventionally"
from Eurocentric, bourgeois, and patriarchal points of view, actually articulate overt and covert common desires and shared dreams that run like a fast-
flowing river through the peaks and valleys, the high points and low points of
African American history, culture, and struggle.

FEMCEES AND NEO-SOUL SISTERS: FEMALE RAPPERS, HIP HOP
FEMINISTS, AND THE HIP HOP WOMEN'S MOVEMENT

Whether or not acknowledged by academics—both female and male, feminist and masculinist—there is a women's rights and women's liberation-

styled movement in progress within the broader Hip Hop Movement. In fact, several women-centered hip hop cultural critics have noted that a new form of feminism—what has been frequently dubbed *hip hop feminism*—has been afoot within the world of hip hop from the very first moment that hyper-masculinism and misogyny reared their ugly heads and hideous horns in rap music and hip hop culture. Neo-soul sisters, female rappers (i.e., "femcees") and, more generally, hip hop women's critical responses to hyper-masculin-ism, misogyny, and patriarchy in rap music and hip hop culture, as well as their critical commentary on and contestations of hyper-masculinism, misog-yny, and patriarchy in mainstream American music, culture, politics, and society, has discursively developed to the extent where their collective *hip hop women-centered rhetoric, poetics, aesthetics, theory, and praxis* can be said to constitute a *Hip Hop Women's Movement*. However, the Hip Hop Women's Movement is about more than merely critiquing hyper-masculin-ism, misogyny, and patriarchy—even more, it is about celebrating hip hop womanhood and hip hop girlhood in all their hues, it is about hip hop women loving each other and learning to unapologetically speak their special truths to each other and the wider world, and, finally, it is about offering viable alternatives to the "video vixen," "skeezer," "gold-digger," "hood rat," "hoo-chie mama," and "baby mama drama" caricatures of African American and other nonwhite hip hop women. [30]

Indeed, new forms of politicization and mobilization have emerged among the African American and other nonwhite women of the Hip Hop Generation that speak to the special ways they have remixed the "personal is political" paradigm of the Women's Liberation Movement of the 1960s and 1970s. Undoubtedly African American and other nonwhite women are not *en masse* embracing the "feminist" label, but this should not be taken as a rejection of feminism on their part as much as it should serve as a sign of their repudiation of feminism as espoused by the conservative feminist and antifeminist forces that co-opted feminism during the Reagan and Bush ad-ministration years between 1980 and 1992. Truth be told, feminism is seen as something foreign to most nonwhite women's *herstories*, cultures, and strug-gles because of the academization and embourgeoisement of feminism in the 1980s and 1990s. [31]

College-educated women are more likely to be exposed to feminism than those women who do not attend college, or those women whose lives are quarantined to their respective nonwhite world. Because nonwhite working-class and working-poor women have to overcome unfathomable obstacles in order to attend college it could be argued that contemporary feminism has, to a certain extent, fallen prey to the political economy of U.S. capitalism. Which is also to sadly say that feminism, although it had such a powerful public presence in the late 1960s and throughout the 1970s, by the 1980s and 1990s it became increasingly privatized and commodified. [32]

It would seem that the women of the Hip Hop Generation do not reject the fundamental tenets of feminism, but rather what has been done or not done in the name of feminism. Here we have come back to the issue of nomenclature. For instance, in my experience of teaching African American studies over the last decade and a half I have found most young black women extremely receptive to black feminist thought in part, I believe, because (within the interdisciplinary and intersectional context of African American studies) they can easily comprehend how a form of antiracist feminism will help them *personally*, and the larger African American community *politically*. In other words, these young women are still working within the "personal is political" paradigm, but doing so from the standpoint of *racially gendered women* from, quite often, working-class and working-poor communities. In *Hip Hop's Inheritance* I observed that almost the exact same remix of cultural feminism and cultural nationalism was advanced by the members of the Black Women's Liberation Movement during the late 1960s and 1970s. One can only speculate how many more young African American women would embrace feminism, womanism, and/or women's liberation if they were exposed to the specific forms of feminist/womanist struggle waged by their black feminist foremothers, and not simply the super-sanitized, whitewashed, one-token-woman-of-color, vanilla version of feminism and the Women's Liberation Movement that is touted and taught in most women's studies classrooms.

In fact, my teaching experiences in African American studies have also exposed me to the fact that many (although certainly not all) young African American men are equally as receptive to feminism when it is refracted through the lens of African American women's lives and struggles. For example, I can distinctly recall that once I gave an assignment where I asked my "Introduction to Hip Hop Studies" class to compare and contrast Rachel Raimist's documentaries *Nobody Knows My Name* (1999) and *A B-Girl Is . . . : A Celebration of Women in Hip Hop* (2005) with a classic black feminist text (e.g., autobiography, novel, collection of poetry, or volume of theory), with the only stipulation being that the "classic black feminist text" had to have been published prior to 1979, which, of course, is the year that most hip hop studies scholars agree hip hop began in earnest. I was truly amazed to see how my students enthusiastically took to the assignment. There were comparisons of the hip hop feminist themes in Raimist's documentaries with texts by Sojourner Truth, Maria Stewart, Anna Julia Cooper, Ida B. Wells, Ella Baker, Dorothy Height, Sonia Sanchez, Rita Dove, and Ntozake Shange, among others. What really struck me, however, was a collaboration between one of my female students and one of my male students where they mixed excerpts of a 1970s speech by Angela Davis with head-bobbing hip hop beats. The young lady rapped about the prison industrial complex, health care, domestic violence, and women's rights in between and often along with Angela Davis's speech, while the young man scratched snatches of the speech on two turntables behind her. It was, to say the least, an absolutely phenomenal performance.

Afterwards I asked them how their collaboration came about, and the young sister said that they had been discussing what they were learning in the class about hip hop feminism with each other and decided they wanted to "put a new face on feminism." She candidly continued: "It does not have to be what it was back in the day, right? We can take it, and just like we did with other things from our past, we can update it, we can remix it, right? Ain't that what you said hip hop was all about the other day in class Professor Rabaka?"

At this point, the young brother chimed in, saying: "Yeah, we wanted to give feminism a facelift! This right here is 'hood feminism! Ghetto feminism! You know what I mean, a feminism for the sisters on the block, like Joan Morgan say. It ain't about hatin' on men. It's about women learning to love, respect, and appreciate themselves. Ain't that what you said? Really though, to be truthful with you, this hip hop feminism stuff made me realize I got some work to do in terms of my own gender politics—I mean, with my moms, my sister, my lady, and even my little daughter." Obviously, this was one of those rare and remarkable moments where a risky assignment paid off, pedagogically speaking. To see both of these students—both of whom just so happened to be underprivileged first-generation college students—so "hyped" about hip hop feminism made me even more determined to expose the connections between classic soul queens and the Women's Liberation Movement and contemporary female rappers, neo-soul sisters, and the Hip Hop Women's Movement.

I have found that exposing my students to hip hop feminism usually makes them more receptive to other forms of feminism, whether it is African American, Chicana/Latina, Native American, or Asian American feminism. Many of us working within women's studies find it extremely troubling that young women and young men can earn their college degrees and have absolutely no working knowledge of women's history, culture, and struggle. Again, whether or not young African American and other nonwhite women refer to themselves as "feminists" is superfluous at this point because, similar to the black women who began embracing the term "womanist" in the early 1980s, the women of the Hip Hop Movement have a right to practice *self-naming, self-definition, and self-determination* on their own terms, and no group of high-handed "old school feminists"—as Joan Morgan (2007, 476) put it—has a right to tell them otherwise.[33]

What needs to be understood here are the ways in which the 1980s and 1990s backlash against feminism defamed the "feminist" label to such a degree that now there is an entire generation of young women and young men who are reluctant to critically engage the history of women's rights and women's liberation movements because they do not want to be typecast as "feminists." This practice is, perhaps, even more prickly in nonwhite communities because of the ways in which nonwhite cultural nationalism has been collapsed into the reductive either/or logic of nonwhite male chauvinism.[34] It would seem to me that those of us currently working in women's studies should open ourselves to the fact that although the women of the Hip Hop Movement's "feminism," "womanism," or what have you, may not resemble our own or our mother or grandmother's "feminism," their contributions are not only valid but extremely valuable for future women's liberation movements.[35]

The nonwhite women of the Hip Hop Movement whose gender consciousness has been heightened as a result of their exposure to feminist ideas within women's studies classrooms often use their newfound knowledge in ways comparably different than most of their contemporary white counterparts, because their daily lives and struggles, their lived experiences and lived endurances demand not only that they be fluent in womanist/feminist theory and praxis, but also in critical race theory, postcolonial theory, and Marxist (and other anticapitalist) theory. Many of these young women are able to detect early on the deficiencies of mainstream feminism as a stand-alone theory, and usually they quickly tire of all of the esoteric "academic talk" of feminism. When they put feminist theory into praxis, they usually turn to the issues and terrain that they feel strongest about and are most familiar with. As a result of their coming of age during a period of intense technological revolution—for instance, from the Sony Walkman to Apple's iPod, from car phones to Apple's iPhone, and from the Commodore 64 computer to Apple's iPad—the young women of the Hip Hop Women's Movement, as with the Hip Hop Movement more generally, have been inundated with the explosion of social media and popular culture that took place between 1980 and the present day. Consequently, social media and popular culture have become important sites of and sources for hip hop feminism, and often these new-fangled feminists (albeit, many would argue, "feminists" nonetheless) make important connections between "old school" grassroots politics and Hip Hop Movement cyber-politics, between 1960s and 1970s-styled politicization and turn-of-the-twenty-first-century new social movement mobilization.[36]

Even if we were to focus our discussion primarily on the hip hop feminists featured in Gwendolyn Pough, Elaine Richardson, Aisha Durham, and Rachel Raimist's groundbreaking edited volume, *Home Girls Make Some Noise!: A Hip Hop Feminism Anthology* (2007), we can deduce that hip hop feminism critically engages music, film, fashion, fiction, poetry, spoken word, dance, theater, and visual art, as well as other aspects of popular culture, as essential arenas for feminist politicization and mobilization. Which is also to say, when compared with the feminist mobilization of the

1960s and 1970s, the majority of hip hop feminist mobilization at the present moment seems to emerge from cyber-social networks, mass media, and popular culture, rather than nationally networked women's organizations based in government, academic, or male-dominated leftist bureaucracies. Undeniably, hip hop culture touches the lives of young nonwhite women—and even the lives of many young white women—more than the feminism coming out of women's studies classes in particular, and the American academy in general.

This means, then, that those of us who would truly like to reach and radicalize the women of the Hip Hop Generation will have to come to the realization that whether or not we like it hip hop feminists have (or, at the very least, they are in the process of), in the words of my student above, *"giving feminism a facelift."* We might even go so far as to say that for many of the women of the Hip Hop Generation their feminist politics reflect the fact that the majority of nonwhite women regularly receive substandard education in the public school system and, therefore, school has ceased to serve as the central place where they learn literacy, sociality, and politics. Instead, for many, if not for most, cyber-social networks, mass media, and popular culture have, literally, become their classroom and, not seeking to sound snooty, little or no distinction is made between uncritical information and authentic critical education.[37]

In observing the fact that hip hop culture currently reaches more young nonwhite women, especially black and brown women, than the feminism found in the academy of the twenty-first century, I am not in any way arguing that hip hop, and specifically rap music and videos, is not full of controversy and contradictions when and where we come to the ways in which women (again, especially black and brown women) are represented or, rather, misrepresented within the world of hip hop. Instead, I am emphasizing the fact that rap music and hip hop culture are malleable and mobile enough to be adapted to a wide range of ideas and actions, a wealth of theories and praxes—some are progressive, while others are regressive; some are truly remarkable, while others are merely mediocre; and some are liberating, while others are incarcerating. Taking into consideration the contradictory ability of hip hop culture to simultaneously imprison and emancipate women, most hip hop feminists' theory and praxis revolves around their relationships with and critiques of the racial-patriarchal-capitalist political economy of cyber-social networks, mass media, and popular culture. All of this makes perfect sense when one contemplates the hyper-masculinism, misogyny, and embourgeoisement seemingly inherent in the most popular expressions of hip hop culture: commercial rap music and videos. Were we to focus specifically on African American women's ragged relationship with rap music and videos, then we would be able to easily see the often conflicted connections many women of the Hip Hop Generation make between hip hop culture, feminism, and antiracism.

It is important here to observe that whether or not hip hop feminists are aware of it, African American women at the turn of the twentieth century faced a similar situation with respect to misrepresentations and gross mischaracterizations of African American women in what was then an emerging mass media and culture industry. As I discussed in detail in *Hip Hop's Amnesia*, Harriet Tubman, Margaret Murray Washington, Frances E.W. Harper, Ida B. Wells, Josephine Ruffin, and Mary Church Terrell established the National Association of Colored Women (NACW) in 1896, which was not only committed to the uplift of African American women, but also preoccupied with repudiating antiblack racist caricatures of black women in the then materializing mass media. Similar to their African American feminist foremothers in the Black Women's Club Movement, then, the members of the Hip Hop Women's Movement find themselves fighting the simultaneously antiblack racist and sexist stereotypes incessantly being hurled at them. Most of the women of the Hip Hop Generation who have been able to engage and ultimately embrace feminism or womanism strongly stress the necessity of sensibly using hip hop culture, especially rap music and videos, as a critical consciousness-raising tool, an antiracist feminist forum to expose the young women (and men) of the Hip Hop Movement to what nonwhite and nonelite feminism has to offer—that is, as I discussed in detail in *Hip Hop's Inheritance*, the very kind of feminism put forward and practiced by most members of the Black Women's Liberation Movement in the 1960s and 1970s.

Most contemporary cultural critics and cultural studies scholars agree that hip hop is the late twentieth-century and early twenty-first-century generation's signature sociocultural contribution (or "damned" deprivation, depending on who you ask), so it should not shock anyone, least of all those of us working in the field of new social movement theory, that a new form of feminism—that is, *hip hop feminism*—has risen from the underbelly or entrails of hip hop culture. In addition, none of this should shock and awe any of us when we bear in mind something that Frantz Fanon demonstrated in his discussion of the ways in which violence, exploitation, and oppression often unwittingly give rise to radical, if not outright revolutionary forms of resistance. Men, least of all the men of the Hip Hop Generation, do not have a monopoly on radicalism or revolutionary thought and praxis. Which is also to say, the hyper-masculinism, misogyny, and male supremacy seemingly at the center of commercial hip hop culture has only intensified many young women's decolonial desire(s) to critique and combat patriarchy or, rather, *patriarchal colonialism*. Were we to "flip the script," to use hip hop lingo, and view commercial hip hop as a kind of racially gendered "colonial world" where women are the central radical/revolutionary anticolonial agents and actresses, then Fanon's caveat in *The Wretched of the Earth* (1968) concerning the "colonized's" right to violent resistance—or, rather, resistance "by any means necessary"—is plausibly even more relevant to the discussion at hand:

> The violence which has ruled over the ordering of the colonial world, which has ceaselessly drummed the rhythm for the destruction of native social forms and broken up without reserve the systems of reference of the economy, the customs of dress and external life, that same violence will be claimed and taken over by the native at the moment when, deciding to embody history in his [or her] own person, he [or she] surges into forbidden quarters. To wreck the colonial world is henceforward a mental picture of action which is very clear, very easy to understand, and which may be assumed by each one of the individuals which constitute the colonized people. (40–41)[38]

That is to say, then, that any woman—regardless of her age, race, class, sexual orientation, or religious affiliation—might at any moment come to a kind of critical feminist/womanist consciousness that compels her to "wreck the [racially gendered] colonial world" of hip hop. Fanon's conception of the "wreck" contained within the process of "true decolonization" can be shown to be connected to the concept of "wreck" prevalent in contemporary hip hop feminist discourse (59). For instance, in her groundbreaking book, *Check It While I Wreck It!: Black Womanhood, Hip Hop Culture, and the Public Sphere* (2004), Gwendolyn Pough explained that within hip hop feminist discourse "wreck" is "a hip hop term that connotes fighting, recreation, skill, boasting, or violence. The hip hop concept of wreck sheds new light on the things blacks have had to do in order to obtain and maintain a presence in the larger public sphere, namely fight hard and bring attention to their skill and right to be in the public sphere" (17). By focusing exclusively on the trials and tribulations of African American women within the world of hip hop we are able to more easily see not only how Pough's hip hop feminist conception of wreck connects with Fanon's decolonialist conception of wreck, but also how, much like the wider Eurocentric, bourgeois, and patriarchal U.S. "public sphere," commercial hip hop culture schizophrenically renders black women's bodies and sexuality hyper-visible even as it renders their social and political struggles utterly invisible.

It is a known fact that women within the world of hip hop have had to "fight hard and bring attention to their skill and right to be" included in the world of hip hop—again, a world they undeniably helped to create and continue to cultivate. Their simultaneous struggles both within *and* without the world of hip hop is what distinguishes hip hop women's form of feminism. Pough importantly continued: "Bringing wreck, for black participants in the public sphere historically, has meant reshaping the public gaze in such a way as to be recognized as human beings—as functioning and worthwhile members of society—and not to be shut out of or pushed away from the public sphere" (17). It would seem that here we have come to the heart of hip hop feminism, and this primarily has to do with African American and other nonwhite women's earnest efforts to refashion the "public gaze" of hip hop culture "in such a way as to be recognized as human beings" and "not to be shut out of or pushed away from" the world of hip hop as a consequence of male hip hoppers hyper-masculinism, misogyny, and male supremacy.

Many of the womenfolk Joan Morgan referred to as "old school feminists" have taken issue with hip hop feminists' use of cyber-social networks, mass media, and popular culture, and because hip hop feminists do not use the more tried-and-true grassroots political methods popularized during the Women's Liberation Movement of the 1960s and 1970s. Because of what they perceive to be hip hop feminists' disregard for the "old school" emphasis on integrating academe, many "old school feminists" have further argued that the Hip Hop Women's Movement is basically misconceived and often mealy-mouthed. Others argue, however, that the women of the Hip Hop Generation with feminist sensibilities are actually dialectically deconstructing and reconstructing the wider Eurocentric, bourgeois, and patriarchal U.S. public sphere, as well as cyber-social networks, mass media, and popular culture, in new womanist ways that are simultaneously novel and necessary. Here, then, it will be important for us to briefly examine how the hip hop feminists themselves define or, rather, radically redefine feminism (*and* womanism) to speak to the special needs of their lives and struggles.

Perhaps one of the first major works on rap music and hip hop culture to provocatively broach the subject of hip hop and feminism was Tricia Rose's pioneering book *Black Noise: Rap Music and Black Culture in Contemporary America* (1994). Although the volume does not seem to directly draw from either the Black Arts Movement or Feminist Art Movement, it is interesting to observe that Rose conceives of, and conceptualizes the work of women rappers loosely using a combination of black aesthetic and feminist aesthetic criteria. As with hip hop culture in general, hip hop feminism often only hints at its influences, past and present. However, here we should unambiguously acknowledge its influences, not only to determine what it has inherited from previous sociopolitical and cultural aesthetic movements, but also to ascertain how it has built on and, in many instances, gone beyond its influences and ancestral movements.

Undoubtedly the work of women rappers forces us to reevaluate our criteria for what constitutes feminist or womanist art, but the same could be said (and actually has been said) about the work of many of the major players in the Feminist Art Movement of the 1960s and 1970s, such as Judy Chicago, Faith Ringgold, Sheila Levrant de Bretteville, Susan Lacy, Dara Birnbaum, June Wayne, Nancy Spero, Mary Kelly, Kate Millett, Martha Rosler, Faith Wilding and, later, the Guerrilla Girls. Just as the artist-activists of the Feminist Art Movement sought to expand the range and meaning of the Women's Liberation Movement by offering up alternative articulations of women's loves, lives, and struggles, so too are the artist-activists of the Hip Hop Women's Movement expanding the range and meaning of contemporary feminism and womanism by offering up either new or alternative expressions of turn-of-the-twenty-first-century women's loves, lives, and struggles. In a sense, hip hop feminists represent important elements of a new avant-garde in both hip hop and contemporary feminist aesthetics, theory, and praxis.[39]

Rose's *Black Noise* offers us an early glimpse of how hip hop feminists have blurred the supposed boundaries between hip hop and feminism, and why the Hip Hop Women's Movement is one of the most salient forms of feminism in contemporary U.S. culture and society. However, having said all of this, it is important to remind my readers that even as hip hop studies scholars acknowledge and critically theorize the Hip Hop Women's Movement, most of the womenfolk we are referring to as "hip hop feminists" do not self-identify as feminists and do not subscribe to each and every "feminist" tenet that has been handed down by their womanist/feminist foremothers. As with so many other arenas of hip hop culture, labeling has been left to those who need such sobriquets in order to make sense of what has long been regarded as nonsense.

After identifying three primary themes prevalent in the work of African American women rappers—"heterosexual courtship, the importance of the female voice, and mastery in women's rap and black female public displays of physical and sexual freedom"—Rose (1994, 147, 149) revealed that by the mid-1990s discussions of women rappers had been separated into two inter-related arguments: "(1) women rappers are feminist voices who combat sexism in rap; and/or (2) the sexist exclusion or mischaracterization of women's participation in rap devalues women's significance and must be countered by evidence of women's contributions." Returning to the idea articulated above concerning the contradictory ability of hip hop culture to simultaneously imprison and emancipate women, the facts and fictions of the one-dimensional argument that all or even most male rappers are sexist and all or even most female rappers are antisexist should be debunked without delay.

First, and most obviously, this kind of lazy logic is nothing but another contribution to the long-standing discourse surrounding the "battle of the sexes," and it situates *female-feminist rappers* in unbending binary opposition to *male-misogynist rappers*—which is also to say, this line of logic also sounds like nothing more than a rearticulation of the age-old male/female dichotomy. It could almost go without saying that many female rappers unflinchingly criticize the misogyny in rap music and hip hop culture, but it is completely incorrect to argue that their relationship with male rappers can be best depicted as one that is in absolute opposition to all or even most male rappers. Needless to say, like hip hop itself, many female rappers' critiques of misogynistic rap music frequently have been contradictory and extremely complicated: contradictory, insofar as many female hip hoppers have a love/hate relationship with hip hop, as discussed by Joan Morgan in *When Chickenheads Come Home to Roost* (1999), and, more recently, by Aya de Leon in "Lyrical Self-Defense and the Reluctant Female Rapper" (2007b) and Shawan Worsley in "Loving Hip Hop When It Denies Your Humanity" (2007); and many female rappers' critiques of misogynistic rap music are frequently extremely complicated when and where we come to the fact that many of the most popular female rappers (e.g., Da Brat, Lil' Kim, Foxy Brown, Gangsta Boo, Trina, Jacki-O, Khia, Shawnna, Remy Ma, and Nicki Minaj) often unrepentantly embrace the hyper-sexualized and licentious images of black women endlessly promoted in commercial rap music and hip hop culture.[40]

Second, the monolith of male-misogynist rappers versus female-feminist rappers also unwittingly overlooks the fact that almost all (hetero)sexual discourse at the turn of the twenty-first century could be said to be complex and contradictory; one, perhaps, need not raise the issue of the ever-increasing (heterosexual) divorce rate in the United States. Were we to turn to the ongoing dialogue between male and female rappers surrounding sex, love, and heterosexual relationships, then, we would probably be able to see that not all male rappers' sexual discourse is sexist and, by the same token, not all female rappers' sexual discourse is feminist and/or outright antisexist. Many of the more commercially successful female rappers, such as the aforementioned Lil' Kim, Foxy Brown, Trina, Jacki-O, Khia, and Nicki Minaj, frequently come across as going out of their way to defend male rappers' misogyny, and at times a lot of their own lyrics reflect and, therefore, ratify misogynistic hip hop masculinity, male supremacist conceptions of mothers, wives, and family life, and the socially accepted (i.e., within a patriarchal society) gender roles of men as protectors, providers, adulterous lovers, brothers, fathers, and husbands.

Quiet as it has been kept, just as there have been female rappers—such as MC Lyte, Queen Latifah, Monie Love, Bahamadia, Medusa, Mystic, Jean Grae, Ursula Rucker, and Sarah Jones—who have critiqued misogynistic rap music, there have been male rappers who have taken men to task for delinquent daddyism, domestic violence, rape, pressuring women to have abortions, and not recognizing and respecting the contributions of African American women to African American history, culture, and struggle. Many pro-women rap songs produced by males have sought to celebrate black womanhood, especially black motherhood.[41] To begin with the most obvious examples, male rappers have produced song after song singing the praises of their mothers: from Tupac Shakur's immortal "Dear Mama," to Mos Def's "Umi Says," to Kanye West's "Hey Mama." Examples of male rappers who have critically engaged rape and domestic violence include: A Tribe Called Quest's "Date Rape," De La Soul's "Millie Pulled a Pistol on Santa," Tupac

Shakur's "Brenda's Got A Baby," NaS's "Black Girl Lost," Common's "Between Me, You & Liberation," Immortal Technique's "Dance With The Devil," and Damian Marley's "Pimpa's Paradise." Several male rappers have also, however tongue-in-cheek and crudely, critiqued stripping, pimping, and prostitution, and here Common's "A Film Called Pimp" (featuring MC Lyte), Wyclef Jean's "Perfect Gentleman," the Roots's "Pussy Galore," and Talib Kweli's "Black Girl Pain" quickly come to mind.

Again, hip hop's sexual politics is complex and contradictory and, therefore, it cannot be reduced to the simple male-misogynist rappers versus female-feminist rappers, or vice versa. Indeed, there is a need to critique the hyper-masculine histories of hip hop that either exclude, co-opt, or devalue women's contributions, but even as we undertake these critiques it is important for us not to negate the contributions of male hip hoppers who have questioned, critiqued, and condemned misogynistic rap music in specific, and hip hop's sexism in general. Additionally, it is equally important for us not to overlook the fact that although, in *Black Studies, Rap, and the Academy* (1993), Houston Baker would have us believe that hip hop culture emerged in the late 1970s and early 1980s as a "resentment of disco culture and a reassertion of black manhood," African American women were undeniably at the heart of hip hop's inauguration and early evolution and it can just as easily be viewed as a new expression of African American womanhood in the aftermath of the Black Women's Liberation Movement and its cultural aesthetic corollary the Black Feminist Art Movement (86).

In arguing that rap music is a "reassertion of black manhood," Baker's analysis collapses rap music into an expression of black masculinity and, in some ways, closes the door to the possibility that it could also be viewed as *an expression of African American women's new-fangled, post-soul, post-funk, post-disco, and post-electro femininity*. What is more, Baker seems to sidestep the notion that rap music specifically, and hip hop culture more generally, could actually represent a transgender forum where African American males *and* females voice their criticisms and put forward their visions of healthy and unhealthy relationships (e.g., intimate, interpersonal, intracommunal, and intercommunal relationships). By turning African American women's actual presence in the emergence of rap music into an absence, in this specific instance the otherwise gender progressive Baker contributes to the age-old male/female dichotomy and negates not only African American women's contributions to the origins and early evolution of rap music and hip hop culture, but he also erases the ways in which female rappers and female hip hop fans might profit and derive pleasure from their participation in rap music and hip hop culture on their own hip hop feminist/womanist terms—à la the African American women artist-activists who participated in both the Black Arts Movement and the Feminist Art Movement.[42]

Although many consider rap the major musical expression of the Hip Hop Movement, just as we did with rock & roll in relationship to the Civil Rights Movement in the previous "remix," it is important for us not to overlook neo-soul as a second major soundtrack for the Hip Hop Movement. Distinguished from the doldrums of digitized 1980s and 1990s rhythm & blues by its incorporation of live instrumentation, as well as elements of rap, jazz, fusion, funk, go-go, gospel, rock, reggae, and various African musics, neo-soul represents a soul music revival movement. As implied by its name (i.e., literally "new soul"), neo-soul music is basically *new century soul music or, rather, twenty-first-century music for the soul*, with undeniable hip hop sensibilities.[43]

In other words, neo-soul is a heterogeneous and hybrid musical form that recenters the autobiographical and sociopolitical singer-songwriter style of classic soul. Consequently, many of its critics have stressed that it has a greater emphasis on lyrical content or "socially conscious" lyrics when compared with the apolitical and pedestrian character of most contemporary rhythm & blues. Also, neo-soul is known to be a concept album-oriented genre that, by establishing and amplifying lyrical and musical recurring themes throughout the course of an album, directly draws from the more "organic" and acoustic musical innovations and production techniques of classic soul music (e.g., Nina Simone's *Wild Is The Wind* [1966], *High Priestess of Soul* [1966], and *Nina Simone Sings the Blues* [1967]; Roberta Flack's *First Take* [1969], *Chapter Two* [1970], *Quiet Fire* [1971], and *Killing Me Softly* [1973]; Curtis Mayfield's *Curtis* [1970], *Roots* [1971], and *Superfly* [1972]; Isaac Hayes's *To Be Continued* [1970], *The Isaac Hayes Movement* [1970], and *Black Moses* [1971]; Bill Withers's *Just As I Am* [1971], *Still Bill* [1972], and *+'Justments* [1974]; Marvin Gaye's *What's Going On?* [1971], *Let's Get It On* [1973], *I Want You* [1976], and the criminally underappreciated *Here, My Dear* [1978]; Smokey Robinson's *Smokey* [1973], *Pure Smokey* [1974], and *A Quite Storm* [1975]; and, finally, Philadelphia International Records's 1970s album catalog almost in its entirety). Neo-soul's concept album orientation is, of course, in stark contrast to most contemporary rhythm & blues, which is a more hit song-oriented genre based on catchy "hooks" (i.e., choruses), cameos from commercial rappers, computerized music, live music samples, and the pop-oriented super-polished sound of a recognized production team.

In an age of hyper-computerized and hyper-commercialized music, neo-soul artists' emphasis on an acoustic "band sound" and message-oriented music offers a much-needed alternative, not only to contemporary rhythm & blues, but also to the blandness of commercial rap. Frequently characterized as "musical bohemians" because their work draws from such a wide range of musical genres (and not all of them distinctly African American musical genres), *Time* magazine writer Christopher John Farley (1998) went so far as

to say that neo-soul artists, such as Lauryn Hill, D'Angelo, Erykah Badu, and
Maxwell, "share a willingness to challenge musical orthodoxy" during an era
(i.e., 1990–2000) dominated by the rise of gangsta rap and hard-core hip hop
culture. Putting forward a provocative working-definition of neo-soul, Farley
wrote further:

> Simply defined, neo-soul describes artists—like song-stylist Erykah Badu—
> who combine a palpable respect for and understanding of the classic soul of
> the '60s and '70s with a healthy appetite for '90s sonic experimentation and
> boundary-crossing. Neo-soul artists tend to create music that's a good deal
> more real, a good deal more edgy than the packaged pop of, say, teen-oriented
> groups like the Spice Girls and Cleopatra. And they tend to write lyrics that are
> more oblique and yet more socially and emotionally relevant than those of
> gangsta rappers. (1)

Farley's work is extremely important in terms of the discussion at hand
because his now "classic" *Time* article candidly captured the musical conceptions of several pioneering neo-soul artists in their own words and at the
height of their popularity in the late 1990s. For instance, directly commenting on how she sought to both develop as an artist and break down barriers
within the world of hip hop, Lauryn Hill said: "Sometimes it's hard to really
make any statements when you know that the industry caters to hit singles
rather than to developing artists," but "I definitely felt like I wanted to push
the envelope of hip hop. It was very important to me that the music be very
raw . . . and there be a lot of live instrumentation."

Echoing Hill, Maxwell criticized the music industry's condescending attitude toward consumers and explicitly stated that he intends his music to be
an alternative to both contemporary rhythm & blues and commercial rap,
remarking: "I think people are a lot smarter than they are credited for being. I
like to challenge what some people think most people will accept and listen
to, particularly African Americans and particularly in the R&B genre. To me,
it's important to reflect the alternative."

And, finally, similar to Hill and Maxwell, D'Angelo likewise emphasized
artistic integrity and musical innovation over all that "synthetic stuff" (his
words), forcefully contending: "The mid-to-late '60s was the golden age of
soul and funk. It wasn't like now, where you have one producer working for
a slew of artists, who all sound the same. Artists are no longer self-contained
and are more prone to conform. In the '60s, people were defying what people
expected. That's what's missing now" (2).

In a sense, then, neo-soul seeks to offer alternatives to and highlight
"what's missing now" in contemporary rhythm & blues and commercial rap
music: edifying message-oriented music, gospel-influenced vocalizations,
acoustic instrumentation, sonic experimentation, unbridled improvisation,
and so forth. Consciously going against the musical grain, neo-soul artists'

work is situated at the crossroads where the black musical past meets the African American (and multicultural) musical present. Which is also to say, although rap music is regularly in the musical limelight and receives more media attention, much of the future of African American music may very well rest on the musical innovations and sonic experimentations of neo-soul artists, who have calmly and quietly become (along with alternative, underground, and political rappers) the conscience, even if not the "official" voices, of the Hip Hop Movement. Where commercial rap music seems to have reached the point where it has begun to incessantly recycle itself (i.e., rhyme after rhyme revolving around money, sex, drinking, drugs, and clubs), neo-soul's sonic experimentations have seemed to grow bolder and bolder with each new album.

Of course, not all of the sonic experiments of neo-soul result in authentic musical innovations, but its fan base remains loyal and seems to greatly appreciate the restless spirit of the genre. In comparing neo-soul with contemporary rhythm & blues, it could be easily argued that by the 1980s and 1990s most rhythm & blues seems to have degenerated into the super-polished computerized and sonic seduction productions of high profile producers and powerful, pop-oriented record companies. Consequently, the uplifting and enlightening messages in classic rhythm & blues, rock & roll, soul, and funk music, not to mention musicianship in general, began to seriously decline, if not disappear altogether for a time. As the noted *Vibe* magazine music critic Dimitri Ehrlich (2002) succinctly observed:

> By definition, neo-soul is a paradox. "Neo" means new. Soul is timeless. All the neo-soul artists, in various ways, perform balancing acts, exploring classic soul idioms while injecting a living, breathing presence into time-tested formulas. They humanize R&B, which has often been reduced to a factory-perfected product. Like sushi, neo-soul is fresh enough to be served raw. (72)

In response to the flash and splash of 1990s and early 2000s digitized rhythm & blues, neo-soul put forward "raw" messages more relevant to the soul of the Hip Hop Movement, especially black ghetto youth and other working-poor nonwhite youth. Indeed, commercial rap music might capture the quasi-political, sexual, and recreational impulses of the Hip Hop Movement, but it was left to neo-soul music to articulate hip hoppers' conceptions of love—and here my research has revealed that as a genre neo-soul music amazingly embodies all five major forms of love (at least as the ancient Greeks conceived of them): *epithumia* (deep desire/passionate longing/lust); *eros* (romantic/sexual love); *storge* (familial love); *phile* (friendship/platonic love); and *agape* (selfless/unconditional love). Therefore, in neo-soul—in contradistinction to the blah-blah-blah and blandness of most contemporary rhythm & blues—love is conceptualized as something that extends well beyond intimate or sexual relationships (i.e., *epithumia*). Neo-soul artists frequently sing about and celebrate *black life, black love, black culture, and the black community*. Following in the musical footsteps of classic soul artists, such as Ray Charles, Etta James, Curtis Mayfield, Aretha Franklin, James Brown, Nina Simone, Smokey Robinson, Otis Redding, Carla Thomas, Bill Withers, Roberta Flack, Donnie Hathaway, Marvin Gaye, Stevie Wonder, Gladys Knight, Al Green, Ann Peebles, Bobby Womack, and the Staple Singers, neo-soul artists do not privilege black sexuality over black spirituality.

Many neo-soul artists are also known to be musical innovators who, from my point of view, represent synthesized elements of the bohemian undergrounds of both contemporary rhythm & blues and rap. Their work, literally, offers more meaningful and deeper messages than contemporary rhythm & blues, and expands the range and meaning of hip hop beyond commercial rap music. In *Songs in the Key of Black Life: A Rhythm and Blues Nation*, Mark Anthony Neal (2003) echoed Ehrlich's above assertion concerning neo-soul being a "paradox" and "perform[ing] balancing acts, exploring classic soul idioms while injecting a living, breathing presence into time-tested formulas," when he asserted:

> Though neo-soul and its various incarnations have helped to redefine the boundaries and contours of black pop, often the most popular of these recordings, like Maxwell's *Urban Hang Suite*, India.Arie's *Acoustic Soul*, and Musiq Soulchild's *Aijuswanaseing*, exist comfortably alongside the trite blah, blah, blah of the 112s and Destiny's Childs of the world. Just a small reminder that "difference" is often valued only when it smells, tastes, and sounds like the same old same old. And even when artists break the mold, as Maxwell did with *Urban Hang Suite* and D'Angelo did with *Brown Sugar*, they are expected to remain true to that formula lest they risk the critical backlash that Maxwell and D'Angelo faced in the aftermath of artistically compelling projects like *Embrya* (1998) and *Voodoo* (2000), respectively. The bottom line is that contemporary R&B and the radio and video programmers responsible for making that music available to listeners and viewers remain trapped in a small black box largely informed by hip hop bottoms and Blige-like histrionics with small traces of Luther and Whitney and enough tone deafness to have Clara Ward, Mahalia Jackson, and Sam Cooke turn twice in their graves about every four and a half minutes. . . . With such a small margin to work with, the seminal hybrid-soul of Lenny Kravitz, the Family Stand, Seal, Corey Glover, Meshell Ndegeocello, Dionne Farris, Michael Franti (both the Disposable Heroes and Spearhead versions), and even Wyclef Jean has been consistently marginalized save an occasional MTV buzz clip and the hordes of "pomobohos" like myself who continue to crave great "black" music even if it don't sound like Marvin Gaye or Aretha Franklin. (117–18)

Neal's comment that neo-soul's "'difference' is often valued only when it smells, tastes, and sounds like the same old same old" should be accented, as it helps to highlight how even as neo-soul seeks to offer alternatives to contemporary rhythm & blues and commercial rap it, too, has been musically colonized and quarantined to a sphere of sonically and socially acceptable "difference" (and, dare I go even further to say, "blackness"). This, of course, makes one wonder how much more "different" or "bohemian" could or would neo-soul be were it not for the incessant pressures placed on neo-soul artists to appeal to the orthodoxy and political economy of a music industry dominated by the excesses and vulgarities of commercial rap? The free expression found in so much classic soul music is often buried beneath a barrage of musical fodder awkwardly aimed at placing neo-soul artists' work within the realm of either contemporary rhythm & blues or commercial rap. Rarely, if ever, is neo-soul appreciated on its own terms—terms which can be easily traced back to the black aesthetic and the classic soul music of the 1960s and 1970s. This is all very problematic for several reasons, but here I would like to emphasize how it ironically also offers a marginalized musical abode where the women of the Hip Hop Movement have been able to create a body of work that offers up black feminist and womanist answers to many of the Hip Hop Movement's most urgent interpersonal, spiritual, cultural, social, and political issues.

THE HIP HOP WOMEN'S MOVEMENT AND ITS WOMEN-CENTERED NEO-SOUL SOUNDTRACK: MOVING BEYOND MALE-CENTERED RAP MUSIC AND HIP HOP CULTURE

Where women have come to be misogynistically marginalized within the rap genre, they have been ever-present and undeniably at the center of the Neo-Soul Movement. Indeed, by centering their discussions almost exclusively on rap music over the past thirty years or so, most hip hop cultural critics have put into play a subtle, and sometimes not-so-subtle, form of sexism that, in keeping with patriarchy, privileges the more male-centered musical genre (i.e., rap) over the more female-centered musical genre (i.e., neo-soul). Moreover, even if one disagrees that neo-soul seems to be more female-centered (especially considering the popularity of neo-soul Romeos, such as D'Angelo, Maxwell, Musiq Soulchild, Rahsaan Patterson, Anthony Hamilton, Donnie, Raheem DeVaughn, Raphael Saadiq, Van Hunt, John Legend, Bilal, Dwele, Eric Benét, Calvin Richardson, Lyfe Jennings, Anthony David, Martin Luther, and Jesse Boykins III), at the very least, a convincing case could be made that it is far more female-friendly when compared with commercial rap. The unprecedented accomplishments of several neo-soul divas—such as Lalah Hathaway, Mary J. Blige, Des'ree, Angie Stone, Lauryn Hill, Erykah Badu, Les Nubians, India.Arie, Jill Scott, Macy Gray, Amel Larrieux, Conya Doss, Sunshine Anderson, Syleena Johnson, Jaguar Wright, Georgia Anne Muldrow, Alicia Keys, Floetry, Marsha Ambrosius, N'dambi,

Nneka, Estelle, Chrisette Michele, Ledisi, Goapele, Corinne Bailey Rae, Ayo, Malia, Leela James, Hil St. Soul, and Janelle Monáe—lends even more credence to this line of logic.

While it may very well be the case that none of the aforementioned neo-soul divas considers their work "feminist" or "womanist," and certainly not in the often arcane sense in which these terms are currently hurled around the American academy, it is still important for us to acknowledge that collectively their work (1) significantly contributes to hip hop culture and the over-arching Hip Hop Movement; (2) exposes hip hop men and non-hip hop men and women to many of the central issues impacting hip hop women's lives; and (3) indeed does unapologetically critique and offer viable alternatives to rap music and hip hop culture's hyper-masculinism, misogyny, and male supremacy. Again, they may not use fly feminist theory terms, such as "patriarchy," "hyper-masculinism," "misogyny," and "male supremacy" in their songs and interviews, but if one listens to and really hears both the romantic *and* political messages in their music it is almost impossible to argue that the neo-soul sisters of the Hip Hop Movement have not critiqued and combated commercial rap's hyper-masculinism, misogyny, and male supremacy. Recall, classic soul queens frequently used their music to counter the high levels of testosterone, hyper-masculinism, misogyny, and male supremacy in rhythm & blues, rock & roll, soul, and funk in the 1960s and 1970s.

Hyper-masculinist interpretations of hip hop have been regarded as the rule for quite some time, but here I would like to touch on one of the more egregious examples to briefly give my readers a sense of what most of the lopsided and lame male-centered analyses of rap music and hip hop culture look and sound like. Making Houston Baker's lapse into the age-old male/female dichotomy above almost seem miniscule, in *Hip Hop America* (1999) none other than noted music critic Nelson George infamously wrote:

> Hip hop has produced no Bessie Smith, no Billie Holiday, no Aretha Franklin. You could make an argument that Queen Latifah has, as a symbol of female empowerment, filled Aretha's shoes for rap, though for artistic impact Latifah doesn't compare to the Queen of Soul. Similarly, you can make a case that Salt-N-Pepa's four platinum albums and clean-cut sexuality mirror the Supremes' pop appeal, though neither of the two MCs or their beautiful DJ Spinderella is ever gonna be Diana Ross. In twenty-plus years of hip hop history on record, a period that has produced black vocalists Chaka Khan, Whitney Houston, Anita Baker, Tracy Chapman, Mary J. Blige, and Erykah Badu, there are no women who have contributed profoundly to rap's artistic growth. Aside from Latifah and Salt-N-Pepa, MC Lyte has recorded for over a decade and Yo-Yo has garnered some respect. So has longtime spinner and mixtape star DJ Jazzy Joyce. In the late '90s Foxy Brown and Lil' Kim have proven that raw language and sex sells, but no one is mistaking them for innovators. (184; see also George 1989)

When George wrote, "there are no women who have contributed profoundly to rap's artistic growth" and, concerning those he deems the most noteworthy female rappers, "no one is mistaking them for innovators," one wonders what criteria he used to measure whether these female rappers have "contributed profoundly to rap's artistic growth." Let's "keep it real" here, as we say within the hip hop community. It ain't like measuring aesthetic contributions is some sort of exact, empirical science. This, of course, gives us grounds to critically call into question George's "hip hop aesthetic," which seems to be completely oblivious to the black feminist aesthetic and the womanist art world.

George dropped the names of several female rappers, but, as we witnessed in the quote above, he claimed that none of them have significantly impacted "rap's artistic growth." This is primarily so, according to George, because "[t]here is an adolescent quality to hip hop culture that makes it clear that most of its expressions are aimed to please teenage boys, and this usually excludes women from the dialogue. The dynamics of *adult* relationships are the backbone of blues and soul music, in which both women and men tell stories of love, hate, infidelity, and lust," whereas hip hop's "typical narrator is a young, angry, horny male who is often disdainful of or, at least, uninterested in commitments of any kind." In fact, he continued, for most of hip hop's history, "it has been a truism that the male rap consumer, white and black, simply won't accept female rappers" (185, emphasis in original). What is truly amazing here, however, is the fact that George does not in anyway critically interrogate the reasons why female rappers are "exclude[d] . . . from the dialogue" and why "the male rap consumer, white and black, simply won't accept female rappers."

By not critically interrogating the reasons why female rappers are "exclude[d] . . . from the dialogue," isn't George himself continuing to quarantine them to a space outside of the world of rap music, thus silencing or, at the least, significantly disparaging female rappers and their contributions to rap music and hip hop culture? Building on the women-centered soul aesthetic bequeathed by the classic soul queens to hip hop women, here instead of simply observing rap music and hip hop culture's gender problems (e.g., the misogyny of both male rappers *and* male rap consumers) couldn't we offer a solution by suggesting a *hip hop feminist aesthetic* (or, rather, *hip hop womanist aesthetic*)? As someone who has been listening to rap music and an avid student of hip hop culture since I first heard "Rapper's Delight" blast out of my older brother's boom box speakers on a basketball court in 1979, it would seem to me that although it has often gone unacknowledged and, therefore unnamed, a "hip hop feminist aesthetic" indeed has historically and currently continues to exist and, as a matter of fact, it stretches all the way back to the origins and early evolution of rap music and hip hop culture.

Even if the current "male rap consumer, white and black, simply won't accept female rappers," it does not mean that male rappers and male rap consumers have not previously—especially before rap music's mid-1980s crossover success—accepted and respected the skills and contributions of female rappers. How else can we explain female MCs' (or the inclusion of female MCs on so many) early hit rap records (in fact, "rap classics!"), for instance: Paulette Tee and Sweet Tee, "Vicious Rap" (1978) and "Rhymin' and Rappin'" (1979); Lady B, "To the Beat Y'All!" (1979); Funky 4+1 More (featuring Sha Rock), "Rappin' and Rockin'" (1979), "That's the Joint!" (1981), "Do You Want to Rock (Before I Let You Go)?" (1982), and "Feel It!" (1984); Afrika Bambaataa & the Cosmic Force (featuring Lisa Lee), "Zulu Nation Throwdown!" (1980); Blondie, "Rapture" (1981); Sylvia, "It's Good to Be the Queen" (1982); Us Girls (featuring Sha Rock, Lisa Lee, and Debbie Dee), "Us Girls" (1984); and, of course, the Sequence, "Funk You Up!" (1979), "Monster Jam" (1980), "And You Know That" (1980), "Funky Sound" (1981), "Simon Says" (1982), "I Don't Need Your Love" (1982), "Here Comes the Bride" (1982), "I Just Want to Know" (1983), "Funk You Up '85" (1984), and "Control" (1985)?

However, even as we discuss the existence of a hip hop feminist aesthetic and the conventional hyper-masculine histories of rap music and hip hop culture, female rappers' vexed rejection of the term "feminist" must be raised, as it sheds more light on hip hop's contradictory and complex character. For example, in *Black Noise* (1994), Tricia Rose wrote, "during my conversation with Salt, MC Lyte, and Queen Latifah it became clear that these women were uncomfortable with being labeled feminist and perceived feminism as a signifier for a movement that related specifically to white women," which—as I discussed in *Hip Hop's Inheritance*—eerily echoes the views of many members of the Black Women's Liberation Movement in the 1960s and 1970s (176). Rose further explained, "[t]hey also thought feminism involved adopting an antimale position, and although they clearly express frustrations with men, they did not want to be considered or want their work to be interpreted as antiblack male" (176).

As it was with the women of the Black Women's Club Movement at the turn of the twentieth century and the members of the Black Women's Liberation Movement during the 1960s and 1970s, most African American female rappers have a filial connection with African American men that stems from their shared experience of antiblack racism, economic exploitation, and cultural colonization. We should be clear here, as Rose pointed out, black women "clearly express frustrations with [black] men," but—to paraphrase Frantz Fanon in *Black Skin, White Masks* (1967)—it is the "lived-experience of the black" or, rather, the "fact of [their] blackness" in a simultaneously white *and* male supremacist capitalist society that has brought generation after generation of black women to the confounding conclusion that black men's sufferings as a result of antiblack racism (from the African Holocaust and the Middle Passage to racial colonialism and enslavement, through to twenty-first-century segregation and ongoing American apartheid) binds them to black men ideally as allies and comrades in struggle. This, of course, is also a sentiment that has been routinely echoed in the love and protest songs of virtually all of the neo-soul divas.

For many black women siding with black men in antiracist struggle, even though many antiracist black men are yet and still sexist, is like reluctantly choosing between the lesser of two evils. Black feminist foremothers have handed down invaluable lessons concerning multicultural and transcultural feminist/womanist alliances: from the memoirs of Black Women's Club Movement pioneers, such as Ida B. Wells (1969, 1970, 1991, 1993, 1995) and Mary Church Terrell (1932, 1940), to the history-making theory and praxis of the Black Women's Liberation Movement arguably best embodied in the work of SNCC's Black Women's Liberation Committee, which broke away from SNCC in 1968 to form an independent group initially named the Black Women's Alliance and later the Third World Women's Alliance (1968–1980); the National Black Feminist Organization (1973–1975); the National Alliance of Black Feminists (1976–1980); the Combahee River Collective (1975–1980); and, lastly, Black Women Organized for Action (1973–1980). Moreover, the recurring theme of denial and betrayal, which has long been at the heart of black feminist writings, whether that denial and betrayal is at the hands of black men or white women (or both), continues to haunt the Hip Hop Women's Movement. Which is to say, a similar suspicion characterizes female rappers, neo-soul sisters, and other hip hop women's perception of and fractured relationships with feminism. Rose (1994, 177) intrepidly asserted:

> For these women rappers, and many other black women, feminism is the label for members of a white women's social movement that has no concrete link to black women or the black community. Feminism signifies allegiance to historically specific movements whose histories have long been the source of frustration for women of color. Similar criticisms of women's social movements have been made vociferously by many black feminists. As they have argued, race and gender are inextricably linked for black women. This is the case for both black and white women. However, in the case of black women, the realities of racism link black women to black men in a way that challenges cross-racial sisterhood. Sisterhood among and between black and white women will not be achieved at the expense of black women's racial identity.

As was witnessed above, most black women historically have been just as committed to women's liberation as white feminists. However, it has been their lived-experience of white women's "feminist racism" that has caused them to consistently recoil from Eurocentric and bourgeois white women-

Remix 3

centered conceptions of feminism and women's liberation. African American women should not be expected to embrace a form of feminism or a women's movement that is rhetorically aimed at their liberation while in reality it contributes to and continues their racial oppression, economic exploitation, and cultural colonization. Herein lies the frequently commented on frustration and terse tension between black and white feminists, as well as the reason why the vapid male-misogynist rappers versus female-feminist rappers, or vice versa, is quite simply not applicable to the Hip Hop Women's Movement. To speak here specifically about black women rappers, it is important to observe the recurring themes of black identity and black unity that runs throughout most of their music. This means, then, if many of them perceive feminism to be antiblack male, it stands to reason that feminism is not seen as a viable option for black women or contemporary black liberation.

African American women rappers are not simply in dialogue with the women of the Hip Hop Movement. They are also in dialogue with the men of the Hip Hop Movement, and it is their shared lived-experience and shared lived-endurance of antiblack racism, antiblack economic exploitation, and antiblack cultural colonization, which they suffer along with black men, that makes them simultaneously critical of black men's misogyny, but also sympathetic to and appreciative of black men's ongoing efforts to combat antiblack racism, antiblack economic exploitation, and antiblack cultural colonization. Joan Morgan, in *When Chickenheads Come Home to Roost: A Hip Hop Feminist Breaks It Down* (1999), brilliantly articulated the seemingly inexplicable relationship between black women, feminism, and black men:

> White girls don't call their men "brothers" and that made their struggle enviably simpler than mine. Racism and the will to survive it creates a sense of intra-racial loyalty that makes it impossible for black women to turn our backs on black men—even in their ugliest and most sexist of moments. I needed a feminism that would allow us to continue loving ourselves *and* the brothers who hurt us without letting race loyalty buy us early tombstones. (36, emphasis in original)

Like generation after generation of black women before them, hip hop feminists find themselves in a situation where they understand it to be "impossible for black women to turn our backs on black men." Consequently, it will never be enough for black and other nonwhite women to desegregate white feminist discourse or, furthermore, for white feminists to finally (and paternalistically) allow *the racially gendered other* to speak. Much more, a systematic deconstruction and reconstruction of feminism and women's liberation should be carried out and, even more specifically, one that takes into serious consideration the ways in which race, culture, class, religion, sexuality, and nationality discursively destabilize gender as a putatively autonomous analytical category within women's life-worlds and life-struggles.

Noted hip hop feminist Heather Humann (2007) went so far as to say, "[a]lthough women's rights are undoubtedly important, a point of view that *only* considers gender can become problematic, because it mistakenly pits women against men instead of realizing that the system itself is flawed and encourages exploitation and oppression of large numbers of people" (101–2, emphasis in original). The emergence of intersectional studies (especially the critique of the ways in which race, gender, class, spirituality, and sexuality overlap and intermesh) during the late 1970s, 1980s, and 1990s must be taken into consideration here, or else it will be very difficult to comprehend hip hop feminism and the overarching Hip Hop Women's Movement. In other words, hip hop feminists critically comprehend that mass media interpretations of hip hop, as well as the mass media's widely disseminated distorted stories about hip hop, are actually part and parcel of *the ongoing social construction and maintenance of mainstream Eurocentric, bourgeois, and patriarchal racial, gender, class, religious, sexual, and national, among other, identities.*

All of this is to say, *hip hop feminism is much more than feminism, and it focuses on more than feminist issues, misogyny, and patriarchy.* Hip hop feminists use hip hop culture as one of their primary points of departure to highlight serious social issues and the need for political activism aimed at eradicating racism, sexism, capitalism, and heterosexism as overlapping and interlocking systems of oppression. In this sense, then, hip hop feminism displays the influence of not only feminism, but several of the new theories that have emerged within the last three decades and, even more, it arguably represents the most visible recent reminder that for feminism to really find footing in the twenty-first century and truly speak to the special needs of the women of the Hip Hop Movement it will have to epistemically open itself to the theoretical and practical advances of several of the new theories and praxes that have emerged in the aftermath of the various progressive movements of the 1960s and 1970s. For example, some of the new theories that hip hop feminism has regularly drawn from and critically dialogued with include: womanist theory, mestiza consciousness theory, critical race theory, critical race feminist theory, Africana critical theory, postcolonial theory, subaltern theory, queer theory, transnationalism, democratic socialism, and black Marxism.

Hip hop feminism is not only critical of white women-centered feminism, but also *super-strong black women-centered feminism.* Discursively building on Michele Wallace's classic *Black Macho and the Myth of the Superwoman* (1979), Joan Morgan's (1999) work helps to highlight hip hop feminists' repudiation of the myth of the super-strong, self-sacrificing, and long-suffering black woman (83–112; see also James and Busia 1993). As was the case with the members of the Black Women's Liberation Movement of the 1960s and 1970s, hip hop feminists are much less likely to embrace the myth of the super-strong black woman. In fact, hip hop feminists are highly critical of those black and other nonwhite women who resist the notion that, in so many words, the "personal is political," insofar as those women who demur and refuse to give full and uninhibited voice to their needs and deep desires, their strengths and weaknesses not only perpetuate the myth of the super-strong, self-sacrificing, and long-suffering black woman, but they also impede black women's liberation and authentic African American emancipation.

In their own way, hip hop feminists seem to be asking the very same question that so many of their foremothers in the Black Women's Club Movement and Black Women's Liberation Movement asked: Can authentic black liberation be achieved if black women, who roughly constitute half of the black folk in the United States, remain enslaved and imprisoned as a result of patriarchal gender roles and racially gendered social rules? To state it outright: black women's liberation is (or, rather, *should be*) an integral part of authentic African American emancipation. African Americans cannot and will not achieve true decolonization and lasting human liberation if black women are not freed from gender domination and discrimination in the midst of the overarching struggle for racial, social, and economic justice in the United States.

In the United States patriarchy is predicated on masculinist popular culture as much as it is on male-centered politics, economics, and social conventions, and this is one of the reasons hip hop feminists find it necessary to carry out their critiques within the wider world of mass media and popular culture.[44] However, and this is where the "old school feminists'" concerns critically come into play, it is quite often difficult to discern whether hip hop feminists in particular, and the women of the Hip Hop Generation in general, are creating a new form of feminism and a new wing of the Women's Liberation Movement to meet the novel needs of their generation, or simply being insidiously entertained by sexism's new, even more seductive, twenty-first-century soundtrack. Within the world of hip hop many hip hoppers, female and male, with feminist sensibilities and antisexist politics live anguished existences, torn between the latest hip hop fad and radical antiracist feminism. Many of us (myself included, to speak candidly) are guilty of being enamored with hip hop artists and their commercial and/or alternative cultural products, avowing the power, beauty, and—with a yelping "yeah!"—the ugliness of their poetry and artistry each and every time we mouth the wise/wack words of their rhymes, mimic their seductive dances moves, and bounce with abandon to their bodacious beats. It is as if we know but wanna hide the fact from ourselves that we have embraced a form of *hip hop bad faith*, because all of the murder-mouthing, mean-mugging, and rotund rump-shaking in contemporary hip hop culture regularly reminds us that no matter how hype hip hop used to be, no matter how it may have raised our consciousness and made us aware of important social and political issues in the past, now it frequently leaves us numb and desensitized to the pain and suffering of the present—and, especially, the pain and suffering of the women and girls of the Hip Hop Generation.

I will openly admit that I have long been offended by the insults and indifference of most of what is taken to be hip hop in the world of popular music and popular culture. However, even as I write all of this I manage to steer clear of a deep depression in light of the fact that at this very moment I am in the process of deconstructing and reconstructing hip hop culture. I refuse to be imprisoned by the distorted and disturbing images of what it means to be a relatively young man who loves and is inspired by hip hop culture. There quite simply is no eleventh commandment that has been handed down that says that all males who are hip hoppers must be hyper-masculinist, misogynist, and/or male supremacist. Instead of leading the youth to mindlessly adopt the most misogynistic thought and behavior available, "real hip hop," what is commonly called "conscious" and/or "alternative" hip hop, can cause hip hoppers to call into question unjust social conventions, conservative politics, and the carpetbagger nature of corporate capitalism. What is more, when and where we agree that conscious hip hop has and continues to raise our awareness about pressing issues is precisely when and where we acknowledge that hip hop has the ability to highlight, critique, and disrupt power relations. Within the world of intersectional theory and praxis, power relations are not simply predicated on race and class, but gender and sexuality also play a pivotal role here, and this is where feminism and sexuality studies importantly come into play.

A simultaneously intersectional and interdisciplinary critical theory of hip hop culture highlights the multidimensionality and polyvocality of hip hop identities and, it should be emphasized, hip hop identities are as racially gendered as any other social and/or cultural identity in the United States. Consequently, hip hop feminism focuses on and forces hip hoppers to acknowledge the racially gendered discursive formations and discursive practices of hip hop culture, as well as the wider social, political, and cultural world. Which is to say, hip hoppers' conceptions of manhood and womanhood or, rather, masculinity and femininity did not miraculously fall from the sky, and an intersectional and interdisciplinary critical theory of hip hop culture enables hip hoppers to cogently connect the dots between preexisting race, gender, class, and sexual orientation oppression and their current forms within the world of hip hop. Instead of viewing hip hop as nothing more than another site where a simultaneously patriarchal and "pathological" culture distracts young women (and men) from feminist theory and praxis, hip hop feminism "wrecks" patriarchal power relations in hip hop by juxtaposing

commercial and conscious hip hop and the ways in which women are represented and/or misrepresented in both.

Of course, there are few if any authentic feminist spaces within the world
of popular culture in patriarchal societies, but for hip hop feminists this is all
beside the point. The point is to offer the women and girls of the Hip Hop
Generation feminist and womanist alternatives to the patriarchal
(mis)representations of womanhood and girlhood incessantly spewing out of
the U.S. culture industries. As Gwendolyn Pough (2004, 74) pointed out,
because hip hop's sexism is so prevalent, and because there is only so long
that the women and girls of the Hip Hop Generation can embrace either the
super-strong black woman or video vixen identities, hip hop feminists have
"found ways to deal with these issues within the larger public sphere and the
counter-public sphere of hip hop by bringing wreck to stereotyped images
through their continued use of expressive culture."[45]

Patriarchs do not now and have never had a monopoly on popular or
expressive culture, and the hip hop feminists "flip the script" by using hip
hop culture as a medium to raise awareness about women's life-worlds and
life-struggles. By critically studying and participating in hip hop culture, hip
hop feminists bring their intimate knowledge of hip hop to bear on the ways
in which patriarchy plays itself out within the world of hip hop and the wider
social, political, and cultural world. Contradictory and controversial, in the
final analysis hip hop feminism challenges both hip hop *and* feminism, and
the work of the hip hop feminists discussed above, among others, offers
positive proof that U.S. feminism is not now and never has been the prime
property or exclusive domain of middle-class white or college-educated
women. In both the past and the present, women's rights and women's liberation movements in the United States have been built and maintained by
women from a wide range of backgrounds who comprehend feminist theory
to be an indispensable tool (albeit often inadequate when it comes to the
critique of racism, capitalism, and heterosexism) in their efforts to critically
understand and explain their lived-experiences with, and lived-endurances of
misogyny and patriarchy.

As was the case with the members of the Black Women's Liberation
Movement of the 1960s and 1970s, most black women continue to reject
bourgeois and white women-centered conceptions of feminism that, from
black women's point of view, have absorbed several of the signatures of
American society, such as Jeffersonian individualism, Jacksonian democracy, bourgeois materialism, allusive antiblack racism, and hedonism. As a
strain of feminist theory and praxis primarily inspired by past nonwhite
women's antiracist and anticapitalist feminism, hip hop feminism can be said
to offer both a critique of and a corrective for contemporary conceptions and
articulations of U.S. feminism. It must be openly admitted, however, because
the women of the Hip Hop Generation are also members of U.S. society,

similar to many of the feminists who have gone before them, they too have been influenced by and often embrace Eurocentric, patriarchal, bourgeois, and hetero-normative views and values—hence, my above characterization of hip hop feminism as "contradictory and controversial." With one foot in hip hop culture and one foot in feminism, even as hip hop feminism endeavors to critique hip hop *and* feminism it often shows itself to be culturally and conceptually incarcerated: critical of hip hop, yet basking in its boldness, and critical of "old school feminism," yet extremely appreciative (and often in awe) of its audacious commitment to women's rights, women's decolonization, and women's liberation.

Truth be told, most nonwhite youth have been socialized to want the "American dream" (i.e., a "good" job, fancy clothes, shiny jewelry, a flashy car, and a big house with a two-car garage) just like their mainstream white counterparts. This means, then, that the young women of the Hip Hop Generation are not immune to Americanisms, and hip hop feminism not only harbors many of the contradictions of hip hop and feminism, but also many of the contradictions of American history, culture, politics, and society. This fact should not shock anyone, least of all the "old school feminists" of the previous generation. Because, as quiet as it has been kept, their theories and praxes are also deeply rooted in Americanisms, even though they are undeniably critical of patriarchy in U.S. history, culture, politics, and society. By not denying the contradictions of hip hop culture, and by emphasizing the ways in which sexism overlaps and intersects with race, class, sexuality, spirituality, and nationality in U.S. popular culture, hip hop feminists are simultaneously expanding the range and uses of intersectional theory and complicating what it means to be both a hip hopper and a feminist.

At this point it would seem that the Hip Hop Women's Movement has laid to rest the question of whether it is possible for one to be both a hip hopper and a feminist. Unapologetically courting controversy, the Hip Hop Women's Movement represents a revitalization of feminism from working-poor nonwhite women's perspectives, and a much-needed deconstruction and reconstruction of hip hop culture from an antiracist feminist perspective. Consequently, hip hop and feminism, both of which have historically marginalized, colonized, and co-opted the contributions of nonwhite women, have been and are being transformed by the poetry, artistry, intellectualism, and activism of nonelite and nonwhite women.

For most of the women of the Hip Hop Generation, then, their lived-experiences and lived-endurances resoundingly reaffirm that, however different from their feminist foremothers, *the personal is still political*, and the political continues to be bound up with patriarchal and racially gendered notions of "a woman's place" in U.S. culture and society. Even with all of its contradictions and seeming callousness toward other forms of feminism, hip hop feminism is innovatively continuing the Women's Liberation Movement and Feminist Art Movement. Whether we agree or disagree with hip hop feminists' articulations of hip hop or feminism—or, even more, *hip hop feminism*—is all beside the point: The point, to put it plainly, is that they are critically interpreting and explicating hip hop and feminism on their own terms and from their own distinct standpoints as both hip hoppers *and* feminists. And, I honestly believe, both hip hop culture and feminism have been and will continue to be enriched as a result of the seminal syntheses and critical contributions of hip hop feminism and the Hip Hop Women's Movement.

In many ways mirroring the interstitial expressive culture surrounding soul, although not nearly as female-friendly or women-centered as the classic soul discussed above, in the late 1960s and throughout the 1970s classic funk provided black America with a unique mouthpiece through which to articulate *alternative, post-Civil Rights Movement and post-soul views and values.* Growing out of both the black aesthetic and soul aesthetic, classic funk expressed the disdain and desperation of African American youth in the aftermath of Martin Luther King's assassination and the demise of the Civil Rights Movement. As prone to partying as it was to politicking, funk brazenly built on every form of black popular music that preceded it: from the spirituals and the blues through to rock & roll and soul.

However, like rhythm & blues in relationship to the Civil Rights Movement, it also—often tongue-in-cheek—expressed the evolving politics and social visions of the Black Power Movement. As soul began to soften as a consequence of its commercialization in the mid- to late-1970s, funk captured the harder and heavier, the bolder and blacker intra-communal politics and social visions that were being increasingly muted in soul as the 1970s progressed and disco rose to national (and international) prominence. An undeniable offshoot of soul and in many senses the second major soundtrack of the Black Power Movement, classic funk factors into the origins and evolution of rap music and hip hop culture as no other music does because it was the black popular cultural and musical form that immediately preceded the emergence of rap music and hip hop culture in the late 1970s and early 1980s.

Even though funk served as the foundation for most "old school" rap classics, it remains something of a mystery to most hip hoppers. In our ongoing efforts to critically explore "hip hop's inheritance" from as well as "hip hop's amnesia" surrounding previous black popular musics and black popular movements, it is important to chronicle and critique the first post-soul form of black popular music and black popular culture, *funk*. Consequently, the subsequent "remix" will be devoted to exploring funk as a second soundtrack for the Black Power Movement and its distinct contributions to rap music, hip hop culture, and the cultural politics of the Hip Hop Movement.

NOTES

1. For further discussion of soul music, and for the most noteworthy works that informed my interpretation here, see Awkward (2007), Bowman (1997), Garland (1969), Guralnick (1986), Haralambos (1975), Hirshey (1984), Hoskyns (1987), J.A. Jackson (2004), R. Larkin (1970), Mason (1992), Pruter (1991), Ward (1998), and Werner (2004, 2006).

2. *Brown v. the Board of Education* (1954), as is well known, desegregated public schools. *Gideon v. Wainwright* (1963) granted accused individuals the right to an attorney. Prior to *Gideon v. Wainwright* an attorney was provided by the state only in cases that could result in the death penalty. *Heart of Atlanta v. the United States* (1964) stipulated that any business which participated in interstate commerce was required to observe all federal civil rights legislation. The Civil Rights Act of 1964 stopped racial segregation and discrimination in all public accommodations; gave the U.S. attorney general the authority to intervene on behalf on the victims of civil rights violations; and made it forbidden for employers to discriminate against people based on their race. The Twenty-Fourth Amendment (1964) outlawed poll taxes in all fifty states. In other words, states could no longer charge people in exercising their right to vote. And, finally, the Voting Rights Act of 1965 essentially guaranteed the Fifteenth Amendment to the U.S. Constitution, which prohibited U.S. citizens from being denied the right to vote based on their race. The Voting Rights Act also ended literacy tests and provided the U.S. attorney general with the authority to intervene on behalf of those voters who had been discriminated against based on their race. For further discussion of 1950s, 1960s, and 1970s civil rights legislation and its impact on post-Civil Rights Movement America, and for the most noteworthy works that informed my interpretation here, see Blackmon (2008), Haney-Lopez (1996), S. Kennedy (1990, 2011), Spann (1993), and M.S. Weiner (2006).

3. My interpretation of the Black Power Movement and Black Power studies has been primarily informed by Collier-Thomas and Franklin (2001), Glaude (2002), J.L. Jeffries (2002), C. Johnson (2007), Joseph (2001, 2002, 2006a, 2010), Ogbar (2004), and Van Deburg (1992, 1997, 2001, 2004).

4. For further discussion of my conception of *revolutionary re-Africanization*, see Rabaka (2008, 2009, 2010b).

5. For further discussion of Stokely Carmichael's conception of Black Power and its enormous influence on the Black Power Movement, and for the most noteworthy works that informed my interpretation here, see Carmichael (2003, 2007), Joseph (2008), McCormack (1973), C.J. Stewart (1998), and Thelwell (1999).

6. In *Forms of Fanonism*, to use Fanon as an example of the ways in which there seems to be a double standard when it comes to *the violence of domination* and *the violence of liberation* or, rather, *the violence of the oppressor* and *the violence of the oppressed*, I wrote: "What is most often missing from the harangues about Fanon's views on violence are any serious discussions of *how* and *why* he advocated *self-defensive antiracist, anticolonialist, anticapitalist, and antisexist violence.* No mention is made of the interminable imperialist violence that the wretched of the earth have been barbarically forced to endure at the hands of the white supremacist patriarchal colonial capitalist world. No mention is made of the holocausts, genocides, enslavements, racializations, colonizations, segregations, pogroms, and lynchings that the wretched of the earth have long had to live and labor through. No mention is made of the many millions of ways in which the white supremacist patriarchal colonial capitalists have repeatedly robbed the wretched of the earth of their human rights, civil rights, voting rights, and any other kind of 'rights.' This is all brushed aside with a subtle and brisk brutality which has caused a couple of European critical theorists with serious social consciences to question the ways in which Europe has narcissistically and racistly quarantined 'humanism' to include 'whites only' and 'nonviolence' to involve 'nonwhites only'" (Rabaka 2010b, 275). In essence, to put it plainly, nonwhites who are not nonviolent in the face of their suffering and social misery deviate from the "model minority" model that whites have long encouraged them to embrace if they are to have a future in the United States (and the wider world). It is interesting to observe that some of this same sentiment has been handed down from the movements of the 1960s and 1970s to the Hip Hop Generation, with contemporary "urban" nonwhite youth being seen as more violent than "suburban" white youth. In fact, there are several ways in which the motifs of

minstrelism discussed in chapter 2 of *Hip Hop's Inheritance* continue to haunt how the Hip Hop Generation is interpreted or, more correctly, misinterpreted. For further discussion of Fanon's views on violence, as well as those of Jean-Paul Sartre and Herbert Marcuse, see "Revolutionary Humanist Fanonism" in *Forms of Fanonism* (Rabaka 2010b, 271–304). And, for a more detailed discussion of blackface minstrel motifs in rap music and hip hop culture, see Rabaka (2011, 49–82).

7. My discussion of Malcolm X's thought here has been informed by Cone (1991), Conyers and Smallwood (2008), Goldman (1979), Malcolm X (1989, 1990, 1991a, 1991b, 1992a, 1992b, 1992c), Marable (2011), and Terrill (2010).

8. Beyond Van Deburg's work, my analysis here has greatly benefited from Cedric Johnson's judicious research in *Revolutionaries to Race Leaders: Black Power and the Making of African American Politics* (2007), where he audaciously "calls into question those modes of political engagement that have become hegemonic within black public life since the late sixties" (xxiii). In many ways updating the work of Harold Cruse in his classic *The Crisis of the Negro Intellectual: A Historical Analysis of the Failure of Black Leadership* (1967), which critically surveyed the evolution of black political and intellectual culture from the 1920s to the 1960s, Johnson's book examines the transition from black radical to black reformist politics from the mid-1960s to the mid-1990s. Although relatively underdiscussed in African American studies circles, Johnson (2007) highlights how the "evolution of Black Power as a form of ethnic politics limited the parameters of black public action to the formal political world. Insurgent demands for black indigenous control converged with liberal reform initiatives to produce a moderate black political regime and incorporate radical dissent into conventional political channels" (xxiii). His narrative captures both the conceptual and political shifts along the "winding historical path from the defiant calls for systemic transformation and radical self-governance during the Civil Rights and Black Power Movements toward the consolidation of a more conservative politics predicated on elite entreaty, racial self-help, and incremental social reforms" (xxiii). This means, then, that at the very moment that many of the Black Power proponents were, for the lack of a better word, "integrating" into mainstream American culture, politics, and society circa the mid-1970s, rap music and hip hop culture were beginning to take shape as the dominant mediums through which to express the "new" (i.e., post-Civil Rights Movement, post-Black Power Movement, post-Vietnam War Movement, etc.) politics and aesthetics of the generation born between 1963 and 1993. This should be borne in mind as we explore what both the Black Power Movement and Black Arts Movement bequeathed to the Hip Hop Movement and, in turn, the Hip Hop Movement's arguably more "mainstream" and "multicultural" politics and aesthetics compared to both the Black Power Movement and Black Arts Movement.

9. My interpretation of the Black Arts Movement has been primarily informed by Clarke (2005), Collins and Crawford (2006), Jarrett (2005), L.P. Neal (1968, 1989), Phelps (2013), Rambsy (2011), Smethurst (2005), D.L. Smith (1991), Traylor (2009), and Widener (2010). And, for further discussion of the Black Power Movement and Black Arts Movement's impact on college campuses between 1965 and 1975, see I.H. Rogers (2012), F. Rojas (2007), Rooks (2006), and Williamson (2003).

10. It is important here to observe that Black Power and Black Arts radicals' view that the masses of black folk during the 1960s and 1970s had little or no lasting contact with white bourgeois culture and values was more than likely influenced by Fanon's *The Wretched of the Earth* (1968, 111–12, 129–40). For instance, calling his readers' attention to the intense inferiority complex and the burgeoning embrace of bourgeois views and values on the part of the African proletariat and, for that matter, most Africans who came into regular contact with white colonizers and their culture, Fanon pointed to the African peasantry and those who had the least direct and daily contact with racial colonialism and its political economy. However, it should be pointed out that it was not the rural radicalism of the African peasantry alone that constituted the singular revolutionary democratic socialist force of change in Africa for Fanon, but a creative coalition and alliance of anticolonialist, anticapitalist, and antiracist rural, urban and, even, suburban sociopolitical classes with a shared interest in Africa's development, as well as the distinct development of their respective nations, cities, towns, rural regions, and local cultures. This means, then, that Fanon did not completely reject the active and important radical

political participation of the African proletariat as much as he emphasized its embourgeoise-ment when compared and contrasted with the lived-experiences, life-struggles, and, more im-portantly, the anti-imperialist and potential revolutionary consciousness (if provided with prop-er "political education") of the lumpenproletariat and peasantry of Africa. For further discus-sion, my readers are urged to see my analysis in *Forms of Fanonism*, especially in "form" 3, "Marxist Fanonism" (Rabaka 2010b, 145–216). Fanon's influence on the cultural aesthetics of the Black Arts movement is discussed in greater detail below.

11. For further discussion of Fanon's theory of radical political education and contributions to critical pedagogy, see Rabaka (2010b, 161–69).

12. The Black Studies Movement emerged within the context of other 1960s and 1970s sociopolitical movements, such as the Civil Rights Movement, Black Power Movement, Wom-en's Liberation Movement, Third World Liberation Movement, Free Speech Movement, and Anti-War Movement. Where the Black Arts Movement is commonly conceived of as the cultural aesthetic arm of the Black Power Movement, the Black Studies Movement may be taken as its intellectual and educational outlet. As a movement and *interdisciplinary discipline* black studies, which is now known as either *African American studies* or increasingly *Africana studies*, evolved out of the Black Power Movement's strong stress on black self-definition, black self-determination, culturally relevant education, cultural pluralism, and student activism. The first efforts to establish a black Studies department began in 1966 at San Francisco State College (now known as San Francisco State University), where black students, according to Maulana Karenga (2002, 14), "[i]nfluenced by the writings of the African revolutionary Frantz Fanon's [*The Wretched of the Earth*] and the emphasis on Third World solidarity by Third World Liberation Movements . . . issued fifteen demands which served as a model for other Black Studies struggles." It is interesting to observe that other nonwhite student groups at San Francisco State joined with the Black Student Union to form the "Third World Front" of student groups who struggled for black studies. Included among these student groups were the Mexican American Student Confederation, the Latin American Student Organization, the Asian American Political Alliance, the Intercollegiate Chinese for Social Action, and the Phi-lippine American Collegiate Endeavor. After two years of student protest for black studies, University of Chicago-trained sociologist Nathan Hare was appointed the coordinator of black studies in February of 1968 and charged with the task of formulating an autonomous academic department devoted to systematically and critically studying African American history, culture, and struggle. After several delays by the board of trustees and other administrators, as well as further student protests, the first department of black studies was established at San Francisco State College in November of 1968. Here emphasis should be placed not only on the fact that what we now know as Africana studies was inaugurated during the Black Power period, but also that it took African Americans in alliance with other oppressed and racially colonized groups to found the field. This is equally important when we bear in mind the often one-dimensional interpretations of the Black Power period as a time of "black supremacy" where African Americans advanced "reverse racism," and also the undeniable fact that rap music and hip hop culture, in their own unique way, have continued many of the coalitions and alliances established during the 1960s and 1970s student movements. The literature on Africana studies, which currently in its most comprehensive sense has come to include African studies, African diasporan studies, African American studies, Afro-Asian studies, Afro-European studies, Afro-Islamic studies, Afro-Jewish studies, Afro-Latino studies, Afro-Native American studies, Car-ibbean studies, Pan-African studies, Black British studies and, of course, black studies, is diverse and extensive. The most noteworthy overviews and critical analyses that influenced my interpretation here include Aldridge and James (2007), Aldridge and Young (2000), Anderson and Stewart (2007), Asante and Karenga (2006), Azevedo (2005), Ba Nikongo (1997), Bobo and Michel (2000), Bobo, Hudley, and Michel (2004), Gordon and Gordon (2006a, 2006b), Johnson and Henderson (2005), Johnson and Lyne (2002), Kopano and Williams (2004), F. Rojas (2007), Rooks (2006), and Whitten and Torres (1998).

13. For further discussion of the black aesthetic, especially as an outgrowth of the Black Arts Movement, and for the most noteworthy works that informed my interpretation here, see H.A. Baker (1980, 1988), Bodunde (2001), Gayle (1969, 1970, 1971), Karenga (1968, 1972, 1997), L.P. Neal (1968, 1989), Ongiri (2010), Shockley (2011), and W.D. Wright (1997).

14. As is well known, Benjamin Quarles's *Black Abolitionists* (1969) has long been regarded as a classic and one of the cornerstone texts in African American Abolitionist studies. Although not explored as often as other areas in African American history, culture, and struggle, over the years since Quarles's study a steady stream of black abolitionist research has been published. For example, Blackett (1983), Mabee (1970), McKivigan and Harrold (1999), Sanneh (1999), Stauffer (2001), Wu (2000), and Yee (1992). For further examples of and critical commentary on the body of literature produced by enslaved Africans and now commonly called "slave narratives," please see Andrews and Gates (1999, 2000), Fisch (2007), and Y. Taylor (1999a, 1999b).

15. For further discussion of mainstream American avant-gardism, and for the most noteworthy works that informed my interpretation here, see Arthur (2005), J.M. Harding (2012), Hobbs (1997), Maconie (2012), Nel (2002), and Yu (2009).

16. What I have termed here the *"low-down folk culture" link* between the Black Arts movement and the Niggerati of the Harlem Renaissance connects with hip hoppers' obsession with "ghetto-fabulous" life and culture and continues to have currency among African American studies scholars. Most works in what is currently called "black popular culture studies" in one way or another engage contemporary black folk culture or, rather, black vernacular culture. For example, see Basu and Lemelle (2006), Bolden (2008), Bracey (2003), Dent (1992), Iton (2008), M.A. Neal (1998, 2002, 2003), H.B. Shaw (1990), and Tucker (2007).

17. For further discussion of the culture, aesthetics, and politics surrounding soul music in the 1960s and 1970s, and for the most noteworthy works that informed my interpretation here, see Guillory and Green (1998), Mason (1992), Maultsby (1983), Merlis and Seay (1997), A. Shaw (1970), R.W. Stephens (1984), Van Deburg (1992, 1997), Ward (1998), and Werner (2004, 2006).

18. My interpretation of Curtis Mayfield has been informed by Burns (2003), G. Freeland (2009), Pruter (1991), and Werner (2004).

19. My interpretation of Aretha Franklin has been informed by Barnard (2001), Bego (1990), A. Cohen (2011), Dobkin (2006), A. L. Franklin (1999), and P.J. Greene (1995).

20. For further discussion of women-centered soul, and for the most noteworthy works that informed my interpretation here, see Awkward (2007), D. Freeland (2001), P.J. Greene (1995), Hirshey (1984), and Nathan (1999).

21. For a more detailed discussion of the connections between classic blues queens and neo-soul sisters and women-centered rappers, see "remix" 2, "'Lifting As We Climb!': Classic Blues Queens and the Black Women's Club Movement, Neo-Soul Sistas and the Hip Hop Women's Movement," in Rabaka (2012, 19–98).

22. Unfortunately there are not very many reliable sources (i.e., scholarly books or articles) on Mary J. Blige. However, I was able to glean much of value from D. Bailey (2009), T. Brown (2008), Maimone (2011), and Torres (2008).

23. As is well known, Blige's rap alias is "Brook Lynn." She is not by any means a bad rapper. However, we would all much rather her focus on her heart-stirring and jaw-dropping old-sounding, new soul singing.

24. My interpretation of Meshell Ndegeocello's music and politics has been informed by D.A. Brooks (2007), Clay (2007a, 2007b), N. Lewis (2006), Linden (2004), and Mockus (2007).

25. For further discussion of Nina Simone's life and legacy, and for the most noteworthy works that informed my interpretation here, see Acker (2004), Brun-Lambert (2009), Cohodas (2010), S. Hampton (2004), Simone (1991), and R. Williams (2002).

26. For further discussion of Aunt Jemima and the mammy archetype, and for the most noteworthy works that informed my interpretation here, see Goings (1994), Kern-Foxworth (1994), Manring (1998), D. Roberts (1994), and Wallace-Sanders (2008).

27. For further discussion of the "tragic mulatto" trope, "miscegenation," and colorism within American history, literature, popular culture and politics, and for the most noteworthy works that informed my interpretation here, see Berzon (1978), Bost (2003), Manganelli (2012), McLendon (1995), Raimon (2004), Russell-Cole, Wilson, and Hall (1992), Sherrard-Johnson (2007), Sollors (1997), and Zackodnik (2004).

28. For more detailed discussion of African American women's contributions to and enormous influence on the origins and evolution of the Black Power Movement, see Breines (2006), Clarke (2005), Collier-Thomas and Franklin (2001), Gore, Theoharis, and Woodard (2009), Joseph (2006a), Springer (2005), and Weber (1981).

29. For further discussion of black women's stereotypes and the politics surrounding black women's stereotypes, and for the most noteworthy works that informed my interpretation here, see L.M. Anderson (1997), Harris-Perry (2011), James and Busia (1993), L.D. Johnson (2012), and Jones and Shorter-Gooden (2003).

30. For further discussion of hip hop feminism and the Hip Hop Women's Movement, and for the most noteworthy works that informed my interpretation here, see A. Anderson (2003), R.N. Brown (2008), Brown and Kwakye (2013), Champlain (2010), Craft (2010), Durham (2007), Guillory (2005), Lust (2011), J. Morgan (1995, 1999, 2007), Pough (2002, 2003, 2004), Pough, Richardson, Durham, and Raimist (2007), and Sharpley-Whiting (2007).

31. For further discussion of the conservative feminist and antifeminist forces that co-opted feminism during the Reagan and Bush administration years between 1980 and 1992, and for the most noteworthy works that informed my interpretation here, see Burack and Josephson (2003), Heywood and Drake (1997), Lynn (1992), Põldsaar (2006), and Schreiber (2008).

32. For further discussion of post-Women's Liberation Movement feminism in the 1980s and 1990s, and for the works that factored into my analysis here, see Dow (1996), Maglin and Perry (1996), and Oakley and Mitchell (1997). My conception of the origins and evolution of the Women's Liberation Movement of the 1960s and 1970s, as well as its aftermath in the 1980s and 1990s, is primarily based on the work of Verta Taylor and her colleagues (see Rupp and Taylor, 1986, 1991; Schmidt and Taylor, 1997; Staggenborg and Taylor, 2005; Taylor and Rupp, 1991). In this section, along with Taylor and her collaborators' work, my analysis has been influenced by Berkeley (1999), Dicker (2008), S. Evans (1979), Ferree and Martin (1995), Freeman (1975), and Giardina (2010).

33. For further discussion of womanist theory or, rather, womanism, and for the most noteworthy works that informed my interpretation here, see Eaton (2008), Heilmann (2003), M.G. Hill (2012), Houston and Davis (2002), Hudson-Weems (1995, 1997, 2004), Kolawole (1997), Maparyan (2011), L. Phillips (2006), and Prince, Silva-Wayne, and Vernon (2004).

34. It is almost impossible to critically discuss hip hop feminism without also connecting it to and critically engaging hip hop hyper-masculinism, which is, whether consciously or unconsciously, based on the brashness and braggadocio of Black Power Movement hyper-masculinism. As a matter of fact, Charise Cheney's groundbreaking *Phallic/ies and Hi(s)stories: Masculinity and the Black Nationalist Tradition, from Slave Spirituals to Rap Music* (1999) and *Brothers Gonna Work It Out!: Sexual Politics in the Golden Age of Rap Nationalism* (2005) both astutely illustrate several of the ways in which past forms of black nationalist masculinism inform present forms of black nationalist masculinism, especially "rap nationalism." Other noteworthy works on hip hop masculinity that have directly influenced my analysis here include J.S. Greene (2008), Hardy (2010), Hopkinson and Moore (2006), Hurt (2006), Osayande (2008), J.K. Smith (2002), and M. White (2011).

35. My interpretation of the new forms of feminism and the Women's Liberation Movement after 1980 and at the dawn of the twenty-first century, especially among Hip Hop Generation women, has been informed by Berger (2006), Dicker and Piepmeier (2003), Hernández and Rehman (2002), Heywood and Drake (1997), Karaian, Rundle, and Mitchell (2001), Labaton and Martin (2004), and Reger (2005).

36. Important explorations of the new (i.e., 1980s onward) forms of feminist politics and social organization include R.A. Bernard (2009), Incite! Women of Color Against Violence (2006), M. Rojas (2009), and Sharpley-Whiting (2007).

37. My conception of hip hop epistemologies and pedagogies has been informed by Alridge, Stewart, and Franklin (2010), Brown and Kwakye (2013), Dimitriadis (2001), M.L. Hill (2009), Parmar (2009), and Runell and Diaz (2007).

38. For those skeptical of my use of Fanon's critical theory in the interest of women's decolonization and women's liberation, it is important to acknowledge feminists' and womanists' long-standing critical relationship with his radical politics and revolutionary humanist praxis. Admittedly, Fanon has a contradictory, controversial, and regularly contested relation-

ship with feminism, womanism, and women's studies (Dubey 1998; Fuss 1995; Gopal 2002; McClintock 1995; Sharpley-Whiting 1997). As the growing body of criticism on Fanon's "feminism" demonstrates, it would be extremely difficult to deny his contributions—again, however contradictory, controversial, and contested—to women's quest to decolonize their distinct life-worlds and lived-experiences in the male supremacist world in which they find themselves. As I argued in *Forms of Fanonism: Frantz Fanon's Critical Theory and the Dialectics of Decolonization*, Fanon's commitment to women's liberation was deeply connected to, and, even more, inextricable from his commitments to revolutionary decolonization, democratic socialism, and human liberation, and, as with each of the aforementioned, his theory of women's liberation has progressive and retrogressive aspects (Rabaka 2010b). There has long been a knee-jerk tendency among theorists, both male and female, who engage Fanon's contributions to feminism, womanism, and women's liberation to argue *either* that Fanon was gender progressive *or* that Fanon was gender regressive. I openly acknowledge, in all intellectual honesty, that Fanon was *both*: in his texts he seems to be schizophrenically, at times, a staunch advocate for women's rights and women's liberation, and, at other times, completely oblivious of his "Freudian slips" and blind-spots with regard to gender justice and the ways in which his work—that is, his own words—speak to, not the *decolonization* of women's life-worlds and lived-experiences, but the *recolonization* of women's life-worlds and lived-experiences. In a sense, then, Fanon's contributions to feminism prefigure and mirror much of the contradictory and controversial character of hip hop feminism by containing some progressive and some retrogressive elements.

39. For further discussion of feminist art and the Feminist Art Movement of the 1970s and 1980s, and for the most noteworthy works that informed my interpretation here, see Broude and Garrard (1994, 2005), Deepwell (1995), Elliot and Karras (2011), Gaulke and Klick (2012), Linton, Maberry, and Pulsinelli (2011), Lippard (1976, 1980, 1995), and Raven, Langer, and Fruech (1988).

40. For further discussion of "femcees" (i.e., female rappers), and for the most noteworthy works that informed my interpretation here, see Babb (2002), Biferie (1993), Bost (2001), Celious (2002), de Leon (2007a), Desnoyers-Colas (2003), Goodall (1994), S. Jackson (2010), Oware (2009), Peoples (2007), Reid-Brinkley (2008), R. Roberts (1991, 1994), Sharpley-Whiting (2007), Skeggs (1993), G. Thomas (2007, 2009), and Troka (2002).

41. While it can be considered progressive for men to recognize women's life-struggles, it is extremely problematic when "genuine" womanhood is quickly collapsed into motherhood. When one carefully and critically listens to male rappers' odes to their mothers from a womanist and/or black feminist perspective what one mostly hears are mythic idealizations of the maternal. In other words, it often seems as though male rappers' mothers (and other older women) are somehow exceptions to hip hop's hyper-masculinist and misogynist rules that regularly reduce young women to "baby mamas," "gold diggers," "skeezers," "bitches," and "hoes." African American men's mythic idealization of the maternal did not begin with the men of the Hip Hop Generation but, interestingly, this species of thought can be shown to extend all the way back to the men of the New Negro Movement and Harlem Renaissance. Engaging this issue by focusing on a specific New Negro Movement/Harlem Renaissance luminary, I have treated W.E.B. Du Bois's simultaneous contributions to and critique of the mythic idealization of black motherhood in my book *W.E.B. Du Bois and the Problems of the Twenty-First Century*, see especially chapter 5, "Du Bois and 'The Damnation of Women': Critical Social Theory and the Souls of Black Female Folk" (Rabaka 2007, 137–87).

42. For further discussion of the ways in which female rappers and female hip hop fans might profit and derive pleasure from their participation in rap music and hip hop culture on their own hip hop feminist/womanist terms, see A. Anderson (2003), Babb (2002), Balton (1991), Biferie (1993), Bost (2001), Celious (2002), DeBerry (1995), Desnoyers-Colas (2003), S. Jackson (2010), Latifah (2000), Lust (2011), D. Perkins (2000), Pough (2004), Pough, Richardson, Durham, and Raimist (2007), Souljah (1996), and G. Thomas (2009).

43. My interpretation of the origins and evolution of neo-soul has been informed by T. Brooks (2007), C. Campbell (2009), Cunningham (2010), Furman and Furman (1999), C.S. Harris (2004), T. Harrison (2011), Jenkins (2008), Kajikawa (2012), J. King (1999), McIver (2002), Nickson (1999), Planer (2002), Rucker (2011), Samuels (2001), and Whaley (2002).

44. As is well known, hip hop feminists are not the only group of contemporary feminists whose feminist critique centers on the ways that patriarchy plays itself out in mass media and popular culture (see Buszek 2006; S.J. Douglas 1994, 2010; Genz 2009; Gillis and Hollows 2009; Hollows 2000; Hollows and Moseley 2006; Milestone and Meyer 2012; Tasker and Negra 2007; Worsley 2010; Zeisler 2008). However, hip hop feminism is distinguished by its use of hip hop culture as its primary point of departure in its efforts to develop a new-fangled antiracist feminist critique of, not simply contemporary popular culture, but also contemporary politics, economics, and society.

45. For further discussion of hip hop feminists' critique of "stereotyped images through their continued use of [black popular and] expressive culture," see A. Anderson (2003), Brown and Kwakye (2013), Champlain (2010), Craft (2010), Durham (2007), jamila (2002), Lust (2011), J. Morgan (1999), Pough (2002, 2003), Pough, Richardson, Durham, and Raimist (2007), and Sharpley-Whiting (2007).

Remix 4

Funk

From P-Funk to G-Funk

The childlike, "dirty" nature of some funk lyrics is also a deliberate return to an uninhibited state of mind, a state of childlike innocence and wonder, as a part of an adult state of sexual release and a state of African-rooted balance between Western and African opposites. Comedian Richard Pryor's phenomenal success in the early 1970s as a stand-up comic was precisely due to his use of vulgar language and imagery, which black folks found hilarious because of its pungent truth in their lives. Whether it is a symbol, metaphor, or the real thing, there is no reason why funk should not be associated with "dirtiness" and sex.

—Rickey Vincent, *Funk: The Music, the People, and the Rhythm of the One*

INTRODUCTION: FUNK MUSIC, AESTHETICS, POLITICS, AND CULTURE

Similar to classic soul, classic funk is frequently disassociated from the politics, aesthetics, and culture of the Black Power Movement and Black Arts Movement, respectively. However, even though it is primarily known as "dance music" and "party music," like a lot of rap, musically and lyrically classic funk was as wide-ranging and wide-reaching as classic soul. For instance, recurring themes in classic funk include "partying" and "hanging loose," as well as spirituality, sexuality, love, lust, cultural celebration, social commentary, and political critique. [1]

Musically classic funk borrowed frenzy-filled African American church-influenced vocalizations from gospel; full-throated tales of broken hearts and busted dreams from the blues; jaw-dropping improvisations and a reinvented, off-kilter sense of swing from jazz; bustling basslines and blaring Stax-styled

221

horn arrangements from rhythm & blues; extended explorations of black sexuality and black spirituality, as well as a kind of tongue-in-cheek political critique and social commentary, from soul; flamboyant guitar solos from psychedelic rock; outrageous costumes, hairstyles, makeup, platform-soled boots, and over-the-top theatrics from glam rock; polyrhythmic drum patterns and other "exotic" sounds from African music; and auxiliary percussion instrumentation and drum patterns from Latin music. Initially popularized by jazz, rhythm & blues, and soul musicians, funk can be further contrasted with rhythm & blues and soul in that it was primarily a band-based music, where rhythm & blues and soul eventually came to be dominated by charismatic solo artists and vocal groups for the most part.

Generally speaking, funk bands composed, produced, and sang their own songs and, similar to jazz bands, worked hard to create a distinct band sound. In fact, as with jazz, funk emphasized improvisation, favoring extended "jams" which ultimately made it one of the first forms of black popular music to almost completely sidestep the 45-rpm single (three minute and thirty seconds) format. In the midst of the extended jams the messages in classic funk most often revolved around a series of jarring juxtapositions: love *and* lust, comedy *and* tragedy, optimism *and* pessimism; and Martin Luther King-style integrationism *and* Malcolm X-style black nationalism. Consequently, when classic funk is resituated within the milieu in which it emerged it can be viewed as more than merely a rhythmically harder form of rhythm & blues and a psychedelic brand of soul preoccupied with romancing, dancing, and partying, but a second soundtrack for the much-misunderstood Black Power Movement that simultaneously converged with and diverged from both classic rhythm & blues and classic soul.

Similar to classic soul, classic funk registered the shift from the moderatism of the Civil Rights Movement to the militantism of the Black Power Movement. The unhinged happiness that is easily detected in most classic funk is largely a consequence of African Americans' optimism in light of what were initially perceived as the successes of the Civil Rights Movement (e.g., the Civil Rights Act of 1964, the Voting Rights Act of 1965, the Fair Housing Act of 1968, and other Great Society legislation). Indeed, with the establishment of affirmative action programs in the early 1970s it appeared as though American apartheid would finally be put to rest, and funk, in a sense, would provide the long overdue epitaph.

However, African American optimism quickly turned to pessimism, African American happiness to sadness, as scores of black skilled laborers were either laid off or lost their relatively "good-paying" jobs in the 1970s as a consequence of America's transition from an industrial to a technological and service-oriented economy. The once booming factories that employed working-class and working-poor African Americans eventually shut down and moved their operations elsewhere. At the same time, the government's fiscal conservatism in the 1970s slashed funding for education, job training, social programs, and creative arts initiatives aimed at improving the conditions of working-class and working-poor African Americans who had borne the brunt of more than a century of Jim Crow laws and other manifestations of modern American apartheid.

In essence, affirmative action programs were met with antiaffirmative action programs almost immediately. And, no matter how long and how loudly conservative and liberal legislators and citizens wrangled over the merits or demerits of affirmative action, from the mid-1970s onward the "subaltern" souls, the folk at the low end of the social ladder, continued to suffer and endure unspeakable social misery. As a matter of fact, by the mid-1970s there was such a strong backlash against the civil rights legislation of the 1960s that conservative and liberal whites alike regularly claimed that they were victims of "reverse discrimination" and, in essence, being held hostage to the "radical" civil rights social policies of the 1960s. In light of this backlash the high hopes that African Americans entered into the 1970s with eventually turned into resentment and unrepentant displays of black radicalism. Funk, similar to classic soul, registered both the regressivism and progressivism, the resentment and new forms of black radicalism that came to characterize African American life in the 1970s.[2]

Classic funk continued the hard and heavy, driving rhythms that characterized classic soul at its inception but, by the mid-1970s, were regularly being reduced to the soft sounding middle-of-the-road (MOR) music primed for the commercial radio format. Funk was a deeper and darker "underground" sound that initially found few white fans in its "pure" and "uncut" form (to paraphrase funkmaster George Clinton in "P-Funk [Wants To Get Funked Up]"). With its references to pimps, players, prostitutes, drugs, drinking, other worlds, extraterrestrials, spaceships, parties, poverty, and black cultural politics, at its inception funk captured the experiences of economically impoverished African Americans in ways that few other forms of black popular music have. Reflecting African American optimism, pessimism, and hedonism between the late 1960s and the late 1970s, *lyrically and musically classic funk provided a foundation for rap in much the same way that classic soul provided a foundation for neo-soul.*

Rap not only continues to explore many of the lyrical themes introduced by funk, but it often does so using a modified *funk aesthetic*. Funk, to reiterate, drew from almost every major form of black popular music that preceded it: from the spirituals and the blues through to rock & roll and soul. Similarly, rap draws from and, literally, *recycles and remixes* all previous forms of black popular music. Rap's recycling and remixing of earlier forms of black popular music not only links it to the funk aesthetic, but also to an often overlooked—albeit extremely important—aspect of the overarching African American aesthetic and its preoccupation with originality, authenticity, and hybridity. In "Characteristics of Negro Expression," which was originally published in 1934, revered Harlem Renaissance writer Zora Neale Hurston observed that "[w]hat we really mean by originality is the modification of ideas." For example, she continued, even "[t]he most ardent admirer of the great Shakespeare cannot claim first source even for him. It is his treatment of the borrowed material"—old myths, legends, folk tales, and other stories—that has garnered him a high place in human history (Hurston 1995, 838).

Hurston helps us reconceive of both funk and rap as *black popular music based on "borrowed material."* Here originality has more to do with what one does with the "borrowed material" rather than the "first source[s]" or origins of the material. Acknowledging that much of African American culture was forged from "borrowed material[s]" from either Africa or "white civilization," she furthered shared:

> So if we look at it squarely, the Negro is a very original being. While he lives and moves in the midst of a white civilization, everything that he touches is reinterpreted for his own use. He has modified language, mode of food preparation, practice of medicine, and most certainly the religion of his new country. . . . Everyone is familiar with the Negro's modification of the whites' musical instruments, so that his interpretation has been adopted by the white man himself and then reinterpreted. . . . Thus has arisen a new art in the civilized world, and thus has our so-called civilization come. (838)

Foreshadowing both the funk and rap aesthetics, Hurston hinted at the ways in which pre-funk and pre-rap African American musicians recycled and remixed the accoutrements of white America to such an innovative, sophisticated, and intriguing extent that their "interpretation has been adopted by the white man himself and then reinterpreted. . . . Thus has arisen a new art in the civilized world, and thus has our so-called civilization come." Instead of conceiving of black popular music as "nigger noise" (what she mockingly termed "niggerism"), Hurston understood African American music to be part of the reinterpretation and reinvention process that African Americans have been involved in since the dark days of their enslavement. Funk was emblematic of African Americans' reinterpretation and reinvention process in the post-Civil Rights Movement and Black Power Movement 1970s.

Building on and going beyond the reinterpretation and reinvention process of the 1920s and 1930s Jazz Age and Harlem Renaissance, funk brought together a spellbinding tangle of the musical *and* radical political impulses between the late 1960s and the late 1970s. Similar to rhythm & blues and soul before it, funk was not merely a reaction to white music, culture, and politics—although, truth be told, it did have its fair share of reactionary and regressive elements. Yet and still, it existed on its own contradictory and often off-kilter terms, for the most part, free from the trappings of Eurocentrism and the crossover craze to which soul was slowly succumbing in the mid- to late-1970s.[3]

Funk was audacious in its affirmation of post-Civil Rights Movement African American issues and ills, and unapologetically aimed at working-class and poor black folk who were in desperate need of its expressions of both reality *and* fantasy. As one of the major foundations of rap, funk handed down more than most hip hoppers may realize, and it may not be going too far to suggest that rap cannot be adequately understood without a working knowledge of not only funk's major figures (e.g., James Brown, Sly Stone, and George Clinton) and classic funk beats, but also the spiritual, sexual, cultural, social, and political messages that collectively permeate their music and that uniquely reflect the wider spiritual, sexual, cultural, social, and political world of African America in the 1970s. Consequently, this "remix" will examine the origins and evolution of funk; its meaning, function, and significance for African Americans in the 1970s; and its enormous influence on the origins and evolution of rap music, hip hop culture, and the Hip Hop Movement.

PRE-FUNK: HARD BOP—THE RADICAL POLITICAL AND MUSICAL ROOTS OF FUNK

In *Flash of the Spirit: African & Afro-American Art & Philosophy* (1983), Robert Farris Thompson suggested that the etymology of the word "funk" may be traced back to a Kikongo word, "*lu-fuki*," which essentially means "bad body odor." Noting the inversion of the term within the African American colloquial context of the 1950s and 1960s, he furthered stated:

> The slang term "funky" in black communities originally referred to strong body odor, and not to "funk," meaning fear or panic. The black nuance seems to derive from the Kikongo *lu-fuki*, "bad body odor," and is perhaps reinforced by contact with *fumet*, "aroma of food and wine," in French Louisiana. But the Kikongo word is closer to the jazz word "funky" in form and meaning, as both jazzmen and Bakongo use "funky" and *lu-fuki* to praise persons for the integrity of their art, for having "worked out" to achieve their aims. In Kongo today it is possible to hear an elder lauded in this way: "like, there is a really funky person!—my soul advances toward him to receive his blessing" (*yati, nkwa lu-fuki! Ve miela miami ikwenda baki*). Fu-Kiau Bunseki, a leading native authority on Kongo culture, explains: "Someone who is very old, I go to sit with him in order to feel his *lu-fuki*, meaning, I would like to be blessed by him." For in Kongo the smell of a hardworking elder carriers luck. This Kongo sign of exertion is identified with the positive energy of a person. Hence "funk" in black American jazz parlance can mean earthiness, a return to fundamentals. (104–5)

In other words, similar to *lu-fuki* in Africa, in African America "funk" signifies "the positive energy of a person." Hence, "funk" in black popular music parlance most often signifies "soulfulness," "earthiness," and "a return to fundamentals." Additionally, because the word "funk" can mean both "bad body odor" *and* the "positive energy of a person" within African American vernacular culture it can also be connected to the Yoruba spiritual concept *asé*. In Yoruba *asé* essentially means "divine energy" or "positive energy," "life-force" in English or "force-vitale" in French, and it is reportedly strongest in body fluids, especially tears, sweat, saliva, semen, breast milk, blood, and urine.[4] Bearing in mind that almost every funk band of repute had some kind of connection to jazz, Thompson's conception of *lu-fuki*/funk and my emphasis on its conceptual connections to *asé* accent not only the African origins of funk—etymologically, spiritually, culturally, philosophically, and musically speaking—but also, and equally important here, the ways in which funk was part of an African American musical and cultural continuum that reached back to the heyday of hard bop between 1955 and 1965.[5]

Although several jazz historians have suggested that hard bop emerged as a reaction to the whitened and lightened, softer sounds of cool jazz in the early- to mid-1950s, it was actually part of the internal evolution of bebop and a heartfelt response to Charlie Parker's untimely death in March of 1955. Coming of age in the post-World War II period between 1945 and 1955 in which both bebop and rhythm & blues rose to unprecedented popularity, hard bop was essentially a synthesis of these two musics with enough snatches of gospel and blues to lead noted jazz historian James Lincoln Collier in *The Making of Jazz: A Comprehensive History* (1978) to suggest that hard bop was an attempt to reclaim jazz and "return [it] to [its] fundamentals" (435–53). In an interview with Dean Schaffer (2010), Michael Cuscuna spoke about the transition from bebop to hard bop, stating:

> Both Art [Blakey] and Horace [Silver] were very, very aware of what they wanted to do. They wanted to get away from the jazz scene of the early '50s, which was the Birdland scene—you hire Phil Woods or Charlie Parker or J.J. Johnson, they come and sit in with the house rhythm section, and they only play blues and standards that everybody knows. There's no rehearsal, there's no thought given to the audience. Both Horace and Art knew that the only way to get the jazz audience back and make it bigger than ever was to really make music that was memorable and planned, where you consider the audience and keep everything short. They really liked digging into blues and gospel, things with universal appeal. So they put together what was to be called the Jazz Messengers. (1)

Because it sought to "get the jazz audience back and make it bigger than ever," hard bop generously drew from jump blues and rhythm & blues, the preeminent black popular musics between 1945 and 1965. Moving beyond the "blues and standards" bebop style of the mid- to late-1940s and early 1950s, hard bop musicians such as Horace Silver, Art Blakey, Charles Mingus, Miles Davis, Sonny Rollins, Max Roach, Clifford Brown, Sonny Clark, Lou Donaldson, Hank Mobley, Jackie McLean, Benny Golson, Lee Morgan, and Cannonball Adderley created a new, earthier, and more accessible form of bebop that featured melodies that tended to be simpler and frequently more "soulful" sounding. The hard bop rhythm section was usually looser, with the bassist not as tightly confined to playing four beats to the bar, as was the case with bebop. The endlessly improvising hard bop bassist would eventually morph into the nonstop grooving, slapping, and thumping funk bassist in the 1970s, which included iconic bass players such as Larry Graham (of Sly & the Family Stone and Graham Central Station), William "Bootsy" Collins (of James Brown's original J.B.'s band, Parliament, Funkadelic, and Bootsy's Rubber Band), Marvin Isley (of the Isley Brothers), Verdine White (of Earth, Wind & Fire), Marshall "Rock" Jones (of the Ohio Players), Robin Duhe (of Maze), Louis Johnson (of the Brothers Johnson), Mark "Mr. Mark" Adams (of Slave), and Nate Phillips (of Pleasure).

Hard bop also displayed a strong gospel influence and incorporated "amen chords" (i.e., the plagal cadence) and triadic harmonies into its sound. As discussed in the previous "remix," the gospel sound increasingly crept its way into rhythm & blues, and ultimately the synthesis of rhythm & blues and gospel, among other musics, gave way to the emergence of soul. This is to say, it was hard bop that first turned to gospel and helped to popularize the gospel sound in black popular music. And, lastly, along with mixing gospel elements with bebop, hard bop horn men and pianists also demonstrated their nuanced familiarity with early rhythm & blues. Writing of the interplay between jazz and rhythm & blues in the 1950s that laid the foundation for both soul and funk in *Hard Bop: Jazz and Black Music, 1955–1965* (1992), David Rosenthal observed:

> For a while, it was hard to see what the future of black jazz might be. The early fifties saw an extremely dynamic rhythm & blues scene take shape, including a succession of brilliant doo-wop combos like the Ravens, the Clovers, and the Orioles; a New Orleans school centering on Fats Domino, Professor Longhair, Shirley & Lee, and others; the urban blues of the Muddy Waters and Bobby Bland-type; and much else besides. This music, and not cool jazz, was what chronologically separated bebop and hard bop in ghettos. Young jazz musicians, of course, enjoyed and listened to these R&B sounds which, among other things, began the amalgam of blues and gospel that would later be dubbed "soul music." And it is in this vigorously creative black pop music, at a time when bebop seemed to have lost both its direction and its audience, that some of hard bop's roots may be found. (24)

While many music critics have noted the influence of gospel and soul on funk, their work has frequently overlooked the ways in which jazz, and particularly hard bop, contributed to the origins and evolution of funk. Going back to the etymology of the word funk in black vernacular culture, it is interesting to observe that it was hard bop musicians who popularized the term. As Paul Tanner, David Megill, and Maurice Gerow noted in *Jazz* (1992), initially hard bop was called "funky hard bop" (112–21). As a matter of fact, several hard bop songs featured the word "funk" or "funky" in their titles, most famously Horace Silver's "Opus de Funk" (1952), Cannonball Adderley's "Blue Funk" (1958), Kenny Drew's "Funk-Cosity" (1960), Hank Mobley's "Funk in the Deep Freeze" (1957) and "Barrel of Funk" (1956), Donald Byrd's "Pure D. Funk" (1960) and "Sudwest Funk" (1958), Patti Bown's "Waltz de Funk" (1960), the Jazz Crusaders' "Big Hunk of Funk" (1962), Rahsaan Roland Kirk's "Funk Underneath" (1961) and, finally, Grant Green's "Hip Funk" (1962).

Similar to the funk musicians of the 1970s, the hard bop funk musicians of the 1950s and 1960s drew from the panorama of black popular music between 1945 and 1965 to create their new form of jazz. In this sense, bebop—with its fast tempos, complex harmonies, intricate melodies, and airtight rhythm sections that maintained steady beats based on four-beats-to-the-bar bass playing and the drummer's ride cymbal—was merely one of many forms of music on hard boppers' much-broadened musical palette. Hard bop funksters broke with what they perceived to be the "old school" formulas of bebop and the softness and symphonic sounds of cool jazz. Hence, hard bop funk can be viewed as both a funnel and forum where blues, jazz, gospel, and rhythm & blues came together in creative dialogue, and it was this dynamic dialogue that reemerged as what is now known as "funk" roughly between 1969 and 1979.

Almost fifty years later we might look back at the years between 1955 and 1965 as the last period in which jazz effortlessly attracted the hippest young African American musicians—which is to say, the most musically advanced, those with the most solid technical and improvisational skills, and those with the strongest cultural sense of themselves, not only as entertainers but as distinctly *African American* artists. As David Rosenthal emphasized in "Jazz in the Ghetto: 1950–1970" (1988b), it was during the turbulent decade between 1955 and 1965 that hard bop was the dominant jazz style in the poverty-stricken neighborhoods where the majority of these youngsters lived. To them, hard bop was hip and expressed the inexpressible feelings of what it meant to be "young, gifted, and black" in the midst of the Civil Rights Movement.

At times hard bop was bluesy, bleak, and sorrow-filled, but—like gospel, blues, bebop, rhythm & blues, and soul—it transformed and transfigured those pent-up feelings by both exorcising them and reinterpreting them through a Civil Rights Movement-centered worldview, undaunted verve, and history-making musical acumen. In a way, then, hard bop was the 1960s funk of the Civil Rights Movement, where the James Brown/Sly Stone/George Clinton-style funk was the 1970s funk of the Black Power Movement. In keeping with the inversions that are so common within African American colloquial communities, hard bop was "bad" music. Meaning "bad" in the sense that James Brown was a "baaad-mother-*you-betta-shut-yo-mouth*!," hard bop was simultaneously cathartic to blacks and seemingly threatening to whites. Similar to 1970s funk, hard bop funk refused to fit into nice and neat little categories created by Eurocentric music critics and their minions, and herein lies part of the reason it was so threatening to whites.

The word "hard" in hard bop suggests that the music offered an outlet for hard feelings, thoughts, and political points of view that might have been otherwise suppressed in light of the soft sounds and crossover craze that preoccupied Motown and the Brill Building in the 1960s. Hard bop classics such as Art Blakey's "Message from Kenya" (1957), "The Freedom Rider" (1961), and "Freedom Monday"(1965); Horace Silver's "Safari" (1953), "The Preacher" (1955), "Pyramid" (1958), "The Baghdad Blues" (1959), "The Tokyo Blues" (1962), "The Cape Verdean Blues" (1965), "The African Queen" (1965), "Mexican Hip Dance" (1966), "Rain Dance" (1968), and "Serenade to a Soul Sister" (1968); Wayne Shorter's "The Back Sliders" (1961), "Tell It Like it Is" (1961), and "Those Who Sit and Wait" (1961); Lee Morgan's "The Witch Doctor" (1961), "Search for the New Land" (1964), "Mr. Kenyatta" (1964), "Cornbread" (1965), "The Rajah" (1966), and "Zambia" (1966); Cedar Walton's "The Promised Land" (1962) and "Afreaka" (1967); Curtis Fuller's "Arabia" (1961), "The High Priest" (1963), and "The Egyptian" (1965); Jackie McLean's "116th and Lenox" (1959), "Appointment in Ghana" (1960), "Medina" (1960), "Street Singer" (1960), and "Let Freedom Ring" (1962); and, finally, John Coltrane's "Dakar" (1957), "Bahia" (1958), "Black Pearls" (1958), "Dial Africa" (1958), "Gold Coast" (1958), "Tanganyika Strut" (1958), "Liberia" (1960), "Africa" (1961), "Dahomey Dance" (1961), "Tunji" (1962), "Spiritual" (1962), "India" (1963), and "Alabama" (1963) all in one way or another speak to hard bop's broadened political palette and cultural identification, not only with the Civil Rights Movement, but also with the struggles of other oppressed people around the world. Obviously hard boppers connected African Americans' culture and struggles for freedom with continental African cultures and struggles for freedom.[6]

As if picking up where some of Billie Holiday's protest songs, Bud Powell's tortured piano playing, and Charles Mingus's thunderous bass plucking left off in the 1950s, between the early- to mid-1960s hard bop audaciously expressed deeper thoughts and darker feelings—thoughts and feelings that frequently and unrepentantly conveyed moral outrage and malicious irony, as well as political depression and social despair that often mirrored the suffering and setbacks of the Civil Rights Movement. However, as Ingrid Monson argued in *Freedom Sounds: Civil Rights Call Out to Jazz and Africa* (2007), jazz in general, and the hard bop of the 1950s and 1960s in particular, sonically registered more than the politics of the Civil Rights Movement—it was also aurally indicative of more than a century of struggle against American apartheid:

> Any account of the politics of race in jazz during the 1950s and 1960s must surely begin with a recognition of the structural significance of Jim Crow policies for the music world. To begin with, the history of this music called jazz, from its origins through the golden age, is coextensive with the history of Jim Crow segregation. In this sense, Jim Crow functioned as a structural condition over which the emergence of the genre took place, and its effects were not limited to the South. Shortly after *Plessy vs. Ferguson* (1896)—the Supreme Court decision that established the doctrine of "separate but equal"— Buddy Bolden's band dazzled New Orleans with a distinctive sound that heralded the synthesis of ragtime, blues, spirituals, classical music, marches, and popular songs that became jazz. At the other end of the period under study, the passage of the Civil Rights Act of 1964 and the Voting Rights Act of 1965 (which dismantled the legal basis for racial segregation) saw the recording of John Coltrane's *A Love Supreme*, the flourishing of Miles Davis's second great quintet, and the experimentalism of Sun Ra's *Heliocentric World*. This is not to suggest that Jim Crow *caused* jazz but to recognize that, throughout the establishment and flourishing of the genre, discriminatory practices in the music industry and society indelibly shaped everyday life for musicians and their audiences. Segregation also concentrated a great deal of African American musical talent in the "racially expected" genres of jazz, blues, and gospel since the opportunities in other genres, such as classical music, were limited. (6–7, emphasis in original)

Hard bop funk, as with the Black Power funk of the 1970s that would follow in its wake, was a form of both *sonic contestation* and *social contestation*. Similar to the emergence of jazz, which was in part a response to *Plessy vs. Ferguson*, hard bop funk arose in the midst of the social and political upheavals that led to and fueled the Civil Rights Movement. It was able to convey social messages and make political statements that both rhythm & blues and rock & roll had to skirt around precisely because it was, for the most part, a nonverbal or lyricless form of music that was open to multiple interpretations. Connected to the above contention that hard bop frequently expressed deeper thoughts and darker feelings is the notion that its nonverbal communication, and often its song titles, actually spoke loud and quite clearly about how hard boppers felt about "discriminatory practices in the music industry and society."

Hard bop's deeper thoughts and darker feelings were frequently expressed in its preference for slower tempos, extensive use of the minor mode, gospel chords, and blues-based phrasing. Hence, if the popular image of beboppers (wearing berets and horn-rimmed glasses, as well as sporting meerschaum pipes) suggested the aloof intellectual and political dissident, the brash image of hard boppers reached all the way back to the roots of black popular music, specifically gospel and blues, while simultaneously synthesizing those hallowed roots with rhythm & blues musicians and civil rights workers' African American modernist ethos between 1955 and 1965. This new synthesized gospel, blues, and rhythm & blues-based jazz prompted a new relationship with those aspects of African American culture there were looked down on and dismissed by white America and the black bourgeoisie. As a result, even though "funk" initially meant an unpleasant odor, within the vibrant vernacular world of hard bop it was transfigured into a musical *and* cultural metaphor that ultimately came to convey African American history, culture, and struggle-centered originality, authenticity, and hybridity. Just as the Civil Rights Movement sought to upset the established social and political order, the first wave of funk between 1955 and 1965 sought to upset the established musical and cultural order by emphasizing aspects of African American history and culture that hard bop funksters believed should be shared and used in the ongoing struggle to achieve civil rights, social justice, and artistic innovation.

Foreshadowing 1970s funk in relationship to the Black Power Movement, hard bop—again, the funk of the 1950s and 1960s—was more than merely music, and it frequently reflected the major breakthroughs and setbacks of the Civil Rights Movement. Describing hard bop as "music of cultural burial and cultural awakening" in *Freedom Is, Freedom Ain't: Jazz and the Making of the Sixties* (2003), Scott Saul effectively argued that hard bop channeled the artistic, political, and spiritual impulses of the Civil Rights Movement:

> Hard bop was the music of a generation, born in the 1920s and early 1930s, who imaginatively tried to recapture the roots of jazz in gospel and the blues while extending its ambition in the realm of art, politics, and spirituality (and often some combination of the three). Flowing in the post-war period out of cities like Chicago, Indianapolis, Pittsburgh, Detroit, and New York, it was unabashedly urban music, music that had a gem-like toughness and brilliance, a balance of glamour and grit. Jazz before had been "hot" or "cool," but hard bop was intense, soulful, unfussy, insistent—too agitated to be simply hot, too moody to be simply cool. The music crystallized in tandem with the Civil Rights Movement and was in many ways its sonic alter ego. Like the movement, it grounded new appeals for freedom in older idioms of black spirituality, challenging the nation's public account of itself and testifying to the black community's cultural power. And, like the movement again, it worked through a kind of orchestrated disruption—a musical version of what civil rights workers called "direct action," which jazz musicians experienced as a rhythmic

assertiveness and a newly taut relation between the demands of composition
and the possibilities of improvisation. (2–3)

The funk of the Black Power Movement could be said to sonically capture
not only African Americans' artistic, political, and spiritual impulses in the
1970s, but also African Americans' intellectual (in light of the Black Studies
Movement), cultural (in light of black nationalism), and sexual (in light of
the Sexual Liberation Movement) impulses in the 1970s. This is not to say
that hard bop did not express African Americans' intellectual, cultural, and
sexual impulses in the 1950s and early- to mid-1960s, but that by the late
1960s and throughout the 1970s these collective urges were more pronounced as a result of the radical rhetoric, politics, and aesthetics that characterized the Black Power Movement. Consequently, right alongside rhythm &
blues, rock & roll, and soul, hard bop provided a major musical *and* political
model for 1970s funk. And, when Saul suggested that hard bop was in many
senses the "sonic alter ego" of the Civil Rights Movement, his work seems to
hint at the ways in which hard bop, by speaking a special truth that was not
conveyed by rhythm & blues, rock & roll, soul, or prominent civil rights
leaders, also harbored some of the tension and turbulence of times.

As a matter of fact, when we seriously consider the assertion that hard
bop was in essence the "sonic alter ego" of the Civil Rights Movement, we
are able to reinterpret the decidedly deeper thoughts and darker feelings of
the hard bop funksters as, however culturally coded, corollaries of the rhetoric, political values, and desegregated social visions of Martin Luther King,
Ella Baker, Malcolm X, Fannie Lou Hamer, Bayard Rustin, Septima Clark,
the National Association for the Advancement of Colored People (NAACP),
the National Urban League (NUL), the Congress of Racial Equality (CORE),
the Southern Christian Leadership Conference (SCLC), the Student Nonviolent Coordinating Committee (SNCC), and National Council of Negro Wom-
en (NCNW), among others. As with the work of each of these individuals
and organizations during the Civil Rights Movement, hard bop harbored the
hurt and articulated the excruciating angst African Americans experienced
during the decade-long struggle against American apartheid that began with
the 1955 Montgomery Bus Boycott and ended with the passage of the Voting
Rights Act of 1965.

Truth be told, tension and turbulence are actually at the heart of hard bop,
and it can be easily heard *and* heartfelt in Art Blakey's earth-shaking kick
drum and clamoring press-rolls; in the pioneering funky piano grooves put
down by Horace Silver; in the mercurial and trenchant muted trumpet of
Miles Davis; in the roaring and seemingly always over-the-top saxophonic
brilliance of Sonny Rollins; in the take-no-prisoners protest songs that Nina
Simone never tired of singing; in the alluring "ugly beauty" of Thelonious
Monk's rhythmically complex and dissonance-filled piano playing; in the

gutbucket blues-influenced simultaneously "Negro spiritual" and "Eastern" spirituality sound John Coltrane seemed to effortlessly coax from his saxophone; in the endless squeaking and slightly sharp notes Jackie McLean seemed to slip into each and every one of his alto saxophone solos; in the volcanic drumming that drove Max Roach's great quintet with Clifford Brown to play like their lives depended on it night after night; in the hair-curling screams and improvisational genius that made it appear as though Charles Mingus was preaching while plucking and often pounding his bass; and, finally, in the histrionic and frequently harsh singing of Abbey Lincoln that seemed to eerily invoke the protest songs of Ma Rainey, Bessie Smith, and Billie Holiday.

The main point of convergence for the hard boppers was, on the one hand, their use of their music to express the hard lives and harsh conditions under which most African Americans lived from day to day during the Civil Rights Movement. On the other hand, and part of what made the music more accessible than bebop, by imaginatively synthesizing jazz with gospel and openly borrowing from rhythm & blues, hard bop explored the highs and lows of African American life in the 1950s and 1960s. It could convey some of the sanctity of the spirituals and gospel on Sunday morning while simultaneously alluding to the latest rhythm & blues hit that had everyone bumping and grinding in the juke joint on Saturday night. This same sonic range, from black spirituality to black sexuality, can be found in 1970s funk. And, whether one turns to the sensuous sounds of the Ohio Players on albums such as *Pain* (1971), *Pleasure* (1972), *Ecstasy* (1973), *Climax* (1974), *Skin Tight* (1974), *Fire* (1975) and *Honey* (1975), or the musical mysticism of Earth, Wind & Fire on albums such as *Last Days and Time* (1972), *Head to the Sky* (1973), *Open Your Eyes* (1974), *That's the Way of the World* (1975), *Gratitude* (1975), *Spirit* (1976), and *All & All* (1977), themes of both black spirituality and black sexuality continued to characterize funk in the 1970s.

As it continued to evolve in the 1960s, hard bop was increasingly influenced by soul. Similar to its incorporation of aspects of rhythm & blues into its sound in the 1950s, hard bop became more "soulful" in the 1960s, and hit songs such as Herbie Hancock's "Watermelon Man" (1962), Lee Morgan's "The Sidewinder" (1963), Donald Byrd's "Cristo Redentor" (1963), Horace Silver's "Song for My Father" (1964), Duke Pearson's "Wahoo!" (1964), and Cannonball Adderley's "Mercy, Mercy, Mercy" (1966) often sound like jazz versions of popular soul songs. In fact, Saul (2003) went so far to say, hard bop "was always tying together aesthetics and ethics, the style of soul and the mandate of soul." However, with its unmediated Civil Rights Movement-centered social messages and political statements, at its heart hard bop "hoped to evoke a new mobilization of black energy." And, through this "new mobilization of black energy," it aspired to "galvanize a larger 'Freedom Movement' that extended from the early stirrings of the Civil Rights

Movement through the late-sixties' mobilizations of the black community under the signs of "Black Power" and "Soul Power" (3).

All of this is to say, along with being "music of cultural burial and cultural awakening" (*burying* the setbacks of the Civil Rights Movement and the pop music pretensions of the 1960s, and *birthing* a harder and rhythmically heavier sound to coincide with the radical politics of the Black Power Movement), 1970s funk amazingly carried over and captured elements of both the moderatism and militantism, integrationism and suppressed nationalism of the Civil Rights Movement.

JAMES BROWN: FROM THE FOUNDATIONS OF FUNK TO THE RHYTHMS AND RHYMES OF RAP

Similar to the hard boppers of the 1950s and early 1960s, by the mid-1960s soul artists' work began to show the influence of the burgeoning Black Power Movement. One of the first major soul artists to get "funky" and open their music to the rhetoric and politics of the Black Power Movement was undoubtedly James Brown. Born on May 3, 1933, in Barnwell, South Carolina, to Susie Brown and Joseph Gardner, Brown grew up in abject poverty. When he was two years old, his parents separated and eventually divorced after his mother left his father for another man. His mother subsequently abandoned the family and until the age of six he lived with his father and his father's live-in girlfriends. By the age of seven he was abandoned by his father and sent to live with his aunt, who ran a whorehouse. Dropping out of school in the seventh grade, like many hip hoppers, Brown learned his lessons in the streets, hanging out, hustling, shining shoes, sweep store floors, washing cars and dishes, and, most importantly, singing and dancing. [7]

In trouble with the law, at the age of sixteen Brown was convicted of armed robbery and sent to a juvenile detention center in Toccoa, which is in upstate Georgia, in 1949. In jail, he focused on singing and dancing, and he also learned to play guitar, piano, and drums. By 1955 he was out of jail and the lead singer of a gospel group called the Gospel Starlighters, which eventually morphed into a rhythm & blues group called the Flames. Deeply influenced by Louis Jordan, Ray Charles, Roy Brown, Little Willie John, Wynonie Harris, Clyde McPhatter, Jackie Wilson, Hank Ballard, and Little Richard, Brown obsessively soaked up as much of the 1950s rhythm & blues scene as he possibly could, studying the lyrics, music, dance moves, and showmanship of his idols. It was not long before Brown began to produce hit songs, including "Please, Please, Please" (1956), "Try Me" (1958), "I'll Go Crazy" (1960), "Think" (1960), "Lost Someone" (1961), "Night Train" (1961), and "Prisoner of Love" (1963).

By 1964 Brown had grown restless. Constantly touring during the Civil Rights Movement, he saw firsthand how African Americans were being mistreated and the harsh conditions under which they worked and lived—conditions very similar to the ones he grew up in. Which is to say, he and his band were not immune to American apartheid. They experienced segregation and racial discrimination just like working-class and underclass African Americans. Enough was enough. He made up his mind: more than sweaty love songs were needed. Brown ingeniously sought to sonically capture the new rhymes and new rhythms of African America. Almost as if responding to the March on Washington, which took place on August 28, 1963, in July of 1964 Brown released a twelve-bar blues titled "Out of Sight."

Seeming to sonically replicate the marching, cheering, and call-and-response singing of the March on Washington, "Out of Sight" featured stuttering, lockstep staccato dance rhythms and blaring horn blasts that were in essence the polyrhythmic alter ego of the increasingly pop-oriented and soft sounding songs that were beginning to pass for rhythm & blues in the mid-1960s. With "Out of Sight," Brown virtually single-handedly rerooted rhythm & blues in the African rhythms and the blues that had always distinguished black popular music from mainstream popular music. Reflecting on his breakthrough in his autobiography, *James Brown: The Godfather of Soul* (1986), he wrote:

> "Out of Sight" was another beginning, musically and professionally. My music—and most music—changed with "Papa's Got a Brand New Bag," but it really started on "Out of Sight," just like the change from R&B to soul started with "Think" and "I'll Go Crazy." You can hear the band and me start to move in a whole other direction rhythmically. The horns, the guitar, the vocals, everything was starting to be used to establish all kinds of rhythms at once. On that record you can hear my voice alternate with the horns to create various rhythmic accents. I was trying to get every aspect of the production to contribute to the rhythmic patterns. What most people don't realize is that I had been doing the multiple rhythm patterns for years on stage, but . . . I had agreed to make the rhythms on the records a lot simpler. (149)

By refusing to rhythmically dumb down his music any longer, Brown's game-changing rhythmic experiments were in essence the polyrhythmic equivalent to Curtis Mayfield's Civil Rights Movement-centered lyrical experiments on songs such as "It's All Right" (1963), "Keep on Pushing" (1964), "Amen" (1965), and "People Get Ready" (1965). Recorded in February of 1965, Brown's "Papa's Got a Brand New Bag" was in many ways a musical response to Malcolm X's assassination on February 21, 1965, and a sonic harbinger of the five days of fury that have come to be called the "Watts Riots," which rocked Los Angeles from August 11–15, 1965, and resulted in 34 deaths, 1,032 injuries, 3,438 arrests, and over $40 million in property damage. Released on July 17, 1965, "Papa's Got a Brand New Bag" reached *Billboard*'s Hot R&B Singles top slot on August 14, 1965, in the midst of the Watts Riots and held that position for an astonishing eight weeks. It was also Brown's first song to make it into the Top Ten of *Billboard*'s Hot 100, peaking at number eight.

"Papa's Got a Brand New Bag" was, indeed, a "new bag." Building on the polyrhythmic experiments initiated with "Out of Sight," "Papa's Got a Brand New Bag" had all of the hallmarks of what would soon be recognized as "funk" with its propulsive percussiveness extending to Brown's voice and every instrument. Waves of rhythms hit the listeners, hinting at funk's roots in earlier forms of black popular music. It was gospel and blues, jazz and rhythm & blues, rock & roll and soul all rolled into one, and it had enough moxie to make even the most stoic and stiff-necked listeners get up and dance. Using a series of incredibly talented post-bop and soul musicians, Brown's funk stripped down the harmonic and melodic aspects of his music, which consequently exposed the complex rhythmic core of black popular music.

Brown's funk remixed the rhythms of various forms of black popular music and placed them together, simultaneously jumping and bumping, swinging and sweating to one overarching—albeit most often polyrhythmic—beat. *Where other pioneers in rhythm & blues and soul built on the lyrical, harmonic, and melodic breakthroughs of previous forms of black popular music, Brown's music was arguably the first to focus on the rhythmic contributions of previous forms of black popular music and synthesize them into a completely new form of black popular music*: funk. In a sense, Brown's emphasis on the distinct rhythms of black popular music means that at the exact moment that African Americans were seeking to *re-Africanize* themselves by reconnecting with their African heritage during the Black Power Movement he contributed to *the re-Africanization process* by highlighting the importance of reconnecting with the distinctly African musical elements of African Americans' African heritage. Rhythm has always been associated with the African aspects of African American music, and Brown *re-Africanized* black popular music in the 1960s and 1970s by "establish[ing] all kinds of rhythms at once" and by "get[ting] every aspect of the production to contribute to the rhythmic patterns."[8]

By emphasizing rhythm over melody, proto-rap-styled chanting over Motown black pop-styled singing, Brown and his band, literally, laid the foundation for funk. After the phenomenal success of "Papa's Got a Brand New Bag," Brown went on to release a series of socially relevant songs that were in clear contrast to the dance ditties and yearning ballads of his early rhythm & blues years. Songs such as "Money Won't Change You" (1966), "Don't Be a Dropout" (1966), "Get It Together" (1967), "Give It Up or Turn It a Loose" (1968), "I Don't Want Nobody to Give Me Nothing (Open Up the

Door and I'll Get It Myself)" (1969), "Talkin' Loud & Sayin' Nothing" (1970), "Get Up, Get Into It, and Get Involved" (1970), "Soul Power" (1971), "King Heroin" (1972), "Public Enemy #1" (1972), "Get on the Good Foot" (1972), "I Got a Bag of My Own" (1972), "The Payback" (1974), "Papa Don't Take No Mess" (1974), and "Funky President (People It's Bad)" (1974) unambiguously reflect both the rhetoric and political radicalism of the Black Power Movement.

Brown's funk formula ultimately featured a panoply of heavy poly-rhythms, choppy guitar riffs, bustling basslines, Stax-styled horn blasts, and hard bop-inspired improvisations that were offset by his gritty, gravel-voiced *gospelisms* and frenzy-filled screeches, which seemed to simultaneously reach back to jazz and jump blues and push forward to rap and neo-soul. His music was the heartbeat of black America during the Black Power Move-ment, and arguably none of his songs drives this point home better than his immortal Black Power anthem "Say It Loud—I'm Black and I'm Proud." Recorded and released in the aftermath of Martin Luther King's assassination on April 4, 1968, "Black and Proud" was preceded by the sentimental sound-ing "America Is My Home" in June of 1968. Disillusioned, morally outraged, and still reeling after King's assassination, black America would have none of Brown's "America Is My Home" schmaltz. The song flopped, and he caught a lot of flack from the swelling ranks of black radicals. By July of 1968 Brown wanted to demonstrate that he was still committed to *black empowerment* and deeply outraged by what seemed to be an all-out govern-ment-sanctioned assault on black America.

"Black and Proud" was a career-defining moment for James Brown and a turning point in black popular music. As if channeling Martin Luther King and Malcolm X's high-sounding and hyperbole-filled rhetoric, Brown's "Black and Proud" was a mixture of socially relevant lyrics and funky rhythms. Moreover, the song's call-and-response could be said to signify that both King and Malcolm were African American preachers who consistently used antiphony in both their sermons and political speeches. More specifical-ly, "Black and Proud" invoked Malcolm with its emphasis on black pride and black self-determination. It conjured up the spirit of King and the social vision of the Civil Rights Movement with its clever reference to the spiritual "I've Been 'Buked"—paraphrasing the song to emphasize how African Americans have been "'buked" and been "scorned," and how they have "been treated bad," and "talked about as sure as you're born." Like the funksters and political rappers who would follow in his footsteps, Brown sought to make his music speak to the special needs of African Americans, especially the African American underclass. As a consequence, many in white America denounced him for making such a bold statement concerning black pride. Consequently, for all intents and purposes, white America la-beled Brown a rabble-rouser and, from his point of view, "blacklisted" him and banned his records from the pop charts. Writing candidly of this difficult period in his autobiography, Brown (1986) sternly stated:

> You shouldn't have to tell people what race you are, and you shouldn't have to teach people they should be proud. But it was necessary to teach pride then, and I think the song did a lot of good for a lot of people. That song scared people, too. Many white people didn't understand it any better than many Afro-Americans understood "America Is My Home." People called "Black and Proud" militant and angry—maybe because of the line about dying on your feet instead of living on your knees. . . . The song cost me a lot of my crossover audience. The racial makeup at my concerts was mostly black after that. I don't regret recording it, though, even if it was misunderstood. It was badly needed at the time. It helped Afro-Americans in general and the dark-skinned man in particular. I'm proud of that. (200)

In the musical aftermath of "Black and Proud" direct references to race, racism, the ghetto, and poverty became much more prevalent in black popular music. Hence, along with being an innovator in terms of expanding the polyrhythmic palette of rhythm & blues and soul, Brown is also a lyrical innovator—unrepentantly expressing the raw emotions and long-repressed radicalism of black America as it transitioned from the Civil Rights Movement to the Black Power Movement, from rhythm & blues and rock & roll to soul and funk. Both lyrically and musically, most soul artists followed Brown's lead and began to produce funkier, more militant and socially relevant songs, for example: Curtis Mayfield's "Mighty Mighty (Spade and Whitey)" (1969); Sly & the Family Stone's "Don't Call Me Nigger, Whitey" (1969); the Staple Singers' "When Will We Be Paid?" (1969); the Temptations' "Message From a Black Man" (1969); Donny Hathaway's "The Ghetto" (1970); Marvin Gaye's "Inner-City Blues (Makes Me Wanna Holler)" (1971); Funkadelic's "America Eats Its Young" (1972); Eddie Kendricks' "My People . . . Hold On" (1972); Stevie Wonder's "Living for the City" (1973); Smokey Robinson's "Just My Soul Responding" (1973); and Willie Hutch's "Brother's Gonna Work It Out" (1973).

Brown continued to evolve his pioneering funk in the 1970s with classic albums such as *Ain't It Funky* (1970), *Sho' Is Funky Down Here* (1971), *Get on the Good Foot* (1972), *Black Caesar* (1973), *Slaughter's Big Rip-Off* (1973), *The Payback* (1974), *Hell* (1975), and *Reality* (1975). However, by 1976 he seems to have lost steam, as his music became quite formulaic, almost as if he retreated from the funky polyrhythms he pioneered in favor of softer, simpler, disco-friendly beats. Influencing everyone from Motown to Miles Davis, the Isley Brothers to the Ohio Players, and Parliament/Funkadelic to Earth, Wind & Fire, as the 1970s and disco came to an end and the 1980s and the funk-based rap phenomenon began, James Brown's influence was seemingly ubiquitous.

After openly acknowledging Brown and recording the rap track "Unity" with him in 1984, it could be argued that it was Afrika Bambaataa who "hipped" the Hip Hop Generation to James Brown. It was as if Brown came back with a vengeance, as many of the most memorable and groundbreaking rap songs of the 1980s and 1990s featured either classic James Brown songs or classic James Brown-produced songs. For instance, Brown's once controversial "Say It Loud—I'm Black and I'm Proud" (1968) was sampled in: Eric B. & Rakim's "Move the Crowd" (1987); MC Shan's "Down By Law" (1987); Big Daddy Kane's "Long Live the Kane" (1988); Public Enemy's "Fight the Power" (1989); MC Lyte's "Throwin' Words at U" (1989); N.W.A.'s "100 Miles and Runnin'" (1990); Ice Cube's "Jackin' for Beats" (1990); Brand Nubian's "Dedication" (1990) and "I'm Black and I'm Proud" (1998); Salt-N-Pepa's "Do You Want Me?" (1990); Intelligent Hoodlum's "Black and Proud" (1990); Run-D.M.C.'s "Naughty" (1990); Grand Puba's "Lickshot" (1992); and Cypress Hill's "Insane in the Brain" (1993), among many others.

Brown's "Funky Drummer" (1970) was sampled in: Grandmaster Flash's "Fastest Man Alive" (1986); Sweet Tee and Jazzy Joyce's "It's My Beat" (1986); Boogie Down Productions' "South Bronx" (1987); Public Enemy's "Bring the Noise" (1987), "Rebel Without a Pause" (1987), "She Watch Channel Zero?!" (1988), "Fight the Power" (1989), and "Hazy Shade of Criminal" (1992); Big Daddy Kane's "Somethin' Funky" (1987); Run-D.M.C.'s "Beats to the Rhyme" (1988) and "Run's House" (1988); Stetsasonic's "We're the Band" (1988) and "Sally" (1988); J.J. Fad's "Let's Get Hyped" (1988) and "Comin' Correct" (1988); Slick Rick's "The Moment I Feared" (1988); the Beastie Boys' "Shadrach" (1989) and "Three MC's and One DJ" (1998); Paris's "I Call Him Mad" (1989) and "The Devil Made Me Do It" (1989); Mellow Man Ace's "River Cubano" (1989); the Geto Boys' "Mind of a Lunatic" (1989) and "Read the Nikes" (1989); 2 Live Crew's "Coolin'" (1989); Kool Moe Dee's "I'm Blowin' Up" (1989) and "Knowledge Is King" (1989); the D.O.C.'s "Let the Bass Go!" (1989); LL Cool J's "Nitro" (1989), "Mama Said to Knock You Out" (1990), "The Boomin' System" (1990), and "Who's Afraid of the Big Bad Wolf?" (1991); and EPMD's "I'm Mad" (1990), among many others.

Brown's "Get Up, Get Into It, Get Involved" (1970) was sampled in: Eric B. & Rakim's "Eric B. Is President" (1986); Public Enemy's "Bring the Noise" (1987), "Party for Your Right to Fight" (1988), "Brother's Gonna Work It Out" (1990), and "Can't Truss It" (1991); Big Daddy Kane's "Get Into It" (1987) and "Set It Off" (1988); 2 Live Crew's "Drop the Bomb" (1988); MC Shan's "Juice Crew Law" (1988); the Beastie Boys' "The Sound of Science" (1989); Gang Starr's "Got U" (1989); LL Cool J's "Mr. Good Bar" (1990); Run-D.M.C.'s "Bounce" (1993); and Organized Konfusion's "Maintain" (1994), among many others. By not only placing a greater em-

phasis on rhythm, but also by proto-rapping about the ongoing harsh realities
African Americans faced in the post-Civil Rights Movement period, James
Brown and his pioneering funk became one of the core models for rappers
and rap music. But, long before the rappers raised him up and revered his
music and uncompromising messages in the 1980s and 1990s, Brown's contemporaries recognized his musical and less-is-more lyrical genius. It could
be said that Brown's soulful funk helped to update the black popular music
aesthetic and turn it away from the crossover craze and pop pretentions that
many believe black popular music was being held hostage to in the mid- to
late-1960s.

As Brown's music grew lyrically and rhythmically heavier in the late
1960s, whites who had been moved by the funky sounds of "Out of Sight"
and "Papa's Got a Brand New Bag" continued to crave the new music, but
since Brown had alienated his white audience with "Black and Proud" there
was an opening for one of his at this point legions of aural acolytes. Finding
his way into the fray, Sylvester Stewart, who is better known by his stage
name Sly Stone, was certainly not a musically reincarnated James Brown.
However, by the time Sly & the Family Stone released their more soul than
funk debut, *A Whole New Thing*, in July of 1967, he had absorbed enough of
Brown's funk, Motown's uptown soul, Stax's southern soul, and psychedelic
rock to jump-start a more white folk-friendly form of funk that would popularize funk in ways that James Brown probably never imagined.

SLY & THE FAMILY STONE: FROM PSYCHEDELIC SOUL
TO PSYCHEDELIC FUNK

Born in Denton, Texas, on March 15, 1943, Sylvester Stewart moved with
his family to San Francisco, California, when he was nine years old. A
musical prodigy, by the time he was seven he had mastered the piano. By
eleven he had mastered the guitar, bass, and drums as well. Prior to his high
school years he put his musical talent to use in his family's gospel group,
"The Stewart Four," an experience which profoundly shaped his musical
vision and throaty gospel-influenced vocals for the rest of his life. After high
school he played in several unsuccessful local bands.

Frustrated and in need of a consistent paycheck to make ends meet, Stewart went to radio school and eventually became one of the first DJs on the
new black radio station KSOL in 1966. That same year he formed a new
group, "The Stoners," a name which hinted at his increasing fascination with
drugs. From the beginning, the Stoners were different. The core of the band
featured two black women (Cynthia Robinson on trumpet and Sly's sister
Rose Stone on piano); two whites (Jerry Martini on saxophone and Gregg
Errico on drums); and three black men (Sly Stone on piano, organ, guitar,

bass, harmonica, etc., Larry Graham on bass, and Sly's brother Freddie Stone on guitar). As they morphed from Sly & the Stoners into Sly & the Family Stone, Sly recruited his younger sister's gospel group, the Heavenly Tones, which featured Vaetta Stewart (a.k.a. Vet Stone), Mary McCreary, and Elva Mouton, and affectionately rechristened them "Little Sister" to handle background vocals.[9]

After the disappointing sales of their debut album in 1967, Sly & the Family Stone went back into the studio determined to make an album that would reach across the chasms of race and class, as well as the increasingly rigid musical categories that racialized rock as "white music" and soul as "black music." In essence, playing the part of the more conciliatory and integrationist-oriented Martin Luther King-style musical genius to James Brown's more militant and black nationalist-oriented Malcolm X-style musical genius, Sly & the Family Stone's second album, *Dance to the Music* (1968), was filled with inventiveness and youthful exuberance. With *Dance to the Music* the world got its first glimpse of Sly Stone's genius, as he articulated his Civil Rights Movement-centered vision of peace, brotherly love, and antiracism over a mind-boggling blend of psychedelic rock, soul, and funk that was every bit as moving as James Brown's more jazz, rhythm & blues, and soul-based funk.

By smoothing out the rough edges of both psychedelic rock and soul, and simultaneously synthesizing it with a more polished and pop-sounding version of James Brown's pioneering funk, *Dance to the Music*, especially the title track, helped to establish a new subgenre within soul: *psychedelic soul*. Drawing on Jimi Hendrix's psychedelic rock, James Brown's funk, and his own eclectic gospel-soul genius, Stone's new psychedelic soul sound emphasized Motown-like pop-soul songwriting; Stax-styled blaring horns; heavily distorted organ; fuzz, wah-wah, phaser, and reverb guitar effects; pulsing, popping, slapping, and speaker-rattling basslines; funky backbeat drumming; African and other "exotic" percussion, especially congas, bongos, and chimes; and "trippy" recording studio sound effects and production techniques.

A *Billboard* Pop Singles Top 10 hit, "Dance to the Music" almost immediately influenced and altered the sound of soul. As a matter of fact, the influence of Sly & the Family Stone's psychedelic soul sound can be easily detected on: the Temptations' "Cloud Nine" (1968), "Runaway Child, Running Wild" (1969), "Psychedelic Shack" (1969), "Ball of Confusion (That's What the World Is Today)" (1970), "You Make Your Own Heaven and Hell Right Here on Earth" (1970), "Ungena Za Ulimwengu (Unite the World)" (1971), "Papa Was a Rollin' Stone" (1972), and "Masterpiece" (1973); Curtis Mayfield's "(Don't Worry) If There's a Hell Below, We're All Going to Go" (1970), "Move on Up" (1970), "Get Down" (1971), "Beautiful Brother of Mine" (1971), "Superfly" (1972), "Pusherman" (1972), "Freddie's Dead"

(1972), and "Future Shock" (1973); the Supremes' "Love Child" (1968) and "Stoned Love" (1970); Edwin Starr's "War" (1970); the 5th Dimension's *Stoned Soul Picnic* (1968), *The Age of Aquarius* (1969), and *Portrait* (1970); and the Undisputed Truth's "What It Is?" (1971), "Smiling Faces Sometimes (Tell Lies)" (1971), "Mama I Got A Brand New Thing" (1972), "Law of the Land" (1973), "Help Yourself" (1974), "I'm a Fool For You" (1974), "Spaced Out" (1975), "U.F.O.'s" (1975), and "Higher Than High" (1975).

Continuing in the psychedelic soul and pop-funk vein, Sly & the Family Stone released *Life* in September of 1968. Somewhere between the explosive tentativeness of *A Whole New Thing* and the commercial inventiveness of *Dance to the Music*, *Life* was not a commercial success, but it was a much more cohesive slice of psychedelic soul and pop-funk than its predecessors. The album featured better songwriting, tighter and funkier grooves, and an even heavier dose of sonic psychedelics. To state it outright, Sly & the Family Stone sounded like a band (albeit a genre-jumping psychedelic rock-soul-funk band), and their singing and playing on *Life* reflected the unity they passionately sang about on songs like "Fun," "Harmony," "Life," and "Love City." Boldly building on *Life*, Sly & the Family Stone's fourth album, *Stand!* (1969), focused almost exclusively on the themes of unity, brotherly love, and integration, but it also importantly added hate, racism, sex, and the resilience of the human spirit in the aftermath of the Civil Rights Movement to the mix.

Stand! was a turning point for Sly & the Family Stone. To begin, it had a different lyrical and musical feel than the previous Sly & the Family Stone albums. On *Life*, Stone balanced the heavier political or message tracks "Fun," "Harmony," "Life," and "Love City" with lighter, almost innocuous tracks like "Dynamite!," "Chicken," and "M'Lady." On *Stand!* every track, except for "Sex Machine," revealed a more militant-minded Sly Stone with progressive and often extremely provocative thoughts about serious social and political issues. With even better songwriting on *Stand!*, Stone's lyrical wit was infectious, and with each song displaying a rare funk-based rhythmic brilliance, the grooves were relentless. It was virtually impossible to play the album and not both think deeply *and* dance with abandon. As a matter of fact, it seemed that *Stand!* had something for everyone: blistering black pride anthems ("Stand!" and "Don't Call Me Nigger, Whitey!"); an uplifting Mo-town-like pop-soul melody ("Everyday People"); dirty dance floor funk ("Sing a Simple Song"); much-needed optimism ("You Can Make It If You Try"); a commentary on the escalating COINTELPRO-induced paranoia within the Black Power Movement ("Somebody's Watching You"); and an epic thirteen-minute rhythm & blues-based bump-and-grind track where Sly's fuzz-filled harmonica playing sounds like Little Walter on LSD ("Sex Machine").[10]

Instead of the joyousness and playfulness that characterized most of their previous music, each song on *Stand!* was conceptually linked by its seriousness and social relevance. Hence, following in the footsteps of Jimi Hendrix's groundbreaking theme-oriented psychedelic rock albums *Are You Experienced?* (1967), *Axis: Bold as Love* (1967), and *Electric Ladyland* (1968), it could be argued that Stone helped to steer funk (and to a certain extent soul as well) toward the concept album format.[11] Essentially commenting on the entire social, political, and cultural landscape of black America in the late 1960s, *Stand!* was universal, yet centered on distinctly African American sociopolitical issues. It was broad, but narrow enough to appeal to black nationalist sentiments. It was celebratory and simultaneously solemn. It was frequently lighthearted, yet somehow consistently heavy-hearted. It was too black and too funky to be psychedelic rock, too optimistic and dance-inducing to be the blues, and too psychedelic and anarchic to be soul. By running a black life-based theme through each track, and by finally developing his songwriting to the point where his lyrics perfectly matched the soaring heights and dirty, deep funk depths of his innovative amalgam of psychedelic rock, soul, and funk, Sly Stone garnered a place right alongside Jimi Hendrix and James Brown as a quintessential influence on the evolution of funk in the 1970s.

However, even as he increasingly became the popular face of funk after Brown was blacklisted as a consequence of "Black and Proud," Stone was equally influential on the evolution of soul in the 1970s. As a matter of fact, the move toward concept albums in soul can be directly attributed to the impact of Stone's *Stand!* For example, soul concept albums such as: Isaac Hayes's *To Be Continued* (1970), *The Isaac Hayes Movement* (1970), and *Black Moses* (1971); Marvin Gaye's *What's Going On?* (1971), *Let's Get It On* (1973), *I Want You* (1976), and *Here, My Dear* (1978); Stevie Wonder's *Where I'm Coming From* (1971), *Music of My Mind* (1972), *Talking Book* (1972), *Innervisions* (1973), *Fulfillingness' First Finale* (1974), and *Songs in the Key of Life* (1976); Bill Withers's *Just As I Am* (1971), *Still Bill* (1972), and *+'Justments* (1974); the O'Jays' *Back Stabbers* (1972), *Ship Ahoy* (1973), *Family Reunion* (1975), *Survival* (1975), and *Message in the Music* (1976); and Smokey Robinson's *Smokey* (1973), *Pure Smokey* (1974), and *A Quiet Storm* (1975) all bear traces of Stone's influence by threading black love, black life, and black struggle-based recurring themes throughout the course of their albums.

As the 1960s ended and the 1970s began black America seems to have reached a crossroad. The high hopes of the Civil Rights Movement no longer seemed realistic in the aftermath of the setbacks of the late 1960s, especially Martin Luther King's assassination and most of white America's apparent indifference to ongoing black suffering and political struggles. Widespread disenchantment and disarray worked its way through the Black Power Movement: King's assassination; Black Panther Party leader Huey Newton's September 1968 conviction for fatally shooting Oakland police officer John Frey; Black Panther Party leader Bobby Seale's March 1969 indictment and conviction for conspiracy, inciting a riot, and other charges related to his participation in the protests outside of the 1968 Democratic National Convention in Chicago; and Angela Davis's October 1970 through June 1972 jail time for her suspected involvement in the Soledad Brothers' August 1970 abduction—all in many ways foreshadowed that the 1970s would be *a decade of disintegration as opposed to the long-hoped for decade of integration and cultural pluralism.* [12]

With most African Americans continuing to be socially segregated and economically exploited, the 1970s was a decade of deep disappointment, and black popular music, especially funk, registered this desperation and frustration. As if retreating to survey the social and political scene, Sly Stone did not release a followup album to *Stand!* in 1970; instead he produced three game-changing psychedelic funk singles in August and December of 1969 that raced up the charts and helped to hold his fan base. The first single was a dazzling psychedelic soul-style doo-wop-based ballad called "Hot Fun in the Summertime." With its dreamy lyrics and gently swinging, almost breezy syncopated beat, "Hot Fun" not only captured much of black America's lingering optimism like only chocolate-covered flower child Sly Stone could, but it also stood in stark contrast to a lot of the lyrical heaviness of *Stand!* Almost as if reassuring his white fan base that he could still be lyrically lighthearted, the flip side of the "Hot Fun" single featured "Fun" from the Family Stone's third album *Life*.

Sly & the Family Stone's last release of the 1960s was "Thank You (Falettinme Be Mice Elf Agin)," with "Everybody Is a Star" on the flip side. Many critics consider "Thank You" the first sonic salvo announcing the beginning of the Family Stone's second era, during which their music grew more militant and began to privilege heavy funk over psychedelic rock, creating a darker and deeper funk sound. Lyrically the song packed a punch, with every word harboring multiple meanings, and the meanings become even more meaningful when Sly's tortured lead vocals merged with the gospel choir background vocals of Rose Stone, Freddie Stone, Larry Graham, and Little Sister.

Musically the song churned and chugged along like a runaway train metaphorically heading away from white America and back to the heart of black America. With its darker and deeper funk sound, "Thank You" could be read as Sly Stone saying thank you to black America for supporting him and accepting him on his own psychedelic rock-soul-funk terms. The song can also be interpreted as Stone's aural assertion that *there quite simply is no single and definitive way to be black.* Indeed, he was black but had a serious relationship with psychedelic rock, the Hippie Movement, and other ele-

ments of white counterculture. The self-assertiveness of "Thank You" ingeniously gave way to the joyous celebration of difference on its flip side, the
aptly titled "Everybody Is a Star."

Sharing the lead vocals with Rose Stone, Freddie Stone, and Larry Graham, on "Everybody Is a Star," Sly Stone synthesized Motownesque pop-
soul with gritty Stax-style southern soul and produced a secular gospel sound
that was at once exuberant and edifying. Seeming to tap into the ethos of both
moderate and militant black America at the dawn of the 1970s, lyrically and
vocally Stone remixed his psychedelic soul concept and incorporated more
gospelisms into his overall sound. With its emphasis on the uniqueness and
humble dignity of each person, in a way with "Everybody Is a Star" Stone
demonstrated that whether his listeners were a part of moderate black America or militant black America, or white America in general, he still loved
"everyday people" and deeply believed that all people needed to be empowered and freed from repressive social, political, and cultural restrictions. It
was a message that re-emerged as the central motif of Sly & the Family
Stone's fifth album, the provocatively titled *There's a Riot Goin' On* (1971).

Originally titled *Africa Talks to You*, Sly retitled the album in response to
Marvin Gaye's *What's Going On?*, which was released to critical acclaim six
months before *There's a Riot Goin' On*. According to Miles Marshall Lewis
in his book-length commentary on the album, *Sly & the Family Stone's
There's a Riot Goin' On* (2006), "Sly's title was meant to answer Marvin
Gaye's rhetorical question" (69–118). Hence, Marvin rhetorically asked,
"What's going on?," and Sly rhetorically answered, "There's a riot goin' on."

Whatever vestiges of optimism that continued to linger in Stone's music
on *Stand!* and the three late 1969 singles had all but disappeared by the time
Riot was released. The pop-funk sound had been replaced by an eerie, fore-
boding deep funk sound. The beloved band sound of Sly & the Family Stone
had been replaced by the heavily overdubbed, multi-tracked, brooding and
often moody sounds of Sly Stone the psychedelic drug-taking and lyric-
slurring erratic solo artist. The Family Stone contributed here and there, but
overall, as Lewis noted, most critics "consider *There's a Riot Goin' On* Sly's
first solo album" (97).

Sly's heavy drug use, the pressures of superstardom, and the unprecedented tidal wave of black pride, black nationalism, and Pan-Africanism sweeping across African America in the early 1970s all contributed to his new,
even funkier sound, lyrical outlook, and social vision—as well as, unfortunately, the Family Stone's disbanding. As a consequence of Sly missing
countless concerts, or showing up too high to perform when he did drag
himself out of his drug-induced stupor, as well as repeatedly missing recording dates to work on their new album, the Family Stone began to painfully
drift apart. Embracing both the post-hippie hedonism and black radicalism of
the early 1970s, Sly's one-man *Riot*, similar to its predecessor *Stand!*, was

lyrically and musically sprawling, but there was one big difference according to Lewis: "[n]ever before on a Sly & the Family Stone album were songs open to so much interpretation and, even more so, dripping with cynicism. On the other hand you can hardly hear what he's saying for most of the album" (72).

When placed within the historical and musical context in which it emerged, it is conceivable that the bulk of *Riot*'s lyrics are intentionally indecipherable because—as Sly seemed to be saying at the time—"there's a riot goin' on," and riots are nothing if not full of sights and sounds that are difficult to comprehend. Riots are not rational and do not recognize the rules and regulations of civil society, and perhaps that was precisely the point of Sly's cryptic lyrics. In essence, he produced an album that mirrored the tension and turmoil, the contradictions and confusion ominously engulfing America in the early 1970s, and his muddy vocals and the sweat-drenched, mysterious, almost menacing sound of his solo funk was as intriguing as it was unsettling, as innovative as it was eerie, as esoteric as it was obviously anarchic. Lewis importantly explained:

> Like Radiohead's *Kid A* or even the Rolling Stones' *Exile on Main St.* more recent to the time, a murkiness in the mix of the record inhibits complete comprehension of the words. Sly reportedly "auditioned" random women in the studio to sing on *Riot*, then erased their vocals from the master recordings the morning after they, shall we say, danced to the music. This constant over-dubbing and erasure eventually created a muddy sound on the reel-to-reel tapes that left many of his vocals practically inaudible. Which means people looking for simple platitudes like *everybody is a star* of the past were left straining to decipher what Sly was now saying, what he meant by what he was saying, or what they thought they heard him saying. Again, fans of *Exile on Main St.* had the same problem. But it was much more rare, really totally unheard of, for a black artist to consciously create such a dilemma for his listeners. (73, emphasis in original) [13]

Similar to the funksters and rappers who would soon follow his lead, Sly's message-oriented music placed him at the heart of both American popular culture and American political culture. He was seen as an *artist* and an *activist* and, as a consequence, his new darker and, for the most part, deeper lyrics and music altered his long-standing image among his white fan base as the sagacious, uplifting, peaceful, and fun-loving "freaky" black bohemian. Moreover, at the exact tension-filled moment when "the public still believed that music could save and/or change the world—with evidence to the contrary only just surfacing—Sly Stone, if anyone, was expected to bring his universal optimism and acerbic social observations to the table and help everyone make heads or tails of what was happening to the country," asserted Lewis (72).

Stripped of the buoyancy that was so integral to the success of *Stand!*, *Riot* was the sound of youthful idealism embittered and often enraged. It was the sound of black America's disillusionment with how little things had really and truly changed for the black masses in the aftermath of the Civil Rights Movement. It was also Sly Stone's personal rejection of the "black hippie" stereotype—a rejection that actually reached back to "Thank You (Falettinme Be Mice Elf Agin)"—that seemed to place him, along with his contemporary Jimi Hendrix, in the new, post-Civil Rights Movement "colored section" reserved for "freaky" black rock artists.

Writing about Sly's refusal to be a psychedelic Uncle Tom and his evolving relationship with his white audience, Greil Marcus (1975) observed: "With *Riot*, Sly gave his audience—particularly his white audience—exactly what they didn't want. What they wanted was an upper, not a portrait of what lay behind the big freaky black superstar grin that decorated the cover of the album" (89). Consequently, *Riot* revealed that part of Sly's increasing reclusiveness was not merely eccentric behavior on the part of a "black hippie" superstar, but a reaction to the unrealistic and often antiblack racist, blackface minstrelesque demands of his white audience. Sly's response to post-Civil Rights Movement antiblack racism virtually traveled along the same path as that of the rest of black America at the time, and—again, like the rest of black America—it was soul and funk as opposed to psychedelic rock and pop-oriented rhythm & blues that spoke to him in a special way, and soothed him and helped him get in touch with what was happening internally and externally.

As revealed in Joel Selvin's *Sly & the Family Stone: An Oral History* (1998), Sly became quite close with the Black Panther Party in the late 1960s and his however subtle embrace of Panther ideology led him to produce a blacker, funkier, more militant music that in many ways reflected the rhetoric and politics of the Black Power Movement in particular, and black America at the dawn of the 1970s in general (94–98). Consequently, in tune with his loose interpretation of Panther ideology, as well as the general sentiment in black America in the early 1970s, *Riot* reflected the decline of the Civil Rights Movement and the rise of the social disillusionment and political disarray of the Black Power Movement. Recurring references to police brutality and political assassinations on *Riot* obviously pointed to his association with the Panthers. For instance, the FBI's infamous Counter Intelligence Program (COINTELPRO) was primarily aimed at disrupting and spreading dissension within the Black Panther Party in the late 1960s and early 1970s, as well as disinformation between the Black Panthers and other black nationalist organizations.

With regard to assassinations, Panthers Bobby Hutton, Arthur Glen Morris, Anthony Coltrale, Robert Lawrence, Steve Bartholomew, Tommy Lewis, Sidney Miller, and Frank Diggs, among others, were assassinated in 1968.

And, Panthers Nathaniel Clark, Walter "Toure" Pope, Mark Clark, and Fred Hampton, among others, were assassinated in 1969. However, *Riot*'s references to police brutality and political assassinations were also indicative of Sly's long pent-up feelings concerning the assassinations of Malcolm X, Medgar Evers, Martin Luther King, John Kennedy, and Bobby Kennedy, among many others.[14]

Where his music prior to *Riot* was the epitome of optimistic pop radio-friendly funk, on *Riot* optimism was replaced with cynicism, joy with misery, and enthusiasm with unambiguous apathy. Seeming not particularly interested in black popular music if it didn't have that familiar pop or crossover sound and make them wanna dance with abandon or have ferocious (and "freaky") sex, most of white America at the time closed their ears to Sly's new music *and* message. Similar to James Brown, soon Sly, too, was blacklisted and abruptly returned to the post-Civil Rights Movement "colored section" reserved for black musicians who articulated their moral outrage and deep despair regarding African Americans' ongoing social segregation and economic exploitation in the aftermath of the Civil Rights Movement.

Despite the fact that *Riot* produced three hit singles (i.e., "Family Affair," "Runnin' Away," and "[You Caught Me] Smilin'"), ultimately it alienated many of the white fans who had lionized Sly and fondly thought of him as a "freaky," funky, and fun-loving black apostle of psychedelic soul. However, these same white fans who had previously held Sly in such high esteem, Dave Marsh (1985) maintained, were often not "prepared for such a harsh, direct look at the black experience" (59). Truth be told, this eventually became the fundamental problematic at the heart of white reactions to black popular music, which could be extremely intense and passion-filled, and white compassion toward, comprehension, and sincere consideration of the diverse post-Civil Rights Movement realities of African American history, culture, and struggle, which have been for the most part rarely more than superficial.

Black popular music in the 1970s continued to be ardently admired when it satisfied romanticized white presumptions concerning black overindulgence in, and black effortlessness with respect to pleasure, leisure, singing, dancing, partying, drinking, eating, and, of course, sex. But, these romanticized white presumptions did not require any genuine respect for, heartfelt empathy with, authentic historical knowledge of, or sincere commitment to ending, the quite often unromantic conditions, nightmarish situations, and dehumanizing circumstances in which these supposedly distinctly "black characteristics" developed. Consequently, when Sly passionately shared some of the angst, disarray, and resentment which perplexed African America's collective consciousness in the midst of the Black Power Movement's accelerating disintegration on *Riot*, most of his former white fans seemed absolutely apathetic.

Lyrically and thematically building on the bold *soul music as social commentary* model innovatively explored by Marvin Gaye on *What's Going On?*, with *Riot* Sly offered *soulful deep funk music as social commentary*, in turn helping to establish a trend in 1970s black popular music where soulsters and funksters explored, commented on, and often acerbically critiqued the underbelly and ongoing struggles of black America. *Riot*'s black life-centered and Black Power Movement-influenced deep funk tracks, such as "Luv n' Haight," "Africa Talks to You (The Asphalt Jungle)," "Brave & Strong," and "Thank You for Talkin' to Me Africa," stood in stark contrast to the trippy and hippie psychedelic soul that Sly & the Family Stone pioneered on their previous albums. Although white America may have, for the most part, closed its ears to Sly's new *riotous funk*, most of black America's ears were wide open and deeply moved by the soulful sounds and heartfelt funk they heard on *Riot*. In one of the best discussions of Stone's *Riot* ever published, Greil Marcus (1975) wrote of its enormous and game-changing impact on black popular music in the 1970s:

> Some months after *Riot* was released—from the middle of 1972 through early 1973—the impulses of its music emerged on other records, and they took over the radio. I don't know if I will be able to convey the impact of punching buttons day after day and night after night to be met by records as clear and strong as Curtis Mayfield's "Superfly" and "Freddie's Dead," the Staple Singers' "Respect Yourself" and the utopian "I'll Take You There," the O'Jays' "Back Stabbers," War's astonishing "Slipping Into Darkness" and "The World Is a Ghetto," the Temptations' "Papa Was a Rolling Stone," Johnny Nash's "I Can See Clearly Now," Stevie Wonder's "Superstition," for that matter the Stones' *Exile on Main St.* (the white *Riot*)—records that were surrounded, in memory and still on the air as recent hits, by Marvin Gaye's deadly "Inner-City Blues," by Undisputed Truth's "Smiling Face Sometimes (Tell Lies)," by the Chi-Lites' falsetto melancholy, by *Riot* itself. Only a year before such discs would have been curiosities; now, they were all of a piece: one enormous answer record. Each song added something to the others, and as in a pop explosion, the country found itself listening to a new voice. (79–80)

The new voice of "heavy" or "deep" funk, as it was called, morphed and moved in many different directions as the 1970s wore on. By rejecting the crossover pop-soul sound Motown perfected in the 1960s, by reconnecting with the roots of black popular music in gospel, blues, and jazz, and by making music that was in tune with and an expression of African Americans' post-Civil Rights Movement struggles, James Brown, Jimi Hendrix, and Sly Stone—yes, even Jimi Hendrix when we seriously consider his *Electric Ladyland* (1968), *Band of Gypsys* (1970), and *The Rainbow Bridge Concert* (1971) albums—laid the foundation for what we now know as funk.[15] However, unlike Brown or Hendrix, Stone arguably went the furthest in articulating the aspirations and frustrations of African Americans at the dawn of the

1970s because he expressed those aspirations and frustrations over the course of an entire album, as opposed to a random track or two here and there (à la Brown and Hendrix). Sly's next album, *Fresh* (1973), was even more of a masterpiece than *Riot*, featuring more explicit social commentary and slightly tighter and brighter deep funk grooves. Songs such as "If You Want Me to Stay" and "Frisky" demonstrated that Sly was still a master pop-funk songwriter. However, other tracks such as "In Time," "Let Me Have It All," "Thankful n' Thoughtful," "Skin I'm In," "If It Were Left Up to Me," and "Babies Makin' Babies" also indicated that the *soulful deep funk music as social commentary* motif of *Riot* was more than a mere psychedelic drug-induced fluke.

Fresh is arguably better than *Riot* because of its close-to-the-chest cynicism, more explicit social commentary, beautiful gospel-soul soaked ballads, and slightly more accessible deep funk rhythms. But, because his music was no longer considered optimistic and, therefore, not pop-radio friendly, for all intents and purposes, Sly began a long drug-induced decline that he has yet to musically recover from. Even though his post-*Fresh* albums, such as *Small Talk* (1974), *High on You* (1975), *Heard Ya Missed Me, Well I'm Back* (1976), and *Back on the Right Track* (1979), all featured a track or two of solid social commentary and beautifully sung soul-funk ballads, Sly Stone's legacy primarily rests on his work between 1967 and 1973—which is to say, between *A Whole New Thing* and *Fresh*. Moreover, it has been primarily through these groundbreaking albums that he has contributed to rap music and the Hip Hop Movement. For example, beginning with World Class Wreckin' Cru's "Mission Impossible" (1986), which sampled "Dance to the Music" (1968), Sly & the Family Stone have been regularly sampled and, therefore, have consistently contributed to rap's musical and lyrical lexicon. After the World Class Wreckin' Cru hipped the Hip Hop Generation to Sly & the Family Stone it seemed that the floodgates burst open and Sly was, once again, helping a generation of young folk, literally, "dance to the music."

One of the most sampled artists in hip hop history, Sly's classic psychedelic soul and psychedelic funk hits have been, however surreptitiously, woven into the lyrical and musical fabric of rap music and hip hop culture. For instance, after the World Class Wreckin' Cru sampled "Dance to the Music" it was subsequently sampled in: N.W.A.'s "Something 2 Dance 2" (1988); the Beastie Boys' "Egg Man" (1989); Queen Latifah's "Dance for Me" (1989); DJ Jazzy Jeff & the Fresh Prince's "The Reverend" (1989); and Will.i.am's "Dance to the Music" (2006). Stone's "Everyday People" was sampled in: Full Force's "Old Flames Never Die" (1986) and Arrested Development's Grammy Award-winning "People Everyday" (1992). Stone's "Sing a Simple Song" (1968) has been sampled more than one hundred times, most memorably in: Eazy-E's "Eazy-Duz-It" (1988); Public Enemy's "Fight the Power" (1988), "Party for Your Right to Fight" (1988), "Get the

Fuck Out of Dodge" (1990), and "Can't Truss It" (1991); Stetsasonic's "It's My Song" (1988); the Jungle Brother's "J-Beez Comin' Through" (1989) and "Simple as That" (1993); Digital Underground's "The Humpty Dance" (1989) and "Return of the Crazy One" (1993); De La Soul's "Eye Know" (1989); Kid Rock's "Genuine Article" (1990); LL Cool J's "Mama Said to Knock You Out" (1990) and "How I'm Comin'" (1993); Tone Loc's "Funky Westside" (1991); Ice-T's "Ricochet" (1991); A Tribe Called Quest's "Jazz (We've Got)" (1991); Paris's "Check It Out Ch'all" (1992); Pete Rock & C.L. Smooth's "For Pete's Sake" (1992) and "Anger in the Nation" (1992); Mellow Man Ace's "Me La Pelas" (1992); Das EFX's "Mic Checka" (1992), "Hard Like a Criminal" (1992), and "Check It Out" (1993); Redman's "Blow Your Mind" (1992); Common's "Blows to the Temple" (1992); Arrested Development's "Revolution" (1992) and "Mr. Wendal" (1992); Tupac Shakur's "Souljah's Revenge" (1993), "Peep Game" (1993), and "Temptations" (1995); Run-D.M.C.'s "In the House" (1993); KRS-One's "Sound of Da Police" (1993); Ice Cube's "Really Doe" (1993); and J Dilla's "Hey Hey Hey Heyyyyy" (2005), among many others.

Stone's "Thank You (Falettinme Be Mice Elf Agin)" (1969) was sampled in: Schoolly D's "Housing the Joint" (1987) and Janet Jackson's multiple award-winning "Rhythm Nation" (1989). Ice Cube sampled "Don't Call Me Nigger, Whitey" in "Horny Lil' Devil" (1991). Pharoahe Monch sampled "I Want to Take You Higher" in "Let's Go" (2007). Hence, Sly Stone has undeniably influenced the musical and lyrical lexicon of rap music and hip hop culture, and even a pop funk message song like "You Can Make It If You Try" (1969) seems to resonate with rappers and other hip hoppers decades after it captivated and inspired black radicals and white hippies alike in the late 1960s and early 1970s. "You Can Make It If You Try" was famously sampled in: Stetsasonic's "Talkin' All That Jazz" (1988); the Jungle Brothers' "Because I Got It Like That" (1988); Ice Cube's "The Product" (1990), "True to the Game" (1991), and "Wicked" (1992); and Ice-T's "New Jack Hustler" (1991), among others.

By incorporating aspects of James Brown's funk and Jimi Hendrix's psychedelic rock into his own distinct brand of *psychedelic funk*, Sly Stone began a sonic synthesis that, much like fusion jazz in the 1970s, opened funk to the innovations of other, more recent music. Just as Sly began his descent into drugs in the mid-1970s one of his many musical followers rose to prominence with one of the most storied and bizarre funk collectives in history: George Clinton and Parliament/Funkadelic. Perhaps more than any other funksters Parliament/Funkadelic (or "P-Funk" colloquially) wrote lyrics, created a "cosmic" sound, dressed, and performed in a way that reflected the loves, lusts, lives, and ongoing struggles of working-class and underclass African Americans in the 1970s. Parliament/Funkadelic's music and messages reveal a great deal about black America in the 1970s and, even though often off kilter, their musical, cultural, and sexual politics frequently reflected the political idealism *and* social realism, the optimism *and* pessimism, the comedy *and* tragedy swirling through black America during the Black Power Movement and its immediate aftermath.

P-FUNK: GEORGE CLINTON, PARLIAMENT/FUNKADELIC, PSYCHEDELIC ROCK, PSYCHEDELIC SOUL, AND PSYCHEDELIC FUNK

Born in an outhouse in Kannapolis, North Carolina, on July 22, 1941, George Clinton grew up extremely poor. The oldest of nine, his mother struggled to raise her children without a father and consequently, looking after his many siblings, young George developed many of the organizational skills that would make him the mastermind behind three of the greatest funk bands of the 1970s: Parliament, Funkadelic, and Bootsy's Rubber Band. The Clinton family's difficulties led them to seek better opportunities up north in Plainfield, New Jersey, where a fifteen-year-old George formed a doo-wop group called the Parliaments in 1956. Working as a hairdresser in one of the most popular barbershops in Plainfield, he came into contact with talented local vocalists and musicians and began rehearsing in the back room of the barbershop. The original Parliaments doo-wop group featured Clinton, Calvin Simon, Grady Thomas, Clarence "Fuzzy" Haskins, and Raymond Davis. [16]

By the early 1960s Clinton was more interested in making music than cutting, coloring, and straightening hair. As the Parliaments evolved from a doo-wop group into a rhythm & blues group, he became fascinated with the Motown sound and believed that the Motor City hit record company was the perfect place for his burgeoning group. After moving to Detroit he had a less-than-stellar audition at Motown and, as a result, instead of recording for Motown the Parliaments only managed a few moderate singles on the small Detroit-based Revilot Records. However, their hard work seems to have paid off by 1967 when their single "I Wanna Testify" became a top three R&B hit. Unfortunately, their success was short lived, as Revilot Records went bankrupt (many believe due to Motown's instigation), and Clinton temporarily lost his group's name in the first of many legal snafus that would plague him throughout his storied career.

Although Motown was not interested in the Parliaments, it was interested in Clinton's quirky and frequently flippant songwriting—a unique style of songwriting that would provide Parliament, Funkadelic, Bootsy's Rubber Band, Parlet, and the Brides of Funkenstein with an impressive string of hits in the mid- to late-1970s. Serving as a staff songwriter for Motown, Clinton managed to land his "Can't Shake It Loose" (1968) with Diana Ross & the Supremes and "I'll Bet You" (1970) with the Jackson 5. But, he didn't want to spend the rest of his life writing hits for others. He wanted his own band so that he could explore new lyrical and musical directions, many of which were inspired by his time in Detroit, and especially his experiences at Motown.

After initially forming a backing band with Detroiters Frankie Boyce, Richard Boyce, and Langston Booth, eventually Clinton recruited New Jerseyites Bernie Worrell on keyboards and synthesizers, Eddie Hazel on lead guitar, Lucius "Tawl" Ross on rhythm guitar, Billy "Bass" Nelson on bass, and Ramon "Tiki" Fulwood on drums to accompanying the Parliaments, which is to say that his late 1960s group consisted of five vocalists and five instrumentalists. It was this new self-contained band that signed with Westbound Records in 1968 and synthesized James Brown's funk, Jimi Hendrix's psychedelic rock, and Sly Stone's psychedelic soul into what they famously dubbed "Funkadelic." Because the Parliaments, at least in name, were still signed to the defunct Revilot Records, Clinton and his new band began to record under the intriguing Funkadelic tag.

As Matt Rogers discussed in *Funkadelic's Maggot Brain* (2013), Funkadelic's first three albums—*Funkadelic* (1970), *Free Your Mind . . . And Your Ass Will Follow* (1970), and *Maggot Brain* (1971)—were a combination of guitar-driven psychedelic rock and bass-heavy psychedelic funk. By the time they recorded the *America Eats Its Young* (1972) double album only Clinton and Worrell remained of the original lineup. Tawl Ross left the band after he overdosed on LSD and needed rehabilitation. Eddie Hazel and Billy Nelson quit the band because of money disputes—another issue that would consistently plague both Parliament and Funkadelic until their acrimonious disbanding in the early 1980s.

Clinton and Worrell recorded *America Eats Its Young* with two separate bands, the House Guests and United Soul (U.S.), and it was this aggregate of new musicians and bohemians that would ultimately combine and become the core of Parliament/Funkadelic. The Cincinnati, Ohio-based House Guests brought bassist William "Bootsy" Collins, guitarist Phelps "Catfish" Collins, drummer Frank "Kash" Waddy, trumpeter Clayton "Chicken" Gunnells, and saxophonist Robert McCullough into the Parliament/Funkadelic fold, while the United Souls placed guitarist Garry Shider and bassist Cordell Mosson in the P-Funk ranks. With its slightly more soulful and funkier sound, as opposed to the psychedelic funk rock sound featured on their first three albums, *America Eats Its Young* touched on a wide range of political topics, but it did so from Funkadelic's unique point of view: for instance, the title track, "America Eats Its Young," commented on the ways in which war, political corruption, and miseducation demoralize the youth; "Biological Speculation" and "Balance" stressed nature's ability to right wrongs and bring order; and "Wake Up" was about being political aware.

Along with releasing the first Funkadelic album in 1970, Clinton managed to release the first "Parliament" (as opposed to "the Parliaments") album on former Motown songwriting and production team Holland-Dozier-Holland's Invictus Records. With a sound closer to early Funkadelic than the one associated with Parliament from the mid-1970s forward, *Osmium* (1970) provided a blueprint for future Parliament albums, even if it was a musically raw and lyrically sprawling affair. From the lunatic lyrics on songs like "Moonshine Heather" and "My Automobile" to the subtle social commentary on songs like "Oh Lord, Why Lord/Prayer" and "Livin' the Life," *Osmium* demonstrated the duality of Clinton's musical vision.

In 1973 Clinton signed Parliament to a new recording contract with Casablanca Records. Using the same cast of characters recording under the Funkadelic name, including the newly added "Horny Horns" (which featured former James Brown band trombonist Fred Wesley and saxophonist Maceo Parker, as well as trumpeters Larry Hatcher and Richard "Kush" Griffith, among others), Clinton brilliantly re-created his defunct Parliament psychedelic soul-funk concept. Fred Wesley and the Horny Horns, however, added a hard bop funk and Sun Ra "Arkestra" psychedelic jazz dimension to the mushrooming Parliament/Funkadelic sound and, as a result, mid- to late-1970s Parliament albums took on some of the spacey, astrological, and intergalactic rhetoric that Sun Ra and his avant-garde jazz "Arkestra" popularized on classic albums such as *The Nubians of Plutonia* (1959), *The Futuristic Sounds of Sun Ra* (1961), *Cosmic Tones for Mental Therapy* (1963), *Other Planes of There* (1964), *The Heliocentric World of Sun Ra* (1965), *Outer Spaceways Incorporated* (1968), *Atlantis* (1969), *Astro-Black* (1972), *Space is the Place* (1972), *Cosmo-Earth Fantasy* (1974), *Pathways to Unknown Worlds* (1975), *Cosmos* (1976), *A Quiet Place in the Universe* (1977), *Lanquidity* (1978), *Space Probe* (1978), and *On Jupiter* (1979), among many others.[17]

Instead of basing it out of doo-wop and rhythm & blues, the new Parliament would essentially be a jazz horn-driven, gospel soul-influenced funk group. Hence, ultimately Clinton (and his outrageous alter egos "Starchild" and "Dr. Funkenstein," etc.) envisioned Funkadelic as his psychedelic rock funk band, and Parliament as his psychedelic soul funk band. Solidifying both bands' sounds on Funkadelic's *Cosmic Slop* (1973) and *Standing on the Verge of Getting It On* (1974) and Parliament's *Up for the Down Stroke* (1974) and *Chocolate City* (1975), by the mid-1970s Clinton and Parliament/Funkadelic were quickly moving from the musical margins to the musical center. When Parliament's *Mothership Connection* (1976) was certified platinum for selling more than one million albums Clinton and Parliament/Funkadelic quickly became a major force within the American music industry. By developing a radio-friendly funk group (i.e., Parliament) and continuing to record and release his more avant-garde, psychedelic rock funk group (i.e., Funkadelic), Clinton not only became one of the towering figures of black popular music in the 1970s, but he also demonstrated the wide range and reach of black popular music in the 1970s.

During the extraordinarily creative period between 1975 and 1980, Parliament and Funkadelic released a series of albums and hit singles that revolutionized black popular music in the 1970s and helped to lay the foundation for black popular music in the 1980s. Parliament/Funkadelic's proto-hip hop aesthetic enabled them to absorb, honor, play with, and frequently parody an extraordinary range of musical styles, flinging them back at the musical universe with a frightening freakiness and flamboyance that usually resulted in some of the most deranged yet danceable psychedelic rock-soul-funk songs of the mid- to late-1970s. However, it was not simply their musical range that distinguished Parliament/Funkadelic, but also the remarkable social, political, and cultural range of their often parody and satire-filled lyrics that made them stand out among the crowd of critically acclaimed funk bands in the 1970s.

For instance, Parliament's *Chocolate City* was in many ways a response to the rise of black majorities in several U.S. cities, as well as the election of a number of black mayors in both large and small cities across the nation in the early 1970s. A short list of the most noted among the African American mayors elected in "chocolate cities" between 1970 and 1975, the year *Chocolate City* was released, includes: Kenneth Gibson in Newark, New Jersey; James McGee in Dayton, Ohio; A. Price Woodard in Wichita, Kansas; Robert Caldwell in Salina, Kansas; Lyman Parks in Grand Rapids, Michigan; James Ford in Tallahassee, Florida; Coleman Young in Detroit, Michigan; Clarence Lightner in Raleigh, North Carolina; Maynard Jackson in Atlanta, Georgia; Thomas Bradley in Los Angeles, California; Doris Davis in Compton, California; and Walter Washington in Washington, D.C. Therefore, celebrating the changing sociopolitical landscape in the early- to mid-1970s, Clinton literally *rapped* about "chocolate cities" *and* their "vanilla suburbs," the latter of which was a reference to "white flight," in the 1970s.[18]

Taking all manner of artistic license, Clinton traded "D.C." for "C.C."—meaning "chocolate city," of course. The album cover featured a chocolate Lincoln Memorial, Washington Monument, and Capitol Hill melting, presumably (and metaphorically) from the new black social, political, and cultural heat burning during the Black Power Movement. "Chocolate City's" lyrics reimagined an entirely African American U.S. federal government, where famous African American musical and cultural icons lead the nation in a new social, political, and cultural direction: Muhammad Ali was designated as the president; Aretha Franklin was the first lady; Ike Turner would serve as the secretary of the treasury; Stevie Wonder would be the secretary of fine arts; and Richard Pryor the minister of education.

Between lively chants of "gainin' on ya!," Clinton referenced "forty acres and a mule" and then he stated "you don't need the bullet when you got the ballot," which was a not-so-obscure reference to Malcolm X's famous 1964 "The Ballot or the Bullet" speech. After mentioning marches and protests, Clinton advised his listeners to make sure they have their "James Brown pass," perhaps referencing Brown's ability to get black folk to cease much of the urban unrest in the aftermath of Martin Luther King's assassination. Consequently, all of this points to the fact that Parliament/Funkadelic's political universe was as broad and off-beat as their musical universe, and after *Chocolate City*—especially on their classic concept albums *Mothership Connection* (1976), *The Clones of Dr. Funkenstein* (1976), *Funkentelechy vs. the Placebo Syndrome* (1977), *Motor Booty Affair* (1978), *Gloryhallastoopid* (1979), and *Trombipulation* (1980)—Clinton used parody and satire to offer his social commentary and political critique. As Amy Wright importantly observed in "A Philosophy of Funk: The Politics and Pleasure of a Parliafunkadelicment Thang!" (2008), "[r]ather than openly critiquing political leaders, Clinton used humor to propose a black counter-hegemony"—meaning, a new, essentially post-Civil Rights Movement *and* post-Black Power Movement form of black radical politics and black social organization that would provide an accessible alternative to the dominant middle-class white world African Americans were then suffering through and barely surviving in (42).

With regard to the song "Chocolate City" in particular, Wright asserted, "[i]nstead of replacing white officials with black leaders of the Civil Rights Movement and Black Power Movement, he [i.e., Clinton] placed black artists in charge of this new imagined nation, recognizing the significance of popular culture in an increasingly conservative political climate. With a void in leadership that many would argue has persisted until today, Clinton recognized that the black population held popular culture figures in higher regard and had more faith in their abilities to lead than black elected officials or black activists" (42–43). In light of black America's disillusionment with civil rights leaders and other black politicians in the 1970s, Parliament/Funkadelic's music could be said to serve as the sounds of black freakiness and black radicalness in dialogue with U.S. politics and society, as well as the popular culture and popular music of the time. Parliament/Funkadelic gave voice to working-class and underclass African Americans' thoughts and feelings, their frustrations and aspirations that had been ignored by the mostly middle-class leaders of the Civil Rights Movement, Women's Liberation Movement, Anti-War Movement, and New Left Movement.

Undeniably one of the groups hit the hardest by the devastating economic effects of the Vietnam War and deindustrialization, the black working-class identified with the off-beat alternatives P-Funk offered. In fact, Clinton composed several explicit social commentaries on black popular culture, poverty, and post-Civil Rights Movement racism. For example, almost the entire *America Eats Its Young* double album, "Cosmic Slop," "Chocolate City," "Funky Dollar Bill," and "You and Your Folks, Me and My Folks" provided stinging social commentary and political critique. Strange as it may seem, Parliament/Funkadelic emphasized and seemed to sincerely believe in music's redemptive, rejuvenating, and transcendent powers, which appeared to only underscore the Sun Ra-inspired outlandish Africanesque extraterrestrials, weird worlds, surreal universes, and alternative realities Clinton invented and incessantly explored in his work between 1976 and 1981. "Through their progressive lyrics, their wild stage show, their crazy appearance, their innovative sound, and their philosophy of funk," Wright wrote, Parliament/Funkadelic "confronted and collapsed whites' stereotypes of blacks while producing an alternative sound and style" (38). In other words, when viewed from the standpoint of the African American working class and underclass of the 1970s, Parliament/Funkadelic was much more than gobbledygook or insane black outer-space blather, for all intents and purposes, they were much-needed post-Black Power Movement black superheroes valiantly fighting both musically and in many other ways metaphorically on behalf of the everyday average black folk in the streets, clubs, churches, and mom-and-pop businesses that continue to be the backbone of black America.

In myriad ways, Parliament/Funkadelic offered the black working class and underclass both earthly and unearthly—literally, *otherworldly*—alternatives, and there is a sense in which *Mothership Connection* can be interpreted as their critique of what they understood to be the weakening and whitening of funk and the interloping emergence of disco, as well as their effort to provide African Americans with alternatives to the ongoing segregation, oppression, exploitation, and depression they faced day after day on Earth. It is interesting to observe that at the same time that P-Funk was developing their musical intergalactic tales an emerging form of African American fiction that combined elements of science fiction, fantasy, and horror began taking shape in the 1970s.

Arguably one of the most influential writers within African American science fiction was Octavia Butler, whose first novel *Patternmaster* (1976) was published the same year as *Mothership Connection*. Detailing a secret history that spanned from ancient Egypt to a period far into the future, *Patternmaster* imaginatively dealt with telepathic mind control as well as an extraterrestrial plague. Her other novels, such as *Mind of My Mind* (1977), *Survivor* (1978), *Wild Seed* (1980), and *Clay's Ark* (1984), collectively mirrored many of the themes being explored by Clinton and Parliament/Funkadelic in the late 1970s and early 1980s. Because most of the works in African American science fiction involve fantasy, science, technology, and time travel, as in Butler's *Kindred* (1979), in the 1990s this literary movement was dubbed "Afro-futurism." Other writers identified with either African American science fiction or "Afro-futurism" include Samuel Delany, Nalo Hopkinson, Nnedi Okorafor, N.K. Jemisin, Andrea Hairston, Nisi Shawl, and Ken Sibanda, among others.[19]

Musically, however, Clinton and Parliament/Funkadelic were not alone in looking to and exploring ancient Egypt, outer space, and other worlds for funky inspiration. Other funk musicians also tapped into the "Afro-futurism" and otherworldliness circulating throughout black America in the 1970s, especially as the Black Power Movement, for all intents and purposes, came to an end in 1975 as the Black Panther Party buckled under COINTELPRO repression, incarceration, disorganization, and increased drug addiction. Funksters like LaBelle, Earth, Wind & Fire, Betty Davis, the Sylvers, the Isley Brothers, the Commodores, and, late in the decade, Rick James all donned Afro-futuristic-looking sparkling space suits with oversized shoulder pads, super-high glittering platform boots, and over-the-top exotic hairstyles that smacked of a special spacey topsy-turvy black pride that hinted at a "brand new funk" (à la James Brown) from some other, more black folk-friendly planet or universe. As a matter of fact, Earth, Wind & Fire went so far as to solicit the services of high-profile magicians David Copperfield and Doug Henning to help them develop a spectacle-filled concert that could rival P-Funk's 1976 Earth Tour, which featured colorful futuristic space suits and a jaw-dropping oversized spaceship (i.e., the "mothership") landing on-stage each night.

Where Parliament/Funkadelic toyed with psychedelia, interplanetary travel, and "Afronauts" (as opposed to astronauts) descending to the Earth, Earth, Wind & Fire's stage show combined Egyptology, African spirituality, and interplanetary travel in their efforts to demonstrate that their extremely successful and incredibly distinctive brand of jazz horn-driven gospel-soul-funk did not recognize borders or boundaries of any sort, whether temporal, spatial, spiritual, musical, cultural, or racial. Hence, although often over-looked, there are a series of themes revolving around *escapism, utopianism, and futurism* that run through most 1970s funk that could be more or less interpreted as a musical and cultural response to the various crises confront-ing the Black Power Movement in particular, and 1970s black America in general. Culturally and historically, the escapism, utopianism, and futurism in 1970s funk are important in light of the fact that apparently life for black folk had become so unlivable that it was only in outer space or in some other world summoned up by psychedelic drugs, mysticism, magic, or via some quasi-black nationalist vision of a lost Atlantis-like African paradise that it seemed possible for African Americans to finally live in peace and be re-spected by other people. Socially and politically, the escapism, utopianism, and futurism in mid- to late-1970s funk symbolized African Americans' retreat, even if only temporarily, from the political radicalism and social vision of the Black Power Movement, and their turn inward, to each other, to their churches and mosques, and to those aspects of African and other non-European cultures that might enable them to, once again, weather the conservative storm and antiblack racist onslaught that characterized the late 1970s and the 1980s.

Although hip hoppers were initially drawn to the infectious, electro-funk of Clinton's post-Parliament/Funkadelic early- to mid-1980s hits such as "Atomic Dog" (1982) and "Do Fries Go with That Shake?" (1985), it wasn't until the Real Roxanne's "Roxanne's Back Side (Scratch It)" (1984), where she sampled Funkadelic's "Get Off Your Ass and Jam," and LL Cool J's "Dear Yvette" (1985), where he sampled Clinton's "Atomic Dog," that hip hoppers really began to develop what would come to be called *Parliament/ Funkadelic rap* or, rather, *P-Funk rap*. Over the years the Parliament/Funkadelic catalog has played a pivotal role in the evolution of rap music, and many of their 1970s funk hits repeatedly turned up on the rap hits of the 1980s and 1990s. For example, Funkadelic's "Good Old Music" was sampled in: the Jungle Brothers' "Jimbrowski" (1988); MC Lyte's "Survival of the Fittest (Remix)" (1989); Biz Markie's "She Not Just Another Woman" (1989); the D.O.C.'s "The D.O.C. & the Doctor" (1989); Mellow Man Ace's "Mas Pingon" (1989); Monie Love's "Pups Lickin' Bone" (1990); Run-D.M.C.'s "Bob Your Head" (1990); Scarface's "Good Girl Gone Bad" (1991); Big Daddy Kane's "Death Sentence" (1991); Common's "Tricks Up My Sleeve" (1992); and the Coup's "The Blunt" (1993).

Parliament's "Come In Out of the Rain" (1972) was sampled in: the Jungle Brothers' "I'm in Love with Indica" (1993); De La Soul's "Paul's Revenge" (1993); NaS's "One Love" (1994); and OutKast's "Elevators (ONP 86 Mix)" (1996). Funkadelic's "Cosmic Slop" helped to fuel the subtle funk of the D.O.C.'s "Beautiful But Deadly" (1989) and Ice Cube's "Doing Dumb Shit" (1991), and Paliament's "Chocolate City" swirled underneath the booming beats of Salt-N-Pepa's "He's Gamin' on Ya" (1991) and Ice Cube's "I Wanna Kill Uncle Sam" (1991). Finally, Funkadelic's "Get Off Your Ass and Jam" was sampled in: Public Enemy's "Bring the Noise" (1987) and "Contract on the World Love Jam" (1990); Eazy-E's "Eazy-Duz-It" (1988); Tone Loc's "Funky Cold Medina" (1989); N.W.A.'s "100 Miles and Runnin'" (1990); A Tribe Called Quest's "Rhythm (Devoted to the Art of Moving Butts)" (1990) and "The Pressure" (1996); Schoolly D's "King of New York" (1990); Tupac Shakur's "Holler If Ya Hear Me" (1993); and Xzibit's "What U See Is What U Get" (1998). With over one thousand samples of his music, or music he produced, floating through the beats and rhymes of rap music, right along with James Brown and Sly Stone, George Clinton's P-Funk helped to lay the foundation for rap music and hip hop culture.

Sampling serious funksters such as James Brown, Lynn Collins, Sly & the Family Stone, the Ohio Players, the Bar-Kays, and Cymande on their debut *3 Feet High & Rising* (1989), it was probably De La Soul's "Me, Myself & I" (1989) that did the most to raise Parliament/Funkadelic's profile within the world of rap in the late 1980s. Essentially using the chorus from Funkadelic's "(Not Just) Knee Deep" (1979) as the chorus for "Me, Myself & I," De La Soul did not bury P-Funk's flamboyant funkiness deep in the mix the way most rappers had previously. On "Me, Myself & I" one gets a sonic glimpse of the sheer beauty and the powerful gospel-like lunacy of Parliament/Funkadelic.

De La Soul and P-Funk were a black bohemian match made in musical heaven, and soon other rappers came clamoring for the Parliament/Funkadelic catalog in pursuit of a similar musical magic. However, once turned on to P-Funk's 1970s hits, rappers and their productions teams usually went back even further to James Brown and Sly & the Family Stone's late-1960s funk. Brown and Stone's funk usually inspired enthusiastic explorations of other 1970s funk innovators, and these explorations, these intense "funk studies" eventually yielded a new form of funk-based rap or, more simply, *funk rap*, and funk rap ultimately provided the foundation for the busy keyboard bass-lines and half-sung hooks of gangsta rap.

G-FUNK: FROM FUNK RAP TO GANGSTA RAP

Perhaps the most noted of the early funk rap groups was the Oakland, California-based Digital Underground, which featured leader Greg "Shock G" Jacobs (a.k.a., "Humpty Hump") and a constantly changing cast of characters including Money-B, Jeremy "DJ-JZ" Jackson, DJ Nu-Stylez, Cleetis "Clee" Mack, 2Fly Eli, DJ Fuze, Chopmaster J, Kent Racker, Mystic, Boni Boyer, Nzazi Malonga, and Saafir. Initially known as "Rackadelic," Shock G began his career in hip hop culture as an album cover cartoonist and liner note writer deeply influenced by legendary Parliament/Funkadelic album cover cartoonist and liner note writer Pedro Bell. As the Parliament/Funkadelic and hip hop influences grew on Shock G he eventually founded Digital Underground in 1987. At first Digital Underground was conceived of as a funky Black Panther Party-styled rap group but, after the meteoric rise of Public Enemy, Shock G took the group in a more lighthearted, comedic, and Parliament/Funkadelic-influenced direction.[20]

Digital Underground's debut, *Sex Packets* (1990), was a perfect mix of comedy rap and party rap riding P-Funk rhythms. As imaginative and festive as most Parliament/Funkadelic albums between 1975 and 1980, Digital Underground directly borrowed from Clinton's P-Funk blueprint and updated it, broadened it, and customized it for hip hop culture. *Sex Packets'* two big hits were virtually Clinton productions *in absentia*: "Doowutchyalike" (1990) sampled Parliament's "Flashlight" (1977) and "Agony of Defeet" (1980), as well as Clinton's "Atomic Dog" (1982). Likewise, "Humpty Dance" sampled Parliament's "Theme from the Black Hole" (1979) and

"Let's Play House" (1980), as well as major P-Funk influence Sly & the Family Stone's "Sing a Simple Song" (1968). Clinton and P-Funk's influence on *Sex Packets* was not purely musical, but lyrical as well. Ultimately revolving around a fictitious drug that supposedly allowed its partakers to experience sex without actually having sex, which sounds a lot like an early form of virtual reality long before it was in vogue, *Sex Packets* was often as silly as it was sexy—just like a lot of P-Funk music in the 1970s (e.g., *Funkentelechy vs. the Placebo Syndrome, Motor Booty Affair, Gloryhallas-toopid, Trombipulation, One Nation Under a Groove, Uncle Jam Wants You, Stretchin' Out in Bootsy's Rubber Band, Ahh . . . The Name Is Bootsy, Baby!*, and *Bootsy? Player of the Year*).

Digital Underground's second album was a six-song EP unimaginatively titled *This is an EP Release* (1991) and is primarily noted because future rap superstar Tupac Shakur made his debut on the classic tracks "Same Song" and "The Way We Swing (Remix)." Once again offering a comedy rap and party rap alternative to the quickly growing gangsta rap genre, *This is an EP Release* continued to build on Clinton's P-Funk aesthetic, featuring samples of Parliament's "Flashlight" (1977) on "Arguin' on the Funk" and samples of their "Theme from the Black Hole" (1979) on "Same Song." Moreover, "Same Song" brought an inventive Bernie Worrell-meets-Jimmy Smith-meets-John Medeski synth-organ solo into the funky mix, making it one of the first rap hits to successfully combine live instruments with music samples—a hip hop production technique that would in many ways become standard practice for rap, rhythm & blues, and neo-soul producers from the early 1990s onward.

Sons of the P (1991) was Digital Underground's third album and it continued the P-Funk comedy rap and party rap vibe of their previous releases but importantly added a strain of political or message rap to the mix. For instance, "No Nose Job" provided a critique of African American celebrities who had had cosmetic surgery to alter their appearance to look European, and both "Heartbeat Props" and "The Higher Heights of Spirituality" offered social commentary and demonstrated that, much like Parliament/Funkadelic, Digital Underground was as concerned about the social and political conditions of African Americans as they were about being humorous and making people dance. Again, like P-Funk in the 1970s, Digital Underground incorporated some of the laughing-to-keep-from-crying aesthetic into their, however humorous, truth-telling rhymes. Going even further in their homage to P-Funk, the title track, "Sons of the P," was cowritten by and featured the unmistakable gospel soul-soaked vocals of funkmaster George Clinton. Hence, the "sons of the P"—meaning, literally, the sons of the P-Funk or the sons of the "pure funk"—were acknowledged by their musical and spiritual father (i.e., "Dr. Funkenstein").

Other tracks on *Sons of the P* were steeped in P-Funk hits, as well as other classic funk hits. For example: "Kiss You Back" sampled Funkadelic's "(Not Just) Knee Deep" (1979) and James Brown's "Funky President" (1974); "Flowin' on the D-Line" sampled Parliament's "Aqua Boogie" (1978) and the Honey Drippers' "Impeach the President" (1973); and "Tales of the Funky" sampled Funkadelic's "One Nation Under a Groove" (1978). However, Digital Underground's obsession with P-Funk was once again more than musical. The back-cover art of *Sons of the P* featured a P-Funk-style comic strip that recast Digital Underground as the funky offspring of "Dr. Funkenstein" (i.e., Clinton), which conceptually linked *Sons of the P* with not only *The Clones of Dr. Funkenstein*, but also other classic Parliament/Funkadelic albums such as *Cosmic Slop*, *Tales of Kidd Funkadelic*, *Mothership Connection*, *Funkentelechy vs. the Placebo Syndrome*, *One Nation Under a Groove*, *Motor Booty Affair*, *Uncle Jam Wants You*, *Gloryhallastoopid*, and *Trombipulation*.

Before Digital Underground began to sample P-Funk classics and other funk hits with their unique blend of comedy rap and party rap, gangsta rappers had begun to increasingly turn to Parliament/Funkadelic classics and other funk hits. As mentioned above, both Eazy-E's "Eazy-Duz-It" (1988) and N.W.A.'s "100 Miles and Runnin'" (1990) sampled Funkadelic's "Get Off Your Ass and Jam," and both the D.O.C.'s "Beautiful But Deadly" (1989) and Ice Cube's "Doing Dumb Shit" (1991) sampled Funkadelic's "Cosmic Slop." However, it was not until legendary hip hop producer and rapper André Romell Young, who is better known as "Dr. Dre," broke with Eazy-E and N.W.A. and released *The Chronic* in December of 1992 that the gangsta rap and funk fusion reached epic proportions and redefined the sound of rap music in the 1990s.

With a stage name that pays homage to Dr. Funkenstein (i.e., George Clinton), Dr. Dre twisted and turned the dense sonic collages of EPMD and Public Enemy's production team, the Bomb Squad, into his own unique gang life-inspired and classic funk-influenced style of rap. However, gangsta rap's infamous gritty and grimy lyrics can be traced back to several "old school" sources. Although often overlooked, Oakland, California-based rapper Too $hort's early albums *Don't Stop Rappin'* (1983), *Players* (1985), *Raw, Uncut, and X-Rated* (1986), *Born to Mack* (1987), and *Life Is . . . Too Short* (1988) were in many senses what we would presently dub "gangsta rap" before the genre had a proper name. Above and beyond all others, Too $hort should probably be acknowledged as the first gangsta rapper, but because his first three albums were poorly distributed his work was not widely known until *Born to Mack*, which was released a year after two East Coast early gangsta rappers came on the scene.[21]

Obviously Philadelphia, Pennsylvania-based rapper Schoolly D's proto-gangsta rhymes on classic albums such as *Schoolly D* (1986), *Saturday*

Night!: The Album (1987), *Smoke Some Kill* (1988), and *Am I Black Enough for You?* (1989) are foundational for the genre. Moreover, the same could be said about New York City-based rapper Just-Ice's early gangsta rhymes on classic albums such as *Back to the Old School* (1986), *Kool & Deadly* (1987), and *The Desolate One* (1989). Even still, it was not until Los Angeles-based rappers such as Ice-T and Eazy-E got into the rap game in the late 1980s that gangsta rap really took off and became a force to be reckoned with.

Musically, gangsta rap did not seem to have a distinct sound until Dr. Dre worked his hip hop production wizardry in the early 1990s, most often radically reworking Dr. Funkenstein's P-Funk brew into his own distinct gangsta rap/funk fusion known as "G-funk"—which is to say, *gangsta funk*. Stylistically, G-funk is distinguished from other genres of rap in light of its heavy use of P-Funk samples, multilayered synthesizers (especially, high-pitched Bernie Worrellesque *portamento* sine wave synthesizer leads), slow hypnotic grooves, deep bass, and soulful female background vocals (à la Parliament/Funkadelic's Parlet and the Brides of Funkenstein). Employing a slower and often intentionally slurred rap style in their efforts to sonically signify California colloquialisms, punctuate choice words, and maintain rhythmic cadence, G-funk rappers usually rap about money, sex, clubs, drugs, drinking, violence, gang life, and their love for their friends and hometowns. A short list of some of the more prominent G-funk rap artists includes: Dr. Dre; Snoop Dogg; Warren G; Ice Cube; Tupac Shakur; Tha Dogg Pound; Da Brat; Nate Dogg; DJ Quik; Mack 10; Bone Thugs-N-Harmony; Compton's Most Wanted; the Lost Boyz; Above the Law; the Lady of Rage; 213; Suga Free; and Cosmic Slop Shop.[22]

Instead of packing as many samples as possible into a song—à la EPMD and the Bomb Squad's late-1980s production techniques—G-funk usually used fewer, for the most part, unaltered classic funk samples in each song. In fact, G-funk is often distinguished from other forms of rap in that, similar to neo-soul, it employs a bevy of live instruments. According to Adam Krims in *Rap Music and the Poetics of Identity* (2000), G-funk can be characterized as "a style of generally West Coast rap whose musical tracks tend to deploy live instrumentation, heavy on bass and keyboards, with minimal (sometimes no) sampling and often highly conventional harmonic progressions and harmonies" (74). Which means, then, in the early 1990s Dr. Dre was essentially an anomaly within the world of rap music in light of the fact that he consistently used live musicians to re-create the P-Funk and other classic funk hits that served as the basis for the gritty and frequently gruesome Los Angeles-centered gangsta rhymes he and his cohort favored. It was this innovative technique that enabled him to produce a distinct sound that deviated from the sample-heavy sounds of most other (especially East Coast- or New York City-centered) rap music at the time.

Beginning with "Alwayz into Somethin'" (from N.W.A.'s *Efil4zaggin* [1991], which is "niggaz 4 life" spelled backwards), Dre began to use a steady stream of P-Funk and other funk classics as the basis of his production work. "Alwayz into Somethin'" sampled Parlet's "Help from My Friends" (1980) and James Brown's "Stoned to the Bone" (1973), but it is extremely important to note the flashes of funk that Dre sampled as early as N.W.A.'s *N.W.A. and the Posse* (1987) album: "Boyz-n-the-Hood" sampled Jean Knight's "Mr. Big Stuff" (1971) and the Staple Singers' "I'll Take You There" (1972); "Dope Man" sampled the Ohio Players' "Funky Worm" (1972); and "L.A. is the Place" sampled Earth, Wind & Fire's "Brazilian Rhyme (Beijo)" (1977) and Bootsy's Rubber Band's "Hollywood Squares" (1978). That is to say, five years before the phenomenal success of *The Chronic*, between 1987 and 1992 Dre produced countless classic funk-based gangsta rap tracks that enabled him to hone his production techniques and perfect his signature G-funk sound.

Building on the 1970s blaxploitation films and their primarily funky soul soundtracks (e.g., *Shaft* [1971], *Superfly* [1972], *Across 110th Street* [1972], *Trouble Man* [1972], *Black Caesar* [1973], *Coffy* [1973], *The Mack* [1973], *Truck Turner* [1974], *Together Brothers* [1974], *Let's Do It Again* [1975], and *Sparkle* [1976]), *The Chronic* was instrumental in bringing the braggadocio, brashness, and broken dreams theme of the declining years of the Black Power Movement and its aftermath into the world of rap music and hip hop culture. Sampling and radically reworking (again, with live instruments) Parliament's "The Big Bang Theory" (1979), Funkadelic's "(Not Just) Knee Deep" (1979), and George Clinton's "Atomic Dog" (1982) on "Dre Day"; James Brown's "Funky Drummer" (1970), Parliament's "Mothership Connection" (1976) and "Swing Down, Sweet Chariot" (1977) on "Let Me Ride"; Parliament's "Color Me Funky" (1979) on "The Chronic (Intro)"; and Parliament's "P-Funk (Wants to Get Funked Up)" (1975) on "The Roach (The Chronic Outro)," Dre's sonically detailed production on *The Chronic* popularized the Parliament/Funkadelic-based fat beats, soulful background vocals, blaxploitation film-inspired cinematic storylines, and live instrumentation with walking basslines and whiny synths that became known as the G-funk sound. In some senses surpassing his primary inspiration, George Clinton, in his ability to come up with tighter and catchier hooks that combined soul, funk, and hip hop sensibilities, similar to Digital Underground and DJ Quik (especially on his *Quik is the Name* [1991], *Way 2 Fonky* [1992], and *Safe & Sound* [1995]), Dre built on Dr. Funkenstein's sonic blueprint, ingeniously updated it, extended it, expanded it, and customized it for his pioneering gangsta rap/funk fusion.

Selling more than eight million copies and earning Dre his first Grammy Award in 1994, *The Chronic*, with its gangsta rhymes and funky rhythms, altered the sound and direction of rap music in the 1990s; in the process it popularized a darker, more disturbing brand of rap music and hip hop culture that represented the harshness, frustrations, and ongoing ills of black America in the last two decades of the twentieth century. But, this rougher and rawer form of rap had been a part of rap music and hip hop culture virtually since its inception. It simply didn't receive the kind of airplay or critical acclaim that other forms of early rap, such as comedy rap, party rap, or rock rap, did until the emergence of Too $hort's *Born to Mack* (1987) and *Life Is . . . Too Short* (1989), Ice-T's *Rhyme Pays* (1987) and *Power* (1988), N.W.A.'s *N.W.A. and the Posse* (1987) and *Straight Outta Compton* (1988), Eazy-E's *Eazy-Duz-It* (1988), and the D.O.C.'s *No One Can Do It Better* (1989). Furthermore, one of the things that ties all of these albums together is obviously their vivid tales of gang life, police brutality, crime, poverty, violence, sex, drugs and drinking, but also, and equally important, the fact that each consistently used classic funk samples as the basis of their overall "gangsta" sound.

Most hip hoppers openly acknowledge classic funk's influence on N.W.A. and its offshoot artists (e.g., Eazy-E, Ice Cube, the D.O.C., MC Ren, and, of course, Dr. Dre), but few have noted Ice-T's indebtedness to classic funk. For instance, his *Rhyme Pays'* track "409" sampled the Commodore's "The Assembly Line" (1974) and his "Make It Funky (Remix)" sampled James Brown's "Make It Funky" (1971), "Hot Pants" (1971), and "Get on the Good Foot" (1972). *Power's* "I'm Your Pusher" sampled Curtis Mayfield's "Pusherman" (1972), "Heartbeat" sampled War's "Heartbeat" (1975), and the title track, "Power," sampled James Brown's "I Don't Want Nobody to Give Me Nothing (Open Up the Door I'll Get It Myself)" (1969). At its inception, then, funk was woven into the musical fabric of gangsta rap, and, consequently, Dr. Dre's G-funk was actually the culmination of half a decade of sonic experimentation and aural innovation between 1987 and 1992.

G-funk, and gangsta rap in general, did not merely borrow rhythms and beats from classic funk, but also some of the gritty ghetto realism that distinguished funk from other genres of black popular music in the 1970s. In fact, to my ears most gangsta rap lyrics are frequently nothing more than contemporary updates of classic funk's lyrical themes; and, according to Rickey Vincent in *Funk: The Music, the People, and the Rhythm of the One* (1996), this is primarily because funk and rap are essentially the products of the same class of "outcast musicians from the black underclass in America" (30). Much like the "hot jazz," "jungle rhythms," and jive of Louis Armstrong, Duke Ellington, and Cab Calloway in the 1920s and 1930s, for many folk funk music is associated with slang, sex, and the sordid side of black life in the 1970s. Additionally, further confusion surrounding the word "funk" abounds "because of its auditory proximity to the word *fuck*, and the many potential implications of the words. This is in fact one of the very legitimizations of the music, for black culture in its unassimilated form is not burdened by Western distinctions of what is nasty or crude." Vincent went on to say, "[f]unk—and even 'fuck music'—is therefore quite legitimate if one considers that music is a part of life and sex is a shameless and special part of life" (24, emphasis in original).

When gangsta rappers discuss money, sex, clubs, drugs, and drinking, we should not forget that they are in many ways following in the footsteps of classic soulsters and funksters like James Brown, Sly Stone, George Clinton, Curtis Mayfield, LaBelle, Donny Hathaway, Marvin Gaye, Stevie Wonder, Parlet, Isaac Hayes, Barry White, Betty Davis, the Isley Brothers, the Ohio Players, the Brides of Funkenstein, the Bar-Kays, and War, all of whom produced songs that took the ghetto, lust, sex, drugs, drinking, and clubbing as topics in their music. Moreover, when gangsta rappers use profanity in their songs, we would do well to recall George Clinton and Parliament/ Funkadelic's consistent use of "nasty" and "dirty" words as "part of a rebellious repudiation of the West's concept of formality." As a matter of fact, Vincent strongly stressed:

> The childlike, "dirty" nature of some funk lyrics is also a deliberate return to an uninhibited state of mind, a state of childlike innocence and wonder, as a part of an adult state of sexual release and a state of African-rooted balance between Western and African opposites. Comedian Richard Pryor's phenomenal success in the early 1970s as a stand-up comic was precisely due to his use of vulgar language and imagery, which black folks found hilarious because of its pungent truth in their lives. Whether it is a symbol, metaphor, or the real thing, there is no reason why funk should not be associated with "dirtiness" and sex. (24)

Truth be told, many of the themes found in rap in general, and gangsta rap in particular, can be found in classic 1970s funk and blaxploitation films. Everything from drug abuse and drinking to pimping and promiscuity so often associated with rap music was likewise an integral part of the topical and lyrical universe of blaxploitation films and classic funk in the decade leading up to the emergence of rap music and hip hop culture. [23]

Hence, instead of deviating from and representing the "bastard child" of the black popular music tradition, rap can actually be "legitimately" and easily explained as the culmination of black popular music from the pathos of the blues through to the festive vibes of funk. In this sense, many rappers feel a special kinship with funk because they deeply identify not only with the pounding polyrhythms of funk, but also with the polyvocal ghettocentric messages conveyed in funk. Rappers' unwavering identification with funk is primarily because, when viewed from a musicological, sociological, and political perspective that is sensitive to the intricacies of African American history, culture, and struggle, the real and raw truth is that funk was invented and evolved by the very same underclass of people who ingeniously invented and initially evolved rap music and hip hop culture as the 1970s gave way to the 1980s: black ghetto youth. What is more, it was black ghetto youth's uncanny combination of regressive politics *and* progressive politics, poverty *and* artistic wealth, lust *and* love, as well as ill will *and* goodwill that laid the foundation for every seemingly hyper-schizophrenic form of rap music that has intrigued and offended listeners all over the world for close to three and a half decades.

Needless to say, by the late 1980s rap had evolved into much more than party rap, comedy rap, and rock rap, and while the West Coast had its funk-influenced gangsta rap, the East Coast had its own distinct style of rap that captured the post-Civil Rights Movement disillusionment and despair that engulfed black America in the last quarter of the twentieth century. Both the East Coast and West Coast forms of rawer, harder, and "realer" rap in the late 1980s eventually came to be identified as "reality rap" and "gangsta rap," respectively. Moreover, and however politically incorrect, both of these forms of rap seem to have emerged from the same source and represent much more than a pervasive pathology that plagued funk-influenced black ghetto youth in the 1980s and 1990s. But, more tellingly, reality and gangsta rap during this period was in many ways symptomatic of the same frustration and outrage over Civil Rights Movement and Black Power Movement broken promises and flagrant filibustering that fueled the funk explosion and blaxploitation films of the 1970s.

The term "hard-core hip hop" generally refers to those aspects of hip hop culture, especially gangsta rap and non-gangsta-related "reality" rap, which highlight and harangue the "hard-core" or harsh conditions of ghetto life and struggles. It is essentially a subgenre within the world of rap that first developed on the West Coast "gang-banging" and crack-infested hip hop scene—again, Too $hort's proto-gangsta and occasional reality rhymes on *Don't Stop Rappin'* (1983), *Players* (1985), and *Raw, Uncut, and X-Rated* (1986), although often overlooked, arguably provided the earliest examples of the gangsta/reality rap *modus operandi*. The gangsta/reality rap style quickly spread to the East Coast hip hop scene, and by the mid-1980s both Schoolly D and Just-Ice had produced early gangsta rap classics.[24]

Often characterized as "confrontational," "aggressive," and "angry"— that is, lyricwise, beatwise, and with its inclusion of "noisy" P-Funk-inspired sampling and production—included among the pioneers of hard-core rap music and hip hop culture are acclaimed rap artists, such as the aforementioned Too $hort, Schoolly D, and Just-Ice, as well as Spoonie Gee, Kool G Rap, Run-D.M.C., Ice-T, Boogie Down Productions, Public Enemy, N.W.A., Slick Rick, and Big Daddy Kane.[25] Emerging in the midst of Reaganism, hard-core hip hop's confrontational lyricism and decidedly political poetics mostly mirrored the lives and struggles of black male ghetto youth, providing a long-muted and long-thought to be mindless mass with a national—and soon international—voice. Hard-core hip hop culture spawned two major genres of rap: conscious rap and gangsta rap.

As a precursor to conscious and gangsta rap, in the 1980s what was then called "hard-core rap" eschewed the early rap and hip hop fascinations with, and themes of partying and bragging (à la the Sugarhill Gang, the Sequence, Grandmaster Flash & the Furious Five, the Treacherous Three, Whodini, U.T.F.O., Kurtis Blow, and Roxanne Shanté). Hard-core rappers in the 1980s rhymed about the harsh reality, grim experiences, and bleak future prospects of black youth life in the ghettos they grew up in and, for the most part, still lived in. They rhymed about reality, *their* reality, which was filled with nagging parents (mostly mothers), players, pimps, prostitutes, preachers, prisoners, schoolteachers, drug dealers, hustlers, and hoodlums. Their rhymes reflected an America—a *black America*—that Ronald Reagan and his right-wing cronies consistently turned a blind eye to and woefully turned their backs on.[26]

hard-core rap was both *streetwise* and *beatwise*—meaning, it had high-quality lyrics and bumping, head-banging beats. It was in-your-face tough talk backed by big, booty-shaking and trunk-rattling rhythms. Much of it was menacing and mean spirited, but a lot of it was also quite humorous. Which is also to say, in its own way 1980s hard-core rap continued the African American tragicomic tradition that—as I discussed in *Hip Hop's Inheritance* and *Hip Hop's Amnesia*—harks back to our enslaved ancestors' work songs and field hollers, as well as classic blues, classic jazz, and bebop.

Although gangsta rap is currently the most famous—or, rather, the most infamous (to put it poorly)—contemporary manifestation of hard-core rap, not all hard-core rap revolves around or relies on gangsta themes—which is to say, primarily *the ghetto-gangsta-nigga-pimp-hoe-thug theme*. However, it should be emphasized, much of it overlaps with the reality rap lyrics of most "conscious," "message," or "political" rap. Moving away from party rhymes and braggadocio, and big boasts about their microphone skills and sexual prowess, 1980s hard-core rappers' music and lyrics eventually began to re-flect the gritty and most often grating inner-city surroundings in which it was created and initially enjoyed.

Prior to the gangsta rap *ghetto-gangsta-nigga-pimp-hoe-thug theme* for-mula that found fame and fortune in the 1990s—back when Boogie Down Productions released *Criminal Minded*, Public Enemy dropped *Yo! Bum Rush the Show!*, Too $hort blew up the block with *Born to Mack*, and Ice-T hit hard with *Rhyme Pays*, all in 1987—the lyrical lines between gangsta and conscious rap were extremely blurred. The common thread between all these albums has to do with the fact that each contains more or less political rhymes and what would now be considered "gangsta" rhymes. For instance, even Public Enemy, a group noted for the progressive nature of most of their work, had seemingly gangsta-themed tracks on their debut *Yo! Bum Rush the*

Show!—just listen to the songs such as "Sophisticated Bitch," "Miuzi Weighs A Ton," and "Timebomb."[27]

All of this is to say, even in its first decade of development rap music and hip hop culture harbored serious political contradictions and sordid social thoughts, as well as seemingly *sadomasochistic and schizophrenic progressive/regressive tendencies.* On the one hand, 1980s hard-core rappers understood themselves to be exposing the harsh realities of life in the ghetto or, rather, *in the hood.* By exposing the issues and ills of the ghetto many hard-core rappers honestly believed that more people, especially those folk who did not live in the ghetto and who could relatively easily access much-needed resources, would get involved and altruistically work to change the "Third World" or "underdeveloped" country-like conditions most African Americans lived in. On the other hand, hard-core rappers also felt the need to make connections between what was happening in the ghetto and what was happening in the wider public sphere (i.e., increasing unemployment, rising crime rates, the slashing of social services, and the underfunding of public education—in short, virtually *a war on the poor*).[28]

In other words, 1980s hard-core rappers offered up their own homespun superstructural critique and political commentary on rising antiblack racism and increased economic exploitation during the right-wing-dominated Reagan and Bush years. Additionally, hard-core rappers also sought to deliver messages directly to ghetto youth and express their own distinct ghettocentric worldviews. Undeniably, their worldviews seemed to be preoccupied with money, sex, clubs, drugs, drinking, guns, violence, and profanity, and so forth. But, almost the exact same thing could be said about suburban white youth in the 1980s and 1990s. We have to be careful here not to demonize black ghetto youth for the exact same things that the larger society gives white suburban youth a pass on and pat on the wrist for.[29]

Admittedly, I can understand why so many on both the "right" and the "left" have accused rap music of promoting profanity, promiscuity, drug abuse, alcoholism, sexism, and heterosexism, among other issues and ills. But, I cannot in good conscience understand why so many obviously intelligent adults have a tendency to make little or no distinctions between gangsta rap and the plethora of other genres of rap music—especially, "conscious," "political," "message," "alternative," "underground," or "reality" rap.[30] Furthermore, it really sickens me that many of the same "obviously intelligent adults" hypocritically rail against youth who do not make distinctions between, say, the progressive jazz of John Coltrane and the smooth jazz of Kenny G, or the progressive rock of Led Zepplin and the pop rock of the Bee Gees, but yet insult the whole of the Hip Hop Generation by belittling and making a mockery of a music that clearly means so much to us and says so much about the world as we are experiencing (or, rather, *enduring*) it.

As quiet as it has been kept, similar to funk in the 1970s, gangsta rap and hard-core hip hop actually say a great deal about American culture, politics, society, race relations, gender discrimination, class struggle, and sexuality between the late 1980s and the present. For instance, in *Rap Music and the Poetics of Identity* (2000), music scholar Adam Krims contended that the years between 1988 and 1996 constituted the "classic gangsta rap" era (46–92). If nothing else, then, late 1980s and 1990s gangsta rap provides us with a window into rap music and hip hop culture's evolution at a time when black popular music and black popular culture unrepentantly reflected the underbelly and undesirable elements of late-twentieth-century America's on-going apartheid, oppression of women, exploitation of its workers, and dastardly disregard for its poor.

In often complex ways, the issues and ills as a consequence of a combination of destructive government policies and programs, devastating deindustrialization, intense political disaffection, persistent poverty, unabating unemployment, putrid police repression, the rise of the prison industrial complex, the drug trade, and increased gang activity all, in one way or another, informed the subjects, sights, sounds, semantics, and sadomasochism of gangsta rap and its correlate hard-core hip hop culture. Early gangsta rap classics—including Too $hort's *Life Is . . . Too Short* (1988), *Short Dog's in the House* (1990), *Shorty the Pimp* (1992), *Get in Where You Fit In* (1993), and *Cocktails* (1995); Ice-T's *Power* (1988), *The Iceberg/Freedom of Speech* (1989), and *O.G.: Original Gangster* (1991); N.W.A.'s *Straight Outta Compton* (1988) and *Niggaz4Life* (1991); the D.O.C.'s *No One Can Do It Better* (1989); Ice Cube's *AmeriKKKa's Most Wanted* (1990), *Death Certificate* (1991), and *The Predator* (1992); Dr. Dre's *The Chronic* (1992); Tupac Shakur's *2Pacalypse Now* (1991), *Strictly 4 My Niggaz* (1993), *Me Against the World* (1995), *All Eyez on Me* (1996), and *The Don Killuminati: The 7 Day Theory* (1996); the Notorious B.I.G.'s *Ready to Die* (1994) and *Life After Death* (1997); and, of course, Snoop Dogg's *Doggystyle* (1993) and *Tha Doggfather* (1996)—all in their own unique way seem to eerily reflect black ghetto youth's experiences, if not the traumatic experiences of black America as a whole, during the dark days of the Reagan and Bush administrations and, indeed, at the end of the twentieth century. As Krims contended, "there was frequently explicitly political commentary on institutions (such as the police, the various levels of government, and racism itself) which had failed inner-city African Americans" floating through the gangsta rap produced between 1987 and 1997 (82). In a sense, by the time Bill Clinton was elected president in November of 1992 and Dr. Dre released *The Chronic* in December of 1992 gangsta rap, with its funk-influenced homespun hip hop-style cultural criticism, hedonism, and sadomasochism, was all but considered part and parcel of rap music and hip hop culture, and Snoop's game-changing *Doggystyle* ushered in a whole new, even higher pop culture profile for gangsta rap and hard-core hip hop.

The irony here, of course, is that black ghetto youth's harrowing experiences during the Reagan and Bush years between 1980 and 1992, along with a penchant for classic rhythm & blues, classic soul, classic funk, classic gangster films, classic kung fu films, and classic blaxploitation films, provided the first wave of gangsta rappers with the provocative prose, poetic license, and captivating commentary that they ingeniously "remixed" and translated into a "multi-billion-dollar-a-year global industry, influencing fashion, lifestyles and language while selling everything from SUVs to personal computers," as Steve Jones and Edna Gundersen asserted in their *USA Today* article "Can Rap Regain Its Crown?" (2007, 2). It has been said that crime pays, but here it would seem that poetically licensed lyrical rhymes about crime, violence, poverty, money, sex, clubs, drugs, and drinking over blaring funk-based beats is what really pays. Consequently, from its debut in 1987 under the guise of the above-mentioned hard-core or proto-gangsta rap albums by Too $hort, Schoolly D, Just-Ice, Boogie Down Productions, Public Enemy, Ice-T, and N.W.A. through to the assassinations of Tupac Shakur in 1996 and the Notorious B.I.G. in 1997, gangsta rap and hard-core hip hop were an extraordinary commercial success. Their sudden and, for most highbrow music critics, inexplicable success thrust them to the center of, not only the music industry, but of the wider world of the U.S. entertainment, film, and culture industries.

It became quite common for gangsta rap albums to achieve "gold," "platinum," or very often "multiplatinum" sales status during its heyday between 1987 and 1997. Albums by classic gangsta rap artists—such as Too $hort, Ice-T, N.W.A., Ice Cube, Dr. Dre, the D.O.C., Snoop Dogg, Tupac Shakur, Compton's Most Wanted, Above the Law, the Geto Boys, Scarface, the Notorious B.I.G., Bone Thugs-N-Harmony, Da Lench Mob, DJ Quik, and Master P.—sold by the hundreds of thousands, some even sold by the millions, in essence, eclipsing almost all other forms of rap music in the public eye. For instance, even if we were to focus exclusively on Death Row Records, undeniably the leading gangsta rap record label in the 1990s, their extraordinary album sales mirror the emergence and staying power of gangsta rap in the 1990s: Dr. Dre's *The Chronic* (1992), Snoop Dogg's *Doggystyle* (1993) and *Tha Doggfather* (1996), the *Above the Rim* (1994) soundtrack, the *Murder Was the Case* (1994) soundtrack, Tha Dogg Pound's *Dogg Food* (1995), Tupac's *All Eyez On Me* (1996) and *The Don Killuminati* (1996), and the *Gang-Related* (1997) soundtrack were all certified "multiplatinum" by the Recording Industry Association of America (RIAA).[31]

Between 1987 and 1997 gangsta rap registered as more than merely a new, decidedly more decadent direction in rap music and hip hop culture. It also, however morally repugnant and roguishly, represented African

American youth's—especially black ghetto youth's—increasing frustration
with what they perceived to be the antiquated and incessant employment of
the Civil Rights Movement model in the interest of achieving social justice at
the turn of the twenty-first century. Eithne Quinn, in *Nuthin' But a "G"
Thang: The Culture and Commerce of Gangsta Rap* (2005), asserted that
gangsta rap between 1987 and 1997 was "a self-conscious, timely (though
largely non-progressive) rejection of traditional modes of cultural and political protest" (13).

The question begs: Why would turn-of-the-twenty-first-century black
ghetto youth reject "traditional modes of cultural and political protest,"
whether they were being put forward by white or black "adult" America?
Because, gangsta rap seems to emphasize with each and every rhyme, it was
"adult" America's august "traditions" and "social conventions" that created
the crippling cauldron, the socially segregated, derisively and greatly despised ghettos and slums black ghetto youth were imprisoned and callously
left to rot in by both the black and white bourgeoisies, by both black and
white politicians, and by both black and white preachers and teachers.

Gangsta rap is nothing else if it is not *African American youth angst* and a
telltale semantic and sonic sign that black ghetto youth think and feel very
deeply about the wicked world they inherited from their political predecessors, social movement ancestors, pop culture precursors, and, of course, musical antecedents. By poeticizing, packaging, and mercilessly marketing "the
ghetto," gangsta entrepreneurs "ironically created a saleable product out of
their own region's de-industrialization," contended Quinn (13). In the 1980s
and 1990s gangsta rap was "grounded in difficult and extreme material conditions," but, Quinn continued, "it was also deeply informed by topical discourses and sensational images of urban America."

Between 1980 and 1992, both Ronald Reagan and George H.W. Bush
"exploited poor black Americans by mobilizing opportunist discourses of
race, and, in a circular move, used such discourses to justify their policies of
federal withdrawal and penal escalation" (13). From Reagan and Bush's
hard-core Republican points of view, at least based on the policies and programs their respective administrations put forward, black America in the
1980s and early 1990s seemed like and was, thus, treated like a long-lost
wasteland or deindustrialized desert. Furthermore, along with the critical,
hyper-critical, and sometimes even hateful responses by Jesse Jackson, Louis
Farrakhan, and Khalid Muhammad, among many others, gangsta rappers
registered post-Civil Rights Movement black America's riposte to the rising
tide of extreme right-wing Republicanism and carpetbagger capitalist racism
sweeping across the United States between 1980 and 2000.

Once gangsta rap is situated within the callous and crippling 1980s and
early 1990s context in which it initially emerged and evolved, when we
sincerely take to heart the above contention that gangsta rap represents

African American youth angst and a sure semantic and sonic sign that black ghetto youth think and feel very deeply about the decadent and divisive world they inherited, then, and perhaps only then, does gangsta rap reveal itself to be an expression of the Hip Hop Generation's skewed and schizophrenic, hedonistic and extremely problematic aesthetics *and*—most importantly here—politics. Admittedly, gangsta rap's politics may not look or sound like the Civil Rights Movement's politics as expressed through 1950s and 1960s rhythm & blues and rock & roll. Moreover, gangsta rap's politics may not look or sound like the Black Power Movement's politics as expressed through 1960s and 1970s soul and funk. But, even though its politics often seem to be in outright opposition to the politics of the Civil Rights Movement and Black Power Movement, no mistake should be made about it, gangsta rap is—however sick and twisted—an expression of the Hip Hop Generation's aesthetics *and* politics. Helping to corroborate this contention, and continuing her expert "gangsta" analysis, Quinn importantly observed:

> With its confrontational and darkly humorous themes, the form [i.e., gangsta rap] elicited great affective investment from its fan base, but also outraged and affronted others. Discursively, then, gangsta's importance rested on its generation a staggering amount of controversy, leading to intense soul-searching and outcry. The genre provoked sharp debate both within and beyond the black community, from the FBI's writing an official letter in 1989 to express concern about NWA's single "Fuck tha Police" (from *Straight Outta Compton*) to the 1993 bulldozing of rap CDs by Calvin Butts III, black minister of the Abyssinian Baptist Church in Harlem, and the 1995 congressional hearings on censorship, which focused on Death Row Records. In the face of heightened public and political responses, gangsta rappers drew attention to, toyed with, and often purposefully exacerbated social divisions. Such discursive reflection helped energize gangsta's artistry. . . . In content and form, gangsta rap lyrics explore how groups and individuals negotiate their social positioning and, as artists, their own roles as cultural mediators, commercial producers, and musical personas. (12)

As an understandable consequence of its hyper-masculinity, hyper-misogyny, hyper-materialism, and frequent hyper-homophobia, gangsta rap is rarely probed for the ways in which its *texts* shrewdly reflect its *contexts*.[32] What I seek to do here is bring gangsta rap's aesthetics and politics together, exploring why and to what extent classic gangsta rap's content and form were ambivalent, self-conscious, possibly progressive on certain issues, regrettably regressive on others, and all the while trenchantly transgressive in the *context* of 1980s and 1990s America (à la classic funk in the *context* of 1960s and 1970s America). By looking at gangsta rappers as artists, not simply "high school drop-out hoodlums," "street hustlers," and "unredeemable thugs" we can calmly come to understand why Quinn contended that "[i]n the face of heightened public and political responses, gangsta rappers drew attention to, toyed with, and often purposefully exacerbated social divisions" (again, similar to classic funksters). Lots of artists "push buttons" and controversially raise issues that society seeks to gloss over or sweep under the rug. It is undeniable that America—yes, even after the Civil Rights Movement, Women's Liberation Movement, and Lesbian, Gay, Bisexual & Transgender Liberation Movement—continues to have several serious "social divisions" that are horribly (albeit often realistically) reflected in gangsta rap and, however unheralded and unflattering, have come to haunt the Hip Hop Generation as a whole.[33]

What if Quinn is really and truly onto something when she asserted that gangsta rap lyrics "explore how groups and individuals negotiate their social positioning and, as artists, their own roles as cultural mediators, commercial producers, and musical personas?" I would like to audaciously suggest that the same could be said about each and every form of rap music. In its own often warped and often wicked way rap music reflects both the Hip Hop Generation's aesthetics *and* politics. In many ways it is sort of the "Rosetta Stone" of the wider Hip Hop Movement, possibly providing future interpreters of hip hop culture with a key to discursively decipher the many mysteries (and countless controversies and contradictions) of hip hop as both music *and* movement.

Whether or not we like it, gangsta rappers are artists. Indeed, they are "cultural mediators, commercial producers, and musical personas." However, what frequently distinguishes them from other American and non-American artists is the fact that they and their beloved artistry—that is to say, their aesthetic *texts*—initially emerged and evolved within the unforgiving *context* of U.S. ghettos, hoods, barrios, slums, and government housing projects. There is, indeed, a cruel and heartbreaking irony to be poor and extremely poverty-stricken in a country that for so long has been said to be the most affluent and politically progressive on the face of God's green earth. As with the *amnesia* hip hoppers have been plagued with, narcissism is not the Hip Hop Generation's alone. If nothing else, America is a narcissistic nation chock-full of folk who hold extremely gnarly beliefs about how much better they are than the hard-working and humble humanity who make up the majority of the human species.

Often within the world of the ghetto the issues and ills of the larger society play themselves out in the extreme: for example, instead of masculinity there is hyper-masculinity; instead of misogyny there is hyper-misogyny; instead of materialism there is hyper-materialism; instead of heterosexism there is hyper-heterosexism; and instead of violence there is hyper-violence, etc. However, bear mind that much of the ghetto's "hyper-ness," if you will, is informed by its ragged relationship with mainstream and moneyed America. The ghetto does not exist in a vacuum, and, although most folk in America suffer from an acute form of *amnesia* when and where we come to the ghetto, rappers—and, yes, even the most morally repugnant and ethically reprehensible gangsta rappers—frequently develop schizophrenic progressive/regressive ghettocentric discourses that far outrun abstract academic and *bourgeois chic* discourses concerning "the ghetto problem" and "the immigration issue" in America.[34] In "Listening to Learn and Learning to Listen: Popular Culture, Cultural Theory, and American Studies" (1990a), George Lipsitz suggested that it is often artists, rather than scholars and critics, who are "the most sophisticated cultural theorists in America":

> Indeed, one might argue that the most sophisticated cultural theorists in America are neither critics nor scholars, but rather artists—writers Toni Morrison, Leslie Marmon Silko, Rudolfo Anaya, and Maxine Hong Kingston or musicians Laurie Anderson, Prince, David Byrne, and Tracy Chapman. Their work revolves around the multiple perspectives, surprising juxtapositions, subversions of language, and self-reflexivities explored within cultural theory. It comes from and speaks to contemporary cultural crises about subjectivity and nationality. Issues that critics discuss abstractly and idealistically seem to flow effortlessly and relentlessly from the texts of popular literature and popular culture. (627)[35]

Following Lipsitz's lead I would like to suggest that similar to classic funksters, contemporary rappers' work "revolves around the multiple perspectives, surprising juxtapositions, subversions of language, and self-reflexivities explored within cultural theory." Also, it "comes from and speaks to contemporary cultural crises about subjectivity and nationality." Moreover, "[i]ssues that critics discuss abstractly and idealistically seem to flow effortlessly and relentlessly from the texts" of rap music, and hip hop culture more generally. When hip hop's aesthetics and politics are brought together and placed in critical dialogue with the wider political cultures of both turn-of-the-twenty-first-century African America and mainstream America, then hip hop music and the broader Hip Hop Movement may be interpreted as a grassroots youth movement. That is to say, in many senses, the Hip Hop Movement is *simultaneously an aesthetic, cultural, social, and political multi-issue movement* in the interests of Sly & the Family Stone's "Everyday People" *and* Arrested Development's remixed "People Everyday," replete with their collective references to peace, love, freedom, freakiness, fairness, and justice.

To push this line of logic even further, I am suggesting that even the most controversial forms of rap music, in this instance gangsta and hard-core rap, are simultaneously a dissident kind of "everyday people's" political expression—with trappings of the age-old "hidden transcript" of racially colonized communities—*and*, rather ironically, a hyper-visible and hyper-corporatized mainstream commercial musical form. Above and beyond all of the above, yet and still, rap loudly and often rudely registers as contemporary black popular music. It contains both the traditional subversions of authority that grew out of African Americans' history of racial oppression and economic exploitation, and it also offers a highly commodifiable and sometimes pseudo-radical chic variety of youth protest, early-twenty-first-century youth angst, and African American youth's ongoing antiracist rebellion and search for social justice.

The fact that rap music is marketed and hyper-consumed, and that even the most masculinist, misogynist, materialist, and heterosexist rappers requisition the folklore, tales, toasts, jive, jokes, colloquialisms, mannerisms, and musics of the long-honored "old school" African American rhetorical and musical traditions for explicitly commercial ends, remixes, perhaps even distorts and "dumbs down," but does not in any way whatsoever negate, the rich colloquial and cultural traditions deeply embedded within it. All of this, of course, might be one of the main reasons rap music has not been *European Americanized* and overrun by a bunch of modern-day Elvis Presleys, Bill Haleys, Buddy Hollys, and countless other blond-haired and blue-eyed rock and soul Romeos (and jigging Juliets).

Perhaps one of the reasons the deceptively deep and sometimes hidden history of rap music's "remixed" archetypal representations have been often-overlooked in even the most scholarly and critical treatments of the music is the simple but frequently ignored fact that overly academic engagements of rap music have routinely downplayed and diminished *the sociopolitical dimensions of hip hop discourse*. In other words, when hip hop is acknowledged as both *a new form of music* and *a new form of sociopolitical movement*, then we can easily see that rap music's "remixed" archetypal representations of poor black folk come uncomfortably close to the conventional antiblack racist categories that poverty-stricken black people have long been cast in by "conservative," "liberal," and sometimes even allegedly "radical" white America. These extremely controversial *colored-Negro-nigger-black-African American archetypes* once commercially constructed—not in the black ghetto but in the bourgeois boardrooms of corporate America, and then sent out to lily-white suburban audiences gleefully on *inner-city safari* far removed from the initial point of aesthetic origin and political performance (à la Edward Said's [1999, 2000] "traveling theory")—discursively and dangerously overlap with long-standing racial myths and sexual stereotypes about African Americans.

At the center of the more searing claims leveled against rap, especially gangsta rap, is its purported reinforcing of negative and "niggardly" stereotypes about African Americans. Although corporate America is certainly complicit in spreading "negative and 'niggardly' stereotypes about African Americans" via rap music, what makes gangsta rap stand out and extra explosive, even among other contentious forms of rap music, is that it is primarily young, poor, black males who conjure up and recreate the extremely controversial *colored-Negro-nigger-black-African American archetypes* that lie at the heart of gangsta rap and hard-core hip hop culture. Gangsta rap complicates the conventional critiques coming out of African American studies, American studies, ethnic studies, critical race studies, cultural studies, and postcolonial studies concerning misrepresentations of black folk and blackness predominantly generated by Eurocentric and bourgeois white male theorists, critics, artists, and producers. For instance, even the negative and "niggardly" representations of black folk and blackness incessantly circulated in 1970s blaxploitation films, for the most part, could be chalked up to the radical chic and erstwhile exploitative practices of wealthy white male screenwriters, directors, and producers.

However, and this is one of the reasons it is so controversial, rap—especially gangsta rap—offered one of the first mainstream consumer-friendly and mass commercial forms in which mostly young black cultural workers generated images that were often blatantly associated with antiblack racist myths and sexual stereotypes about black folk and blackness. By flagrantly courting controversy, in its own sick and twisted way, rap music deftly demonstrates that the Hip Hop Generation's politics are probably just as—if not even more—complicated and contradictory as its music and overarching aesthetics. Hence, here I am strongly suggesting that it is time to acknowledge hip hop for what it really is or, at the least, for what it has actually heuristically become over the last three and a half decades of its existence: both *a new form of music* and *a novel form of sociopolitical movement*—that is to solemnly say, *the Hip Hop Movement*.

There is a very serious sense in which rap music's controversies and contradictions are actually emblematic of the wider Hip Hop Movement's controversies and contradictions. Consequently, even as I summon the Hip Hop Generation to move beyond its seemingly incessant and extremely narcissistic celebrations of its sexual prowess, "sick whips," music, money, movies, and mansions, at the very same moment I openly and honestly admit the contradictions and controversies of my most beloved generation. In fact, I would go so far to say that the Hip Hop Generation seems prone to contradiction and controversy, and this propensity for contradiction and controversy manifests itself loud and clear in the Hip Hop Movement's sometimes progressive and sometimes regressive and extremely problematic politics and social visions.

Just as rappers—the "unofficial" mouthpieces of the Hip Hop Movement—routinely send schizophrenic progressive/regressive mixed messages, frequently on the same song, the Hip Hop Movement's politics and social visions seem to constantly and chameleonically shift. For instance, it is quite common for rappers to one moment feign a posture of peace, benevolence, and nonviolence, then the next moment metaphorically mean-mug and sonically saber-rattle so as to invoke the black buck/badman/trickster black folk hero who is seemingly always unerringly heading down a murderous blood-bath warpath. Rappers often one moment mercilessly critique American capitalism and all of its ills, then the very next moment boldly brag about their rags-to-riches unapologetic embrace of the American Dream and their extraordinary Booker T. Washington-style-bootstrap-uplift achievements, replete with copious references to multiple mansions, Maybachs, "baby-mamas," and other material (and, let it be said, sadomasochistic) comforts. Moreover, rappers are renown for one moment praising their mothers and grandmothers, but then in the very next moment calling seemingly almost all Hip Hop Generation women "hood rats," "hoochie mamas," "chickenheads," "skeezers," "tricks," "tramps," "gold-diggers," "hussies," "heifers," "bitches," and "hoes." In what has now become a characteristic double move in the rap game (if not in hip hop culture in general), the Hip Hop Movement's overtly "radical" gestures and "political" posturing are frequently as self-conscious, self-serving, and even opportunist as its often reactionary, antiliberal, and at times even antiradical wrongheaded assertions.

Rappers—again, representing the "unofficial" mouthpieces of the Hip Hop Movement—in their own often-unwitting ways frequently register the Hip Hop Movement's very serious problems with the discernible decrease in nationally networked African American protest movements and social justice struggles between 1980 and the present. In this sense, it could be said that rap music reveals that the Hip Hop Movement's real political energies and ongoing efforts actually lay in the struggle to come to terms with an age in which there has been a dramatic decline in popular protest politics, and this has been all the more devastating and dispiriting in light of African Americans' long history of political protest and freedom fighting: from the Abolitionist Movement and Black Women's Club Movement, to the New Negro Movement and Harlem Renaissance; from the Bebop Movement and Civil Rights Movement to the Black Power Movement and Black Women's Liberation Movement.

Most rap music, to a certain extremely salient extent, may reflect hip hoppers' post-Civil Rights Movement, post-Black Power Movement, post-Women's Liberation Movement, and post-Lesbian, Gay, Bisexual & Transgender Liberation Movement inertia and disappointment. Can it be honestly denied that inertia, anger, angst, disappointment, and even antiradicalism have come to be part and parcel of most rap music, and—however unnerving this all may be for many of us—this discontent and exasperation is somehow as aesthetically and politically important and inexplicably invigorating as the music's more obvious expressions of ambition, optimism, radicalism, and other progressive pronouncements? Rap music does more than merely convey the hyper-misogyny and hyper-materialism of the Hip Hop Generation. It also communicates extremely important social and political thought that frequently reflects the sociopolitical pulse of the Hip Hop Movement. Moreover, rap exhibits an acute awareness—often buried beneath a barrage of braggadocio, bourgeoisism, profanity, misogyny, homophobia, and banging beats—of the promises that have not been fulfilled in the aftermaths of the Civil Rights Movement, Black Power Movement, Women's Liberation Movement, and Lesbian, Gay, Bisexual & Transgender Liberation Movement. In short, at its core rap music is a *discourse on declension*—which is to say, it is a discourse on *political decline, social decay, cultural crisis, sexual subversion, and moral deterioration.*

Continuing to explore rap music and hip hop culture as a post-Civil Rights Movement, post-Black Power Movement, post-Women's Liberation Movement, and post-Lesbian, Gay, Bisexual & Transgender Liberation Movement *discourse on declension* between 1980 and the present, the fifth and final "remix" to follow identifies and critically analyzes the ways in which rap music and hip hop culture articulate the—however sprawling and unconventional—politics and social visions of the Hip Hop Movement, what these politics and social visions tell us about the Hip Hop Generation and contemporary society, and how hip hoppers' unconventional politics and social visions over the last three and a half decades have been shaped by (even as they have undeniably shaped) the turn-of-the-twenty-first-century social, political, cultural, and musical world. When "remixes" 1 through 4 are taken into serious consideration—which is to say, when the politics and social visions of classic rhythm & blues, rock & roll, soul, and funk are taken into serious consideration—rap music registers as more than merely the "sick and twisted" songs and tall tales of turn-of-the-twenty-first-century black ghetto youth (and misguided white suburban youth), but creative expressions of the broader and still brewing Hip Hop Movement's politics and social justice agendas. We turn now, then, to the much-mangled and much-misunderstood, often hated and frequently celebrated *post-Civil Rights Movement, post-Black Power Movement, post-Women's Liberation Movement, and post-Lesbian, Gay, Bisexual & Transgender Liberation Movement forms of black popular culture and black popular music-based politics and social movement* that have collectively and increasingly come to be called *the Hip Hop Movement.*

NOTES

1. My interpretation of funk has been primarily informed by Bolden (2008), M.P. Brown (1994), Danielsen (2006), Lornell and Stephenson (2001, 2009), Maultsby (2001), Morant (2011), Ripani (2006), A. Stewart (2000), D. Thompson (2001), and R. Vincent (1996).

2. For more detailed discussion of affirmative action, and for the most noteworthy works that informed my interpretation here, see T.H. Anderson (2004), Cahn (1995), Curry (1996), Katznelson (2005), Kellough (2006), and Wise (2005).

3. For further discussion of the "softening" of soul music in the mid- to late-1970s, and for the most noteworthy works that informed my analysis here, see Bayles (1994), Bowman

(1997), George (1988), Hirshey (1984), J.A. Jackson (2004), Maultsby (1983), M.A. Neal (1997, 2005b), Phinney (2005), Pruter (1991), R.W. Stephens (1984), Ward (1998), and Werner (2006).

4. My interpretation of Yoruba/Ifa religion, and specifically the concept of *asé*, has been informed by Bascom (1969), Beier (1980), Hallen (2000), Hallgren (1995), J.M. Murphy (1993), and Neimark (1993). And, my interpretation of African American vernacular culture, and black popular music patois in particular, has been informed by Nielsen (1997, 2004), Rickford (1999), Rickford, Mufwene, Bailey, and Baugh (1998), Rickford and Rickford (2000), and Smitherman (1975, 1986, 2000, 2006).

5. For further discussion of hard bop and post-bop, and for the most noteworthy works that informed my analysis below, see DeVeaux (1991), Goldsher (2002), Henry (2004), Mathieson (2002), Rosenthal (1988a, 1992), G. Sales (1984), and Saul (2003).

6. For more detailed discussion of hard boppers' politics and the politics of hard bop, and for the most noteworthy works that informed my analysis here, see Henry (2004), R.D.G. Kelley (2012), Monson (2007), Rosenthal (1992), Saul (2003), and P. Thomas (2012).

7. My interpretation of James Brown's life and musical legacy has been informed by G. Brown (2008), J. Brown (1986, 2005), George and Leeds (2008), Scannell (2012), Silverman and Slutsky (1997), R.J. Smith (2012), J. Sullivan (2008), and Wolk (2004).

8. My interpretation of African music, in the most general sense, has been informed by Agawu (2003), Bebey (1999), Bender (1991), Chernoff (1979), Ewens (1992), Nketia (1974), Stone (2008), and Tenaille (2002).

9. My interpretation of Sly & the Family Stone has been informed by P.S. Jones (1993), Kaliss (2008), M.M. Lewis (2006), Marsh (1985), Ripani (2006), Santiago (2008), and Selvin (1998).

10. For further discussion of the FBI's infamous Counter Intelligence Program (COINTEL-PRO), especially its assault on black America from the beginning of World War I in 1914 to the end of the Vietnam War in 1975, and for the most noteworthy works that informed my analysis here, see Blackstock (1988), Churchill and Wall (1988, 2002), J.K. Davis (1992), Drabble (2004, 2007, 2008), Jeffreys-Jones (2007), O'Reilly (1983, 1989, 1994), and T. Weiner (2012).

11. It is extremely important not to overlook Jimi Hendrix's enormous influence on funk, especially the mind-boggling music of major funkmasters Sly Stone, George Clinton and Parliament/Funkadelic, the Isley Brothers, War, and Betty Davis. For further discussion of Hendrix and his pionerring guitar-centered *funk rock*, see C.R. Cross (2005), D. Henderson (2008), C.S. Murray (1989), J. Perry (2004), Roby and Schreiber (2010), and Shapiro and Glebbeek (1991).

12. For further discussion of the setbacks of the Civil Rights Movement in the late 1960s and the despair at the dawn of the Black Power Movement, and for the most noteworthy works that informed my analysis here, see Fergus (2009), Gore, Theoharis, and Woodard (2009), J.L. Jeffries (2006), C. Johnson (2007), Joseph (2006a, 2006b), Ogbar (2004), Ongiri (2010), and Van Deburg (1992).

13. I could not agree more with Lewis's comparison of Sly Stone's *There's a Riot Goin' On* with the Rolling Stones' *Exit on Main St.* (1972) double-album, which, following the blues-soaked bleakness and weariness of *Beggars Banquet* (1968), *Let It Bleed* (1969), and *Sticky Fingers* (1971), seemingly took the advances of their previous work to the extreme by burying Mick Jagger's throaty blues rock vocals deep in the mix while simultaneously accenting the groundbreaking guitar alchemy of Keith Richards and Mick Taylor. For the first time, at least to my ears, the Rolling Stones' forays into blues, country, soul, and even gospel didn't sound forced, and actually came across as organic and heartfelt for the most part. There simply is no denying the blues rock beauty of classic songs such as "Rocks Off," "Tumbling Dice," "Torn and Frayed," "Happy," "Let It Loose," and "Shine a Light." However, even in light of *Exit on Main St.*'s undeniable sonic beauty, lyrically *There's a Riot Goin' On* seemingly touches on a wider range of the pressing issues impacting America—indeed, *black* America—at the dawn of the 1970s. Yet and still, both albums seemed to prefigure future work in rock and funk, respectively. For further discussion of the Rolling Stones' *Exit on Main St.*, and for the most noteworthy works that informed my analysis here, see Elliott (2012), Greenfield (2006), Janovitz (2005), J. Perry (1999), Sandford (2012), and Tarlé (2001).

14. My analysis here has been undergirded by a number of critical works in Black Panther Party studies, most importantly among them Alkebulan (2007), C.J. Austin (2006), Bloom and Martin (2013), Churchill and Wall (1988), Cleaver and Katsiaficas (2001), Lazerow and Williams (2006, 2008), and Rhodes (2007).

15. For further discussion of Jimi Hendrix's later genre-jumping funk rock albums, such as *Electric Ladyland* (1968), *Band of Gypsys* (1970), *The Rainbow Bridge Concert* (1971), and *The Cry of Love* (1971), see McDermott (1992), C.S. Murray (1989), J. Perry (2004), Roby and Schreiber (2010), and Shapiro and Glebbeek (1991).

16. My interpretation of George Clinton and Parliament/Funkadelic has been informed by L. Bradley (2006), B. Cooper (1980), Danielsen (2006), Doleac (2011), Drisdel (2011), M. Fox (1990), Himes (1979, 1980, 1986), Maxile (2011), McLeod (2003), Mills (1998), Morant (2011), M. Rogers (2013), Vickers (1976), and C.M. Young (1978).

17. For further discussion of the incomparable Sun Ra and his avant-garde jazz "Arkestra," including his enormous influence on black popular music beyond the jazz genre as well as 1960s and 1970s black aesthetic and political culture more generally, see Bischoff (2012), Corbett, Elms, and Kapsalis (2006, 2010), Kreiss (2008), Lock (1999), Ra (2006), Szwed (1997), and Trent (1997).

18. For more detailed discussion of black mayors between 1970 and 1975, and for the most noteworthy works that informed my analysis here, see Atwater (2010), Eisinger (1979), Haskins (1972), Nelson and Meranto (1977), Poinsett (1970), Rich (1996), and J.P. Thompson (2006).

19. For further discussion of Octavia Butler's pioneering science fiction, see O.E. Butler (2010), G.J. Hampton (2010), Holden (1998), Levecq (2000), Luckhurst (1996), Omry (2005), Ramirez (2002), Salvaggio (1984), Schwab (2006), and Thaler (2010). And, for critical treatments of African American science fiction and Afro-futurism more generally, see David (2007), Grayson (2003), Jackson and Moody-Freeman (2011), Kilgore (2003), Lavender (2011), Nama (2008), A. Nelson (2002), and Yaszek (2006).

20. Michael Small's *Break It Down: The Inside Story from the New Leaders of Rap* (1992) remains one of the best sources on Digital Underground, among many other late-1980s and early-1990s rap acts, along with Bynoe (2006), Price (2006), and P. Shapiro (2005a).

21. For further discussion of Dr. Dre, G-funk, and the formative years of gangsta rap, and for the most noteworthy works that informed my analysis here, see Borgmeyer and Lang (2007), J. Brown (2006), Kenyatta (2000), E. Quinn (2005), Ro (1996, 1998, 2007), and B. Williams (2008).

22. My interpretation of G-funk has been informed by Boyd (1997), Canton (2006), Evil (2005), E. Quinn (2005), Ro (1996, 1998), W. Shaw (2000a, 2000b, 2000c), and Villard (2000).

23. For further discussion of black exploitation (i.e., "blaxploitation") films and archetypical characters, and for the most noteworthy works that informed my analysis here, see Dunn (2008), Guerrero (1993), J. Howard (2007), D. James (1995), Koven (2001, 2010), N. Lawrence (2008), Martinez, Martinez, and Chavez (1998), Rome (2004), Sévéon (2008), Sieving (2011), Sims (2006), and Walker, Rausch, and Watson (2009). Hip hop's "inheritance" from blaxploitation films was also discussed in my chapter, "'Say It Loud!—I'm Black and I'm Proud!': From the Black Arts Movement and Blaxploitation Films to the Conscious and Commercial Rap of the Hip Hop Generation," in Rabaka (2011, 83–128).

24. For further discussion of West Coast rap music and hip hop culture, and for the most noteworthy works that informed my analysis here, see Basu (1992), B. Cross (1993), Grant (2002), A.K. Harrison (2009), Hess (2010), Jiménez (2011), R.D.G. Kelley (1994), Loza, Santiago, Alvarez, and Moore (1994), Mayne (2000), Miller, Vandome, and McBrewster (2011), M.H. Morgan (2009), E. Quinn (2005), W. Shaw (2000a, 2000b, 2000c), and T.L. Williams (2002).

25. For further discussion of these, among other, primarily East Coast pioneers of hard-core rap music and hip hop culture, and for the most noteworthy works that informed my analysis here, see Bynoe (2006), Hess (2010), McCoy (1992), Nelson and Gonzales (1991), Price (2006), P. Shapiro (2005a), M.W. Small (1992), Wang (2003), and Woodstra, Bush, and Erlewine (2008).

26. For further discussion of the Reagan administration's impact on black America, and for the most noteworthy works that informed my analysis here, see Bothmer (2010), Brownlee and Graham (2003), Bunch (2009), Detlefsen (1991), Ehrman (2005), Hudson and Davies (2008), Laham (1998), Martin (2011), Rousseas (1982), Schaller (1992), and Shull (1993).

27. For further discussion of Public Enemy, their early gangsta-themed songs, and popularization of what we now call "conscious rap," and for the most noteworthy works that informed my analysis here, see Chuck D (1997), Danielsen (2008), Eiswerth (1996), Hamrick (1991), Kowalewski (1993), Myrie (2008), Shabazz (1999), Walser (1995), and Weingarten (2010).

28. For further discussion of the "war on the poor" (as opposed to what is commonly called the "war on poverty"), and for the most noteworthy works that informed my analysis here, see E. Anderson (1981, 1990, 1999, 2008), Farmer (2003), Gans (1995), M.B. Katz (1989), Sidel (1996), and Stricker (2007).

29. My interpretation of Hip Hop Generation white suburban youth's thought and behavior has been influenced by Clark (2011), Epstein (1998), Giroux (1998), Kitwana (2005), R.W. Larkin (1979), Medovoi (2005), Pitts (2001), and Wooden and Blazak (2001).

30. For further discussion of the various genres of rap music, and for the most noteworthy works that informed my analysis here, see Bogdanov, Woodstra, Erlewine, and Bush (2003), A. Bradley (2009), Bradley and DuBois (2010), Bynoe (2006), Hess (2007a, 2007b, 2010), Krims (2000), Lena (2003, 2004, 2006), Price (2006), and P. Shapiro (2005a).

31. For further discussion of Death Row Records and its dominance of the gangsta rap genre in the 1990s, and for the most noteworthy works that informed my analysis here, see J. Brown (2002), Knight (2003), Miller, Vandome, and McBrewster (2011), Ro (1996, 1998), Savidge (2001), and R. Sullivan (2002).

32. My emphasis here on *rap texts* being reflective of *hip hop contexts*—and broader *U.S. economic, social, political, and cultural contexts*—has been undeniably influenced by Murray Forman's brilliant book *The Hood Comes First: Race, Space, and Place in Rap and Hip Hop* (2002), as well as several other cutting-edge works in cultural geography and racial geography, such as Dwyer and Bressey (2008), Flint (2004), Harvey (1989, 1996, 2006, 2009), McKittrick and Woods (2007), Schein (2006), and N. Smith (1984).

33. For further discussion of the politics of gangsta rap or, rather, gangsta rap's politics, and for the most noteworthy works that informed my analysis here, see Adams and Fuller (2006), Bowser (2012), Boyd (1997), Canton (2006), Dyson (1997, 2002), Elafros (2005), Grant (2002), M.L. Johnson (2011), Kitwana (1994), Kubrin (2005a, 2005b), Martinez (1997), Riley (2005), Rose-Robinson (1999), R.J. Walker (1996), Watts (1997), and M. White (2011).

34. My analysis here has been informed by several noteworthy works in the sociology of the ghetto—or, rather, "ghetto studies"—that primarily focus on African American life and struggles in the ghetto. For example, see Hannerz (1969), Hilfiker (2002), N. Jones (2010), Meier (1976), Stanley-Niaah (2010), Venkatesh (2000), R.L. Warren (2008), D. Wilson (2007), and Winant (2001).

35. For George Lipsitz's more detailed book-length analyses of artists, writers, and musicians as critical and cultural theorists of contemporary society, see Lipsitz (1990b, 1994, 2007). The influence of Lipsitz's work on my analysis of the—again, however unorthodox—politics of gangsta rap simply cannot be overstated.

III

The Soundtracks and Social Visions of the Hip Hop Movement, 1980–Present

Remix 5

The Hip Hop Movement

From Black Popular Music and Black Popular Culture to a Black Popular Movement

In many ways, hip hop represents a particular species of social movement. The movement is made possible by new social and economic arrangements, technological innovations, and the global dissemination of U.S. popular media cultures. Sociologists broadly define social movements as collective efforts to produce social change. Any attempt to discuss hip hop as a movement demands careful delineation because it is variously preoccupied with style, performance, opposition, leisure, consumption, representation, and entrepreneurship.

—S. Craig Watkins, *Representing: Hip Hop Culture and the Production of Black Cinema*

INTRODUCTION: POST-CIVIL RIGHTS MOVEMENT AND POST-BLACK POWER MOVEMENT POLITICS, POPULAR MUSIC, AND POPULAR CULTURE

To invoke hip hop as a "movement," rather than merely a "generation," is to conjure up and consciously conceive of hip hop as *the accumulated politics and aesthetics of each and every African American movement and musical form that preceded it*. To speak of hip hop as a "movement" also means circumventing the long-standing—and, at this point, very tired—tendency to privilege hip hop's aesthetics and other accoutrements, especially rap music and videos, over hip hop's politics and social visions. Just as it would be absurd to attempt to reduce the Civil Rights Movement to classic rhythm & blues or the Black Power Movement to classic soul, it is ridiculous to reduce

285

the Hip Hop Movement to rap music, especially the two most popular forms of rap at the present moment: commercial and gangsta rap. As discussed in the previous "remixes," commercial and gangsta rap are only two of the more than three dozen subgenres of rap music, including African rap; alternative rap; avant-garde rap; battle rap; British rap; chopped & screwed; Christian rap; conscious rap; country rap; crunk; Dirty South rap; East Coast rap; electro-rap; freestyle rap; French rap; funk rap; German rap; G-funk rap; hard-core rap; heavy metal rap; hyphy rap; jazz rap; Latin rap; Mafioso rap; message rap; Miami bass rap; Midwest rap; Muslim rap; nerdcore rap; old school rap; opera rap; party rap; political rap; pop rap; ragamuffin rap; reggae rap; Reggaeton; rock rap; snap rap; Spanish rap; Southern rap; turntablism; underground rap; and, of course, West Coast rap.[1]

Commercial and gangsta rap are simply two of a variety of rap styles that serve as soundtracks for the Hip Hop Movement. As such, just like the other rap subgenres discussed throughout this book, as well as in *Hip Hop's Inheritance* and *Hip Hop's Amnesia*, commercial and gangsta rap capture and convey many of the Hip Hop Generation's contradictions, but also many of its contributions. No matter how troubling many of us may find various aspects of rap music it is important for us not to perfunctorily and hyper-critically lump all rappers and rap music together. Whether or not we are willing to acknowledge it, in its own off-kilter and extremely unorthodox way the Hip Hop Movement builds on the good *and* the bad, the progressive *and* the regressive aspects of the Civil Rights Movement and Black Power Movement, among other movements. Hence, instead of cherry-picking those elements of previous black popular movements and black popular musics that have been raised up and revered by the moderates of the Civil Rights Movement and the militants of the Black Power Movement and deemed most representative of their respective movements, the Hip Hop Movement has often indiscriminately and quite cavalierly drawn from everything and anything, whether deemed "good" or "bad," from the past in its efforts to critique and give voice to black ghetto youths' (and their multiracial allies') ongoing sufferings, social misery, worldviews, and all-around angst.

The failure to acknowledge and seriously understand just what the Hip Hop Movement is and is not, truth be told, is not solely the fault of hip hoppers' parents and grandparents. Many of the misunderstandings surrounding the Hip Hop Movement not only stem from their elders' overemphasis on the ills of commercial and gangsta rap, but also on hip hoppers' own confusion and collective failure to articulate an identifiable agenda and set of goals. For instance, in his critical ethnography *Thug Life: Race, Gender, and the Meaning of Hip Hop* (2011), Michael Jeffries painfully admitted, "while respondents' contributions failed to provide evidence that the Hip Hop Movement is explicitly concerned with a specific set of social issues or political topics, there is plenty of evidence that suggests respondents use hip hop to understand their social worlds" (27). It may very well be in hip hoppers'—not merely rappers, but the wider world of hip hoppers—collective "use [of] hip hop to understand their social worlds" that we are able to glean some semblance of the agenda and goals of the Hip Hop Movement.

Admittedly, by no means a "movement" in the same manner the Civil Rights Movement or Black Power Movement were movements, but, make no mistake about it, the Hip Hop Movement is indeed a *movement* nonetheless. To understand the Hip Hop Movement as a new social and political movement it is important to—in the most Fanonian and Foucaultian fashion imaginable—temporarily suspend the constant comparisons with the Civil Rights Movement or Black Power Movement. In fact, if "remixes" 1 through 4 revealed anything they demonstrated that the black popular movements and the black popular musics of the past not only harbored contradictions and ignited countless controversies, but they also, however unheralded, bequeathed a great many of those contradictions and controversies to rap music and the Hip Hop Movement. Where rhythm & blues could be said to have grown out of the emergence of the Civil Rights Movement ("remix" 1), and funk the emergence of the Black Power Movement ("remix" 4), to a certain extent, it could be said that the Hip Hop Movement (although *not* hip hop culture) was spawned by the politics and popularization of rap music in the early- to mid-1980s. "Although hip hop encompasses more than rap music," Lester Spence insightfully observed in *Stare in the Darkness: The Limits of Hip Hop and Black Politics* (2011), "rap music is not only the most consumed aspect of hip hop but is arguably the easiest form to infuse with politics" (5). No matter where we fall in the heated debates concerning the merits and demerits of rap, it is hard to deny that it most often "represents a powerful critique of contemporary black urban circumstances."[2]

In the most unprecedented manner imaginable, the Hip Hop Movement inverts *the black popular music as an outgrowth of the black popular movement tradition* and, perhaps, starts a new tradition where black popular movements may in fact spring from the cultural crises, alienation, political expressions, and social visions conveyed in black popular music in particular and black popular culture in general. As the first black popular movement to emerge in the aftermath of the Civil Rights Movement and Black Power Movement, the Hip Hop Movement simultaneously builds on and breaks with the politics and social visions of the previous black popular movements. In many ways following in the footsteps of the militants of the Black Power Movement and Black Arts Movement, hip hoppers emphasize the political nature of black popular culture in general and black popular music in particular. Hence, those who quickly quip that invoking a "Hip Hop Movement" is quite simply "hogwash" should bear in mind that the Hip Hop Generation is not the first generation of black youth to not only note the political nature of black popular culture, but also to earnestly attempt to use the politics and

social visions embedded in black popular culture in the interest of political
activism and social organization.[3]

Those who doubt whether political activism and social organization can
actually grow out of rap music and hip hop culture should bear in mind the
work of several sociologists, musicologists, and cultural critics who argue
that popular culture and popular music, generally speaking, can and has
historically influenced the way we view ourselves and the world.[4] Moreover,
those still skeptical of the notion that a unique form of politics and a distinct
social vision are buried in the beats and rhymes of rap music and the wider
word of hip hop completely ignore the fact that "a variety of individuals
connect rap and hip hop to black politics," Spence declared, ultimately "arguing either that it is the biggest internal threat African Americans face or
that it has the greatest potential to build a new black politics" (3). All of this
is to say, rap music and hip hop culture cannot be both "mindless" and
"meaningless" noise (*not* "real music") primarily produced by black ghetto
youth *and* "the biggest internal threat African Americans face" at the turn of
the twenty-first century.

Obviously rap music and hip hop culture carry a great deal of political
weight and cultural clout if, indeed, many of the former moderates of the
Civil Rights Movement and militants of the Black Power Movement understand them to be serious impediments to African Americans' search for social justice, political parity, and cultural pluralism in the present. However,
as with rhythm & blues and rock & roll during the Civil Rights Movement
("remixes" 1 and 2), or soul and funk during the Black Power Movement
("remixes" 3 and 4), rap music and hip hop culture are not automatically and
unalterably negative or somehow predestined to be detrimental to the development of a post-Civil Rights Movement black popular movement. To state
it outright: *Rap music and hip hop culture are merely the tools of choice used
by the Hip Hop Movement. And, if rap music and hip hop culture can be and,
truth be told, have been used to degrade and destroy, then it should also be
acknowledged that they can and have been used to elevate and educate.*
Spence importantly explained:

> MCs, activists, pundits, and citizens alike believe that rap lyrics communicate
> politics; they believe that hip hop can be used to circulate and generate a new
> form of political activism, and they believe that rap consumption shifts politi-
> cal attitudes. Rap and hip hop are not only "Black America's CNN"; they are
> also the key to generating a new black political movement. They are spaces in
> which blacks create new meanings of "blackness" and develop critiques that
> offer alternatives to the status quo. (3)[5]

When we move away from the constant comparisons with the Civil Rights
Movement and Black Power Movement, the politics and social visions expressed in the Hip Hop Movement's music and overarching culture can actu-

ally be conceived of as *a new, post-Civil Rights Movement and post-Black Power Movement form of black popular culture and black popular music-based politics and social movement.* However, even as we acknowledge the political nature of black popular culture and black popular music it should be emphasized yet again that they do not in and of themselves constitute politics in the traditional sense. Usually politics involves socially authorized and, therefore, socially acceptable efforts aimed at gaining and maintaining power. With respect to conventional African American political history and culture, great care must to be taken to distinguish between, for instance, Rosa Parks's decision to remain seated on a segregated Montgomery city bus in the 1950s and Aretha Franklin's decision to passionately sing "Respect" in the 1960s. Both decisions were undeniably political acts that are open to all sorts of political interpretations, but I would be the first to note the distinct differences between Parks and Franklin's political acts: Parks's political act played itself out in the social and political world, where Franklin's political act played itself out in the world of popular music and popular culture. That being said, I still believe that it is important for us to acknowledge that both of these political acts were actually part of the same continuum, one that connected the Civil Rights Movement to the New Negro Movement, and likewise classic soul to classic jazz.[6]

The Hip Hop Movement has inherited much from both the politics and aesthetics of previous black popular movements and black popular musics, and as with the previous movements and musics the Hip Hop Movement and rap music have helped black ghetto youth and their multiracial allies get in touch with their feelings and organize their thoughts on a wide range of topics from social justice and sexuality to racism and religious intolerance. Instead of juxtaposing aesthetics against politics or, rather, privileging politics over aesthetics, the Hip Hop Movement seeks to understand how the two inform each other. In other words, *the Hip Hop Movement is as much a political movement as it is an artistic movement.* Rather than the conventional *either/or* approach to politics and popular culture, the Hip Hop Movement has a unique *both/and* approach that refuses to privilege politics over popular culture, or popular culture over politics.

In this "remix" the central question is not whether there are politics and social visions buried beneath the beats and rhymes of rap music, or within the world of contemporary black popular culture in general. Popular music and popular culture are teeming with political critiques and social commentaries "that offer alternatives to the status quo" and traditional political science. Rather, the core concern here has more to do with the ways in which rap music and hip hop culture articulate the—however sprawling and unconventional—politics and social visions of the Hip Hop Movement, what these politics and social visions tell us about the Hip Hop Generation and contemporary society, and how hip hoppers' unconventional politics and social visions over the last three and a half decades have been shaped by (even as they have undeniably shaped) the turn-of-the-twenty-first-century social, political, and cultural world. Perhaps one of the main reasons that rap music and the Hip Hop Movement's politics and social visions have been ignored and erased is because most social commentators, political analysts, and cultural critics have been surreptitiously, albeit eagerly, awaiting the second coming of the Civil Rights Movement, and, similar to the Black Power Movement, the Hip Hop Movement has simply refused to play second fiddle and be forced to fit into the mold of previous black popular movements—no matter how great those previous movements and how much those movements may have inspired, even if unwittingly, the Hip Hop Movement.

THE HIP HOP MOVEMENT: A BLACK POPULAR MUSIC AND BLACK POPULAR CULTURE-BASED BLACK POPULAR MOVEMENT

Most hip hop scholars, critics, and fans will readily concede that rap music and hip hop culture have inherited much from previous black popular musics and black popular cultures. However, few of these scholars, critics, and fans have been willing to acknowledge the ways in which rap music and hip hop culture have been influenced by previous black popular movements, such as the Black Women's Club Movement, New Negro Movement, Civil Rights Movement, Black Power Movement, and Black Women's Liberation Movement. In other words, there is a curious amnesia surrounding the ways in which previous black popular movements have influenced the politics and social visions of rap music and the Hip Hop Movement. Because the influence of previous African American social and political movements on rap music and hip hop culture is often ignored, it is extremely difficult for many (including many hip hoppers) to conceive of rap music and hip hop culture as expressions of a broader Hip Hop Movement. But, building on James Scott's groundbreaking work in *Domination and the Arts of Resistance: Hidden Transcripts* (1990), Tricia Rose distinguished between the "public transcripts" of the powerful and the "hidden transcripts" of the powerless in *Black Noise: Rap Music and Black Culture in Contemporary America* (1994).

Applying Scott's analysis to rap music and hip hop culture, Rose (1994, 100) explained that the "dominant public transcripts are maintained through a wide range of social practices and are in a constant state of production." She continued, "[p]owerful groups maintain and affirm their power by attempting to dictate the staging of public celebrations, by feigning unanimity among groups of powerholders to make such social relations seem inevitable, by strategically concealing subversive or challenging discourses, by preventing access to the public stage, by policing language and using stigma and euphemism to set the terms of public debate or perception." In the aftermath of the Civil Rights Movement and Black Power Movement African Americans began to be marginalized, silenced, and policed in new "postmodern" ways that upheld the old, in many senses, pre-Civil Rights Movement antiblack racist and segregationist "public transcripts." As discussed in "remix" 4, the frustration, depression, and disillusionment of the dark days of the Black Power Movement ultimately gave way to the escapism, utopianism, and futurism of funk during the 1970s.

It was funk that consistently captured and conveyed the lives, loves, losses, and struggles of black America in the period immediately following the painful demise of the Black Power Movement (circa 1975 to 1980). As if purposely moving away from the traditional black popular movement model, the Hip Hop Movement initially took many of its cues from black popular music and black popular culture, which—beginning with the spirituals and the blues during and immediately after African American enslavement—historically had always contained "hidden transcripts" and coded critiques of white America's religion, culture, aesthetics, politics, and society. Rather than attempt to stubbornly re-create the Civil Rights Movement or Black Power Movement in the 1980s, the Hip Hop Movement began by drawing from both the frustration and futurism of funk, the hipness and sexiness of classic soul, the calculated callousness of classic black gangster films, and the skewed expressions of black pride swirling through blaxploitation films.

Taken together, each of these ingredients from 1960s and 1970s black popular music and black popular culture enabled early hip hoppers to develop their own distinct style of protest music and, ultimately, their own unique version of sociopolitical movement, which Rose, among others, argues constitute a series of "hidden transcripts" that have allowed hip hoppers' to engage in "symbolic and ideological warfare with institutions and groups that symbolically, ideologically, and materially oppress African Americans." In her own percipient words:

> Rap music is, in many ways, a hidden transcript. Among other things, it uses cloaked speech and disguised cultural codes to comment on and challenge aspects of current power inequalities. Not all rap transcripts directly critique all forms of domination; nonetheless, a large and significant element in rap's discursive territory is engaged in symbolic and ideological warfare with institutions and groups that symbolically, ideologically, and materially oppress African Americans. In this way, rap music is a contemporary stage for the theater of the powerless. On this stage, rappers act out inversions of status hierarchies, tell alternative stories of contact with police and the education process, and draw portraits of contact with dominant groups in which the hidden transcript inverts/subverts the public, dominant transcript. Often rendering a nagging critique of various manifestations of power via jokes, stories,

gestures, and song, rap's social commentary enacts ideological insubordination. (100–101)

Initiated by African American and other nonwhite working-class and working-poor youth, the Hip Hop Movement may not embody the "best" and "brightest" ideals contemporary African America has to offer, but, in its own off-kilter and unconventional way, it undeniably "inverts/subverts the public, dominant transcript." Flying in the face of the traditional African American leadership model that mostly looks to moderate, middle-aged, middle-class, and churchgoing African Americans to lead, the Hip Hop Movement's leaders historically have been and, for the most part, remain black ghetto youth. Instead of basing their movement solely on the politics and social visions of previous black popular movements, especially the Civil Rights Movement and Black Power Movement, hip hoppers' use a spellbinding combination of black political culture, black popular culture, and black popular music to upend "status hierarchies, tell alternative stories of contact with police and the education process, and draw portraits of contact with dominant groups in which the hidden transcript inverts/subverts the public, dominant transcript."

Rap music and hip hop culture have enabled black ghetto youth to create their own social, political, and cultural world that counters the daily violence, crime, poverty, and alienation that haunt them in the inner cities, slums, barrios, and ghettos. When we suspend the juxtapositions of the Hip Hop Movement with the Civil Rights Movement and Black Power Movement, then we can easily detect the ways in which it not only diverges from previous movements, but also converges and continues the politics and social justice agendas of previous movements. Indeed, several hip hop scholars have pointed out how rap music is a contemporary variant of "playing the dozens" and "signifying."[7] Others have observed rap's use of song, poetry, and spoken word to tell alternative, ghettocentric stories, "kick reality rhymes," and teach "life lessons," all of which can be traced back to continental African *griots*.[8]

The *griots* were essentially oral historians who, generation after generation, passed down the history, culture, and folklore of the community via song, storytelling, and poetry, all the while spicing their tales with parables, proverbs, and sometimes even prophecy. In *The New Beats: Exploring the Music, Culture, and Attitudes of Hip Hop* (1994), arguably one of the earliest works to make the connection between African griots and African American rappers, Stephen Fernando asserted, "[e]ndowed with this much prized oral skill, the griot enjoyed a very respected position within his community, just like many modern-day microphone personalities" (255). In a sense, most rappers are *urban griots*, using their rhymes to give voice to the often hidden hurts and daily horrors that shape black ghetto youths' lives. In this way, rap music and hip hop culture also build on the African American tradition of using poetry and song to "tell it like it is" and protest social injustices.

Whether we turn to the spirituals during African American enslavement or the blues during Reconstruction and post-Reconstruction, whether we turn to rhythm & blues and rock & roll during the Civil Rights Movement or soul and funk during the Black Power Movement, Amiri Baraka's axiom in *Blues People* (1963) about black popular music revealing special, bitter, and long-buried truths about both black *and* white America continues to ring true with rap and other forms of hip hop music. Furthermore, according to renowned musicologist Jon Michael Spencer in *Re-searching Black Music* (1996), beginning with the blues black popular music has consistently reflected African Americans' "hell on earth" and experience of American apartheid (xiv). Similar to the biblical tales of trials and tribulations poignantly captured in the spirituals, black popular music—from the blues and jazz through to soul, funk, and now rap and neo-soul—is essentially a diverse collection of songs that "reveal the nitty-gritty details of life as it is lived at the underside of society and the underbelly of history."

In essence continuing the black protest music tradition at the very moment that black protest movements seemed to be things of the past and many of the traditional moderate, middle-aged, middle-class, and churchgoing African American leaders appeared politically exhausted, rap music's often politically incorrect politics and social visions initially symbolized and indeed eventually summoned a post-Civil Rights Movement and post-Black Power Movement social and political movement, *the Hip Hop Movement*. Rather than reading the 1980s and the advent of rap music as the nadir of the black popular movement and black popular music traditions, at this point it is plausible to reinterpret the period ending the twentieth century and beginning the twenty-first century between 1980 and 2010 as an era in which both the black popular movement and black popular music traditions morphed and mutated into *a new black popular music and black popular culture-based black popular movement—the Hip Hop Movement*. When we move away from the mostly mainstream media-inspired overemphasis on commercial and gangsta rap music and videos and bear in mind the more than three dozen subgenres of rap and other forms of hip hop music identified throughout this volume (as well as *Hip Hop's Inheritance* and *Hip Hop's Amnesia*), then, and perhaps only then, can we conceive of rap music and hip hop culture as expressions of a wider Hip Hop Movement.

Whether or not hip hoppers' parents and grandparents are aware of it, a lot of rap and other forms of hip hop music have helped to politicize (and frequently radicalize) the Hip Hop Generation, and it is important for hip hoppers' elders to understand that, similar to the African griots, as Katina Stapleton contended in "From the Margins to Mainstream: The Political Power of Hip Hop" (1998), "what makes hip hop artists such successful purveyors of cultural and political information is that they relay messages of importance to youth in a form that they enjoy" and easily understand (220). As a matter of fact, being the most popular form of hip hop culture, rap music "has proven its ability to both capture the ear of those who listen to it for aesthetic reasons and those who look to the genre for deeper meaning. From its rough and tumble forms to the most commercial jams, hip hop has been able to raise awareness among African Americans and the general public about the issues that face black youth on a day-to-day basis." Thus, it would seem that most hip hoppers' parents and grandparents make little or no distinction between those hip hoppers who "listen to it for aesthetic reasons and those who look to the genre for deeper meaning."

When rap music and other elements of hip hop culture are explored for their "deeper meaning[s]," especially noncommercial forms of rap music and hip hop culture, then rap music and hip hop culture almost invariably re-emerge as: (1) arguably one of the most provocative forms of black protest music in African American music history; (2) a unique educational and informational arena where hip hoppers identify social, political, and cultural problems and offer solutions to those problems (à la critical theory of contemporary society); and (3) expressions of *a new black popular music and black popular culture-based black popular movement—the Hip Hop Movement.* Even though they may not have dubbed it the "Hip Hop Movement" the way I have here, over the years several hip hop scholars and critics have made veiled references to—for lack of a better word—a social, political, and cultural *movement* among post-Civil Rights Movement and post-Black Power Movement African American (among other multiracial and multicultural) youth. For example, Stapleton went so far as to say:

> Music has always been a major source of cultural identity within the African American community. Rap music is no exception. As part of the larger hip hop culture, rap music has served to form a cohesive bond among urban youth. Through the mass distribution of hip hop records and videos, hip hop has also been able to at least partially erase lines between young people of different socio-economic backgrounds and vastly different geographic locations. Equally important, hip hop culture has established itself as a powerful informational tool and means of resistance. It is not an overstatement to say that despite its faults, hip hop has provided America with one of its only hard-hitting indictments of the social conditions that continue to be a harsh reality for African American young people. Hip hop has shown itself to be both the site of political controversy and a means of more than one type of political action. (231–32)

In light of the unique relationship between black popular movements and black popular music it seems fairly safe to say that confrontational, deliberative, and pragmatic political theory and praxis can and, indeed, has materialized whenever and wherever black popular music is produced and consumed. As a consequence, black popular movements and black popular music should not be conceived of in strict sociological or musicological terms, or as being separate from or mutually exclusive of each other. Rather, they are and historically have been intensely intertwined, constantly overlapping and intersecting, inspiring and influencing one another—with black popular movements frequently displaying a deep musical dimension, and black popular music often displaying a deep political dimension. In fact, if *Hip Hop's Inheritance*, *Hip Hop's Amnesia*, and the present volume have illustrated anything it is the simple fact that the remarkable relationship between black popular movements and black popular music has historically and currently continues to be arguably one of the most distinctive features of African American politics and social movements. When we turn to the Hip Hop Movement it could be said that the foregoing connection is especially true.

THE HIP HOP MOVEMENT: A SOCIAL, POLITICAL, AND CULTURAL MOVEMENT

While it is undeniably one of the major sources of political education and political action within the world of hip hop, rap music should not be considered the only source of political education and political action within the Hip Hop Movement. The Hip Hop Movement has regularly turned to poetry, spoken word, neo-soul and other forms of hip hop music, alternative radio, alternative television, documentaries, radical journalism, cultural criticism, scholarly books, novels, plays, social media, cyber-politics, grassroots political organizing, and the church in its quest to reveal and resist African America's—especially black ghetto youths'—ongoing racial oppression, cultural colonization, and economic exploitation, among other ills, during the post-Civil Rights Movement and post-Black Power Movement period between 1980 and the present. Although not following all the "rules and regulations" for many of the more highbrow and hard-nosed academic critics to acknowledge it as a new social movement, it is important for us not to allow our disdain for commercial and gangsta rap to blind us to one of the most significant social movements since the Civil Rights Movement that has, as Stapleton contended above, consistently "provided America with one of its only hard-hitting indictments of the social conditions that continue to be a harsh reality for African American young people" in the post-Civil Rights Movement period. Corroborating Stapleton and my assertion that rap music and hip hop culture are actually expressions of one of the most important social, political, and cultural movements since the Civil Rights Movement and Black Power Movement, in his watershed work *Representing: Hip Hop Culture and the Production of Black Cinema* (1998), S. Craig Watkins stated:

In many ways, hip hop represents a particular species of social movement. The movement is made possible by new social and economic arrangements, technological innovations, and the global dissemination of U.S. popular media cultures. Sociologists broadly define social movements as collective efforts to produce social change. Any attempt to discuss hip hop as a movement demands careful delineation because it is variously preoccupied with style, performance, opposition, leisure, consumption, representation, and entrepreneurship. First, this particular movement takes place on the field of popular culture, a site not immediately discerned as political, or capable of producing social change. Second, hip hop is invigorated by the creative labor of a constituency not ordinarily regarded as interested in effecting social change: youth. Third, like social movements in general, hip hop enables its participants to imagine themselves as part of a larger community; thus, it produces a sense of collective identity and agency. To be sure, this particular movement constitutes a distinct mode of intervention in the social world. (65)

Despite what most contemporary musicologists, sociologists, and political scientists seem to believe, then, there are a growing number of scholars, critics, social organizers, and political activists who have long understood rap music and hip hop culture to be a part of post-Civil Rights Movement and post-Black Power Movement youths' "collective efforts to produce social change." In *Social Movements, 1768–2004* (2004), noted political sociologist Charles Tilly essentially argued that social movements are most often made up of ordinary people, rather than members of the politically powerful and elite, and it is these "ordinary people," these "organic intellectuals"—à la Antonio Gramsci's provocative work in his *Prison Notebooks*—who collectively think, act, and speak in the best interest of, and in concert with everyday average people—the so-called "masses." Gramsci (1971, 9) famously contended that "[a]ll men are intellectuals," but "not all men have in society the function of intellectuals." It is extremely important to emphasize this point because neither black youth nor the ghettos they have been callously quarantined to have been recognized for their intellectual activities and positive cultural contributions.

Although "one can speak of intellectuals," Gramsci declared, "one cannot speak of non-intellectuals, because non-intellectuals do not exist." In point of fact, "[t]here is no human activity from which every form of intellectual participation can be excluded: *homo faber* cannot be separated from *homo sapiens*," which is to say, the "primitive man" (*homo faber*) cannot be completely divorced from the evolution of the much-vaunted "wise man" (*homo sapiens*). Intellectuals do not simply inhabit college campuses and highbrow cafés, then; they can also be found in each and every community in this country, including the slums, ghettos, and barrios. Right along with "philosophers" and "men of taste," Gramsci included artists in his conception of "organic intellectuals," contending: "Each man, finally, outside his professional activity, carries on some form of intellectual activity, that is, he is a 'philosopher,' an artist, a man of taste, he participates in a particular conception of the world, has a conscious line of moral conduct, and therefore contributes to sustain a conception of the world or to modify it, that is, to bring into being new modes of thought" (9; see also 3–43).[9]

It is not only rappers, but hip hoppers in general, whether they consider themselves philosophers, artists, sophisticates, or gangsters, who participate in a distinct "conception of the world," have a "conscious line of moral [and frequently immoral] conduct," and who, consequently, contribute "to sustain a conception of the world or to modify it, that is, to bring into being new modes of thought." Many of the "new modes of thought" and political practices that the Hip Hop Movement has brought into being do not stem from one central issue (e.g., class struggles and other material interests) à la the "old" social movement model, but often arise from myriad social, political, and cultural issues. This conception of social movements is in clear contrast to those who embrace what could be termed the "old" conception of social movements, which holds that social movements and social protest are almost exclusively motivated by class interests and carried out by members who share the same class status. Generally the goals of "old" social movements revolve around institutional changes that yield political and economic redistribution along class lines.[10]

The "new" social movement model offers several correctives for the limitations of the "old," essentially Eurocentric social movement model which, from critical race, womanist, feminist, postcolonialist, pacifist, and queer theorists and activists' points of view, did not adequately engage social issues and injustices stemming from racism, sexism, heterosexism, war, and religious intolerance, among other issues. According to Rhys Williams in "The Cultural Contexts of Collective Action: Constraints, Opportunities, and the Symbolic Life of Social Movements" (2004):

> As a whole, new social movements scholarship emerged as a response to and interpretation of contemporary European social movements, such as the Greens, that were focused on cultural, moral, and identity issues, rather than on economic distribution. Much post-war European sociology was more influenced by Marxist theory than was its American counterpart; as such, it had often assumed that collective action came out of material interests and that collective actors were economic classes. "The social movement," for many European scholars, was the labor-socialist movement. By contrast, NSMs [i.e., new social movements] were often thought to be more like "moral crusades," and as such appeared as a new phenomenon that needed to be theorized distinctly for the historical moment in which they occurred. Thus the cultural component of new social movement theory had to do with the *content* of movement ideology, the *concerns motivating activists*, and the *arena* in which collective action was focused—that is, cultural understandings, norms, and identities rather than material interests and economic distribution. New social movement theory was generally macro in orientation, and retained the tradi-

tional Marxian concern with articulating the ways in which societal infrastruc-
tures produced and are reflected by culture and action. New social movement
theory garnered attention, support, and critique from scholars. Many North
American critics, not surprisingly, questioned whether the social movements
themselves, or the social conditions that helped to produce them, were in fact
"new." (92, all emphasis in original)

It is important to emphasize that new social movements usually focus on
"cultural understandings, norms, and identities" rather than solely on class
struggles or material interests à la "old" social movements. Additionally,
Williams's emphasis on the cultural aspects of new social movement theory,
which revolve around the "*content* of movement ideology, the *concerns mo-
tivating activists*, and the *arena* in which collective action [is] focused,"
seems to directly speak to the Hip Hop Movement's qualifications as a new
social movement. The Hip Hop Movement distinguishes itself from other
African American (if not other American) popular movements in light of its
unique use of black popular music, black popular culture, social media, cyber-politics, grassroots political organizing, and more traditional forms of
social activism in its efforts to establish and express its post-Civil Rights
Movement and post-Black Power Movement "movement ideology," encap-
sulate the "concerns" of its organic intellectual activists, and engage the new
social, political, and cultural "arena" at the turn of the twenty-first century.

Drawing from a wide range of new social movement scholarship, the
defining characteristics of new social movements can be essentially summar-
ized as: (1) identity, autonomy, and self-realization; (2) defense rather than
offense; (3) politicization of everyday life; (4) working-class *and* underclass
(as opposed to merely middle-class) mobilization; (5) self-exemplification
(organizational forms and styles that reproduce and circulate the ideology of
the movement); (6) unconventional means (as opposed to conventional
means such as voting); and (7) partial and overlapping commitments (a web
of intermeshing memberships rather than traditional party loyalty).[11] In many
ways what I am wont to call the "Hip Hop Movement" resembles a "new"
social movement much more than it does an "old" social movement, and this,
almost in and of itself, may go far to explain why so many "old school"
musicologists, sociologists, political scientists, and cultural critics have
failed to acknowledge the movement going on right before their eyes (and
ears) between 1980 and the present.

Here it is important to observe that both the new social movement scholars and hip hop scholars emphasize *collective identity and agency* as being
central to their respective fields' critical inquiry, with Watkins going so far as
to say, "like social movements in general, hip hop enables its participants to
imagine themselves as part of a larger community; thus, it produces a sense
of collective identity and agency." Obviously the Hip Hop Movement's "po-

liticization of everyday life," its "unconventional means" of using black popular music and black popular culture to educate, decolonize and politicize, its
"partial and overlapping commitments" to the strategies, tactics, and goals of
both "old" *and* "new" popular movements, its "working-class *and* underclass
(as opposed to merely middle-class) mobilization," and, perhaps most importantly, its "self-exemplification" and emphasis on "self-realization" all speak
volumes about its clear qualifications as a "new" social, political, and cultural movement and also the ways in which it brazenly promotes a unique post-
Civil Rights Movement and post-Black Power Movement collective identity
and form of agency.

Collective identity, as Francesca Polletta and James Jasper asserted in
"Collective Identity and Social Movements" (2001), is "an individual's cognitive, moral, and emotional connection with a broader community, category,
practice, or institution. It is a perception of a shared status or relation, which
may be imagined rather than experienced directly, and it is distinct from
personal identities, although it may form part of a personal identity" (285).
Collective identities, they continued, "are expressed in cultural materials—
names, narratives, symbols, verbal styles, rituals, clothing, and so on—but
not all cultural materials express collective identities. Collective identity
does not imply the rational calculus for evaluating choices that 'interest'
does. And unlike ideology, collective identity carries with it positive feelings
for other members of the group" (285).

Indeed, it is possible to have an individual identity that is not directly tied
to that of the broader collective and, as a result, one may argue that simply
defining oneself does not in and of itself constitute a politically significant
act or serve as adequate evidence of a social movement. Watkins's warning
above that "[a]ny attempt to discuss hip hop as a movement demands careful
delineation because it is variously preoccupied with style, performance, opposition, leisure, consumption, representation, and entrepreneurship" should
be taken to heart here. However, as Scott Hunt and Robert Benford in "Collective Identity, Solidarity, and Commitment" (1994) asserted, "[b]y virtue
of constructing and elaborating a sense of who they are, movement participants and adherents also construct a sense of who they are not" (443). Needless to say, this process of differentiation is an extremely important one, and
obviously registers as a politically significant act when we recall the unconventional politics, counterculture, and defensive posture of, as well as the
emphasis on both self-realization and self-exemplification in, new social
movements discourse discussed above.

In *Social Movements: A Cognitive Approach* (1991), Ron Eyerman and
Andrew Jamison famously conceived of social movements as "forms of cognitive praxis which are shaped by both external and internal political processes" (4; see also 45–65). They went on to elaborate:

Social movements express shifts in the consciousness of actors as they are articulated in the interactions between activists and their opposition(s) in historically situated political and cultural contexts. The content of this consciousness, what we call the cognitive praxis of a movement, is thus socially conditioned: it depends upon the conceptualization of a problem which is bound by the concerns of historically situated actors and on the reactions of their opponents. In other words, social movements are the result of an interactional process which centers around the articulation of a collective identity and which occurs within the boundaries of a particular society. Our approach thus focuses upon the process of articulating a movement identity (cognitive praxis), on the actors taking part in this process (movement intellectuals), and on the contexts of articulation (political cultures and institutions). (4)

Throughout this study my focus has been on the process through which hip hopper's have articulated a post-Civil Rights Movement and post-Black Power Movement *Hip Hop Movement identity*, on the principle actors or *Hip Hop Movement organic intellectual-activists*—primarily rappers, but also other hip hop heavyweights—who have contributed to the evolution of the Hip Hop Movement, and on the social, political, and cultural contexts that have influenced the Hip Hop Movement and its preferred medium of political articulation and cultural expression: rap music. No matter how one may view rap music it is difficult to deny the way that it has helped the Hip Hop Movement "express shifts in the consciousness of [post-Civil Rights Movement and post-Black Power Movement] actors" and in myriad ways symbolized the "cognitive praxis" of the Hip Hop Movement. As a matter of fact, as Eyerman and Jamison continued their groundbreaking research on social movements they made a remarkable discovery concerning the relationship between music and social movements.

Similar to Stapleton and Watkins above, Eyerman and Jamison linked collective identity and agency to the interconnections between popular music and popular movements in their sequel to *Social Movements*, the acclaimed *Music and Social Movements: Mobilizing Traditions in the Twentieth Century* (1998). In *Music and Social Movements* Eyerman and Jamison (1998, 23) argued that music is essentially a cognitive phenomenon with enormous potential to influence the politics and culture of social movements in light of its "knowledge-bearing" and "identity-giving qualities" (see also 48–73). Which means, then, that hip hoppers' emphasis on the ways in which rap music and other aspects of hip hop culture have enlightened them, politicized them, socialized them, and provided them with a deeper understanding of themselves, their communities and respective societies, as well as the wider world, is not out of the ordinary or merely juvenile gibberish.

Discursively developing their conception of "exemplary action," Eyerman and Jamison contended that it can be conceived of as a "specification of the symbolic action" and the "cognitive praxis of social movements." Moreover, the "exemplary action of cognitive praxis is symbolic in several senses," but it is also, they strongly stressed, "'more' than merely symbolic. As real cultural representations—art, literature, songs—it is artifactual and material, as well." Which is to say, the music and other artistic expressions of popular sociopolitical movements are more than merely ideational and traditional art. Indeed, they are art in every sense of the word "art," but they are also "knowledge-bearing" and "identity-giving" social, political, cultural, intellectual, and spiritual expressions that are simultaneously symbolic *and* factual, if not often literal representations and articulations of the life-worlds and life-struggles of popular movement participants and adherents. Eyerman and Jamison went further to explain:

> What we are attempting to capture with the term [i.e., exemplary action] is the exemplary use of music and art in social movements, the various ways in which songs and singers can serve a function akin to the exemplary works that Thomas Kuhn [in *The Structure of Scientific Revolutions* (1970)] characterized as being central to scientific revolutions: the paradigm-constituting entities that serve to realign scientific thinking and that represent ideal examples of fundamentally innovative scientific work. The difference between culture and science, however, is that the exemplary action of music and art is lived as well as thought: it is cognitive, but it also draws on more emotive aspects of human consciousness. As cultural expression, exemplary action is self-revealing and thus a symbolic representation of the individual and the collective which are the movement. It is symbolic in that it symbolizes all the movement stands for, what is seen as virtuous and what is seen as evil. In the age of symbols, an age of electronic media and the transmission of virtual images, the exemplary action of a movement can serve an educative function for many more than the participants and their immediate public. This exemplary action can also be recorded, in film, word, and music. (23)

Again, Eyerman and Jamison help to highlight that hip hoppers are not alone in viewing their beloved music and art—which is to say, rap music and other aspects of hip hop culture—as having more than merely aesthetic implications. As we witnessed in each of the previous "remixes," music and other art created in the context of or inspired by social movements, political struggles, and cultural crises most often take on multiple meanings—some aesthetic and cultural meanings, and other more social and political meanings. Rap and other hip hop culture-inspired art forms are not exceptions to these rules. Moreover, when Eyerman and Jamison contended above that "songs and singers can serve a function akin to the exemplary works that Thomas Kuhn characterized as being central to scientific revolutions: the paradigm-constituting entities that serve to realign scientific thinking and that represent ideal examples of fundamentally innovative scientific work," it is possible for us to transpose Kuhn's conception of scientific revolutions and apply it to rap music, hip hop culture, and countercultural revolutions.

Where Kuhn conceived of scientific "paradigm-constituting entities" and "scientific revolutions," it is possible for us to conceive of *black popular music and black popular culture-constituting entities* and *countercultural revolutions* that historically have and currently continue to "serve to realign [social, political, and cultural] thinking and that represent ideal examples of fundamentally innovative [social, political, and cultural] work"—à la George Lipsitz's collective contentions in his volumes *Time Passages: Collective Memory and American Popular Culture* (1990b), *Dangerous Crossroads: Popular Music, Postmodernism, and the Poetics of Place* (1994), *The Possessive Investment in Whiteness: How White People Profit from Identity Politics* (1998), *American Studies in a Moment of Danger* (2001), *Footsteps in the Dark: The Hidden Histories of Popular Culture* (2007), and *How Racism Takes Place* (2011). In applying Kuhn's conception of scientific revolutions to the relationship between black popular music and black popular movements in general, and rap music and the Hip Hop Movement in specific, it is relatively easy to see how black popular "songs and singers can serve a function akin to the exemplary works that Thomas Kuhn characterized as being central to scientific revolutions." However, within the context of black popular music and black popular movements the focus logically shifts from natural science to the human, cultural, and social sciences, from scientific revolutions to social, political, and cultural revolutions. In this sense it would be difficult for anyone knowledgeable of the history of black popular music to deny the ways in which its unique dialogical and pedagogical relationship with black popular movements has consistently helped to "realign" and reinvigorate social, political, and cultural thinking and "represent ideal examples of fundamentally innovative" social, political, and cultural work either inspired by or emerging from black popular movements.

Hence, when rap music and hip hop culture are viewed as part of the "symbolic action" and "cognitive praxis" of the Hip Hop Movement a qualitatively different and more constructive conversation emerges. As both cultural expressions and "exemplary actions" of the Hip Hop Movement, rap and other genres of hip hop music are simultaneously "knowledge-bearing," "identity-giving," and "self-revealing" and, as a result, they constitute "symbolic representation[s]" of hip hop individuals and the hip hop collective which, taken together, expose us to many of the core concerns, political views, and social visions of the Hip Hop Movement. Furthermore, the representational nature of rap and other forms of hip hop music in many senses "symbolizes all the movement stands for, what is seen as virtuous and what is seen as evil"—from the comedy rap of the Fat Boys and the party rap of the Beastie Boys to the more recent Dirty South rap of Lil' Wayne and gangsta rap of Rick Ross.

As Eyerman and Jamison (1998, 23–24) observed, "art and music—culture—are forms of both knowledge and action," they are "part of the frameworks of interpretation and representation produced within social movements and through which they influence the broader societal culture. As such, they are much more than functional devices for recruitment or resources to be mobilized." In other words, even though it often appears that rap music and hip hop culture do not have a political agenda or viable social vision in the traditional social movement sense, because the Hip Hop Movement is actually *a black popular music and black popular culture-based social and political movement* the bulk of its cultural concerns, political views, and social visions are in its cultural expressions and "exemplary actions," including its music, dance, literature, art, theater, film, fashion, and forays into more mainstream cultural conversations, social movements, and political struggles.[12]

However, even as we acknowledge the ways in which hip hop "art and music—[hip hop] culture—are forms of both knowledge and action" and "part of the frameworks of interpretation and representation produced within [the Hip Hop Movement] and through which [it] influence[s] the broader societal culture," it is important for us not to overlook the myriad instrumental uses of black popular music in both "old" and "new" African American social and political movements. Tempering their discussion of the extramusical functions of music within the context of social movements, Eyerman and Jamison maintained, "[i]t is not our intention to deny that there are instrumental uses of music in social movements and elsewhere, but, to the extent that social movements are able to transcend these instrumental (and commercial) usages, music as exemplary action becomes possible" (24). When we make critical distinctions between commercial and gangsta rap and the myriad other forms of rap—especially conscious, political, message, alternative, and underground rap—then the ways that rap "transcend[s] . . . instrumental (and commercial) usages" and simultaneously serves instrumental, intellectual, spiritual, cultural, social, and political functions is even more evident.

Many aspects of hip hop culture—not merely rap and other forms of hip hop music—reflect the political views and social visions of the Hip Hop Movement. But, along with Eyerman and Jamison, I believe that music is an especially powerful political and pedagogical tool in relationship to modern social movements in light of the fact that, as Watkins noted above, it is essentially inextricable from and at the heart of hip hop "style, performance, opposition, leisure, consumption, representation, and entrepreneurship." Continuing this line of logic, Eyerman and Jamison stated:

> As cognitive praxis, music and other forms of cultural activity contribute to the ideas that movements offer and create in opposition to the existing social and cultural order. Perhaps more effectively than any other form of expression, music also recalls a meaning that lies outside and beyond the self. In that sense it can be utopian or pre-modern. In saying this we do not mean to imply that

such truth-bearing is inherent in music, part of some transcendent and meta-
physical fundament. Our argument is more modest in that we restrict our claim
to music in relation to social movements. In social movements, even mass-
produced popular music can take on a truth-bearing significance. (24)

As we witnessed with rhythm & blues and rock & roll during the Civil Rights
Movement and soul and funk during the Black Power Movement, as a "cognitive praxis" emerging from within the context of the Hip Hop Movement
the myriad genres of rap music have consistently conveyed the collective
"ideas that [the Hip Hop Movement has] offer[ed] and create[d] in opposition
to the existing social and cultural order" which continues to ideologically
enslave, racially colonize, and economically exploit African America at the
turn of the twenty-first century. If nothing else, then, this study has demonstrated how "even mass-produced [and mass-consumed] [black] popular music can take on a truth-bearing significance" and serve instrumental, intellectual, spiritual, cultural, social, and political functions within the context of
black popular movements. Moreover, this study has also taken great pains to
point out the ways past black popular movements' relationships with past
black popular musics have been handed down to the Hip Hop Movement and
essentially recreated in its relationship with rap and other forms of hip hop
music.

   African American movements historically have been and unrepentantly
remain much more complicated and complex than most historians, sociologists, and political scientists of social movements have been willing to concede. All of this is to say that here when I write of the "Hip Hop Movement,"
I am invoking a momentous movement that is much like the mid-twentieth-
century African American movements which, whether acknowledged or not,
have provided the Hip Hop Generation with not merely its aesthetics, musical or otherwise, but with the firm foundations upon which it has built its
pioneering post-Civil Rights Movement and post-Black Power Movement
history, culture, politics, and social justice agendas. Moreover, here by sum-
moning the "Hip Hop Movement" I wish to move the conversation concerning hip hop culture forward, above and beyond critiques—constructive or
otherwise—about rap music's bourgeoisism, sexism, and heterosexism, and
turn our attention anew toward the ways in which one-dimensional discussions that crudely collapse the whole of hip hop culture into rap music, or
vice versa, erase or, at the very least, render invisible not only hip hop's other
major artistic areas (e.g., visual art, dance, theater, film, fashion, literature,
etc.), but also its distinct politics and social justice agendas.

THE HIP HOP MOVEMENT: A MULTICULTURAL, MULTIRACIAL, MULTINATIONAL, MULTILINGUAL, AND MULTIRELIGIOUS MULTI-ISSUE MOVEMENT

In one the first scholarly books on rap music, *Black Noise: Rap Music and Black Culture in Contemporary America* (1994), Tricia Rose asserted that rap music "brings together a tangle of some of the most complex social, cultural, and political issues in contemporary American society" (2). As was discussed in the previous "remixes," something very similar could be said about classic rhythm & blues, rock & roll, soul, and funk. African American music, even in its earliest manifestations (e.g., the spirituals and the blues), registers the complexities and contradictions of African American life and struggles in ways that few other art forms have been able to, or conceivably can. Much has been made of the contradictions of hip hop culture, especially rap music, which, on the one hand, has been undeniably used to raise the Hip Hop Generation's historical, cultural, social, and political consciousness, but, on the other hand, has been also used to big-up bourgeoisism, celebrate sexism, and hail heterosexism.

However, as Rose emphasized, "[r]ap's contradictory articulations are not signs of absent intellectual clarity" or political naïveté on the part of hip hoppers. Rather, truth be told, "they are a common feature of community and popular cultural dialogues that always offer more than one cultural, social, or political viewpoint. These unusually abundant polyvocal conversations seem irrational when they are severed from the social contexts where everyday struggles over resources, pleasure, and meanings take place" (2).

Special mention should be made of Rose's contention that rap's contradictions are actually "a common feature of community and popular cultural dialogues that always offer more than one cultural, social, or political viewpoint." This means that *there is no single and central point of view that each and every African American adheres to or operates from*, and hip hoppers must be granted artistic license just as the most controversial artists historically have been. Think about the state of aesthetic realism and fantasy if, say, Shakespeare's raunchier plays (e.g., *Much Ado About Nothing*, *A Midsummer Night's Dream*, or *The Taming of the Shrew*) had been censored as opposed to celebrated, or Picasso's *Guernica* had been banned because it controversially depicted the fascist bombing of a small Basque town in April of 1937, or Leon Golub's *Interrogation III* had been disallowed in the early 1980s because it depicted two ominous-looking male tormentors dressed in military clothes standing beside a hooded nude woman strapped to a chair with her legs cocked open so as to reveal her genitals.

Let's be real here: a lot of rap is okay, more of it is good, but very little of it is genuinely great or will one day be considered "classic" music. However, the same could be truthful said about any genre of music, especially any genre of black popular music. We must bear in mind here that all forms of African American music (including the spirituals) have been assailed from both within and without—that is to say, attacked from both inside and outside of African America at one time or another. [13]

If nothing else, "remixes" 1 through 4 illustrated that classic rhythm & blues, rock & roll, soul, and funk were all at one time or another perceived as indecent, immoral, and irreligious influences on U.S. youth, especially black ghetto and white suburban youth. In other words, black popular music and black popular culture have long been considered corrupting forces, furiously fueling the wildfires and untamed youthful passions of America's "impressionable" and "troubled" youth. Therefore, it is important for hip hoppers' parents and grandparents to steer clear of *African American musical nostalgia*, which is to say, *the now common custom of claiming that earlier forms of black popular music were somehow free from controversy and contradiction.* To put it plainly, *African American musical nostalgia* entails waxing poetic and nostalgic about a time when African American music allegedly offered a "purer" aesthetic and a "higher" moral vision—it is, quite simply, to yearn for a time in African American history and culture, musical or otherwise, that has never really existed.

To break this down even further, I am saying as simply and sincerely as I possibly can that all forms of black popular music seem to have an innovative aesthetic appeal and insightful moral visions that, initially and with ironic regularity, are either overlooked or assailed from both within and without African America. But, it must be observed, the same music that is criticized and demonized in its infancy is usually eventually seen as a serious aural innovation and cultural contribution. Hence, when the formerly disliked and demonized genre falls from the lofty heights of musical popularity among black youth ultimately it too is bemoaned, if not mourned, and in time juxtaposed and privileged over the following newfangled, supposedly "degenerate" and demonized form of black popular music.

Just as African American political thought and social movements seem to come and go in cycles, so too does black popular music seem to come and go in cycles, albeit *sonic cycles*. This is, in part, I honestly believe, because African American music and African American movements are much more inextricable and intensely intertwined than most African American music critics and African American movement scholars have fully fathomed. [14] What is truly distinctive about the Hip Hop Movement, especially when compared and contrasted with previous African American movements, is the widespread consciousness of the centrality and passionate belief in the singularity of its newfangled music in relationship to its overarching social, political, and cultural movement. [15]

Where many of the more conservative members of the Civil Rights Movement railed against the new expressions of black sexuality in rhythm &

blues and rock & roll, and where many of the more militant members of the Black Power Movement perceived certain aspects of soul and funk to be nothing more than corporate America's continued commercialization and commodification of black popular music, most members of the Hip Hop Movement openly embrace some form of rap music, whether old school rap, party rap, pop rap, political rap, jazz rap, gangsta rap, conscious rap, alternative rap, rock rap, reggae rap, Latin rap, Reggaeton, Christian rap, Dirty South rap, Midwest rap, West Coast rap, underground rap, or hard-core rap. When the various forms of mid-twentieth-century black popular music are carefully placed within the context of the major African American movements of their specific moment of musical popularity we are able to calmly conclude that the classic rhythm & blues and rock & roll women were the equivalent of contemporary female rappers, neo-soul divas, b-girls and, yes, video vixens.[16] Classic rhythm & blues and rock & roll men equate to contemporary rappers, neo-soul Romeos, b-boys and, yes, hip hop "hoodlums."[17]

Likewise, classic rhythm & blues and rock & roll, with their raunchy-to-respectable meteoric rise, initially occupied a place very similar to contemporary rap music in mid-twentieth-century America's social imagination. For instance, it will be recalled that in "remix" 2 the Right Reverend John Carroll exclaimed, "[r]ock & roll inflames and excites youth like jungle tom-toms." Moreover, as Jack Lait and Lee Mortimer maintained in *U.S.A. Confidential* (1952), classic rhythm & blues and its whitened and lightened offshoot rock & roll were both overburdened "with tom-toms and hot jive and ritualistic orgies of erotic dancing, weed-smoking and mass mania, [replete] with African jungle background" (37). All of this is to say that almost all of the mid-twentieth-century black popular music that is now raised up and highly revered as undeniably noble expressions of African American—if not mainstream American—culture were, in their own unique ways during their heydays, once understood to be notorious—and, let it be said openly and honestly, notorious "nigger noise," as U.S. historical and cultural records reveal.[18]

As with the musics and movements discussed in the previous "remixes," rap music and hip hop culture as a whole undeniably harbor many controversies and contradictions. However, instead of placing hip hop outside of the African American movement orbit, these "controversies and contradictions," conversely, place it squarely within the African American movement tradition. As Rose remarked, the "unusually abundant polyvocal conversations" that historically have been and remain at the heart of African American movements "seem irrational when they are severed from the [distinct] social," political, historical, and cultural contexts that gave rise to them and fueled their forward motion. As the major soundtrack for the contemporary African American movement, the Hip Hop Movement, rap music registers African Americans' ambitions in and frustrations with post-Civil Rights

Movement, post-Black Power Movement, post-Women's Liberation Movement, postfeminist, and, indeed, postmodern America.[19]

A lot of rap music—especially what is variously called "conscious" rap,
"political" rap, or "message" rap—critiques ongoing antiblack racism and
questions the social, political, and economic gains of the Civil Rights Movement and Black Power Movement. In this sense, although often overlooked,
rap also voices hip hoppers' intraracial critiques of both Civil Rights Movement moderates and Black Power Movement militants. Instead of the pros-
perity and remixed democracy they believed they were promised by Civil
Rights moderates and Black Power militants many hip hoppers experienced
firsthand new, virtually unprecedented forms of callousness and poverty as
they came of age in the last quarter of the twentieth century.[20] Directly
commenting on the generational and "intraracial class division" between the
Civil Rights moderates, Black Power militants, and hip hoppers, in *Reflecting Black: African American Cultural Criticism* (1993), Michael Eric Dyson
declared:

> In this regard, rap music is emblematic of the glacial shift in aesthetic sensibil-
> ities between blacks of different generations, and it draws attention to the
> severe economic barriers that increasingly divide ghetto poor blacks from
> middle- and upper-middle-class blacks. Rap reflects the intra-racial class divi-
> sion that has plagued African American communities for the last thirty years.
> The increasing social isolation, economic hardship, political demoralization,
> and cultural exploitation endured by most ghetto poor communities in the past
> few decades have given rise to a form of musical expression that captures the
> terms of ghetto poor existence. I am not suggesting that rap has been limited to
> the ghetto poor, but only that its major themes and styles continue to be drawn
> from the conflicts and contradictions of black urban life. (7)

Whether we like it or not, taken as a whole rap music represents the aspirations and idiosyncrasies of the Hip Hop Generation, as well as the ambitions
and eccentricities of the wider world of African America between 1980 and
the present. This is a point that should not be glossed over to please the
"siddity" whims and wishes of the contemporary black bourgeoisie, who
have long been embarrassed and enraged by rap music (especially gangsta
rap and hard-core hip hop), if not the whole of the Hip Hop Generation. But,
as emphasized above, hip hop culture should not be roguishly reduced to rap
music, and especially not gangsta rap and hard-core hip hop. Without in any
way disavowing or diminishing the sonic or social significance of gangsta
rap and hard-core hip hop it is important to unequivocally state that these
forms of rap music and hip hop culture, with their unambiguous embrace of
the ghetto-gangsta-nigga-pimp-hoe-thug theme and junior high school-like
smutty and slutty sadomasochistic fantasies, seem to have eclipsed all other

elements of hip hop culture, especially hip hop's politics and more progressive poetics.

The Hip Hop Generation is not the first generation of young black folk to be raised up and called out as especially egregious examples of what is outright wrong with African America, if not America in general. In "remixes" 1 and 2, we witnessed the controversies surrounding classic rhythm & blues and rock & roll during the Civil Rights Movement. In "remixes" 3 and 4, we observed the contentious relationship most Americans, including many African Americans, had with the expressions of black pride and black self-determination in soul and funk during the Black Power Movement. In each instance cited here it was—to employ Dyson's words from the passage above—the rise of a "form of musical expression that capture[d] the terms of ghetto poor existence" that caused controversy.

Furthermore, it was—as allegedly with the soulsters and funksters—the supposed celebration of "ghetto poor existence" that was frowned on by the black and white upper and middle classes. Even though the black and white upper and middle classes historically have only seemed willing to help the ghetto poor when it has been convenient for them (i.e., the black and white upper and middle classes), which is very rarely, notice how they have had a great deal of disdain toward the ghetto poor when they, the poor and poverty-stricken, have creatively expressed their lives and loves, their ambitions and frustrations, their trials and tribulations on their own terms. We have here, then, another one of the major issues the Hip Hop Movement (again, as opposed to merely the Hip Hop Generation) seeks to address: the ghetto, and the poor and poverty-stricken, working class and underclass who, often humbly and enduring many hardships, dwell therein.

The Hip Hop Movement's politics should not be expected to mindlessly mirror the Civil Rights Movement or the Black Power Movement's politics. At first issue is the simple fact that such a position is nostalgic in the worst way, yearning for an era that currently only exists in history books. The Hip Hop Movement must be allowed to emerge in its own time and on its own terms. However, as was witnessed with the emergence of rhythm & blues during the Civil Right Movement years and funk during the Black Power Movement years, the impulse on the part of nostalgic African American elders and black bourgeois conservatives to control and quarantine African American youth militancy is not new and, in truth, as I discussed in detail in *Hip Hop's Amnesia*, has been a repetitive part of African American history, culture, and struggle reaching all the way back to the Black Women's Club Movement and the New Negro Movement. In fact, what is strikingly new and novel about the Hip Hop Movement when compared with the Civil Rights Movement and the Black Power Movement is that it registers as both an African American movement *and* an unprecedented *multicultural, multi-*

racial, multinational, multilingual, and multireligious multi-issue move-ment.[21]

The Hip Hop Movement is obviously an African American movement insofar as its primary points of departure are previous African American movements and many of its goals are identical to those of previous African American movements. As argued throughout this study, whether consciously or unconsciously, the Hip Hop Movement has indeed inherited a great deal from the major mid-twentieth-century African American movements: from rhythm & blues, rock & roll, and the Civil Rights Movement to soul, funk, and the Black Power Movement. The Hip Hop Movement's roots in the Civil Rights Movement and Black Power Movement, consequently, should be more readily acknowledged. However, even when and where its emergence in the aftermath of the Civil Rights Movement and Black Power Movement is acknowledged, few have taken the time to do more than merely mention or make passing references to these historic connections.

What is needed now, especially in light of the hyper-commercialization of rap music and hip hop culture, are more nuanced archaeologies and alternative histories of hip hop's origins and evolution. Where *Hip Hop's Inheritance* offered an alternative history of hip hop by focusing on the cultural aesthetic movements that provided it with its artistic foundation, *Hip Hop's Amnesia* engaged early-twentieth-century African American social and political movements, as well as their respective soundtracks, which provided the Hip Hop Movement with its musical, cultural, and political foundations. *The Hip Hop Movement* has examined the Hip Hop Generation's "inheritance" from, and "amnesia" with regard to classic rhythm & blues, rock & roll and the Civil Rights Movement, and classic soul, funk and the Black Power Movement. In other words, *The Hip Hop Movement* has explored what rap music and hip hop culture have inherited from the major African American musics and movements of the second half of the twentieth century, essentially covering the major black popular movements and major black popular musics between 1945 and 1980. From 1980 through to the present black popular music and black popular culture have achieved a high level of visibility and, in several senses, respectability that ushered in an entirely new ethos in both contemporary popular culture *and* contemporary political culture.

THE WHITE NEGRO REVISITED AND REMIXED: WHITE SUBURBAN YOUTH AND THE HIP HOP MOVEMENT

Almost as if picking up right where the Lost Generation of the 1920s, the Beat Generation of the 1950s, and the hippies of the 1960s left off, the white suburban youth of the Hip Hop Generation might be called "the new white

Negroes," to borrow from Norman Mailer's infamous *The White Negro: Superficial Reflections on the Hipster* (1957). At this point it could almost go without saying that the meteoric rise and "crossover" success of rap music and hip hop culture resonated with white suburban youth coming of age in post-Civil Rights Movement America. Herein lies one of the great ironies of rap music and hip hop culture: it not only sonically symbolizes the aspirations and frustrations of black ghetto youth, but also, and rather ironically I believe, it has been used to channel the angst and alienation of white suburban youth at the turn of the twenty-first century.[22]

No matter how my more black nationalist-minded readers may feel about this, 1980s and 1990s "gold" (at least half a million albums sold), "platinum" (one million albums sold), and "multiplatinum" (two million or more albums sold) album sales speak volumes about the ways in which white suburban youth identified—albeit often from an antiblack racist exotic and erotic frame of reference—with rap music and hip hop culture. In other words, here I wish to openly acknowledge that rap music and hip hop culture have both particular *and* universal elements—which is to say, elements that simultaneously speak to the special epochal needs of black ghetto youth *and* white suburban youth, among others. The duality of hip hop discourse, in my mind, lucidly demonstrates the continued centrality of African American thought, culture, and struggles within the wider context of contemporary American culture, politics, and society.

As with the more moderate Civil Rights Movement youth and the more militant Black Power Movement youth, Hip Hop Movement youth must be allowed to develop strategies and tactics that they believe directly speak to their specific cultural, social, and political struggles. The social and political problems of the past, quite simply said, are not the social and political problems of the present, and the ongoing centrality of African American thought, culture, and struggles within the Hip Hop Movement speaks volumes about the ways in which hip hoppers, in their own unique way, are raising awareness about historic and current issues impacting African America. "Instead of corrupting young whites," optimistically exclaimed Bakari Kitwana in *Why White Kids Love Hip Hop: Wankstas, Wiggers, Wannabes, and the New Reality of Race in America* (2005), "hip hop is helping usher in a new racial politics that has come into its own with the post-Baby Boom Generation" (19). Hip hop, Kitwana continued, is a "framework," a "culture that has brought young people together and provides a public space that they can communicate within unrestricted by the old obstacles" (78).

The "old obstacles" Kitwana hints at here obviously have something to do with pre-Hip Hop Generation racial segregation, economic exploitation, and perhaps even gender domination. As they come to maturity the Hip Hop Generation is coming to realize that it is *the first generation of U.S. citizens not born into or forced to come of age in a racially segregated U.S. society.*

There is a palpable new freedom in the air, and even our most hard-nosed cultural critics and political pundits have been forced to concede that "young whites are engaging with black youth culture just as corporate culture has become a tool for marketing everything, even blackness, via pop culture. In short, America has changed" (78–79). In many ways what I am wont to call the "Hip Hop Movement" is preoccupied with many of the exact same issues—racial, cultural, sexual, gender, and economic issues—that engrossed its musical antecedents and movement ancestors. However, what truly distinguishes the Hip Hop Movement from previous African American musics and movements might actually have more to do with the unique historical moment in which it emerged and rapidly evolved.

Although the Hip Hop Movement is arguably preoccupied with either the exact same or extremely similar issues as previous major African American movements, what ultimately distinguishes it is its unique use of digital and telecommunications technology, new forms of social networking, social media and cyber-politics, and—many might argue, most importantly—the hard historical fact that the gains of the Civil Rights Movement and Black Power Movement seem to have hit some kind of reset button that has miraculously enabled an entire generation of U.S. citizens to sidestep the unspeakable horrors, hindrances, and hard feelings that have historically accompanied enslavement, racial colonization, racial segregation, lynching, Jim Crow laws, Black Codes, and outright American apartheid. It is undeniable that many hip hoppers—especially, ironically, both political *and* gangsta rappers—feel that contemporary society is particularly discouraging for and inhospitable to working-class and poor black people, especially black ghetto youth. However, many of these same hip hoppers are quick to concede that if things are bad for black people now, then they were worse prior to the Civil Rights Movement and Black Power Movement. Indeed, as was exclaimed above, "America has changed," but not enough to where institutional racism or antiblack economic exploitation are things of the past or somehow artifacts that only exist in history books and the dated footage featured in historical documentaries.

Perhaps what has really changed has more to do with white suburban youth's open admission of their fascination with black ghetto youths' popular music and popular culture. Whether we agree or disagree with white suburban youths' hyper-consumption of black ghetto youth's popular music and popular culture, the fact remains that there is indeed a "new racial reality" in America. Kitwana importantly identified what he understood to be the "five primary variables" that helped to usher in the Hip Hop Movement's "new racial politics":

A new racial politics has been unfolding in the post-Baby Boom Generation that before now has not been adequately discussed. Five primary variables helped create the climate for this new racial politics to emerge: the rise of the global economy and a resulting sense of alienation among young whites in the 1980s and 1990s; significant ruptures in the popular music scene; a further shifting American economy at the turn of the millennium, which was accompanied by a declining sense of white privilege; the institutionalization of key aspects of the Civil Rights Movement; and finally the sociopolitical range of post-1960s black popular culture. (23)

Here it is important to observe Kitwana's emphasis on race, culture, politics, and economics. From his point of view, the breakthroughs of the Civil Rights Movement, the "sociopolitical range of post-1960s black popular culture," and the "rise of the global economy" all factor into the Hip Hop Movement's "new racial politics." Notice that Kitwana was careful not to overaestheticize hip hop culture's roots. Deftly demonstrating that hip hop culture is much more than rap music, by highlighting the Hip Hop Movement's roots in the Civil Rights Movement he turned his readers' attention to the often underdiscussed fact that the Civil Rights Movement not only altered African Americans' relationship with the U.S. government and legal system, but also African Americans' relationship with white America, especially white youth. Kitwana importantly continued his discourse on the Hip Hop Movement's "new racial reality":

This new reality influenced the degree to which white youth have engaged hip hop. The narratives of the Civil Rights Movement in history textbooks, the telling and re-telling of the same in documentaries and feature films, the endless replaying of audio and video footage of [Martin Luther] King's speeches on radio and television year after year (following the establishment of the King holiday and strong pockets of resistance to it) have all helped familiarize white kids with distant or unknown aspects of black culture. For the first time, most young white Americans came of age with a fair degree of awareness of African American culture. At the same time, public acceptance of old stereotypical assumptions was diminishing. (38)

Although I do not share Kitwana's belief that "[f]or the first time, most young white Americans came of age with a fair degree of awareness of African American culture," because I believe it is important to critically question which aspects of African American culture white youth are familiar with (i.e., mostly black popular music and black popular culture), I do agree with his assertion that the Civil Rights Movement has garnered a singular place within contemporary American culture, politics, and society. In addition, even though I disagree with Kitwana's contention that "public acceptance of old stereotypical assumptions [is] diminishing," because even a cursory listen to the latest gangsta, hard-core, commercial, or pop rap—for example, 50 Cent's *Before I Self-Destruct* (2009), Kanye West's *My Beautiful Dark Twisted Fantasy* (2010), Snoop Dogg's *Doggumentary* (2011), The

Game's *The R.E.D. Album* (2011), Lil' Wayne's *Tha Carter IV* (2011), Drake's *Take Care* (2011), Nicki Minaj's *Pink Friday: Roman Reloaded* (2012), Rick Ross's *God Forgives, I Don't* (2012), or 2 Chainz's *Based on a T.R.U. Story* (2012)—will demonstrate loudly and clearly that many of the main motifs of blackface minstrelism, 1970s blaxploitation films, and the pimpisms of Dolemite, Blowfly, Iceberg Slim, and, of course, Donald Goines continue to haunt rap music, hip hop culture, and the Hip Hop Movement.

In my own experience speaking to, literally, thousands of white students and fans of rap music and hip hop culture over the past fifteen years, I have come to the conclusion that it has been rap music and hip hop culture—and rap music and hip hop culture alone—that has exposed these (mostly suburban) white youth to African American culture, and African Americans in general, for that matter. Undoubtedly, there is an extremely knowledgeable and frequently critical core of white hip hop fans who have a broad comprehension and deep appreciation of African American history, culture, and struggle, and who are for the most part self-reflexive and highly critical of their own white privilege within the world of hip hop and in U.S. society at large. Indeed, it is this cadre of white hip hop youth that many black and other nonwhite hip hoppers regard as *authentic antiracist allies* in the Hip Hop Movement.

However, truth be told, most white hip hop fans (often through no direct fault of their own) know virtually nothing about the African American social, political, intellectual, cultural, and spiritual traditions out of which rap music and hip hop culture emerged. Most white hip hop fans are woefully bereft of the most basic facts about African American history and culture, for instance: how the long-term effects of enslavement, racial segregation, and other aspects of American apartheid continue to plague African America in the twenty-first century; how African American women and girls' experience of several centuries of antiblack racist rape and other forms of antiblack racist sexual violence during enslavement continues to influence the images, myths, and stereotypes about African American women and girls in the twenty-first century; how U.S. ghettos came into being and why most working-class and working-poor black folk consider them concentration camps; why African American youth are, for the most part, uninspired and often outright angry about going to school and learning about white history and white culture but virtually nothing about black history and black culture—of course, other than the fact that African Americans were enslaved and then, once freed by President Abraham Lincoln, robbed of their reparations of "forty acres and a mule"; why, even after the Civil Rights Movement and affirmative action, African Americans continue to struggle for civil rights and social justice; and, lastly, how and why elements of whiteness—more specifically, white hip hop fans' racial identities and privileges—are a consequence of African American enslavement, racial oppression, cultural colonization, and economic exploitation and the unprecedented expressive culture all of this unheralded and horrid history paradoxically produced.

In the courses I teach on hip hop, black popular music, and black popular culture, I am regularly astonished by my white students' seemingly sincere appreciation of rap music and hip hop culture and their simultaneous ignorance of the particular history, culture, and struggles that spawned, swirl around, and float through rap music and hip hop culture and that, however unwittingly, deeply influences their enthusiastic investment in black popular music and black popular culture. As I crisscross the country each academic year to deliver countless lectures on rap music and hip hop culture I meet throngs of well-meaning liberal white students (much like the ones I lovingly teach in Boulder, Colorado) raised in and attending college in cushy suburban settings where African Americans, African American history, African American culture, and African American struggles are more of an idea than a reality, more abstract figments than concrete figures. Frequently these students admit that they have had virtually no experience with more than a handful of African Americans in their short privileged lives and that even though they attended the best college-preparatory schools in their city, state, or region, they learned little or nothing about African Americans, African American history, African American culture, and African American struggles.

Even as these well-meaning liberal white college students admit they know virtually nothing about African Americans, African American history, African American culture, and African American struggles beyond black popular music and black popular culture, they are quick to defensively invoke all the rap music they have listened to and all the rap videos they have watched, and how rap music and videos have essentially taught them everything they need to know about African American life and culture. "NaS is from the projects, so he knows what's happening in the hood," a white male student once stuttered. "Yeah," another immediately chimed in, "I have everything Jay-Z ever released, including all his mixtapes. He tells it like it is. He spits fire! And, he went from rags to riches. He's the new American Dream."

A white female student quickly joined the clamoring chorus, "I'm from the South, and when I listen to Lil' Wayne I really *feel* him." She passionately emphasized the word "feel" the way only a young liberal white woman can with her voice trembling as if she were on the verge of either crying or fainting, or both. She quickly regained her composure and continued, "He's putting New Orleans on the rap map. People need to know what's going on down South. It's not just about East Coast and West Coast anymore. Rap is the voice of the Hip Hop nation, Hip Hop America!"

NaS, Jay-Z, and Lil' Wayne's actual fidelity to the facts of ghetto life and culture aside, I could not help but wonder how these students came to accept such limited and deeply distorted articulations of black ghetto life and culture with such uncomplicated and uncritical confidence? I also wondered why they were so certain that NaS, Jay-Z, and Lil' Wayne were "telling it like it is," *like it really is*, given my students' admittedly limited knowledge of African American life and culture? It is as if NaS, Jay-Z, and Lil' Wayne, among other popular rappers, are to many white hip hop fans what African American historians, sociologists, political scientists, and cultural critics—for example, Cornel West, bell hooks, Michael Eric Dyson, Tricia Rose, Mark Anthony Neal, Joan Morgan, and Robin D.G. Kelley—are to many black hip hop fans, especially hip hop organic intellectual activists.

Without a working knowledge of African American history, culture, and struggles, and without being self-reflexive and highly critical of their own white privilege within the world of hip hop, as well as in U.S. society, politics, economics, and culture at large, most white hip hop fans invariably end up embracing "old school" and often pre-Civil Rights Movement conceptions of race, class, sexuality, spirituality, and African America in general. As a result, instead of positively and progressively contributing to the Hip Hop Movement, most white hip hop fans are, even if unintentionally, re-creating and perpetuating the long and extremely ugly history of *racial tourism* which demands that black people distort and deform themselves to conform to whites' antiblack racist desires in order to be successful in *the mainstream white desire/leisure/pleasure-driven marketplace*. As quiet as it has been kept, rap music and hip hop culture have been central to *the mainstream white desire/leisure/pleasure-driven marketplace* between 1980 and the present even as many rappers and hip hoppers more generally have sought to simultaneously rupture their relationships with mainstream American popular music, popular culture, aesthetics, politics, and economics.

So, instead of white hip hoppers having "a fair degree of awareness of African American culture," as Kitwana asserted above, most white youth actually have an extremely ahistorical and apolitical understanding of what little they actually know about African America. But, this was not always the case. As a matter of fact, in the early years of rap music and hip hop culture's evolution it was no small feat for whites who did not live near African Americans or have close relations with African Americans to listen to and keep up with rap music and hip hop culture.

To be a white hip hop fan in the 1980s most often meant, literally, leaving the suburbs or some other lily-white locale and traveling to a predominantly nonwhite slum, ghetto, or barrio. It meant voluntarily sharing physical and cultural space with working-class and poor nonwhites on their own terms and, however temporarily, being a "minority" in the midst of a black majority. In the 1980s and throughout what has been variously termed the "Golden Age of Rap" between 1987 and 1999, the stories and images of black hip hoppers were much more complex and complicated because conscious, message, and political rap frequently shared the same sonic and social spaces as commercial and gangsta rap. For example, the average white hip hop fan in the early 1990s was just as likely to own copies of Public Enemy's *Fear of a Black Planet* (1990), A Tribe Called Quest's *The Low End Theory* (1991), and Arrested Development's *3 Years, 5 Months & 2 Days in the Life Of . . .* (1992) right alongside their much-coveted copies of Ice Cube's *Death Certificate* (1991), Dr. Dre's *The Chronic* (1992), and Snoop Dogg's *Doggystyle* (1993).

As a consequence, 1990s conscious, message, and political rap often countered the antiblack racist myths and stereotypes about blacks and other nonwhites that most white Americans had been reared and raised on and, truth be told, were being increasingly exposed to via commercial and gangsta rap. Most white hip hop fans in the 1980s and 1990s had qualitatively different kinds of relationships with rap music and hip hop culture compared to most white hip hop fans between 2000 and the present, because between 1980 and 2000 white appreciation of or participation in rap music and hip hop culture required, if not historical and cultural knowledge, certainly familiarity with extramusical and other nonaesthetic aspects of African American life and culture, as well as a willingness to fluently articulate a shared respect for the real life, flesh and blood black folk, artist or otherwise, who welcomed them into the dank, dark world of the ghetto and who were in many senses their goads and guides through African America between 1980 and 2000.[23]

By the time rap began to solidly outsell rock in the first decade of the twenty-first century, white hip hop fans' immersion in extramusical African American life and culture was perceived as an "old school" and seemingly "odd" part of rap music and hip hop culture's colorful past. Between 2000 and the present rap has become so popular among white youth that most rap concerts are no longer convened in African American communities and clubs, but mostly held in posh suburban concert halls and venues, which essentially means that for the most part black hip hoppers are "minorities" in cultural and sonic spaces they, literally, created to combat their angst, alienation, and exploitation. At this point, rap music and hip hop culture and contemporary "American popular music" and contemporary "American popular culture" are in many senses one and the same.

Ironically, however, the more popular rap music and hip hop culture became with white youth and the more it was commodified by corporate America, the more it became quite common to be a white fan of hip hop who knew all the latest "hot" rap songs and "tricked-out" trends in hip hop culture but who had little or no extramusical contact with African Americans and, again, who knew virtually nothing about African American history, culture, and struggle. Candidly discussing the white desire/leisure/pleasure-driven popular music and popular culture marketplace in relationship to rap music and hip hop culture in *The Washington Post*, Maryland legislator and white hip hopper Justin Ross (2007, 1) wrote with a rare self-reflexive and brutal honesty:

> In the current debate over whether hip hop has become degrading to women and harmful to race relations, I've heard quite a bit from black activists, some of whom have fought for years against the sort of lyrics I'm writing about, and I've gotten several earfuls from black rap artists. But I haven't heard a peep from the white fans who essentially underwrite the industry by purchasing more than 70 percent of the rap music in this country, according to Mediamark Research, Inc. I don't presume to tell any artist, studio executive or record label what to record or not record. But I will presume to ask young white customers: Why are we buying this stuff?
>
> Across the country, white kids in comfortable suburban neighborhoods (mine was Greenbelt) sit in their cars or bedrooms or studio apartments, listening to the latest rap music that glorifies violence, peddles racist stereotypes and portrays women as little more than animals. We look through the keyhole into a violent, sexy world of "money, hoes and clothes." We're excited to be transported to a place where people brag about gunplay, use racial epithets continually and talk freely about dealing drugs. And then we turn off whatever we're listening to and return to our comfy world in time for dinner.

Ross's comments help us critically connect the rise of *the ghetto-gangsta-nigga-pimp-hoe-thug theme* that has dominated most commercial rap over the last twenty years with white youths' ever-increasing hyper-consumption of gangsta rap and hard-core hip hop culture. Because they are not self-reflexive and highly critical of their white privilege and unwitting internalization of white supremacy, most white fans of rap music and hip hop culture fail to see that the hip hop-style "ghettos," "gangstas," "niggas," "pimps," "hoes," and "thugs" are actually figments of white America's antiblack racist imaginations and not necessarily indicative of the real aspirations and frustrations of African American youth. These mostly corporate white man-made "ghettos," "gangstas," "niggas," "pimps," "hoes," and "thugs" only exist in the commercial rap music and videos concocted specifically for white suburban youth and their culturally misoriented "colored" friends' hyperconsumption. As make-believe, whitewashed, and Eurocentric as most Hollywood movies, commercial and gangsta rap are as shackled and chained to modern antiblack racist myths and stereotypes as African Americans' ancestors were, literally, shackled and chained to antiblack racist myths and stereotypes during their more than four hundred years of enslavement between 1441 and 1865.

There are those who are saying to themselves, "Why is he making rap music about race? It ain't a 'black thang.' Rap is for everybody. It's just good, clean fun. He is reading too much into rap. It's not that deep. History, politics, sociology, and literary theory have no place in the world of hip hop. It ain't academic. It's about beats, rhymes, and keepin' it real." I respond to their "racism is a thing of the past" rhetoric and "you people need to get over slavery" slurs by reminding them that, as Ross observed above, white hip hop fans purchase "more than 70 percent of the rap music in this country," and that the "ghetto," "gangsta," "nigga," "pimp," "hoe," and "thug" antiblack racist myths and stereotypes of black ghetto youth that white suburban youth consume almost every time they listen to rap or watch a rap video are in many ways identical to the antiblack racist myths and stereotypes of African Americans that made blackface minstrel shows America's first national popular culture and also provided America with its first national popular music. It would seem that Jean-Baptiste Alphonse Karr's famous nineteenth-century saying, "*plus ça change, plus c'est la même chose*" (translation: "the more things change, the more things stay the same"), continues to ring true in the twenty-first century, especially with regard to antiblack racism in America.[24]

Antiblack racism has been central to if not the motor inside the wicked machine I have dubbed the "white desire/leisure/pleasure-driven popular music and popular culture marketplace." And, for those who continue to doubt the antiblack racist and blackface minstrelesque subtext of much of the rap music white hip hop fans consume, I return to Ross, who insightfully and in true antiracist ally fashion ingeniously wondered aloud what would happen if rap artists inverted their ghettocentric narratives and instead developed *suburbcentric* rhymes about "selling dope in the suburbs, or shooting white people or beating down white men. Would rap's comfortable white fans continue to consume it?" Moreover, I have often pondered whether white youth would hyper-consume rap if instead of hearing the insidious word "nigga" a dozen or more times in seemingly each and every song rappers incessantly hurled antiwhite racial epithets, such as "ofay," "honky," "cracker," "peckerwood," "redneck," and "gringo." Indeed, "[w]ould rap's comfortable white fans continue to consume it?"

Ross importantly concluded, "I suspect the record companies wouldn't even sell it. Like the majority of people who buy rap music, the majority of people who get rich off it are white [and male]." A form of rap that turns its foul-mouthed musings, sonic sadomasochism, violent fantasies, and critical sociopolitical attention toward powerful people in the suburbs, as opposed to powerless people in the ghetto, "might hit a little too close to home for hip hop's fans and profiteers" (1). So much for those who continue to stubbornly believe that rap music and hip hop culture are "just good, clean fun." They very well may be to ahistorical and apolitical hyper-privileged white suburban youth, but most black and other nonwhite ghetto youth obviously have a very different relationship with rap music and hip hop culture.

Above Kitwana asserted that in the post-Black Power Movement period between 1975 and 2005, "For the first time, most young, white Americans came of age with a fair degree of awareness of African American culture. At the same time, public acceptance of old stereotypical assumptions was diminishing." On principle, I respectfully disagree with this contention, not because I lack faith in the white youth of the Hip Hop Generation (believe me, there is probably no one on the planet who would like to see them rid themselves of antiblack racism more than I), but because I am solemnly committed to telling my students and colleagues, as well as my family and friends, the truth as opposed to flattering them by telling them what they want to hear and filling their heads full of fictions and fantasies.

As a *hip hop radical humanist* I would like to openly and honestly say that I love white hip hoppers unconditionally and endlessly. I would like to see them grow and develop to their fullest potential just as much as I would like to see black and other nonwhite hip hoppers grow and develop to their fullest potential. But, deep in my heart, in that place where I hold sacred truths, I know that none of us will be able to rescue and reclaim our hard-won humanity until we are all willing to be self-reflexive and self-critical—in the most Fanonian and Foucaultian fashions imaginable—about the ways we individually and collectively perpetuate and constantly re-create interlocking systems of oppression, exploitation, and violence such as racism, sexism, heterosexism, bourgeoisism, capitalism, and colonialism.[25]

Rap music and hip hop culture are not black ghetto youth's alone; white and other nonwhite youth have been consistent contributors to, and participants in rap music and hip hop culture. But, when the negative aspects of hip hop are brought up, when hip hop is singled out as an especially deplorable or "niggardly" form of popular culture black ghetto youth are most often betrayed and abandoned by white and other nonwhite hip hop youth. It is time for white and other nonwhite hip hoppers to make up their minds and decide whether they are going to be posers and part of hip hop's problem or organic intellectual artist-activists and part of hip hop's solution. All hip hoppers, not merely black hip hoppers, are responsible for the state of hip hop culture and, likewise, all hip hoppers—again, not merely black hip hoppers—must make whatever sacrifices and learn whatever lessons necessary to make their special contributions to the Hip Hop Movement.

To be fair to Kitwana, who is a much-respected colleague and comrade of mine, it should be pointed out that he only engaged gangsta rap and hard-core hip hop in passing in *Why White Kids Love Hip Hop*. However, this could be seen, yet and still, as a problematic omission in a book provocatively titled *Why White Kids Love Hip Hop*. Call me pessimistic, if you must, but I'm not sufficiently convinced that "white kids'" relationship with hip hop actually constitutes "love" (and certainly not "real love," in a Mary J. Blige hip hop soul sense), as much of it looks, sounds, smells, tastes, and feels a lot like *lust*—of course, *love* and *lust* are both four-letter words that begin with the letter "l," but, needless to say, there is a big, yawning chasm of difference between them. To invoke "lust" here also takes us back to African American enslavement (e.g., recall the systematic antiblack racist rape of enslaved black girls and black women by oppressing, exploiting, and violating white men); the Lost Generation invasion (seeking sexual gratification) of uptown nightclubs and other haunts during the Harlem Renaissance years; white America's obsession with jazz music and jazz dance during the so-called "Jazz Age" of the 1920s; the Beat Generation (and later the Beatniks') fascination with bebop music and the militant politics of the Bebop Movement during the 1950s; and much of white America's association of early rhythm & blues and rock & roll with sex and sordid behavior during the Civil Rights Movement years.

After teaching hip hop studies courses over the last fifteen years, I remain suspicious of what white youth really and truly know about African American culture *beyond black popular music and black popular culture*. Indeed, I will readily agree with Kitwana that white youth seem to have sound-bite knowledge of the Civil Rights Movement, but when I press them—as I on principle always do—in my classes and in my lectures around the country, most often white youth's knowledge of the Civil Rights Movement seems to have been gathered from what they were able to glean from Google, *Wikipedia*, Twitter, Facebook, MySpace, miscellaneous blogs, prime-time sitcoms, the nightly news, or Hollywood movies. Here I am faithfully following W.E.B. Du Bois, bell hooks, Frantz Fanon, Malcolm X, Paulo Freire, Gloria Ladson-Billings, Henry Giroux, and Peter McLaren by making a critical distinction between *information* and bona fide *education*: information is most often desultory and superficial, where education is deep and significant.

Truth be told, most white youth have a superficial or referential relationship with the Civil Rights Movement, and almost every other aspect of African American culture, because "mature" mainstream white America—meaning, their ancestors, great-grandparents, grandparents, and parents—historically have had and currently continue to have artificial and often antiblack racist relationships with African American history, culture, and struggle. In other words, I am saying as simply and sincerely as I possibly can, that what I have elsewhere called *hip hop's amnesia* is not wholly or inherently the Hip Hop Generation's alone, but it has been, however unheralded, handed down from previous generations and movements to the Hip Hop Generation and, by default, the newfangled Hip Hop Movement.

HIP HOP'S AMNESIA AND THE AMNESIA SURROUNDING HIP HOP: THE POLITICS AND SOCIAL VISIONS OF RAP MUSIC AND THE HIP HOP MOVEMENT

In many ways the Hip Hop Generation's angst seems to be connected more to the much-misunderstood Black Power Movement and its correlate Black Arts Movement than the Civil Rights Movement. Recall that many hip hoppers' discontent and political depression revolves around the excruciating feelings of abandonment, frustration, and repulsion discussed in "remixes" 3 and 4. Clearly, Black Power militants felt that the Civil Rights Movement did not go far enough in its efforts to eradicate antiblack racism and antiblack economic exploitation at the hands of U.S. capitalism and bourgeoisism.

As witnessed in myriad rappers'—especially conscious, message, or political rappers'—rhymes, similar to the Black Power militants, the Hip Hop Generation has articulated almost identical sentiments concerning the advances *and* setbacks of the Civil Rights Movement. For instance, in *The Hip Hop Generation: Young Blacks and the Crisis in African American Culture* (2002), Bakari Kitwana contended that hip hoppers' frustrations with the Civil Rights Movement stem from what they understand to be "America's unfulfilled promise of equality and inclusion" (xx). After all of the demonstrations, protests, marches, sit-ins, and freedom rides of the 1960s, the Hip Hop Generation, similar to the Black Power proponents, have recurringly called into question the concrete gains of the Civil Rights Movement. As a matter of fact, Kitwana claimed, African Americans in the twenty-first century continue to be plagued by racism and the crude antiblack racist calculus of U.S. capitalism that the 1950s and 1960s civil rights struggle was valiantly waged against.

All too often various forms of *amnesia* seem to rear their heads when and where discussions concerning the gains of the 1950s and 1960s civil rights struggle fail to acknowledge the truly troubling state of African America since the late 1960s. "Ignored is the grim reality," Kitwana cautioned, "that concrete progress within the civil rights arena has been almost nil for nearly four decades. Neither acknowledged are the ways persisting institutionalized racism has intensified for Hip Hop Generationers despite 1950s and 1960s civil rights legislation" (xx–xxi).

With all due respect, then, politically conscious and progressive hip hoppers have refused to romanticize and mythologize the social gains of the Civil Rights Movement because they know all too well that those advances were not the end-all and be-all in terms of African Americans' ultimate achievement of a truly democratic and culturally pluralistic society free from racism, patriarchy, heteorsexism, religious intolerance, and the evils of capitalist political economy. In other words, it seems that the politically conscious among the hip hoppers have come to the uncomfortable conclusion that no matter how "great" and "groundbreaking" the Civil Rights Movement's achievements were, African Americans' search for social justice must go on unabated in the twenty-first century—*a luta continua*, to solemnly invoke the motto of the FRELIMO Movement during Mozambique's war for independence (circa 1962 to 1975). Highlighting how the hip hoppers' struggles against racism and capitalism differ from those of both the Civil Rights moderates and Black Power militants, Kitwana sternly stated:

> The 1950s and 1960s brought many changes in law, and the early 1970s ushered in an age of black elected officials, but the 1980s and 1990s were void of any significant movement around which young blacks could organize at the national level. For us, in part due to the previous generation's victories, today's "enemy" is not simply white supremacy or capitalism. White supremacy is a less likely target at a time when lynchings aren't commonplace (in the traditional sense) and when blacks can vote and are not required by law to sit in the back of the bus. To deem capitalism the enemy when financial success and the righteousness of the free market have become synonymous with patriotism is hardly popular. (148–49)

It is understood, then, that the Hip Hop Generation has its own distinct versions of racism and capitalism that it must critique and contend with. What is less understood, however, is that many of the strategies and tactics of past social movements do not automatically offer viable solutions to our problems in the present. Obviously there are myriad ways in which the racism and capitalism of the twenty-first century are inextricable from the racism and capitalism of the twentieth century. But, simply acknowledging how they are inextricable without also critically acknowledging their *ideological evolution* over the last fifty years does not help hip hop organic intellectual artist-activists *identify*, *critique*, and *contend with* contemporary—often even more insidious and abominable—forms of racism and capitalism (and, not to mention, sexism and heterosexism as well).[26]

This means, then, that in the final analysis even the Black Power Movement and its aesthetic arm, the Black Arts Movement, can only provide the Hip Hop Movement with paradigms and points of departure that raise our awareness of *why* the preceding generation struggled and *what* they struggled against. It is up to hip hoppers to determine *when*, *where*, and *how* we will struggle against the most pressing issues of our epoch. However, the main point is that *there must be ongoing and increased insurgent struggle*, not merely rhetorical radicalism, vocal acrobatics, and word wizardry about the new struggles of African Americans and the other wretched of the earth in the twenty-first century.

As Kitwana bemoaned above, "the 1980s and 1990s were void of any significant movement [in the traditional social movement sense] around which young blacks could organize at the national level," and, sadly, something very similar could be said for young folk of other colors and cultures. How has coming of age in an era "void of any significant [national] move- ment" depoliticized or, at the least, politically depressed the Hip Hop Gener- ation? Or, at the very least, how has it caused hip hoppers' entire approach to politics and social movement to be drastically different from any generation of Americans, especially African Americans, in post-Civil War history?

Eithne Quinn (2005, 37) went so far as to say that even gangsta rappers "are nothing if not charged symbols of post-Civil Rights malaise." Growing up in the long shadow cast by our grandparents and parents' Civil Rights moderatism and Black Power militantism, respectively and respectfully, most hip hoppers' "malaise" has caused them to resent and reject traditional forms of African American political protest and social movement. However, as Kitwana (2002, 149) astutely observed, even though the Hip Hop Genera- tion does not have a "broad national movement, we are not without smaller- scale activist movements." Thus, as it often seems to me, more than any other segment of the hip hop community it historically has been and remains the rappers who have consistently taken up the responsibility to boldly speak the special truth of contemporary black ghetto youth. Rappers, although often ridiculed, register hip hoppers' anger, angst, and rejection of the more mod- erate elements of our grandparents and parents' youth culture, politics, and social visions, as well as the more mainstream conventions and values that dehumanize black and other nonwhite marginalized people.

Even though it has been often ignored, as rap music has matured it has also been used as a tool to constructively critique and comment on the major issues and ills of the Hip Hop Movement. It is interesting to observe that among the "smaller-scale activist movements" that Kitwana asserted that the Hip Hop Movement is composed of several of these micro-movements have produced rappers (and spoken-word artists) who have offered up their partic- ular micro-movement's (and often micro-movements', in the plural sense) valuable criticisms of the wider Hip Hop Movement, its more mainstream rap music and version of hip hop culture. Hence, the Hip Hop Movement's myriad mini-movements articulate the Hip Hop Generation's political cri- tiques and social commentary in terms of U.S. culture, politics, and society as a whole *and* frequently do the same with respect to the more popular versions of hip hop culture, politics, and community.[27]

"It seems logical that a force from within hip hop cultural movement," quipped Kitwana, "would be the most sound vehicle to bring the Hip Hop Generation's political interest into the mainstream political process" (187). However, it is additionally important for us not to overlook the ways in which the Hip Hop Generation also constructively or, rather, self-reflexively critiques its own exacerbation and perpetuation of many of the issues and ills it is critical of in the wider world of U.S. culture, politics, and society. As is quite well known, for instance, the Hip Hop Movement has, however inchoate, collectively articulated critiques of racism; sexism; heterosexism; capitalism; class struggle; electoral politics; government bias in favor of the rich; government disaster response with respect to poor nonwhite communities; the military's overrecruitment of the poor, especially poor nonwhites; war and American imperialism abroad; employment discrimination; housing discrimination; the horrors of low-income housing; the immigration issue; environmental racism; corporate corruption; police brutality; and the prison industrial complex (especially, mandatory minimum sentencing and the death penalty) within the world of mainstream U.S. culture, politics, and society.

The Hip Hop Movement has matured to the point where it has a, however unheralded, highly developed self-reflexive critical culture. Of all its critics, ironically it would seem that the hip hoppers themselves have consistently offered rap music and hip hop culture the most useful evaluations of both its contradictions *and* its authentic contributions. For example, as I discussed in *Hip Hop's Inheritance*, insightful criticisms from the Hip Hop Women's Movement have been given voice by incomparable rappers (a.k.a., "femcees") and spoken-word artists, such as Sarah Jones, Mecca the Ladybug, Eve, Michelle Tea, Missy Elliott, Lenelle Moïse, Lauryn Hill, Aya de León, Leah Harris, Jill Scott, Jessica Care Moore, Bahamadia, Meliza Bañales, Alix Olson, Queen Latifah, Ursula Rucker, Medusa, Mystic, Jean Grae, and, of course, Meshell Ndegeocello. Moreover, as I discussed in *Hip Hop's Amnesia*, criticism aimed at the wider Hip Hop Movement emerging from the Homosexual Hip Hop Movement has been articulated by extraordinarily gifted rappers and spoken-word artists, such as Aggracycst, Alicia Leafgreen (a.k.a., White Lesbian Rapper [WLR]), Code Red, DaLyrical, Damashai, Deadlee, Deep Dickollective, Buttaflysoul, Dutchboy, God-dess & She, Hissy Fitt, Johnny Dangerous, Juba Kalamka, Jwahari, Katastrophe, Mack Mistress, Miss Money, Q-Boy, QPid (a.k.a., Yung Shortee), Smokey Da Bandit, Smut Stud, Storietella the Female Beast, Sugur Shane, Tim'm West, and Tori Fixx.

Needless to say, as *Hip Hop's Inheritance*, *Hip Hop's Amnesia*, and the previous "remixes" of the present volume have illustrated, homosexual hip hoppers are concerned with more than merely hip hop's homophobia and heterosexism, just as hip hop feminists are concerned with more than rap music's misogyny and incessant pandering to patriarchy. At this point, hip hop's internal politics and self-reflexive critical culture play themselves out in ways that challenge most conventional conceptions of politics, social movement, and self-reflexivity. Similar to most rap music, hip hop's politics frequently touch on a wide range of topics and, truth be told, the novel ways hip hop has both collapsed and combined pressing social problems has confounded several of the more sophisticated contemporary social and political theorists, who brazenly insist on using twentieth-century social movement models and political paradigms in their efforts to interpret the Hip Hop Movement's unprecedented and solidly twenty-first-century *multicultural, multiracial, multinational, multilingual, multireligious, and extremely multi-issue politics and social movement.* Again, Kitwana offered his expert insight on this issue:

> Influence of popular culture aside, the gains of the Civil Rights/Black Power generation were so large and transformative that that historic period has come to define what activism is. The Civil Rights Movement is extensively debated and taught in our schools and is commemorated during holidays and observances like Martin Luther King Jr. Day and Black History Month, year after year. Future movements are impossible to conceive and activism that produced significant social gains prior to the 1950s and 1960s has been all but forgotten. Current forms of struggle that go outside of the civil rights box are ignored or deemed meaningless. (153)

Indeed, a major part of the problem most pre-Hip Hop Generation folk have with rap music and hip hop culture has something to do with its seemingly incessant celebrations of sex, sexism, drugs, alcoholism, and materialism, among other ills. But, by lopsidedly focusing almost all of their attention on gangsta and commercial rap music and the other more popular aspects of hip hop culture (e.g., hip hop slang, film, fashion, dance, graffiti, and body art, etc.), hip hop's unequivocal critics often downplay and diminish hip hop's political culture and, by default, the multi-issue politics and social movement of the broader Hip Hop Movement altogether. This is not simply unfortunate, but it is also extremely disingenuous, as it negates the principled and politically progressive elements of hip hop culture—again, not to mention the broader much-misunderstood Hip Hop Movement.

In so many words, in *The Hip Hop Generation* Kitwana seems to be saying that Civil Rights and Black Power generationers, if not Baby Boomers in general, seem to be suffering from an acute case of *political nostalgia.* For most folk born after World War II the Civil Rights Movement represents the *condicio sine qua non*, which is to say, the only "real" and "right" way to wage a struggle for civil rights and social justice. All social movements before and after do not register because they were not or, as in the case of the Hip Hop Movement, they absolutely are not the Civil Rights Movement—or one of the other "great" and groundbreaking movements of the 1960s (e.g., the Women's Liberation Movement, New Left Movement, Anti-War Movement, Chicano Movement, Hippie Movement, and Lesbian, Gay, Bisexual & Transgender Liberation Movement, etc.).

As Kitwana correctly put it, movements that emerged in the aftermath of the Civil Rights Movement—such as the myriad mini-movements that make up the Hip Hop Movement—or, even further, post-Hip Hop Movement future movements, "are impossible to conceive." And, what is more, "activism that produced significant social gains prior to the 1950s and 1960s"—a lot of which I critically engaged in *Hip Hop's Amnesia*—"has been all but forgotten." This, of course, is to say that the Abolitionist Movement, Women's Suffrage Movement, Black Women's Club Movement, New Negro Movement, Harlem Renaissance, Lost Generation, Bebop Movement, and Beat Generation, for all intents and purposes, have been "all but forgotten" by most hip hoppers' grandparents and parents, who seem to remain preoccupied with the Civil Rights Movement of the 1950s and 1960s. Here we have in black and white, and in clear and concise prose, precisely and exactly what I referred to in my previous volume as *hip hop's amnesia*. Again, *hip hop's amnesia* is not simply about what the Hip Hop Generation has forgotten but should remember, but also about what generations prior to ours—and possibly even what the generations that will surely follow after ours—have forgotten, or will forget, but should remember about rap music, hip hop culture, and the unique historical, cultural, social, political, and economic moment in which this novel music and culture emerged and unnerved.

Kitwana could not have hit the nail on its head any harder than when he asserted, "[c]urrent forms of struggle that go outside of the civil rights box are ignored or deemed meaningless." How much of the Hip Hop Movement, which obviously goes "outside of the civil rights box," is for all intents and purposes either altogether "ignored or deemed meaningless?" How has this "benign neglect"—in the Moynihanian and Nixonian senses—further complicated and continued the contradictions and crises of the Hip Hop Movement's already complicated *multicultural, multiracial, multinational, multilingual, multireligious, and extremely multi-issue politics and social movement*?[28] How might *hip hop's amnesia* and the *amnesia surrounding hip hop* be remedied by openly acknowledging not only the Civil Rights Movement, but also the Abolitionist Movement, Women's Suffrage Movement, Black Women's Club Movement, New Negro Movement, Harlem Renaissance, American Labor Movement, Lost Generation, Bebop Movement, Beat Generation, Black Power Movement, Hippie Movement, Free Speech Movement, Women's Liberation Movement, New Left Movement, Anti-War Movement, Sexual Liberation Movement, American Indian Movement, Chicano Movement, Asian American Movement, Lesbian, Gay, Bisexual & Transgender Liberation Movement, Political Prisoners Movement, Disability Rights Movement, Animal Rights Movement, and Environmental Justice Movement, among many others too numerous to name? Each of the aforementioned generations and movements contributed to the Hip Hop Movement's aesthetics, poetics, and politics.

The Hip Hop Movement, when it is all said and done, is *simultaneously a multicultural, multiracial, multinational, multilingual, multireligious, and extremely multi-issue musical and sociopolitical macro-movement composed of several often seemingly uncoordinated micro-movements*. In its own sometimes warped and sometimes wicked ways, it embodies both what might be considered the "best" and the "worst" of the historic movements mentioned above. Moreover, it is important here to bear in mind something that Robin D.G. Kelley perceptively asserted in *Freedom Dreams: The Black Radical Imagination* (2002), where he wrote, "the desires, hopes, and intentions of the people who fought for change cannot be easily categorized, contained, or explained" (ix).

Let's face it. Social and political movements are not nice and neat affairs, they are invariably messy. Each movement mentioned above had its "messy"—if not, outright anarchic and maddening—moments. The Hip Hop Movement, being composed of several mini-movements, might be messier and more maddening than any previous movement; this much I am willing to humbly concede. But, what I am not willing to concede or overlook is the historical fact that there were high levels of almost each and every major allegedly "negative" or "vulgar" aspect of rap music and hip hop culture at the heart of most, if not all, of the aforementioned movements: from the use of profanity to widespread and well-documented promiscuity; from sexism to materialism; and from alcoholism to drug addiction.

The Hip Hop Movement admittedly may be unlike any previous social movement in its composition and seemingly uncoordinated political aspirations, but, make no mistake about it, it is a movement nonetheless. Furthermore, for those who would quickly and flippantly label the Hip Hop Movement a bravura flop, I want to caution them to keep in mind Kelley's caveat when he warned us against judging whether a movement was a "success" or a "failure" based on whether it was able to achieve *all* of its goals. To speak candidly here, serious social and political movements, as well as insurgent cultural aesthetic movements, are often not so much about eradicating each and every ill on their respective agendas as much as they are about critical consciousness-raising and decolonizing, politicizing, and radicalizing the wretched of the earth, inspiring them to begin their processes of self transformation *and* social transformation. Kelley insightfully contended:

> Unfortunately, too often our standards for evaluating social movements pivot around whether or not they "succeeded" in realizing their vision rather than on the merits or power of the visions themselves. By such a measure, virtually every radical movement failed because the basic power relations they sought to change remain pretty much intact. And yet it is precisely these alternative visions and dreams that inspire new generations to continue to struggle for change. (ix)

I would be one of the first to solemnly admit the Hip Hop Movement's "failures." But, even as we observe what hip hoppers did not do, it is extremely important to point to what they did—and, even more, what they are doing now. The focus on "failure" is connected to the all-too-American tendency to sanctimoniously stand tall and tell the world what we are *against* but never really state what we are *for*, what we really and truly believe in. Undeniably, the Hip Hop Movement has inherited a great deal of political ambivalence from the preceding sociocultural movements, and there are lists long enough to wrap around the surface of the globe several times detailing each and every despicable and dastardly deed committed in the name of the "Hip Hop Generation" or, rather, the "Hip Hop Movement."

Yet and still, I honestly believe there will come a time in the not too distant future when there will be a reappraisal of rap music, hip hop culture, and the overarching Hip Hop Movement, and, if nothing else, it will be acknowledged for its contributions to both aesthetics *and* politics—which is to say, it will finally be recognized as *a musical and sociopolitical multi-issue movement*. For instance, according to my colleague Adam Bradley, in *Book of Rhymes: The Poetics of Hip Hop* (2009), "[t]hanks to the engines of global commerce, rap is now the most widely disseminated poetry in the history of the world" (xiii). He went further to incisively observe:

> Of course, not all rap is great poetry, but collectively it has revolutionized the way our culture relates to the spoken word. Rappers at their best make familiar the unfamiliar through rhythm, rhyme, and wordplay. They refresh the language by fashioning patterned and heightened variations of everyday speech. They expand our understanding of human experience by telling stories we might not otherwise hear. The best MCs—like Rakim, Jay-Z, Tupac, and many others—deserve consideration alongside the giants of American poetry. We ignore them at our own expense. (xiii)[29]

However strange it might seem for us to admit it, there are people who have never read or even heard of William Wordsworth and Walt Whitman, or Pablo Neruda and Langston Hughes, but who can recite to you verbatim and with little difficulty the latest Lil' Wayne, Nicki Minaj, Drake, or Rick Ross rhyme. Rap music and hip hop culture have definitely had an impact on America, if not the world, and that impact has not been always and everywhere negative or vulgar. This is where hip hop's critics demonstrate the lopsided and often lame nature of many of their blanket condemnations of rap music, where they frequently refuse to give credence to any form of rap.

For many of rap music's more wild-eyed and, I am wont to say, "hardcore" critics there quite simply is no difference between Will Smith and Lil' Wayne, Lauryn Hill and Lil' Kim, or Common and 2 Live Crew. Rap music, as has been long said of the ghetto youth who invented and initially evolved it, is all the same, filled with cliché rhyme after cliché rhyme concerning the ghetto, guns, hot girls, drinking, and drugs. The fact that rap music, and hip hop culture in general, is actually much more nuanced and its politics much more complicated and complex than the simple "what you see is what you get" figments of "mature"—and mostly upper- and middle-class—folks' imaginations seems to rarely dawn on them.

In other words, rap music is seemingly a soundtrack to an underworld that the well-to-do and relatively wealthy in American want nothing whatsoever to do with—unless, of course, it is a Friday or Saturday night and they are downtown at a party or up in a club. Then, and perhaps only then, do the well-to-do and relatively wealthy wanna hang out in the hood and kick it with the "hoodlums" of the Hip Hop Generation. Needless to say, the "thug passion" is palpable even all the way up here from the cultural confines of, and ongoing twenty-first-century American apartheid-like conditions in Denver and Boulder, Colorado.

As the most popular expression of hip hop culture, rap music's resonance with the wider public speaks volumes about the ways in which the Hip Hop Movement has impacted the contemporary public sphere. To go back to the statement that rap essentially "expand[s] our understanding of [the] human experience by telling stories we might not otherwise hear," is it equally important to acknowledge that not all of the stories that rap shares are negative or about the ghetto, guns, hot girls, drinking, and drugs. As a matter of fact, rap has consistently proven to be a provocative tool to push the envelope and press issues that might have otherwise fallen through the cracks and crevices of contemporary "polite" culture, politics, and society (e.g., see Common's *One Day It'll All Make Sense* [1997], *Like Water for Chocolate* [2000], *Be* [2005], *The Dreamer/The Believer* [2011], or the Roots' *The Tipping Point* [2004], *Game Theory* [2006], *Rising Down* [2008], and *Undun* [2011], or Lupe Fiasco's *Food & Liquor* [2006], *The Cool* [2007], *Lasers* [2011], and *Food & Liquor II* [2012]). In its own unique way rap also registers as the Hip Hop Generation's deconstruction and reconstruction of what it means to be black or white, male or female, rich or poor, heterosexual or homosexual, etcetera, at the turn of the twenty-first century. However, while rap is undeniably "new school" music, it also undeniably remains "old school" poetry.

Most of rap's fans and critics seem to have forgotten that at its core *rap is poetry*, and poetry is a textual and, at times, oral form that can lyrically express both love *and* hate, the sacred *and* the secular, comedy *and* tragedy, and ecstasy *and* agony. Rap's fans and critics would do well to remember that "[r]ap is public art," Bradley (2009, xiii) insisted, and that "rappers are perhaps our greatest public poets, extending a tradition of lyricism that spans continents and stretches back thousands of years." He candidly continued:

> Rap is poetry, but its popularity relies in part on people not recognizing it as such. After all, rap is for good times; we play it in our cars, hear it at parties and at clubs. By contrast, most people associate poetry with hard work; it is something to be studied in school or puzzled over for hidden insights. Poetry

stands at an almost unfathomable distance from our daily lives, or at least so it seems given how infrequently we seek it out. (xii)

Here, then, it is important for us to emphasize *hip hop's amnesia* and the *amnesia surrounding hip hop* with respect to the highbrow approach to poetry and the lowbrow interpretation of rap. This obvious highbrow/lowbrow double standard seems to almost perfectly mirror how hip hop's multi-issue politics are treated or, rather, ill-treated. Compared to previous movements' politics, the Hip Hop Movement's multi-issue politics are juxtaposed as merely "juvenile gibberish" and not worthy of being taken seriously, even though hundreds and hundreds of conscious, political, and message rappers—not to mention neo-soulsters—have innovatively articulated hip hop culture's complex and complicated multi-issue politics and social movement in searing song after song. But, the fact that there are increasingly more and more books being written that explore "rap as poetry" or the "poetic dimensions of rap" bodes well for hip hop's aesthetics, even if, truth be told, much of this work is extremely ambivalent with respect to hip hop's multi-issue politics and social movement beyond rap music and hip hop's poetics.

That being said, here it is important for us to conclude our discussion—and this book—by emphasizing what might be loosely termed "rap's radical side" or, rather, the "rhetorical radicalism of rap music." In terms of internal critiques of the Hip Hop Generation's hyper-materialism and general bourgeois radicalism (if one must refer to it as "radicalism" at all), several conscious, message, political, democratic socialist, and democratic socialist-sounding (or, rather, pseudo-democratic socialist) rappers have rhetorically put hip hop's bourgeoisisms and capitalist pretensions on blast. Inspired by 1960s and 1970s political poets and spoken-word artists, such as Amiri Baraka, Sonia Sanchez, Haki Madhubuti, Nikki Giovanni, the Last Poets, the Watts Prophets, Jayne Cortez, and Gil Scott-Heron, "message rap" took its name from Grandmaster Flash & the Furious Five's 1982 rap classic "The Message."

As discussed in the first "remix" of the present volume, "The Message's" first verse seems to deftly demonstrate why it resonated, and continues to resonate, so deeply with black ghetto youth. Rapping about poverty, crime, and drug addiction, Flash & the Furious Five documented black ghetto youth's alienation and frustration in the early 1980s. It would seem that "mature" and mainstream America frequently focuses more on violence, misogyny, and homophobia in rap music and hip hop culture than on the cries of desperation and perceptive critiques of the crushing and crippling nature of ghetto life emanating from "conscious," "political," and "message" rap music.

As anyone who has earnestly read the previous "remixes" will be able to calmly comprehend, the need to critique violence, misogyny, and homophobia in rap music and hip hop culture remain paramount. However, I honestly believe that it is also just as important for us to acknowledge the ways in which hip hoppers have been politically progressive and continue to offer principled critiques of both hip hop *and* America's violence, hyper-masculinism, hyper-heterosexism, hyper-materialism, and open embrace of capitalist vampirism. "The Message" influenced countless early rappers, and the genre (i.e., "message rap") that the song spawned continues to the present moment—although corporate America obviously does not believe that message rap is as profitable as violent, materialistic, misogynistic, and homophobic rap.

Arguably more than any other form of rap music, message rap articulates the Hip Hop Movement's mission and multi-issue sociopolitical agenda. Even as I write all of this, however, I know all too well that I must proceed with caution, that rejecting each and every aspect of rap music and hip hop culture that doesn't jibe with some high-falutin, "polite," and "politically correct" conception of culture, politics, and society will leave us with a very short list of "principled" and "progressive" rap music and hip hop culture. But, by the same token, we have to honestly ask ourselves whether there has ever been a social or political movement with perfect or pristine politics, especially in America? As we witnessed in the previous "remixes" neither the Civil Rights Movement nor the Black Power Movement can claim to have had perfect and always and everywhere "principled" and "progressive" politics. The exact same thing could be said about the Hippie Movement, Anti-War Movement, New Left Movement, Women's Liberation Movement, and Lesbian, Gay, Bisexual & Transgender Liberation Movement, among the many other movements that followed in their wake.

We have to ask ourselves whether it is purely a coincidence that many of the more principled and politically progressive rap artists have turned to producing, packaging, marketing, and distributing their own work because they simply do not want to deal with the backwards bourgeois culture and incessantly antiblack racist super-exploitative practices of corporate America? Or, whether contemporary corporate America has been stuck on stupid so long that they honestly cannot see how unbalanced and lyrically lopsided their artist rosters are, with gangsta, commercial, and pop rappers almost exclusively having access to high-profile production teams, high-end marketing programs, and prestigious concert venues that only corporate-connected music industry moguls can lavish their artists with. Even though I whole heartedly agree with Kitwana (2002, 188) when he declared, "to date most [of hip hop's politics] have been steeped in political naïveté, partisan politics, or petty-bourgeois radicalism," yet and still, I believe it is important for us to acknowledge those rap artists and hip hoppers who have broken with and boldly gone beyond the old moderatism of the Civil Rights Movement and the angry militantism of the Black Power Movement, as well as the inertia and complacency that seem to have so many hip hoppers in a social and political holding pattern.

Although controversial and contradictory—similar to almost every other aspect of hip hop culture—conscious, political, and message rappers have consistently challenged, decolonized, and repoliticized the Hip Hop Movement, if not much of post-Civil Rights Movement and post-Black Power Movement America. Like the gangsta rappers, message rappers have primarily focused on black ghetto youth, and poverty-stricken people in general. This is important to point out because there has been a long-standing tendency for both the white and black bourgeoisies to turn a blind eye to the high levels of human suffering and social misery emerging from deep within the bowels of the barrios, slums, and ghettos.

Arguably beginning with Public Enemy's *Yo! Bum Rush the Show* in 1987 and KRS-One and Boogie Down Production's *By All Means Necessary* in 1988, message rap exploded. It rhetorically rallied (and continues to rally) on behalf of ghetto youth, collectively combining an innovative—and often extremely unnerving for many—mix of black nationalism, anarchism, Marxism, Leninism, Maoism, Fanonism, Guevaraism, Castroism, Zapatistaism, Buddhism, socialism, feminism, and womanism, among many other political and ideological perspectives. The remarkable political and ideological range and reach of conscious, political, and message rappers deftly demonstrates the Hip Hop Movement's unique *multicultural, multiracial, multinational, multilingual, multireligious, and extremely multi-issue politics and social visions.*

Obviously what qualifies such a varied group of artists and activists as rappers or hip hoppers is their unyielding use of rap music and hip hop culture as their primary points of departure. Along with other subgenres of rap music, such as "alternative," "underground," and "jazz" rap, one of the major preoccupations of conscious, political, and message rappers has been their emphasis on political critique and social commentary. However, one thing that clearly distinguishes most conscious, political, and message rappers from alternative, underground, and jazz rappers is the fact that frequently the former group of rappers embrace and articulate what might be deemed "radical" political views and agendas, in contrast to the more generalized kind of "drive-by" political critique and social commentary typical of the latter.

In other words, most conscious, political, and message rappers also double as political activists or, rather, *raptivists* (i.e., rappers *and* sociopolitical activists), whose rhymes reflect specific "radical" plans or progressive political programs aimed at transforming—not merely "drive-by" critiquing or cleverly commenting on—contemporary society, especially what is happening in the slums, barrios, and ghettos coast to coast. This is precisely where and why conscious, political, and message rappers can be said to connect with the wider world of contemporary radical politics and social movements. After all, didn't Karl Marx quip in his *Theses on Feuerbach*: "The philosophers have only interpreted the world in various ways, but the damned point is to change it?"

How many seemingly hundreds and hundreds of rappers are merely "interpret[ing] the world in various ways" without coming to the realization that "the damned point is to change it?" Here, I am once again, in the most heartfelt manner imaginable, hailing the Hip Hop Movement. I honestly believe that when taken together—and when we do not summarily disqualify folk simply because we do not agree with each and every thing they call or claim to be "hip hop"—we are so much more than merely a "generation" in some sort of generalized or sociologically succinct and academically acceptable way.

Unlike the commercial and pop rappers whose work, for the most part, often seems to glamorize the ghetto, most conscious, political, and message rappers understand themselves to be "telling it like it is" and "kickin' reality" in their rhymes. Indeed, they rhyme about the ghetto, guns, hot girls, drinking, and drugs arguably just as much as gangsta, commercial, and pop rappers. But, the difference is that conscious, political, and message rappers rhyme about these things to raise awareness, to remind the ghetto, the nation, and even the globe that 150 years after President Abraham Lincoln issued the Emancipation Proclamation African Americans continue to be enslaved and shackled and chained by antiblack racism, poverty, poor housing, horrid health care, unabated unemployment, ongoing substandard education, over-representation in the armed services, and penal escalation.[30]

In short, socially and politically conscious rappers, in their own often-warped and often-wicked ways, actually represent the conscience of the Hip Hop Movement. The messages in their music often have morals and provide principles without being overly didactic. As a matter of fact, the best and most provocative conscious, political, and message rappers are the ones whose politics and social visions *challenge* and *change* their audiences surreptitiously—that is to say, in seemingly secretive and unwitting ways via the power of their poetry and wordplay.

Major conscious, political, and message rappers include: Arrested Development; Basehead; Big Will; the Blue Scholars; Boogie Down Productions; Brand Nubian; Browny Loco; Commendante; Common (a.k.a., Common Sense); the Coup; Dead Prez; Def Jef; Del tha Funkee Homosapien; De La Soul; Digable Planets; the Disposable Heroes of Hiphoprisy; Divary; Dream Warriors; Dred Scott; Dudley "Declaime" Perkins; Elegal; Missy Elliott; Michael Franti; Freestyle Fellowship; the Fugees; Gang Starr; Guru; Genocide; the Goats; Goodie Mob; Cee-Lo Green; Lauryn Hill; Immortal Technique; Intelligent Hoodlum; Sick Jacken & Cynic; Wyclef Jean; Jedi Mind Tricks; Sarah Jones; the Jungle Brothers; Jurassic 5; K'naan; Kemo the Blaxican; KRS-One; Little Brother; Lupe Fiasco, Main Source; Mos Def; MRK; the Native Guns; Sole; Talib Kweli; the Narcicyst; Olmeca; Outkast; Paris; the Perceptionists; the Pharcyde; Pharoache Monch; Phonté; Poor Righteous Teachers; Public Enemy; Psycho Realm; Queen Latifah; Q-Tip; Rage Against the Machine; Rakim; Rebel Diaz; Zack de la Rocha; Rockin' Squat; the Roots; Hasan Salaam; Lakim Shabazz; Sister Souljah; Spearhead; Strate Crooked; Success-N-Effect; Amir Sulaiman; Tohil; Tolteca; A Tribe Called Quest; the Visionaries; Saul Williams, and X-Clan, among many others. Obviously this is not a list of conscious, political, and message rappers that would be acceptable to those who wish to listen to rap music completely free from *the ghetto-gangsta-nigga-pimp-hoe-thug theme* that seems to saturate so many aspects of contemporary hip hop culture.

Again, cutting loose each and every rapper who, however momentarily, gives in to *the ghetto-gangsta-nigga-pimp-hoe-thug theme* will ultimately leave us with an extremely limited and short playlist. I honestly believe that what is most important here is for us to not only listen for the negative and vulgar in rap music, but also the positive, the edifying, and the uplifting. We need to begin to listen for the love as opposed to the hate, and develop the ability to not simply critique but also appreciate rap music on its own terms.

I can say with some certainty that anyone who sincerely listens to any of the above conscious, political, and message rappers will hear sonic decon-structions of *the ghetto-gangsta-nigga-pimp-hoe-thug theme* and aural recon-structions of what it means to be African American and poor, African American and male, African American and female, African American and heterosexual, African American and homosexual, African American and Christian, African American and Muslim, African American and from a specific city, state, or region, and, even more, what it means to transcend the tried and true conceptions of what it means to be *African in America*. All of this is to say, that very often it is not gangsta, commercial, or pop rap that reveals what lies at the heart of the Hip Hop Movement but—seemingly unbeknownst to all but the most ardent critics, fans, and students of hip hop culture—conscious, political, and message rap. In short, conscious, political, and message rap frequently challenges both external and internal misconcep-tions about what it means to be a hip hopper and, most importantly here, what it means to be relatively young, struggling, humble, and hard-working human beings who are valiantly confronting the various issues and ills facing black folk and the Hip Hop Generation as a whole at the turn of the twenty-first century.

The Hip Hop Movement may not even remotely resemble previous social and political movements, but it is a movement. The Hip Hop Movement may not have all the hallmarks of a "progressive" movement, but—as the con-scious, political, and message rap noted above reveals—there are principled and politically progressive hip hoppers—sensitive human souls with un-

quenchable commitments to continuing the fight for freedom that has been
nobly handed down from generation to generation, movement to movement,
and suffering soul to suffering soul. For those of us deeply disturbed by what
is going on in our global warming and war-torn world, for those of us com-
passionately concerned about the perilous path that the Hip Hop Generation
and Obama's America is heading down, for those of us still desperately
searching for solutions to our most pressing social and political problems—
conscious, political, and message rap and socially and politically conscious
hip hop culture remain a beacon of light, boldly illuminating the cold and
corrupt, dark and discontent world we inherited.

Conscious, political, and message rappers cannot rupture the Hip Hop
Generation's relationship with the preexisting violence, racism, sexism,
heterosexism, capitalism, colonialism, militarism, alcoholism, drug addiction, and religious intolerance, etcetera, by themselves. Each and every one
of us must, on the most hallowed humanist principles, make whatever sacrifices necessary to transform ourselves and our society, our kinfolk and our
community, our friends and even, truth be told, our enemies. Real humanism—what I am wont to call "radical humanism"—does not start and stop
with our family and friends, our specific race and gender, our fellow citizens
and soldiers, or our religious brethren and sistren, but transcends all of the
trappings of, literally, "man-made" contemporary nation-states, religions,
languages, politics, economics, culture, and society.

So much of contemporary rap music and hip hop culture seems to revolve
around a constant repetition of the present. We hear again and again, and
over and over about "what's hot!" and "what's not!" It is all about right here
and right now: the next sadomasochistic rendezvous, the next *ménage à trios*,
the next trite tryst, the next train, the next gangbang, and on and on *ad
infinitum*. Meanwhile, hip hoppers are left with no real sense of history, of
their unique heritage, and, consequently, most hip hoppers seem to have no
real prospects for the future—that is to say, the future beyond this Friday's
paycheck and that off-da-hook house party they heard gonna happen over the
weekend.

There is an old adage, frequently attributed to Marcus Garvey, that says:
"If you don't know your past, you will never know your future." I could not
agree with Garvey more. I would only like to add the cold, hard fact that no
real future can evolve out of a present that is incessantly repeating itself over
and over again: cliché rhyme after cliché rhyme, and cliché video after cliché
video about the ghetto, guns, hot girls, drinking, and drugs. As demonstrated
in the discussions in "remixes" 1 through 4, there is so much more to rap
music and hip hop culture.

I honestly believe that we all have our contributions to make to the Hip
Hop Movement, and if I didn't I couldn't have made the innumerable sacrifices necessary to research and write this book. Just as the classic rhythm &

blues and rock & roll youth had their fun but made their contributions to the Civil Rights Movement, and just as the classic soul and funk youth had their fun but made their contributions to the Black Power Movement, hip hoppers can have their fun but need to make sure that they are making serious and seminal contributions—not only sonic and aesthetic contributions, but also social and political contributions to the Hip Hop Movement. At this point we can conclude that each of the previous major forms of black popular music coincided with a broader African American social and political movement. And, it is important to observe that frequently the artist-activists and political activists were often one and the same, if not, at the least, in deep dialogue concerning the most pressing social and political problems facing African America in specific, and the United States in general. Without hip hoppers beginning to consciously come together as a *movement*—again, which is more than merely a "generation"—it is almost certain that the Hip Hop Generation will go down in history as one of the most violent, vulgar, materialistic, misogynistic, and homophobic generations in American history, if not possibly in world history.

To speak candidly here, when I listen to India.Arie, the Roots, Jill Scott, Mos Def, Talib Kweli, Erykah Badu, Common, Nneka, Michael Franti, Meshell Ndegeocello, Dead Prez, Anthony David, Amel Larrieux, Rage Against the Machine, N'dambi, and Lupe Fiasco, among many others, I am uplifted. I am inspired. I am energized and given the strength to continue the struggle for freedom and social justice. However, their more principled, prudent, and progressive work also reminds me that *real struggle grows out of love* or, rather, *real and righteous struggle is love-inspired*: love for God; love for our ancestors; love for our family and friends; love for our culture; love for our community; love for our city, state, and country; love for oppressed and exploited people around the world; and, lastly, a humble and non-narcissistic love for ourselves.

Again, I would like to state as simply and sincerely as I possibly can that each and every one of us has our own distinct contributions to make to the evolution of the Hip Hop Movement and the decolonization and repoliticization of the Hip Hop Generation. Moreover, it should also be emphasized that *hip hop's amnesia* and the *amnesia surrounding hip hop* will never really and truly come to an end unless and until we are all able to make our special contributions to hip hop culture without regard to our race, gender, class, sexual orientation, religious affiliation, or nation of origin. In this sense, I would like to suggest that Dead Prez's searing song "It's Bigger Than Hip Hop!" serve as one of the major mottos of the Hip Hop Movement from this point forward. Indeed, the Hip Hop Movement is "bigger than hip hop" and involves our entire country, if not the entire world. What we do right here and right now will have an impact on the future: our individual future and our collective future.

I have chosen to think, act, teach, research, write, lecture, and engage in critical dialogue because the world we live in desperately requires—more than ever before—that we contribute, however we are best suited, to the ongoing struggle for human freedom, social justice, creativity, and future growth. We must face the world we currently live in and boldly continue to dream of the liberated future world we want and deserve to live in. However, we—and I especially have in mind here members of the Hip Hop Movement—must do more than dream, we must transform our dreams into our reality by doing all that we can to build a world based on freedom, truth, justice, love, respect, and compassion. If rap and other forms of hip hop culture often highlight what is bad or wrong with our world, then it should also be used to accent what is good or right in our world.

From this point forward if whatever we are doing in the name of hip hop is in any way antihuman or violent, then we must stop it and immediately start to embrace a more progressive and pro-human form of hip hop culture. This book was researched, written, and remixed in the spirit of both *critical* and *appreciative love*, as well as the spirit of *affirmational* and *transformational love*, because I am incorrigibly convinced that love and love alone can change and heal humanity. In conclusion, I can honestly say that researching, writing, and remixing this book have changed and healed me, and my most heartfelt prayer is that it will change and heal all those who honor the Hip Hop Generation *and* the Hip Hop Movement by taking the time to read it, debate it, and constructively criticize it, but are ultimately inspired to do something positive, progressive, and pro-human in the name of hip hop and the mostly black ghetto youth who invented and evolved it. In the spirit of African American popular music and popular movements past, present, and future, I conclude solemnly singing the African American national anthem: *Lift Every Voice and Sing.*

NOTES

1. For further discussion of the various subgenres of rap music, and for the most noteworthy works that informed my interpretation here, see Bogdanov, Woodstra, Erlewine, and Bush (2003), Bynoe (2004), Fricke and Ahearn (2002), Hess (2007a, 2007b, 2010), Hewitt and Westwood (1989), M. Katz (2012), Keyes (2002), Krims (2000), Kugelberg (2007), Light (1999), Ogg (2001), Price (2006), T. Rose (1994), P. Shapiro (2005a), and Woodstra, Bush, and Erlewine (2008).

2. Several other hip hop scholars have hinted at or made reference to a "Hip Hop Movement," its aesthetics, politics, and social justice agendas. Consequently, my interpretation here builds on and is in critical dialogue with Alridge (2005), Bernard-Donals (1994), Clay (2006, 2012), Decker (1993), R. Jackson (1994), Kitwana (2002, 2004), Krohn and Suazo (1995), Kun (2002), Shomari (1995), Stapleton (1998), L.Y. Sullivan (1997), Trapp (2005), Usher (2005), and S.C. Watkins (2001, 2005).

3. Along with the present volume, my previous hip hop studies *Hip Hop's Inheritance* and *Hip Hop's Amnesia* essentially emphasized that the "Hip Hop Generation is not the first generation of black youth to not only note the political nature of black popular culture, but also

to earnestly attempt to use the politics and social visions embedded in black popular culture in the interest of political activism and social organization" (see Rabaka 2011, 2012). Hence, whether we turn to classic blues and the Black Women's Club Movement or classic jazz and the New Negro Movement, or classic rhythm & blues and the Civil Rights Movement or classic soul and the Black Power Movement, in each instance black youth in the era under consideration "not only note[d] the political nature of black popular culture, but also . . . earnestly attempt[ed] to use the politics and social visions embedded in black popular culture in the interest of political activism and social organization." In its own off-kilter and frequently crude way, rap music and the Hip Hop Movement are a part of and continuing this tradition.

4. For examples of work by sociologists, musicologists, and cultural critics who argue that popular culture and popular music, generally speaking, can and have historically influenced the way we view ourselves and the world, see Garofalo (1992), Guins and Cruz (2005), Heble and Fischlin (2003), Peddie (2006), Randall (2005), Roy (2010), Storey (2009), Street (1986, 1997, 2012), and Tasker and Negra (2007).

5. Spence's oft-quoted reference to rap being "Black America's CNN" is drawn from Chuck D's *Fight the Power: Rap, Race, and Reality* (1997), where he wrote: "When Public Enemy first came out we used to say, 'Public Enemy, we're agents for the preservation of the black mind. We're media hijackers.' We worked to hijack the media and put it in our own form. That's originally how we came out. Initially rap was America's informal CNN because when rap records came out somebody from far away could listen to a rap record because it uses so many descriptive words and get a visual picture from what was being said. . . . That's why I call rap the Black CNN. Rap is now a worldwide phenomenon. Rap is the CNN for young people all over the world because now you can hear from rappers in Croatia and find out what they talk about and how they're feeling. Rappers in Italy, rappers from Africa. Rap has become an unofficial network of the young mentality. It just has to be directed a lot better than it has" (256).

6. For further discussion of Rosa Parks's life and political legacy, and for the most noteworthy works that informed my interpretation here, see Brinkley (2000), Hanson (2011), and Parks (1992, 1994).

7. For further discussion of rap music as a contemporary variant of "playing the dozens" and "signifying," see Benjamin (2007), Bynoe (2006), Childs (1998), Costello and Wallace (1997), Kulkarni (2004), and Wald (2012).

8. For further discussion of African *griots*, and for the most noteworthy works that informed my interpretation here, see Hale (1998), Hoffman (2000), Jansen (2000), Jegede (1994), J.W. Johnson (1979), Leymarie (1978), and Tang (2007).

9. For further discussion of Antonio Gramsci's life and legacy, especially his conception of the "organic intellectual," and for the works which influenced my interpretation here, see Adamson (1980), Boggs (1976), Fiori (1990), Germino (1990), Gramsci (1977, 1978, 1985, 1995, 2000), Holub (1992), and S.J. Jones (2006).

10. My interpretation of the new social movement model has been influenced by Goodwin and Jasper (2003), Laraña, Johnston, and Gusfield (1994), Marable and Mullings (2009), Morris and Mueller (1992), Porta and Diani (2006), A. Scott (1990), and Snow, Soule, and Kriesi (2004).

11. For examples of the scholarship that influenced my interpretation of the defining characteristics of new social movements, see Dalton and Kuechler (1990), Goodwin and Jasper (2003), Haynes (1997), C.A. Kelly (2001), Laraña, Johnston, and Gusfield (1994), S.H. Lee (2007), McAdam, McCarthy, and Zald (1996), Meyer and Tarrow (1998), Petras (2003), Snow, Soule, and Kriesi (2004), and Sutton (2000).

12. For further discussion of the political nature of popular art, popular music, and popular culture more generally, and for the most noteworthy works that informed my interpretation here, see Combs (1984), Garoian and Gaudelius (2008), Jenkins, McPherson, and Shattuc (2002), Peddie (2006), Randall (2005), Savage and Nimmo (1990), Street (1986, 1997, 2012), Tasker and Negra (2007), Wagnleitner and May (2000), and J.A. Walker (2001).

13. Many may understandably assume that even the great "Negro spirituals" have always been the celebrated and much-sought-after songs that they are today. However, nothing could

be further from the truth. As W.E.B. Du Bois famously and revealingly wrote in *The Souls of Black Folk* (1903):

> Little of beauty has America given the world save the rude grandeur God himself stamped on her bosom; the human spirit in this new world has expressed itself in vigor and ingenuity rather than in beauty. And so by fateful chance the Negro folk-song—the rhythmic cry of the slave—stands to-day not simply as the sole American music, but as the most beautiful expression of human experience born this side the seas. It has been neglected, it has been, and is, half despised, and above all it has been persistently mistaken and misunderstood; but notwithstanding, it still remains as the singular spiritual heritage of the nation and the greatest gift of the Negro people. (251)

Emphasis should be placed on Du Bois's comment that even as late as 1903 African American music—"the Negro folk-song—the rhythmic cry of the slave"—had been shunned by both blacks and whites. For many—especially upper-class and middle-class—blacks it served as an aural embarrassment because it was so closely associated with enslavement. For many whites it sounded like nothing more than "musical primitivism" or, rather, sonic frenetic foolishness. Ultimately, for these reasons, and many more too numerous to mention here, early African American music, including the much revered spirituals and gospel music, was "neglected," it was "half despised, and above all," similar to rap music, it was "persistently mistaken and misunderstood." For further discussion of the origins and evolution of the spirituals, and for the critical research that influenced my analysis here, see Abbington (2001), Cruz (1999), Darden (2004), Epstein (2003), A.C. Jones (1993), Lovell (1972), Mapson (1984), McGregory (2010), J.M. Spencer (1990, 1995), W.T. Walker (1979), and G.S. Warren (1999). Special mention must be made of the critically-acclaimed documentaries on the spirituals and gospel music that indelibly influenced my interpretation here. Along with the scholarly books on the spirituals and gospel music, I would implore my readers to view George Nierenberg's *Say Amen, Somebody!: A History of Gospel Music* (1982), Andrew Dunne and James Marsh's *The Story of Gospel Music* (2004), and Larry Bograd and Coleen Hubbard's *I Can Tell the World: The Spirituals Project* (2010).

14. For further discussion of the (inter)connections between African American music and African American movements (including rap music and the Hip Hop Movement), and for the most noteworthy works that informed my analysis here, see Baraka (1963), Gilroy (1993), Goodman (2009), Guttentag and Sturman (2010), Merlis and Seay (1997), Moten (2003), M.A. Neal (1998, 2002, 2003), Phinney (2005), Ripani (2006), A. Shaw (1986), Spence (2011), Ward (1998), and Werner (2004, 2006).

15. For further discussion of the ways in which rap, neo-soul, and other forms of hip hop music serve as the central soundtracks for the myriad contemporary African American (*and multicultural American*) youth movements (i.e., the overarching Hip Hop Movement between 1980 and the present), and for the most noteworthy works that informed my analysis here, see P. Butler (2009), Bynoe (2004), Goff (2008), C.S. Harris (2004), Hess (2007a, 2007b, 2010), Hill (2009), Keyes (2002), Kowalewski (1993), Krims (2000), Ogbar (2007), I. Perry (2004), T. Rose (1994), Spence (2011), and Watkins (2005).

16. For further discussion of the connections between classic rhythm & blues and rock & roll women and contemporary female rappers, neo-soul divas, b-girls and video vixens, see "remix" 3 in the present volume, as well as Cheney (2005), Harris-Perry (2011), Hayes (2010), Hayes and Williams (2007), S. Lee (2010), I. Perry (2004), Pough (2004), Sharpley-Whiting (2007), and *Vibe Magazine* (2001).

17. For further discussion of the connections between classic rhythm & blues and rock & roll men and contemporary rappers, neo-soul Romeos, b-boys and hip hop "hoodlums," see "remixes" 1 and 2 in the present volume.

18. For further discussion of the ways in which black popular music prior to rap and neo-soul was denigrated, demonized, and frequently referred to as "nigger noise," see Baraka (1963), Floyd (1995), Kempton (2003), Lauterbach (2011), Lhamon (1998), E. Lott (1993),

K.H. Miller (2010), Ogren (1989), Oliver (2006), Peretti (1992), Phinney (2005), and Ramsey (2003).

19. For further discussion of the ways in which rap music registers African Americans' ambitions in, and frustrations with post-Civil Rights Movement, post-Black Power Movement, post-Women's Liberation Movement, postfeminist and, indeed, postmodern America, and for the most noteworthy works that informed my analysis here, see Alridge, Stewart, and Franklin (2010), Boyd (1997, 2002), P. Butler (2009), Bynoe (2004), Cheney (2005), Clay (2012), P.H. Collins (2006), Keyes (2002), Kitwana (2002, 2005), Ogbar (2007), Reeves (2008), T. Rose (2008), Stover (2009), D. Sullivan (2011), and Watkins (1998, 2001, 2005).

20. For more detailed discussions of the racial, social, political, economic, and cultural climate during rap music and hip hop culture's formative years between 1975 and 2000, and for the most noteworthy works that informed my analysis here, see M. Alexander (2010), Bonilla-Silva (2001, 2003), Bonilla-Silva and Doane (2003), Bulmer and Solomos (2004), Essed and Goldberg (2001), Goldberg (1990, 1993, 1994, 1997, 2001, 2008), Goldberg and Solomos (2002), Massey and Denton (1993), Oliver and Shapiro (1995), Omi and Winant (1994), and Winant (1994, 2001, 2004). Moreover, here I specifically have in mind what renowned black feminist sociologist Patricia Hill Collins (1998, 2000, 2005, 2006) dubbed the "new racism" that emerged at the turn of the twenty-first century.

21. With regard to my contention that the Hip Hop Movement actually registers as both an African American movement *and* an unprecedented *multicultural, multiracial, multinational, multilingual, and multireligious multi-issue movement,* my interpretation here is based on a number of scholarly works in "global hip hop studies," or, rather, "international hip hop studies," including Alim, Ibrahim, and Pennycook (2009), Basu and Lemelle (2006), Fernandes (2011), Forman and Neal (2012), A.K. Harrison (2009), Higgins (2009), Kato (2007), Mitchell (2001), Neate (2004), Osumare (2007), Spady, Alim, and Meghelli (2006), Terkourafi (2010), and Toop (1991, 2000). Moreover, I have consulted more geographically and culturally specific scholarly research, for instance, in Native American/American Indian hip hop studies (Browner 2002, 2009; Hisama and Rapport 2005; Miles and Holland 2006; Sheffield 2011; Teves 2011); Chicano and Latino hip hop studies (G. Baker 2011; Dennis 2011; Fernandes 2006, 2011; Flores 2000; MacWeeney 2008; McFarland 2008; Pardue 2008, 2011; Pulido 2008; Rivera 2003; Rivera, Marshall, and Hernandez 2009); African and Caribbean hip hop studies (Charry 2012; C.J. Cooper 2004; Diouf and Nwankwo 2010; Henriques 2011; Hinds 2002; Ntarangwi 2009; Osumare 2007, 2012; Saucier 2011; Stolzoff 2000; Wanguhu 2007; Weiss 2009); Asian, South Asian, and Islamic hip hop studies (Condry 2006; Cooke and Lawrence 2005; Malik 2009; Nair and Balaji 2008; Neate 2004; Nieuwkerk 2011; Sharma 2010); and European hip hop studies (Durand 2002; Feiereisen and Hill 2011; Kaya 2001; Lapiower 1997; I. Maxwell 2003; Pacoda 2000; Toop 2000).

22. My interpretation of white suburban youths' relationship with rap music and hip hop culture has been informed by Armstrong (2004), Bucholtz (2011), Calhoun (2005), Cobb and Boettcher (2007), Cutler (2003), Diner (2006), Ford (2004), Fraley (2009), Harkness (2011), Hess (2005), Kitwana (2005), Rizzo and McCall (2005), J. Scott (2004), V. Stephens (2005), Tanz (2007), G. Taylor (2005), and Yousman (2003).

23. Among the myriad works my analysis of white hip hop fans' relationship with rap music and hip hop culture between 1980 and 2000 has drawn from here, Cutler (2003), Gan, Zillman, and Mitrook (1997), Hess (2005), Johnson, Trawalter, and Dovidio (2000), J. Scott (2004), Tanz (2007), and Yousman (2003) are especially noteworthy.

24. For further discussion of a lot of commercial and gangsta rap's roots in and, even if unconscious, undeniable relationship with blackface minstrelism, see my critique in *Hip Hop's Inheritance* (49–62).

25. For further discussion of my conception of *hip hop radical humanism,* see my more detailed treatments in *Hip Hop's Inheritance* (72–78) and *Hip Hop's Amnesia* (209–24).

26. For further discussion of the *ideological evolution* of the various forms of racism and capitalism—as well as sexism and heterosexism—that are in many ways specific to the Hip Hop Generation and turn-of-the-twenty-first-century America, and for the most noteworthy works that informed my analysis here, see Alexander (2010), Bonilla-Silva (2001, 2003), P.H. Collins (2005, 2006), Desmond and Emirbayer (2010) Gallagher (2008), D.T. Goldberg (1997,

2001, 2008), Marable (1983), Oliver and Shapiro (1995), Omi and Winant (1994), R.C. Smith (1995), and Winant (2004).

27. For further discussion of what has been termed "contemporary African American micro-politics," as well as the ways in which the Hip Hop Movement's new "micro-movement politics" fit within the wider world of "contemporary African American micro-politics," see Ali (2008), C.J. Cohen (2010), Gillespie (2010), Goff (2008), A.K. Harrison (2009), M.P. Jeffries (2011), C. Johnson (2007), Johnson and Stanford (2002), Junn and Haynie (2008), Laraña, Johnston, and Gusfield (1994), Ogbar (2007), R.C. Smith (1996), and Spence (2011).

28. By "benign neglect" here, I wish to invoke the insidious policy that was introduced by New York Senator Daniel Patrick Moynihan. Serving as an adviser on "urban affairs," in 1970 Moynihan sent a memorandum to President Richard Nixon suggesting that "the issue of race could benefit from a period of 'benign neglect.'" He went on to say: "The subject has been too much talked about" and "[w]e may need a period in which Negro progress continues and racial rhetoric fades." Obviously, the "benign neglect" policy was put forward to quell the ongoing racial conflicts and national crisis in the aftermath of the Civil Rights Movement. As the heightened militantism of the Black Power Movement surely showed, African Americans knew full well that civil rights legislation, especially the Civil Rights Act of 1964 and the Voting Rights Act of 1965, meant little or nothing until they were implemented and actually trickled down to working-class and poverty-stricken black folk. In light of the Watts Rebellion in 1965 and the allegedly "widespread arson" in the South Bronx and Harlem in the late 1960s and early 1970s, Moynihan argued that firemen should not have to risk their lives in a "futile war" fighting fires in inner-city neighborhoods. In so many words, he suggested that urban arson was one of the many social pathologies caused by the heated "racial rhetoric" of Black Power militants. Senator Moynihan ultimately believed that his "benign neglect" policy would not only curb the heated "racial rhetoric," but also cure the overcrowding of the ghettos by forcing poor people to flee as a result of arson or the ever-looming threat of arson at the time. For further discussion of the Moynihanian and Nixonian policy of "benign neglect," see Bartol (1992), Eichengreen (2000), Entman and Rojecki (2000), L. Harris (1973), Upchurch (2008), and Wills (1970).

29. For further discussion of rap as poetry and the poetics of hip hop, and for the most noteworthy works that informed my analysis here, see Adler (1991), Bradley and DuBois (2010), Buckholtz (2011), Dorsey (2000), Hart (2012), Parmar (2005), Pate (2010), I. Perry (2004), Sitomer and Cirelli (2004), L.A. Stanley (1992), and T.L. Stanley (2009).

30. For further discussion of the ways in which African Americans continue to be enslaved and shackled and chained by antiblack racism, poverty, poor housing, horrid health care, unabated unemployment, ongoing substandard education, overrepresentation in the armed services, and penal escalation, and for the most noteworthy works that informed my analysis here, see M. Alexander (2010), Blackmon (2008), Massey and Denton (1993), Oliver and Shapiro (1995), T.M. Shapiro (2004), and W.J. Wilson (1987, 1997, 1999, 2009).

Bibliography

NOTE ON THE BIBLIOGRAPHY

The simultaneously musicological and sociological, interdisciplinary and intersectional nature of this book necessitated idiosyncratic authorial and bibliographic decisions—decisions that will not make any self-respecting environmentalist shudder. My personal commitment to our fragile ecology and the economic realities of making this volume affordable demanded economy of expression and citation wherever possible. As a consequence, I have eliminated citations that are obvious. For example, popular music and popular film citations in most instances have been omitted. Musicologists and film studies scholars are likely to cringe, but I suspect nonacademic intellectuals, artists, and activists will greatly appreciate a more affordable and eco-friendly volume.

Abbington, James. (Ed.). (2001). *Readings in African American Church Music and Worship.* Chicago, IL: GIA Publications, Inc.

Abbott, Kingsley. (Ed.). (2000). *Calling Out Around the World: A Motown Reader.* London: Helter Skelter.

Abbott, Lynn. (1992). "'Play That Barber Shop Chord': A Case for the African American Origin of Barbershop Harmony." *American Music* 10 (3), 289–25.

Abbott, Lynn, and Seroff, Doug. (2002). *Out of Sight: The Rise of African American Popular Music, 1889–1895.* Jackson: University Press of Mississippi.

Abromeit, John. (2011). *Max Horkheimer and the Foundations of the Frankfurt School.* Cambridge: Cambridge University Press.

Acker, Kerry. (2004). *Nina Simone.* Philadelphia: Chelsea House Publishers.

Adams, Terri, and Fuller, Douglas. (2006). "The Words Have Changed but the Ideology Remains the Same: Misogynistic Lyrics in Rap Music." *Journal of Black Studies* 36 (6), 938–57.

Adamson, Walter L. (1980). *Hegemony and Revolution: A Study of Antonio Gramsci's Political and Cultural Theory.* Berkeley: University of California Press.

Adler, Bill. (1987). *Tougher than Leather: The Authorized Biography of Run-DMC.* New York: New American Library.

———. (1991). *Rap: Portraits and Lyrics of a Generation of Black Rockers.* New York: St. Martin's Press.

———. (2002). *Tougher than Leather: The Rise of Run-DMC.* Los Angeles, CA: Consafos.

Adler, Bill, and Charnas, Dan. (2011). *Def Jam Recordings: The First 25 Years of the Last Great Record Label.* New York: Rizzoli.

Adorno, Theodor W. (1991). *The Culture Industry: Selected Essays on Mass Culture.* (Jay M. Bernstein, Ed.). New York: Routledge.

———. (1994). *Adorno: The Stars Down to Earth and Other Essays on the Irrational in Culture* (Stephen Crook, Ed.). New York: Routledge.

———. (1997). *Aesthetic Theory.* Minneapolis: University of Minnesota Press.

———. (2000). *The Adorno Reader* (Brian O'Connor, Ed.). Malden, MA: Blackwell.

Agawu, V. Kofi. (2003). *Representing African Music: Postcolonial Notes, Queries, Positions.* New York: Routledge.

Aldridge, Daniel W. (2011). *Becoming American: The African American Quest for Civil Rights, 1861–1976.* Wheeling, IL: Harlan Davidson.

Aldridge, Delores P., and James, E. Lincoln. (Eds.). (2007). *Africana Studies: Philosophical Perspectives and Theoretical Paradigms.* Pullman, WA: Washington State University Press.

Aldridge, Delores, and Young, Carlene. (Eds.). (2000). *Out of the Revolution: An Africana Studies Anthology.* Lanham, MD: Lexington Books.

Alexander, Michelle. (2010). *The New Jim Crow: Mass Incarceration in the Age of Color-Blindness.* New York: New Press.

Alford, Lucy. (Ed.). (1984). *Break-Dancing.* London: Hamlyn.

Ali, Omar H. (2008). *In the Balance of Power: Independent Black Politics and Third-Party Movements in the United States.* Athens: Ohio University Press.

Alim, H. Samy, Ibrahim, Awad, and Pennycook, Alastair. (Eds.). (2009). *Global Linguistic Flows: Hip Hop Cultures, Youth Identities, and the Politics of Language.* New York: Routledge.

Alkebulan, Paul. (2007). *Survival Pending Revolution: The History of the Black Panther Party.* Tuscaloosa: University of Alabama Press.

Allen, Ernest, Jr. (1996). "Making the Strong Survive: The Contours and Contradictions of Message Rap." In William E. Perkins (Ed.), *Droppin' Science: Critical Essays on Rap Music and Hip Hop Culture* (159–91). Philadelphia: Temple University Press.

Alridge, Derrick P. (2005). "From Civil Rights to Hip Hop: Toward a Nexus of Ideas." *Journal of African American History* 90 (3), 226–52.

Alridge, Derrick P., Stewart, James B., and Franklin, V.P. (Eds.). (2010). *Message in the Music: Hip Hop, History, and Pedagogy.* Washington, DC: Association for the Study of African American Life and History/ASALH Press.

Altschuler, Glenn C. (2003). *All Shook Up: How Rock & Roll Changed America.* New York: Oxford University Press.

Anderson, Adrienne. (2003). *Word!: Rap, Politics and Feminism.* Lincoln: Writers Club Press.

Anderson, Elijah. (1981). *Place on the Corner.* Chicago: University of Chicago Press.

———. (1990). *Streetwise: Race, Class, and Change in an Urban Community.* Chicago: University of Chicago Press.

———. (1999). *Code of the Street: Decency, Violence, and the Moral Life of the Inner-City.* New York: Norton.

———. (Ed.). (2008). *Against the Wall: Poor, Young, Black, and Male.* Philadelphia: University of Pennsylvania Press.

Anderson, Jervis. (1973). *A. Philip Randolph: A Biographical Portrait.* New York: Harcourt Brace Jovanovich.

Anderson, Lisa M. (1997). *Mammies No More: The Changing Image of Black Women on Stage and Screen.* Lanham, MD: Rowman & Littlefield.

Anderson, Talmadge, and Stewart, James B. (2007). *Introduction to African American Studies: Transdisciplinary Approaches and Implications.* Baltimore, MD: Black Classic Press.

Anderson, Terry H. (2004). *The Pursuit of Fairness: A History of Affirmative Action.* New York: Oxford University Press.

Andrews, William L., and Gates, Henry Louis. (Eds.). (1999). *The Civitas Anthology of African American Slave Narratives.* Washington, DC: Civitas/Counterpoint.

———. (Eds.). (2000). *Slave Narratives.* New York: Library of America.

Andriote, John-Manuel. (2001). *Hot Stuff: A Brief History of Disco.* New York: HarperEntertainment.

Appell, Glenn, and Hemphill, David. (2006). *American Popular Music: A Multicultural History.* Belmont, CA: Thomson Wadsworth.

Aquila, Richard. (2000). *That Old-Time Rock & Roll: A Chronicle of an Era, 1954–1963.* Urbana: University of Illinois Press.

Armstrong, Edward G. (2004). "Eminem's Construction of Authenticity." *Popular Music and Society* 27 (3), 335–55.

Arnesen, Eric. (2002). *Black Protest and the Great Migration: A Brief History with Documents.* Bedford: St. Martin's Press.

Arthur, Paul. (2005). *Line of Sight: American Avant-Garde Film since 1965.* Minneapolis: University of Minnesota Press.

Asante, Molefi K., and Karenga, Maulana. (Eds.). (2006). *The Handbook of Black Studies.* Thousand Oaks, CA: Sage.

Asante, Molefi Kete, and Mazama, Ama. (Eds.). (2005). *Encyclopedia of Black Studies.* Thousand Oaks, CA: Sage.

Askin, Allan Bradley. (1970). "An Economic Analysis of Black Migration." Ph.D. dissertation, Massachusetts Institute of Technology, Cambridge, MA.

Atwater, Deborah F. (2010). *The Rhetoric of Black Mayors: In Their Own Words.* Lanham: University Press of America.

Austin, Curtis J. (2006). *Up Against the Wall: Violence in the Making and Unmaking of the Black Panther Party.* Fayetteville: University of Arkansas Press.

Austin, Joe. (2001). *Taking the Train: How Graffiti Art Became an Urban Crisis in New York City.* New York: Columbia University Press.

Averill, Gage. (2010). *Four Parts, No Waiting: A Social History of American Barbershop Harmony.* New York: Oxford University Press.

Awkward, Michael. (2007). *Soul Covers: Rhythm & Blues Remakes and the Struggle for Artistic Identity (Aretha Franklin, Al Green, Phoebe Snow).* Durham: Duke University Press.

Azevedo, Mario. (Ed.). (2005). *Africana Studies: A Survey of Africa and the African Diaspora.* Durham, NC: Carolina Academic Press.

Babb, Tracie. (2002). *The Treatment of Women in the Hip Hop Community: Past, Present, and Future.* New York: Fordham University Press.

Back, Les. (2000). "Voices of Hate, Sounds of Hybridity: Black Music and the Complexities of Racism." *Black Music Research Journal* 20 (2), 127–49.

Bailey, Beth, and Farber, David. (1993). "The 'Double-V' Campaign in World War II Hawaii: African Americans, Racial Ideology, and Federal Power." *Journal of Social History* 26 (4), 817–43.

Bailey, Diane. (2009). *Mary J. Blige.* New York: Rosen.

Baker, Geoffrey. (2011). *Buena Vista in the Club: Rap, Reggaeton, and Revolution in Havana.* Durham: Duke University Press.

Baker, Houston A., Jr. (1980). *The Journey Back: Issues in Black Literature and Criticism.* Chicago: University of Chicago.

———. (1988). *Afro-American Poetics: Revisions of Harlem and the Black Aesthetic.* Madison: University of Wisconsin.

———. (1993). *Black Studies, Rap, and the Academy.* Chicago: University of Chicago Press.

Baldwin, Davarian L. (2007). *Chicago's New Negroes: Modernity, the Great Migration & Black Urban Life.* Chapel Hill: University of North Carolina Press.

Ball, Jared A. (2005). "The Mixtape: A Case Study in Emancipatory Journalism." Ph.D. dissertation, University of Maryland, College Park, MD.

———. (2009). "FreeMix Radio: The Original Mixtape Radio Show." *Journal of Black Studies* 39 (4), 614–34.

———. (2011). *I Mix What I Like!: A Mixtape Manifesto.* New York: AK Press.

Balton, Chris. (Director). (1991). *Sisters in the Name of Rap*. Los Angeles, CA: PolyGram Video.

Banfield, William C. (2010). *Cultural Codes: Makings of a Black Music Philosophy—An Interpretive History from Spirituals to Hip Hop*. Lanham, MD: Scarecrow Press.

———. (2011). *Representing Black Music Culture: Then, Now, and When Again?* Lanham, MD: Scarecrow Press.

Ba Nikongo, Nikongo. (Ed.). (1997). *Leading Issues in African American Studies*. Durham, NC: Carolina Academic Press.

Baptista, Todd R. (2000). *Group Harmony: Echoes of the Rhythm & Blues Era*. New Bedford, MA: TRB Enterprises.

Baraka, Amiri. (1963). *Blues People: Negro Music in White America*. New York: Morrow.

———. (1969). *Black Magic: Collected Poetry, 1961–1967*. Indianapolis: Bobbs-Merrill.

———. (1987). *The Music: Reflections on Jazz and Blues*. New York: Morrow.

———. (1994). *Conversations with Amiri Baraka* (Charlie Reilly, Ed.). Jackson: University Press of Mississippi.

———. (2009). *Digging: The African American Soul of American Classical Music*. Berkeley: University of California Press.

Barnard, Stephen. (2001). *Aretha Franklin*. London: Unanimous.

Bartol, Frank R. (1992). *A Season of Benign Neglects and Other Essays*. Munising, MI: Bayshore Press.

Bascom, William R. (1969). *The Yoruba of Southwestern Nigeria*. New York: Holt, Rinehart & Winston.

Basu, Dipannita. (1992). "Rap Music, Hip Hop Culture, and the Music Industry in Los Angeles." *The Center for Afro-American Studies Report* 15 (1 and 2), 20–25.

Basu, Dipannita, and Lemelle, Sidney J. (Eds.). (2006). *The Vinyl Ain't Final: Hip Hop and the Globalization of Black Popular Culture*. London: Pluto Press.

Batey, Angus. (1998). *Rhyming & Stealing: A History of the Beastie Boys*. London: Independent Music Press.

Batt-Rawden, Kari, and DeNora, Tia. (2005). "Music and Informal Learning in Everyday Life." *Music Education Research* 7 (3), 289–304.

Baughan, Brian. (2012). *The Story of Def Jam Records*. Philadelphia: Mason Crest.

Bayles, Martha. (1994). *Hole in Our Soul: The Loss of Beauty and Meaning in American Popular Music*. New York: Free Press.

Bebey, Francis. (1999). *African Music: A People's Art*. New York: Lawrence Hill Books.

Beckman, Janette, and Adler, Bill. (1991). *Rap: Portraits and Lyrics of a Generation of Black Rockers*. New York: St. Martin's Press.

Becton, Julius. (Ed.). (2008). *The Exclusion of Black Soldiers from the Medal of Honor in World War II: The Study Commissioned by the United States Army to Investigate Racial Bias in the Awarding of the Nation's Highest Military Decoration*. Jefferson, NC: McFarland & Co.

Bego, Mark. (1990). *Aretha Franklin: The Queen of Soul*. New York: St. Martin's Press.

Beier, Ulli. (1980). *Yoruba Myths*. Cambridge: Cambridge University Press.

Bell, Robert I. (2007). *The Myth of Rock & Roll: The Racial Politics of American Popular Music, 1945–2005*. Philadelphia, PA: Robell Publishing.

Bender, Wolfgang. (1991). *Sweet Mother: Modern African Music*. Chicago: University of Chicago Press.

Benhabib, Seyla, Bonss, Wolfgang, and McCole, John. (Eds.). (1993). *On Max Horkheimer: New Perspectives*. Cambridge, MA: MIT Press.

Benjamin, Bobby J. (2007). "'You can bat yo' eyes and stomp yo' feet': The History and Discourse of Signifying, Toastin', Rappin', and Playin' the Dozens." M.A. thesis, Northwestern State University of Louisiana, Natchitoches, LA.

Benjaminson, Peter. (1979). *The Story of Motown*. New York: Grove Press.

Bennett, Andy, Shank, Barry, and Toynbee, Jason. (Eds.). (2005). *The Popular Music Studies Reader*. New York: Routledge.

Berger, Melody. (Ed.). (2006). *We Don't Need Another Wave: Dispatches from the Next Generation of Feminists*. Emeryville, CA: Seal Press.

Berkeley, Kathleen C. (1999). *Women's Liberation in America.* Westport, CT: Greenwood Press.

Bernard, Regina A. (2009). *Black & Brown Waves: The Cultural Politics of Young Women of Color and Feminism.* Boston: Sense Publishers.

Bernard-Donals, Michael. (1994). "Jazz, Rock & Roll, Rap and Politics." *Journal of Popular Culture* 28 (2), 127–38.

Berry, Mary Frances. (1994). *Black Resistance, White Law: A History of Constitutional Racism in America.* New York: Penguin.

Bertrand, Michael T. (2000). *Race, Rock, and Elvis.* Urbana: University of Illinois Press.

Berzon, Judith R. (1978). *Neither White nor Black: The Mulatto Character in American Fiction.* New York: New York University Press.

Best, Steven. (1995). *The Politics of Historical Vision: Marx, Foucault, Habermas.* New York: Guilford.

Best, Steven, and Kellner, Douglas. (1991). *Postmodern Theory: Critical Interrogations.* New York: Guilford.

Biferie, Michelle J. (1993). "Gender, Race, Class and the Problem of Meaning: Black Female Rappers as a Site for Resistance." M.A. thesis, Florida Atlantic University, Boca Raton, FL.

Bischoff, David. (2012). *Young Sun Ra and the Strange Celestial Roads.* Chicago: Hotspur Publishing.

Blackett, Richard J. M. (1983). *Building an Anti-Slavery Wall: Black Americans in the Atlantic Abolitionist Movement, 1830–1860.* Baton Rouge: Louisiana State University Press.

Blackmon, Douglas A. (2008). *Slavery by Another Name: The Re-Enslavement of Black Americans from the Civil War to World War II.* New York: Doubleday.

Blackstock, Nelson. (1988). *COINTELPRO: The FBI's Secret War on Political Freedom.* New York: Pathfinder.

Blake, John. (2004). *Children of the Movement.* Chicago: Lawrence Hill Books.

Blocker, Jack S. (2008). *A Little More Freedom: African Americans Enter the Urban Midwest, 1860–1930.* Columbus: Ohio State University Press.

Bloom, Joshua, and Martin, Waldo E. (2013). *Black Against Empire: The History and Politics of the Black Panther Party.* Berkeley: University of California Press.

Bobo, Jacqueline, Hudley, Cynthia, and Michel, Claudine. (Eds.). (2004). *The Black Studies Reader.* New York: Routledge.

Bobo, Jacqueline, and Michel, Claudine. (Eds.). (2000). *Black Studies: Current Issues, Enduring Questions.* Dubuque, IA: Kendall/Hunt.

Bodunde, Charles. (2001). *Oral Traditions and Aesthetic Transfer: Creativity and Social Vision in Contemporary Black Poetry.* Bayreuth, Germany: Bayreuth University.

Bogdanov, Vladimir, Woodstra, Chris, and Erlewine, Stephen T. (Eds.). (2002). *All Music Guide to Jazz: The Definitive Guide to Jazz Music.* San Francisco, CA: Backbeat Books.

———. (Eds.). (2003a). *All Music Guide to Blues: The Definitive Guide to Blues.* San Francisco, CA: Backbeat Books.

———. (Eds.). (2003b). *All Music Guide to Soul: The Definitive Guide to R&B and Soul.* San Francisco, CA: Backbeat Books.

Bogdanov, Vladimir, Woodstra, Chris, Erlewine, Stephen T., and Bush, John. (Eds.). (2003). *All Music Guide to Hip Hop: The Definitive Guide to Rap & Hip Hop.* San Francisco, CA: Backbeat Books.

Boggs, Carl. (1976). *Gramsci's Marxism.* London: Pluto Press.

Bograd, Larry, and Hubbard, Coleen. (Directors). (2010). *I Can Tell the World: The Spirituals Project.* Los Angeles, CA: Vanguard.

Bolden, Tony. (2008). *The Funk Era and Beyond: New Perspectives of Black Popular Culture.* New York: Palgrave Macmillan.

Bond, Julian, and Wilson, Sondra K. (Eds.). (2000). *Lift Every Voice and Sing: A Celebration of the Negro National Anthem.* New York: Random House.

Bonilla-Silva, Eduardo. (2001). *White Supremacy and Racism in the Post-Civil Rights Era.* Boulder, CO: Lynne Rienner.

———. (2003). *Racism Without Racists: Color-Blind Racism and the Persistence of Racial Inequality in the United States.* Lanham, MD: Rowman & Littlefield.

Bonilla-Silva, Eduardo, and Doane, Ashley. (Eds.). (2003). *White Out: The Continuing Significance of Racism*. New York: Routledge.

Borgmeyer, John, and Lang, Holly. (2007). *Dr. Dre: A Biography*. Westport, CT: Greenwood Press.

Bost, Suzanne. (2001). "'Be deceived if ya wanna be foolish': (Re)constructing Body, Genre, and Gender in Feminist Rap." *Postmodern Culture* 12 (1). http://pmc.iath.virginia.edu/issue.901/12.1bost.html.

———. (2003). *Mulattas and Mestizas: Representing Mixed Identities in the Americas, 1850–2000*. Athens: University of Georgia Press.

Bothmer, Bernard von. (2010). *Framing the Sixties: The Use and Abuse of a Decade from Ronald Reagan to George W. Bush*. Amherst: University of Massachusetts Press.

Bottomore, Tom. (1984). *The Frankfurt School*. New York: Tavistock.

———. (2002). *The Frankfurt School and Its Critics*. New York: Routledge.

Bowman, Robert M.J. (1997). *Soulsville, U.S.A.: The Story of Stax Records*. New York: Schirmer Books.

Bowser, Benjamin P. (2012). *Gangster Rap and Its Social Cost: Exploiting Hip Hop and Using Racial Stereotypes to Entertain America*. Amherst, NY: Cambria Press.

Boyd, Todd. (1997). *Am I Black Enough for You?: Popular Culture from the 'Hood and Beyond*. Indianapolis: Indiana University Press.

———. (2002). *The New H.N.I.C.: The Death of Civil Rights and the Reign of Hip Hop*. New York: New York University Press.

———. (2003). *Young, Black, Rich, and Famous: The Rise of the NBA, the Hip Hop Invasion and the Transformation of American Culture*. New York: Doubleday.

Braceland, Francis. (1956). "Rock & Roll Called a Communicable Disease." *New York Times* (March 28), 8.

Bracey, Earnest N. (2003). *On Racism: Essays on Black Popular Culture, African American Politics, and the New Black Aesthetics*. Lanham, MD: University Press of America.

Brackett, David. (Ed.). (2005). *The Pop, Rock, and Soul Reader: Histories and Debates*. New York: Oxford University Press.

Brackett, Nathan, and Hoard, Christian David (2004). *The New Rolling Stone Album Guide: Completely Revised and Updated 4th Edition*. New York: Simon & Schuster.

Bradley, Adam. (2009). *Book of Rhymes: The Poetics of Hip Hop*. New York: Basic/Civitas.

Bradley, Adam, and DuBois, Andrew. (Eds.). (2010). *The Anthology of Rap*. New Haven: Yale University Press.

Bradley, Lloyd. (2006). *George Clinton: The Authorized Biography of George Clinton*. Edinburgh: Canongate.

Brahinsky, Rachel. (2008). "5 Questions with Michael Franti." *Performing Songwriter* 16 (112), 54.

Bramwell, David, and Green, Jairus. (2003). *Breakdance: Hip Hop Handbook*. New York: Street Style Publications.

Branch, Taylor. (1988). *Parting the Waters: America in the King Years, 1954–63*. New York: Simon & Schuster.

———. (1998). *Pillar of Fire: America in the King Years, 1963–65*. New York: Simon & Schuster.

———. (2006). *At Canaan's Edge: America in the King Years, 1965–68*. New York: Simon & Schuster.

Brandt, Nat. (1996). *Harlem at War: The Black Experience in WWII*. Syracuse: Syracuse University Press.

Breines, Winifred. (2006). *Trouble Between Us: An Uneasy History of White and Black Women in the Feminist Movement*. New York: Oxford University Press.

Brennan, Tim. (1994). "Off the Gangsta Tip: A Rap Appreciation, or Forgetting about Los Angeles." *Critical Inquiry* 20 (4), 663–93.

Brinkley, Douglas. (2000). *Rosa Parks: A Life*. New York: Viking.

Brooks, Daphne A. (2007). "'All That You Can't Leave Behind': Black Female Soul Singing and the Politics of Surrogation in the Age of Catastrophe." *Meridians: Feminism, Race, Transnationalism* 8 (1), 180–204.

Brooks, TaKeshia. (2007). *Dream Factory Deferred: Black Womanhood, History and Music Video.* Bloomington, IN: iUniverse.

Broude, Norma, and Garrard, Mary D. (Eds.). (1994). *The Power of Feminist Art: The American Movement of the 1970s, History and Impact.* New York: H.N. Abrams.

———. (Eds.). (2005). *Reclaiming Female Agency: Feminist Art History After Postmodernism.* Berkeley: University of California Press.

Broven, John. (1974). *Walking to New Orleans: The Story of New Orleans Rhythm & Blues.* Bexhill-on-Sea, East Sussex, UK: Blues Unlimited.

———. (1978). *Rhythm and Blues in New Orleans.* Gretna, LA: Pelican.

———. (2009). *Record Makers and Breakers: Voices of the Independent Rock & Roll Pioneers.* Urbana: University of Illinois Press.

Brown, Courtney. (2008). *Politics in Music: Music and Political Transformation from Beethoven to Hip Hop.* Atlanta, GA: Farsight Press.

Brown, Geoff. (2008). *The Life of James Brown: A Biography.* London: Omnibus.

Brown, Jake. (2002). *Suge Knight: The Rise, Fall, and Rise of Death Row Records —The Story Marion "Suge" Knight.* Phoenix, AZ: Colossus Books.

———. (2006). *Dr. Dre in the Studio: From Compton, Death Row, Snoop Dogg, Eminem, 50 Cent, the Game, and Mad Money: The Life, Times, and Aftermath of the Notorious Record Producer, Dr. Dre.* Phoenix, AZ: Colossus.

———. (2009). *Rick Rubin: In the Studio.* Toronto: ECW Press.

Brown, James. (1986). *James Brown: The Godfather of Soul* (with Bruce Tucker). New York : Macmillan.

———. (2005). *I Feel Good: A Memoir of a Life of Soul* (with Marc Eliot). New York: New American Library.

Brown, Matthew P. (1994). "Funk Music as Genre: Black Aesthetic, Apocalyptic Thinking and Urban Protest in Post-1965 African American Pop." *Cultural Studies* 8 (3), 484–508.

Brown, Ruth Nicole. (2008). *Black Girlhood Celebration: Toward a Hip Hop Feminist Pedagogy.* New York: Peter Lang Publishing.

Brown, Ruth Nicole, and Kwakye, Chamara Jewel. (Eds.). (2013). *Wish to Live: The Hip Hop Feminism Pedagogy Reader.* New York: Peter Lang.

Brown, Terrell. (2007). *Reverend Run.* Broomall, PA: Mason Crest.

———. (2008). *Mary J. Blige.* Broomall, PA: Mason Crest.

Browner, Tara. (2002). *Heartbeat of the People: Music and Dance of the Northern Pow-Wow.* Urbana: University of Illinois Press.

———. (Ed.). (2009). *Music of the First Nations: Tradition and Innovation in Native North America.* Urbana: University of Illinois Press.

Brownlee, W. Elliot, and Graham, Hugh Davis. (Eds.). (2003). *The Reagan Presidency: Pragmatic Conservatism and Its Legacies.* Lawrence: University Press of Kansas.

Brun-Lambert, David. (2009). *Nina Simone: The Biography.* London: Aurum.

Bucholtz, Mary. (2011). *White Kids: Language, Race and Styles of Youth Identity.* Cambridge: Cambridge University Press.

Bullard, Sara. (1993). *Free at Last: A History of the Civil Rights Movement and Those Who Died in the Struggle.* New York: Oxford University Press.

Bulmer, Martin, and Solomos, John. (Eds.). (2004). *Researching Race and Racism.* New York: Routledge.

Bunch, William. (2009). *Tear Down this Myth: How the Reagan Legacy Has Distorted Our Politics and Haunts Our Future.* New York: Free Press.

Burack, Cynthia, and Josephson, Jyl J. (Eds.). (2003). *Fundamental Differences: Feminists Talk Back to Social Conservatives.* Lanham, MD: Rowman & Littlefield.

Burnim, Mellonee V., and Maultsby, Portia K. (Eds.). (2006). *African American Music: An Introduction.* New York: Routledge.

———. (Eds.). (2012). *African American Music: An Introduction* (2nd ed.). New York: Routledge.

Burns, Peter. (2003). *Curtis Mayfield: People Never Give Up.* London: Sanctuary.

Buszek, Maria Elena. (2006). *Pin-Up Grrrls: Feminism, Sexuality, Popular Culture.* Durham: Duke University Press.

Butler, Octavia E. (1976). *Patternmaster.* Garden City, NY: Doubleday.
———. (1977). *Mind of My Mind.* Garden City, NY: Doubleday.
———. (1978). *Survivor.* Garden City, NY: Doubleday.
———. (1979). *Kindred.* Garden City, NY: Doubleday.
———. (1980). *Wild Seed.* Garden City, NY: Doubleday.
———. (1984). *Clay's Ark.* New York: St. Martin's Press.
———. (2010). *Conversations with Octavia Butler* (Conseula Francis, Ed.). Jackson: University Press of Mississippi.
Butler, Paul. (2009). *Let's Get Free!: A Hip Hop Theory of Justice.* New York: New Press.
Bynoe, Yvonne. (2004). *Stand and Deliver: Political Activism, Leadership, and Hip Hop Culture.* Brooklyn, NY: Soft Skull Press.
———. (Ed.). (2006). *Encyclopedia of Rap and Hip Hop Culture.* Westport, CT: Greenwood Press.
Bynum, Cornelius L. (2010). *A. Philip Randolph and the Struggle for Civil Rights.* Urbana: University of Illinois Press.
Cahn, Steven M. (Ed.). (1995). *The Affirmative Action Debate.* New York: Routledge.
Calhoun, Lindsay R. (2005). "'Will the Real Slim Shady Please Stand Up?': Masking Whiteness, Encoding Hegemonic Masculinity in Eminem's Marshall Mathers LP." *Howard Journal of Communication* 16 (4), 267–94.
Campbell, Chris. (2009). *The Essential Neo-Soul.* Fairway, KS: Metro Jazz Media & Progressive Underground Publications.
Campbell, Gregory A. (2006). "A Beautiful, Shining Sound Object: Contextualizing Multi-instrumentalism in the Association for the Advancement of Creative Musicians." D.M.A. dissertation, University of Washington, Seattle, WA.
Campbell, Michael. (2007). *Rock & Roll: An Introduction* (with James Brody). New York: Schirmer.
Canton, David A. (2006). "The Political, Economic, Social, and Cultural Tensions in Gangsta Rap." *Reviews in American History* 34 (2), 244–57.
Caponi-Tabery, Gena. (1999). "Jump for Joy: The Jump Trope in African America, 1937–1941." *Prospects* 24, 521–74.
———. (2008). *Jump for Joy: Jazz, Basketball, and Black Culture in 1930s America.* Amherst: University of Massachusetts Press.
Carasik, Diane Sue. (1972). "Motown Record Corporation and the Revival of Rhythm and Blues Music." M.A. thesis, Boston University, Boston, MA.
Carawan, Guy, and Carawan, Candie. (Eds.). (2007). *Sing for Freedom: The Story of the Civil Rights Movement through its Songs.* Montgomery, AL: New South Books.
Carmichael, Stokely. (2003). *Ready for Revolution!: The Life and Struggles of Stokely Carmichael (Kwame Ture)* (with Ekwueme Michael Thelwell). New York: Scribner.
———. (2007). *Stokely Speaks: From Black Power to Pan-Africanism.* Chicago, IL: Lawrence Hill Books.
Carmichael, Stokely, and Hamilton, Charles V. (1967). *Black Power: The Politics of Liberation in America.* New York: Vintage Books.
Carroll, John. (1956). "Rock & Roll Inflames and Excites the Youth." *Variety* (April 23), 32.
Carson, Clayborne, Garrow, David J., Gill, Gerald, Harding, Vincent, and Hine, Darlene Clark. (Eds.). (1997). *The Eyes on the Prize Civil Rights Reader.* New York: Penguin.
Carter, David C. (2009). *The Music Has Gone Out of the Movement: Civil Rights and the Johnson Administration, 1965–1968.* Chapel Hill: University of North Carolina Press.
Castleman, Craig. (1982). *Getting Up: Subway in New York.* Cambridge: Massachusetts Institute of Technology Press.
Castleman, Harry, and Podrazik, Walter J. (2003). *Watching TV: Six Decades of American Television.* Syracuse: Syracuse University Press.
Celious, Aaron Kabir. (2002). "Blaxploitation Blues: How Black Women Identify with and are Empowered by Female Performers of Hip Hop Music." Ph.D. dissertation, University of Michigan, Ann Arbor, MI.
Cepeda, Raquel. (Ed.). (2004). *And It Don't Stop: The Best American Hip Hop Journalism of the Last 25 Years.* New York: Faber & Faber.

Champlain, Kalyana. (2010). "'Who you callin' a bitch?': Women in Hip Hop and Spoken-word as a Means to Expand and Validate a Postcolonial Feminist Rhetorical Theory." M.A. thesis, University of Rhode Island, Kingston, RI.

Chang, Jeff. (2003). "Even Our Enemies Deserve Music." *New Internationalist* 359, 14.

———. (2005). *Can't Stop Won't Stop: A History of the Hip Hop Generation.* New York: St. Martin's Press.

———. (Ed.). (2006). *Total Chaos: The Art And Aesthetics of Hip Hop.* Cambridge, MA: Basic/Civitas Books.

Charnas, Dan. (2010). *The Big Paycheck: The History of the Business of Hip Hop.* New York: New American Library.

Charry, Eric S. (Ed.). (2012). *Hip Hop Africa: New African Music in a Globalizing World.* Bloomington: Indiana University Press.

Cheney, Charise L. (1999). *Phallic/ies and Hi(s)stories: Masculinity and the Black Nationalist Tradition, From Slave Spirituals to Rap Music.* Champaign: University of Illinois Press.

———. (2005). *Brothers Gonna Work It Out!: Sexual Politics in the Golden Age of Rap Nationalism.* New York: New York University Press.

Chernoff, John Miller. (1979). *African Rhythm and African Sensibility: Aesthetics and Social Action in African Musical Idioms.* Chicago: University of Chicago Press.

Childs, Dennis Ray. (1998). "Signifying Badmen: The Outlaw Poetics of NaS, Goodie Mob, and the Coup." M.A. thesis, University of California, Los Angeles.

Chilton, John. (1992). *Let the Good Times Roll: The Story of Louis Jordan and His Music.* Ann Arbor : University of Michigan Press.

Chong, Dennis. (1991). *Collective Action and the Civil Rights Movement.* Chicago: University of Chicago Press.

Chuck D. (1997). *Fight the Power: Rap, Race, and Reality* (with Yusuf Jah). New York: Delacorte Press.

Churchill, Ward, and Wall, Jim V. (1988). *Agents of Repression: The FBI's Secret Wars Against the Black Panther Party and the American Indian Movement.* Boston: South End.

———. (Eds.). (2002). *The COINTELPRO Papers: Documents from the FBI's Secret Wars Against Domestic Dissent.* Boston: South End.

Clark, Chap. (2011). *Hurt 2.0: Inside the World of Today's Teenagers.* Grand Rapids, MI: Baker Academic.

Clarke, Cheryl. (2005). *"After Mecca": Women Poets and the Black Arts Movement.* New Brunswick: Rutgers University Press.

Clay, Andreana. (2006). "'All I Need Is One Mic': Mobilizing Youth for Social Change In the Post-Civil Rights Era." *Social Justice* 33 (2), 105–21.

———. (2007a). "'I Used to be Scared of the Dick': Queer Women of Color and Hip Hop Masculinity." In Gwendolyn D. Pough, Elaine Richardson, Aisha Durham, and Rachel Raimist (Eds.), *Home Girls Make Some Noise!: The Hip Hop Feminism Anthology* (148–). Mira Loma, CA: Parker Publishing.

———. (2007b). "Like an Old Soul Record: Black Feminism, Queer Sexuality, and the Hip Hop Generation." *Meridians: Feminism, Face, Transnationalism* 8 (1), 53–73.

———. (2012). *The Hip Hop Generation Fights Back!: Youth, Activism, and Post-Civil Rights Politics.* New York: New York University Press.

Cleaver, Kathleen, and Katsiaficas, George N. (Eds.). (2001). *Liberation, Imagination, and the Black Panther Party: A New Look at the Panthers and their Legacy.* New York: Routledge.

Cobb, Michael D., and Boettcher, William A. (2007). "Ambivalent Sexism and Misogynistic Rap Music: Does Exposure to Eminem Increase Sexism?" *Journal of Applied Social Psychology* 37 (12), 3025–42.

Cohen, Aaron. (2011). *Aretha Franklin's Amazing Grace.* New York: Continuum.

Cohen, Cathy J. (2010). *Democracy Remixed: Black Youth and the Future of American Politics.* New York: Oxford University Press.

Cohen, Rich. (2004). *Machers and Rockers: Chess Records and the Business of Rock & Roll.* New York: W.W. Norton.

Cohodas, Nadine. (2000). *Spinning Blues into Gold: The Chess Brothers and the Legendary Chess Records.* New York: St. Martin's Press.

————. (2010). *Princess Noire: The Tumultuous Reign of Nina Simone.* New York: Pantheon Books.

Coleman, Brian. (2007). *Check the Technique: Liner Notes for Hip Hop Junkies.* New York: Villard.

Collier, James Lincoln. (1978). *The Making of Jazz: A Comprehensive History.* Boston: Houghton Mifflin.

Collier-Thomas, Betty, and Franklin, V.P. (Eds.). (2001). *Sisters in the Struggle: African American Women in the Civil Rights-Black Power Movement.* New York: New York University Press.

Collins, Ann V. (2012). *All Hell Broke Loose: American Race Riots from the Progressive Era through World War II.* Santa Barbara, CA: Praeger.

Collins, Lisa Gail, and Crawford, Margo Natalie. (Eds.). (2006). *New Thoughts on the Black Arts Movement.* New Brunswick: Rutgers University Press.

Collins, Patricia Hill. (1990). *Black Feminist Thought: Knowledge, Consciousness, and the Politics of Empowerment.* New York: Routledge.

————. (1998). *Fighting Words: Black Women and the Search for Social Justice.* Minneapolis: University of Minnesota Press.

————. (2000). *Black Feminist Thought: Knowledge, Consciousness, and the Politics of Empowerment* (2nd ed.). New York: Routledge.

————. (2005). *Black Sexual Politics: African Americans, Gender, and the New Racism.* New York: Routledge.

————. (2006). *From Black Power to Hip Hop: Racism, Nationalism, and Feminism.* Philadelphia: Temple University Press.

Collis, John. (1998). *The Story of Chess Records.* New York: Bloomsbury Publishing.

Combs, James E. (1984). *Polpop: Politics and Popular Culture in America.* Bowling Green, OH: Bowling Green University Popular Press.

Condry, Ian. (2006). *Hip Hop Japan: Rap and the Paths of Cultural Globalization.* Durham: Duke University Press.

Cone, James H. (1991). *Martin & Malcolm & America: A Dream or A Nightmare.* Maryknoll, NY: Orbis.

Conyers, James L., and Smallwood, Andrew P. (Eds.). (2008). *The Malcolm X Critical Reader.* Durham, NC: Carolina Academic Press.

Cooke, Miriam, and Lawrence, Bruce B. (Eds.). (2005). *Muslim Network from Hajj to Hip Hop.* Chapel Hill: University of North Carolina Press.

Cooper, Barry. (1980). "The Gospel According to Parliament." *Village Voice* (January 14), 69–70.

Cooper, Carolyn J. (1995). *Noises in the Blood: Orality, Gender, and the "Vulgar" Body of Jamaican Popular Culture.* Durham: Duke University Press.

————. (2004). *Sound Clash: Jamaican Dancehall Culture at Large.* New York: Palgrave Macmillan.

Cooper, Martha, and Chalfant, Henry. (1984). *Subway Art.* New York: Holt, Rinehart & Winston.

Corbett, John, Elms, Anthony, and Kapsalis, Terri. (Eds.). (2006). *Pathways to Unknown Worlds: Sun Ra, El Saturn, and Chicago's Afro-futurist Underground, 1954–1968.* Chicago: WhiteWalls.

————. (Eds.). (2010). *Sun Ra: Traveling the Spaceways: The Astro-Black and Other Solar Myths.* Chicago: University of Chicago Press.

Costello, Mark, and Wallace, David F. (1997). *Signifying Rappers: Rap and Race in the Urban Present.* New York: Ecco Press.

Craft, Chanel R. (2010). "Where My Girls At?: The Interpellation of Women in Gangsta Hip Hop." M.A. thesis, Department of Women's Studies, Georgia State University, Atlanta, GA.

Crazy Horse, Kandia. (Ed.). (2004). *Rip It Up: The Black Experience in Rock & Roll.* New York: Palgrave Macmillan.

Cross, Brian. (1993). *It's Not About a Salary: Rap, Race, and Resistance in Los Angeles.* New York: Verso.

Cross, Charles R. (2005). *Room Full of Mirrors: A Biography of Jimi Hendrix.* New York: Hyperion.

Cruse, Harold. (1967). *The Crisis of the Negro Intellectual: A Historical Analysis of the Failure of Black Leadership.* New York: Quill.

Cruz, Jon. (1999). *Culture on the Margins: The Black Spiritual and the Rise of American Cultural Interpretation.* Princeton: Princeton University Press.

Cunningham, Phillip L. (2010). "'There's nothing really new under the sun': The Fallacy of the Neo-Soul Genre." *Journal of Popular Music Studies* 22 (3), 240–58.

Curry, George E. (Ed.). (1996). *The Affirmative Action Debate.* Cambridge, MA: Basic Books.

Cutler, Cecilia. (2003). "'Keepin' It Real': White Hip Hoppers' Discourses of Language, Race, and Authenticity." *Journal of Linguistic Anthropology* 13 (2), 211–33.

———. (2007). "The Co-Construction of Whiteness in an MC Battle." *Pragmatics: Journal of the International Pragmatics Assocation* 17 (1), 9–22.

Dagbovie, Pero Gaglo. (2005). "'Of All Our Studies, History Is Best Qualified to Reward Our Research': Black History's Relevance to the Hip Hop Generation." *Journal of African American History* 90 (3), 299–23.

———. (2006). *Black History: "Old School" Black Historians and the Hip Hop Generation.* Troy, MI: Bedford Publishers.

Dahl, Bill. (2001). *Motown: The Golden Years, The Stars and Music That Shaped a Generation.* Iola, WI: Krause.

Dalton, Russell J., and Kuechler, Manfred. (Eds.). (1990). *Challenging the Political Order: New Social and Political Movements in Western Democracies.* New York: Oxford University Press.

Daniel, Pete. (2000). *Lost Revolutions: The South in the 1950s.* Chapel Hill: University of North Carolina Press.

Danielsen, Anne. (2006). *Presence and Pleasure: The Funk Grooves of James Brown and Parliament.* Middletown, CT: Wesleyan University Press.

———. (2008). "The Musicalization of 'Reality': Reality Rap and Rap Reality on Public Enemy's Fear of a Black Planet." *European Journal of Cultural Studies* 11 (4), 405–21.

Darden, Bob. (2004). *People Get Ready!: A New History of Black Gospel Music.* New York: Continuum.

David, Marlo. (2007). "Afrofuturism and Post-Soul Possibility in Black Popular Music." *African American Review* 41 (4), 695–708.

Davis, Daniel S. (1972). *Mr. Black Labor: The Story of A. Philip Randolph, Father of the Civil Rights Movement.* New York: E.P. Dutton.

Davis, Jack E. (Ed.). (2001). *The Civil Rights Movement.* Malden, MA: Blackwell.

Davis, James K. (1992). *Spying on America: The FBI's Domestic Counterintelligence Program.* New York: Praeger.

Davis, Nathan T. (1996). *African American Music: A Philosophical Look at African American Music in Society* (with Ursula Broschke-Davis). Needham Heights, MA: Simon & Schuster.

Davis, Sharon. (1988). *Motown: The History.* Enfield, Middlesex: Guinenss Publishing.

DeBerry, Stephen. (1995). "Gender Noise: Community Formation, Identity and Gender Analysis in Rap Music." M.A. thesis, Graduate School of Education & Information Studies, University of California, Los Angeles.

Decker, Jeffrey L. (1993). "The State of Rap: Time and Place in Hip Hop Nationalism." *Social Text* 34, 53–84.

Deepwell, Katy. (Ed.). (1995). *New Feminist Art Criticism: Critical Strategies.* Manchester: Manchester University Press.

Deffaa, Chip. (1996). *Blue Rhythm: Six Lives in Rhythm & Blues.* Urbana: University of Illinois Press.

de Jong, Nanette T. (1997). "Chosen Identities and Musical Symbols: The Curaçaoan Jazz Community and the Association for the Advancement of Creative Musicians." Ph.D. dissertation, University of Michigan, Ann Arbor, MI.

de Leon, Aya. (2007a). "If Women Ran Hip Hop." In Gwendolyn D. Pough, Elaine Richardson, Aisha Durham, and Rachel Raimist (Eds.), *Home Girls Make Some Noise!: The Hip Hop Feminism Anthology* (185–86). Mira Loma, CA: Parker Publishing.

———. (2007b). "Lyrical Self-Defense and the Reluctant Female Rapper." In Alix Olson (Ed.), *Word Warriors: 35 Women Leaders in the Spoken-Word Revolution* (63–72). Emeryville, CA: Seal Press.

Delmont, Matthew F. (2012). *The Nicest Kids in Town: American Bandstand, Rock & Roll, and the Struggle for Civil Rights in 1950s Philadelphia.* Berkeley: University of California Press.

Demers, Joanna. (2003). "Sampling the 1970s in Hip Hop." *Popular Music* 22 (1), 41–56.

Dennis, Christopher. (2011). *Afro-Colombian Hip Hop: Globalization, Transcultural Music, and Ethnic Identities.* Lanham, MD: Lexington Books.

Dent, Gina. (Ed.). (1992). *Black Popular Culture.* Seattle: Bay Press.

De Schweinitz, Rebecca. (2009). *If We Could Change the World: Young People and America's Long Struggle for Racial Equality.* Chapel Hill: University of North Carolina Press.

Desmond, Matthew, and Emirbayer, Mustafa. (2010). *Racial Domination, Racial Progress: The Sociology of Race in America.* New York: McGraw-Hill Higher Education.

Desnoyers-Colas, Elizabeth F. (2003). "Sista MC Droppin' Rhymes with a Beat: A Fantasy Theme Analysis of Songs Performed by African American Female Rap Artists." Ph.D. dissertation, Regent University, Virginia Beach, VA.

Detlefsen, Robert R. (1991). *Civil Rights Under Reagan.* San Francisco, CA: ICS Press.

DeVeaux, Scott. (1991). "Constructing the Jazz Tradition: Jazz Historiography." *Black American Literature Forum* 25 (3), 525–60.

Devenish, Colin. (2001). *Rage Against the Machine.* New York: St. Martin's/Griffin.

Dicker, Rory. (2008). *History of U.S. Feminism.* Berkeley, CA: Seal Press.

Dicker, Rory, and Piepmeier, Alison. (Eds.). (2003). *Catching a Wave: Reclaiming Feminism for the 21st century.* Boston: Northeastern University Press.

Dierenfield, Bruce J. (2008). *The Civil Rights Movement.* New York: Pearson Longman.

Dimitriadis, Greg. (Ed.). (2001). *Performing Identity/Performing Culture: Hip Hop as Text, Pedagogy, and Lived Practice, Vol. 1.* New York: Peter Lang.

Diner, Robyn. (2006). "'The Other White Meat': Princess Superstar, Irony, Sexuality, and Whiteness in Hip Hop." *Canadian Review of American Studies* 36 (2), 195–209.

DiNovella, Elizabeth A. (2002). "Louder than Bombs: A Profile of Michael Franti." *The Progressive* 66 (2), 39.

Diouf, Mamadou, and Nwankwo, Ifeoma Kiddoe. (Eds.). (2010). *Rhythms of the Afro-Atlantic World: Rituals and Remembrances.* Ann Arbor: University of Michigan Press.

DjeDje, Jacqueline C., and Meadows, Eddie S. (Eds.). (1998). *California Soul: Music of African Americans in the West.* Berkeley: University of California Press.

Dobkin, Matt (2006). *I Never Loved a Man The Way I Love You: Aretha Franklin, Respect, and the Making of a Soul Music Masterpiece.* New York: St. Martin's Griffin.

Dodson, Howard, and Diouf, Sylviane A. (Eds.). (2004). *In Motion: The African American Migration Experience.* Washington, DC: National Geographic Books.

Doleac, Benjamin Grant. (2011). "'Ready to spread': P-Funk and the Politics of Signifyin(g)." M.A. thesis, University of Alberta, Edmonton, Alberta, Canada.

Donahue, Matthew A. (2001). "The Message Behind the Beat: Social and Political Attitudes Expressed in American Rap and Punk Rock Music of the 1980s and Early 1990s." Ph.D. dissertation, Bowling Green State University, Bowling Green, OH.

Dorsey, Brian. (2000). *Spirituality, Sensuality, Literality: Blues, Jazz, and Rap as Music and Poetry.* Vienna, Austria: Braumüller.

Douglas, Susan J. (1994). *Where the Girls Are: Growing Up Female with the Mass Media.* New York: Times Books.

———. (2010). *The Rise of Enlightened Sexism: How Pop Culture Took Us from Girl Power to Girls Gone Wild.* New York: St. Martin's Griffin.

Dow, Bonnie J. (1996). *Prime-Time Feminism: Television, Media Culture, and the Women's Movement since 1970.* Philadelphia, PA: University of Pennsylvania Press.

Drabble, John. (2004). "To Ensure Domestic Tranquility: The FBI, COINTELPRO-WHITE HATE and Political Discourse, 1964–1971." *Journal of American Studies* 38 (2), 297–328.

———. (2007). "From White Supremacy to White Power: The FBI, COINTELPRO-WHITE HATE, and the Nazification of the Ku Klux Klan in the 1970s." *Journal of American Studies* 48 (3), 49–74.

———. (2008). "Fighting Black Power-New Left Coalitions: Covert FBI Media Campaigns and American Cultural Discourse, 1967–1971." *European Journal of American Culture* 27 (2), 65–91.

Driscoll, Kevin Edward. (2009). "Stepping Your Game Up: Technical Innovation Among Young People of Color in Hip Hop." M.A. thesis, Department of Comparative Media Studies, Massachusetts Institute of Technology, Cambridge, MA.

Drisdel, Derrick. (2011). *George Clinton Double O.G.* New York: Icon Books.

Dubey, Madhu. (1998). "The 'True Lie' of the Nation: Fanon and Feminism." *differences: A Journal of Feminist Cultural Studies* 10 (2), 1–29.

Du Bois, W.E.B. (1903). *The Souls of Black Folk: Essays and Sketches.* Chicago: A.C. McClurg.

———. (1924). *The Gift of Black Folk: The Negroes in the Making of America.* Boston: Stratford.

———. (1939). *Black Folk: Then and Now: An Essay in the History and Sociology of the Negro Race.* New York: Henry Holt.

Dunn, Stephane. (2008). *Baad Bitches and Sassy Supermamas: Black Power Action Films.* Urbana: University of Illinois Press.

Dunne, Andrew, and Marsh, James. (Directors). (2004). *The Story of Gospel Music: The Power in the Voice.* Burbank, CA: BBC/Warner Home Video.

Dunson, Josh. (1965). *Freedom in the Air: Song Movements of the Sixties.* New York: International Publishers.

Durand, Alain-Philippe. (Ed.). (2002). *Black, Blanc, Beur: Rap Music and Hip Hop Culture in the Francophone World.* Lanham, MD: Scarecrow Press.

Durham, Aisha S. (2007). "Homegirl Going Home: Hip Hop Feminism and the Representational Politics of Location." Ph.D. dissertation, University of Illinois at Urbana-Champaign.

Dwyer, Claire, and Bressey, Caroline. (Eds.). (2008). *New Geographies of Race and Racism.* Burlington, VT: Ashgate.

Dyson, Michael Eric. (1993). *Reflecting Black: African American Cultural Criticism.* Minneapolis: University of Minnesota Press.

———. (1997). *Between God and Gangsta Rap: Bearing Witness to Black Culture.* New York: Oxford University Press.

———. (2002). *Holler If You Hear Me: Searching for Tupac Shakur.* New York: Basic Civitas.

———. (2005). *Is Bill Cosby Right?: Or Has the Black Middle-Class Lost Its Mind?* New York: Basic Civitas.

———. (2006). *Come Hell or High Water: Hurricane Katrina and the Color of Disaster.* New York: Basic Civitas.

———. (2007). *Know What I Mean?: Reflections on Hip Hop.* New York: Basic Civitas.

Dyson, Michael Eric, and Daulatzai, Sohail. (Eds.). (2010). *Born to Use Mics: Reading Nas's Illmatic.* New York: Basic Civitas.

Early, Gerald L. (2004). *One Nation Under a Groove: Motown and American Culture.* Ann Arbor: University of Michigan Press.

Eastman, Ralph. (1989). "Central Avenue Blues: The Making of Los Angeles Rhythm and Blues, 1942–1947." *Black Music Research Journal* 9 (1), 19–33.

Eaton, Kalenda C. (2008). *Womanism, Literature, and the Transformation of the Black Community, 1965–1980.* New York: Routledge.

Echols, Alice. (2010). *Hot Stuff: Disco and the Remaking of American Culture.* New York: W.W. Norton.

Edgerton, Gary R. (2007). *The Columbia History of American Television.* New York: Columbia University Press.

Edgerton, Robert B. (2001). *Hidden Heroism: Black Soldiers in America's Wars.* Boulder, CO: Westview Press.

Ehrlich, Dimitri. (2002). "Young Soul Rebels." *Vibe* (February), 72.

Ehrman, John. (2005). *The Eighties: American in the Age of Reagan.* New Haven: Yale University Press.

Eichengreen, Barry J. (2000). *From Benign Neglect to Malignant Preoccupation: U.S. Balance-of-Payments Policy in the 1960s.* Cambridge, MA: National Bureau of Economic Research.

Eisinger, Peter K. (1979). *Black Mayors and the Politics of Racial Economic Advancement.* Madison: University of Wisconsin Press.

Eiswerth, Joseph P. (1996). "Rap Music as Protest: A Rhetorical Analysis of Public Enemy's Lyrics." M.A. thesis, University of Nevada, Las Vegas.

Elafros, Athena. (2005). "'Revolutionary But Gangsta": An Examination of Message raps and Gangsta Raps in the late 1980s." M.A. thesis, Queen's University at Kingston, Kingston, ON, Canada.

Elliot, Marguerite, and Karras, Maria. (Eds.). (2011). *The Woman's Building & Feminist Art Education, 1973–1991: A Pictorial Herstory.* Los Angeles: Otis College of Art & Design Press.

Elliott, Martin. (2012). *The Rolling Stones: Complete Recording Sessions, 1962–2012.* London: Cherry Red.

Ellison, Mary. (1985). "Consciousness of Poverty in Black Music." *Popular Music &Society* 10 (2), 17–46.

Ellison, Ralph. (1964). *Shadow and Act.* New York: Random House.

———. (1995a). *Collected Essays of Ralph Ellison* (John F. Callahan, Ed.). New York: Modern Library.

———. (1995b). *Conversations with Ralph Ellison* (Maryemma Graham and Amritjit Singh, Eds.). Jackson: University Press of Mississippi.

———. (2001). *Living With Music: Ralph Ellison's Jazz Writings* (Robert G. O'Meally, Ed.). New York: Modern Library.

Ellison, Ralph, and Murray, Albert. (2000). *Trading Twelves: The Selected Letters of Ralph Ellison and Albert Murray* (John F. Callahan, Ed.). New York: Modern Library.

Entman, Robert M., and Rojecki, Andrew. (2000). *The Black Image in the White Mind: Media and Race in America.* Chicago: University of Chicago Press.

Epstein, Dena J. (2003). *Sinful Tunes and Spirituals.* Urbana: University of Illinois Press.

Epstein, Jonathon S. (1998). *Youth Culture: Identity in a Postmodern World.* Malden, MA: Blackwell.

Escott, Colin. (1991). *Good Rockin' Tonight: Sun Records and the Birth of Rock & Roll* (with Martin Hawkins). New York: St. Martin's Press.

———. (1999). *All Roots Lead to Rock: Legends of Early Rock & Roll: A Bear Family Reader.* New York: Schirmer.

Essed, Philomena, and Goldberg, David Theo. (Eds.). (2001). *Race Critical Theories: Texts and Contexts.* Malden, MA: Blackwell.

Evans, Sara. (1979). *Personal Politics: The Roots of Women's Liberation in the Civil Rights Movement.* New York: Vintage Books.

Evil, Pierre. (2005). *Gangsta Rap.* Paris: Flammarion.

Ewens, Graeme. (1992). *Africa O-Ye!: A Celebration of African Music.* New York: Da Capo.

Executive Order 8802. (1941, June 25). General Records of the United States Government; Record Group 11. Washington, DC: National Archives.

Eyerman, Ron, and Jamison, Andrew. (1991). *Social Movements: A Cognitive Approach.* University Park, PA: Pennsylvania State University Press.

———. (1995). "Social movements and cultural transformation: Popular music in the 1960s." *Media Culture Society* 17 (3), 449–86.

———. (1998). *Music and Social Movements: Mobilizing Traditions in the Twentieth Century.* Cambridge: Cambridge University Press.

Fanon, Frantz. (1965). *A Dying Colonialism.* New York: Grove.

———. (1967). *Black Skin, White Masks.* New York: Grove.

———. (1968). *The Wretched of the Earth.* New York: Grove.

———. (1969). *Toward the African Revolution.* New York: Grove.

———. (2005). *The Wretched of the Earth* (Richard Philcox, Trans.). New York: Grove.

————. (2008). *Black Skin, White Masks* (Richard Philcox, Trans.). New York: Grove.

Farley, Christopher John. (1998). "Music: Neo-Soul on a Roll." *Time.* Available online at: http://www.time.com/time/magazine/article/0,9171,988672,00.html [Retrieved on May 9, 2010].

Farmer, Paul. (2003). *Pathologies of Power: Health, Human Rights, and the New War on the Poor.* Berkeley: University of California Press.

Feiereisen, Florence, and Hill, Alexandra M. (Eds.). (2011). *Germany in the Loud Twentieth Century: An Introduction.* Oxford: Oxford University Press.

Felisbret, Eric, and Felisbret, Luke. (2009). *Graffiti New York.* New York: Abrams.

Fergus, Devin. (2009). *Liberalism, Black Power, and the Making of American Politics, 1965–1980.* Athens: University of Georgia Press.

Fernandes, Sujatha. (2006). *Cuba Represent!: Cuban Arts, State Power, and the Making of New Revolutionary Cultures.* Durham: Duke University Press.

————. (2011). *Close to the Edge: In Search of the Global Hip Hop Generation.* New York: Verso.

Fernando, Stephen H. (1994). *The New Beats: Exploring the Music, Culture, and Attitudes of Hip Hop.* New York: Anchor/Doubleday.

————. (1999). "Back in the Day: 1975–1979." In Alan Light (Ed.), *The Vibe History of Hip Hop* (13–15). New York: Random House.

Ferree, Myra Marx, and Martin, Patricia Y. (Eds.). (1995). *Feminist Organizations: Harvest of the New Women's Movement.* Philadelphia: Temple University Press.

Finley, Laura L. (2002). "The Lyrics of Rage Against the Machine: A Study in Radical Criminology?" *Journal of Criminal Justice and Popular Culture* 9 (3), 150–66.

Fiori, Giuseppe. (1990). *Antonio Gramsci: Life of a Revolutionary.* New York: Verso.

Fisch, Audrey. (Ed.). (2007). *The Cambridge Companion to the African American Slaves Narrative.* Cambridge: Cambridge University Press.

Fisher, Marc. (2007). *Something in the Air: Radio, Rock, and the Revolution that Shaped a Generation.* New York: Random House.

Fleming, Robert E. (1987). *James Weldon Johnson.* Boston: Twayne.

Flint, Colin. (Ed.). (2004). *Spaces of Hate: Geographies of Discrimination and Intolerance in the U.S.A.* New York: Routledge.

Flores, Juan. (2000). *From Bomba to Hip Hop: Puerto Rican Culture and Latino Identity.* New York: Columbia University Press.

Flory, Jonathan Andrew. (2006). "I Hear a Symphony: Making Music at Motown, 1959–1979." Ph.D. dissertation, University of North Carolina at Chapel Hill, Chapel Hill, NC.

Floyd, Samuel A. (1995). *The Power of Black Music: Interpreting its History from Africa to the United States.* New York: Oxford University Press.

Ford, Larry. (1971). "Geographic Factors in the Origin, Evolution, and Diffusion of Rock and Roll Music." *Journal of Geography* 70 (8), 455–64.

Ford, Ryan. (2004). "Hip Hop Whitewash: The Impact of Eminem on Rap Music and Music Industry Economics." *Socialism and Democracy* 18 (2), 127–34.

Forman, Murray. (2000). "'Represent': Race, Space and Place in Rap Music." *Popular Music* 19, 65–90.

————. (2002). *The Hood Comes First: Race, Space, and Place in Rap and Hip Hop.* Middletown, CT: Wesleyan University Press.

Forman, Murray, and Neal, Mark Anthony. (Eds.). (2004). *That's the Joint!: The Hip Hop Studies Reader.* New York: Routledge.

————. (Eds.). (2012). *That's the Joint!: The Hip Hop Studies Reader* (2nd ed.). New York: Routledge.

Foucault, Michel. (1971). *The Order of Things: An Archaeology of the Human Sciences.* New York: Pantheon.

————. (1973). *Madness and Civilization: A History of Insanity in the Age of Reason.* New York: Vintage.

————. (1974). *The Archaeology of Knowledge and the Discourse on Language.* New York: Pantheon.

―――. (1977). *Language, Counter-Memory, Practice: Selected Essays and Interviews by Michel Foucault* (Donald F. Bouchard, Ed.). Ithaca: Cornell University Press.

―――. (1979). *Discipline and Punish: The Birth of the Prison.* New York: Vintage.

―――. (1980). *Power/Knowledge: Selected Interviews and Other Writings, 1972–1977* (Colin Gordon, Ed.). New York: Pantheon.

―――. (1979). *Discipline and Punish: The Birth of the Prison.* New York: Vintage.

―――. (1984). *The Foucault Reader* (Paul Rabinow, Ed.). New York: Pantheon.

―――. (1988). *Politics, Philosophy, Culture: Interviews and Other Writings, 1977–1984* (Lawrence D. Kritzman, Ed.). New York: Routledge.

―――. (1990a). *The History of Sexuality, Volume 1: The Will to Knowledge.* New York: Vintage.

―――. (1990b). *The History of Sexuality, Volume 2: The Use of Pleasure.* New York: Vintage.

―――. (1990c). *The History of Sexuality, Volume 3: The Care of the Self.* New York: Vintage.

―――. (1994). *The Birth of the Clinic: An Archaeology of Medical Perception.* New York: Vintage.

―――. (1996). *Foucault Live: Interviews, 1961–1984* (Sylvère Lotringer, Ed.). New York: Semiotext(e).

―――. (2009). *The History of Madness in the Classical Age.* New York: Routledge.

Fox, Kamal. (2002). "Mixed Feelings: Notes on the Romance of the Mixed Tape." *rhizomes* 05. www.rhizomes.net/issue5/fox.html.

Fox, Marisa. (1990). "George Clinton: Unslave Yo Self!" *Village Voice* (January 16), 86–89.

Fraley, Todd. (2009). "I Got a Natural Skill . . . : Hip Hop, Authenticity, and Whiteness." *Howard Journal of Communications* 20 (1), 37–54.

Francese, Carl, and Sorrell, Richard S. (2001). *From Tupelo to Woodstock: Youth, Race, and Rock & Roll in America, 1954–1969.* Dubuque, IA: Kendall/Hunt.

Franklin, Aretha Louise. (1999). *Aretha: From These Roots* (with David Ritz). New York: Villard Books.

Franklin, Eric N., and Watkins, William H. (1984). *Breakdance.* Chicago: NTC/Contemporary Publishing.

Franklin, John Hope. (1947). *From Slavery to Freedom: A History of American Negroes.* New York: Knopf.

Franklin, Vincent P. (1984). *Black Self-Determination: A Cultural History of the Faith of the Fathers.* Westport, CT: Lawrence Hill.

Franti, Michael. (2006). *Food for the Masses: Lyrics & Portraits.* San Rafael, CA: Insight Editions.

Freeland, David. (2001). *Ladies of Soul.* Jackson: University Press of Mississippi.

Freeland, Gregory. (2009). "'We're a Winner': Popular Music and the Black Power Movement." *Social Movement Studies* 8 (3), 261–88.

Freeman, Joreen. (1975). *Politics of Women's Liberation: A Case Study of an Emerging Social Movement and Its Relation to the Policy Process.* New York: Longman.

Frere-Jones, Sasha. (1999). "Run-DMC." In Alan Light (Ed.), *The Vibe History of Hip Hop* (61–68). New York: Random House.

Fricke, Jim, and Ahearn, Charlie. (Eds.). (2002). *Yes Yes Y'all!: The Experience Music Project Oral History of Hip Hop's First Decade.* New York: Da Capo Press.

Friedlander, Paul. (2006). *Rock & Roll: A Social History.* Boulder, CO: Westview Press.

Friedman, Douglas E., and Gribin, Anthony J. (2003). *Who Sang Our Songs?: The Official Rhythm & Blues and Doo-wop Songography.* West Long Branch, NJ: Harmony Songs Publications.

Fuller, Graham, and Mack, Lorrie. (Eds.). (1985). *The Motown Story.* London: Orbis.

Furman, Leah, and Furman, Elina. (1999). *Heart of Soul: The Lauryn Hill Story.* New York: Ballantine Books.

Fuss, Diana. (1995). *Identification Papers: Readings on Psychoanalysis, Sexuality, and Culture.* New York: Routledge.

Galiana, Jota Martínez. (1997). *Rage Against the Machine = Furia Contra el Sistema.* Valencia, España: Editorial La Máscara.

Gallagher, Charles A. (Ed.). (2008). *Racism in Post-Race America: New Theories, New Directions.* Chapel Hill, NC: Social Forces Publishing.

Gan, Su-lin, Zillmann, Dolf, and Mitrook, Michael. (1997). "Stereotyping Effect of Black Women's Sexual Rap on White Audiences." *Basic and Applied Social Psychology* 19 (3), 381–99.

Gans, Herbert J. (1995). *The War Against the Poor: The Underclass and Anti-Poverty Policy.* New York: Basic Books.

Garland, Phyl. (1969). *The Sound of Soul.* Chicago: H. Regnery Book Co.

Garofalo, Reebee. (1990). "Crossing Over: 1939–1989." In Jannette L. Dates and William Barlow (Eds.), *Split Image: African Americans in the Mass Media* (57–130). Washington, DC: Howard University Press.

———. (1992). *Rockin' the Boat: Mass Music and Mass Movements.* Boston: South End Press.

———. (2011). *Rockin' Out: Popular Music in the U.S.A.* Upper Saddle River, NJ: Pearson/Prentice Hall.

Garoian, Charles R., and Gaudelius, Yvonne. (2008). *Spectacle Pedagogy: Art, Politics, and Visual Culture.* Albany: State University of New York Press.

Garrow, David J. (2004). *Bearing the Cross: Martin Luther King, Jr., and the Southern Christian Leadership Conference.* New York: Perennial Classics.

Gastman, Roger, and Neelon, Caleb. (2010). *The History of American Graffiti.* New York: Harper Design.

Gaulke, Cheri, and Klick, Laurel. (Eds.). (2012). *Feminist Art Workers: A History.* Los Angeles: Otis College of Art and Design Press.

Gayle, Addison. (Ed.). (1969). *Black Expression: Essays By and About Black Americans in the Creative Arts.* New York: Weybright & Talley.

———. (Ed.). (1970). *Black Situation.* New York: Horizon Press.

———. (Ed.). (1971). *Black Aesthetics.* Garden City, NY: Doubleday.

Gayle, Raymond. (Director). (2010). *Electric Purgatory: The Fate of the Black Rocker.* San Francisco, CA: Microcinema International.

Geller, Jennifer. (2008). "A Mixtape DJ's Drama: An Argument for Copyright Preemption of Georgia's Unauthorized Reproduction Law." *Chicago-Kent Journal of Intellectual Property* 8 (1), 1–40.

Genz, Stéphanie. (2009). *Postfemininities in Popular Culture.* New York: Palgrave Macmillan.

George, Nelson. (1985). *Where Did Our Love Go?: The Rise & Fall of the Motown Sound.* New York: St. Martin's Press.

———. (1988). *The Death of Rhythm & Blues.* New York: Pantheon Books.

———. (1989). "Rap's Tenth Birthday." *Village Voice* 24, 40.

———. (Ed.). (1990). *Stop the Violence: Overcoming Self-Destruction.* New York: Pantheon.

———. (1992). *Buppies, B-Boys, Baps & Bohos: Notes on Post-Soul Black Culture.* New York: HarperCollins.

———. (1994). *Blackface: Reflections on African Americans and the Movies.* New York: HarperCollins.

———. (1999). *Hip Hop America.* New York: Viking.

———. (2007). *Where Did Our Love Go?: The Rise and Fall of the Motown Sound.* Urbana: University of Illinois Press.

George, Nelson, and Leeds, Alan. (Eds.). (2008). *The James Brown Reader: 50 Years of Writing about the Godfather of Soul.* New York: Plume.

Germino, Dante L. (1990). *Antonio Gramsci: Architect of a New Politics.* Baton Rouge: Louisiana State University Press.

Geschwender, James A. (1971). *The Black Revolt: The Civil Rights Movement, Ghetto Uprisings, and Separatism.* Englewood Cliffs, NJ: Prentice-Hall.

Giardina, Carol. (2010). *Freedom for Women: Forging the Women's Liberation Movement, 1953–1970.* Gainesville: University Press of Florida.

Giddings, Paula. (1984). *When and Where I Enter: The Impact of Black Women on Race and Sex in America.* New York: Quill.

Gill, Flora. (1975). "Economics and the Black Exodus: An Analysis of Negro Emigration from the Southern United States, 1910–1970." Ph.D. dissertation, Department of Economics, Stanford University, Stanford, CA.

Gillespie, Andra. (2010). *Whose Black Politics?: Cases in Post-Racial Black Leadership.* New York: Routledge.

Gillet, Charlie. (1996). *The Sound of the City: The Rise of Rock & Roll.* London: Souvenir Press.

Gillis, Stacy, and Hollows, Joanne. (Eds.). (2009). *Feminism, Domesticity, and Popular Culture.* New York: Routledge.

Gilroy, Paul. (1993). *Small Acts: Thoughts on the Politics of Black Cultures.* New York: Serpent's Tail.

Ginwright, Shawn A. (2004). *Black in School: Afrocentric Reform, Urban Youth & the Promise of Hip Hop Culture.* New York: Teachers College Press.

———. (2006). "Toward a Politics of Relevance: Race, Resistance and African American Youth Activism." *Youth Activism: A Web Forum Organized by the Social Science Research Council.* http://ya.ssrc.org/african/Ginwright/.

Ginwright, Shawn, and James, Taj. (2002). "From Assets to Agents of Change: Social Justice, Organizing, and Youth Development." *New Directions for Youth Development* 96, 27–46.

Giroux, Henry A. (1998). *Channel Surfing: Racism, the Media, and the Destruction of Today's Youth.* New York: St. Martin's Griffin.

Glasgow, Douglas G. (1981). *The Black Underclass: Poverty, Unemployment, and Entrapment of Ghetto Youth.* New York: Vintage Books.

Glaude, Eddie S., Jr. (Ed.). (2002). *Is it Nation Time?: Contemporary Essays on Black Power and Black Nationalism.* Chicago: University of Chicago Press.

Goff, Keli. (2008). *Party Crashing: How the Hip Hop Generation Declared Political Independence.* New York: Basic Books.

Goings, Kenneth W. (1994). *Mammy and Uncle Mose: Black Collectibles and American Stereotyping.* Bloomington: Indiana University Press.

Goldberg, David Theo. (Ed.). (1990). *Anatomy of Racism.* Minneapolis: University of Minnesota Press.

———. (1993). *Racist Culture: Philosophy and the Politics of Meaning.* Cambridge, MA: Blackwell.

———. (Ed.). (1994). *Multiculturalism: A Critical Reader.* Cambridge, MA: Blackwell.

———. (1997). *Racial Subjects: Writing on Race in America.* New York: Routledge.

———. (2001). *The Racial State.* Malden, MA: Blackwell.

———. (2008). *The Threat of Race: Reflections on Racial Neoliberalism.* Malden, MA: Blackwell-Wiley.

Goldberg, David Theo, and Solomos, John. (Eds.). (2002). *A Companion to Racial and Ethnic Studies.* Malden: Blackwell.

Goldman, Peter L. (1979). *The Death and Life of Malcolm X.* Urbana: University of Illinois Press.

Goldsher, Alan. (2002). *Hard Bop Academy: The Sidemen of Art Blakey and the Jazz Messengers.* Milwaukee: Hal Leonard.

Goodall, Nataki H. (1994). "Depend on Myself: T.L.C. and the Evolution of Black Female Rap." *Journal of Negro History* 79 (1), 85–93.

Goodman, Jon. (Director). (2009). *Let Freedom Sing: How Music Inspired the Civil Rights Movement.* Fairfax, VA: Time-Life Video.

Goodwin, Jeff, and Jasper, James M. (Eds.). (2003). *Rethinking Social Movements: Structure, Meaning, and Emotion.* Lanham, MD: Rowman & Littlefield.

Goosman, Stuart L. (1992). "The Social and Cultural Organization of Black Group Vocal Harmony in Washington, D.C. and Baltimore, Maryland, 1945–1960." Ph.D. dissertation, University of Washington, Seattle, WA.

———. (1997). "The Black Authentic: Structure, Style, and Values in Group Harmony." *Black Music Research Journal* 17 (1), 81–99.

———. (2005). *Group Harmony: The Black Urban Roots of Rhythm & Blues.* Philadelphia: University of Pennsylvania Press.

Gopal, Priyamvada. (2002). "Frantz Fanon, Feminism, and the Question of Relativism." *New Formations* 47, 38–42.

Gordon, Lewis R., and Gordon, Jane Anna. (Eds). (2006a). *A Companion to African American Studies*. Malden, MA: Blackwell.

———. (Eds.). (2006b). *Not Only the Master's Tools: African American Studies in Theory and Practice*. Boulder, CO: Paradigm.

Gordy, Berry. (1994). *To be Loved: The Music, the Magic, the Memories of Motown: An Autobiography*. New York: Warner Books.

Gore, Dayo F., Theoharis, Jeanne, and Woodard, Komozi. (Eds.). (2009). *Want to Start a Revolution?: Radical Women in the Black Freedom Struggle*. New York: New York University Press.

Gourse, Leslie. (Ed.). (1997). *The Billie Holiday Companion: Seven Decades of Commentary*. New York: Schirmer Books.

Govenar, Alan B., and Joseph, Benny. (2004). *The Early Years of Rhythm & Blues*. Atglen, PA: Schiffer.

Gramsci, Antonio. (1971). *Selections from the Prison Notebooks of Antonio Gramsci* (Quintin Hoare and Geoffrey Nowell-Smith, Eds.). New York: International.

———. (1977). *Selections from the Political Writings, 1910–1920* (Quintin Hoare, Ed.). New York: International.

———. (1978). *Selections from the Political Writings, 1921–1926* (Quintin Hoare, Ed.). New York: International.

———. (1985). *Selections from the Cultural Writings* (David Forgacs and Geoffrey Nowell-Smith, Eds.). Cambridge: Harvard University Press.

———. (1995). *Antonio Gramsci: Further Selections from the Prison Notebooks* (Derek Boothman, Ed.). Minneapolis: University of Minnesota Press.

———. (2000). *The Antonio Gramsci Reader: Selected Writings, 1916–1935* (David Forgacs, Ed.). New York: New York University Press.

Grant, Elizabeth. (2002). "Gangsta Rap, the War on Drugs and the Location of African American Identity in Los Angeles, 1988–1992." *European Journal of American Culture* 21 (1), 4–15.

Grayson, Sandra M. (2003). *Visions of the Third Millennium: Black Science Fiction Novelists Write the Future*. Trenton, NJ: Africa World Press.

Greenberg, Steve. (1999). "Sugar Hill Records." In Alan Light (Ed.), *The Vibe History of Hip Hop* (23–33). New York: Random House.

Greene, Jasmin S. (2008). *Beyond Money, Cars, and Women: Examining Black Masculinity in Hip Hop Culture*. Newcastle, NE, UK: Cambridge Scholars.

Greene, Pamela J. (1995). "Aretha Franklin: The Emergence of Soul and Black Women's Consciousness in the Late 1960s and 1970s." Ph.D. dissertation, Bowling Green State University, Bowling Green, OH.

Greenfield, Robert. (2006). *Exile on Main Street: A Season in Hell with the Rolling Stones*. Cambridge, MA: Da Capo.

Gregg, Melissa. (2002). "Remnants of Humanism." *Continuum* 16 (3), 273–84.

Gregory, James. (2005). *The Southern Diaspora: How the Great Migrations of Black and White Southerners Transformed America*. Chapel Hill: University of North Carolina Press.

Gribin, Anthony J., and Schiff, Matthew M. (1992). *Doo-wop: The Forgotten Third of Rock & Roll*. Iola, WI: Krause Publications.

———. (2000). *The Complete Book of Doo-wop*. Iola, WI: Krause Publications.

Griffin, Gil. (1994). "Michael Franti is No Longer Disposable." *Billboard* 106 (33), 10.

Groh, George W. (1972). *The Black Migration: The Journey to Urban America*. New York: Weybright & Talley.

Groia, Philip. (1983). *They All Sang on the Corner: A Second Look at New York City's Rhythm & Blues Vocal Groups*. West Hempstead, NY: P. Dee Enterprises.

Grossman, James R. (1991). *Land of Hope: Chicago, Black Southerners, and the Great Migration*. Chicago: University of Chicago Press.

Gueraseva, Stacy. (2005). *Def Jam, Inc.: Russell Simmons, Rick Rubin, and the Extraordinary Story of the World's Most Influential Hip Hop Label*. New York: One World/Ballantine.

Guerrero, Edward. (1993). *Framing Blackness: The African American Image in Film.* Philadelphia: Temple University Press.

Guillory, Monique, and Green, Richard C. (Eds.). (1998). *Soul: Black Power, Politics, and Pleasure.* New York: New York University Press.

Guillory, Nichole Ann. (2005). "Schoolin' Women: Hip Hop Pedagogies of Black Women Rappers." Ph.D. dissertation, Louisiana State University, Baton Rouge, LA.

Guins, Raiford, and Cruz, Omayra Zaragoza. (Eds.). (2005). *Popular Culture: A Reader.* Thousand Oaks, CA: Sage.

Gulla, Bob. (Ed.). (2008). *Icons of R&B and Soul: An Encyclopedia of the Artists Who Revolutionized Rhythm* (2 vols.). Westport, CT: Greenwood.

Guralnick, Peter. (1986). *Sweet Soul Music: Rhythm & Blues and the Southern Dream of Freedom.* New York: Harper & Row.

———. (1989). *Lost Highway: Journeys & Arrivals of American Musicians.* New York: Harper & Row.

———. (1999). *Feel Like Going Home: Portraits in Blues and Rock 'n' Roll.* Boston: Little Brown.

Guttentag, Bill, and Sturman, Dan. (Directors). (2010). *Soundtrack for a Revolution.* New York: Docurama Films/New Video.

Haa, Erikka. (1997). *Soul.* New York: Friedman/Fairfax Publishers.

Haden-Guest, Anthony. (1997). *The Last Party: Studio 54, Disco, and the Culture of the Night.* New York: William Morrow.

Hagedorn, John. (2008). *World of Gangs: Armed Young Men and Gangsta Culture.* Minneapolis: University of Minnesota Press.

Hager, Steven. (1984). *Hip Hop: The Illustrated History of Break-Dancing, Rap Music, and Graffiti.* New York: St. Martin's Press.

Hahn, Steven. (2003). *A Nation Under Our Feet: Black Political Struggles in the Rural South, from Slavery to the Great Migration.* Cambridge, MA: Harvard University Press.

Hale, Thomas A. (1998). *Griots and Griottes: Masters of Words and Music.* Bloomington: Indiana University Press.

Hallen, Barry. (2000). *The Good, the Bad, and the Beautiful: Discourse about Values in Yoruba Culture.* Bloomington: Indiana University Press.

Hallgren, Roland. (1995). *The Vital Force: A Study of Àṣẹ in the Traditional and Neo-Traditional Culture of the Yoruba People.* Lund, Sweden: University of Lund.

Halpern, Rick. (1997). *Down on the Killing Floor: Black and White Workers in Chicago's Packinghouses, 1904–1954.* Urbana: University of Illinois Press.

Halpern, Rick, and Horowitz, Roger. (1996). *Meatpackers: An Oral History of Black Packinghouse Workers and Their Struggle for Racial and Economic Equality.* New York: Twayne Publishers.

Hamm, Mark S., and Ferrell, Jeff. (1994). "Rap, Cops, and Crime: Clarifying the 'Cop Killer' Controversy." *Academy of Criminal Justice Sciences/ACJS Today* (May/June), 25–32.

Hampton, Gregory J. (2010). *Changing Bodies in the Fiction of Octavia Butler: Slaves, Aliens, and Vampires.* Lanham, MD: Lexington.

Hampton, Sylvia. (2004). *Nina Simone: Break Down & Let It All Out* (with David Nathan). London: Sanctuary.

Hamrick, Kevin Robert. (1991). "'Fight the Power!': An Ideographic Analysis of the Rhetoric of Public Enemy." M.A. thesis, Department of Speech Communication and Theater Arts, Wake Forest University, Winston-Salem, NC.

Haney-López, Ian. (1996). *White by Law: The Legal Construction of Race.* New York: New York University Press.

Hannerz, Ulf. (1969). *Soulside: Inquiries into Ghetto Culture and Community.* New York: Columbia University Press.

Hannusch, Jeff. (1985). *I Hear You Knockin': The Sound of New Orleans Rhythm and Blues.* Ville Platte, LA: Swallow Publications.

———. (2001). *The Soul of New Orleans: A Legacy of Rhythm and Blues.* Ville Platte, LA: Swallow Publications.

Hanson, Joyce Ann. (2011). *Rosa Parks: A Biography.* Santa Barbara, CA: Greenwood.

Haralambos, Michael. (1975). *Soul Music: The Birth of a Sound in Black America.* New York: Da Capo.

Harding, James M. (2012). *Cutting Performances: Collage Events, Feminist Artists, and the American Avant-Garde.* Ann Arbor: University of Michigan Press.

Harding, Vincent. (1981). *There Is A River: The Black Struggle for Freedom in America.* New York: Harcourt Brace Jovanovich.

Hardy, Antoine. (2010). *Loving the Cool: A Rhetorical Study of Black Masculinity and Contemporary Hip Hop "Love Songs."* Saarbrücken, Germany: VDM Verlag Dr. Müller GmbH & Co.

Harkness, Geoff. (2011). "Backpackers and Gangstas: Chicago's White Rappers Strive for Authenticity." *American Behavioral Scientist* 55 (1), 57–85.

Harris, Christopher S. (2004). "Rappin', Riffin', Resistin': The Revolutionary Poetics of Underground Rap Music and Neo-Soul." M.PS. thesis, Cornell University, Ithaca, NY.

Harris, Laurie Lanzen. (2012). *The Great Migration North, 1910–1970.* Detroit: Omnigraphics, Inc.

Harris, Louis. (1973). *The Anguish of Change.* New York: Norton.

Harrison, Alferdteen. (Ed.). (1991). *Black Exodus: The Great Migration from the American South.* Jackson: University Press of Mississippi.

Harrison, Anthony Kwame. (2009). *Hip Hop Underground: The Integrity and Ethics of Racial Identification.* Philadelphia: Temple University Press.

Harrison, Thomas. (2011). *Music of the 1990s.* Santa Barbara, CA: Greenwood.

Harris-Perry, Melissa V. (2011). *Sister Citizen: Shame, Stereotypes, and Black Women in America.* New Haven: Yale University Press.

Hart, Austin Harold. (2012). "One Love: Collective Consciousness in Rap and Poetry of the Hip Hop Generation." M.A. thesis, East Carolina University, Greenville, NC.

Harvey, David. (1989). *The Urban Experience.* Baltimore: Johns Hopkins University Press.

———. (1996). *Justice, Nature, and the Geography of Difference.* Cambridge, MA: Blackwell.

———. (2006). *Spaces of Global Capitalism.* New York: Verso.

———. (2009). *Social Justice and the City.* Athens: University of Georgia Press.

Haskins, James. (1972). *A Piece of the Power: Four Black Mayors.* New York: Dial Press.

Haugen, Jason D. (1998). "Some Socio-Cultural Functions of Deixis in Gangsta Rap Discourse." *Texas Linguistic Forum* 42, 145–57.

———. (2003). "'Unladylike Divas': Language, Gender, and Female Gangsta Rappers." *Popular Music & Society* 26 (4), 429–44.

Hayes, Eileen M. (2010). *Songs in Black and Lavender: Race, Sexual Politics, and Women's Music.* Urbana: University of Illinois Press.

Hayes, Eileen M., and Williams, Linda F. (Eds.). (2007). *Black Women and Music: More Than the Blues.* Urbana: University of Illinois Press.

Haynes, Jeffrey. (1997). *Democracy and Civil Society in the Third World: Politics and New Political Movements.* Malden, MA: Blackwell.

Hazzard-Gordon, Katrina. (1990). *Jookin': The Rise of Social Dance Formations in African American Culture.* Philadelphia: Temple University Press.

Heatley, Michael. (Ed.). (1999). *The Beastie Boys: In Their Own Words.* London: Omnibus.

Heble, Ajay, and Fischlin, Daniel. (Eds.). (2003). *Rebel Musics: Human Rights, Resistant Sounds, and the Politics of Music Making.* Montréal: Black Rose Books.

Heilmann, Ann. (2003). *Feminist Forerunners: New Womanism and Feminism in the Early Twentieth Century.* London: Pandora.

Held, David. (1980). *Introduction to Critical Theory: Horkheimer to Habermas.* Berkeley: University of California Press.

Hendershott, Heidi A. (2004). "School of Rap: The Politics and Pedagogies of Rap Music." Ph.D. dissertation, Pennsylvania State University, University Park, PA.

Henderson, David. (2008). *'Scuse Me While I Kiss the Sky: Jimi Hendrix: Voodoo Child.* New York: Atria.

Henderson, Errol A. (1996). "Black Nationalism and Rap Music." *Journal of Black Studies* 26 (3), 308–39.

Henriques, Julian. (2011). *Sonic Bodies: Reggae Sound Systems, Performance Techniques, and Ways of Knowing*. New York: Continuum.

Henry, Lucas Aaron. (2004). "Freedom Now!: Four Hard Bop and Avant-Garde Jazz Musicians' Musical Commentary on the Civil Rights Movement, 1958–1964." M.A. thesis, Department of History, East Tennessee State University, Johnson City, TN.

Hernández, Daisy, and Rehman, Bushra (Eds.). (2002). *Colonize This!: Young Women of Color on Today's Feminism*. New York: Seal Press.

Hess, Mickey. (2005). "Hip Hop Realness and the White Performer." *Critical Studies in Media Communication* 22 (5), 372–89.

———. (Ed.). (2007a). *Icons of Hip Hop: An Encyclopedia of the Movement, Music, and Culture* (2 vols.). Westport, CT: Greenwood.

———. (2007b). *Is Hip Hop Dead?: The Past, Present, and Future of America's Most Wanted Music*. Westport, CT: Praeger.

———. (2010). *Hip Hop in America: A Regional Guide* (2 vols). Santa Barbara, CA: Greenwood.

Hewitt, Paolo, and Westwood, Tim. (Eds.). (1989). *Rap Beats to the Rhyme*. London: Omnibus.

Heywood, Leslie, and Drake, Jennifer. (Eds.). (1997). *Third Wave Agenda: Being Feminist, Doing Feminism*. Minneapolis: University of Minnesota Press.

Higgins, Dalton. (2009). *Hip Hop World*. Berkeley, CA: Groundwood Books.

Hildebrand, Lee. (1994). *Stars of Soul and Rhythm & Blues: Top Recording Artists and Show-Stopping Performers, from Memphis and Motown to Now*. New York: Billboard Books.

Hilfiker, David. (2002). *Urban Injustice: How Ghettos Happen*. New York: Seven Stories Press.

Hill, Marc Lamont. (2009). *Beats, Rhymes, and Classroom Life: Hip Hop Pedagogy and the Politics of Identity*. New York: Teachers College Press.

Hill, MarKeva Gwendolyn. (2012). *Womanism Against Socially-Constructed Matriarchal Images: A Theoretical Model Toward a Therapeutic Goal*. New York: Palgrave Macmillan.

Himes, Geoffrey. (1979). "'Uncle Jam': Fulfilling the Promise of Funk." *The Washington Post* (November 21), B4.

———. (1980). "The Funk Mob's Big Splash." *The Washington Post* (December 7), H1.

———. (1986). "George Clinton's Ghetto Funk." *The Washington Post* (July 17), B2.

Hinds, Selwyn Seyfu. (2002). *Gunshots in My Cook-up: Bits and Bites from a Hip Hop Caribbean Life*. New York: Atria Books.

Hine, Darlene Clark, and Thompson, Kathleen. (1998). *A Shining Thread of Hope: The History of Black Women in America*. New York: Broadway Books.

Hirshey, Gerri. (1984). *Nowhere to Run: The Story of Soul Music*. New York: Times Books.

Hisama, Ellie M., and Rapport, Evan. (Eds.). (2005). *Critical Minded: New Approaches to Hip Hop Studies*. Brooklyn, NY: Institute for Studies in American Music.

Hobbs, Stuart D. (1997). *End of the American Avant-Garde*. New York: New York University Press.

Hoffman, Barbara G. (2000). *Griots at War: Conflict, Conciliation, and Caste in Mande*. Bloomington: Indiana University Press.

Holden, Rebecca J. (1998). "The High Costs of Cyborg Survival: Octavia Butler's *Xenogenesis* Trilogy." In *Foundation: The International Review of Science Fiction* 72, 49–56.

Holiday, Billie. (1956). *Lady Sings the Blues* (with William Dufty). New York: Penguin.

Hollows, Joanne. (2000). *Feminism, Femininity, and Popular Culture*. Manchester: Manchester University Press.

Hollows, Joanne, and Moseley, Rachel. (Eds.). (2006). *Feminism in Popular Culture*. New York: Berg.

Holub, Renate. (1992). *Antonio Gramsci: Beyond Marxism and Postmodernism*. New York: Routledge.

Hope, Richard O. (1979). *Racial Strife in the U.S. Military: Toward the Elimination of Discrimination*. New York: Praeger.

Hopkinson, Natalie, and Moore, Natalie Y. (2006). *Deconstructing Tyrone: A New Look at Black Masculinity in the Hip Hop Generation*. San Francisco: Cleis Press.

Horkheimer, Max. (1972). *Critical Theory: Selected Essays*. New York: Continuum.

——. (1974a). *Eclipse of Reason*. New York: Continuum.

——. (1974b). *Critique of Instrumental Reason: Lectures and Essays Since the End of World War II*. New York: Continuum.

——. (1978). *Dawn and Decline: Notes, 1926–1931 and 1950–1969*. New York: Continuum.

——. (1993). *Between Philosophy and Social Science: Selected Early Writings*. Cambridge: MIT Press.

Horkheimer, Max, and Adorno, Theodor W. (1995). *Dialectic of Enlightenment*. New York: Continuum.

Hoskyns, Barney. (1987). *Say It One Time for the Broken-Hearted: The Country Side of Southern Soul*. London: Fontana Collins.

Houston, Marsha, and Davis, Olga I. (Eds.). (2002). *Centering Ourselves: African American Feminist and Womanist Studies of Discourse*. Cresskill, NJ: Hampton Press.

Howard, Josiah. (2007). *Blaxploitation Cinema: The Essential Reference Guide*. Guildford: FAB.

Howard-Pitney, David. (2004). *Martin Luther King, Malcolm X, and the Civil Rights Struggle of the 1950s and 1960s: A Brief History with Documents*. Boston: Bedford/St. Martin's.

Hudson, Cheryl, and Davies, Gareth. (Eds.). (2008). *Ronald Reagan and the 1980s: Perceptions, Policies, Legacies*. New York: Palgrave Macmillan.

Hudson-Weems, Clenora. (1995). *Africana Womanism: Reclaiming Ourselves*. Boston: Bedford.

——. (1997). "Africana Womanism and the Critical Need for Africana Theory and Thought." *Western Journal of Black Studies* 21 (2), 79–84.

——. (2004). *Africana Womanist Literary Theory*. Trenton, NJ: Africa World Press.

Huhn, Tom. (Ed.). (2004). *The Cambridge Companion to Adorno*. Cambridge: Cambridge University Press.

Humann, Heather D. (2007). "Feminist and Material Concerns: Lil' Kim, Destiny's Child, and Questions of Consciousness." In Gwendolyn D. Pough, Elaine Richardson, Aisha Durham, and Rachel Raimist (Eds.), *Home Girls Make Some Noise!: The Hip Hop Feminism Anthology* (94–105). Mira Loma, CA: Parker Publishing.

Hunt, Scott A., and Benford, Robert D. (2004). "Collective Identity, Solidarity, and Commitment." In David A. Snow, Sarah Anne Soule, and Hanspeter Kriesi (Eds.), *The Blackwell Companion to Social Movements* (433–57). Malden, MA: Blackwell.

Hunter, Marcus Anthony. (2010). "The Nightly Round: Space, Social Capital, and Urban Black Nightlife." *City and Community* 9 (2), 165–86.

Huntington, Carla S. (2007). *Hip Hop Dance: Meanings and Messages*. Jefferson, NC: McFarland & Co.

Huntley, Horace, and Montgomery, David. (2004). *Black Workers' Struggle for Equality in Birmingham*. Urbana: University of Illinois Press.

Hurst, Fannie. (1933). *Imitation of Life*. New York: Harper.

Hurston, Zora Neale. (1995). *Folklore, Memoirs, and Other Writings* (Cheryl A. Wall, Ed). New York: Library of America.

Hurt, Byron. (Director). (2006). *Hip Hop: Beyond Beats & Rhymes*. Northampton, MA: Media Education Foundation and God Bless the Child Productions.

Ianniello, Lynne. (1965). *Milestones Along the March: Twelve Historic Civil Rights Documents, from World War II to Selma*. New York: F.A. Praeger.

Ice-T. (1994). *The Ice Opinion: Who Gives a Fuck?* (with Heidi Sigmund). New York: St. Martin's Press.

——. (2011). *Ice: A Memoir of Gangster Life and Redemption—From South Central to Hollywood* (with Douglas Century). New York: One World/Ballantine Books.

Incite! Women of Color Against Violence. (Eds.). (2006). *Color of Violence: The Incite! Anthology*. Cambridge, MA: South End Press.

Ipiotis, Celia. (Director). (1984). *Popular Culture in Dance: the World of Hip Hop*. New York: ARC Videodance.

Israel. (Director). (2002). *The Freshest Kids: A History of the B-Boy*. Los Angeles: QD3 Entertainment.

Iton, Richard. (2008). *In Search of the Black Fantastic: Politics and Popular Culture in the Post-Civil Rights Era.* New York: Oxford University Press.

Jabbaar-Gyambrah, Tara Aminah. (2007). "Hip Hop, Hip Life: Global Sistahs." Ph.D. dissertation, State University of New York at Buffalo.

Jackson, Buzzy. (2005). *A Bad Woman Feeling Good: Blues and the Women Who Sing Them.* New York: W.W. Norton.

Jackson, John A. (2004). *House on Fire: The Rise and Fall of Philadelphia Soul.* New York: Oxford University Press.

Jackson, Oscar A. (1995). *Bronzeville: A History of Chicago Rhythm & Blues.* Chicago: Heno.

Jackson, Robert. (1994). *The Last Black Mecca, Hip Hop: A Black Cultural Awareness Phenomena and Its Impact on the African American Community* (James Williams, Ed.). Chicago, IL: Research Associates.

Jackson, Sandra, and Moody-Freeman, Julie E. (Eds.). (2011). *The Black Imagination, Science Fiction, Futurism and the Speculative.* New York: Peter Lang.

Jackson, Sharon. "Sha Rock." (2010). *Luminary Icon: The Story of the Beginning and End of Hip Hop's First Female MC* (with Lesha Brown). Virginia Beach, VA: Outta Da Blue Publishing.

James, Darius. (1995). *That's Blaxploitation!: Roots of the Baadasssss 'Tude (Rated X by an All-Whyte Jury).* New York: St. Martin's Griffin.

James, Etta. (1995). *Rage to Survive: The Etta James Story* (with David Ritz). New York Villard Books.

James, Stanlie, and Busia, Abena. (Eds.). (1993). *Theorizing Black Feminism: The Visionary Pragmatism of Black Women.* New York: Routledge.

jamila, shani. (2002). "Can I Get a Witness?: Testimony from a Hip Hop Feminist." In Daisy Hernández and Bushra Rehman (Eds.), *Colonize This!: Young Women of Color on Today's Feminism* (279–94). New York: Seal Press.

Janovitz, Bill. (2005). *Exile on Main St.* New York: Continuum.

Jansen, Jan. (2000). *The Griot's Craft: An Essay on Oral Tradition and Diplomacy.* Piscataway, NJ: Transaction Publishers.

Jarrett, Gene Andrew. (2005). "The Black Arts Movement and Its Scholars." *American Quarterly* 57 (4), 1243–51.

Jay, Martin. (1985). *Adorno.* Cambridge, MA: Harvard University Press.

———. (1996). *The Dialectical Imagination: A History of the Frankfurt School and the Institute of Social Research, 1923–1950.* Berkeley: University of California Press.

Jaynes, Gerald David. (1986). *Branches Without Roots: Genesis of the Black Working-Class in the American South, 1862–1882.* New York: Oxford University Press.

Jefferson, Robert F. (2008). *Fighting for Hope: African American Troops of the 93rd Infantry Division in World War II and Postwar America.* Baltimore: Johns Hopkins University Press.

Jeffreys-Jones, Rhodri. (2007). *The FBI: A History.* New Haven: Yale University Press.

Jeffries, Judson L. (2002). *Huey P. Newton: The Radical Theorist.* Jackson: University Press of Mississippi.

———. (Ed.). (2006). *Black Power in the Belly of the Beast.* Urbana: University of Illinois.

Jeffries, Michael P. (2011). *Thug Life: Race, Gender, and the Meaning of Hip Hop.* Chicago: University of Chicago Press.

Jegede, Tunde. (1994). *African Classical Music and the Griot Tradition.* London: Diabaté Arts.

Jenkins, Henry, McPherson, Tara, and Shattuc, Jane. (Eds.). (2002). *Hop on Pop: The Politics and Pleasures of Popular Culture.* Durham: Duke University Press.

Jenkins, Rasheedah. (2008). "The Songs of Black (Women) Folk: Music, Politics, and Everyday Living." Ph.D. dissertation, Louisiana State University, Baton Rouge, LA.

Jiménez, Gabriela. (2011). "'Something 2 Dance 2': Electro Hop in 1980s Los Angeles and Its Afro-Futurist Link." *Black Music Research Journal* 31 (1), 131–44.

Johnson, Cedric. (2007). *Revolutionaries to Race Leaders: Black Power and the Making of African American Politics.* Minneapolis: University of Minnesota Press.

Johnson, Daniel M., and Campbell, Rex R. (1981). *Black Migration in America: A Social Demographic History.* Durham: Duke University Press.

Johnson, E. Patrick, and Henderson, Mae G. (Eds.). (2005). *Black Queer Studies: A Critical Anthology.* Durham: Duke University Press.

Johnson, James D., Trawalter, Sophie, and Dovidio, John F. (2000). "Converging Interracial Consequences of Exposure to Violent Rap Music on Stereotypical Attributions of Blacks." *Journal of Experimental Social Psychology* 36, 233–51.

Johnson, James Weldon. (1933). *Along This Way: The Autobiography of James Weldon Johnson.* New York: Viking Press.

———. (2000). *The Complete Poems* (Sondra K. Wilson, Ed.). New York: Penguin.

———. (2004). *Writings: The Autobiography of an Ex-Colored Man; Along This Way; New York Age Editorials; Selected Essays; Black Manhattan; Selected Poems.* New York: Penguin Books.

Johnson, John William. (1979). *Griots in Pre-Modern Mali.* Waltham, MA: African Studies Association.

Johnson, Lakesia D. (2012). *Iconic: Decoding Images of the Revolutionary Black Woman.* Waco, TX: Baylor University Press.

Johnson, Maurice L. (2011). "A Historical Analysis: The Evolution of Commercial Rap Music." M.A. thesis, Florida State University, Tallahassee, FL.

Johnson, Ollie A., and Stanford, Karin L. (Eds.). (2002). *Black Political Organizations in the Post-Civil Rights Era.* New Brunswick: Rutgers University Press.

Johnson, Vernon, and Lyne, Bill. (Eds.). (2002). *Walkin' the Talk: An Anthology of African American Studies.* Upper Saddle River, NJ: Prentice Hall.

Jones, Alan, and Kantonen, Jussi. (2000). *Saturday Night Forever: The Story of Disco.* Chicago: A Cappella Books.

Jones, Arthur C. (1993). *Wade in the Water: The Wisdom of the Spirituals.* Maryknoll, NY: Orbis Books.

Jones, Charisse, and Shorter-Gooden, Kumea. (2003). *Shifting: The Double-Lives of Black Women in America.* New York: HarperCollins.

Jones, Ebony Elizabeth. (2008). "Motown and the Movement." M.A. thesis, University of Toledo, Toledo, OH.

Jones, Ferdinand, and Jones, Arthur C. (2001). *The Triumph of the Soul: Cultural and Psychological Aspects of African American Music.* Westport, CT: Praeger.

Jones, Nikki. (2010). *Between Good and Ghetto: African American Girls and Inner-City Violence.* New Brunswick: Rutgers University Press.

Jones, Patricia Spears. (1993). "Sly & the Family Stone under the Big Tit: Atlanta, 1973." *Kenyon Review* 15 (4), 66–68.

Jones, Roberta. (2003). "Staying Human on the Left Coast: Michael Franti and Spearhead have become a musical and political force on the West Coast." *Political Affairs* 82 (8), 8.

Jones, Steve, and Gundersen, Edna. (2007). "Can Rap Regain Its Crown?" *USA Today* (June 15), 1–6. Retrieved from http://www.usatoday.com/life/music/news/2007-06-14-rap-decline_N.htm.

Jones, Steven J. (2006). *Antonio Gramsci.* New York: Routledge.

Joseph, Peniel E. (Ed.). (2001). "Black Power Studies I." *The Black Scholar* 31, 3–4.

———. (2006a). *Black Power Movement: Rethinking the Civil Rights-Black Power Era.* New York: Routledge.

———. (2006b). *Waiting 'Til the Midnight Hour: A Narrative History of Black Power in America.* New York: Henry Holt.

———. (2008). "Revolution in Babylon: Stokely Carmichael and America in the 1960s." *Souls: A Critical Journal of Black Politics, Culture, and Society* 9 (4), 281–301.

———. (2010). (Ed.). *Neighborhood Rebels: Black Power at the Local Level.* New York: Palgrave Macmillan.

Junn, Jane, and Haynie, Kerry L. (Eds.). (2008). *New Race Politics in America: Understanding Minority and Immigrant Politics.* New York: Cambridge University Press.

Kajikawa, Loren. (2012). "D'Angelo's *Voodoo* Technology: African Cultural Memory and the Ritual of Popular Music Consumption." *Black Music Research Journal* 32 (1), 137–59.

Kaliss, Jeff. (2008). *I Want to Take You Higher: The Life and Times of Sly & the Family Stone.* New York: Hal Leonard/Backbeat Books.

Kamin, Jonathan. (1975). "Parallels in the Social Reactions to Jazz and Rock." *The Black Perspective in Music* 3 (3), 278–98.

Kaplan, Max. (1993). *Barbershopping: Musical and Social Harmony*. Rutherford, NJ: Fairleigh Dickinson University Press.

Karaian, Lara, Rundle, Lisa Bryn, and Mitchell, Allyson. (Eds.). (2001). *Turbo Chicks: Talking Young Feminisms*. Toronto: Sumach Press.

Karenga, Maulana. (1968). "Black Art: A Rhythmic Reality of Revolution." *Negro Digest* 3, 5–9.

———. (1972). "Black Cultural Nationalism." In Addison Gayle Jr., (Ed.), *The Black Aesthetic* (32–38). Garden City, NY: Doubleday.

———. (1997). "Black Art: Mute Matter Given Force and Function." In Henry Louis Gates Jr. and Nellie Y. McKay (Eds.), *The Norton Anthology of African American Literature* (1972–1977). New York: W.W. Norton.

———. (2002). *Introduction to Black Studies* (3rd ed.). Los Angeles, CA: University of Sankore Press.

Kato, M. T. (2007). *From Kung Fu to Hip Hop: Globalization, Revolution, and Popular Culture*. Albany: State University of New York Press.

Katz, Mark. (2012). *Groove Music: The Art and Culture of the Hip Hop DJ*. New York: Oxford University Press.

Katz, Michael B. (1989). *The Undeserving Poor: From the War on Poverty to the War Welfare*. New York: Pantheon Books.

Katznelson, Ira. (2005). *When Affirmative Action was White: An Untold History of Racial Inequality in Twentieth Century America*. New York: W.W. Norton.

Kaya, Ayhan. (2001). *Sicher in Kreuzberg/Constructing Diasporas: Turkish Hip Hop Youth in Berlin*. Piscataway, NJ: Transaction Publishers.

Kelley, Norman. (2002). *R&B, Rhythm and Business: The Political Economy of Black Music*. New York: Akashic.

Kelley, Robin D.G. (1994). *Race Rebels: Culture, Politics, and the Black Working-Class*. New York: Free Press.

———. (1997). *Yo' Mama's Disfunktional!: Fighting the Culture Wars in Urban America*. Boston: Beacon.

———. (2002). *Freedom Dreams: The Black Radical Imagination*. Boston: Beacon.

———. (2012). *Africa Speaks, America Answers: Modern Jazz in Revolutionary Times*. Cambridge: Harvard University Press.

Kelley, Robin D.G., and Lewis, Earl. (Eds.). (2000). *To Make Our World Anew: A History of African Americans*. New York: Oxford University Press.

Kellner, Douglas. (1989). *Critical Theory, Marxism, and Modernity*. Baltimore: Johns Hopkins University Press.

———. (1990a). "Critical Theory and Ideology Critique." In Ronald Roblin (Ed.), *Critical Theory and Aesthetics* (85–123). Lewistown: Edwin Mellen Press.

———. (1990b). "Critical Theory and the Crisis of Social Theory." *Sociological Perspectives* 33 (1), 11–33.

———. (1993). "Critical Theory and Social Theory: Current Debates and Challenges." *Theory, Culture, and Society* 10 (2), 43–61.

Kellough, J. Edward. (2006). *Understanding Affirmative Action: Politics, Discrimination, and the Search for Justice*. Washington, DC: Georgetown University Press.

Kelly, Brian. (2001). *Race, Class, and Power in the Alabama Coalfields, 1908–1921*. Urbana: University of Illinois Press.

Kelly, Christine A. (2001). *Tangled Up in Red, White, and Blue: New Social Movements in America*. Lanham, MD: Rowman & Littlefield.

Kempton, Arthur. (2003). *Boogaloo: The Quintessence of American Popular Music*. New York: Pantheon Books.

Kennedy, Stetson. (1990). *Jim Crow Guide: The Way It Was*. Boca Raton: Florida Atlantic University Press.

————. (2011). *Jim Crow Guide to the U.S.A.: The Laws, Customs and Etiquette Governing the Conduct of Non-whites and Other Minorities as Second-Class Citizens.* Tuscaloosa: University of Alabama Press.

Kenyatta, Kelly. (2000). *You Forgot about Dre!: The Unauthorized Biography of Dr. Dre and Eminem: From NWA to Slim Shady (A Tale of Gangsta Rap, Violence, and Hit Records).* Los Angeles: Busta Books.

Kern-Foxworth, Marilyn. (1994). *Aunt Jemima, Uncle Ben, and Rastus: Blacks in Advertising, Yesterday, Today, and Tomorrow.* Westport, CT: Greenwood Press.

Kersten, Andrew Edmund. (2007). *A. Philip Randolph: A Life in the Vanguard.* Lanham, MD: Rowman & Littlefield.

Keyes, Cheryl L. (2000). "Empowering Self, Making Choices, Creating Spaces: Black Female Identity via Rap Music Performance." *Journal of American Folklore* 113 (449), 255–69.

————. (2002). *Rap Music and Street Consciousness.* Urbana: University of Illinois Press.

Kilgore, De Witt Douglas. (2003). *Astrofuturism: Science, Race, and Visions of Utopia in Space.* Philadelphia: University of Pennsylvania Press.

Kimbrough, Natalie. (2007). *Equality or Discrimination?: African Americans in the U.S. Military during the Vietnam War.* Lanham, MD: University Press of America.

King, Deborah K. (1988). "Multiple Jeopardy, Multiple Consciousness: The Context of a Black Feminist Ideology." *Signs* 14 (1), 42–72.

King, Jason. (1999). "When Autobiography Becomes Soul: Erykah Badu and the Cultural Politics of Black Feminism." *Women & Performance: A Journal of Feminist Theory* 10 (1 & 2), 211–43.

King, Martin Luther, Jr. (1986). *A Testament of Hope: The Essential Writings of Martin Luther King, Jr.* (James Melvin Washington, Ed.). San Francisco: Harper & Row.

————. (1992). *I Have a Dream: Writings and Speeches That Changed the World* (James Melvin Washington, Ed.). San Francisco: Harper.

————. (2001). *A Call to Conscience: The Landmark Speeches of Dr. Martin Luther King, Jr.* (Clayborne Carson and Kris Shepard, Eds.). New York: Warner Books.

Kirby, David. (2009). *Little Richard: The Birth of Rock & Roll.* New York: Continuum.

Kitwana, Bakari. (1994). *The Rap on Gangsta Rap, Who Run It?: Gangsta Rap and Visions of Black Violence.* Chicago: Third World Press.

————. (2002). *The Hip Hop Generation: Young Blacks and the Crisis in African American Culture.* New York: Basic/Civitas.

————. (2004). "The State of the Hip Hop Generation: How Hip Hop's Cultural Movement is Evolving into Political Power." *Diogenes* 51 (3), 115–20.

————. (2005). *Why White Kids Love Hip Hop: Wangstas, Wiggers, Wannabes, and the New Reality of Race in America.* New York: Basic/Civitas.

————. (Ed.). (2012). *Hip Hop Activism in the Obama Era: Essays and Interviews.* Chicago: Third World Press.

Knight, Suge. (2003). *American Nightmare, American Dream.* New York: Riverhead.

Knowles, Christopher. (2010). *The Secret History of Rock & Roll: The Mysterious Roots of Modern Music.* Berkeley, CA: Viva Editions.

Kochman, Thomas. (1972). *Rappin' and Stylin' Out: Communication in Urban Black America.* Urbana: University of Illinois Press.

Kolawole, Mary Ebun Modupe. (1997). *Womanism and African Consciousness.* Trenton, NJ: Africa World Press.

Kopano, Baruti N., and Williams, Yohuru R. (Eds.). (2004). *Treading Our Ways: Selected Topics in Africana Studies.* Kendall/Hunt Publishing.

Koven, Mikel J. (2001). *The Pocket Essential Blaxploitation Films.* Harpenden: Pocket Essentials.

————. (2010). *Blaxploitation Films.* Harpenden: Kamera.

Kowalewski, Zbigniew. (1993). *The Revolutionary Message of Rap Music.* San Francisco, CA: Walnut Publishing.

Kreiss, Daniel. (2008). "Appropriating the Master's Tools: Sun Ra, the Black Panthers, and Black Consciousness, 1952–1973." *Black Music Research Journal* 28 (1), 57–82.

Krims, Adam. (2000). *Rap Music and the Poetics of Identity.* Cambridge: Cambridge University Press.

Krohn, Franklin B., and Suazo, Frances L. (1995). "Contemporary Urban Music: Controversial Messages in Hip Hop and Rap Lyrics." *ETC.: A Review of General Semantics* 52 (2), 139–55.

Kubrin, Charis E. (2005a). "Gangstas, Thugs, and Hustlas: Identity and the Code of the Street in Rap Music." *Social Problems* 52 (3), 360–78.

———. (2005b). "'I See Death Around the Corner': Nihilism in Rap Music." *Sociological Perspectives* 48 (4), 433–59.

Kugelberg, Johan. (Ed.). (2007). *Born in the Bronx: A Visual Record of the Early Days of Hip Hop.* New York: Rizzoli.

Kuhn, Thomas S. (1970). *The Structure of Scientific Revolutions* (2nd ed.). Chicago: University of Chicago Press.

Kulkarni, Neil. (2004). *Hip Hop: Bring the Noise—The Stories Behind the Biggest Songs.* New York: Thunder's Mouth Press.

Kun, Josh. (2002). "Two Turntables and a Social Movement: Writing Hip Hop at Century's End." *American Literary History* 14 (3), 580–92.

Kusmer, Kenneth L. (1976). *A Ghetto Takes Shape: Black Cleveland, 1870–1930.* Urbana: University of Illinois Press.

Labaton, Vivien, and Martin, Dawn L. (Eds.). (2004). *Fire This Time!: Young Activists and the New Feminism.* New York: Anchor Books.

Laham, Nicholas. (1998). *The Reagan Presidency and the Politics of Race: In Pursuit of Colorblind Justice and Limited Government.* Westport, CT: Praeger.

Lait, Jack, and Mortimer, Lee. (1952). *U.S.A. Confidential.* New York: Crown Publishers.

Lamaison, Jean-Louis. (1977). *Soul Music.* Paris: Albin Michel.

Lapiower, Alain. (1997). *Total Respect: La Generation Hip Hop en Belgique.* Brussels: Fondation Jacques Gueux/EVO.

Laraña, Enrique, Johnston, Hank, and Gusfield, Joseph R. (Eds.). (1994). *New Social Movements: From Ideology to Identity.* Philadelphia: Temple University Press.

Larkin, Ralph W. (1979). *Suburban Youth in Cultural Crisis.* New York: Oxford University Press.

Larkin, Rochelle. (1970). *Soul Music: The Sound, the Stars, the Story.* New York: Lancer Books.

Larsen, Nella. (1929). *Passing.* New York: Alfred A. Knopf.

Latifah, Queen. (2000). *Ladies First: Revelations of a Strong Woman.* New York: Perennial Currents.

Lauterbach, Preston. (2011). *The Chitlin' Circuit: And the Road to Rock & Roll.* New York: W.W. Norton.

Lavender, Isiah. (2011). *Race in American Science Fiction.* Bloomington: Indiana University Press.

Lawrence, Novotny. (2008). *Blaxploitation Films of the 1970s: Blackness and Genre.* New York: Routledge.

Lawrence, Tim. (2003). *Love Saves the Day: A History of American Dance Music Culture, 1970–1979.* Durham: Duke University Press.

Lawson, R.A. (2010). *Jim Crow's Counterculture: The Blues and Black Southerners, 1890–1945.* Baton Rouge: Louisiana State University Press.

Lawson, Steven F., and Payne, Charles M. (2006). *Debating the Civil Rights Movement, 1945–1968.* Lanham, MD: Rowman & Littlefield.

Lazerow, Jama, and Williams, Yohuru R. (Eds.). (2006). *In Search of the Black Panther Party: New Perspectives on a Revolutionary Movement.* Durham: Duke University Press.

———. (Eds.). (2008). *Liberated Territory: Untold Local Perspectives on the Black Panther Party.* Durham: Duke University Press.

Lee, Benson. (Director). (2008). *Planet B-Boy: Break-Dancing Has Evolved.* New York: Arts Alliance America.

Lee, Harper. (1960). *To Kill a Mockingbird.* Philadelphia: Lippincott.

Lee, Shayne. (2010). *Erotic Revolutionaries: Black Women, Sexuality, and Popular Culture.* Lanham, MD: Hamilton Books.

Lee, Su H. (2007). *Debating New Social Movements: Culture, Identity, and Social Fragmentation.* Lanham, MD: University Press of America.

Lemann, Nicholas. (1991). *The Promised Land: The Great Black Migration and How It Changed America.* New York: Vintage.

Lena, Jennifer C. (2003). "From 'Flash' to 'Cash': Producing Rap Authenticity, 1979 to 1995." Ph.D. dissertation, Columbia University, New York.

———. (2004). "Meaning and Membership: Samples in Rap Music, 1979 to 1995." *Poetics* 32 (3–4), 297–310.

———. (2006). "Social Context and Musical Content: Rap Music, 1979–1995." *Social Forces* 85 (1), 479–95.

LeRoy, Dan. (2006). *The Beastie Boys' Paul's Boutique.* London: Continuum.

Levecq, Christine. (2000). "Power and Repetition: Philosophies of (Literary) History in Octavia E. Butler's *Kindred.*" *Contemporary Literature* 41 (1), 525–53.

Levine, Ellen. (1993). *Freedom's Children: Young Civil Rights Activists Tell Their Own Stories.* New York: Putnam.

Levine, Lawrence. (1977). *Black Culture and Black Consciousness: Afro-American Folk Thought from Slavery to Freedom.* New York: Oxford University Press.

Levy, Eugene D. (1973). *James Weldon Johnson: Black Leader, Black Voice.* Chicago: University of Chicago Press.

Lewis, Andrew B. (2009). *The Shadows of Youth: The Remarkable Journey of the Civil Rights Generation.* New York: Hill & Wang.

Lewis, George. (2008). *A Power Stronger Than Itself: The AACM and American Experimental Music.* Chicago: University of Chicago Press.

Lewis, George H. (1973). "Social Protest and Self-Awareness in Black Popular Music." *Popular Music and Society* 2 (4), 327–33.

Lewis, Jerry M., and Looney, John G. (1983). *The Long Struggle: Well-Functioning Working-Class Black Families.* New York: Brunner/Mazel.

Lewis, Miles Marshall. (2006). *Sly & the Family Stone's There's a Riot Goin' On.* New York: Continuum.

Lewis, Nghana. (2006). "'You Sell Your Soul like You Sell a Piece of Ass': Rhythms of Black Female Sexuality and Subjectivity in Meshell Ndegeocello's *Cookie: The Anthropological Mixtape.*" *Black Music Research Journal* 26 (1), 111–30.

Lewis-Colman, David M. (2008). *Race Against Liberalism: Black Workers and the UAW in Detroit.* Urbana: University of Illinois Press.

Leymarie, Isabelle. (1978). "The Role and Function of the Griots among the Wolof of Senegal." Ph.D. dissertation, Columbia University, New York.

Lhamon, W.T. (1998). *Raising Cain: Blackface Performance from Jim Crow to Hip Hop.* Cambridge, MA: Harvard University Press.

———. (Ed.). (2003). *Jump Jim Crow: Lost Plays, Lyrics, and Street Prose of the First Atlantic Popular Culture.* Cambridge, MA: Harvard University Press.

Light, Alan. (Ed.). (1999). *The Vibe History of Hip Hop.* New York: Random House.

———. (2000). *Always on Vacation: The Beastie Boys.* London: Little Brown.

———. (2005). *The Skills to Pay the Bills: The Story of the Beastie Boys.* New York: Three Rivers Press.

Lightfoot, Claude M. (1968). *Ghetto Rebellion to Black Liberation.* New York: International Publishers.

Linden, Amy. (2004). "The Last Maverick: Me'Shell Ndegeocello and the Burden of Vision." In Kandia Crazy Horse (Ed.), *Rip It Up: The Black Experience in Rock & Roll* (185–89). New York: Palgrave Macmillan.

Linton, Meg, Maberry, Sue, and Pulsinelli, Elizabeth. (Eds.). (2011). *Doin' It in Public: Feminism and Art at the Woman's Building.* Los Angeles: Otis College of Art and Design Press.

Lippard, Lucy R. (1976). *From the Center: Feminist Essays on Women's Art.* New York: Dutton.

———. (Ed.). (1980). *Issue: Social Strategies by Women Artists.* London: Institute of Contemporary Arts.

———. (1995). *The Pink Glass Swan: Selected Essays on Feminist Art.* New York: New Press.

Lipsitz, George. (1990a). "Listening to Learn and Learning to Listen: Popular Culture, Cultural Theory, and American Studies." *American Quarterly* 42 (4), 615–36.

———. (1990b). *Time Passages: Collective Memory and American Popular Culture.* Minneapolis: University of Minnesota Press.

———. (1994). *Dangerous Crossroads: Popular Music, Postmodernism, and the Poetics of Place.* New York: Verso.

———. (1998). *The Possessive Investment in Whiteness: How White People Profit from Identity Politics.* Philadelphia: Temple University Press.

———. (2001). *American Studies in a Moment of Danger.* Minneapolis: University of Minnesota Press.

———. (2007). *Footsteps in the Dark: The Hidden Histories of Popular Culture.* Minneapolis: University of Minnesota Press.

———. (2011). *How Racism Takes Place.* Philadelphia: Temple University Press.

Lock, Graham. (1999). *Blutopia: Visions of the Future and Revisions of the Past in the Work of Sun Ra, Duke Ellington, and Anthony Braxton.* Durham: Duke University Press.

Lornell, Kip. (1995). *Happy in the Service of the Lord: African American Sacred Vocal Harmony Quartets in Memphis.* Knoxville: University of Tennessee Press.

———. (Ed.). (2010). *From Jubilee to Hip Hop: Readings in African American Music.* Upper Saddle River, NJ: Prentice Hall.

Lornell, Kip, and Stephenson, Charles C. (2001). *The Beat: Go-Go's Fusion of Funk and Hip Hop.* New York: Billboard Books.

———. (2009). *The Beat!: Go-Go Music from Washington, D.C.* Jackson: University Press of Mississippi.

Lott, Eric. (1993). *Love and Theft: Blackface Minstrelsy and the American Working-Class.* New York: Oxford University Press.

Lovell, John. (1972). *Black Song: The Forge and the Flame—The Story of How the Afro-American Spiritual was Hammered Out.* New York: Macmillan.

Loza, Steven, Santiago, Josefina, Alvarez, Milo, and Moore, Charles. (1994). "Los Angeles Gangsta Rap and the Aesthetics of Violence." *Selected Reports in Ethnomusicology* 10, 149–61.

Luck, Richard. (2002). *The Beastie Boys.* Harpenden: Pocket Essentials.

Luckhurst, Roger. (1996). "'Horror and Beauty in Rare Combination': The Miscegenate Fictions of Octavia Butler." *Women: A Cultural Review* 7 (1), 28–38.

Lust, Alexandria Leah. (2011). "'Understanding the depth of the '90s women': TLC's Political, Musical, and Artistic Complexities of Hip Hop Feminist Thought, 1991–2002." M.A. thesis, Sarah Lawrence College, Bronxville, NY.

Lüthe, Martin. (2010). "Color-line and Crossing-over Motown and Performances of Blackness in 1960s American Culture." Ph.D. dissertation, Justus Liebig University, Giessen, Germany.

Lynn, Susan. (1992). *Progressive Women in Conservative Times: Racial Justice, Peace, and Feminism, 1945 to the 1960s.* New Brunswick: Rutgers University Press.

Mabee, Carleton. (1970). *Black Freedom: The Nonviolent Abolitionists from 1830 through the Civil War.* New York: Macmillan.

Maconie, Robin. (2012). *Avant-Garde: An American Odyssey from Gertrude Stein to Pierre Boulez.* Lanham, MD: Scarecrow Press.

MacWeeney, India. (2008). *Imagining the Real: Chicano Youth, Hip Hop, Race, Space and Authenticity.* London: University of London.

Maglin, Nan Bauer, and Perry, Donna. (Eds.). (1996). *"Bad Girls"/"Good Girls": Women, Sex, and Power in the Nineties.* New Brunswick, NJ: Rutgers University Press.

Magoun, Alexander B. (2007). *Television: The Life Story of a Technology.* Westport, CT: Greenwood Press.

Mahon, Maureen. (2000). "Black Like This: Race, Generation, and Rock in the Post- Civil Rights Era." *American Ethnologist* 27 (2), 283–311.

———. (2004). *Right to Rock: The Black Rock Coalition and the Cultural Politics of Race.* Durham: Duke University Press.

Mailer, Norman. (1957). *The White Negro: Superficial Reflections on the Hipster.* San Francisco: City Lights Books.

Maimone, Sofia Z. (2011). *Mary J. Blige.* New York: Gareth Stevens.

Malcolm X. (1971). *The End of White World Supremacy: Four Speeches.* Merlin House/Seaver Books.

———. (1989). *Malcolm X: The Last Speeches.* New York: Pathfinder.

———. (1990). *Malcolm X Speaks: Selected Speeches and Statements.* New York: Grove Weidenfeld.

———. (1991a). *Malcolm X Speeches at Harvard* (Archie Epps, Ed.). New York: Paragon House.

———. (1991b). *Malcolm X Talks to Young People: Speeches in the U.S., Great Britain, and Africa.* New York: Pathfinder.

———. (1992a). *The Autobiography of Malcolm X* (with Alex Haley). New York: Ballantine Books.

———. (1992b). *By Any Means Necessary.* New York: Pathfinder.

———. (1992c). *The Final Speeches, February 1965.* New York: Pathfinder.

Malik, Abd Al. (2009). *Sufi Rapper: The Spiritual Journey of Abd al Malik.* New York: Inner-Traditions.

Manganelli, Kimberly S. (2012). *Transatlantic Spectacles of Race: The Tragic Mulatta and the Tragic Muse.* New Brunswick: Rutgers University Press.

Manring, M. M. (1998). *Slave in a Box: The Strange Career of Aunt Jemima.* Charlottesville: University Press of Virginia.

Maparyan, Layli Phillips. (2011). *The Womanist Idea.* New York: Routledge.

Mapson, J. Wendell. (1984). *Ministry of Music in Black Church.* Valley Forge, PA: Judson Press.

Marable, Manning. (1980). "A. Philip Randolph and the Foundations of Black American Socialism." *Radical America* 14, 7–29.

———. (1983). *How Capitalism Underdeveloped Black America.* Boston: South End.

———. (2011). *Malcolm X: A Life of Reinvention.* New York: Viking.

Marable, Manning, and Mullings, Leith. (Eds.). (2000). *Let Nobody Turn Us Around: Voices of Resistance, Reform, and Renewal—An African American Anthology.* Lanham, MD: Rowman & Littlefield.

———. (Eds.). (2009). *New Social Movements in the African Diaspora: Challenging Global Apartheid.* New York: Palgrave Macmillan.

Marcus, Greil. (1975). *Mystery Train: Images of America in Rock 'n' Roll Music.* New York: E.P. Dutton.

Margolick, David. (2000). *Strange Fruit: Billie Holiday, Café Society, and an Early Cry for Civil Rights.* Philadelphia: Running Press.

Markovitz, Jonathan. (2004). *Legacies of Lynching: Racial Violence and Memory.* Minneapolis, MN: University of Minnesota Press.

Marks, Carole. (1989). *Farewell, We're Good and Gone: The Great Black Migration.* Bloomington: Indiana University Press.

Marsh, Dave. (1985). "Sly & the Family Stone." In Dave Marsh, *Fortunate Son: Criticism and Journalism by America's Best-Known Rock Writer* (55–60). New York: Random House.

Marshall, Lee. (2003). "For and Against the Record Industry: An Introduction to Bootleg Collectors and Tape Traders." *Popular Music* 22 (1), 57–72.

Martin, Bradford D. (2011). *The Other Eighties: A Secret History of America in the Age of Reagan.* New York: Hill & Wang.

Martinez, Gerald, Martínez, Diana, and Chavez, Andres. (1998). *What It Is, What It Was!: The Black Film Explosion of the '70s in Words and Pictures.* New York: Hyperion.

Martinez, Theresa A. (1997). "Popular Culture as Oppositional Culture: Rap as Resistance." *Sociological Perspectives* 40 (2), 265–86.

Mason, Phillip L. (1992). "Soul in the Culture of African Americans." *Music Educators Journal* 79 (3), 49–52.

Massey, Douglas S., and Denton, Nancy A. (1993). *American Apartheid: Segregation and the Making of the Underclass.* Cambridge: Harvard University Press.

Mathieson, Kenny. (2002). *Cookin': Hard Bop and Soul Jazz, 1954–65.* Edinburgh: Canongate.

Mattern, Mark. (1998). *Acting in Concert: Music, Community, and Political Action.* New Brunswick: Rutgers University Press.

Maultsby, Portia K. (1983). "Soul Music: Its Sociological and Political Significance in American Popular Culture." *Journal of Popular Culture* 17, 51–60.

———. (2001). "Funk Music: An Expression of Black Life in Dayton, Ohio and the American Metropolis." In Hans Krabbendam, Marja Roholl, and Tity De Vries (Eds.), *The American Metropolis: Image and Inspiration* (197–213). Amsterdam: Vu University Press.

Maultsby, Portia K., and Burnim, Mellonee V. (1987). "From Backwoods to City Streets: The Afro-American Musical Journey." In Geneva Gay and Willie Baber (Eds.), *Expressively Black: The Cultural Basis of Ethnic Identity* (109–36). New York: Praeger Press.

Maxile, Horace. (2011). "Extensions on a Black Musical Tropology: From Trains to the Mothership (and Beyond)." *Journal of Black Studies* 42 (4), 593–608.

Maxwell, Ian. (2003). *Phat Beats, Dope Rhymes: Hip Hop Down Under Comin' Upper.* Middletown, CT: Wesleyan University Press.

Mayfield, Curtis. (1969). "The Message in Soul Music." *Soul* (September 22), 16.

Mayne, Heather J. (2000). "The Wild, Wild West: Images of California in Contemporary Rap Music." *California History* 79 (1), 70–75.

McAdam, Doug, McCarthy, John D., and Zald, Mayer N. (Eds.). (1996). *Comparative Perspectives on Social Movements: Political Opportunities, Mobilizing Structures, and Cultural Framings.* New York: Cambridge University Press.

McClintock, Anne. (1995). *Imperial Leather: Race, Gender, and Sexuality in the Colonial Conquest.* New York: Routledge.

McCord, William Maxwell. (1969). *Life Styles in the Black Ghetto.* New York: Norton.

McCormack, Donald J. (1973). "Stokely Carmichael and Pan-Africanism: Back to Black Power." *Journal of Politics* 35 (2), 386–409.

McCourt, Tom. (1983). "Bright Lights, Big City + A Brief History of Rhythm & Blues, 1945–1957." *Popular Music & Society* 9 (2), 1–18.

McCoy, Judy. (1992). *Rap Music in the 1980s: A Reference Guide.* Metuchen, NJ: Scarecrow Press.

McDaniels, Darryl. (2001). *King of Rock: Respect, Responsibility, and My Life with Run-DMC* (with Bruce Haring). New York: St. Martin's Press.

McDermott, John. (1992). *Hendrix: Setting the Record Straight* (with Eddie Kramer). New York: Warner Books.

McFarland, Pancho. (2008). *Chicano Rap: Gender and Violence in the Post-Industrial Barrio.* Austin: University of Texas Press.

McGregory, Jerrilyn. (2010). *Downhome Gospel: African American Spiritual Activism in Wiregrass Country.* Jackson: University Press of Mississippi.

McIver, Joel. (2002). *Erykah Badu: The First Lady of Soul.* London: Sanctuary Publishing.

McKittrick, Katherine, and Woods, Clyde Adrian. (Eds.). (2007). *Black Geographies and the Politics of Place.* Cambridge, MA: South End Press.

McKivigan, John R., and Harrold, Stanley. (Eds.). (1999). *Anti-Slavery Violence: Sectional, Racial, and Cultural Conflict in Antebellum America.* Knoxville: University of Tennessee Press.

McLendon, Jacquelyn Y. (1995). *The Politics of Color in the Fiction of Jessie Fauset and Nella Larsen.* Charlottesville: University Press of Virginia.

McLeod, Ken. (2003). "Space Oddities: Aliens, Futurism and Meaning in Popular Music." *Popular Music* 22 (3), 337–55.

Medovoi, Leerom. (2005). *Rebels: Youth and the Cold War Origins of Identity.* Durham: Duke University Press.

Meier, August. (1976). *From Plantation to Ghetto.* New York: Hill & Wang.

Meister, Richard J. (1972). *The Black Ghetto: Promised Land or Colony?* Lexington, MA: Heath.

Merlis, Bob, and Seay, Davin. (1997). *Heart & Soul: A Celebration of Black Music Style in America, 1930–1975.* New York: Stewart, Tabori & Chang.

Meyer, David S., and Tarrow, Sidney G. (Eds.). (1998). *The Social Movement Society: Contentious Politics for a New Century.* Lanham, MD: Rowman & Littlefield.

Miles, Tiya, and Holland, Sharon P. (Eds.). (2006). *Crossing Waters, Crossing Worlds: The African Diaspora in Indian Country.* Durham: Duke University Press.

Milestone, Katie, and Meyer, Anneke. (2012). *Gender and Popular Culture.* Cambridge: Polity.

Miller, Calvin Craig. (2005). *A. Philip Randolph and the African American Labor Movement.* Greensboro, NC: Morgan Reynolds Publishing.

Miller, Doug. (1995). "The Moan within the Tone: African Retentions in Rhythm & Blues Saxophone Style in Afro-American Popular Music." *Popular Music* 14, 155–74.

Miller, Frederic P., Vandome, Agnes F., and McBrewster, John. (Eds.). (2011). *Rap West Coast.* Paris: Alphascript Publishing.

Miller, Jim. (1999). *Flowers in the Dustbin: The Rise of Rock & Roll, 1947–1977.* New York: Simon & Schuster.

Miller, Karl Hagstrom. (2010). *Segregating Sound: Inventing Folk and Pop Music in the Age of Jim Crow.* Durham: Duke University Press.

Mills, David. (1998). *George Clinton & P-Funk: An Oral History* (Dave Marsh, Ed.). New York: Avon.

Mitchell, Tony. (Ed.). (2001). *Global Noise: Rap and Hip Hop Outside the USA.* Hanover, NH: University Press of New England.

Mittleman, David. (1996). "The Association for the Advancement of Creative Musicians and the College of Sociology: Avant-Garde Collectives in Contact." M.A. thesis, Claremont Graduate School, Claremont, CA.

Mockus, Martha. (2007). "Me'Shell Ndegeocello: Musical Articulations of Black Feminism." In Christa D. Acampora and Angela L. Cotton (Eds.), *Unmaking Race, Remaking Soul: Transformative Aesthetics and the Practice of Freedom* (81–102). Albany: State University of New York Press.

Monson, Ingrid T. (2007). *Freedom Sounds: Civil Rights Call Out to Jazz and Africa.* New York: Oxford University Press.

Moore, Thurston. (2004). *Mixtape: The Art of Cassette Culture.* New York: Universe Publishing.

Morant, Kesha M. (2011). "Language in Action: Funk Music as the Critical Voice of a Post-Civil Rights Movement Counterculture." *Journal of Black Studies* 42 (1), 71–82.

Morgan, Joan. (1995). "Fly-Girls, Bitches, and Hoes: Notes of a Hip Hop Feminist." *Social Text* 45, 151–57.

———. (1999). *When Chickenheads Come Home to Roost: A Hip Hop Feminist Breaks It Down.* New York: Simon & Schuster.

———. (2007). "Afterword." In Gwendolyn D. Pough, Elaine Richardson, Aisha Durham, and Rachel Raimist (Eds.), *Home Girls Make Some Noise!: The Hip Hop Feminism Anthology* (475–80). Mira Loma, CA: Parker Publishing.

Morgan, Johnny. (2011). *Disco: The Music, The Times, The Era.* New York: Sterling.

Morgan, Marcyliena H. (2005). "Hip Hop Women Shredding the Veil: Race and Class in Popular Feminist Identity." *South Atlantic Quarterly* 104 (3), 425–44.

———. (2009). *The Real Hip Hop: Battling for Knowledge, Power, and Respect in the L.A. Underground.* Durham: Duke University Press.

Morris, Aldon. (1981). "Black Southern Student Sit-in Movement: An Analysis of Internal Organization." *American Sociological Review* 46 (6), 744–67.

———. (1984). *The Origins of the Civil Rights Movement: Black Communities Organizing for Change.* New York: Free Press.

Morris, Aldon D., and Mueller, Carol M. (Eds.). (1992). *Frontiers in Social Movement Theory.* New Haven: Yale University Press.

Morrow, Bruce. (2007). *Doo-wop: The Music, the Times, the Era* (with Rich Maloof). New York: Sterling Publishing.

Morrow, Raymond A. (1994). *Critical Theory and Methodology* (with David D. Brown). Thousands Oaks, CA: Sage.

Morse, David. (1971). *Motown and the Arrival of Black Music.* New York: Macmillan.

Moten, Fred. (2003). *In the Break: The Aesthetics of the Black Radical Tradition.* Minneapolis: University of Minnesota Press.

Müller-Doohm, Stefan. (2005). *Adorno: A Biography.* Cambridge, UK: Polity Press.

Murphy, Joseph M. (1993). *Santeria: African Spirits in America.* Boston: Beacon.

Murray, Albert. (1973). *The Hero and the Blues.* Columbia: University of Missouri Press.

———. (1976). *Stomping the Blues.* New York: McGraw-Hill.

———. (1996). *The Blue Devils of Nada: A Contemporary American Approach to Aesthetic Statement.* New York: Pantheon Books.

———. (1997). *Conversations with Albert Murray* (Roberta S. Maguire, Ed.). Jackson: University Press of Mississippi.

Murray, Charles Shaar. (1989). *Crosstown Traffic: Jimi Hendrix and the Post-War Rock &Roll Revolution.* New York: St. Martin's Press.

Murray, Dufferin A. (1998). "From the Word Up: The Poetic Message of Rap Music." Ph.D. dissertation, University of Western Ontario, London, ON, Canada.

Myrie, Russell. (2008). *Don't Rhyme for the Sake of Riddlin': The Authorized Story of Public Enemy.* New York: Canongate Books.

Nair, Ajay, and Balaji, Murali. (Eds.). (2008). *Desi Rap: Hip Hop and South Asian America.* Lanham, MD: Lexington Books.

Naison, Mark. (2004). "From Doo-wop to Hip Hop: The Bittersweet Odyssey of African Americans in the South Bronx." *Socialism & Democracy* 18 (2), 37–49.

Nama, Adilifu. (2008). *Black Space: Imagining Race in Science Fiction Film.* Austin: University of Texas Press.

Nathan, David. (1999). *The Soulful Divas: Personal Portraits of Over a Dozen Divine Divas — from Nina Simone, Aretha Franklin & Diana Ross to Patti LaBelle, Whitney Houston & Janet Jackson.* New York: Billboard Books.

Neal, Larry P. (1968). "The Black Arts Movement." *Drama Review* 12 (4), 29–39.

———. (1989). *Visions of a Liberated Future: Black Arts Movements Writings* (Michael Schwartz, Ed.). New York: Thunder's Mouth Press.

Neal, Mark Anthony. (1997). "Sold Out on Soul: The Corporate Annexation of Black Popular Music." *Popular Music and Society* 21 (3), 117–35.

———. (1998). *What the Music Said: Black Popular Music and Black Public Culture.* New York: Routledge.

———. (2002). *Soul Babies: Black Popular Culture and the Post-Soul Aesthetic.* New York: Routledge.

———. (2003). *Songs in the Key of Black Life: A Rhythm and Blues Nation.* New York: Routledge.

———. (2005a). *New Black Man: Rethinking Black Masculinity.* New York: Routledge.

———. (2005b). "Rhythm and Bullshit: The Slow Decline of R&B (Rhythm & Blues)." ALTERNET.ORG.   http://www.alternet.org/story/23384/rhythm_and_bullshit_the_ slow_decline_of_r%26b.

Neate, Patrick. (2004). *Where You're At?: Notes from the Frontline of a Hip Hop Planet.* New York: Riverhead Books.

Negus, Keith. (1999). *Music Genres and Corporate Cultures.* New York: Routledge.

Neimark, Philip J. (1993). *The Way of the Orisa: Empowering Your Life through the Ancient African Religion of Ifa.* San Francisco: Harper.

Nel, Philip. (2002). *Avant-Garde and American Postmodernity: Small Incisive Shocks.* Jackson: University Press of Mississippi.

Nelson, Alondra. (Ed.). (2002). *Afrofuturism. Social Text* 20 (2/71).

Nelson, Havelock, and Gonzales, Michael A. (1991). *Bring the Noise: A Guide to Rap Music and Hip Hop Culture.* New York: Harmony Books.

Nelson, William E., and Meranto, Philip J. (1977). *Electing Black Mayors: Political Action in the Black Community.* Columbus: Ohio State University Press.

Nevels, Cynthia S. (2007). *Lynching to Belong: Claiming Whiteness Through Racial Violence.* College Station: Texas A&M University Press.

Nickson, Chris. (1999). *Lauryn Hill: She's Got That Thing.* New York: St. Martin's Press.

Nielsen, Aldon Lynn. (1997). *Black Chant: Languages of African American Postmodernism.* Cambridge: Cambridge University Press.

———. (2004). *Integral Music: Languages of African American Innovation.* Tuscaloosa: University of Alabama Press.

Nierenberg, George T. (Director). (1982). *Say Amen, Somebody!* Carmel, CA: Pacific Arts Video Records.

Nieuwkerk, Karin van. (Ed.). (2011). *Muslim Rap, Halal Soaps, and Revolutionary Theater: Artistic Developments in the Muslim World.* Austin: University of Texas Press.

Nketia, J.H. Kwabena. (1974). *The Music of Africa.* New York: W.W. Norton.

Ntarangwi, Mwenda. (2009). *East African Hip Hop: Youth Culture and Globalization.* Urbana: University of Illinois Press.

Oakley, Ann, and Mitchell, Juliet. (Eds.). (1997). *Who's Afraid of Feminism?: Seeing Through the Backlash.* New York: New Press.

O'Brien, Gail Williams. (1999). *The Color of the Law: Race, Violence, and Justice in the Post-World War II South.* Chapel Hill: University of North Carolina Press.

Ogbar, Jeffrey O.G. (2004). *Black Power: Radical Politics and African American Identity.* Baltimore: Johns Hopkins University Press.

———. (2007). *The Hip Hop Revolution: The Culture and Politics of Rap.* Lawrence: University of Kansas Press.

Ogg, Alex. (2001). *The Hip Hop Years: A History of Rap* (with David Upshal). New York: Fromm International.

———. (2002). *The Men Behind Def Jam: The Radical Rise of Russell Simmons and Rick Rubin.* London: Omnibus.

Ogren, Kathy J. (1989). *The Jazz Revolution: Twenties America & the Meaning of Jazz.* New York: Oxford University Press.

Oliver, Melvin L., and Shapiro, Thomas M. (1995). *Black Wealth/White Wealth: A New Perspective on Racial Equality.* New York: Routledge.

Oliver, Paul. (2006). *Broadcasting the Blues: Black Blues in the Segregation Era.* New York: Routledge.

Olson, Alix. (Ed.). (2007). *Word Warriors: 35 Women Leaders in the Spoken-Word Revolution.* Emeryville, CA: Seal Press.

Omi, Michael, and Winant, Howard. (1994). *Racial Formation in United States: From the 1960's to the 1990's.* New York: Routledge.

Omry, Keren. (2005). "A Cyborg Performance: Gender and Genre in Octavia Butler." *Phoebe: Journal of Gender and Cultural Critiques* 17 (2), 45–60.

Ongiri, Amy Abugo. (2010). *Spectacular Blackness: The Cultural Politics of the Black Power Movement and the Search for a Black Aesthetic.* Charlottesville: University of Virginia Press.

O'Reilly, Kenneth. (1983). *Hoover and the Un-Americans: The FBI, HUAC, and the Red Menace.* Philadelphia: Temple University Press.

———. (1989). *Racial Matters: The FBI's Secret File on Black America, 1960–1972.* New York: Free Press.

———. (1994). *Black Americans: The FBI Files.* (David Gallen, Ed.). New York: Carroll & Graf.

Osayande, Ewuare X. (2008). *Misogyny & The Emcee: Sex, Race & Hip Hop.* Philadelphia, PA: Talking Drum Communications.

Osborne, Jerry, and Hamilton, Bruce. (1980). *Blues, Rhythm & Blues, Soul.* Phoenix: O'Sullivan Woodside.

Osofsky, Gilbert. (1996). *Harlem, The Making of a Ghetto: Negro New York, 1890–1930.* Chicago: Ivan R. Dee.

Osumare, Halifu. (2007). *The Africanist Aesthetic in Global Hip Hop.* New York: Palgrave Macmillan.

———. (2012). *The Hiplife in Ghana: The West African Indigenization of Hip Hop.* New York: Palgrave Macmillan.

Othello, Jeffrey. (2004). *The Soul of Rock & Roll: A History of African Americans in Rock Music.* Oakland, CA: Regent Press.

Oware, Matthew. (2009). "A 'Man's Woman'?: Contradictory Messages in the Songs of Female Rappers, 1992–2000." *Journal of Black Studies* 39 (5), 786–802.

Owens, Michael Leo. (2007). *God and Government in the Ghetto: The Politics of Church-State Collaboration in Black America.* Chicago: University of Chicago Press.

Pacoda, Pierfrancesco. (2000). *Hip Hop Italiano: Suoni e Scanari del Posse Power.* Torino: Einaudi.

Palmer, Robert. (1991). "The Church of the Sonic Guitar." *South Atlantic Quarterly* 90, 649–73.

———. (1995). *Rock & Roll: An Unruly History.* New York: Harmony Books.

———. (1996). *Dancing in the Street: A Rock & Roll History.* London: BBC Books.

Pardue, Derek. (2008). *Ideologies of Marginality in Brazilian Hip Hop.* New York: Palgrave Macmillan.

———. (2011). *Brazilian Hip Hoppers Speak from the Margins: We's on Tape.* New York: Palgrave Macmillan.

Parks, Rosa. (1992). *Rosa Parks: My Story* (with James Haskins). New York: Dial.

———. (1994). *Quiet Strength: The Faith, the Hope, and the Heart of a Woman who Changed a Nation* (with Gregory J. Reed). Grand Rapids, MI: Zondervan Publishing House.

Parmar, Priya. (2005). "Cultural Studies and Rap: The Poetry of an Urban Lyricist." *Taboo: The Journal of Culture and Education* 9 (1), 5–15.

———. (2009). *Knowledge Reigns Supreme: The Critical Pedagogy of Hip Hop Activist KRS-ONE.* Rotterdam, The Netherlands: Sense Publishers.

Pate, Alexs D. (2010). *In the Heart of the Beat: The Poetry of Rap.* Lanham, MD: Scarecrow Press.

Payne, Charles M., and Green, Adam. (Eds.). (2003). *Time Longer Than Rope: A Century of African American Activism, 1850–1950.* New York: New York University Press.

Peddie, Ian. (Ed.). (2006). *The Resisting Muse: Popular Music and Social Protest.* Aldershot, England: Ashgate.

Peoples, Whitney A. (2007). "'Under Construction': Identifying Foundations of Hip Hop Feminism and Exploring Bridges Between Black Second-Wave and Hip Hop Feminisms." *Meridians: Feminism, Race, Transnationalism* 8 (1), 19–52.

Peretti, Burton W. (1992). *The Creation of Jazz: Music, Race, and Culture in Urban America* Urbana: University of Illinois Press.

———. (2009). *Lift Every Voice: The History of African American Music.* Lanham, MD: Rowman & Littlefield Publishers.

Perkins, Danila. (Director). (2000). *Miss M.C.: Women in Rap.* Thousand Oaks, CA: Ventura Distribution.

Perkins, William E. (Ed.). (1996). *Droppin' Science: Critical Essays on Rap Music and Hip Hop Culture.* Philadelphia: Temple University Press.

Perry, Earnest L. (2002a). "A Common Purpose: The Negro Newspaper Publishers Association's Fight for Equality During World War II." *American Journalism* 19 (2), 34–37.

———. (2002b). "It's Time to Force a Change: The African American Press' Campaign for a True Democracy during World War II." *Journalism History* 28 (2).

Perry, Imani. (2004). *Prophets of the Hood: Politics and Poetics in Hip Hop.* Durham: Duke University Press.

Perry, John. (1999). *Exile on Main St.: The Rolling Stones.* New York: Schirmer Books.

———. (2004). *Jimi Hendrix's Electric Ladyland.* New York: Continuum.

Peterson, Shani H., Wingood, Gina M., DiClemente, Ralph J., Harrington, Kathy, and Davies, Susan. (2007). "Images of Sexual Stereotypes in Rap Videos and the Health of African American Female Adolescents." *Journal of Women's Health* 16 (8), 1157–64.

Petigny, Alan C. (2009). *The Permissive Society: America, 1941–1965.* New York: Cambridge University Press.

Petras, James F. (2003). *The New Development Politics: The Age of Empire Building and New Social Movements*. Aldershot, England: Ashgate.

Pfeffer, Paula F. (1990). *A. Philip Randolph: Pioneer of the Civil Rights Movement*. Baton Rouge: Louisiana State University Press.

Phelps, Carmen L. (2013). *Visionary Women Writers of Chicago's Black Arts Movement*. Jackson: University Press of Mississippi.

Phillips, Kimberley L. (1999). *AlabamaNorth: African American Migrants, Community, and Working-Class Activism in Cleveland, 1915–1945*. Urbana: University of Illinois Press.

———. (2012). *War!, What is it Good For?: Black Freedom Struggles and the U.S. Military from World War II to Iraq*. Chapel Hill: University of North Carolina Press.

Phillips, Layli. (Ed.). (2006). *The Womanist Reader*. New York: Routledge.

Phillips, Susan A. (1999). *Wallbangin': Graffiti and Gangs in L.A.* Chicago: University of Chicago Press.

Phinney, Kevin. (2005). *Souled American: How Black Music Transformed White Culture*. New York: Billboard Books.

Pierrepont, Alexandre. (2007). "'This Magnificent Musical Procession Called Life': The Association for the Advancement of Creative Musicians (AACM)." Ph.D. dissertation, Université Paris Descartes, Paris, France.

Pitts, John. (2001). *The New Politics of Youth Crime: Discipline or Solidarity?* New York: Palgrave.

Planer, Rhonda. (2002). "Jill Scott: Words and Wisdom from a Neo-Soul Princess." *Black Collegian* 32, 2. Available online at: http://www.black-collegian.com/issues/2ndsem02/jill-scott2002-2nd.shtml [Retrieved December 9, 2003].

Poinsett, Alex. (1970). *Black Power: Gary Style, The Making of Mayor Richard Gordon Hatcher*. Chicago: Johnson Publishing Co.

Põldsaar, Raili. (2006). *Critical Discourse Analysis of Anti-Feminist Rhetoric as a Catalyst in the Emergence of the Conservative Universe of Discourse in the United States in the 1970s–1980s*. Tartu: Tartu University Press.

Polikoff, Alexander. (2005). *Waiting for Gautreaux: A Story of Segregation, Housing, and the Black Ghetto*. Evanston, IL: Northwestern University Press.

Polletta, Francesca, and Jasper, James M. (2001). "Collective Identity and Social Movements." *Annual Review of Sociology* 27, 283–305.

Porta, Donatella Della, and Diani, Mario. (2006). *Social Movements: An Introduction*. Malden, MA: Blackwell.

Posner, Gerald L. (2002). *Motown: Music, Money, Sex, and Power*. New York: Random House.

Potter, Russell A. (1995). *Spectacular Vernaculars: Hip Hop and the Politics of Postmodernism*. Albany: State University of New York Press.

Pough, Gwendolyn. (2002). "Love Feminism But Where's My Hip Hop?: Shaping a Black Identity." In Daisy Hernández and Bushra Rehman (Eds.), *Colonize This!: Young Women of Color on Today's Feminism* (85–98). New York: Seal Press.

———. (2003). "Do the Ladies Run This . . . ?: Some Thoughts on Hip Hop Feminism." In Rory Dicker and Alison Piepmeier (Eds.), *Catching a Wave: Reclaiming Feminism for the 21st Century* (232–43). Boston: Northeastern University Press.

———. (2004). *Check It While I Wreck It!: Black Womanhood, Hip Hop Culture, and the Public Sphere*. Boston: Northeastern University Press.

Pough, Gwendolyn D., Richardson, Elaine, Durham, Aisha, and Raimist, Rachel. (Eds.). (2007). *Home Girls Make Some Noise!: The Hip Hop Feminism Anthology*. Mira Loma, CA: Parker Publishing.

Price, Emmett G. (2006). *Hip Hop Culture*. Santa Barbara, CA: ABC-CLIO.

Price, Emmett G., Kernodle, Tammy L., and Maxile, Horace J. (Eds.). (2011). *Encyclopedia of African American Music* (vols. 1–3). Santa Barbara, CA: ABC-CLIO.

Price, Kenneth M., and Oliver, Lawrence J. (Eds.). (1997). *Critical Essays on James Weldon Johnson*. New York: G.K. Hall.

Prince, Althea, Silva-Wayne, Susan, and Vernon, Christian. (Eds.). (2004). *Feminisms and Womanisms: A Women's Studies Reader*. Toronto: Women's Press.

Pruter, Robert. (1991). *Chicago Soul.* Urbana: University of Illinois Press.

———. (1996). *Doo-Wop: The Chicago Scene.* Urbana: University of Illinois Press.

———. (Ed.). (1993). *The Blackwell Guide to Soul Recordings.* Cambridge, MA: Blackwell.

Pulido, Isaura Betzabe. (2008). "Knowledge-The Fifth element of Hip Hop Music: Mexican and Puerto Rican Youth Engagement of Hip Hop as Critically Rac(ed) Education Discourse." Ph.D. dissertation, University of Illinois at Urbana-Champaign.

Quarles, Benjamin. (1969). *Black Abolitionists.* Oxford: Oxford University Press.

Quinn, Eithne. (2000a). "Black British Cultural Studies and the Rap on Gangsta." *Black Music Research Journal* 20 (2), 195–216.

———. (2000b). "'Who's the Mack?': The Performativity and Politics of the Pimp Figure in Gangsta Rap." *Journal of American Studies* 34 (1), 115–36.

———. (2005). *Nuthin' But a "G" Thang: The Culture and Commerce of Gangsta Rap.* New York: Columbia University Press.

Quinn, Michael. (1996). "'Never Shoulda Been Let out the Penitentiary': Gangsta Rap and the Struggle over Racial Identity." *Cultural Critique* 34, 65–89.

Ra, Sun. (2006). *The Wisdom of Sun Ra: Sun Ra's Polemical Broadsheets and Streetcorner Leaflets* (John Corbett, Ed.). Chicago: WhiteWalls.

Rabaka, Reiland. (2007). *W.E.B. Du Bois and the Problems of the Twenty-First Century: An Essay on Africana Critical Theory.* Lanham, MD: Lexington Books.

———. (2008). *Du Bois's Dialectics: Black Radical Politics and the Reconstruction of Critical Social Theory.* Lanham, MD: Lexington Books.

———. (2009). *Africana Critical Theory: Reconstructing the Black Radical Tradition, from W.E.B. Du Bois and C.L.R. James to Frantz Fanon and Amilcar Cabral.* Lanham, MD: Lexington Books.

———. (2010a). *Against Epistemic Apartheid: W.E.B. Du Bois and the Disciplinary Decadence of Sociology.* Lanham, MD: Lexington Books.

———. (2010b). *Forms of Fanonism: Frantz Fanon's Critical Theory and the Dialectics of Decolonization.* Lanham, MD: Lexington Books.

———. (Ed.). (2010c). *W.E.B. Du Bois: A Critical Reader.* Surrey, UK: Ashgate Publishing.

———. (2011). *Hip Hop's Inheritance: From the Harlem Renaissance to the Hip Hop Feminist Movement.* Lanham, MD: Lexington Books.

———. (2012). *Hip Hop's Amnesia: From Blues and the Black Women's Club Movement to Rap and the Hip Hop Movement.* Lanham, MD: Lexington Books.

———. (forthcoming). *The Neo-Soul Movement: From Classic Soul to Hip Hop Soul.* Lanham, MD: Lexington Books.

Rahn, Janice. (2002). *Painting Without Permission: Hip Hop Graffiti Subculture.* Westport, CT: Bergin & Garvey.

Raimon, Eve A. (2004). *The "Tragic Mulatta" Revisited: Race and Nationalism in Nineteenth Century Anti-slavery Fiction.* New Brunswick: Rutgers University Press.

Rainwater, Lee. (2006). *Behind Ghetto Walls: Black Families in a Federal Slum.* New Brunswick: Transaction Publishers.

Rajakumar, Mohanalakshmi. (2012). *Hip Hop Dance.* Santa Barbara, CA: Greenwood.

Rambsy, Howard. (2011). *The Black Arts Enterprise and the Production of African American Poetry.* Ann Arbor: University of Michigan Press.

Ramey, Lauri. (2008). *Slave Songs and the Birth of African American Poetry.* New York: Palgrave Macmillan.

Ramirez, Catherine S. (2002). "Cyborg Feminism: The Science Fiction of Octavia Butler and Gloria Anzaldua." In Mary Flanagan and Austin Booth (Eds.), *Reload: Rethinking Women and Cyberculture* (374–402). Cambridge: MIT Press.

Ramsey, Guthrie P. (2003). *Race Music: Black Cultures from Be-Bop to Hip Hop.* Berkeley: University of California Press.

Randall, Annie Janeiro. (Ed.). (2005). *Music, Power, and Politics.* New York: Routledge.

Ransby, Barbara. (2003). *Ella Baker and the Black Freedom Movement: A Radical Democratic Vision.* Chapel Hill: University of North Carolina Press.

Raven, Arlene, Langer, Cassandra L., and Fruech, Joanna. (Eds.). (1988). *Feminist Art Criticism: An Anthology.* Ann Arbor, MI: UMI Research Press.

Redd, Lawrence N. (1974). *Rock is Rhythm & Blues: The Impact of Mass Media.* East Lansing: Michigan State University Press.

———. (1985). "Rock!: It's Still Rhythm and Blues." *The Black Perspective in Music* 13 (1), 31–47.

Reddy, Chandan. (2011). *Freedom with Violence: Race, Sexuality, and the US State.* Durham: Duke University Press.

Redmond, Mike, and Goldberg, Marv. (1975). "The Doo-Wah Sound: Black Pop Groups of the 1950s." *Yesterday's Memories* 1 (1), 22–26.

Reed, Ishmael, Franti, Michael, and Adler, Bill. (1992). "Hiphoprisy: A Conversation with Ishmael Reed and Michael Franti." *Transition* 56, 152–65.

Reed, T.V. (2005). *The Art of Protest: Culture and Activism from the Civil Rights Movement to the Streets of Seattle.* Minneapolis: University of Minnesota Press.

Reeves, Marcus. (2008). *Somebody Scream!: Rap Music's Rise to Prominence in the Aftershock of Black Power.* New York: Faber & Faber.

Reger, Jo. (Ed.). (2005). *Different Wave-lengths: Studies of the Contemporary Women's Movement.* New York: Routledge.

Reid-Brinkley, Shanara R. (2008). "The Essence of Res(ex)pectability: Black Women's Negotiation of Black Femininity in Rap Music and Music Video." *Meridians: Feminism, Race, Transnationalism* 8 (1), 236–60.

Reilly, April. (1973). "The Impact of Technology on Rhythm & Blues. *The Black Perspective in Music* 1 (2), 136–46.

Resnick, Michael. (2006). "BurnList: The Digital 'Mix Tape' Comes of Age." Retrieved from http://www.events-in-music.com/burnlist-mix-tapes.html.

Rhodes, Jane. (2007). *Framing the Black Panthers: The Spectacular Rise of a Black Power Icon.* New York: New Press.

Rich, Wilbur C. (1996). *Black Mayors and School Politics: The Failure of Reform in Detroit, Gary, and Newark.* New York: Garland.

Rickford, John R. (1999). *African American Vernacular English: Features, Evolution, Educational Implications.* Malden, MA: Blackwell.

Rickford, John R., Mufwene, Salikoko S., Bailey, Guy, and Baugh, John. (Eds.). (1998). *African American English.* New York: Routledge.

Rickford, John R., and Rickford, Russell J. (2000). *Spoken Soul: The Story of Black English.* New York: Wiley.

Riley, Alexander. (2005). "The Rebirth of Tragedy Out of the Spirit of Hip Hop: A Cultural Sociology of Gangsta Rap Music." *Journal of Youth Studies* 8 (3), 297–311.

Ripani, Richard J. (2006). *The New Blue Music: Changes in Rhythm & Blues, 1950–1999.* Jackson: University Press of Mississippi.

Rivera, Raquel Z. (2003). *New York Ricans from the Hip Hop Zone.* New York: Palgrave Macmillan.

Rivera, Raquel Z., Marshall, Wayne, and Hernandez, Deborah P. (Eds.). (2009). *Reggaeton.* Durham: Duke University Press.

Rizzo, Albertina, and McCall, Amanda. (2005). *Hold My Gold: A White Girl's Guide to the Hip Hop World.* New York: Simon & Schuster.

Ro, Ronin. (1996). *Gangsta: Merchandizing the Rhymes of Violence.* New York: St. Martin's Press.

———. (1998). *Have Gun Will Travel: The Spectacular Rise and Violent Fall of Death Row Records.* New York: Doubleday.

———. (2005). *Raising Hell: The Reign, Ruin, and Redemption of Run-D.M.C. and Jam Master Jay.* New York: Amistad.

———. (2007). *Dr. Dre: The Biography.* New York: Thunder's Mouth Press.

Roach, Hildred. (1973). *Black American Music: Past and Present.* Boston: Crescendo Publishing Co.

Roberts, Diane. (1994). *The Myth of Aunt Jemima: Representations of Race and Region.* New York: Routledge.

Roberts, Robin. (1991). "Music Videos, Performance and Resistance: Feminist Rappers." *Journal of Popular Culture* 25 (2), 141–52.

———. (1994). "Ladies First: Queen Latifah's Afrocentric Feminist Music Video." *African American Review* 28 (2), 245–57.

Roby, Steven, and Schreiber, Brad. (2010). *Becoming Jimi Hendrix: From Southern Cross-roads to Psychedelic London, The Untold Story of a Musical Genius.* Philadelphia: Da Capo Press.

Rocco, John. (Ed.). (2000). *The Beastie Boys Companion* (with Brian Rocco). New York: Schirmer.

Rodman, Gilbert B. (2006). "Race . . . and Other Four Letter Words: Eminem and the Cultural Politics of Authenticity." *Popular Communication* 4 (2), 95–121.

Rogers, Charles E. (1996). "Franti's Spearhead Rap's Crucial Consciousness." *New York Amsterdam News* 87 (50), 24.

Rogers, Ibram H. (2012). *The Black Campus Movement: Black Students and the Racial Reconstitution of Higher Education, 1965–1972.* New York: Palgrave Macmillan.

Rogers, Matt. (2013). *Funkadelic's Maggot Brain.* New York: Continuum.

Rojas, Fabio. (2007). *From Black Power to Black Studies: How a Radical Social Movement Became an Academic Discipline.* Baltimore: Johns Hopkins University Press.

Rojas, Maythee. (2009). *Women of Color and Feminism.* Berkeley, CA: Seal Press.

Roll, Jarod. (2010). *Spirit of Rebellion: Labor and Religion in the New Cotton South.* Urbana: University of Illinois Press.

Rome, Dennis. (2004). *Black Demons: The Media's Depiction of the African American Male Criminal Stereotype.* Westport, CT: Praeger.

Rooks, Noliwe M. (2006). *White Money/Black Power: The Surprising History of African American Studies and the Crisis of Race in Higher Education.* Boston: Beacon Press.

Rosalsky, Mitch. (Ed.). (2000). *Encyclopedia of Rhythm & Blues and Doo-Wop Vocal Groups.* Lanham, MD: Scarecrow Press.

Rose, Harold M. (1971). *The Black Ghetto: A Spatial Behavioral Perspective.* New York: McGraw-Hill.

———. (Ed.). (1972). *Geography of the Ghetto: Perceptions, Problems, and Alternatives.* DeKalb: Northern Illinois University Press.

Rose, Tricia. (1994). *Black Noise: Rap Music and Black Culture in Contemporary America.* Middletown, CT: Wesleyan University Press.

———. (2008). *The Hip Hop Wars: What We Talk About When We Talk About Hip Hop— and Why It Matters.* New York: Basic/Civitas.

Rosenthal, David H. (1988a). "Hard Bop and Its Critics." *The Black Perspective in Music* 16 (1), 21–29.

———. (1988b). "Jazz in the Ghetto: 1950–1970." *Popular Music* 7 (1), 51–56.

———. (1992). *Hard Bop: Jazz and Black Music, 1955–1965.* New York: Oxford University Press.

Rosenthal, Rob, and Flacks, Richard. (2011). *Playing for Change: Music and Musicians in the Service of Social Movements.* Boulder, CO: Paradigm Publishers.

Rose-Robinson, Sia. (1999). "A Qualitative Analysis of Hardcore and Gangsta Rap Lyrics, 1985–1995." Ph.D. dissertation, Howard University, Washington, DC.

Ross, Justin D. (2007). "Offended?: The Rap's on Me." *Washington Post* (September 9). Available at: http://www.washingtonpost.com/wp-dyn/content/article/2007/09/07/AR2007090702048.html.

Rounds, Dwight. (2007). *The Year the Music Died, 1964–1972: A Commentary on the Best Era of Pop Music, and an Irreverent Look at the Musicians and Social Movements of the Time.* Austin, TX: Bridgeway Books.

Rousseas, Stephen William. (1982). *The Political Economy of Reagonomics: A Critique.* Armonk, NY: M.E. Sharpe.

Rowe, Mike. (1975). *Chicago Blues: The City & the Music.* New York: Da Capo Press.

Roy, William G. (2010). *Reds, Whites, and Blues: Social Movements, Folk Music, and Race in the United States.* Princeton: Princeton University Press.

Rubin, Rachel, and Melnick, Jeffrey Paul. (Eds.). (2001). *American Popular Music: New Approaches to the Twentieth Century.* Amherst: University of Massachusetts Press.

Rublowsky, John. (1971). *Black Music in America.* New York: Basic Books.

Rucker, Ali C. (2011). "'Penitentiary Philosophy' and 'Untitled': Transgression in the Neo-Soul Sensibility of Erykah Badu and D'Angelo." Honors thesis, Wellesley College, Wellesley, MA.

Rudel, Anthony J. (2008). *Hello, Everybody!: The Dawn of American Radio.* Orlando: Harcourt.

Rudman, Laurie A., and Lee, Matthew R. (2002). "Implicit and Explicit Consequences of Exposure to Violent and Misogynous Rap Music." *Group Processes Intergroup Relations* 5 (2), 133–50.

Runell, Marcella, and Diaz, Martha. (2007). *The Hip Hop Education Guidebook: Volume 1.* New York: Hip Hop Association Publications.

Runowicz, John Michael. (2010). *Forever Doo-wop: Race, Nostalgia, and Vocal Harmony.* Amherst: University of Massachusetts Press.

Rupp, Leila J., and Taylor, Verta. (1986). "The Women's Movement: Strategies and New Directions." In Robert H. Bremner, Richard Hopkins, and Gary W. Reichard (Eds.), *American Choices: Social Dilemmas and Public Policy Since 1960* (75–104). Columbus: Ohio State University Press.

———. (1991). "Women's Culture and the Continuity of the W Women's Movement." In Tayo Andreasen (Ed.), *Moving On: New Perspectives on the Women's Movement* (68–89). Aarhus, Denmark: Aarhus University Press.

Russell-Cole, Kathy, Wilson, Midge, and Hall, Ronald E. (1992). *The Color Complex: The Politics of Skin Color Among African Americans.* New York: Harcourt Brace Jovanovich.

Sachdev, Chhavi, and Freeman, Karen. (2005). "The Entertainment Enlightenment." *Science & Spirit* 16 (6), 26–27.

Said, Edward W. (1999). "Traveling Theory Reconsidered." In Nigel C. Gibson (Ed.), *Rethinking Fanon* (197–214). Amherst, NY: Humanity Books.

———. (2000). "Traveling Theory." In Moustafa Bayoumi and Andrew Rubin (Eds.), *The Edward Said Reader* (195–217). New York: Vintage.

Salem, James M. (1999). *The Late, Great Johnny Ace and the Transition from R&B to Rock & Roll.* Urbana: University of Illinois Press.

Sales, Grover. (1984). *Jazz: America's Classical Music.* New York: Da Capo.

Sales, William W. (1994). *From Civil Rights to Black Liberation: Malcolm X and the Organization of Afro-American Unity.* Boston: South End Press.

Salvaggio, Ruth. (1984). "Octavia Butler and the Black Science Fiction Heroine." *Black American Literature Forum* 18 (2), 78–81.

Samuels, Allison. (2001). "Jill Scott and the Rise of 'Neo-Soul'." *Newsweek* 137 (15), 56.

Sandford, Christopher. (2012). *The Rolling Stones: Fifty Years.* New York: Simon & Schuster.

Sanger, Kerran L. (1995). *"When the Spirit Says Sing!": The Role of Freedom Songs in the Civil Rights Movement.* New York: Garland.

Sanjek, Russell, and Sanjek, David. (1996). *Pennies from Heaven: The American Popular Music Business in the Twentieth Century.* New York: Da Capo Press.

Sanneh, Lamin O. (1999). *Abolitionists Abroad: American Blacks and the Making of Modern West Africa.* Cambridge, MA: Harvard University Press.

Santiago, Abraham J., and Dunham, Steven J. (2006). *Acappella Street Corner Vocal Groups: A Brief History and Discography of 1960s Singing Groups.* Glencoe: Mellow Sound Press.

Santiago, Eddie. (2008). *Sly: The Lives of Sylvester Stewart and Sly Stone.* New York: Lulu.com.

Saucier, Paul Khalil. (Ed.). (2011). *Native Tongues: An African Hip Hop Reader.* Trenton, NJ: Africa World Press.

Saul, Scott. (2003). *Freedom Is, Freedom Ain't: Jazz and the Making of the Sixties.* Cambridge: Harvard University Press.

Savage, Robert L., and Nimmo, Dan D. (1990). *Politics in Familiar Contexts: Projecting Politics through Popular Media.* Norwood, NJ: Ablex Publishing.

Savidge, Leigh. (Director). (2001). *Welcome to Death Row.* Santa Monica, CA: Xenon Pictures.

Scannell, John. (2012). *James Brown.* Oakville, CT: Equinox Publishing.

Schaffer, Dean. (2010). "Secrets of the Blue Note Vault: Michael Cuscuna on Monk, Blakey, and Hancock." *Collector's Weekly* (August 20). http://www.collectorsweekly .com/articles/secrets-of-the-blue-note-vault-michael-cuscuna-on-monk-blakey-and-the-one-that-got-away/.

Schaller, Michael. (1992). *Reckoning with Reagan: American and Its President in the 1980s.* New York: Oxford University Press.

Schein, Richard H. (Ed.). (2006). *Landscape and Race in the United States.* New York: Routledge.

Schenbeck, Lawrence. (2012). *Racial Uplift and American Music, 1878–1943.* Jackson: University Press of Mississippi.

Schloss, Joseph G. (2004). *Making Beats: The Art of Sample-Based Hip Hop.* Middletown, CT: Wesleyan University Press.

———. (2009). *Foundation: B-Boys, B-Girls and Hip Hop Culture in New York.* New York: Oxford University Press.

Schmidt, James. (2007). *Theodor Adorno.* Aldershot, England: Ashgate.

Schmidt, Martha, and Taylor, Verta. (1997). "Women's Movements." In Janet J. Montelaro and Patricia M. Ulbrich (Eds.), *Introduction to Women's Studies* (1–9). New York: McGraw-Hill.

Schreiber, Ronnee. (2008). *Righting Feminism: Conservative Women and American Politics.* Oxford: Oxford University Press.

Schulz, David A. (1969). *Coming Up Black: Patterns of Ghetto Socialization.* Englewood Cliffs, NJ: Prentice-Hall.

Schwab, Gabriele. (2006). "Ethnographies of the Future: Personhood, Agency and Power in Octavia Butler's *Xenogenesis.*" In William Maurer and Gabriele Schwab (Eds.), *Accelerating Possession* (204–28). New York: Columbia University Press.

Scott, Alan. (1990). *Ideology and the New Social Movements.* London: Unwin Hyman.

Scott, James C. (1990). *Domination and the Arts of Resistance: Hidden Transcripts.* New Haven: Yale University Press.

Scott, Jonathan. (2004). "Sublimating Hip Hop: Rap Music in White America." *Socialism and Democracy* 18 (2), 135–55.

Scott, Lawrence P., and Womack, William M. (1998). *Double V: The Civil Rights Struggle of the Tuskegee Airmen.* East Lansing: Michigan State University Press.

Scrivani-Tidd, Lisa M., Markowitz, Rhonda, Smith, Chris, Janosik, MaryAnn, and Gulla, Bob. (Eds.). (2006). *The Greenwood Encyclopedia of Rock History.* (6 vols.). Westport, CT: Greenwood.

Sell, Mike. (2008). *Avant-Garde Performance and the Limits of Criticism: Approaching the Living Theatre, Happenings/Fluxus, and the Black Arts Movement.* Ann Arbor: University of Michigan Press.

Selvin, Joel. (1998). *Sly & the Family Stone: An Oral History* (Dave Marsh, Ed.). New York: Avon Books.

Sévéon, Julien. (2008). *Blaxpoitation: 70s Soul Fever.* Paris: Bazaar & Co.

Shabazz, David L. (1999). *Public Enemy Number One: A Research Study of Rap Music, Culture, and Black Nationalism in America.* Clinton, SC: Awesome Records.

Shapiro, Harry, and Glebbeek, Caesar. (1991). *Jimi Hendrix: Electric Gypsy.* New York: St. Martin's Press.

Shapiro, Herbert. (1988). *White Violence and Black Response: From Reconstruction to Montgomery.* Amherst: University of Massachusetts Press.

Shapiro, Peter. (Ed.). (2001). *Hip Hop: The Mini-Rough Guide.* London: Rough Guides.

———. (Ed.). (2005a). *The Rough Guide to Hip Hop* (2nd ed.). London: Rough Guides.

———. (2005b). *Turn the Beat Around: The Secret History of Disco.* New York: Faber and Faber.

Shapiro, Thomas M. (2004). *The Hidden Cost of Being African American: How Wealth Perpetuates Inequality.* New York: Oxford University Press.

Sharma, Nitasha Tamar. (2010). *Hip Hop Desis: Asian Americans, Blackness, and a Global Race Consciousness.* Durham: Duke University Press.

Sharpley-Whiting, Tracy Denean. (1997). *Frantz Fanon: Conflicts and Feminisms.* Lanham, MD: Rowman & Littlefield.

———. (2007). *Pimps Up, Ho's Down: Hip Hop's Hold on Young Black Women.* New York: New York University Press.

Shaw, Arnold. (1969). *The Rock Revolution.* New York: Crowell-Collier Press.

———. (1970). *The World of Soul: Black America's Contributions to the Pop Music Scene.* New York: Cowles Book Co.

———. (1978). *Honkers and Shouters: The Golden Years of Rhythm & Blues.* New York: Macmillan.

———. (1986). *Black Popular Music in America: From the Spirituals, Minstrels, and Ragtime to Soul, Disco, and Hip Hop.* New York: Schirmer Books.

———. (1987). *The Rockin' Fifties '50s: The Decade that Transformed the Pop Music Scene.* New York: Da Capo Press.

Shaw, Harry B. (Ed.). (1990). *Perspectives of Black Popular Culture.* Bowling Green, OH: Bowling Green State University Popular Press.

Shaw, William. (2000a). *Westsiders: Stories of Boys in the Hood.* London: Bloomsbury.

———. (2000b). *Westside: The Coast-to-Coast Explosion of Hip Hop.* New York: Cooper Square Press.

———. (2000c). *Westside: Young Men and Hip Hop in L.A.* New York: Simon & Schuster.

Sheffield, Carrie L. (2011). "Native American Hip Hop and Historical Trauma: Surviving and Healing Trauma on the 'Rez.'" *Studies in American Indian Literatures* 23 (3), 94–110.

Sherrard-Johnson, Cherene. (2007). *Portraits of the New Negro Woman: Visual and Literary Culture in the Harlem Renaissance.* New Brunswick: Rutgers University Press.

Shockley, Evie. (2011). *Renegade Poetics: Black Aesthetics and Formal Innovation in African American Poetry.* Iowa City: University of Iowa Press.

Shomari, Hashim A. (1995). *From the Underground: Hip Hop Culture as an Agent of Social Change.* Fanwood, NJ: X-Factor Publications.

Shull, Steven A. (1993). *A Kinder, Gentler Racism?: The Reagan-Bush Civil Rights Legacy.* Armonk, NY: M.E. Sharpe.

Sidel, Ruth. (1996). *Keeping Women and Children Last: America's War on the Poor.* New York: Penguin.

Sieving, Christopher. (1998). "Cop Out?: The Media, 'Cop Killer,' and the Deracialization of Black Rage." *Journal of Communication Inquiry* 22 (4), 334–53.

———. (2011). *Soul Searching: Black-Themed Cinema from the March on Washington to the Rise of Blaxploitation.* Middletown, CT: Wesleyan University Press.

Silverman, Chuck, and Slutsky, Allan. (1997). *The Funkmasters the Great James Brown Rhythm Sections, 1960–1973.* Miami, FL: Warner Bros. Publications.

Simien, Evelyn M. (2011). *Gender and Lynching: The Politics of Memory.* New York: Palgrave Macmillan.

Simmons, Joseph. (2000). *It's Like That: A Spiritual Memoir* (with Curtis L. Taylor). New York: St. Martin's Press.

Simmons, Russell. (2001). *Life and Def: Sex, Drugs, Money, and God* (with Nelson George). New York: Crown Publishers.

Simone, Nina. (1991). *I Put a Spell on You: The Autobiography of Nina Simone* (with Stephen Cleary). New York: Pantheon Books.

Sims, Yvonne D. (2006). *Women of Blaxploitation: How the Black Action Film Heroine Changed American Popular Culture.* Jefferson, NC: McFarland.

Singh, Nikhil Pal. (2004). *Black Is A Country: Race and the Unfinished Struggle for Democracy.* Cambridge: Harvard University Press.

Singleton, Raynoma Gordy. (1990). *Berry, Me, and Motown: The Untold Story* (with Bryan Brown and Mim Eichler). Chicago: Contemporary Books.

Sitomer, Alan L., and Cirelli, Michael. (Eds.). (2004). *Hip Hop Poetry and the Classics: Connecting Our Classic Curriculum to Hip Hop Poetry Through Standards-Based Language Arts Instruction.* Beverly Hills, CA: Milk Mug.

Skågeby, Jörgen. (2011). "Slow and Fast Music Media: Comparing Values of Cassettes and Playlists." *Transformations Journal of Media & Culture* 20, 1–23.

Skeggs, Beverley. (1993). "Two Minute Brother: Contestation Through Gender, 'Race' and Sexuality." *Innovation: The European Journal of Social Sciences* 6 (3), 299–323.

Small, Christopher. (1998a). *Music of the Common Tongue: Survival and Celebration in African American Music.* Hanover, NH: University Press of New England.

———. (1998b). *Musicking: The Meanings of Performing and Listening.* Hanover, NH: Wesleyan University Press.

Small, Michael W. (1992). *Break It Down: The Inside Story from the New Leaders of Rap.* New York: Carol Publishing.

Smethurst, James Edward. (2005). *The Black Arts Movement: Literary Nationalism in the 1960s and 1970s.* Chapel Hill: University of North Carolina Press.

Smith, David Lionel. (1991). "The Black Arts Movement and Its Critics." *American Literary History* 3 (1), 93–110.

Smith, Jason K. (2002). *Counter-Hegemonic Masculinity in Hip Hop Music: An Analysis of the Roots, Construction of Masculinity in their Music and in the Media Culture.* Hartford, CT: University of Hartford Press.

Smith, Neil. (1984). *Uneven Development: Nature, Capital, and the Production of Space.* New York: Blackwell.

Smith, R.J. (2012). *The One: The Life and Music of James Brown.* New York: Gotham Books.

Smith, Robert C. (1995). *Racism in the Post-Civil Rights Era: Now You See It, Now You Don't.* Albany: State University of New York Press.

———. (1996). *We Have No Leaders: African Americans in the Post-Civil Rights Era.* Albany: State University of New York Press.

Smith, Suzanne E. (1999). *Dancing in the Street: Motown and the Cultural Politics of Detroit.* Cambridge: Harvard University Press.

Smitherman, Geneva. (1975). *Black Language and Culture: Sounds of Soul.* New York: Harper & Row.

———. (1986). *Talkin and Testifyin: The Language of Black America.* Detroit: Wayne State University Press.

———. (2000). *Talkin That Talk: Language, Culture and Education in African America.* New York: Routledge.

———. (2006). *Word from the Mother: Language and African Americans.* New York: Routledge.

Smith-Shomade, Beretta E. (2003). "'Rock-a-Bye, Baby!': Black Women Disrupting Gangs and Constructing Hip Hop Gangsta Films." *Cinema Journal* 42 (2), 25–40.

Snow, David A., Soule, Sarah Anne, and Kriesi, Hanspeter. (Eds.). (2004). *The Blackwell Companion to Social Movements.* Malden, MA: Blackwell.

Sollors, Werner. (1997). *Neither Black Nor White Yet Both: Thematic Explorations of Interracial Literature.* New York: Oxford University Press.

Souljah, Sister. (1996). *No Disrespect.* New York: Vintage Books.

Southern, Eileen. (1997). *Music of Black Americans: A History.* New York: W.W. Norton.

Spady, James G., Alim, H. Samy, and Meghelli, Samir. (Eds.). (2006). *The Global Cipha: Hip Hop Culture and Consciousness.* Philadelphia, PA: Black History Museum Press.

Spady, James G., Dupres, Stefan, and Lee, Charles G. (Eds.). (1995). *Twisted Tales: In the Hip Hop Streets of Philly.* Philadelphia, PA: UMUM/LOH Publishers.

Spady, James G., Lee, Charles G., and Alim, H. Samy. (1999). *Street Conscious Rap.* Philadelphia, PA: Black History Museum Press/LOH Publishers.

Spann, Girardeau A. (1993). *Race Against the Court: The Supreme Court and Minorities in Contemporary America.* New York: New York University Press.

Spear, Allan H. (1967). *Black Chicago: The Making of a Negro Ghetto, 1890–1920.* Chicago: University of Chicago Press.

Spence, Lester K. (2011). *Stare in the Darkness: The Limits of Hip Hop and Black Politics.* Minneapolis: University of Minnesota Press.

Spencer, Jon Michael. (1990). *Protest & Praise: Sacred Music of Black Religion.* Minneapolis: Fortress Press.

———. (1995). *The Rhythms of Black Folk: Race, Religion, and Pan-Africanism.* Trenton, NJ: Africa World Press.

———. (1996). *Re-Searching Black Music*. Knoxville: University of Tennessee Press.

Springer, Kimberly. (2005). *Living for the Revolution: Black Feminist Organizations, 1968–1980*. Durham: Duke University Press.

Staggenborg, Suzanne, and Taylor, Verta. (2005). "Whatever Happened to the Women's Movement?" *Mobilization: International Journal of Theory and Research About Social Movements and Collective Behavior* 10, 37–52.

Stamz, Richard. (2010). *Give 'em Soul, Richard!: Race, Radio, and Rhythm & Blues in Chicago* (with Patrick A. Roberts). Urbana: University of Illinois Press.

Stanley, Lawrence A. (Ed.). (1992). *Rap: The Lyrics*. New York: Penguin.

Stanley, Tarshia L. (Ed.). (2009). *Encyclopedia of Hip Hop Literature*. Westport, CT: Greenwood.

Stanley-Niaah, Sonjah Nadine. (2010). *Dancehall: From Slave Ship to Ghetto*. Ottawa: University of Ottawa Press.

Stapleton, Katina R. (1998). "From the Margins to Mainstream: The Political Power of Hip Hop." *Media Culture Society* 20 (2), 219–34.

Stauffer, John. (2001). *Black Hearts of Men: Radical Abolitionists and the Transformation of Race*. Cambridge: Harvard University Press.

Stebbins, Robert A. (1996). *The Barbershop Singer: Inside the Social World of a Musical Hobby*. Toronto: University of Toronto Press.

Stenning, Paul. (2008). *Rage Against the Machine: Stage Fighters*. Church Stretton, Shropshire, England: Independent Music.

Stephens, Robert W. (1984). "Soul: A Historical Reconstruction of Continuity and Change in Black Popular Music." *The Black Perspective in Music* 12 (1), 21–43.

Stephens, Vincent. (2005). "Pop Goes the Rapper: A Close Reading of Eminem's Genderphobia." *Popular Music* 24 (1), 21–36.

Stewart, Alexander. (2000). "'Funky Drummer': New Orleans, James Brown and the Rhythmic Transformation of American Popular Music." *Popular Music* 19 (3), 293–318.

Stewart, Charles J. (1998). "The Evolution of a Revolution: Stokely Carmichael and the Rhetoric of Black Power." *Communication Abstracts* 21 (6), 429–46.

Stewart, Earl L. (1998). *African American Music: An Introduction*. New York: Schirmer.

Stewart, Earl, and Duran, Jane. (1999). "Black Essentialism: The Art of Jazz Rap." *Philosophy of Music Education Review* 7 (1), 49–54.

Stewart, James B. (2005). "Message in the Music: Political Commentary in Black Popular Music from Rhythm and Blues to Early Hip Hop." *Journal of African American History* 90 (3), 196–225.

Stirk, Peter M.R. (1992). *Max Horkheimer: A New Interpretation*. Hemel Hempstead, UK: Harvester Wheatsheaf.

Stolzoff, Norman C. (2000). *Wake the Town and Tell the People!: Dancehall Culture in Jamaica*. Durham: Duke University Press.

Stone, Ruth M. (Ed.). (2008). *The Garland Handbook of African Music*. New York: Garland.

Storey, John. (2009). *Cultural Theory and Popular Culture: A Reader*. Athens: University of Georgia Press.

Stover, A. Shahid. (2009). *Hip Hop Intellectual Resistance*. Philadelphia, PA: Xlibris.

Street, John. (1986). *Rebel Rock: The Politics of Popular Music*. New York: Blackwell.

———. (1997). *Politics and Popular Culture*. Philadelphia: Temple University Press.

———. (2012). *Music and Politics*. Cambridge: Polity Press.

Stricker, Frank. (2007). *Why America Lost the War on Poverty—And How to Win It*. Chapel Hill: University of North Carolina Press.

Stuessy, Joe, and Lipscomb, Scott. (2012). *Rock & Roll: Its History and Stylistic Development* (7th ed.). Englewood Cliffs, NJ: Prentice Hall.

Sullivan, Denise. (2011). *Keep On Pushing: Black Power Music from Blues to Hip Hop*. Chicago: Lawrence Hill Books.

Sullivan, James. (2008). *The Hardest Working Man: How James Brown Saved the Soul of America*. New York: Gotham Books.

Sullivan, Lisa Y. (1997). "Hip Hop Nation: The Undeveloped Social Capital of Black Urban America." *National Civic Review* 86 (3), 235–43.

Sullivan, Rachel E. (2003). "Rap and Race It's Got a Nice Beat, but What about the Message?" *Journal of Black Studies* 33 (5), 605–22.

Sullivan, Randall. (2002). *LAbyrinth: A Detective Investigates the Murders of Tupac Shakur and Notorious B.I.G., The Implication of Death Row Records' Suge Knight, and the Origins of the Los Angeles Police Scandal.* New York: Grove Press.

Sutton, Philip W. (2000). *Explaining Environmentalism: In Search of a New Social Movement.* Aldershot, England: Ashgate.

Szatmary, David P. (2010). *Rockin' in Time: A Social History of Rock & Roll.* Upper Saddle River, NJ: Prentice Hall.

Szwed, John F. (1997). *Space is the Place: The Lives and Times of Sun Ra.* New York: Pantheon Books.

———. (1999). "The Real Old School." In Alan Light (Ed.), *The Vibe History of Hip Hop* (3–12). New York: Random House.

Tabb, William K. (1970). *The Political Economy of the Black Ghetto.* New York: Norton.

Tang, Patricia. (2007). *Masters of the Sabar: Wolof Griot Percussionists of Senegal.* Philadelphia: Temple University Press.

Tanner, Paul, Megill, David W., and Gerow, Maurice. (1992). *Jazz.* Dubuque, IA: William C. Brown Publishers.

Tanz, Jason. (2007). *Other People's Property: A Shadow History of Hip Hop in White America.* New York: Bloomsbury.

Tarlé, Dominique. (2001). *Exile: The Making of Exile on Main St.* Guildford: Genesis.

Tarr, Zoltan. (2011). *The Frankfurt School: The Critical Theories of Max Horkheimer and Theodor W. Adorno.* New Brunswick, NJ: Transaction Publishers.

Tasker, Yvonne, and Negra, Diane. (Eds.). (2007). *Interrogating Post-Feminism: Gender and the Politics of Popular Culture.* Durham: Duke University Press.

Tatum, Elinor. (1995). "Spearhead Aims Toward AIDS Education through Music." *New York Amsterdam News* 86 (33), 30.

Taylor, Gary. (2005). *Buying Whiteness: Race, Culture, and Identity from Columbus to Hip Hop.* New York: Palgrave Macmillan.

Taylor, Verta, and Rupp, Leila. (1991). "Researching the Women's Movement: We Make Our Own History, But Not Just As We Please." In Mary Margaret Fonow and Judith A. Cook (Eds.), *Beyond Methodology: Feminist Scholarship as Lived Research* (119–32). Bloomington: Indiana University Press.

Taylor, Yuval. (Ed.). (1999a). *I Was Born a Slave: An Anthology of Classic Slave Narratives—Volume 1, 1772–1849.* Chicago, IL: Lawrence Hill Books.

———. (Ed.). (1999b). *I Was Born a Slave: An Anthology of Classic Slave Narratives—Volume 2, 1849–1866.* Chicago, IL: Lawrence Hill Books.

Tenaille, Frank. (2002). *Music is the Weapon of the Future: Fifty Years of African Popular Music.* Chicago: Lawrence Hill.

Terkourafi, Marina. (2010). *The Languages of Global Hip Hop.* New York: Continuum.

Terrell, Mary Church. (1932). *Colored Women and World Peace.* Philadelphia, PA: Women's International League for Peace and Freedom Press.

———. (1940). *A Colored Woman in a White World.* Salem, NH: Ayer.

Terrell, Tom. (1999). "The Second Wave: 1980–1983." In Alan Light (Ed.), *The Vibe History of Hip Hop* (43–52). New York: Random House.

Terrill, Robert E. (Ed.). (2010). *The Cambridge Companion to Malcolm X.* Cambridge: Cambridge University Press.

Teves, Stephanie Nohelani. (2011). "'Bloodline is all I need': Defiant Indigeneity and Hawaiian Hip Hop." *American Indian Culture and Research Journal* 35 (4), 73–101.

Thaler, Ingrid. (2010). *Black Atlantic Speculative Fictions: Octavia E. Butler, Jewelle Gomez, and Nalo Hopkinson.* New York: Routledge.

Thelwell, Ekwueme Michael. (1999). "Stokely Carmichael to Kwame Ture (1941–1998): 'Infinitely Political, Infinitely Human.'" *Massachusetts Review* 40 (3), 325–41.

Thigpen, David E. (2003). *Jam Master Jay: The Heart of Hip Hop.* New York: Pocket Star Books.

Thomas, Greg. (2007). "Queens of Consciousness & Sex-Radicalism in Hip Hop: On Erykah Badu & The Notorious K.I.M." *Journal of Pan-African Studies* 1 (7), 23–37.

———. (2009). *Hip Hop Revolution in the Flesh: Power, Knowledge, and Pleasure in Lil' Kim's Lyricism.* New York: Palgrave Macmillan.

Thomas, Lorenzo. (2008). *Don't Deny My Name: Words and Music and the Black Intellectual Tradition* (Aldon Lynn Nielsen, Ed.). Ann Arbor: University of Michigan Press.

Thomas, Pat. (2012). *Listen, Whitey!: The Sights and Sounds of Black Power, 1965–1975.* New York: W. W. Norton.

Thompson, Dave. (2001). *Funk.* San Francisco: Backbeat Books.

Thompson, J. Phillip. (2006). *Double Trouble: Black Mayors, Black Communities, and the Call for a Deep Democracy.* New York: Oxford University Press.

Thompson, Robert Farris. (1983). *Flash of the Spirit: African & Afro-American Art & Philosophy.* New York: Random House.

———. (1996). "Hip Hop 101." In William E. Perkins (Ed.), *Droppin' Science: Critical Essays on Rap Music and Hip Hop Culture* (211–19). Philadelphia: Temple University Press.

Tilly, Charles. (2004). *Social Movements, 1768–2004.* Boulder: Paradigm Publishers.

Tollemer, Brice. (2009). *Rage Against the Machine: Ennemis Publics.* Rosières-en-Haye: Camion Blanc.

Tolnay, Stewart E., and Beck, E.M. (1992). "Racial Violence and Black Migration in the American South, 1910 to 1930." *American Sociological Review* 57 (1), 103–16.

Toop, David. (1991). *Rap Attack 2: African Rap to Global Hip Hop.* London: Serpent's Tail.

———. (2000). *Rap Attack 3: African Rap to Global Hip Hop.* London: Serpent's Tail.

Torres, Jennifer. (2008). *Mary J. Blige.* Hockessin, DE: Mitchell Lane.

Tosches, Nick. (1999). *Unsung Heroes of Rock & Roll: The Birth of Rock in the Wild Years Before Elvis.* New York: Da Capo Press.

Trapp, Erin. (2005). "The Push and Pull of Hip Hop: A Social Movement Analysis." *American Behavioral Scientist* 48 (11), 1482–95.

Traylor, Eleanor W. (2009). "Women Writers of the Black Arts Movement." In Angelyn Mitchell and Danille K. Taylor (Eds.), *The Cambridge Companion to African American Women's Literature* (50–70). Cambridge: Cambridge University Press.

Trent, Chris. (1997). *Another Shade of Blue: Sun Ra on Record.* Exeter: Stride Publications.

Troka, Donna. (2002). "'You Heard My Gun Cock': Female Agency and Aggression in Contemporary Rap Music." *African American Research Perspectives* 8 (2), 82–89.

Trotter, Joe William, Jr. (Ed.). (1991). *The Great Migration in Historical Perspective: New Dimensions of Race, Class, and Gender.* Bloomington: Indiana University Press.

Tucker, Linda G. (2007). *Lockstep and Dance: Images of Black Men in Popular Culture.* Jackson: University Press of Mississippi.

Tudor, Dean, and Tudor, Nancy. (1979). *Black Music.* Littleton, CO: Libraries Unlimited.

Upchurch, Thomas. (2008). *Race Relations in the United States, 1960–1980.* Westport, CT: Greenwood.

Usher, Carlton A. (2005). *A Rhyme is a Terrible Thing to Waste: Hip Hop Culture and the Creation of a Political Culture.* Trenton, NJ: Africa World Press.

Van Deburg, William L. (1992). *New Day in Babylon: The Black Power Movement and American Culture, 1965–1975.* Chicago: University of Chicago Press.

———. (1997). *Black Camelot: African American Culture Heroes in Their Times, 1960–1980.* Chicago: University of Chicago Press.

———. (2001). "Villains, Demon, and Social Bandits: White Fear of the Black Cultural Revolution." In Brian Ward (Ed.), *Media, Culture, and the Modern African American Freedom Struggle* (197–210). Gainesville: University Press of Florida.

———. (2004). *Hoodlums: Black Villains and Social Bandits in American Life.* Chicago: University of Chicago Press.

Venkatesh, Sudhir Alladi. (2000). *American Project: The Rise and Fall of a Modern Ghetto.* Cambridge: Harvard University Press.

———. (2006). *Off the Books: The Underground Economy of the Urban Poor.* Cambridge: Harvard University Press.

Vergara, Camilo J. (1995). *The New American Ghetto.* New Brunswick: Rutgers University Press.

Vibe Magazine. (Ed.). (2001). *Hip Hop Divas.* New York: Three Rivers Press.

Vickers, Tom. (1976). "A Journey to the Center of Parliament/Funkadelic." *Rolling Stone* (August 26), 20–21.

Viesca, Victor Hugo. (2004). "The Battle of Los Angeles: The Cultural Politics of Chicana/o Music in the Greater Eastside." *American Quarterly* 56 (3), 719–39.

Villard, Marc. (2000). *Gangsta Rap.* Paris: Gallimard.

Vincent, Rickey. (1996). *Funk: The Music, the People, and the Rhythm of the One.* New York: St. Martin's Griffin.

Wagnleitner, Reinhold, and May, Elaine T. (Eds.). (2000). *Here, There, and Everywhere: The Foreign Politics of American Popular Culture.* Hanover, NH: University Press of New England.

Wald, Elijah. (2009). *How the Beatles Destroyed Rock & Roll: An Alternative History of American Popular Music.* New York: Oxford University Press.

———. (2012). *The Dozens: A History of Rap's Mama.* New York: Oxford University Press.

Waldrep, Christopher. (Ed.). (2001). *Racial Violence on Trial: A Handbook with Cases, Laws, and Documents.* Santa Barbara, CA: ABC-CLIO.

———. (2002). *Many Faces of Judge Lynch: Extralegal Violence and Punishment in America.* New York: Palgrave-Macmillan.

———. (Ed.). (2006). *Lynching in America: A History in Documents.* New York: New York University Press.

———. (2009). *African Americans Confront Lynching: Strategies of Resistance from the Civil War to the Civil Rights Era.* Lanham, MD: Rowman & Littlefield.

Waldschmidt-Nelson, Britta. (2012). *Dreams and Nightmares: Martin Luther King, Jr., Malcolm X, and the Struggle for Black Equality in America.* Gainesville: University Press of Florida.

Walker, David, Rausch, Andrew J., and Watson, Chris. (Eds.). (2009). *Reflections on Blaxploitation: Actors and Directors Speak.* Lanham, MD: Scarecrow Press.

Walker, Jesse. (2001). *Rebels on the Air: An Alternative History of Radio in America.* New York: New York University Press.

Walker, John Albert. (2001). *Art in the Age of Mass Media.* London: Pluto.

Walker, Richard J. (1996). "Taking the Rap: Gangsta Rap Music as a Reflection of Social Conflict in Contemporary American Society." M.A. thesis, George Mason University, Fairfax, VA.

Walker, Wyatt Tee. (1979). *"Somebody's Calling My Name": Black Sacred Music and Social Change.* Valley Forge, PA: Judson Press.

Wallace, Michele. (1979). *Black Macho and the Myth of the Superwoman.* New York: Dial Press.

Wallace-Sanders, Kimberly. (2008). *Mammy: A Century of Race, Gender, and Southern Memory.* Ann Arbor: University of Michigan Press.

Waller, Don. (1985). *The Motown Story.* New York: Scribner.

Walser, Robert. (1995). "Rhythm, Rhyme and Rhetoric in the Music of Public Enemy." *Ethnomusicology: Journal of the Society for Ethnomusicology* 39, 193–217.

Walters, Ronald W. (1993). *Pan-Africanism in the African Diaspora: An Analysis of Modern Afrocentric Political Movement.* Detroit: Wayne State University Press.

Wang, Oliver. (Ed.). (2003). *Classic Material: The Hip Hop Album Guide.* Chicago: ECW Press.

Wanguhu, Michael (Director). (2007). *Hip Hop Colony: The African Hip Hop Explosion.* Chatsworth, CA: Image Entertainment.

Ward, Brian. (1998). *Just My Soul Responding: Rhythm & Blues, Black Consciousness, and Race Relations.* Berkeley: University of California Press.

———. (Ed). (2001). *Media, Culture, and the Modern African American Freedom Struggle.* Gainesville: University Press of Florida.

———. (2004). *Radio and the Struggle for Civil Rights in the South.* Gainesville: University Press of Florida.

Warren, Gwendolin Sims. (1999). *Ev'ry Time I Feel the Spirit: 101 Best-Loved Psalms, Gospel Hymns, and Spiritual Songs of the African American Church*. New York: Henry Holt.

Warren, Roland L. (Ed.). (2008). *Politics and African American Ghettos*. New Brunswick, NJ: Aldine Transaction.

Washburn, Patrick S. (1981). "The 'Pittsburgh Courier's' Double V Campaign in 1942." Paper presented at the Annual Meeting of the Association for Education in Journalism (64th, East Lansing, MI, August 8–11).

———. (1986). "The Pittsburgh Courier's Double V Campaign in 1942." *American Journalism* 3 (2), 73–86.

Watkins, S. Craig. (1998). *Hip Hop Culture and the Production of Black Cinema*. Chicago: University of Chicago Press.

———. (2001). "A Nation of Millions: Hip Hop Culture and the Legacy of Black Nationalism." *Communication Review* 4 (3), 373–98.

———. (2005). *Hip Hop Matters: Politics, Pop Culture, and the Struggle for the Soul of a Movement*. Boston, MA: Beacon.

Watts, Eric K. (1997). "An Exploration of Spectacular Consumption: Gangsta Rap as Cultural Commodity." *Communication Studies* 48 (1), 42–58.

Weber, Shirley N. (1981). "Black Power in the 1960s: A Study of Its Impact on Women's Liberation." *Journal of Black Studies* 11 (4), 483–97.

Weiner, Mark S. (2006). *Americans Without Law: The Racial Boundaries of Citizenship*. New York: New York University Press.

Weiner, Tim. (2012). *Enemies: A History of the FBI*. New York: Random House.

Weingarten, Christopher R. (2010). *Public Enemy's It Takes a Nation of Millions to Hold Us Back*. New York: Continuum.

Weisbrot, Robert. (1990). *Freedom Bound: A History of America's Civil Rights Movement*. New York: Norton.

Weiss, Brad. (2009). *Street Dreams and Hip Hop Barbershops: Global Fantasy in Urban Tanzania*. Bloomington: Indiana University Press.

Wells, Ida B. (1969). *On Lynchings*. New York: Arno Press.

———. (1970). *Crusade for Justice: The Autobiography of Ida B. Wells* (Alfreda Duster, Ed.). Chicago: University of Chicago Press.

———. (1991). *The Selected Works of Ida B. Wells-Barnett* (Trudier Harris, Ed.). New York: Oxford University Press.

———. (1993). *A Red Record: Lynchings in the U.S.* Salem, NH: Ayer & Co.

———. (1995). *The Memphis Dairy of Ida B. Wells* (Miriam Decosta-Willis, Ed.). Boston: Beacon.

Werner, Craig H. (2004). *Higher Ground: Stevie Wonder, Aretha Franklin, Curtis Mayfield, and the Rise and Fall of American Soul*. New York: Crown Publishers.

———. (2006). *Change is Gonna Come: Music, Race & the Soul of America*. Ann Arbor: University of Michigan Press.

West, Cornel. (1993). *Race Matters*. New York: Random House.

Whaley, Deborah E. (2002). "The Neo-Soul Vibe and the Post-Modern Aesthetic: Black Popular Music and Culture for the Soul Babies of History." *American Studies* 43 (3), 75–81.

Wheatland, Thomas. (2009). *The Frankfurt School in Exile*. Minneapolis: University of Minnesota Press.

Whitall, Susan. (1998). *Women of Motown: An Oral History*. New York: Avon Books.

White, Adam. (1985). *The Motown Story*. Boston: Bedford Press.

White, Miles. (2011). *From Jim Crow to Jay-Z: Race, Rap, and the Performance of Masculinity*. Urbana: University of Illinois Press.

Whitten, Norman E., Jr., and Torres, Arlene. (Eds.). (1998). *Blackness in Latin America and the Caribbean: Social Dynamics and Cultural Transformations* (2 vols.). Indianapolis: Indiana University Press.

Widener, Daniel. (2010). *Black Arts West: Culture and Struggle in Post-War Los Angeles*. Durham: Duke University Press.

Wiggerhaus, Rolf. (1995). *The Frankfurt School: Its History, Theories, and Political Significance*. Cambridge: MIT Press.

Wilkerson, Isabel. (2010). *The Warmth of Other Suns: The Epic Story of America's Great Migration.* New York: Random House.

Williams, Bruce. (2008). *Rollin' with Dre: The Unauthorized Account: An Insider's Tale of the Rise, Fall, and Rebirth of West Coast Hip Hop* (with Donnell Alexander). New York: One World.

Williams, Juan. (1987). *Eyes on the Prize: America's Civil Rights Years, 1954–1965.* New York: Viking.

Williams, Justin A. (2010a). "The Construction of Jazz Rap as High Art in Hip Hop Music." *Journal of Musicology* 27 (4), 435–59.

———. (2010b). "Musical Borrowing in Hip Hop Music: Theoretical Frameworks and Case Studies." Ph.D. dissertation, University of Nottingham, Nottingham, UK.

Williams, Rhys H. (2004). "The Cultural Contexts of Collective Action: Constraints, Opportunities, and the Symbolic Life of Social Movements." In David A. Snow, Sarah Anne Soule, and Hanspeter Kriesi (Eds.), *The Blackwell Companion to Social Movements* (91–115). Malden, MA: Blackwell.

Williams, Richard. (2002). *Nina Simone: Don't Let Me Be Misunderstood.* Edinburgh: Canongate Books.

Williams, Todd Larkins. (Director). (2002). *Tha Westside.* San Mateo, CA: Niche Entertainment/Image Entertainment.

Williamson, Joy Ann. (2003). *Black Power on Campus: The University of Illinois, 1965–1975.* Urbana: University of Illinois Press.

Wills, Garry. (1970). *Nixon Agonistes: The Crises of the Self-Made Man.* Boston: Houghton Mifflin.

Wilshire, Peter. (2006). "'I Know I'm Not Alone': A Middle-Eastern Musical Odyssey." *Screen Education* 42, 30–34.

Wilson, David. (2007). *Cities and Race: America's New Black Ghetto.* New York: Routledge.

Wilson, Ross. (2007). *Theodor Adorno.* New York: Routledge.

Wilson, William J. (1987). *The Truly Disadvantaged: The Inner-City, the Underclass, and Public Policy.* Chicago: University of Chicago Press.

———. (1997). *When Work Disappears: The World of the New Urban Poor.* New York: Knopf/Random House.

———. (1999). *The Bridge Over the Racial Divide: Rising Inequality and Coalition Politics.* Berkeley: University of California Press.

———. (2009). *More Than Just Race: Being Black and Poor in the Inner-City.* New York: Norton.

Wimsatt, William Upski. (2003). *Bomb the Suburbs: Graffiti, Race, Freight-Hopping and the Search for Hip Hop's Moral Center.* New York: Soft Skull Press.

Winant, Howard. (1994). *Racial Conditions: Politics, Theory, Comparisons.* Minneapolis: University of Minnesota Press.

———. (2001). *The World is a Ghetto: Race and Democracy Since World War II.* New York: Basic Books.

———. (2004). *The New Politics of Race: Globalism, Difference, Justice.* Minneapolis: University of Minnesota Press.

Wise, Tim J. (2005). *Affirmative Action: Racial Preference in Black and White.* New York: Routledge.

Wolfe, Tom. (1970). *Radical Chic & Mau-Mauing the Flak-Catchers.* New York: Farrar, Straus & Giroux.

Wolk, Douglas. (2004). *Live at the Apollo.* New York: Continuum.

Wolters, Raymond. (1996). *Right Turn: William Bradford Reynolds, the Reagan Administration, and Black Civil Rights.* New Brunswick: Transaction Publishers.

Wood, Amy L. (2009). *Lynching and Spectacle: Witnessing Racial Violence in America, 1890–1940.* Chapel Hill: University of North Carolina Press.

Wood, Joe. (1999). "Native Tongues: A Family Affair." In Alan Light (Ed.), *The Vibe History of Hip Hop* (187–91). New York: Random House.

Wooden, Wayne S., and Blazak, Randy. (2001). *Renegade Kids, Suburban Outlaws: From Youth Culture to Delinquency.* Belmont, CA: Wadsworth.

Woodson, Carter G. (1922). *The Negro in Our History.* Washington, DC: Associated Publishers.

Woodstra, Chris, Bush, John, and Erlewine, Stephen T. (Eds.). (2008). *Old School Rap and Hip Hop.* New York: Backbeat Books.

Worsley, Shawan M. (2007). "Loving Hip Hop When It Denies Your Humanity." In Gwendolyn D. Pough, Elaine Richardson, Aisha Durham, and Rachel Raimist (Eds.), *Home Girls Make Some Noise!: The Hip Hop Feminism Anthology* (274–300). Mira Loma, CA: Parker Publishing.

———. (2010). *Audience, Agency, and Identity in Black Popular Culture.* New York: Routledge.

Wright, Amy. (2008). "A Philosophy of Funk: The Politics and Pleasure of a Parliafunkadelicment Thang!" In Tony Bolden (Ed.), *The Funk Era and Beyond: New Perspectives of Black Popular Culture* (33–50). New York: Palgrave Macmillan.

Wright, Sarah E. (1990). *A. Philip Randolph: Integration in the Workplace.* Englewood Cliffs, NJ: Silver Burdett Press.

Wright, William D. (1997). *Black Intellectuals, Black Cognition, and a Black Aesthetic.* Westport, CT: Praeger.

Wu, Jin-Ping. (2000). *Frederick Douglass and the Black Liberation Movement: The North Star of American Blacks.* New York: Garland.

Wynn, Neil A. (2010). *The African American Experience During World War II.* Lanham, MD: Rowman & Littlefield.

Yaszek, Lisa. (2006). "Afrofuturism, Science Fiction, and the History of the Future." *Socialism & Democracy* 20 (3), 41–60.

Yee, Shirley J. (1992). *Black Women Abolitionists: A Study in Activism, 1828–1860.* Knoxville: University of Tennessee Press.

Young, Charles M. (1978). "Parliament/Funkadelic: Apocalypse Now!" *Rolling Stone* (April 6), 11.

Yousman, Bill. (2003). "Blackophilia and Blackophobia: White Youth, the Consumption of Rap Music, and White Supremacy." *Communication Theory* 13 (4), 366–91.

Yu, Timothy. (2009). *Race and the Avant-Garde: Experimental and Asian American Poetry since 1965.* Stanford, CA: Stanford University Press.

Zackodnik, Teresa C. (2004). *The Mulatta and the Politics of Race.* Jackson: University Press of Mississippi.

Zeisler, Andi. (2008). *Feminism and Pop Culture.* Berkeley, CA: Seal Press.

Zwickel, Jonathan. (2011). *Beastie Boys: A Musical Biography.* Santa Barbara, CA: Greenwood.

Index

McCullough, Robert, 253
McDaniel, Hattie, 184
McDaniels, Darryl "DMC," 88
McGee, James, 255
McLaren, Peter, 321
McLean, Jackie, 226, 229, 232
McNair, Denise, 73, 175
McPhatter, Clyde, 90, 101, 234
MC Lyte, 181, 184, 195, 202, 204, 239, 259
MC Ren, 265
MC Shan, 43, 74, 239
Mecca the Ladybug, 325
Medeski, John, 261
Medusa, 195, 325
Megill, David, 228
Melle Mel, 55, 57, 58
Mellencamp, John, 183
Mellow Man Ace, 239, 250, 259
Messina, Joe, 72
Method Man, 127
Michael, George, 84
Michele, Chrisette, 201
micro-politics, 70, 342
Middle Passage, the, 204
migration (African American), 38, 39, 74, 93, 103
Miles, Buddy, 116, 138
Millennial Anti-War Movement, 10
Miller, Glen, 60
Miller, Karl, 37
Miller, Sidney, 247
Millett, Kate, 193
Millinder, Lucky, 60
Million Man March, 10–11, 124
Million Woman March, 10–11, 124
Mills Brothers, the, 60, 63, 141n18
Minaj, Nicki, 194–195, 313, 329
Mingus, Charles, 226, 229, 232
minstrelism, 4, 113, 130, 133, 313
miscegenation, 106, 178
misogyny, 6, 65, 91, 119–121, 127, 139, 182, 185, 191, 192, 194–195, 202, 203, 206, 207, 210, 274, 278, 325, 331
Miss Money, 325
Mobb Deep, 74
Mobley, Hank, 226, 228
Moïse, Lenelle, 325
Monáe, Janelle, 201

Monica, 171
Monch, Pharoahe, 7, 134, 251
Money-B, 260
Monk, Thelonious, 50, 232
Monson, Ingrid, 229
Montgomery Bus Boycott, 34, 91, 232
Moonglows, the, 65
Moore, Jessica Care, 325
Moore, Johnny, 60
Morello, Mary, 124
Morello, Tom, 121, 124
Morgan, Joan, 188, 193, 194, 206, 207, 315
Morgan, Lee, 226, 229, 233
Morris, Arthur Glen, 247
Morrison, Toni, 275
Mortimer, Lee, 105
Mos Def, 7, 131–138, 157, 195, 334, 337
Mosson, Cordell, 253
Moten, Fred, 159
Mothershed, Thelma, 73
Motown Records, 37, 71, 79
Mouton, Elva, 240
Moynihan, Daniel Patrick, 342
MRK, 334
Muhammad, Elijah, 123
Muhammad, Khalid, 272
Muldrow, Georgia Anne, 157, 179, 181, 183, 201
Mystic, 195, 260, 325

Narcicyst, the, 334
NaS, 6, 39, 43, 74, 157, 195, 259, 315
Nash, Johnny, 249
Nate Dogg, 263
Nation of Islam, 123
National Alliance of Black Feminists, 205
National Association for the Advancement of Colored People (NAACP), 78, 123, 232
National Association of Colored Women (NACW), 191
National Black Feminist Organization, 205
National Council of Negro Women (NCNW), 232
National Lawyer's Guild, 123
National Urban League (NUL), 232
Native Guns, the, 334
Native Tongues Posse, the, 131

About the Author

Reiland Rabaka is an associate professor of African, African American, and Caribbean studies in the Department of Ethnic Studies and the Humanities Program at the University of Colorado at Boulder, where he is also an affiliate professor in the Women and Gender Studies Program and a research fellow at the Center for Studies of Ethnicity and Race in America (CSERA). He also holds graduate faculty appointments in the College of Music, School of Education, Department of Sociology, Department of Religious Studies, and Critical Theory Program at the University of Colorado at Boulder. His research has been published in the *Journal of African American Studies*, *Journal of Black Studies*, *Western Journal of Black Studies*, *Africana Studies Annual Review*, *Ethnic Studies Review*, *Jouvert: A Journal of Postcolonial Studies*, *Socialism & Democracy*, and *Journal of Southern Religion*, among others. He is an editorial board member of the *Journal of African American Studies*, *Journal of Black Studies*, and *Africana Studies Annual Review*.

Dr. Rabaka has published eleven books, including *W.E.B. Du Bois and the Problems of the Twenty-First Century* (2007); *Du Bois's Dialectics: Black Radical Politics and the Reconstruction of Critical Social Theory* (2008); *Africana Critical Theory* (2009); *Forms of Fanonism: Frantz Fanon's Critical Theory and the Dialectics of Decolonization* (2010); *Against Epistemic Apartheid: W.E.B. Du Bois and the Disciplinary Decadence of Sociology* (2010); *Hip Hop's Inheritance: From the Harlem Renaissance to the Hip Hop Feminist Movement* (2011); *Hip Hop's Amnesia: From Blues and the Black Women's Club Movement to Rap and the Hip Hop Movement* (2012); and *The Neo-Soul Movement: From Classic Soul to Hip Hop Soul* (forthcoming). Dr. Rabaka's research has been recognized with several awards, including funding from the National Endowment for the Humanities, the National Endowment for the Arts, the National Science Foundation, the

Eugene M. Kayden Book Award, the Cheikh Anta Diop Book Award, and the National Council for Black Studies' W.E.B. Du Bois-Anna Julia Cooper Award for Outstanding Publications in Africana Studies. His cultural criticism, social commentary, and political analysis has been featured in print, radio, television, and online media venues such as NPR, PBS, BBC, CNN, ABC, NBC, MTV, BET, VH1, the New Books Network, *The Tom Joyner Morning Show*, *The Philadelphia Tribune*, and *The Denver Post*, among others.